D1233525

THE ANGLICAN CHURCH
FROM THE BAY TO THE ROCKIES

THE ANG LICAN ✶✶ CHURCH FROM THE ✶ BAY TO THE ROC KIES

T·C·B·BOON

A HISTORY OF THE ECCLESIASTICAL
PROVINCE OF RUPERT'S LAND AND
ITS DIOCESES FROM 1820 TO 1950

THE RYERSON PRESS TORONTO

ACKNOWLEDGMENTS

This History of the Anglican Church in the Ecclesiastical Province of Rupert's Land is published with the aid of two grants: the first from the Humanities Research Council of Canada from funds provided by the Canada Council, an award that establishes the value and importance of this book as a contribution to the history of Western Canada; the second from the Anglican Foundation of Canada, which indicates the book's usefulness as a record of the development of the Anglican Church in its largest Canadian Ecclesiastical Province.

At the same time I should like to acknowledge grants made to me personally by the Canada Council and from the John S. Ewart Memorial Fund of the University of Manitoba. The first of these enabled me to spend some time in research in the Archives of the great Missionary Societies, and the Hudson's Bay Company in London, England; the second to do similar work in the Public Archives of Canada in Ottawa.

There are others to whom my thanks are also due: Archbishop Barfoot, at whose suggestion this work was first begun in the pages of the *Edmonton Churchman*, and Canon L. A. Dixon of the M.S.C.C., who urged that these articles ought to be made into a book; Archdeacon R. K. Naylor of the Canadian Church Historical Society and Bishop H. R. Hunt (when Executive Secretary of General Synod) who helped to make this possible. I am indebted to Dr. W. L. Morton and Dr. Lorne Pierce for kindly reading the first draft of the typescript; to the Readers of the Humanities Research Council, whose comments were invaluable in revising it; to Dr. T. R. Millman, who not only read the final draft with a critical approach, but gave me the benefit of his experience and technical skill; and to my wife, for her valuable assistance and helpful criticism through more than ten years of work.

No history of the Anglican Church in Rupert's Land could have been written without the willing co-operation of others, who answered questions, made transcripts of manuscripts, lent material from their own files, and read parts of the manuscript. For all their help I am very grateful, and I have ventured to list their names below. I would add that I am also indebted to two men who are now dead: Canon W. B. Heeney, for the collection of material that he made when Archivist of Rupert's Land, and for the inspiration I found in his own historical studies; and Archbishop S. P. Matheson, who during a long friendship, and through his own vivid recollections, linked me with men and events in the past so realistically that I felt impelled to make a further study of them.

THE CHURCH MISSIONARY SOCIETY ARCHIVES
Mr. H. L. Cobb, Miss Grace Belcher, Miss Rosemary Keen

THE SOCIETY FOR THE PROPAGATION OF THE GOSPEL ARCHIVES
Mrs. W. M. Landers, Miss E. Rendall, Miss Caroline Merion

THE SOCIETY FOR THE PROMOTION OF CHRISTIAN KNOWLEDGE
ARCHIVES
Mrs. A. Henderson-Howatt

THE HUDSON'S BAY COMPANY
Miss A. M. Johnson of Beaver House, London; Mrs. Shirley Smith of Hudson's
Bay House, Winnipeg; and Mr. C. P. Wilson, when Editor of THE BEAVER

DIOCESAN OFFICERS IN THE PROVINCE OF RUPERT'S LAND
Mr. R. H. Pook of Rupert's Land, Mrs. T. A. Norris of Athabasca, Mr. G. W.
Pickett of Qu'Appelle, Bishop H. R. Ragg and Archdeacon R. Axon of Calgary, the
late Archdeacon Walter Leversedge, Archdeacon S. F. Tackaberry of Edmonton,
Bishop D. B. Marsh and Mrs. V. Holmes of The Arctic, and Bishop Tom
Greenwood of The Yukon.

OTHERS IN ENGLAND AND CANADA
The Editor of Crockford's CLERICAL DIRECTORY, the Vicar General of the Province
of Canterbury, Miss B. I. Wolfendale of the Methodist Missionary Society, Dr. W.
Kaye Lamb of the Public Archives of Canada and the staff of the Manitoba Legislative Library.

AMONG MY PERSONAL FRIENDS: Canon W. J. Merrick, formerly of St.
John's College, Winnipeg; Mrs. A. N. Wetton of North Battleford, Saskatchewan;
Mr. Harry Shave, Archivist of St. John's Cathedral, Winnipeg; Rev. W. de V.
Angus Hunt, formerly Canon of the Diocese of Edmonton. Others, now deceased:
Mrs. W. J. Garton, Rev. P. A. Northam, formerly of Moosonee, and Canon A. R.
Kelley of General Synod Archives.

T. C. B. BOON

PREFACE

To write this history of the Anglican Church in Rupert's Land has been no easy task. This is the first time such an attempt has been made on so large a scale or to cover so long a period, for the Ecclesiastical Province of this name is the largest in Canada, extending as it does over all of the central and western territory associated with "The Governor and Company of Adventurers of England trading into Hudson's Bay." Books have been written on the political, economic and social developments that have taken place since Hudson's Bay Company rule ceased, but mention of the Anglican Church in such volumes is often only incidental. Shorter studies have been made of Anglican bishops and missionaries who have served in Rupert's Land, but many of these papers are buried in the records of historical societies, or in archives and libraries, unavailable to the ordinary person. Often such studies, when reminiscent of a dimming past, may be just in estimate of character and achievement, but suffer from historical inaccuracy. The Anglican of today knows too little of the history of his own diocese, let alone the Ecclesiastical Province, to be proud of the accomplishments of the past; the serious student often has little idea of where to begin his studies. This book seeks in some measure to remedy this situation and bring history into its proper relation with the present, as the basis of inspiration and action for the future. It may be added that it has taken more than twenty-five years to assemble, study and select the material upon which this work is based, and ten years to prepare the manuscript.

From 1820 to 1870 the path of the Church followed the canoe routes of the Hudson's Bay Company. Progress is centred upon the efforts of individual missionaries, and finally brought coherently together through the founding of the Diocese of Rupert's Land. With 1870, the complication of civil organization emerged; four years later the founding of the Ecclesiastical Province broke up the area into dioceses, each with its individual focus. Within ten years the railway development across the prairies had realigned the population and forced new planning of the Church's work. The formation of General Synod in 1893 brought a conflict between centralized and Provincial authority, in which the influence of the latter was gradually weakened, although the number of its dioceses continued to grow, each diocese trying to solve its own problems as best it could. And so the writer passes from the early diaries and letters of the first period to the journals of Diocesan and Provincial Synods, to those meetings of General Synod and reports from its departments.

I have made free use of Charges by Metropolitans and Bishops to their

Synods because these are coherent and illuminating documents, if read in the light of synodical discussions and resolutions, and they are generally accurate in fact and singularly free from bias in outlook. If I have been less critical of Bishops than some think I should have been, it is simply that from my own experience I have come to the conclusion that local diocesan criticism fades out when one tries to look at development from an all-over or provincial point of view.

I have purposely avoided comment upon any difference in types of churchmanship that may be found in the Province of Rupert's Land. Each diocese has gone its own individual way in this respect; every parish has its own traditions for that matter, but it does not seem to have had any significant effect upon the general progress of the Church. Nor have I made any attempt to discuss the relationship of the Anglican Church with other denominations; however in the areas of social work and education, resolutions passed at Synods often express a desire for co-operation on matters in which it has been felt that the Churches should speak with a united voice.

I have tried to place some emphasis upon the development of the Indian work, which was indeed the original objective of the Anglican Church in Rupert's Land, and, with our work in the Arctic, is still the most provocative problem we face in the Home Mission field. I have tried to do justice to the men and women who have built up the Church in missions and parishes, and to revive recollection of these pioneers, to whose devoted work we now owe so much. I have also tried to draw particular attention to the translational work of the early missionaries, a remarkable achievement that has been such an effective instrument in the spread of the Gospel, and to the founding and progress of our educational institutions. Through the years they have been the powerhouses of the Church.

To write this book has made me very conscious of the greatness of our heritage, and the importance of our responsibility to the present and the future. I trust that those who read it will share these feelings with me.

T. C. B. BOON
Archivist to
the Ecclesiastical Province of Rupert's Land

Winnipeg, Manitoba
September 1, 1962

CONTENTS

LIST OF MAPS

How the Church of England Came to Canada

＋·＋◆◆◆＋···◆◆◆＋···◆◆◆＋···◆◆◆＋···◆◆◆＋···◆◆◆＋···◆◆◆＋···◆◆◆＋·

At our first arrival, after the ship rode at anchor, our general, with such company as could well be spared from the ships, in marching order entered the land, having special care by exhortations that at our entrance thereinto we should all with one voice, kneeling upon our knees, chiefly thank God for our safe arrival; secondly, beseech Him that it would please His Divine Majesty, long to continue our Queen, for whom he, and all the rest of our company, in this order took possession of the country; and thirdly, that by our Christian study and endeavour, these barbarous people, trained up in paganry and infidelity, might be reduced to the knowledge of true religion, and to the hope of salvation in Christ our Redeemer. . . .

THE SECOND VOYAGE OF MARTIN FROBISHER,
by Dionise Settle: July 20, 1577

＋·＋◆◆◆＋···◆◆◆＋···◆◆◆＋···◆◆◆＋···◆◆◆＋···◆◆◆＋···◆◆◆＋···◆◆◆＋·

This is the story of how the Church of England came to Rupert's Land, and how it grew from the tiny seed of a single isolated mission to be twelve Dioceses, ten of which now form the Ecclesiastical Province of the same name. But first it is necessary to take a look at Canada as a whole, for the Church of England came to Canada by four different roads, at four different times and under differing circumstances. It is natural to begin with the Atlantic seaboard, for it was there that the Church first permanently established itself.

The Ecclesiastical Province of Canada

The first services of the Church of England in Nova Scotia were held at Annapolis Royal in 1710, primarily for the British Garrison, and there in 1732 the first endowment of the Church was provided, when the Crown made over to the Church the glebe, formerly owned by the Recollets, to maintain the Chaplain, or "if a parish be established, for the parish minister." St. Paul's Church in Halifax was opened in 1750. Charles Inglis, the first Bishop of Nova Scotia, was consecrated in 1787. Gradually, as settlement increased, the Church spread into what is now New Brunswick, into Prince Edward Island, and the S.P.G. sent three French-speaking missionaries into Quebec in 1774.

Eventually four dioceses were organized: Nova Scotia in 1787, Quebec in 1793, Fredericton in 1845, Montreal in 1850. These now, with Newfoundland (1839), form the Ecclesiastical Province of Canada.

The Ecclesiastical Province of Ontario

In a day when the rivers were the principal highways it was natural that the work of the Church should make its way from Quebec and Montreal up the St. Lawrence River, but it was the rumble of the approaching American Revolution that brought settlement to the Upper St. Lawrence valley, caused the founding of the famous Mohawk Church, and directed the efforts of the Reverend John Stuart, "Father of the Church in Upper Canada," to his fruitful work in the neighbourhood of Kingston. In due course the southern and western parts of Ontario developed into six Dioceses, (Toronto, 1839; Huron, 1857; Ontario, 1862; Algoma, 1873; Niagara, 1875; Ottawa, 1896) which separated from the Ecclesiastical Province of Canada in 1912 to form the Ecclesiastical Province of Ontario, under its own Metropolitan. The number was increased to seven in 1933 by the addition of the Diocese of Moosonee.

The Ecclesiastical Province of British Columbia

Francis Drake and his men landed on the west coast of North America in 1578, and stopped for a moment to thank God, "Who had brought them safely thus far on their adventuring." Captain Vancouver explored the Pacific Coast waters in 1792-1794, and enhanced his reputation by his Christian conduct and just dealings with the natives. The Hudson's Bay Company built Fort Vancouver in 1825, and had chaplains there: Reverend H. Beaver (1836-1838) and Reverend R. J. Staines (1849) who, in 1853, asked the Right Reverend David Anderson of Rupert's Land, the nearest Bishop, to go to Vancouver for Confirmation services. Three years later Captain Prevost, R.N., appealed to the Church Missionary Society on behalf of the natives, and so it came about that William Duncan began his work on the coast in 1857. The discovery of gold in the Cariboo in 1858 further impressed the necessity of immediate action. The Reverend George Hills, Vicar of Great Yarmouth, England, was consecrated as first Bishop of Columbia, February 24, 1859. Twenty years later the new Dioceses of Caledonia and New Westminster were erected on the mainland, and the latter was subsequently divided by the formation of the Diocese of Kootenay (1899) and Cariboo (1914). These, together with the Diocese of Yukon (1891) which was added to it in 1941, form the Ecclesiastical Province of British Columbia.

It was the search for the northwest passage by sea that first brought Martin Frobisher and his men to the arctic shores of Rupert's Land, and it is to Master Dionise Settle, who wrote the account printed at the head of this chapter, that we owe the information that in 1577 the sound of Christian Prayer was first heard in Rupert's Land, and the opportunity and necessity of missionary work first recognized. A year later Frobisher again sailed a fleet of little ships into the ice-clogged seas on the northern coasts of Canada, and that summer (1578) on the shore of what is now assumed to be Baffin Island, a rough kind of tent church was erected, a plain wooden table served as the altar, the vessels were brought from the ship, and with Chaplain Master Woolfall as Celebrant, the first service of Holy Communion, according to the Use of the Church of England, was held on Canadian ground, the crew of the *Anne Francis* forming the congregation. Master Woolfall is described as "a true pastor and minister of God's Word, who for the profit of his flock, spared not to venture his own life," words which might well be applied to his missionary successors in those same regions, where Frobisher's men built stone crosses on the hilltops to show that Christians had visited the country and worshipped there. But three hundred years were to elapse before their pious hopes were realized, through the efforts of a missionary who once followed the sea himself, the Reverend E. J. Peck.

Influence of the Hudson's Bay Company

The departure on June 3, 1668, from Gravesend of two small ships, the *Eaglet* and the *Nonsuch*, for the most southerly shores of Hudson Bay, marked the beginning of a new era in the history of western Canada, and ultimately in the history of the great Missionary Societies of the Church of England, for these ships were the forerunners of many belonging to "The Governor and Company of Adventurers of England trading into Hudson's Bay" that were to reach these parts. Nearly a hundred years elapsed before, under increasing competition from fur traders from Montreal, the Company moved inland and began the establishment of many posts, the names of which are so important in the story of the progress of the Church and have become well known through secular history and romance. It was the general policy of the Company and the conduct of its servants in dealing with the native Indians that established the conditions of trust and goodwill which greatly assisted the early missionaries in their work. The punctiliousness with which the Company and its agents kept their word; the impressiveness of "Dress Days" on Sundays, and Festivals when the Church Services were read in public; and the wholesome effect of the many genuinely pious men amongst the Factors in everyday life, each contributed something towards opening the way for the Christian Gospel. The formal resolutions passed by the Council of the Northern Department of Rupert's Land at its meeting at Norway House on June 24, 1836, dealing with the treatment of the natives, Sunday observance, and education, would appear to be a reiteration of the acknowledged customs of the years, not the initiation of a new and improved policy.[1]

Selkirk Settlers come to Red River

Towards the close of the eighteenth century a revision of the Scottish Land Laws caused a disruption of the Highland Clans and the dispossession of many crofters. The unhappy condition of these people appealed to the kindly heart of the young Earl of Selkirk, and he began to take a keen interest in their welfare and to endeavour to assist with schemes of emigration. When at first he failed to enlist the sympathy and assistance of the British Government, he bought land in Prince Edward Island himself and settled a number of the crofters there. In 1805 he arranged for another party of them to go to the neighbourhood of the present town of Chatham in Ontario.[2] But he was a far-sighted man and seems to have had in mind the suitability of the prairie lands of North-West America (as it was commonly called at the time) for permanent settlement. A few years later Lord Selkirk succeeded in interesting the Hudson's Bay Company in his schemes, which were in line with some tentative ones of their own with respect to retiring employees. He greatly strengthened his position with the Company by acquiring some of its stock, and an agreement was reached in May, 1811, which enabled him to set up the Red River Colony.[3]

The first of the new settlers for the Red River valley arrived at York Factory September 24, 1811, and were followed by other parties in subsequent years. The story of their hardships, disappointments and adventures need not be retold here, but among the promises said to have been made to them in Scotland, one that was not kept in actuality, was that they should have a minister of the Presbyterian Church in the Colony. Some suggestions have been advanced for this

[1]Hudson's Bay Company Archives (hereafter H.B.C.A.), Instructions to Captain John Marsh, June 18, 1688. Douglas MacKay, *The Honourable Company* (2nd ed., Toronto, 1949), 219 ff.
[2]This was the Baldoon Farm, near Lake St. Clair.
[3]Full accounts of the establishment of the Red River Colony are to be found in the following: Douglas MacKay, *op. cit.* E. E. Rich, *Hudson's Bay Company, 1670-1870*, I (London, 1960); *Ibid.*, II, *1763-1870*. A. S. Morton, *A History of the Canadian West to 1870* (Toronto, 1939). W. L. Morton, *Manitoba: A History* (Toronto, 1955).

failure: the isolated position of the country; its unsettled condition, owing to the private war between the Hudson's Bay Company and the North West Company; the removal in 1815 of a considerable proportion of the settlers to eastern Canada; the want of missionary spirit and lack of resources for missionary work in the churches in Scotland at that time.

Lord Selkirk visited his settlers in the Red River Valley in the summer of 1817, and when reminded of the promise of a Presbyterian minister, is said to have replied: "Selkirk always keeps his word." The meeting took place close to where the road now turns around the southeast corner of St. John's Cathedral Churchyard in Winnipeg, and it was by way of a pledge that he then, according to Gunn, presented to the settlers two lots, each having a river frontage of ten chains, saying: "This lot on which we are met today shall be for your Church and manse, the next on the south side of the creek, shall be for your school, and for a help to support your teacher, and, in commemoration of your native parish, it shall be called Kildonan."[4] Conditions, however, altered rapidly in the next three years. Selkirk and the Company became entangled in lawsuits, and in the confusion of the times the spiritual necessities of the Red River settlers appear to have been forgotten. Lord Selkirk himself died, April 8, 1820. A minister indeed came out to the Red River Settlement that same summer, but he was not of the promised and expected Presbyterian persuasion.

The Reverend John West, A.M., boarded the Company's ship *The Eddystone,* lying at Gravesend, on May 27, 1820,[5] and thus began the long and adventurous journey that did not end until October 24, 1823, when he again reached the Thames. Mr. West, born at Farnham in Surrey, 1778, was educated at St. Edmund's Hall, Oxford. After his ordination by the Bishop of London on December 20, 1804, he had spent fifteen years in curacies, one of them at White Roding, Essex, to the Reverend Henry Budd. In 1820 he had been collated to the parish of Chettle in northeast Dorset, from which he temporarily absented himself in order to undertake the work in Canada, though it appears that he set out with some intention of settling permanently at Red River, and being later joined by his family, consisting of his wife and five young children.

The fourth road by which the Church of England came to Canada, and by which it reached Rupert's Land, was thus the old Fur Trader's

[4]Donald Gunn and C. H. Tuttle, *History of Manitoba* (1880).

[5]H.B.C.A., *Minutes of the Hudson's Bay Company's Committee,* October 15, 1819. The reasons for sending a chaplain to the Red River Settlement were stated, and Rev. John West was appointed to that position, "as from the time when he shall board the ship at Gravesend."

Road through Hudson Bay. For nearly forty years it was, with but few exceptions, the only road. It was always a lonely road, calling for faith, endurance and courage on the part of all who travelled it, whether missionary or trader. Mr. West was an ardent supporter of the Church Missionary Society, and he had the approbation and warm support of the Society in part of the work he proposed to do, the improvement of the condition of the native Indians and the preaching of the Gospel to them in North-West America.[6]

[6]Church Missionary Society Archives (hereafter C.M.S.A.), *Minutes of the Correspondence Committee*, December 13, 1819. Receipt of a letter from Rev. John West is noted, announcing his appointment as H.B.C. Chaplain, offering to carry out the objects of the Society and establish schools among the natives there. The Committee voted him £100 towards carrying out his plans. *Ibid.*, January 10, 1820: Doubts were recorded concerning the suitability of the Red River site for the Society's work, and instructions were addressed to the secretary to confer with Mr. West about his becoming a missionary of the Society. *Ibid.*, February 14, 1820: A letter from Mr. West stated that under certain circumstances he would consider becoming an agent of the Society.

CHAPTER ONE

John West: Pioneer

❖❖❖❖❖❖❖❖❖❖

In my appointment to the Company, my instructions were to reside at the Red River Settlement, and under the incouragement and aid of the Church Missionary Society, I was to seek the instruction and endeavour to meliorate the condition of the native Indians.[1]

REV. JOHN WEST'S JOURNAL

❖❖❖❖❖❖❖❖❖❖

The voyage itself was not without its anxieties, as well as those pleasant and unpleasant experiences that confront all travellers setting out into the unknown. Mr. West watched the shores of England and Scotland pass by, as he paced the deck of the *Eddystone*: "The thought that I was now leaving all that was dear to me upon earth, to encounter the perils of the ocean and the wilderness, sensibly affected me at times; but my feelings were relieved in the sanguine hope that I was borne on my way under the guidance of a kind protecting Providence, and that the circumstances of the country whither I was bound, would soon admit of my being surrounded by my family."[2] One Sunday had already been spent at sea, and he had held morning and afternoon services on board. The second Sunday was spent in Stromness harbour in the Orkneys, where the singing of the Old Hundredth Psalm attracted the attention of those on other ships lying in the harbour, "a most interesting and gratifying sight." The ships were hardly a hundred miles out into the Atlantic on their way west when they encountered a strong head wind, with the inevitable result: "Several on board with myself were greatly affected by the motion of the ship. It threw me into such a state of languor, that I felt as though I could have willingly yielded to have been cast overboard."[3] On July 22 the *Eddystone* entered Hudson Strait; the first iceberg was seen and the beauty of "iceblink" noted. On Sunday, July 23, West continued: "I preached in the morning, catechized the young people in the afternoon, and had divine service in the evening, as was our custom . . . it afforded me much pleasure to witness the sailors at times in groups reading the life of Newton, or some religious tracts which I put in their hands. The Scotch I found generally well and scripturally informed, and several of them joined the young people in reading to me the New Testament, and answering the catechetical questions."[4]

[1]John West, *The Substance of a Journal* (London, 1827), 1.
[2]*Ibid.*, 2.
[3]*Ibid.*, 4.
[4]*Ibid.*, 6.

During the next three weeks the voyage was much impeded by ice and fog, and progress at times was very slow and hazardous. Towards the end of the month a large flotilla of Eskimo craft was encountered, and Mr. West was able to observe these people for the first time. He would like to have read to them from a copy of the Gospels in Eskimo, which he had with him, and so have ascertained whether they had had any contact with the Moravian missionaries on the Labrador coast, "but such was the haste, bustle and noise of their intercourse with us, that I lost the opportunity."[5]

Arrival at York Factory

On the evening of the 13th (August) the sailors gave three cheers as we got under weigh on the opening of the ice by a strong northerly wind, and left the vast mass which had jammed us in for many days. The next day we saw the land, and came to the anchorage at York Flats the following morning (15th August) with sentiments of gratitude to God for His protecting Providence through the perils of the ice and of the seas, and for the little interruption in the duties of my profession from the state of the weather during the voyage.[6]

Mr. West's reception upon landing was a kindly one. The necessary arrangements were made for the servants of the Company to attend Divine Service twice on the following Sunday, August 20, and thus a Church of England Service was once more conducted on the shores of Hudson Bay by a Church of England clergyman, after a lapse of two hundred and forty-two years. Another thirty-four years were to pass before a permanent mission was established at this "water-gate" to the northwest of Canada. Successive Hudson's Bay Company Chaplains were to visit there in the course of duty; the first Bishop of Rupert's Land was to preach his first sermon in his new Diocese in a great room in this Fort; well-known missionaries and many, whose names and work are now almost forgotten, were to come and go through York, bound on their Master's business; but for the moment the work of the Church lay inland.

The first few days at York Factory were spent in profitable observation, the results of which have travelled along an unbroken line to our own day, for Mr. West had keen perceptions and an ingenious mind, which motivated quick action:

Observing a number of half-breed children running about, growing up in ignorance and idleness; and being informed that they were a numerous offspring of Europeans by Indian women, and found at all the Company's posts: I drew up a plan which I submitted to the Governor, for collecting a certain number of them, to be maintained, clothed and educated upon a regularly organized system. It was transmitted by him to the Committee of the Hudson's Bay Company, whose

[5]*Ibid.*, 9.
[6]*Ibid.*, 11, 12.

benevolent feelings towards this neglected race, had induced them to send several schoolmasters to the country fifteen or sixteen years ago but who were unhappily diverted from their original purpose, and became engaged as fur traders.[7]

The benevolent feelings of the Honourable Company necessarily took time to materialize, owing to the unsettled times through which it was passing, and it was not until after the union with the North West Company that action was taken. The "Minutes of a Temporary Council held at York Factory, Northern Department of Rupert's Land, the Twentieth day of August, 1822," which form part of the "Bulger Correspondence,"[8] reveal (in a letter dated February 27) the anxiety felt by the Governor and Committee regarding the settlement of men with large families, who, under the scheme of amalgamation, would have to be discharged. Concern was also expressed for the numerous half-breed children whose parents had died or deserted them. "We consider that all these people ought to be removed to Red River, where the Catholics will naturally fall under the Roman Catholic Mission, which is established there, and the Protestants and such Orphan Children as fall to be maintained and clothed by the Company may be placed under the Protestant Establishment and Schools under the Rev. Mr. West." Further, in a letter dated March 8, 1822:

With respect to the Orphan Children there will be some expense at first in erecting buildings, etc. But if the elder Boys are employed in cultivation, and the girls and younger children at other works of industry, the expense will not be very considerable and their Religious Instruction and Education may be carried on at the same time. As the children grow up they may be apprenticed to the Respectable Settlers, who will afterwards support them in consideration of their labour for the term of their apprenticeship. Mr. West and his assistants will take charge of this part of the plan.[9]

A letter dated March 27, 1822, confirmed the directions given in the letter of February 27, enclosed a copy of a letter to Mr. West, and a copy of one to him from Mr. Harrison. The Council then passed a series of resolutions to carry out the instructions of the London Committee, directing Chief Factor Clarke to consult with Governor Bulger about commencing the necessary buildings, and to request the co-operation of West. The expenditure of £300 was authorized for

[7]*Ibid.*, 12. *Church Missionary Society Proceedings, 1821-22*, p. 312. Mr. West wrote this recommendation on August 19, 1820. The Governor of York Factory at that time was William Williams. *C.M.S. Proceedings, 1819-20*, p. 357 ff. Appendix xii (a) *Some Account of the Red River Settlement.* (b) *Proposals for the Establishment in the territories of the Hudson's Bay Company, for the instruction of the Indians.*

[8]E. H. Oliver, ed., *The Canadian North-west: Its Early Development and Legislative Records*, Vol. I (Publication of The Canadian Archives, No. 9, Ottawa, 1914), 638-639.

[9]*Ibid.*, 639-640.

the first year, and the employment of as many of the Company's servants as could be spared for the erection of the buildings.

Nothing seems to have come of the scheme, perhaps because of the influence of Governor Simpson, who at that time did not have the friendly attitude to missions, missionaries and education that he was to display ten years and more later. So far nothing has come to light to link this proposed school with the one actually established by West at the Red River Settlement, which is nearly always referred to in the records as "The Missionary School." The one idea that seems feebly to link the two may have been West's own. The pupils of the school were given small plots to cultivate, and West recorded that he "never saw European schoolboys more delighted than they were, in hoeing and planting their separate gardens." It was not until thirty years later that the early conception of practical education materialized in the Industrial School, which flourished at St. Andrew's under the encouraging care of Archdeacon Cockran, the skilled instruction of William West Kirkby and the paternal approval of Bishop Anderson.

First Contacts with Native Indians

West made his first contact with the native Indians at York Factory and was deeply moved by their condition. In his own words:

During my stay at this post, I visited several Indian families and no sooner saw them crowded together in their miserable-looking tents, than I felt a lively interest (as I anticipated) in their behalf. . . . The duty devolved upon me to seek to meliorate their sad condition, so degraded and emaciated, wandering in ignorance, and wearing away a short existence in one continued succession of hardships in procuring food. I was told of difficulties, and some spoke of impossibilities in the way of teaching them Christianity or the first rudiments of settled and civilized life. . . . I determined not to be intimidated. . . . If little hope could be cherished of the adult Indian . . . it appeared to me that a *wide* and *most extensive field,* presented itself for cultivation in the instruction of the native children. With the aid of an interpreter, I spoke to an Indian, Withewacapo, about taking two of his boys to the Red River Colony with me to educate and maintain. He yielded to my request; and I shall never forget the affectionate manner in which he brought the eldest boy in his arms, and placed him in the canoe on the morning of my departure from York Factory. His two wives, sisters, accompanied him to the water's edge, and while they stood gazing on us, as the canoe was paddled from the shore, I considered that I bore a pledge from the Indian that many more children might be found, if an establishment were formed in British Christian sympathy, and British liberality for their education and support. I had to establish the principle, that the North American Indian of these regions would part with his children, to be educated in white man's knowledge and religion. . . .[10]

[10]John West, *The Substance of a Journal,* 13-15. *C. M. S. Proceedings, 1821-22:* Diary of Rev. John West, August 20, 1820.

The little son of Withewacapo apparently grew up successfully in his new environment at Red River, for in the old St. John's Cathedral (Winnipeg) Register, Baptismal Entry No. 200, dated July 21, 1822, reads: "James Hope, an Indian boy about 9 years of age taught in the Missionary School and now capable of reading the New Testament and repeating the Church of England Catechism correctly. John West." Almost a year later,[11] West baptized three more Indian boys, the first of whom was John Hope, the other son of Withewacapo. Entry 273 simply describes him as "an Indian boy in the Church Missionary Establishment." Both boys, when they grew up, entered the service of the Hudson's Bay Company, and there is evidence of their being in the Mackenzie River valley, for a note in the same Register reads: "Marriage at Fort Simpson, 23rd May, 1846, before M. McPherson, J. P. & G. in Indian Territory between John Hope and Arcaise Dujardais." One of the witnesses was James Hope.[12]

By River and Lake to the Settlement

West travelled from York Factory to the Red River Settlement by the usual route of the Hayes River, Steele River and Hill River to Oxford House, but his journal says little of his experiences on the way except to remark upon the shoals, strong currents and the high banks of the Hill River that caused so much trouble to the "trackers" that they were heard "to execrate the man who first found out such way into the interior."[13] The general impression he received was unpleasant: "The blasphemy of the men, in the difficulties they had to encounter was truly painful to me. I had hoped better things of the Scotch, from their known moral and enlightened education, but their horrid imprecations proved a degeneracy of character in an Indian country."[14] Nor did he find their attitude to women any more satisfactory. "They do not admit them as their companions, nor do they allow them to eat at their tables, but degrade them merely as slaves to their arbitrary inclinations; while the children grow up as wild and uncultivated as the heathen."[15]

[11]June 8, 1823.
[12]*Church Missionary Society Record, 1854*, p. 41. James Hope is reported as being at Red Deer Lake in 1853, instructing twenty-five children, and in touch with Rev. Robert Hunt, then in charge of the mission at Lac la Ronge. *Rae's Arctic Correspondence*, Hudson's Bay Record Society: Appendix, p. 399. Biography of James Hope. Thomas Hope, a younger brother of James and John (who also went to the C.M.S. school at Red River) was baptized September 11, 1834, and joined the H.B.C. as a labourer in 1844 (*Ibid.*, 360). Their father, Withewacapo, appears to have settled at the Indian Settlement, Red River, in his later years. He was baptized William Hope, October 1, 1834, and buried on December 15, 1836.
[13]John West, *The Substance of a Journal*, 15.
[14]*Ibid.*, 15.
[15]*Ibid.*, 15-16.

The matter of working on Sunday worried him: "It often grieved me, in our hurried passage, to see the men employed in taking the goods over the carrying places, or in rowing, during the Sabbath."[16] Twenty years later this latter point was to become one of some controversy between the Honourable Company and some of its missionary allies, particularly the early Methodists. It was perhaps easy to keep Sunday at the Fort, but on the trail of the canoe the summer season was short, the journeys long and slow; the natural demand for all the haste that could be made meant long days and continuous effort if the brigades were to make their round trips successfully.

The arrival of the party at Norway House, close by what is now called Warren's Landing, on October 4, was a welcome relief to its members. Here, not only was the scanty stock of provisions replenished for the voyage over "the fine body of water [which] burst on your view in Lake Winnipeg," but more important: "I obtained another boy for education, reported to me as the orphan son of a deceased Indian and a half-caste woman; and taught him the prayer which the other used morning and evening and which he soon learned:— 'Great Father, bless me, through Jesus Christ.' May a gracious God hear their cry, and raise them up as heralds of his salvation in this truly benighted and barbarous part of the world." This prayer was truly answered, for the boy was baptized on July 21, 1822, with the name of Henry Budd; eighteen years later he was to become the first native catechist and teacher at The Pas, and ten years after that the first native deacon to be ordained by the first Bishop of Rupert's Land.

York Factory had been left very early in September, before the seventh. It had taken nearly four weeks to get to Norway House. The snow was on the ground and the weather getting wintry when West's party started out on October 6 in open boats to cross the three hundred and fifty miles of Lake Winnipeg, which lay between them and the mouth of the Red River. The voyage was not without an unpleasant incident. The course taken was always fairly close to the rocky eastern shore, for the sake of camping at night, and on this occasion West's boat struck a rock when in full sail, but fortunately without being wrecked. About sunrise, on October 13, the boats entered the river and proceeded as far up as Netley Creek. Here West met Pegewys (Peguis), the local Salteaux chief, who produced a testimonial from Lord Selkirk stating that he had been "a steady friend of the settlement ever since its first establishment," and who told him he wished that "more of the stumps and brushwood were cleared away for my [West's] feet, in coming to see his country."

The banks of the Red River offered a pleasing contrast to the forest

16 Ibid., 17.

of pine and spruce through which the earlier part of the voyage from York Factory had been made.

On the 14th October we reached the settlement, consisting of a number of huts widely scattered along the margin of the river; in vain did I look for a cluster of cottages, where the hum of a small population at least might be heard as in a village. I saw but few marks of human industry in the cultivation of the soil. Almost every inhabitant we passed bore a gun upon his shoulder and all appeared in a wild and hunter-like state.[17]

First Days at the Red River Settlement

John West had a happy knack of condensation in writing the journal that has been already quoted so often, but no better description of his early days in the Settlement could be written than his own:

There was an unfinished building as a Catholic church, and a small house adjoining, the residence of the priest, but no Protestant manse, Church or school house, which obliged me to take up my abode at the Colony Fort [Fort Douglas] where the "Charge d'Affaires" of the settlement [Alexander McDonnell] resided, and who kindly afforded accommodation of a room for divine service on the sabbath. [October 15, 1820, would be the date of the first Service.] My ministry was generally well-attended by all the settlers; and soon after my arrival I got a log-house repaired about three miles below the Fort, among the Scotch population, where the schoolmaster took up his abode, and began teaching from twenty to twenty-five children.[18]

West was, of course, estimating the distance from Fort Douglas by river; the schoolmaster was George Harbidge, who had come out from England with him. A little more than two years later, for the wedding took place on October 22, 1822, George Harbidge was married to Elizabeth Bowden, when she arrived from England. Mr. and Mrs. Harbidge continued to look after the school until they returned to England in the summer of 1825. The Reverend A. C. Garrioch, grandson of William Garrioch who had become schoolmaster in 1825, quotes with marked approval in his book *The Correction Line* the words of Donald Gunn, well-known Manitoba historian: "We are not prepared to say what progress they made, but this we will say, that the elementary school established by Mr. West for the instruction of a few Indian boys was the germ whence originated all the Protestant schools and colleges in Manitoba at the present time."[19]

Early in December West removed to the farm that had belonged to Lord Selkirk. It lay about three miles west of Fort Douglas, six miles

[17]*Ibid.*, 21.
[18]*Ibid.*, 27. *Church Missionary Society Proceedings 1821-22*, Diary of Rev. John West, November 1, 1820. The log cabin was repaired and opened as a school on November 1, 1820.
[19]Gunn and Tuttle, *History of Manitoba* (1880), 201.

from the school. "Though more comfortable in my quarters, than at the Fort, the distance put me to much inconvenience in my professional duties." Sunday services were continued, presumably still at the Fort, with some result. "Having frequently enforced the moral and social obligation of marriage upon those who were living with, and had families by Indian or half-caste women, I had the happiness to perform the ceremony for several of the more respectable of the settlers, under the conviction *that the institution of marriage and the security of property, were fundamental laws of society.* I also had many baptisms. . . ."[20]

His work, however, was constantly impeded by want of education on the part of those he was trying to instruct:

This difficulty produced in me a strong desire to extend the blessings of education to them; and from this period it became a leading object with me, to erect in a central situation, a substantial building, which would contain apartments for the schoolmaster, afford accommodation for Indian children, be a day-school for the half-caste adult population who would attend, and fully answer the purpose of a church for the present, until a brighter prospect arose in the Colony, and the inhabitants were more congregated. I became anxious to see such a building arise as a Protestant landmark of Christianity in a vast field of heathenism and general depravity of manners, and cheerfully gave my hand and my heart to perfect the work. I expected a willing co-operation from the Scotch settlers, but was disappointed in my sanguine hopes of their cheerful and persevering assistance, through their prejudices against the English Liturgy, and the simple rites of our communion. I visited them however in their affliction, and performed all ministerial duties as their Pastor while my motto was—Perseverance.[21]

Winter Journey to Beaver Creek, Qu'Appelle

Early in 1821 West turned his attention to duties that lay outside the Red River Settlement. As Chaplain to the Hudson's Bay Company his instructions were "to afford religious instruction and consolation to the servants in the active employment of the Hudson's Bay Company, as well as to the Company's retired servants, and other inhabitants of the settlement, upon such occasions as the nature of the country and other circumstances would permit."[22] On January 15 he left the Forks, where the Red River is joined by the Assiniboine, and set out west on his first experience of winter travelling on the wind-swept, snow-covered prairie. The party was a light one. West travelled in a cariole drawn by three dogs, accompanied by a sledge with two dogs to carry the baggage and provisions, and two men as drivers. The fifteen miles covered on the first day brought the party

[20]John West, *The Substance of a Journal*, 25-26.
[21]*Ibid.*, 26-37.
[22]*Ibid.*, 30.

to a bluff about half way between the present villages of Headingley and St. François Xavier.

On January 19 the going was heavy because of drifting snow, but West shot some ptarmigans, which were welcome because provisions were getting short. Traces of buffalo were seen, and wolves followed their trail. Brandon House was reached on January 20, and on the Sunday service was held at eleven o'clock. At six, the chief officer of the post, John Richard McKay, was married and his two children were baptized. The following morning Mr. West saw for the first time an Indian corpse staged, and after commenting upon the Indian customs he remarked: "I could not but reflect that theirs is a sorrow without hope: all is *gross darkness* with them as to futurity: and they wander through life without the consolatory and cheering influence of that gospel which has brought life and immortality to life."[23]

Before leaving Brandon House he married two more of the Company's servants and baptized a number of children. As their parents could read, he left with them Bibles, Testaments and religious tracts. On January 24 he started for Qu'Appelle, McKay sending two armed servants with him as there was a band of Stoney Indians in the neighbourhood who "had acted in a turbulent manner at the post two days before." The Stoney Indians at that time had the reputation of being great thieves and attacking small parties of white people for the sake of plunder.

On the afternoon of January 27 John West arrived at what he described as Beaver Creek, Qu'Appelle, a few miles below the junction of the Qu'Appelle River with the Assiniboine, and only a little south of where later Fort Ellice was established. Here, he saw for the first time the full effect of alcohol on the plains Indian:

About the same time, a large band of Indians came to the fort from the plains with provisions. Many of them rode good horses, caparisoned with a saddle or pad of dressed skins, stuffed with buffalo wool, from which were suspended wooden stirrups; and a leathern thong, tied at both ends to the under jaw of the animal, formed a bridle. When they had delivered their loads, they paraded the fort with an air of independence. It was not long however before they became clamorous for spirituous liquors; and the evening presented such a bacchanalia, as I never before witnessed. Drinking made them quarrelsome, and one of the men became so infuriated, that he would have killed another with his bow, had not the master of the post immediately rushed in and taken it from him.

West spent three days at this Qu'Appelle post, including the Sunday, on which services were held twice; he married several of the Company's

[23]*Ibid.*, 33.

servants to their native or half-breed wives and baptized their children. "I explained to them the nature and obligations of marriage and baptism; and distributed among them some Bibles and Testaments and religious tracts." Before leaving he was introduced to the chief of the tribe of Indians, who welcomed him with a hearty shake of the hand when he learned the object of the missionary's purpose in his country, "while others came round me, and stroked my head, as a fond father would his favourite boy." He was impressed by the fact that they were strong, athletic men, generally well-proportioned; their countenances were pleasing with aquiline noses and beautifully white and regular teeth.[24]

Qu'Appelle was left on January 30 and the night was spent at an encampment of Indians, some of whom were employed by the Hudson's Bay Company as hunters. They welcomed him with much cordiality. "We smoked a calumet as a token of friendship; and a plentiful supply of buffalo tongues was prepared for supper." Here West found another boy for his school at Red River: "As we were starting the next morning I observed a fine looking little boy standing by the side of the cariole, and told his father if he would send him to me at the Settlement by the first opportunity, I would be as a parent to him, clothe him, and feed him, and teach him what I knew would be for his happiness, with the Indian boys I had already under my care." Early that summer the boy's father did bring him to the Settlement and he was one of the last three boys baptized by John West on June 8, 1823, with the name of Joseph Harbidge, just before he left for England. Unhappily, the boy died early in the spring of 1825 and was buried in the Upper Churchyard, a circumstance that will be recalled later.

Brandon House was reached again on February 3 and Sunday was spent there; services were again held and more children baptized. On the morning of the sixth:

I got into the cariole very early, and the rising sun gradually opened to my view the beautiful and striking scenery. All nature appeared silently and impressively to proclaim the goodness and wisdom of God. Day unto day the revolutions of that glorious orb which shed a flood of light over the impenetrable forest and wild wastes that surrounded me uttereth speech. Yet His voice is not heard among the heathen, nor His name known throughout these vast territories by Europeans in general but to swear by. . . . Oh! for wisdom, truly Christian faith, integrity and zeal in my labours as a minister, in this heathen *and moral desert*.[25]

[24]*Ibid.*, 38.
[25]*Ibid.*, 42-43. *Church Missionary Society Proceedings*, 1821-22, Diary of Rev. John West. Entries here confirm his destination as having been Beaver Creek.

The journey was finished in a blizzard, but the farm was reached about five o'clock on February 9, "with grateful thanks to God, for protecting me through a perilous journey, drawn by dogs over the snow a distance of between five and six hundred miles among some of the most treacherous tribes of Indians in this northern wilderness."

Journey to Pembina

March 12, 1821, saw Mr. West getting into his cariole again, this time to attend a meeting of the Settlers at Pembina, more properly Fort Daer, which had been called to consider the best means of protection, and of resisting any attack that might be made by any of the Sioux Indians who had been reported to have hostile intentions against the colony in the spring. "The 18th being the Sabbath, I preached to a considerable number of persons assembled at the fort. They heard me with great attention; but I was often depressed in mind, at the general view of character, and at the spectacle of human depravity and barbarism I was called to witness."[26]

This was only a short trip. "On the 22nd I reached the farm [Lord Selkirk's], and from the expeditious mode of travelling over the snow, I began to think, as is common among the Indians, that one hundred miles was little more than a step, or in fact but a short distance." The pace and endurance of the drivers astonished him, but he was appalled by the way they beat their dogs, by their blasphemous language, and their incessant smoking.

Springtime in the Settlement

With the coming of spring, Mr. West returned to his idea of erecting a permanent building sixty feet by twenty feet for his school and church. The Red River appeared to him to be the most desirable spot for a missionary establishment and schools, from whence Christianity might arise and be projected amongst the numerous tribes of the north. The settlers were busy on their land and he had congregations of more than a hundred on May 20, when their children from the school were present for public examination and gave general satisfaction in their answers to questions from the "Chief Truths of the Christian Religion and Lewis' Catechism."[27] He was cheered by the arrival of the little boy from Qu'Appelle on May 25, which gave him a stimulus towards his proposed building, but "there was but little willing assistance . . . towards this desirable object; as few possessed any active spirit of public improvement; and the general habits of the people being those of lounging and smoking, were but little favourable to voluntary exercise."

[26]John West, The Substance of a Journal, 44.
[27]Ibid., 58-59.

June 20 brought mail from England via Montreal and Lake
Superior, and West learned that his family were all well. "It was my
intention that they should have embarked with me in my mission to
this country, but circumstances prevented it; and now that I was
surrounded with unexpected difficulties, situated in the very heart of
an Indian territory, most difficult of access, and without military protection, I deemed it most advisable that they should defer the voyage,
in the hope that another year might lessen these difficulties, and bring
a better arrangement for the prosperity of the colony. I could undergo
privations, and enter upon any arduous official duty, for the best
interests of the natives and the settlers; but I could not subject Mrs.
West (and infant children) to the known existing trials of the country,
whose useful talents would otherwise have greatly aided me in the
formation and superintendence of schools."[28]

York Factory and the Bible Society

The same purpose for which Mr. West visited Qu'Appelle in January
took him in the summer of 1821 back to York Factory; he wished to
meet as many as possible of the servants of the Company. Moreover,
the late Earl of Selkirk had personally suggested this annual visit to
Norway House and York Factory because "a great number of their
servants are assembled at this place, for a few weeks in summer, and
have no other opportunity for any public religious instruction."[29] He
spent two days at Norway House, holding a service there on August 12,
after which he baptized between twenty and thirty children and
married two of the Company's servants. At Norway House, also, he
met two distinguished men whose names rank high in the history of
the fur trade, and he apparently travelled with them to York Factory.
These two gentlemen were Mr. Nicholas Garry, Deputy Governor
of the Hudson's Bay Company, and Mr. Simon McGillivray, a
prominent member of the North West Company, and one of the
signatories to the Deed of Co-Partnership. They were on their way
to York Factory to execute the delicate and difficult mission of con-
summating the union that had been arranged between the two companies, and to iron out any problems that might arise amongst the fur
traders themselves. Mr. West felt that this coalition between the two
companies would be highly encouraging in the attempt to better the
conditions of the native Indians, and likely to remove many of the
evils that had prevailed during what he mildly described as the
"ardour of opposition."

A noteworthy event took place during Mr. Garry's visit to York

[28]*Ibid.*, 61.
[29]*Ibid.*, 64.

Factory, which is best described in Mr. West's own words: "During my stay at the Factory, several marriages and Baptisms took place; and it was no small encouragement to me in my ministerial labours, to have the patronage and cordial co-operation of the Director I had the pleasure of meeting, in establishing an Auxiliary Bible Society, for Prince Rupert's Land and the Red River Settlement. It was formed with great liberality on the part of the Company's officers, who met on the occasion; and more than one hundred and twenty pounds were immediately subscribed, in aid of an institution (The British and Foreign Bible Society) which justly challenges the admiration of the world."

There is an interesting letter in McGill University written by Mr. James Leith from Fort Chipiwian [sic] on February 7, 1822, to Mr. Robert McVicar, then Chief Trader in charge of the Company's post at Slave Lake. Mr. Leith commended the work of the newly-formed Branch of the Bible Society to the patronage of his friend, remarking that their absence from the meeting had prevented their having their "names and mite registered among the founders of the philanthropic institution in this wild country." Leith and McVicar could then only show that their generosity was equal to that of their friends, "in support of an institution that embraces such universal sentiments of benevolence to the human species, as that of distributing to them the only sacred Records extant, which certainly in the estimation of all rational beings, must exceed all other worldly gifts."[30] This concern for the welfare of the natives Leith continued to feel as time went on, and it was money derived from his estate that enabled the Bishopric of Rupert's Land to be founded.

The return journey to the Red River was an unpleasant one; owing to a boat wreck, in which no lives were lost, the party was detained six or seven days, and ran very short of provisions. Mr. West experienced at times "a most pressing hunger," having scarcely anything else to eat but a little boiled barley. However, Chief Pegewis received them hospitably when they got to his camp near the mouth of the Red River, giving them a good supply of dried sturgeon.

Upon his return to the colony, West was disappointed to find that no progress had been made with the proposed schoolhouse, and that both Mr. Harbidge and his scholars had gone into residence at Upper Fort Garry, where neither the number of scholars was as large, nor did as many attend the services on Sunday, owing to the distance of the fort from the residences of the settlers. He notes with some pleasure that he had found copies of the Scriptures at some of the

[30]Rupert's Land Archives (hereafter R.L.A.), James Leith Correspondence and Papers.

Company's posts, and the Book of Common Prayer, provided through the interest of one of the directors of the Company. The generosity of the Bible Society had enabled him to distribute copies of the Bible amongst the colonists in *English, Gaelic, German, Danish and French,* none receiving them more gratefully than the Highlanders; but there was considerable active opposition by the Roman Catholic priests to this circulation of the Scriptures.

At Christmas that year there was the usual merriment (at times excessive), but "Divine Service was held at the Fort: Text, Luke II, 8 to 11." The Indian boys repeated some hymns and joined in the singing of the Hallelujah! to the "Emmanuel, which being interpreted is, God with us." He adds in his journal, "I meet with many discouraging circumstances in my ministerial labours; but my path is sometimes cheered with the pleasant hope, that they are not altogether in vain; and that the light of Christianity will break in upon the heathen darkness that surrounds me. *The promises of God are sure;* and when cast down, I am not disheartened."[31]

The Winter and Spring of 1822

The early months of 1822 were ones of privation in the Settlement, and Mr. West reports that "Our principal subsistence is from grain boiled into soup"; even fish were unusually scarce. The Swiss immigrants, who had come in 1821, were particularly disheartened, and many of them were planning to leave in the spring for the United States. However, they were appreciative of the Church: "They attended Divine Service on the Sabbath during my stay, and expressed much gratitude for my reading to them the French Testament and the ministerial duties I performed among them." The spring thaw came unexpectedly early, about March 25, and brought general rejoicing in the colony. This joy was considerably increased when it was learned that the settlers would receive seed wheat from the Company, as their own supplies were now exceedingly short. About this time West accompanied to Pembina a small party that set out to prevent a large band of Sioux from coming to the colony. He was quite impressed with these people, but alarmed by their ferocious conduct and the savage fury of their passions, which he felt to be but another argument for the introduction and influence of Christianity.

About the end of May the boats arrived from Qu'Appelle, bringing another boy for the school. West observed in his journal that the interest he was taking in the education of the natives was beginning to excite the fears of some of the chief factors and traders as to the extent to which it might be carried.

[31]John West, *The Substance of a Journal,* 77.

Though a few conversed liberally with me on the subject, there were others who were apprehensive that the extension of knowledge among the natives, and the locating them in agricultural pursuits, where practicable, would operate as an injury to the fur trade. My reply on the contrary was, that if Christian knowledge were gradually diffused among the natives throughout the vast territory of the Hudson's Bay Company, from the shores of the Atlantic to those of the North Pacific, it would best promote the honour and advantages of all parties concerned in the fur trade, and which I was persuaded was the general enlightened opinion of the Directors in London.[32]

First Church in the Settlement

The end of June brought mail from England with good news of his family and information that "A liberal provision had been made, for a missionary establishment at the Red River, for the maintenance and education of native Indian children, by the Church Missionary Society." A few days later Mr. John Halkett arrived, one of the brothers-in-law of the late Earl of Selkirk, executor of his estate and a director of the Hudson's Bay Company. West seems to have spent considerable time with him that summer, as they first went to Pembina together and later to York Factory. Mr. Halkett did much during his visit to improve the conditions of the settlers, and tried to ensure their future prosperity. While he was still in the colony, West took the opportunity of opening, with divine service, the unfinished building that was intended as a schoolhouse and a temporary place for divine worship. At the same time he baptized two of the boys who had been under his charge, one as James Hope, and the other as Henry Budd; they being able "to read the New Testament, repeat the Church Catechism and to understand the chief principles of the Christian religion." This took place, according to the entry in the register, on July 21, 1822. This day, the Seventh Sunday after Trinity in that year, must be regarded as an outstanding date in the history of the Church of England in Rupert's Land.[33]

York Factory Again

Mr. West's annual journey to York Factory that year was taken by a somewhat different route, as the party reached Lake Winnipeg by way of Lake Manitoba and the Dauphin River. He remarked on the "striking and romantic scenery" through which they passed, and speculated upon the possibility of encouraging a tribe of Indians who traversed the area, and had already shown some inclination to settle by growing potatoes and pumpkins, to turn into permanent good

[32]*Ibid.*, 92.
[33]*Ibid.*, 96. Also, St. John's Cathedral, Winnipeg, Registers: Entries Nos. 200 and 201.

settlers under the superintendence of a resident missionary. Twenty years later the experiment was begun when the Reverend Abraham and Mrs. Cowley opened the mission, now known as Fairford, on the Little Dauphin River. This visit of Mr. West to York Factory is of particular interest because it was upon this occasion that he came into close personal association with Captain John Franklin and the members of his expedition to the Coppermine River; at the time they were awaiting the arrival of the ship to take them back to England. Captain Franklin assisted at the first anniversary meeting of the Auxiliary Bible Society, which in its first year had raised the large sum of £200.0.6d., and was well started on its second year's career with another £60 subscribed at the meeting. At this time West saw much of an Eskimo named Augustus, who had been one of Franklin's guides and understood English fairly well, even speaking it a little. Augustus urged that teachers should be sent to his people at Fort Churchill, and after consulting Captain Franklin, who was keenly interested in these people, and Governor Simpson, West determined that he would visit Fort Churchill the following year.

When the ship arrived it brought Miss Elizabeth Bowden who was on her way to Red River, with the consent and blessing of both the Hudson's Bay Company and the Church Missionary Society, to marry Mr. George Harbidge, the schoolmaster. She was to become the first qualified schoolmistress in western Canada, for she had received her training according to the requirements of the time at the Central School in London, England. Mr. West was able to place under her care a little boy and girl from an Indian tent at the Factory, but it appears that the little girl was not altogether Indian, a circumstance that led West to consider what might happen if such children in general remained uneducated and uncared for, and he expressed the fear that if this should happen "it cannot be a matter of surprise, if at any time hereafter they should collectively or in parties, threaten the peace of the country and the safety of the trading Posts."[34]

The return trip from York Factory appears to be the pleasantest that West experienced.

On the 5th of October we reached the encampment of Pigewis, the chief of the Red River Indians, and on pitching our tents for the night a little way farther upon the banks of the river, he came with his eldest son and another Indian and drank tea with me in the evening. It was the first time that I had met with him, since I received the encouraging information from the Church Missionary Society, relative to the Mission School at the Colony, and I was glad of the opportunity of assuring him, through the aid of an interpreter, who

[34]John West, The Substance of a Journal, 100.

was of our party, "that many, very many in my country wished the Indians to be taught white man's knowledge of the Great Spirit, and as a proof of their love to them, my countrymen had told me to provide for the clothing, maintenance, and education of many of their children; and had sent out the young person whom he then saw to teach the little girls who might be sent to the school for instruction. . . . Though not easily persuaded that you act from benevolent motives; he said *it was good!* and promised to tell all his tribe what I said about the children, and that I should have two of his boys to instruct in the Spring, but added, that 'the Indians like to have time to consider about these matters.' We smoked the calumet, and after pausing a short time, he shrewdly asked me what I would do with the children after they were taught what I wished them to know. I told him they might return to their parents if they wished it, but my hope was that they would see the advantage of making gardens, and cultivating the soil, so as not to be exposed to hunger and starvation, as the Indians generally were, who had to wander and hunt for their provisions. The little girls, I observed, would be taught to knit, and make articles of clothing to wear, like those which white people wore; and all would be led to read the Book that the Great Spirit had given to them, which the Indians had not yet known, and which would teach them how to live well and to die happy. I added, that it was the will of the Great Spirit, which he had declared in His Book 'that a man should have but one wife, and a woman but one husband.' He smiled at this information, and said that 'he thought that there was no more harm in Indians having two wives than one of the settlers,' whom he named. I grieved for the depravity of Europeans as noticed by the heathen, and as raising a stumbling block in the way of their receiving instruction, and our conversation closed upon the subject by my observing, that 'there were some very bad white people, as there were some very bad Indians, but that good book condemned the practice.' [35]

The Last Year

On March 17 he left by dog team for the Company's post at Bas la Rivière, close to what is now Fort Alexander, and on his way back had the misfortune to get lost on Lake Winnipeg for nearly two days before the right direction was found. By this time the driver was nearly snow-blind and incapable of driving the dogs, which were exhausted, while the weather was becoming more cold and stormy. But all ended well when they found their way into the river.

In the spring two small houses were added to the Church Missionary

[35]*Ibid.*, 102-104. *Church Missionary Society Proceedings, 1821-22*, 54. On January 28, 1922, the Committee resolved to establish the North West America Mission. *Ibid.*, 211: Memorandum that was presented to this committee by Benjamin Harrison. Society for the Propagation of the Gospel Archives, (hereafter S.P.G.A.), *Minute Books*, XXXIII, 254. Meeting on March 15, 1822: "Read an application by the Governor of the H.B.C. soliciting the aid of the Society in furnishing them with a missionary or in donation for the erection of a church at the Settlement on the Red River at Lake Winnipeg. Agreed to recommend that the Govr. be informed that under the present circumstances of the Society they cannot extend their operations in those regions beyond the Diocese of Quebec."

School as separate sleeping apartments for the Indian children. Great care was taken to encourage the children in gardening, as it was felt that "a child brought up in the love of cultivating a garden will be naturally led to culture of the field as means of subsistence; and educated in the principles of Christianity, he will become stationary to partake of the advantages and privileges of civilization." The Sunday School, by this time, was generally attended by nearly fifty scholars, independent of the Indian children, and the congregation varied in number from one hundred to one hundred and thirty persons.

It is a most gratifying sight to see the colonists, in groups, direct their steps on the Sabbath morning towards the Mission House, at the ringing of the bell, which is now elevated in a spire that is attached to the building. . . . I never witness the Establishment but with peculiar feelings of delight, and contemplate it as the dawn of a brighter day in the dark interior of a moral wilderness. The lengthened shadows of the setting sun cast upon the buildings, as I returned from calling upon some of the settlers a few evenings ago; and the consideration that there was now a landmark of Christianity in this wild waste of heathenism, raised in my mind a pleasing train of thought. . . . I considered it as no small point gained, to have a public building dedicated to religious purposes, whose spire should catch the eye, both of the wandering natives and the stationary colonists.

The End of John West's Ministry at Red River

Mr. West's last Sunday at the Red River Settlement was marked by the baptism of three boys, John Hope, the second son of Withewacapo; James Harbidge and Charles Pratt, who are all described as Indian boys on the Church Missionary Establishment. Reference has already been made to James Harbidge as the first boy from the Qu'Appelle Valley; John Hope lived until 1894 and was for many years Indian Catechist in the neighbourhood of Battleford, Saskatchewan; Charles Pratt spent most of his life in similar work in the Qu'Appelle Valley, Touchwood Hills and the Red Pheasant Reserve. Thus did the seed sown by John West take root and blossom.

The following Tuesday he held a farewell service:

On the 10th, I addressed a crowded congregation, in a farewell discourse, from the pulpit, previous to my leaving the colony for the Factory: and having administered the Sacrament to those who joined cordially with me in prayer, that the Missionary who was on his way to officiate in my absence, might be ten-fold, yea one hundred-fold, more blessed in his ministry than I had been, I parted with those upon the Church Missionary Establishment with tears. It had been a long, and anxious, and arduous scene of labour to me; and my hope was, as about to embark for England that I might return to the

Settlement and be the means of effecting a better order of things.[36]
The weather was favourable on the morning of our departure; and
stepping into the boat the current soon bore us down the river towards
Lake Winnipeg. As the spire of the Church receded from my view,
and we passed several of the houses of the settlers, they hailed me
with their cordial wishes for a safe voyage, and expressed a hope of
better times for the Colony.[37]

First Mission to the Eskimos

It was upon the advice of Captain John Franklin that John West
decided to travel on foot from York Factory to Fort Churchill,
although the distance was over one hundred and eighty miles; it was
thought too hazardous to try to proceed by canoe while the Bay itself
was still choked with ice. West has left an interesting account of his
journey, which began on July eleventh and ended on the twentieth,
and the way in which they had to contend with mosquitoes, cold nights
and depend upon their guns for their supply of food. This portion of
his diary is one of the few places in which he enters into any great
detail as an observer of nature, although on many occasions his
descriptions of Indian life are both pointed and shrewd. In travelling
to Fort Churchill he seems to have enjoyed a special exhilaration:
"I thought it a high privilege to *visit even* the wild inhabitants of the
rocks with the *simple design* of extending the Redeemer's kingdom
among them; and that in a remote corner of the globe, where probably
no Protestant minister had ever placed his foot before."[38] West spent
as much time as possible in the company of Augustus, who was waiting
for his family to arrive from the north, and a family of Eskimos already
there, the chief member of which was named Achshannook, from
whom he seems to have acquired a great many details about Eskimo
life and habits, and to whom he imparted a considerable amount of
Christian instruction, besides pointing out the many advantages of
Christian civilization.[39]

As usual John West's mind turned to the building of a school, and
he seems tentatively to have suggested the erection of one at Knapp's
Bay, about two hundred miles north of Churchill. From Churchill
building materials might be taken; also dry provisions in casks to
maintain the party at the first making of such a settlement, independent of the common resources of the country and of the Eskimo. In
this idea West was undoubtedly a pioneer.[40]

Another Eskimo party came from Chesterfield Inlet and West joined
them for a few days at a point fifty miles north of Churchill, to watch

[36]West, *The Substance of a Journal*, 156-157.
[37]*Ibid.*, 157.
[38]*Ibid.*, 169.
[39]*Ibid.*, 176-179.
[40]*Ibid.*, 179-180.

them spear white whales. Here he was impressed with their cleanliness and friendliness, and in conversation explored their ideas about religion.

On August 12 Fort Churchill was left; York Factory was reached on the morning of the nineteenth, without any new incident having arisen. By this time the ship had arrived from England, and West had the happiness of meeting the Reverend David T. Jones on his way in to take up the work at the Red River Settlement. To his care were commended two little Chipewyan boys for the school, who had come down from Churchill.

John West Returns to England

It is characteristic of John West that his last recorded thoughts before leaving York Factory should have been upon the possibility of establishing a school and church there with a resident missionary; and not only there, but also at each of the important posts of the Company. At such places provisions would always be available for the support of a limited number of half-caste children, whose education and welfare ever were to West a primary problem; "and the most beneficial results might follow the regular performance of Divine Service on the Sabbath, by a clergyman, throughout the summer months at least, in a building erected and appropriated as a chapel.[41]

West left York Factory in the *Prince of Wales* on September 11, and the return home was accomplished by the middle of October, the Thames being reached on the twenty-fourth of that month. "Since my departure from England in May 1820, to this period of my return, not one accident have I met with, nor have I been called to experience a single day's illness. Though in perils oft by land and sea, and exposed to threatened dangers of the ice, and of the desert, still my life has been preserved. Praised be the Lord God of my Salvation."[42]

Envoy: 1823 - 1845

John West never returned to Rupert's Land, though it was evidently his intention to do so when he left York Factory in 1823, for he welcomed David Jones as his future fellow labourer.[43] He did, however, in 1825-1826 visit eastern Canada on behalf of the New England Company, which was at that time interested in the Mohawk Mission

[41]*Ibid.*, 192.
[42]*Ibid.*, 208.
[43]*Ibid.*, 191. E. E. Rich, *Hudson's Bay Company 1670-1870*, II, 454: It is suggested that George Simpson and West did not get on together—differed on important points of policy—and that it was the influence of Simpson with the London Committee that prevented West's return to the Red River. West never mentions Simpson in his Journal, neither does he at any time criticize the policy of the Honourable Company.

on the Grand River in southwestern Ontario. The rest of his life was spent at the Parish of Chettle in Dorsetshire, to which was added the adjoining Parish of Farnham, in 1834, at which time he became Chaplain to Viscount Duncannon. The last years of his life were devoted to the improvement and education of some other wanderers, namely, the English gypsies, for whose children he founded a considerable school in his own parish. A monument to him in the chancel of Chettle Church, erected after his death on December 31, 1845, recalls his work in Canada as the most important in his life.[44]

As the pioneer missionary in Rupert's Land, John West was called upon to lay foundations and meet difficult situations. It must be recognized that amongst the latter was the extreme disappointment felt by the Gaelic-speaking Scots settlers who had been promised a Presbyterian minister, and who did not approve of the forms, ceremonies and government of the Church of England. To these people Mr. West ministered as far as he was able and to the extent to which he was permitted. His two great contributions to the future of the work of the Church in Rupert's Land were his unceasing efforts to raise the moral tone of the whole community, and his care in fostering the religious instruction of the children, regardless of their parentage. The school that he founded in St. John's became the pattern for the parochial school system, which ultimately was to grow into the public school system. It also was the primary model of the modern Indian residential school. It was for his successor to develop an educational institution of another type, which was to have equally far-reaching results.

Few people looking at a picture of John West would suspect the strength of character behind those mild features, or the fertility of imagination in educational matters concealed beneath them, let alone the enthusiasm, energy, courage and persistence of the man himself. God truly raises up men to meet special situations, and the Church must always rejoice that the Gospel was here first preached and the teaching of the young commenced by such a man as John West.

[44]R.L.A., *Gentleman's Magazine* (February, 1846): Obituary Notice of Rev. John West, A.M.

CHAPTER TWO

David Thomas Jones: Evangelism and Education

❖⊷❖⊷❖⊷❖⊷❖⊷❖⊷❖⊷❖⊷❖⊷

It is sometimes profitable to dwell more at length on the history of the earlier Missionaries, their difficulties and their labours, partly that we may have a more clear and definite idea of the mission in all its subsequent workings, and partly that we may thankfully observe how God is pleased to raise up peculiar instruments for peculiar work, bestowing special gifts on those whom He employs in laying the foundations of His Church in a heathen land.

THE RAINBOW IN THE NORTH, *by Sarah Tucker*

❖⊷❖⊷❖⊷❖⊷❖⊷❖⊷❖⊷❖⊷

The Reverend David Thomas Jones, who succeeded the Reverend John West as the Chaplain of the Hudson's Bay Company at Red River, and general missionary in the district, was a Welshman. The first reference to him is found in the Church Missionary Society Committee Minutes of March 27, 1820: "A letter from Mr. Thomas Hassall of Lampeter[1] recommending as a missionary candidate, Mr. David Jones, age 22½, had been 2 years in Lampeter Seminary and hoped to qualify in 2 years. Letter from D. Jones expressing desire to be a missionary in New Zealand." The minutes of May 8 state: "D. Jones interviewed by Committee. Stated age to be 21. Was brought up to farming. RESOLVED: Jones accepted as missionary candidate. Allowed £45 p.a. not able to support himself." On March 26, 1821, it was further reported that Jones had been sent to study under the Reverend William Sharpe of Mattishall in Norfolk. It was to be four years before the establishment of the C.M.S. College at Islington, and in the meantime the Society's probationers were sent to study under the direction of private tutors who were in Orders. Mr. Jones was ordained deacon by the Bishop of London on December 22, 1822,

---

[1]Lampeter here refers to the name of the town or village. It must not be confused with St. David's College, Lampeter, to which reference is often made simply as "Lampeter." St. David's College was founded in 1822, but did not come into operation until 1827. The letters referred to are to be found in the Minutes and Files of The Committee of Correspondence of the Church Missionary Society in its Archives at 6 Salisbury Square, London EC 4. Work on these archives was not begun until about 1950, and the papers connected with the North West America Mission have not yet been reached in the process of arrangement (1961). They are available in the Church Missionary Society Archives (hereafter C.M.S.A.), in London, and a collection of them is on microfilm in the Public Archives of Canada (P.A.C.), Ottawa, and the Public Archives of Manitoba (P.A.M.), Winnipeg, but the only means of identifying any particular item is by its date.

and priested by the Bishop of Bristol by Letters Dismissary at Cambridge on April 13, 1823. He left England on May 31 on the *Prince of Wales* and arrived at the Red River on October 14, 1823, exactly three years to the day after the arrival of John West.

The Reverend David Jones entered upon his work under much more encouraging circumstances than did Mr. West. There was a church-cum-school, with belfry and bell complete, already in existence. The school was flourishing under the care of Mr. and Mrs. George Harbidge, and before he left the settlement Mr. West had arranged for the building of a parsonage close by. It is perhaps interesting to note some of the circumstances attending the latter. On March 1, 1823, Governor Bulger circulated the following:

Memorandum to be communicated to the Scotch Settlers.

All the settlers in the Red River being bound to contribute to the support of a Clergyman, I am of the opinion that such of the Scotch Settlers as do not belong to the Roman Catholic Communion should, while unprovided with a Gaelic Minister, give their assistance to the Protestant Minister, the Reverend Mr. West. He intends commencing on Monday, 10th March, to build a parsonage house, for the use and accommodation of the Protestant Clergyman for the time being; and it will afford me great satisfaction, should I hear that the Scotch Settlers above alluded to contribute towards that undertaking, by giving three days labour, in such manner as may be directed by Mr. West. Signed: A. Bulger.

Apparently progress was a little slow; it was not until May 30 that a contract was signed, reading as follows:

It is hereby agreed that between Robert Sanderson, Captain Bulger and the Reverend John West, that the said Robert Sanderson will put up the parsonage house, raising the side walls, with upper and lower floors grooved and planed; put in the roof, and find what boards may be wanted, with making the doors and window frames and partitions, so as to form four rooms: and the walls, make the chimney, and finish the whole building by the middle of October next ensuing, for the sum of £60.

The colony agreed to find the nails, glass, hooks and any ironwork that was needed, without extra charge to Robert Sanderson.[2]

By the time Mr. Jones arrived in October, Governor Robert Parker Pelly had taken charge of Fort Douglas. Mr. Jones was appointed to a seat on the Council of Assiniboia by the Hudson's Bay Company, but resigned or retired as an active member because the position conflicted with his work as a missionary. Not until 1835 did his name appear as a regular attender at meetings of the council.

For the next two years the work of the Church seems to have gone on quietly and steadily. In the time between the departure

[2]H. Shave, "Parsonage Creek," *Winnipeg Free Press* (June 7, 1953).

of West, and Jones' arrival, social prayer meetings were held in the settlers' houses by the schoolmaster, George Harbidge, who also baptized several children, noting in the register: "It being a case of necessity and owing to the absence of the Minister." Although the Scots settlers professed themselves unhappy that they were still without their hoped for Presbyterian minister, it does not seem to have affected their attendance at church.

New Church at Image Plains

David Jones found his first winter at the Red River a hard one; it weakened his health considerably for a time, but he persevered with his work. First, in 1824, a new self-supporting school was erected at a point about ten miles down the river from The Forks, with Mr. Bunn as schoolmaster. Many of the congregation were then coming from this locality to church with their families, and during the latter part of the year Mr. Jones devoted himself to the erection of a new church at Image Plains (now St. Paul's, Middlechurch), which was opened on January 30, 1825. He held a service there every Sunday, in addition to conducting the large Sunday School and service at the church by Parsonage Creek. His diary reads "March 26th, 1825, Divine Service as usual at Image Plains; the track was so bad that I was obliged to leave my horse, and waded for the last three miles through water lodged on the surface of the ice to the depth of eighteen inches; a crowded congregation as usual: returned to the Service at the Upper Church; in the evening my usual class of Indian boys." In the building of this church Jones is said to have been materially assisted by Governor Simpson and the local settlers. Later he himself said of it, "I had often looked on this Church as a child of my own rearing. I had worked on it many a day with my own hands; and with the aid of the settlers had brought it to a tolerable degree of perfection."[3]

The church itself was so crowded at services that sometimes Mr. Jones had difficulty in reaching the reading desk. Seven or eight nationalities were represented in the district, and he tells of one occasion on which the whole congregation, English, Scots, Swiss, Germans, Canadians, Norwegians, Half-breeds and Indians joined in singing the hymn "Crown Him Lord of all."

The first Indian communicant (an un-named woman) was admitted at the Christmas celebration in 1825. There were thirty-one Indian children in the C.M.S. School (ten Swampy Crees, five Thick-wood Assiniboines, five Crees from Isle à la Crosse and Athabasca, five Chippewyans from Great Bear Lake, three New Caledonian carriers, three from the Columbia), besides some forty children belonging to families of local settlers.

[3]C.M.S.A., Diary of Rev. D. T. Jones, 1825-1826.

Famine and Flood

The year of 1826 has come down in history as one of the most disastrous in the early years of the Colony. Alexander Ross says:

The disaster began in December [1825]. About the 20th of that month, there was a fearful snowstorm, such as had not been witnessed for years. This storm, which lasted several days, drove the buffalo beyond the hunters' reach, and killed most of their horses; but what greatly increased the evil, was the suddenness of the visitation. As the animals disappeared almost instantaneously, no one was prepared for the inevitable famine that followed; the hunters, at the same time, were so scattered that they could render each other no assistance, nor could they so much as discover each other's whereabouts. Some of them were never found. Families here, and families there, despairing of life, huddled together for warmth, and, in many cases, their shelter proved their grave.[4]

The winter continued unusually severe, the snow lying three feet deep, and in the woods from four to five feet. The temperature often dropped to forty-five degrees below zero, and the ice on the river is said to have had the unusual thickness of five feet seven inches. The winter was prolonged and the spring late, but no alarm was felt until the end of April when the flow of water began to be extraordinary.

On the 2nd of May, the day before the ice started, the water rose nine feet perpendicular in twenty-four hours. Such a rise had never been before noticed in Red River. Even the Indians were startled . . . on the 4th the water overflowed the banks of the river, and now spread so fast, that almost before the people were aware of the danger it had reached their dwellings. . . . So level was the country, so rapid the rise of the waters, that on the 5th, all the settlers abandoned their houses and sought refuge on higher ground. . . . The ice now drifted in a straight course from point to point, carrying destruction before it; and the trees were bent like willows by the force of the current. While the frightened inhabitants were collected in groups on any dry spot that remained visible above the waste of the waters, their houses, barns, carriages, furniture, fencing and every description of property, might be seen floating along over the wide extended plain, to be engulfed in Lake Winnipeg. . . . The water continued rising till the 21st, and extended far over the plains; where cattle used to graze, boats were now plying under full sail.[5]

For some little time the parsonage and the Upper Church, being on slightly higher ground, were untouched. The missionaries made an attempt to save some of their own and the Society's property by placing it in the roof of the church; for though the waters had filled the building, the walls still stood firm. A large wooden platform was also built to which a retreat could be made if necessary: "Sunday, May 14th, was a very dismal day. No people assembled to celebrate the Day of Rest, [there was] no Church to go to, but still Service was held on this

⁴Alexander Ross, *The Red River Settlement* (London, 1856), 100.
⁵*Ibid.*, 102-103.

platform with about forty people present."[6] Three days later it had to be abandoned, and they made their way by boat over the submerged fields to the Snake Indian Hills, where they remained till the twelfth of June. One interesting story has come down over the years. A party of settlers paddling over the waters one Sunday morning in their canoes were attracted by the sound of singing. They found on a wooden stage, no more than eighteen inches above the water, a party of half-breed young women singing hymns. The settlers passed on, unwilling to disturb them, but not a little struck at hearing "in the midst of surrounding desolation, the sweet voices of those lately ignorant and degraded beings floating over the waters in songs of praise."[7]

Only three houses were left standing in the settlement, but one was the parsonage, though of this everything was gone except the outer walls. The Upper Church had suffered less than any other building, but the church in Image Plains was in a sad state. "The glass windows were driven out by the current, the seats were shattered and mostly carried away, the pulpit swept from its foundation, the doors battered down, and all the plastering washed off." Mr. Jones took this as a useful lesson, to teach him not to allow his mind to wander from the main objects of his ministry or be affected by external circumstances. He was thankful that they had not been deprived of this church as a place of worship, "and the Gospel will sound as well from behind a table as from my handsome pulpit."[8] The very practical Mr. Cockran took occasion to bring more land under cultivation, acting as his own plowman while he taught two Indian boys to drive the oxen. Privations remained until the crop of 1827 was harvested.

The Founding of the Red River Academy

In the summer of 1828 David Jones returned to England after spending five years in the Red River Settlement. He left it on June 17 and sailed from York Factory about the middle of September, as usual, baptizing children and conducting weddings between the two points. In fact, the old registers of St. John's Cathedral, which cover this period, enable the journeys of the missionaries to be traced from point

[6]C.S.M.A., Diary of Rev. D. T. Jones, 1825-1826.
[7]Sarah Tucker, *The Rainbow in the North* (London, 1856), 43. This little book was first published by James Nesbit and Company of London in 1851. Other editions followed, one being published in New York in 1861 by the Protestant Episcopal Church Book Society. The book is descriptive of the work of the missionaries at Red River, 1820-1850. Miss Tucker draws largely on R. M. Ballantyne's *Hudson's Bay* regarding Indian life and customs, as well as using missionaries' diaries and letters to the C.M.S. There are some inaccuracies, but it has generally been regarded as a fair source book and, no doubt, a hundred years ago excited much interest about the new Diocese of Rupert's Land.
[8]*Ibid.*, 44.

to point and date to date. He spent a year in England on furlough, and while there was married.

The arrival of the Reverend David Jones and his wife in the Settlement in November, 1829, was welcomed. After some preliminary difficulties with the Presbyterians, who were still resentful over the absence of a Presbyterian minister in the Colony, it was admitted by Alexander Ross that Jones became extremely kind and indulgent to them, and among other things "laid aside such parts of the Liturgy and formula of the Episcopalian Church as he knew were offensive to his Presbyterian hearers."[9] He also held prayer meetings among them after the manner of their own Church, without using the Book of Common Prayer at all, which raised him higher than ever in their estimation. "Mr. Jones was a fine and eloquent preacher; tenderhearted, kind and liberal to a fault. And so popular was he on account of the last mentioned trait of his character that he was all but idolized in Red River!"[10] Mrs. Jones, on her own account, seems to have made a special place in the affections of the people in the Settlement by her kindliness and the simplicity of her character.[11] She was a very capable young woman.

Miss Sarah Tucker, in the *Rainbow in the North,* gives some indication of Mrs. Jones' capabilities when she says that by her arrival at the Red River "Mr. Jones was thus relieved of all secular and domestic cares, which as the household, including the schools, amounted to seventy or eighty persons, were neither few nor light."[12] The attitude of Governor Simpson was now more friendly towards the Church Missionary School and education in general than it had been a few years before, and letters were exchanged between the Governor and the Company's Red River chaplain in the summer of 1832, which are both interesting and important as marking the beginning of a new phase in educational progress.[13]

The first of these is from David Jones to Governor Simpson, dated May 8, 1832, in which Mr. Jones begs leave to call the Governor's attention "to a subject which has occupied much of my thoughts since I first held the office of chaplain to the Honble Hudson's Bay Company. . . . The subject I am desirous of accomplishing is to establish

---

[9]Alexander Ross, *The Red River Settlement,* 131.
[10]*Ibid.,* 131.
[11]C.M.S.A., William Cockran, Letter to C.M.S., October 25, 1836.
[12]Sarah Tucker, *op. cit.,* 67.
[13]These letters are in the Archives of the H.B.C.; photostats of them are now in the Rupert's Land Archives. The C.M.S.A. contains copies of them sent to the Society on July 22, 1832, under a covering letter of that date from Mr. Jones, explaining his attitude in the matter and justifying his actions. The C.M.S. evidently was not happy about these proposals, or misunderstood them. There is a letter in the David T. Jones file in the C.M.S.A., dated July 25, 1833, in which he very vigorously defends himself.

a respectable seminary on a large scale in this settlement for the moral improvement, religious instruction and general education of boys; the sons of Gentlemen belonging to the Fur Trade." Mr. Jones then outlined sundry difficulties that had prevented his taking up the matter before; these can be summarized as the uncertainty of the supply of provisions, which the circumstances of the previous few years had now removed, and the healthiness of the Red River countryside, because of which one might feel little risk of sending children to reside there. He continued: "in such an establishment as is now projected the children would be entirely apart from the other natives of the country and would have no opportunity of speaking any other than the English language . . . in the event of this project being worthy of countenance I would undertake to get an Assistant from England, regularly educated and in all respects fully qualified to aid in the details and labours of the object in view." He suggested that the charge for board, washing and education per annum be £20; if clothing were included, £30, and an entrance fee of £5 because there was "always some undefined circumstance connected with the reception of a child into such an institution which cannot be specified under any particular statement." But in this case the entrance fee would be devoted mainly to the expenses of a respectable building. He would have to pay a salary of at least £100 per annum to an assistant, as well as the wages of additional servants; therefore, he suggested that the charges proposed were quite moderate.

Governor Simpson replied from York Factory on July 14 informing Mr. Jones that his letter "was yesterday laid before the Commissioned Gentlemen now at the Depot, and I have to convey to you our best thanks for the warm interest you are pleased to take in the important object in view, while it offers me great satisfaction to be enabled to say that one and all have expressed their unqualified approbation of the whole plan and have bound themselves to offer it their best support." He mentioned the names of eleven parents who were prepared to send about fifteen boys to the school as soon as it could be opened, and this number would be increased to twenty-five or even thirty the next year; "accordingly I have to beg that you will order a Gentleman, such as you described to come out by the Ship of next season to act as an Assistant and that you will make the necessary preparations for the reception of the boys." The Governor then forwarded a suggestion on behalf of the commissioned gentlemen: "We moreover consider it highly desirable that you form an Establishment in a similar principle for the Education of Girls, the daughters of Gentlemen connected with the Fur Trade, and from the very great kindness Mrs. Jones has shown to the young Ladies that have been placed under your joint care and the deep interest she feels in their welfare and improvement, we cannot doubt that you will be pleased to meet our views in reference to that object likewise." Then he proceeded to name ten parents who were prepared to send sixteen girls, and again had not the least doubt that the number would be made up to thirty. "We have therefore to entreat that you and Mrs. Jones may be pleased to give this proposition favourable consideration and that you will order out from England by the next Ship, a Lady regularly bred up to the Situation of Governess, and qualified to instruct the children in the ornamental, as well as the useful, Branches of Education, in short an accomplished and well-bred Lady, capable of teaching music, drawing, etc. etc. of conciliatory disposition and mild temper and if of a certain [age?] of life to guard in some degree against the chance of her changing her condition so much the better." It was to be understood that the school was to be entirely under the supervision of Mr. and Mrs. Jones

The Arrival of John Macallum

The Red River Academy was duly opened in the fall of 1833. The assistant procured from England was John Macallum, a Scotsman, a native of Fortrose, County of Ross, who graduated M.A. at King's College, Aberdeen, on April 2, 1832. There is a tradition in St. John's College, Winnipeg, that he had taught for some time in a school at Blackheath, London. When he came to the Red River he was twenty-seven years of age. The governess was a Mrs. Lowman, a widow, and the worst fears of the Gentlemen of the Company were realized when at the end of six months she became the wife of Chief Factor James Bird. Miss Mary Kennedy, whose mother was one of the girls of the Academy, and is regarded as an authority on its history, said concerning Mrs. Lowman's successor: "One day the children were surprised to hear that Mrs. Ingham was to marry Mr. Logan. Then another teacher had to be secured—a Miss Armstrong, also an English lady. She married a widower, Mr. Pruden. The schools went flat after each wedding for it usually took a year to secure another teacher from overseas. A Miss Allan came out, and at the end of her term she returned to Scotland—there were no more widowers to go around."[14] On February 16, 1836, John Macallum was married to Chief Factor

[14]There are conflicting recollections about the Red River Academy, and particularly regarding the schoolmistresses. Miss Mary Kennedy, in "Pioneer Women played their Part," *Winnipeg Free Press* (May 27, 1933), says Mrs. Lowman did not come to the Red River until after 1836, but the St. John's Cathedral Register, Winnipeg, shows that Mrs. Lowman married Chief Factor Bird in January, 1835. Mrs. Cowan rightly indicates that Mrs. Lowman came in 1833, and disagrees with Miss Kennedy regarding Mrs. Ingham: W. J. Healey, ed., *Women of the Red River* (Winnipeg, 1923), 17-18.

Charles' daughter, Elizabeth (Betsy), a wedding that stirred much interest in the district.

The Red River Academy continued to make progress. The warm appreciation and support of the Hudson's Bay Company is shown by the following extract from the Minutes of a Council of the Northern Department of Rupert's Land, dated June 3, 1835:[15]

76. The very great benefits that are likely to arise connected with the objects of morality, religion and education not only in Red River but through the Country at large, from the highly respectable and admirably conducted Boarding School, lately established for the instruction of the youth of both sexes under the management of the Revd. Mr. Jones, excites feelings of the most lively interest in its favour, and of great solicitude for its prosperity and success, which even in a business point of view are very desirable from the large amount of Capital it brings into circulation while it is highly creditable to the Country and honourable to the Gentlemen who have come forward so handsomely in its support; but it is with unfeigned regret we observe, that owing to the heavy expense incurred by Mr. Jones in erecting the necessary buildings for this Seminary, it cannot possibly, at the present charge for board & education, afford remuneration adequate to the labour bestowed by Mr. Jones upon it and the outlay of money it has occasioned him; and as an increased charge for Board and Education might operate to the prejudice of this Establishment in its infant state, it is Resolved:

77. That an allowance be made to the Revd. Mr. Jones of £100 p. annum in aid of this highly promising establishment subject to the approbation of the Governor and Committee, and it is further Resolved:

78. That a vote of thanks be presented to Mr. & Mrs. Jones, for the readiness with which they entered into the views and wishes of the Gentlemen in the Country, when requested to undertake the formation of such an establishment for the deep and lively interest they take in the improvement, and unremitting attention they pay to the health and comfort of the young folk entrusted to their care.

The impending departure of Mr. Jones necessarily called for a change in management, and in this the Company took a practical interest. The Minutes of the Council of the Northern Department of Rupert's Land held on June 27, 1837, tell their own story:[16]

81. That an allowance be made to the Revd. Mr. Jones in aid of the Boarding Schools under his management for the Current Outfit. The Revd. Mr. Jones having by his letter of 17th June 1837 given notice of his intention to discontinue the management of the Red River Boarding School, and Mr. McCallum having expressed a willingness to undertake that charge provided the Company become the Purchasers of the buildings and will grant him a lease of the same

[15]E. H. Oliver, *Canadian North-West*, II, 721-722.
[16]*Ibid.*, 769.

for a term of five years at a rent of 10 P. Cent per annum on the purchase money; and it being highly desirable that that institution should not be broken up, it is Resolved:

82. That Chief Factor Christie be authorized to purchase the said buildings on account of the Fur Trade from the Revd. Mr. Jones at a sum not exceeding £500 provided Mr. McCallum enters into an agreement to lease the same from the Company for a term of five years at the rent proposed; and to keep and deliver them in thorough repair at the expiration of his Lease.

The Red River Church

By 1831 John West's little church was becoming too small, and also too decayed, for the congregation to worship there. Late in 1832 plans were being made and subscriptions collected towards a new building, which was erected to the north and west of the original church.[17] The foundation stone was laid on May 15 by Henry H. Berens of the Hudson's Bay Company. This was the first Protestant church, built of stone, in western Canada, and of considerable size. The funds that made it possible appear to have come mostly from the settlers themselves, although a large number of them were actually Presbyterians. Jones always referred to this church as the Red River Church, and a bronze plate, which was made at the time to mark the event, calls it "The Protest't Church." The first Wardens, Alexander Ross, Dr. John Bunn and Robert Logan, who held office from 1835-1848, were appointed to their positions by Governor Simpson, not by Mr. Jones. Services were first held in the new church in November, 1834. There were ninety-six pews and eight square seats in it at first, but four pews had to be removed to make room for stoves. The pews were freehold and when the Presbyterians left it in 1851 (after the arrival of the Reverend John Black), there was considerable controversy over their proprietary rights in the church.

The Red River church of 1833 survived until 1861 when Bishop Anderson, on May 19, preached the last sermon ever heard within its walls. It was built by Pierre Le Blanc, who had been brought to the Red River to rebuild the old North West Fort Gibraltar as the first Upper Fort Garry. Like many buildings in the vicinity of what is now Greater Winnipeg, the church suffered considerably from foundation trouble and its walls had to be reinforced with timber buttresses on the outside; yet it seems to have come through the great flood of 1852

[17]C.M.S.A. Letter from D. T. Jones, undated, but apparently written in part early in 1832: (a) "3rd December last. Gov. Simpson, Mr. Ross and myself started out at 5 a.m. with temp. at −20°F to collect subscriptions—returned 'cold and stiff' with promises between £500 and £600. H.B.C. has given £100 and Executors of Lord Selkirk Estate £50," and (b) "Mr. West's old church is now tottering to decay, and I am about to take down the bell for fear the crazy old tower will be . . . before some fall of wind."

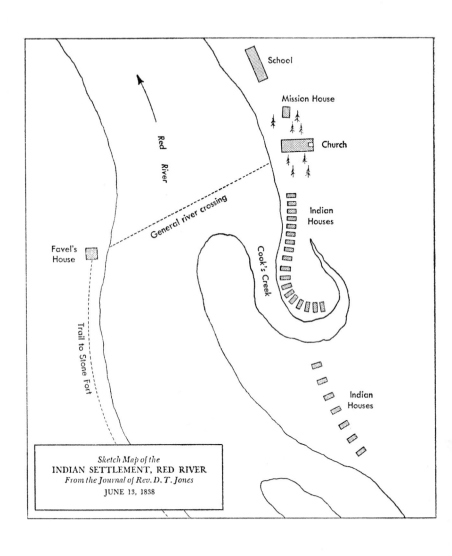

School

Mission House

Church

Red River

General river crossing

Indian Houses

Cook's Creek

Favel's House

Trail to Stone Fort

Indian Houses

Sketch Map of the
INDIAN SETTLEMENT, RED RIVER
From the Journal of Rev. D. T. Jones
JUNE 13, 1838

with some success and to have had much stored in its gallery, as did its little predecessor, in the flood of 1826.[18] This church was consecrated by Bishop Anderson on October 28, 1853, as St. John's Church.

1835 - 1838

During his last three years in the Red River Settlement, David Jones seems to have been kept busy by ministrations and pastoral duties at what were then known as the Upper Church and the Middle Church, and with the superintendency of the Church Missionary Society School and the Red River Academy. There were two boys from the interior of the Province of British Columbia, Kootamey Pelly and Spogan Garry, who came from the Columbia River Valley to the school in 1825 through the interest of Governor Simpson. The former was injured by a fall and unhappily died on Easter Monday, 1830; he was a lad of great promise. Spogan Garry returned to his own people in 1832 and except for a passing reference to him in a letter by Chief Factor Finlayson, little was heard of him until 1837 when three American missionaries, seeking to establish themselves in that part of the country, found a large body of "Spogan Indians" who were already in some measure instructed in the Christian religion, and these missionaries secured Spogan Garry as their interpreter. Cayouse Halket is said to have been a pleasing, thoughtful lad who also came from beyond the Rocky Mountains; he returned there in 1834 but could not adjust himself to the life, and so came back and lived with Mr. Cockran for about two years. A great reader of the Bible and much given to meditation, he gradually went into a decline and finally passed away without any apparent physical cause, from what the Indians themselves call "Thinking Long." Colin Leslie was an Eskimo from Fort Churchill who proved to be a good scholar, but died rather suddenly from influenza. Medical assistance was very primitive in the Red River valley in those days, and though the missionaries did everything in their power to secure to the children under their care a healthy life, never keeping them too long at their books and always insisting that they spend a large part of their time outside, it was not always possible to save some of them when illness came. John Hope, Charles Pratt and James Settee all lived to an advanced age as already has been mentioned.[19]

1836 was a year of sorrow and trouble. Towards the end of August

[18]David Anderson, *Notes on the Flood at the Red River* (London, 1856 and 1873).

[19](a) Sarah Tucker, *op. cit.*, 70 ff., gives a summarized account of these boys.
(b) Thomas E. Jessett, *Chief Spokane Garry* (Minneapolis, 1961), gives a general account of the careers of these boys after their return to their home territory on the Pacific coast.

a severe frost destroyed the gardens and severely injured the other crops; the buffalo hunters returned with empty carts; the boats that had gone to York Factory failed to come back at the usual time, and nothing was heard of them until after winter had set in. Then their crews returned empty-handed, for the supply ships had been driven off by contrary winds and nothing landed from their cargoes, only the mail bags being put ashore. On October 14, Mrs. Jones died unexpectedly after the birth of a child. She was only thirty-one years of age and much loved by the people in the Settlement. Thomas Simpson, the explorer and cousin of the Governor, thought very highly of her and referred to her in one of his letters as "a centre of light." She was buried in the same grave as her little son, David Lloyd, who died in the spring of 1830, and her husband was left with five small children. A monument, which is now in St. John's Cathedral, Winnipeg, was erected to the memory of Mrs. Jones by the girls of the Red River Academy.

David Jones continued with his work, but in the following year he decided to give up the Boarding School. Early in August, 1838, to everybody's regret, he and his little family left the Red River and returned to England, and so passed out of the life of the Colony. On October 8, 1839, he wrote to the Committee of Correspondence of the Church Missionary Society that he had been offered the Professorship of Welsh in St. David's College, with the Curacy of Lampeter attached to it, and on October 22 he further informed the Committee that he had accepted the position. He died in 1844 when he was only forty-five years of age. David Thomas Jones will always be remembered as the builder of St. Paul's Middlechurch, the friend of the Presbyterian community, and the founder of higher education in western Canada.

CHAPTER THREE

The Great Archdeacon

⊹✦⊱⊰✦⊱⊰✦⊱⊰✦⊱⊰✦⊱⊰✦⊱⊰✦⊱⊰✦⊹

This excellent minister was not only a pulpit man; but the plough, the spade, and the hoe, were all familiar to him; few men could be more persevering, more zealous, or more indefatigable. While he kept everyone busy, himself was the busiest of all. One moment called here, another there, handle an axe for one, a hoe for another. Show this one how to dig up a root, another which hand to put foremost; cut a sapling for one, lay a log for another, and a thousand things we cannot name. The next moment, perhaps, spades, hoes, axes, were all thrown aside, and everyone would be seen with his book in his hand; too soon the hour would be up, and twelve long miles to ride in a given time, urged his departure.

THE RED RIVER SETTLEMENT, *by Alexander Ross*

⊹✦⊱⊰✦⊱⊰✦⊱⊰✦⊱⊰✦⊱⊰✦⊱⊰✦⊱⊰✦⊹

"Mr. Cockran is universally regarded in the Colony as the founder of the English Church in Rupert's Land, and from the date of his arrival till 1849, when, on the foundation of the Diocese, individuals were merged into the body, all the principal ecclesiastical business done may be said to have received its impetus from his personal energy." These words are taken from Joseph J. Hargrave's *History of the Red River Settlement,* published only four years after the death of the Venerable Archdeacon Cockran, and they reflect fully the value of his work and opinion of his contemporaries. The evidence of his labours is still with us: the stone churches of St. Andrew's (where he was buried just outside the west door), and St. Peter's at Dynevor near Selkirk, together with St. Mary's, Portage la Prairie, are his enduring monuments.

The Reverend William and Mrs. Cockran with their infant son, Thomas, joined Mr. Jones at the Red River Settlement on October 4, 1825. For forty years Mr. Cockran gave outstanding service to the Church and people of the community and adjoining territory. Physically, he is said to have been a very big and vigorous man, and his early experiences in life seem particularly to have fitted him to meet the situations in the undeveloped country with which he identified himself so closely. The first mention of him is to be found in the minutes of the Committee of Correspondence of the Church Missionary Society, dated August 3, 1824: "Cockran said he was 27 years old, born at

Chillingham, Northumberland. Had been employed in agriculture and helping a school, for last four years had been living in the neighbourhood of Retford (Ordsall), married but no children." (These two latter places were in Nottinghamshire.) Something more about him is learned from a letter to the Society from a gentleman named Brooke, dated March 24, 1824, which described Cockran as a Scottish Presbyterian, and said that he had acted as under-bailiff in Scotland. However, his training and background must have been satisfactory for he was accepted by the Church Missionary Society, ordained deacon on December 19, 1824, by the Bishop of London, and priested on May 29, 1825, barely a week before he and Mrs. Cockran left England on board the *Prince of Wales* on June 4.[1]

First Work at Red River

York Factory was reached on August 15. At the Settlement, Mrs. Cockran took over the work of teaching the girls in the Church Missionary Society's school. Her presence was welcomed by the women already living there, and she will always be remembered as the first minister's wife to reside in western Canada.

Mr. Cockran also took an interest in the school and had a great influence on the boys, although the schoolmaster actually in charge then was William Garrioch, a retired servant of the Company. Years later, in October, 1865, the Reverend James Settee, who was a pupil at the C.M.S. School at the time, said in his report to the Society: "We received intelligence of the death of Archdeacon Cockran. I must acknowledge that it was painful to me. He was worthy of my many tears for the pains he took on my behalf when I was a child; he was my benefactor and my father ever since I was nine years of age. He took me to an Indian tent, and pointed out to me the deplorable condition of the Indian family, and exhorted me to seek after their good."[2] During the absence of Mr. Jones in England (1828-1829), Mr. Cockran undertook the entire responsibility for the services at both churches, and the conduct of the school.

The Grand Rapids

The amalgamation of the Hudson's Bay Company with the North West Company in 1821 naturally resulted in the retirement of a number of servants of both companies, and as many of them had

[1]C.M.S.A., *Minutes of Committee of Correspondence* (August, 1824). Letter from W. Cockran, dated June 24, 1824. R.L.A., *A Brief Sketch of the Life and Labours of Archdeacon Cockran* (London, Religious Tract Society, Tract No. 1029). Undated, but cannot be earlier than 1866, as it contains an account of the funeral, nor later than 1872, as this copy has been covered with part of a report of the West Sussex Hospital for that year.
[2]C.M.S.A., Diary of James Settee of Fairford (October, 1865).

married native wives and had families, the Hudson's Bay Company encouraged them to settle in the lower part of the Red River valley. Mr. Cockran had evidently watched this process with increasing interest, and in the winter of 1828 he held fortnightly prayer meetings in private houses in the neighbourhood, at which sometimes as many as thirty people were present. When David Jones returned in 1829, Mr. Cockran moved to this location, which was about fifteen miles down the river and known by then as The Grand Rapids. Having acquired some land by purchase from the Hudson's Bay Company, he proceeded with the erection of a building that could be used as a house, school and church. According to Donald Gunn there were sixty families living in this district at the time, thirty-six of whom came from Scotland, chiefly from the Orkney Islands.[3] Mr. Cockran observed: "At first my congregation could all be accommodated in a private room in my dwelling house; secondly, in the kitchen; thirdly, in the schoolroom; and by the time we had built and finished our Church, which is fifty feet by twenty-two feet within the walls, and closely pewed, we can fill it well." This church, long known as the Lower Church, was begun in 1831 and dedicated on May 7, 1832.[4]

Mr. Cockran did not confine his attention only to the ministrations of the Church and the pursuit of agriculture, for on November 27, 1831, he opened a day school for the children of the neighbourhood, and the schoolmaster, W. R. Smith, took under his care seventeen boys and six girls, whom he described as "regular in attendance, clean and neat appearing and learning fast." And then, on February 14, 1832, Mr. Cockran began what might be described as industrial activity by introducing six wheels into the school for spinning flax, which he says were "sometimes going and sometimes standing," for the children had never seen anything of the kind before and had no notion about the machine and its movements. "They cannot even manage the treadle with their feet so as to give the wheel motion."

The first Lower Church, which was a frame building, continued in use until 1849, and actually the Right Reverend David Anderson, the First Bishop of Rupert's Land, preached his first sermon in the Settlement within its walls. Five or six years previously it had already proved too small for the congregation and Cockran determined to replace it by a large stone church. A meeting of the congregation was held in December, 1844, to discuss the building of the new church. According to Cockran's journal, "Almost all the males attended. I

[3]Gunn and Tuttle, *History of Manitoba*, 268.
[4]*Church Missionary Society Proceedings 1832-33*, 64. C.M.S.A., Diary of Rev. W. Cockran (May 7, 1832). There was a delay because of the death of George Simpson's infant son on Easter Day, April 22. The exterior of the church was finished on April 21.

addressed them on the zeal and liberality of the Children of Israel, when it was proposed to build the Tabernacle. If Moses found a willing people, the present assembly were equally so. Silver and gold they had none, but stones, lime, shingles, boards, timber and labour were cheerfully contributed, and to such an amount as completely astonished me."[5]

Immediately after the New Year's celebrations of 1845, always a noted occasion amongst the Scottish settlers, the sleighs were made ready to go to the bush. The women worked for days preparing bags of bannocks for the men who spent all the week cutting suitable timber, and only returned home for Sundays and more food. The trees were dressed with the axe into beams and re-sawed into boards; shingles were split and shaved into shape with the drawing knife before being put on with wrought-iron nails; lime kilns were set up on the banks of the river to produce the mortar; and much of the rock in the actual building was obtained from the banks of the river itself, for at that point a limestone formation occurred. When the day for commencing the building work arrived, it is said that Thomas Truthwaite, being ambitious to turn the first sod, started for the church at five o'clock in the morning, but as he came up the hill from the river road he could see the figure of Mr. Cockran, who had already been working there for nearly an hour.

Cockran did not spare himself on this work; he would bring his lunch of bread and cheese with him and drink the Red River water. He was a big and powerful man, and whenever an extra big stone was to be lifted, he would push his way through the crowd saying, "Let me in, men. This is where I shine." The corner-stone was laid on July 4, 1845, by the Reverend John Smithurst, at that time the only other clergyman in the immediate district. The church was eighty-one feet by forty feet, with a tower twenty feet square. It took four years to complete, but it is still a landmark in the district and now the oldest stone church in western Canada.

The Indian Settlement

The same year that Mr. Cockran built the first Lower Church, 1831, his attention was drawn to a band of Salteaux and Swampy Cree Indians whose customary gathering place was at Netley Creek, some ten or twelve miles farther down the river. Their chief was the same Pegewis who had been the friend of John West.[6] He now tried to interest these rather miserable, wandering natives in a settled agricultural life, and assisted by a very hard winter in 1831, he succeeded in

[5]C.M.S.A., Diary of Rev. W. Cockran (December 29, 1844).
[6]*Ibid.* (October 10, 1831).

convincing some of them that such a life would give them comfort and prosperity. The first efforts seem to have been made at Sugar Point,[7] where the river stretches sharply to the east, just above the present town of Selkirk.

About a year later, in 1834, the Sugar Point site was considered unsuitable, and the project moved three or four miles down the river to a situation close to where a creek, since known as Cook's Creek, joins it on the east side. Here a school was established and log houses were built on small river lots. The schoolmaster was Joseph Cook,[8] son of Chief Factor William Hemmings Cook, who was in charge of York Factory when the Selkirk Settlers first landed there. Joseph Cook devoted the rest of his life to the instruction and betterment of these particular Indians. Here, in 1836, sufficient progress had been made to warrant construction of the first church, which was in use until 1854.[9]

Some assistance in building this church was received from the natives themselves when they found that Mr. Cockran was in earnest, but such was the enthusiasm he engendered amongst the people of the Lower Church that many of them willingly trudged the twenty-six mile return journey in order to give their labour towards the building.[10] The work was often slow, for it was hard to settle these wandering people to the regular routine required by agricultural life, and Alexander Ross's words, quoted at the beginning of this chapter, give a fair picture of it in progress. The late Sheriff Colin Inkster, who knew the Archdeacon well in his later years, relates that it was his custom as he rode along the riverside trail, which was then the only road through the Settlement, to dismount if he saw poor work being done and go over to the plowman, talk kindly and encouragingly to him, making any change in the rigging of the plow or the hitching of the oxen he thought necessary, and then test things out with a run or two till all was working satisfactorily.

A year later, writing of the Indian Settlement, Cockran said: "Here we have a comfortable Church which will accommodate about 300 persons. Its white spire, shining through the woods, is a pleasing object. These people have been taken from the chains of heathenism; and are now brought under the sound of the Gospel, to learn the

[7]*Ibid.* (April 18, May 3, May 31, 1832), (July 4, 1833). The earlier entries appear to indicate the location of the Indian Settlement as being in the neighbourhood of Netley Creek itself, but the 1833 entry points conclusively to Sugar Point, just south of the present town of Selkirk, Manitoba. This was near enough to lots owned by retired servants of the H.B.C. to make it a desirable situation for farming, and to provide the land needed by a growing community.
[8]*Ibid.* (June 20, July 4, July 6, August 7, 1833).
[9]C.M.S.A., Letter from Rev. W. Cockran (August 6, 1836).
[10]R.L.A., *A Brief Sketch of the Life and Labours of Archdeacon Cockran* (London, Religous Tract Society, Tract No. 1029), 14.

value of their souls, the evil of sin, the power and love of Christ, of His willingness to save them."[11]

When Mr. Jones paid his last visit to the Indian Settlement on August 9, 1838, an incident of considerable interest occurred.

When service was over," he wrote, "I addressed them in regard to some enemy having sent abroad a report that I was leaving the country in disgust with the Indians and natives in general. After this the Old Chief, Pigwys, stepped into the aisle, and said 'You have spoken to us as you always do, as a father would to his children; I wish all would listen to you. I send by you a letter to the Missionary men in England; tell them not to forget me: I want the Word of life to be always spoken in my land.' He then put the letter herewith sent on the desk. This done, another Indian, seemingly taking the lead among the Muscaigoes [Swampy Crees], got up and spoke to the same purpose, adding with much vehemence and gesture—'Tell them to make haste; time is short, and death is snatching away our friends and relatives very fast. Tell them to make haste.'

The letter is worth quoting in full:

Servants of the great God: We once more call to you for protection and assistance; and hope it will not be altogether unavailing.
You sent us which you call the Word of God, and the Word of Life. We left our hunting-grounds, and came to the Word of Life. When we heard the Word of God, we did not altogether like it; for it told us to leave off getting drunk, to leave off adultery, to keep only one wife, and to cast away our idols, our rattles, drums, and our gods, and all our bad heathen ways; but the Word of God repeatedly telling us, that if we did not leave off all our bad devils, and all our bad heathen ways, that the Great God would send us all to the great devil's fire, by the goodness of your God we seed that the Word of God was true. We now like the Word of God; and we left off getting drunk, left off adultery, cast away our wives—married one, cast away our rattles, drums, idols, and all our bad heathen ways.

Mr. Jones is now going to leave us. Mr. Cockran is talking of leaving us. Must we turn to our idols and gods again? or must we turn to the French Praying-Masters for protection and assistance, where a good few of our children and relations are gone to? We see not less than three French Praying-Masters has arrived in the River, and not one for us. What is this, our friends? The Word of God says, that one soul is worth more than all the world. Surely then, our friends, 300 souls is worthy of one Praying-Master. Can it be expected that once or twice teaching to a child can be sufficient to make him wise, or to enable him to guide himself through life. No, our friends; and we are the same. It is not once or twice a week teaching can be sufficient to make us wise: we have bad hearts, and we hate our bad hearts, and all our evil ways and we wish to cast them all away; and we hope in time, by the help of God, to be able to do it. But have patience, our friends: we hope our children will do better; and expect that once they learn to read the Great God's Book, to go forth to their country people,

[11]C.M.S.A., Letter from Rev. W. Cockran (August 2, 1837).

to tell them the Word of Life: and by this way many will be saved from the devil's great fire.

As Mr. Jones is to be the bearer of this our Letter, we leave him to explain our case more fully.

We once more beg to consider our case; and we hope you will pity us, and hear our cry we make to you, to send us a Father to reside with us here, to teach us, our wives and our children, The Word of God. We thank you all for what you have done for us and our children: we like the Word of Life, and we wish all our country-people should hear of it too.

We all wish to let you know, as Mr. Cockran began with us, we wish him to end with us; he is now well-customed with our oily and fishy smell, and all our bad habits.

We now send you our thanks for the Word of Life you have sent us; and may the Great God be kind to you all, to give you a long life, that you may do good to all the poor Indians! We feel our hearts sore when we think of you all, and those Prayer-Masters that are here. We pray for you and for them; and shall still do so.[12]

The Society responded by sending the Reverend John Smithurst, who, immediately upon his arrival in 1839, took charge of the Indian Settlement entirely, while Mr. Cockran, for the next five years, looked after the Upper, Lower and Middle Churches. In 1841-1842 he had some assistance from the newly-arrived Reverend Abraham Cowley; in 1844 John Macallum was ordained and took charge of the Upper Church. These years of hard work affected Cockran's health, and he became conscious of the strain his activities were laying upon him. In 1839 he wrote to the Church Missionary Society that when he went in the winter to preach at the distant stations, the cold was frequently so severe that he was almost frozen before arriving at his journey's end; and in the church itself, the breath of the congregation froze on the roof of the building, and the hoarfrost gathered on his Bible and Prayer Book.[13]

The Society became concerned about him, and in 1846 he was succeeded at the Lower Church by the Reverend Robert James, and spent a year in Toronto. Upon returning in 1847, Cockran built a house close to the Upper Church known as St. Cross, which in 1866 became part of the revived St. John's College. In addition to assisting Mr. Macallum at the Upper Church, he directed his efforts to the completion of the Lower Church, that it might be ready for the expected Bishop. However, in 1851, when Mr. Smithurst left the Indian Settlement, Mr. Cockran took charge of it and lived there for two years. Here, again, the congregations had increased to such

---

[12]*Church Missionary Society Proceedings 1838-1839*, 125-126. C.M.S.A., Diary of Rev. D. T. Jones (August 9, 1838).
[13]*Church Missionary Society Proceedings 1839-1840*, p. 110.

an extent that they had outgrown the church, which was becoming worn with age. And so, in 1853, Cockran began the building of the present stone church, now known as Old St. Peter's, the foundation stone of which was laid by Bishop Anderson on May 23, but it was completed by Mr. Cockran's successor, the Reverend Abraham Cowley, after he took charge of the Settlement in 1854.

The last year Cockran spent at the Indian Settlement was 1856-1857. In the latter year he moved to Portage la Prairie permanently.

St. Mary's, Portage la Prairie

Up to the year 1850 the efforts of the Church Missionary Society had found their outlet along the waterways of the country, but about that time it was decided to try to advance on the Great Plains, and Cockran was asked to survey the situation. His own report in a letter dated August 4, 1853, may well be recorded:

In the spring of 1850 you authorized me, by the sanction of the Committee, to commence a station towards the west, to the south of Fairford. In the month of March I sent tobacco to the principal Indians who wandered over that quarter, to meet me at certain places in the month of May. At the beginning of this month I set out, with a certain party who were well acquainted with all the rivers and creeks which run into the Assiniboine. We travelled as far west as Beaver Creek, and found no suitable location beyond Portage la Prairie, about seventy-five miles west of the Red River Settlement. To this place we turned our attention, and determined here to plant a settlement.

I went in June 1851, and fixed on a location, and contracted for a schoolroom. The timber was then cut, and hauled to the place, but owing to heavy rains and sickness, with the want of provisions, the original schoolroom was not built, but a smaller one, sufficient to accommodate forty children. In the winter of 1851-52, the Bishop kindly came forward, and assisted to keep the school together.

Having sown the Mission farm at the rapids, I had a good stock of grain, which enabled me to be liberal to the most needy of the settlers, and children who were attending school. In the spring of 1852, though the flood had deprived us of many of our resources, I was still able to extend sufficient help to keep the needy in their houses, and turn their attention to the cultivation of the soil. This spring I furnished them with a liberal supply of seed-wheat. In the winter of 1852-53 the settlement and the school held together. At Christmas Mr. T. Cockran and Mr. Kirkby visited it; in February Mr. Corbett; in March Mr. Chapman. The Indians and settlers have therefore lived in the hope of soon seeing a Missionary placed among them, and they have prepared all the timber for a Church and a grist-mill.

I herewith enclose their petition to the Committee of the Church Missionary Society, believing that you will tenderly sympathize with them in their spiritual wants. The cordial support which I have given to it, through so much opposition, is the best testimony that can be given of my conviction that it is for the glory of God, and the good of man, that Portage la Prairie should be occupied as a Missionary station. There are already 213 souls, who would all profit, and many of them be ultimately saved, through the grace of God, if a Missionary were placed there who would labour for their souls as one "who must give account."

Portage had been a well-known place since the time of La Vérendrye and was a favourite resort of Indians and buffalo hunters. In 1851 a couple of settlers from the Red River moved up to Portage, more went in 1852, and still more in 1853. By 1857 the number had increased to fifteen families. These people were outside the immediate jurisdiction of the Hudson's Bay Company and Governor George Simpson resented the interest Archdeacon Cockran was taking in the district. Pending the erection of a church, "Sunday Services were held in Jack Anderson's dwelling house. . . . It was a log building built twenty feet square. . . . Seats consisted of planks laid across blocks. An eighteen inch aisle led up the centre to the unpainted table which stood at the top and which served as Pulpit, Desk and Altar. There was not much to savour of churchliness until the worshipers and the revered pastor took their places, and then the churchliness was high in the best and highest sense." These are the words of the Reverend A. C. Garrioch in his *First Furrows* and *The Correction Line*. He was taken to worship in that same log house when only six years old.

The first Church of St. Mary's was built in 1855, sixty feet long by twenty-seven feet wide, with side walls about thirteen feet high; at the north end was a tower ten feet square, sixty feet high, with a spire surmounted by a Cross. Constructed of oak logs, it served Portage la Prairie for twenty-two years. It was the work of the people themselves; families made and furnished their own pews, a common model being passed around so that all might be uniform. The pulpits and Communion rail came from the original church in the Indian Settlement, being now unnecessary in the new stone church there.[14]

In 1857, the Archdeacon, as he had become in 1853, moved to Portage la Prairie, which he fathered for the next eight years. By 1860, lands to the east of Portage were being taken up, and the Church of St. Margaret, High Bluff was built in 1861-1862; that of St. Anne, Poplar Point, in the winters of 1862, 1863 and 1864.[15] in 1865, the Archdeacon, feeling worn out by work and worry, and Mrs. Cockran left with the intention of retiring to eastern Canada, but medical treatment in Toronto restored him to his old vigour, and they

[14]A. C. Garrioch, *First Furrows* (Winnipeg, 1923), 89-91. A. C. Garrioch, *The Correction Line* (Winnipeg, 1933), 187-190.
[15]C.M.S.A., Letters from Rev. W. Cockran, August 23, 1860; September 5, 1862; September 25, 1864. The discovery of these letters in August, 1959, removed previous uncertainties about the founding of these churches.

returned. He took charge of Westbourne, then a new settlement fifteen miles northwest of Portage, towards the end of September. Within a few days the Archdeacon contracted a sudden chill, and though taken to his daughter's home in Portage and carefully nursed, he died on October first.

Here we turn to the Journal of the Reverend Abraham Cowley, who was then at the Indian Settlement:

October 7th, 1865. In the early part of the week rumours reached us that Archdeacon Cockran was dead. This made me feel very uncomfortable, though I could hardly rely upon the 'they say' of the Indian who told me of it. On Wednesday afternoon the sight of a note with black-edged envelope and Mr. George's handwriting, confirmed my fears. It contained a statement to the effect, adding a few particulars, and a request to go to St. Andrew's to choose the site for interment. I went on the same afternoon, and, by moonlight, fixed upon a spot where the grave of the Venerable Departed should ever be before the settler coming up to the House of God, that, by it, he being dead may yet speak to young and old.

The story of the way in which the Archdeacon's body was carried from Portage la Prairie to St. Andrew's, a distance of eighty miles, has become an epic in the history of the Church and of Manitoba. It had been the desire of the late Archdeacon that his body should remain at night at each of the missionary churches that he had founded or been associated with, but this was only possible at Poplar Point and St. John's; at some other points a short service was held.[16] The concluding scene may well be taken from Mr. Cowley's Journal:

Yesterday [October 6] several of us, the clergy and people, met to inter the mortal remains of our common friend. It was the desire and plan of the parishioners of St. Andrew's to meet the funeral cortege at the entrance of the parish . . . but as the time appointed was anticipated by those who brought on the dead from above, the people were only able to express their sympathy by being present at the Service. . . . Unfeigned sorrow was very manifest upon the countenance of very many that day, and few who were present will easily forget the solemnity of the occasion. I felt called upon to give up some expression to the feelings by which so many were moved who had known and venerated the dear departed for a period of many years. . . . The labours of our venerable friend are ended. He died in peace. He has entered into his rest. His works do follow him. The remains of a little girl were buried near those of the Archdeacon, at the same time. Was this to remind us that only as a little child the greatest can enter the Kingdom of God?

Alexander Ross says, "Of all the missionaries sent to the Red River in our day, none has laboured more zealously in God's vineyard than

[16]Robert B. Hill, *Manitoba: History of Its Early Settlement, Development and Resources* (Toronto, 1890).

he; none has accomplished so much good; and as a Christian at the bed of sickness, or as a friend to the helpless poor, no minister of the Gospel ever surpassed him."

There is a rugged simplicity about the plain, worn monument just outside the west door of St. Andrew's Church, which seems characteristic of the man.

General Note: Records of lands granted to the Church Missionary Society, Rev. D. T. Jones, Rev. W. Cockran and Bishop David Anderson in the Red River Colony are specified in Register B of the Hudson's Bay Company, which is now in the Company's archives in London, England. This matter is too complicated to make each parcel of land the subject of an individual note, and now in general is only of technical interest.

CHAPTER FOUR

From Mission to Diocese: 1838-1849

.+·+⟨◈⟩+·+·⟨◈⟩+·+·⟨◈⟩+·+·⟨◈⟩+·+·⟨◈⟩+·+·⟨◈⟩+·+·⟨◈⟩+·+·⟨◈⟩+·

> To come upon such a settlement, and to see the Indian children all decently clothed, with their books in their hands, and in their deportment in school or church incomparably more quiet and reverent than I ever saw in an equal number of whites, after having come freshly from the naked or ridiculously tricked-out, and often dirty, heathens . . . does indeed fill the mind with the most thankful emotions of delight and the most earnest longing for the extension, by God's good hand upon the laborers engaged in it, of so blessed a work.
>
> A MEMOIR OF GEORGE JEHOSHAPHAT MOUNTAIN, D.D., D.C.L., LATE BISHOP OF QUEBEC, *by Armine W. Mountain*

.+·+⟨◈⟩+·+·⟨◈⟩+·+·⟨◈⟩+·+·⟨◈⟩+·+·⟨◈⟩+·+·⟨◈⟩+·+·⟨◈⟩+·+·⟨◈⟩+·

The appeal by Chief Pigewis, and the natives of the Indian Settlement on the Red River, was duly transmitted to the Church Missionary Society by the Reverend David T. Jones upon his return to England in the autumn of 1838, with the result that the Society entered into communications with the Hudson's Bay Company through Mr. Benjamin Harrison, then a prominent member of the Committee. The Proceedings of the latter record:

They had the satisfaction to find that the Company was disposed to countenance and promote the formation of a mission station at Cumberland House. The present circumstances of the Society prevent them availing themselves of the opening thus presented, to the extent to which they would otherwise be glad to do. They have, however, set apart one of the ordained students of the institution; who they expect, will proceed to his destination in June next.[1]

The Proceedings of the same year give the following as being received by the Society:

Our friends—when we asked you to send us a Praying Master, we did not expect you would order him to go to another place, but to come here with us; but we hear from the Hudson's Bay Company Traders that the missionary you mentioned in your letter is going to Cumberland; but in your letter you tell us the missionary is coming to us, we therefore intend to keep him here. We thank you for him; and we shall take particular care to do as he tells us. . . . We find the Word of God good: and we intend to follow it to the end of our lives.[2]

[1]*Church Missionary Society Proceedings 1838-1839,* p. 126.
[2]*Church Missionary Society Proceedings 1839-1840,* p. 112.

The missionary sent was the Reverend John Smithurst, a student of the C.M.S. Islington College, who was ordained deacon by the Bishop of London, December 26, 1838, and priested May 26, 1839. He sailed on the *Prince Rupert* early in June, reaching York Factory on August 15, and arrived at Lower Fort Garry late on Friday, September 20. On his way up the river he made a brief stop at the Indian Settlement, and then spent the week-end with Mr. Cockran at the Grand Rapids (St. Andrew's), helping him with his church services and discussing with him his own future work. On the following Monday morning, with Mr. Cockran, he paid an official visit to the Governor, and of this he wrote to his friends in England:

Having been made fully acquainted with the state of things I declined acting according to instructions given me in London. The Indians had applied for a Missionary and had been told in letter via Canada that I was coming to them. I could therefore see no justice in disappointing their expectations and depriving them of a teacher, so necessary in their present circumstances in order to watch over them till they are thoroughly grounded in the faith. I told the Governor I must decline living at the Fort or taking the two Upper Churches: I purposed fixing myself at the Indian Settlement in the house built for me by Mr. Cockran and should devote my undivided attention to the Indians. . . . The consequence is, *I am no longer Chaplain to the H.B.C.* but simply a Missionary.[3]

So eager was Mr. Smithurst to take up his work that he went directly to the Indian Settlement, wishing to be with the people of whom he had charge, and surmising that the house would advance faster with himself around. In a note written some months later, he left one of the few descriptions we have of an early mission dwelling:

My house offers every convenience, having on the ground floor entrance hall, dining-room, sitting-room, study, and a small room which my head servant occupies and where he keeps the earthenware and glass. The two kitchens stand behind the house and are connected with it by a passage. There are cellars under the kitchens and under the dining-room, three rooms upstairs and a long room over the kitchen where we keep grain. I have two good Indian lads as servants (at £12 and £8 a year respectively) most attentive, steady, and clever, both speaking English.[4]

Before November he was already studying the Salteaux language. Mr. Smithurst was at this time about thirty-two years of age, and apparently had had much experience in agricultural work. In 1841 he reported to the Church Missionary Society, "Crops very fine. Barley

[3]*Church Missionary Society Proceedings 1839-1840*, p. 113. R.L.A. MSS: 1101-20C, John Smithurst Papers, "General Information inserted in all Letters home."
[4]*Ibid.*

reaped today, twelve weeks since it was sown. Two hundred bushels of potatoes and abundant corn. Indians are working for winter clothing by clearing ground."

Further Progress at the Indian Settlement

Mr. Smithurst lost no time in settling down to work, as his register bears witness, for beginning with an entry on October 9, 1839, in the course of the next twelve years he took 323 baptisms at the Indian Settlement. His first Communicants' Roll contained fifty-one names, a tribute to the work of Cockran; his last, seventy-nine. Opposite many of the earlier names are the words "Admitted by myself," an obvious indication of the absence of a bishop. First among the marriages that he performed at the Settlement was on October 7, 1840, that of William King (the Chief Pegiwis) to Victoria, and it is interesting to note that at the top of the next page, opposite this first entry, is recorded the marriage between Henry Prince, the youngest son of the Chief, and Sarah Badger.[5]

The progress made in the community may well be illustrated by some further extracts from Smithurst's reports to the Church Missionary Society:

March 6th, 1842, Lord's Day; The Indian Church was filled this morning soon after nine o'clock, so that I did not wait till the regular hour for commencing the Service. I was surprised to see many who had come from Grand Rapids, a distance of 13 miles. There were also many heathen Indians. *March 10th;* I have been engaged myself all the day in the study of the Indian language. I am on the point of completing a translation of the evening Service of our Church, and in a few weeks hope to be able to read it. This will be a great benefit to the old people who do not understand English. *March 23rd;* The Church was very fully attended. After Service, I read over to the communicants my translation of that part of the Communion Service which is now completed. *March 25th;* The Indian Church was filled at an early hour, and the people were remarkably attentive. I afterward administered the Sacrament of the Lord's Supper to 65 persons— 1 European, 3 Half-breeds, 57 Muscaigo Indians and 4 Salteaux.

In his report for the same year, he noted that at the Sunday morning service, when the prayers were in the Indian language, about 250 attended. The attendance at a Wednesday service was from 150 to 250. The Sunday School had 184 scholars, and in addition there were evening lectures from Monday to Friday with an attendance of about eighty. "Many Indians read the Bible fluently, and know the Church Catechism broken into short questions, can say the Collects for the whole year, together with a good part of the Thirty-nine Articles.

[5]T. C. B. Boon, *St. Peter's·Dynevor,* Manitoba Historical Society's Proceedings: Series 3, No. 9, 1952-1953, pp. 22-24.

They converse in English with tolerable ease." In this same year, 1842, a new and enlarged schoolroom was built at the Settlement. Smithurst's work and interest always was first and foremost concerned with the Indian. However, in 1846, a wing of the Sixth Royal Regiment of Foot, a detachment of Royal Engineers, and a detachment of artillery under the command of Colonel Crofton, were ordered to the Settlement under secret instructions from the War Office, and about half the men were quartered at Lower Fort Garry. When Smithurst learned that no arrangements had been made for their spiritual needs, he voluntarily became their chaplain, and throughout the two years these troops were in the Red River Settlement, he travelled seven miles and back every Sunday to hold services at the Lower Fort. During his last two years at the Red River he was a member of the Council of Assiniboia, taking his seat at the same time as the new Bishop of Rupert's Land, on October 12, 1849.

In 1851 Smithurst returned to England, but after about a year he came back to eastern Canada and was appointed to Elora in southern Ontario, now in the Diocese of Niagara. He died in 1867 and is buried at Elora.

In the twelve years he spent in the Indian Settlement of the Red River valley, he made an outstanding contribution to the work of the Church among the natives with his patience, persistence, energy, good temper and courage.

Henry Budd and The Pas

In the summer of 1840, the desire of the Hudson's Bay Company and the hope of the Church Missionary Society to establish a new mission centre at Cumberland House, the oldest inland post of the Company, founded in 1774, was realized in part when Henry Budd was sent there as native catechist. He was the boy brought from Norway House by the Reverend John West, and one of the first two baptized by him. After leaving the C.M.S. school Henry Budd entered the service of the Company, but in 1837 he was invited by Jones and Cockran to teach a school at the Upper Church. In this work he showed such ability that he was considered suitable to undertake this new enterprise on behalf of the Church. He set out for Cumberland House on June 22, 1840, accompanied by his wife and mother.[6] After a short time there, however Henry Budd came to the conclusion that it was

[6]C.M.S.A., Letters from Rev. W. Cockran, June 17, 1840 and August 4, 1841. Diary of Rev. J. Smithurst, June 22, 1840. The first of these letters indicates that the arrangements made in London by the Church Missionary Society and the Hudson's Bay Company for sending out two missionaries (one of whom was to go to Cumberland House) had been abandoned owing to financial difficulties. Henry Budd was chosen to go to Cumberland House as a schoolmaster, and was sent by Cockran and Smithurst.

not a suitable location, and so came back down the river to The Pas. Here, the Saskatchewan River is confined to its banks by high land, and there was already something of a settlement near the site of the old French Fort built by Pierre and Louis-Joseph Vérendrye in 1750. There is a legend still current among the Indians that the cordial reception Budd was given was due to what had already been heard of the Christian story from a remarkable man called Kayanwas. The Pas natives helped Budd to put up a little log house for himself and his family, with a large room that would serve as school and meeting house for the first few years. The spot he selected was a little island in the river at a point called by the Crees W'passkwayaw, the wooded narrows.

In two months he had gathered a Sunday group of thirty-five persons, twenty-four of whom were children.[7] So rapidly did the Gospel spread that in the summer of 1842 it was felt advisable for the Reverend John Smithurst to visit The Pas. Mr. Smithurst left the Indian Settlement on May 30 (a very early date, for the ice is not usually out of Lake Winnipeg at this time) in a boat manned by ten Indians belonging to his congregation. There were delays due to high winds, storms and rough water, and it was not until June 14 that the party reached the mouth of the Saskatchewan River. Here they met a Hudson's Bay Company brigade from the west that was on its way to York Factory. As one of the gentlemen came from a post near the Rocky Mountains, Smithurst was able to make some inquiries about the Reverend Robert T. Rundle, the Wesleyan Methodist missionary who had gone to Edmonton two years previously. He was pleased to find that two boys, who had been educated at the Red River C.M.S. School, had taken the good news of the Gospel to their own neighbourhood near the Rockies when they returned home.

Twenty-six days after leaving the Red River, and not having seen a human habitation, except one encampment of Indians at the Great Falls (now Grand Rapids, Manitoba), Mr. Smithurst wrote:

I cannot well describe the gratification which I felt when, at 4 o'clock p.m., our guide made the pleasing announcement, "Mr. Budd's place is just behind that point of wood." A few minutes brought us within sight of the Mission Establishment, which truly appeared like an oasis in the desert.

The School-house in the centre, Mr. Budd's house on the south side,

[7] J. A. MacKay, "Henry Budd, James Settee, James Hunter," W. B. Heeney, ed., *Leaders of the Canadian Church*, Second Series (Toronto, 1920), 78. Archdeacon MacKay says that he heard the story from the man's widow. Kayanwas ("The Prophet") was a Cumberland Indian. The Archdeacon also states that he regards James Settee as being the real founder of the Lac la Ronge mission. R.L.A., R. B. Horsefield, "The Story of the Pas," *Northern Lights*, IX (December, 1950), 20-28.

and the children's house on the north, appeared respectable buildings for this country; and struck me as reflecting very great credit upon Mr. Budd's industry, considering the very limited means which had been placed at his disposal. A gentle slope from the houses toward the river appeared to have been cleared, but not fenced; and in the rear a neat square field of about an acre was fenced in, and under cultivation.

June 25th, 1842—At 7 o'clock a.m. I preached in the Schoolroom. After Service, I got my crew to work, some in enlarging Mr. Budd's house, and some in fencing-in an additional piece of land in which to plant potatoes.

At 7 p.m. the adult Candidates for Baptism were all assembled in the School-room for examination; and as Mr. Budd had not previously informed me of the number, I was quite astonished to see so many, and began to fear that they were not sufficiently aware of the nature of that Holy Sacrament. I therefore, resolved upon a very searching examination of each individual; but after four hours, I had examined little more than half; and as midnight approached, I concluded with singing and prayer, directing them to assemble again at seven on Lord's-Day morning.

June 26th, 1842: Lord's Day—The Indians assembled at the appointed time this morning, and I preached. After Service, I examined the remainder of the Candidates for Baptism, and did not finish till near 11 o'clock. The result of the examinations was highly satisfactory. . . .

At 2 o'clock in the afternoon, all the Candidates for Baptism were assembled in the School-room. The thirty-eight adults, with their twenty-seven infants, were arranged on benches placed at the two sides and one end of the room. Within these twenty-two school children were arranged, on benches placed in a similar manner, leaving me a passage round the room between the two parties. Prior to commencing the Baptismal Service, I delivered a short address explanatory of its several parts I then baptized—first the adults and infants, and lastly the school children. The whole occupied three hours. . . .

June 27th, 1842—At 7 o'clock this morning I delivered an address in the School-room on the obligations of Marriage. During the forenoon I married thirteen couples.[8]

Mr. Smithurst left The Pas on June 29, and travelling almost night and day, reached the Red River on July 7. He immediately began to urge the claims of this station for a clergyman, and in the summer of 1844 the C.M.S. sent out the Reverend James and Mrs. Hunter.

Fairford and the Reverend Abraham Cowley

On September 28, 1841, another notable missionary arrived at the Red River Settlement. The Reverend Abraham Cowley, the son of a mason, was born at Fairford in Gloucestershire on April 8, 1816, and educated at Fairford Free School, 1821-1828. As a boy he came under

Church Missionary Society Proceedings 1842, 288-297.

the influence of the vicar, the Reverend Canon F. Rice, who later succeeded to the Barony of Dynevor, a title derived from Dynevor Castle, Carmarthenshire in South Wales. The names of Fairford and Dynevor have subsequently become closely associated with the development of Christian work amongst the native Indians of western Canada.[9] Early in 1841 Mr. and Mrs. Cowley sailed to Canada. He was ordained by Bishop George Jehoshaphat Mountain in Christ Church, Montreal, on March 7, and spent a brief curacy at Chateauguay River in the neighbourhood of Huntington, Quebec, the intention being that he should proceed to the Red River Settlement by canoe. Difficulties arose, making it necessary for the Cowleys to return to England, then to sail for Hudson Bay on the *Prince Albert*. They were accompanied by a lay worker of the Society, Mr. J. Roberts, who proceeded to the Indian Settlement to assist Smithurst, while Cowley and his wife settled down at the Lower Church, leaving Cockran freer to look after the Upper and Middle Churches.[10]

Another extension of the work was now planned by Cockran and Smithurst, but not at such a distance as The Pas. The objective this time was on the northwestern shore of Lake Manitoba, the home ground of a large band of Salteaux Indians. To this neighbourhood Cowley went in May, 1842, with a view to finding a suitable location for a new mission. No permanent settlement was made at this time, but Cowley returned early in December and, after enduring considerable discomfort in winter travelling, decided on a place called by the Indians "Pinaymootang" (Pa'rtridge Crop), and there he built a church and school. He did not stay permanently at the time, so a schoolmaster was placed temporarily in charge. For Cowley it was a new kind of undertaking: "As this is without a parallel in all the Society's Missions, I have nothing to guide me save the long and varied experiences of dear Mr. Cockran."[11]

[9]R.L.A., Letter from H. W. Hodges, secretary of the Fairford (Gloucestershire) Parochial Church Council, January 31, 1951. Margaret Arnett MacLeod, ed., *The Letters of Letitia Hargrave* (Toronto, 1947), 173.

[10]*The Church* (Toronto, March 13, 1841). R. M. Ballantyne, *Hudson's Bay* (London, 1848). In this book the Cowleys are referred to as Mr. and Mrs. "G", perhaps because of a misinterpretation of the Gloucestershire-Wiltshire accent.

[11]C.M.S.A., Letter from Rev. Abraham Cowley, December 1, 1842. *Church Messenger* (Toronto, June, 1943): "One Hundred Years Ago" has an extract stating that John Garrioch and Charles Pratt were the first school teachers at the Fairford mission. The abstracts under this heading in the paper, which was issued as an insert for parochial and diocesan magazines, were prepared by the late Professor Young of Toronto and the late Canon A. R. Kelley of Montreal, but the source is not always identified. *The Church Missionary Society Record* (December, 1849), 108, states that the Cowleys moved to Pa'rtridge Crop permanently on August 1, 1844. *Ibid.* (May, 1848), notes the beginnings of agriculture at this mission. *Ibid.* (July, 1848), says that five families owned eleven cattle and four horses among them, and that there were seven houses in this Indian settlement, with two more in the process of building.

The Cowleys laboured at Pa'rtridge Crop for a number of years, the first five of which were said to have afforded no converts; it was proposed that the mission be closed. When this was threatened, however, the natives pleaded that while they themselves were too old and set in their ways to change, their children should be given the opportunity to embrace Christianity. The mission was kept open. Bishop Anderson went to this station early in 1851 and left an account of his visit. While there he "had been permitted by God to Baptize 26 persons, chiefly adult Indians. The place now begins to assume something of the appearance of a Christian Village and I therefore thought it might be well to change its designation from the rather unmeaning name of Pa'rtridge Crop (?) to that of Fairford."[12]

The Cowleys remained there until 1854 when they moved to the Red River to take charge of the Indian Settlement.

Bishop Mountain Visits the Red River Settlement

More than twenty years passed, after 1820, before the missionary districts in the Red River Settlement received their first episcopal visitation, during which time the work had grown and expanded, both amongst the white settlers and the native Indians.

George Jehoshaphat Mountain became Assistant Bishop of Quebec, with the title Bishop of Montreal, in 1836. Although he had the entire supervision of the affairs of the Church in both Upper and Lower Canada, he was aware of the work being done at the Red River Settlement and was anxious to visit this mission. When, or how, Bishop Mountain's desire became known it is hard to say, but both Cockran and Smithurst were in correspondence with him about the matter in the summer of 1840.[13] From their letters it is evident that he had written first, but they both warmly commended the suggestion of an episcopal visit in the near future. Cockran wrote: "The prospect of being honoured with a visit from your Lordship . . . is truly encouraging, as this branch of the Church has been so long without the cognizance of any bishops. Mr. Smithurst and I, assisted by our schoolmasters, shall do as much as we are able to prepare the members of our Church

[12]Eugene Stock, *History of the Church Missionary Society* (London, 1899), I, 364. S.P.G.A., Letter from Right Rev. David Anderson, January 21, 1851.

[13]G. J. Mountain, *The Journal of the Bishop of Montreal during a Visit to Church Missionary Society, North West America Mission* (London, 1845), Appendix, 364. "From the time of his consecration in 1836, Dr. Mountain cherished the intention of visiting this distant branch of the Church of England, and the proposal was heartily seconded by the Society." *Ibid.*: The "Advertisement" which prefaces the text of the *Journal* says, "The Bishop of Montreal having proposed to the Committee of the Church Missionary Society to visit this mission at Red River." Eugene Stock, *op. cit.*, 264, says, "The Society having requested him . . . ." Armine W. Mountain, *Memoir of George Jehoshaphat Mountain, Lord Bishop of Quebec* (Montreal, 1866), 219-220.

for confirmation. We have four congregations, upwards of two thousand Protestants, and about three hundred communicants. The Church Missionary Society will hail your first visit with gratitude, and as far as jurisdiction is concerned I hope no bishop will take any offence."[14] (The Hudson's Bay Company's territory was in the See of the Bishop of London.) Smithurst wrote: "I have intimated your Lordship's intentions to the Indians. . . . we have two schools, one for the Missicaigoes and one for the Saulteaux.[15] The former contains eighty, the latter sixteen day scholars."

Archbishop Howley gave the suggested visit his approval. Writing from Lambeth, September 15, 1840, he told Bishop Mountain:

There can be no impropriety in your visiting the Red River in the Hudson's Bay territory, though not within the limits of your Lordship's jurisdiction, and in your exercising episcopal functions there, such as preaching and exhorting the clergy there, though you would have no power of expressing your authority by law. The clergymen stationed there by the Church Missionary Society would probably be happy to receive you, but I think it would be prudent not to enter the region of misunderstanding by going thither without an intimation to that effect from them. I say this because some difficulty has been made in a similar case in East Indies, which I have reason to think is now removed.

The C.M.S. received the news of the Bishop's intention warmly:

Church Missionary House, London, Salisbury Square, 22nd September, 1840. To the Bishop of Montreal:— We have received with great thankfulness your proposal to visit our North West America Mission. The Committee of this Society is composed of members of the Church of England and it will give them liveliest satisfaction if your Lordship should be enabled to carry into effect your purpose of visiting the missionaries at the Red River.[16]

The plans of the Bishop were delayed year by year, but the journey was at last made in the summer of 1844, with the full co-operation of the Church Missionary Society, which made itself responsible for the expenses. Sir George Simpson, the Governor of the Hudson's Bay Company, seems to have looked upon the proposed journey with some suspicion and very definitely to have declined the suggestion that the Bishop should accompany him personally on one of his own expeditions to the West. In some of the correspondence with the Bishop, Sir George adopted a rather dissuasive attitude: "Unaccustomed as you are to such a mode of travelling, I am apprehensive you will have some difficulty in conducting the march, and in the management of

---

[14]Quebec Diocesan Archives (hereafter Q.D.A.), Series G, Vol. 13, Red River Letters. Letter, June 12, 1840.
[15]*Ibid.*, Letter, June 18, 1840.
[16]*Ibid.* Letter, September 22, 1840.

the crew . . . so that in undertaking this voyage you will have to count, not only on discomfort and inconvenience, but also on a little trial of temper in maintaining proper discipline among your people." Sir George had previously told Mr. Cockran, in discussing the Bishop's journey, that it was easier to project a visit than to perform one. Cockran, commenting on this in a letter to the Bishop, remarked, "Sir George, honest man, thought that none of us would travel as far or as fast after a soul as he would after a rat-skin."[17]

However, some of the advice given by "The Little Emperor" was no doubt good. He pointed out the advantages of using a *Canot-de-maître*, with a crew of fourteen, instead of a *Canot-du-nord* with only a crew of eight. He also told them what to take, how it should be packed, and that linen could be washed frequently en route. In addition, he promised the hospitality of the Company at its posts, and personally selected the crew, including an Indian guide, "A well-conducted Iroquois named Jacques . . . a very expert canoe man. . . . The Indians all spoke French sufficiently for the common purposes of the day. We were thus seventeen persons in the canoe. Our baggage, bedding and provisions, with the equipments of the canoe and the tent, were estimated, I think, at the weight of a ton and a half."[18]

Bishop Mountain left Lachine on May 16, accompanied by his Chaplain, the Reverend P. J. Maning, and a manservant. They followed the route first pioneered through the wilderness of northern Ontario by the fur traders of the old North West Company: up the Ottawa and Mattawa Rivers, across the watershed to Lake Nipissing, and along the north shores of Lake Huron and Lake Superior to Fort William. Here the large canoe was exchanged for two smaller ones in which they made their way to the Lake of the Woods, and by the Winnipeg River to Lake Winnipeg. They reached Lac du Bonnet late in the evening of Friday, June 21. "At 3 a.m., Saturday, Sir George Simpson, Governor, arrived, and stepping from his canoe . . . upon the level rock, 'le petit rocher du bonnet,' upon which the Bishop's party was encamped, greeted the Bishop." There the following letter was written: "My Lord, I understand that Mr. Macallum is desirous of entering Holy Orders, and in the event of his being ordained I intend to recommend his appointment to the office of Assistant Chaplain to the H. B. Co'y. at Red River Settlement." "Geo. Simpson, Governor H. B. Co'y. Territories."[19]

The Bishop was anxious to reach the Indian Settlement by Sunday morning as he could only spare three Sundays at the Red River. His

---

[17]*Ibid.* This is quoted in "Mountain of Quebec," *Canadian Churchman*, LXXI (June 15, 1944), 363-364.
[18]G. J. Mountain, *Journal*, 4-5.
[19]*Ibid.* (June 21, 1844), 41.

party stopped for breakfast at Fort Alexander, then entered Lake Winnipeg, and arrived at the Indian Settlement (St. Peter's) just as the bell was ringing for morning service, a fit ending to the thirty-eight-day journey.

Coming out of the wilderness, Bishop Mountain suddenly found himself in the middle of civilization again. Mr. Smithurst was waiting for him at the door of his house, his native parishioners gathering around him. The children came with their books in their hands, all decently clothed from head to foot. The Bishop noticed a repose and steadiness in the deportment of the people, which seemed to indicate a high and controlling influence upon their characters and hearts. Nor did he find it unpleasing to hear one of his voyageurs remark to another, "There are your Christian Indians: it would be very well if all the whites were as good as they are."[20] Everyone then proceeded to the church, where there was a congregation of two hundred and fifty. The service was in English, the Lessons being translated into Cree by an interpreter. After the service the Bishop visited and addressed the Sunday School, then stayed during the pupils' examination, which consisted of readings from the Bible and questions from the Church Catechism and the Thirty-nine Articles. Bishop Mountain observed: "I do confess I was much disposed to question the profitableness of this last portion of the instruction and asked Mr. S. what the Indian youths would understand by Article 21 on the just subordination of General Councils to Sovereign Princes, but Mr. S. satisfied me on this point."[21] Smithurst noted: "The Indians were quite delighted with the sermon, and said it was not the first time their Chief Praying Father had preached to Indians, for he appeared to know so well what suited them. The next day his lordship drew out a plan for the services during his stay."

Bishop Mountain was received everywhere in the Colony with enthusiasm. Churches were overflowing with officials and employees of the great Company, with hardy Scots settlers, and crowds of native men, women and children. During his stay of less than three weeks, Bishop Mountain held five Confirmation Services and confirmed 846 candidates. At the morning service at the Lower Church (St. Andrew's), 192 women and girls were presented, and in the evening, 150 men and boys. At Middlechurch (St. Paul's), and at the Upper Church (St. John's), there were 150 candidates presented at each service. Finally, at the Indian Settlement (St. Peter's), he confirmed 204 native converts, and remarked in his *Journal* that altogether there would have been about 1,000 candidates, but for the fact that some

[20]*Ibid.*, 48-50.
[21]*Ibid.*, 53-54.

had to go buffalo hunting and others were engaged in the necessary summer voyages of the Company. On June 30, at the Middle Church, he ordained John Macallum, deacon, and on July 7 both Macallum and Cowley priests.

Upon his return to Montreal, Bishop Mountain lost no time in urging the establishment of a permanent Bishopric at the Red River, which he was convinced should be the base and centre of a great missionary effort for Northwest America. "The Church," he said, "in the early days of Christianity was planted in new regions by seating at central point the Bishop with his Cathedral and his College of Presbyters, who ranged the country here and there under his direction. And this, or the nearest approach to this, of which the times are susceptible, is what is wanted now."[22] He pointed out that a visit, such as his, instead of meeting the situation, only served to reveal in strong relief its real character, and the necessity of establishing provision for the exercise of the episcopal functions. He wrote strongly and eloquently, emphasizing that a move should be made at once.[23]

The Archbishops and Bishops who constituted the Colonial Bishoprics' Committee appointed a sub-committee for the purpose of promoting this object and issued a statement in the following year.

The Bishop of Montreal continued to use every exertion within his power until the Bishopric was finally established in 1849. In the meanwhile he did what he could for the oversight of the territory by means of correspondence with the clergy, who seem to have found comfort in seeking his advice, and reporting both progress and difficulties to him.[24] The account sent to the Bishop, for his journey, by Governor Simpson for canoes, wages, supplies, was £410. (The Canot-de-maître cost £33 and the wages were £260.)

Founding of the Bishopric of Rupert's Land

If the journey of Bishop Mountain were instrumental in drawing the attention of the Bishops, clergy and the C.M.S. in England to the necessities and opportunities of the Red River Settlement as a centre of missionary work in northwestern Canada, it was an impulse of good-will born in the country itself that finally made the establishment of the proposed Bishopric possible.

Too little has been said of James Leith, whose generosity provided the main portion of the endowment that was requisite before the Crown could take action. The second son of Alexander Leith of Glenkindie, a Scottish Laird with considerable land holdings in Aberdeen-

[22]*Ibid.*, 173.
[23]*Ibid.*, 178.
[24]Armine W. Mountain, *Memoir*, 247.

shire, James Leith was born in the summer of 1777. In 1801 he came to Montreal with Sir Alexander MacKenzie and the same year entered the firm of Sir Alexander MacKenzie and Company, better known as the X Y Company, as a partner. When this company was amalgamated with the North West Company in 1804, Mr. Leith was described as one of its wintering partners. In 1821, when the amalgamation took place with the Hudson's Bay Company, he was in charge of one of the most important posts of the North West Company, Fort Chipewyan. Because he was implicated in the struggle between the two companies that culminated in the Seven Oaks affair of 1816, he spent a considerable part of his time during the period of law proceedings in Toronto, where he was associated with Bishop Strachan and other prominent Aberdonians resident in York (as it was then) to whom his family was well known. From 1822 to 1829 he was in charge of the Hudson's Bay Company's post at Cumberland House, but returned that year to England owing to ill health, and finally severed his connection with the Company in 1831. Upon his retirement to England, he lived at Torquay in Devonshire until he died on June 19, 1838.[25] By his will, dated February 20, 1835, he left one fourth of his estate to his brother, William Hay Leith; a second undivided fourth part he left to be divided equally among his five sisters.

I give devise and bequeath the remaining Moity or half part of my Lands Heritages personal Estate and Effects not herein before disposed of by this my Will unto my brother the said William Hay Leith and his heirs the Lord Bishop of London for the time being the Reverend the Dean of Westminster for the time being and the Governor and Deputy Governor of the Hudson's Bay Company upon the trusts and for the ends intents and purposes following . . . [to] from time to time expend lay out and dispose of the Interest Dividends and Annual Proceeds arising there from in such manner as to them or the majority of them shall seem most desirable and advantageous for the purpose of establishing propagating and extending the Christian Protestant Religion in and amongst the native aboriginal Indians in that Part of America formerly called Rupertsland but now more generally known as the Hudson's Bay territory. I beg here to remark that I do not consider the Neighbourhood of a Colony a fit place for the commencement of such a work but I wish it to be considered as an observation only as I must leave it to the above named trustees to act according to their own opinions guided by existing circumstances and I trust they will do so as men of honour and understanding. . . . [26]

[25]R.L.A., James Leith Papers, *Memorandum and Notes by James Leith Ross of Ross, Ross and Field, Barristers and Solicitors of 80, King Street West, Toronto,* May 3, 1933. E. E. Rich, *Simpson's Athabasca Journal* (Toronto, 1938), 40.

[26]R.L.A., James Leith Papers. Copy of James Leith's will, provided by James Leith Ross of Ross, Ross and Field, Toronto.

Mr. Leith's will was filed for probate on August 11, 1838, but certain members of the family opposed it and litigation was continued until 1849, when, by a decision of the Master of the Rolls (Lord Langdale), the money was set apart for the endowment of a Bishopric in Rupert's Land. According to Joseph Hargrave, the judgment was partly based on the fact that the Hudson's Bay Company had voluntarily offered to add to the interest from the Leith bequest the sum of £300 sterling per annum in perpetuity. This insured an income of about £700 a year for the Bishop.

The Reverend E. Hawkins, Secretary of the Society for the Propagation of the Gospel, hastened to convey the good news to Bishop Mountain of Montreal. In a letter dated December 1, 1848, he wrote:

Your Lordship will rejoice to hear that there is a fair prospect of the erection of a Bishopric in the Red River Settlement. The treasurers of a fund bequeathed by Mr. Leith having recommended the appropriation of £10,000 to the endowment, the interest of this sum with £300 a year and a house allowed by the Hudson's Bay Company will, it is considered, be a sufficient provision for a Bishop, situated as a Bishop in that remote territory must be. The Episcopal Committee, would, I am sure, be obliged to your Lordship as to any hints for drawing the Patent, the title of the See, the Site, the Cathedral Church, the limits of jurisdiction, perhaps also I may add, the *fit person*.[27]

The Bishop replied on December 21, 1848. He thought the choice of title of the See must lie between Assiniboia and Rupertia: "The whole territory has no name which could be at all proper for a title. . . . It appears to one quite warrantable to create a name for it . . . the territory there being called Prince Rupertsland, I do not see why the See should not be Rupertia." With regard to the Cathedral Church, for example, he wrote: "The Bishop, unless he carries funds with him from England, will probably have to adopt the Church of which the walls have been put up since my visit at The Rapids (of the Red River) a few miles above the Lower Fort, as his Cathedral for the present."[28] He was disposed to recommend the extension of the jurisdiction to make it coincident with the territory proper of the Hudson's Bay Company, but felt that some company posts were really far beyond the limits of their own territory. Land on the other side of the Rocky Mountains should form a separate diocese: that which lay in the wild parts of Upper Canada was already within the limits of the Diocese of Toronto.[29]

[27]S.P.G.A., *Quebec Letters Sent*, 97.
[28]S.P.G.A., *S.P.G. Letters*, G. J. Mountain to Ernest Hawkins, December 21, 1848.
[29]S.P.G.A., *Ibid.*, December 21, 1848.

Bishop Mountain did not name any particular *fit person*, but he did add some recommendations as to the quality of the man who should be selected.

The Bishop must be a person not sparingly endued as with the innocence . . . of the dove, so that the wisdom which may be expected also to be found in him, considering who they are who have the selection. . . . the Protestant population have no ministrations, but those of the Church of England, and the missionaries are greatly beloved, but the first settlers planted by Lord Selkirk were principally Scotch. . . . The task of the Bishop will require a very prudent, moderate and cautious course of proceeding. . . . It is an important object to keep them together and to prolong the unity which has thus far existed.[30]

By the next mail, January 5, 1849, Bishop Mountain added a warning that further consideration had evidently brought to his mind: "As all that has been done in that quarter by our own Church has been done by the Church Missionary Society, and the clergy (at Red River) are all connected with that institution—it appears to me that (since unhappily it cannot be concealed that there are parties within the Church) it would be a matter of prudence to provide in the selection of the Bishop against the probability of any untoward collision—clergymen—exemplary, devoted, much loved, fruitful in their ministry but who may be presumed to hold views characteristic of the Society which supports them."[31]

A letter from the Reverend E. Hawkins to Bishop Mountain, of March 23, 1849, relates:

Your Lordship will be rejoiced to hear that an adequate endowment, chiefly from the bequest of the late James Leith, Esq., having been provided, the Queen has consented to the erection of a Bishopric in Prince Rupertsland; and that the Reverend David Anderson, M.A. of Exeter College, and late theological tutor of St. Bees is nominated to the first Bishop. Mr. Anderson is a widower of about 35, and is a man I am informed, of robust health. The consecration of him as well as of the Bishop of Victoria (Hong Kong) is to take place, in the month of May at Canterbury.[32]

The Royal Letters Patent under the Great Seal, setting up the Diocese of Rupert's Land, was dated May 21, 1849, and the area of the Diocese was made coincident with that drained by all rivers flowing into Hudson's Bay or finding their way to the Arctic Ocean. This same area is now divided into twelve dioceses, ten of which form the present Ecclesiastical Province of Rupert's Land.

[30]S.P.G.A., *Ibid.*, December 21, 1848.
[31]S.P.G.A., *Ibid.*, G. J. Mountain to Ernest Hawkins, January 5, 1849.
[32]S.P.G.A., *Quebec Letters Sent*, March 23, 1849, p. 101. Q.D.A., Series G, Vol. 13, Red River Letters.

On Whitsun Tuesday, May 29, 1849, a bishop was consecrated in Canterbury Cathedral, the first consecration there since the days of Queen Elizabeth I. In fact, two Bishops were consecrated, as indicated by Mr. Hawkins, and both for the C.M.S. mission fields. The Reverend George Smith was consecrated as First Bishop of Victoria (Hong Kong), and the Reverend David Anderson as First Bishop of Rupert's Land (Western Canada).[33]

Cumberland District and Lac la Ronge

Earlier in this chapter reference was made to the work which was begun by Henry Budd, the native catechist at The Pas, and the visit of John Smithurst to this C.M.S. station has also been treated in some detail. In order to preserve the sequence of events it is now necessary to take up the work of the Reverend James Hunter in the Cumberland District, and the extension of the Gospel to Lac la Ronge.

The Reverend James Hunter was born at Barnstaple in North Devon on April 24, 1817. He was educated locally and on leaving school was articled as a conveyancing clerk, afterwards spending some time as a schoolmaster at Tavistock. Here he came under the influence of the Reverend Sir H. Bourchier Wrey of Corffe, and of a Reverend Mr. Jebb, and through these two gentlemen entered the C.M.S. college at Islington to train for Holy Orders. At the same time he acquired some knowledge of medicine in the London hospitals.[34] Mr. Hunter was ordained deacon in 1843 and priest in 1844 by the Bishop of London, and shortly after his ordination, Mrs. Hunter and he sailed for Canada, arriving at The Pas on September 25. Finding there only the limited accommodation provided for Henry Budd, Mr. Hunter proceeded to build more commodious quarters. No doubt the house was used as a school and church as well as parsonage, for he reported fifty-six children in school and an attendance of more than two hundred at the services. Hunter followed the practice of Cockran and Smithurst in encouraging the native Indians to settle on the land and engage in agriculture, himself setting the example in his own mixed farming operations, which were most successful.

The first Christ Church, The Pas, was commenced in 1847. It was sixty-three feet long by twenty-seven feet wide, and had a tower surmounted by a spire, rising over seventy feet.[35] The latter was removed

[33]*Colonial Church Chronicle*, XIII (London, 1850), 38. This gives a full account of the consecration of the Bishops of Victoria and Rupert's Land.

[34]*Paddington, Kensington and Bayswater Chronicle* (London, *ca.* February 13, 1882): Obituary Notice from *The North Devon Herald*. C.M.S.A. Committee of Correspondence Letters: Application from James Hunter, December 30, 1839; replies to Questionnaire, February 8, 1840.

[35]C.M.S.A., James Hunter to Church Missionary Society, July 30, 1850.

in the early eighties because it was thought to be showing signs of being unsafe, but the church itself survived until 1896. Three members of Sir John Richardson's Expedition in search of Franklin, which wintered at Cumberland House in 1847, worked for some weeks on the church and its furnishings.[36]

1847 was also a year of tragedy, for on November 20, Mrs. Hunter died. She was only thirty-two, and has been described as "a lady of devoted piety." She was buried in a vault beneath the church.[37]

On July 10, 1848, James Hunter married Jean Ross, daughter of Donald Ross, Hudson's Bay Company Chief Factor of Norway House. Mrs. Hunter was well acquainted with the Cree language and co-operated with her husband in his work on Cree translations, which covered parts of the Prayer Book and three of the Gospels, besides extensive work on Cree verbs. She also translated hymns and Watt's Catechism into Cree herself.[38] Like Archdeacon Robert McDonald (the expert on the Tukudh language of the Yukon and Lower Mackenzie valleys, whose work was done thirty years later), Mr. Hunter was a strong advocate of the use of Roman letters rather than the syllabic symbols. Because of the sound and understanding scholarship he showed in his studies in the Cree language, he received the Lambeth M.A. in 1854, and the Lambeth D.D. in 1876.

In the meantime, while the work of the Church was prospering at The Pas, it was also steadily expanding in another direction. In 1845, in response to inquiries from the natives, Hunter sent one of the best instructed of his Indian boys at The Pas, James Beardy, to Lac la Ronge, a lake about 200 miles north of Cumberland House. This was only a temporary appointment, for in 1846 a native catechist, James Settee, equally as well known as Henry Budd, was sent to Lac la Ronge, and the reports made were so promising that the Church Missionary Society came to the conclusion that a permanent mission station should be established there.[39]

[36]C.M.S.A., Diary of Rev. James Hunter, December 16, 1847; December 22, 1847; March 18, 1848.
[37]C.M.S.A., James Hunter to Church Missionary Society, November 27, 1847.
[38]Ibid., August 3, 1848.
[39]Ibid., August 4, 1846. C.M.S. Report, August 7, 1847. C.M.S.A. and P.A.C., Diary of Rev. Robert Hunt, being instructions of the Church Missionary Society to him, given May 24, 1849.

CHAPTER FIVE

David Anderson: First Bishop

+-+ଔଲ+-+ଔଲ+-+ଔଲ+-+ଔଲ+-+ଔଲ+-+ଔଲ+-+ଔଲ+-

His Lordship was indeed in its widest sense a man of large humanity,
of a benevolence and goodness, great and untiring; his hand was ever
open as the day to melting charity. . . . The patron and friend of all
schemes of literary advancement, the dispenser of a generous
hospitality, this Christian gentleman has earned with us the guerdon
of a good name—better than riches.

THE NOR'WESTER, *Winnipeg, May 31, 1864*

When the Right Reverend John Medley of Fredericton heard there
was a prospect of a Bishop being sent to the Red River, he thought
there might be some difficulty in finding the right man: "He ought to
have an iron constitution, a loud voice and be able to row, swim, and
do all sorts of rough mechanical work. An unhandy scholar would
never do. Where is to be found Paul the tent maker?"

David Anderson appears to have had none of the qualities suggested,
and yet his initiative, judgment, tact and quiet persistence, which
accepted disappointment without discouragement, laid foundations
upon which the work of the Church has been securely built in the
years that have passed since his time.

David Anderson, son of Captain Archibald Anderson, H.E.I.C.,[1] was
born in London, England, on February 10, 1814. He received a good
classical education at Edinburgh Academy, where one of his classmates
was Archibald Campbell Tait. While still at school, David Anderson
was confirmed by Bishop Sandford of Edinburgh. Later he proceeded
to Exeter College, Oxford, where he took the B.A. degree in 1836.
Exeter was then second only to Christ Church itself in enrolment;
twenty years later (1856), Bishop Anderson was glad to be asked to
lay the foundation stone of the present magnificent chapel. In a
letter to his young friend and former pupil, James Ross (then at the
University of Toronto), dated February 9, 1855, the Bishop wrote of
his Oxford days:

You ask regarding my own university course. I thought you had
known regarding it that my health broke down under study and
that so all my high hopes and those of my tutors for me were disappointed. But this my disappointment at the time when I said all

[1]Honourable East India Company. Incorporated by Charter in 1600, its
powers were curtailed by Act of Parliament in 1858, and it was extinguished in
1873.

too often "all these things are against me" was under God the very cause of my advancement in the Church and mainly contributed to place me at so early an age in that position of which I only feel my own unworthiness. . . . For many months I thought my prospects marred for life as all depended on my own exertions. . . . Instead of a college life as Tutor and Fellow, this led me to the activity of clerical life in a large town. With a curacy in Liverpool, and from pupils of my Rector (all of them now clergymen, save one who died a clergyman) and afterwards when connected with the Clerical College at St. Bees, my mental powers had free scope and I find now that all was in the infinite wisdom of God a preparation for the varied duties, which since have devolved upon me.[2]

David Anderson was ordained deacon by the Right Reverend John Bird Sumner, then Bishop of Chester, on April 23, 1837, at Holy Trinity Church, Clapham, Surrey, England, and priested by the same Bishop on July 8, 1838. His first curacy was at St. Andrew's Church, Liverpool (1837-1838), his second, at St. George's Church, Everton, a suburb of Liverpool, and in 1841 he became Vice-Principal of St. Bees' College in Cumberland, a post he held for six years. In 1841 he married the eldest daughter of Mr. James Marsden of Liverpool. Mrs. Anderson died in 1848, leaving him with three young sons. In 1848 David Anderson became perpetual curate of All Saints', Derby (now the Cathedral Church of that Diocese), but was only there for a few months. In the early spring of 1849 he was nominated as First Bishop of Rupert's Land by the Archbishop of Canterbury (John Bird Sumner), who had ordained him when Bishop of Chester.[3] To accept the position must have been a momentous decision, but according to Bishop Anderson's own account what the Bishop of Montreal had written about the necessities and opportunities of Rupert's Land had a great deal of influence upon him.

The Bishop and the Church Missionary Society

A few days before his consecration, apparently on May 25, 1849, Dr. Anderson (the D.D. degree had been conferred upon him by Oxford University) was present at a meeting of the Church Missionary Society Committee, the ostensible purpose of which was to give instructions and bid farewell to the Reverend Robert and Mrs. Hunt, who were to sail on the same ship with him, and proceed to the Lac la Ronge mission station. The occasion was made an opportunity for reference to the new Bishop of Rupert's Land: "This appointment has relieved the Committee from many anxious responsibilities. It has rendered the task of this day comparatively light. Many questions which the missionaries in their late communications have deferred home will

[2]P.A.M., The Alexander Ross Papers. David Anderson to James Ross, February 9, 1855.
[3]P.A.M., *ibid.*

now be solved by the proper authority. Many injunctions which the Committee would have desired to have impressed upon the missionaries abroad will now be better endorsed by paternal authority."

On the same day, the Committee of Correspondence of the C.M.S. went into practical action, resolving:

1. That adverting to the shortness of time which intervened before the departure of the Bishop to Rupert's Land it is expedient to make an immediate grant out of the Jubilee Fund to the North West America Mission, and that the sum of £500 be apportioned out of that fund for the establishment of a Church Missionary Seminary in Rupert's Land for the education and training of Native Teachers under regulations to be agreed upon between the Committee and the Bishop.

2. That the Committee will be prepared to appoint one of the additional ten Missionaries to be sent out in connexion with the Jubilee Fund to Act as Tutor of the proposed Institution, if a suitable person for that office can be selected.

3. That a limited number of Native Catechists or other pupils be maintained at the proposed Institution at the expense of the Society, with a view to their Ordination and employment in the Mission.[4]

The day before he sailed the Bishop received a copy of this resolution with a long covering letter under the signature of the Reverend Henry Venn, Secretary of the Society, dated June 5.[5] It explained in considerable detail "the general principles upon which the Society conducts its operations in relation to the ecclesiastical authorities connected with its fields of labour." Among the points mentioned was the right of the Committee to dissolve its connection with a missionary, though the latter continued to be licensed by the Bishop; the form of the licence the missionary would receive from the Bishop (a form drawn up by Bishop Heber of Calcutta was recommended); the matter of employing catechists; the advisability of not consecrating churches or chapels as long as they were used for the purposes of missions, as consecration would limit their use as schoolrooms, places for instructing catechumens or congregations of heathen enquirers. It was pointed out that the Society might request the ordination of its agents without title or formal presentations; further, that persons connected with a mission abroad stood in a different relation to the Society from those sent out from home (England). A warning was added that with reference to a native ministry, "the scale [of salary] should have reference to native wants and habits and not to European requirements. The salary ought to be such as a native Church will be ultimately able to provide for the sustentation of its ministers."

[4]C.M.S.A., *Minutes of the Committee of Correspondence*, May 25, 1849.
[5]C.M.S.A., Henry Venn to Bishop David Anderson, June 5, 1849.

The Committee requested that Henry Budd and James Settee and any others of the same rank should be regarded as candidates for Holy Orders, and that Budd would spend the next winter at the Red River under the Bishop's supervision, to enable him to judge the standard of native teachers. The Committee further pointed out that it was the purpose of the Society to establish a seminary at the Red River with a view to training up a native ministry; the £500 that had been voted for this purpose was to be regarded only as a foundation to begin; it would probably be necessary to begin the school or college in a small way and admit general scholars until education became more generally diffused; it was hoped eventually to provide a tutor to assist in this work, but in the meantime Mr. Hunt would be available for some of it. The Committee also suggested the early establishment of a Corresponding Committee at the Red River under the Bishop's presidency, to take into consideration questions of a financial or temporal character: "they pray also that they may be enabled to strengthen your hands to follow up our important opening, under Divine Guidance and blessing, so that a flourishing native Church may be firmly established in that distant land of early promise." This latter expression of goodwill was loyally maintained by the Society over many years.

The Bishop comes to Rupert's Land

Bishop Anderson and his party went aboard the *Prince Rupert* at Gravesend on Wednesday, June 6, 1849. The Reverend Robert Hunt kept a diary[6] of the voyage, from which interesting details can be learned.

Stromness was reached on June 18 and about ten days were spent there. By July 27 the ship had come in sight of Resolution Island, icebergs were abundant, and she was fast in the ice for a time. Towards the end of the voyage they became short of water, though Hunt observed they might have found ice if necessary and melted it. Throughout the voyage he assisted the Bishop at the services on board and found the harmonium a great assistance to their psalmody. On August 16 they landed at York Factory, "all safe and in good health." The next day there was some discussion with Chief Factor Hargrave on the subject of permission having been given by the Company for the location of a missionary at Lac la Ronge, but the matter was settled by pointing out that Mr. Settee had been there for several years.

On August 18 work was begun among the Indians, who were visited in their tents, and subsequently were met in the large hall of the Factory daily during their stay at York. It was in this hall on August 19,

[6] C.M.S.A., P.A.C. and R.L.A., Diary of Rev. Robert Hunt.

1849, that Bishop Anderson preached his first sermon in this diocese, from the text, II Corinthians, X, 14: "We are come as far as to you also in the preaching of Christ."

York Factory was left on August 29, Hunt reports:

Embarked in two boats, handsomely provided and furnished by the Co. . . . *September 1st:* Reached the head of Steel River. *September 4th:* Crossed the first portage (clay exchanged for prim. rocks). *September 10th:* Lake, Jack River. Black Currants. *September 16th: Sunday.* Oxford House. Mr. Robertson, Scotch. *September 23rd:* Last port-[age] before breakfast N-[orway] House, afternoon Evening Service Mr. Hunter. *September 24:* Monday Ross Ville. Mr. Mason and his people. *October 3rd:* Mouth of the River 7 a.m. Ducks, plovers, Indian Settlement 2 p.m. Lower Fort, evening. Found that the Co. had prepared a double house for us, the one part for His Lordship, the other for his Chaplain. . . . Heard that Mr. Macallum had died about 7 o'clock this morning. He had wished to live until the Bishop arrived. I never knew a man more generally beloved.[7]

Mr. and Mrs. Chapman had come to the Diocese with the Bishop under the auspices of the Colonial and Continental Church Society; Chapman was ordained by the Bishop on December 23, and appointed to Middlechurch. The Bishop's first official act was to be present at the funeral of the Reverend John Macallum on October 5, which was taken by Mr. Cockran. The unexpected and much lamented death of John Macallum left the Red River Academy without guidance, and seems to have caused the Bishop to establish himself at the Upper Church (St. John's) rather than at the Lower Church, as he was fully expected to do.[8] It was Macallum's wish that the Bishop should be given the opportunity to purchase the Red River Academy property, and in view of the expressed desire of the Church Missionary Society for the establishment of a school or college, it was natural that the Bishop should accept it.

The Bishop preached for the first time in the Colony itself on Sunday, October 7, in the old St. Andrew's Church, the now treasured stone church not then being quite complete.

David Anderson: The Man Himself

The man who writes a book often, quite unconsciously, writes himself into it. Bishop Anderson in his story of his journey to Moose Factory to ordain John Horden in 1852 (a very rare little volume called *The Net in the Bay*),[9] has done this in no small measure. Here his evangeli-

---

[7]*Ibid.* Quoted because dated accounts of the canoe journey from York Factory to Red River are rare.

[8]C.M.S.A., *In Correspondence.* Letter to Bishop Anderson from the congregation of Grand Rapids, October 20, 1849, and his reply, November 6, 1849.

[9]David Anderson, *The Net in the Bay; or, the Journal of a Visit to Moose and Albany* (London, 1854). A second edition was published in 1873 to promote interest in the newly formed Diocese of Moosonee, and this contains useful and interesting notes by the author.

cal outlook and zeal are revealed as the primary motive of his life. His consideration for the welfare of the Indians; his concern about those of mixed blood living in the vicinity of the H.B.C. posts; his desire to put the work of the mission field upon a solid basis; his energetic use of time and opportunity; his infinite, kindly patience, and his joy when even a little progress had been made, were manifestations of David Anderson's character. Without scientific training in the modern sense, he was a keen observer of nature, and sincerely regretted the lack of knowledge that prevented his making more of his opportunities. He had a companionableness about him that made him welcome not only at the H.B.C. Fort, but around the camp fire and in the Indian's tent as well. He loved music, especially sacred music, noting from time to time the hymns sung at the services en route and how well they went, how the Indians joined in and particularly the musical evenings he enjoyed at Moose Factory, in company with "gentlemen in the service." "My men assisted, while our young friends at the Fort furnished some sweet trebles."

His reading was wide—the library he left at Bishop's Court, Winnipeg, became the nucleus of the present St. John's College Library—and *The Net in the Bay* is illuminated with quotations from Latin and Greek authors, and the works of now forgotten poets.

David Anderson was a man of his age. He was a convinced evangelical churchman, cultured, kindly, singularly modest. The solidity of the foundations he laid has perhaps been obscured by the greater structures built upon them by others who worked under more fortunate circumstances and with greater opportunities; nevertheless, by his quiet courageous persistence he opened up the whole of western Canada to the Gospel. There has been much filling in of vacant spaces since his time, but it was only the actual shores of the Arctic Ocean that were not reached. Of him it may be truly said that he was not disobedient to the vision that had come to him. After the priesting of John Horden at Moose Factory, August 24, 1852, he wrote:

The depth and meaning of the Ordination Service, I had felt more than ever today. The one word, from which I had before been almost inclined to shrink, I now felt to be true, though very humbly and depressingly—the term "Father" and "Father in God." As I heard the Indian use it, and with hope and confidence speak of me "Our Father" —as I looked on my two young friends, the one especially my own son in the ministry, and received their tokens of affection and respect—as I looked on those baptized and confirmed during my stay, I felt that, however unworthy of the title, the design of the office was that I should be as a father to many.

St. John's School and Cathedral

When Bishop Anderson arrived at the Red River it was his own, and everybody else's, intention that he should make the Lower Church

(St. Andrew's) the centre of his activities. But in October, 1849, the immediate and most pressing problem was the welfare of the Red River Academy and the nearby Upper Church, left destitute of both academic and pastoral care by the death of Mr. Macallum. The Bishop took over the supervision of the school, and Miss Anderson, his sister, the care of the pupils, all arrangements being completed by October 26.

In his Charge to his clergy at the end of 1850, the Bishop said with respect to his taking up this educational work, that God seemed to direct him not to refuse the opportunity to do so:

It has laid upon me more of labour, but that labour has had its own reward. To it, in anticipation of the future, I have given the name of "St. John's Collegiate School." Should I be permitted to rebuild the Church there it would be St. John's, my own Cathedral Church, called after the Apostle whom we think of today. Near it would be rebuilt then, if circumstances permit, with more of architectural plan, the Collegiate School. As a part of it, at present and hereafter, it may be a separate building, would be the institution for the training of a native ministry, St. John's College. . . . And over all . . . I would inscribe as the motto of duty and hope, "In Thy light shall we see light."[10]

The Bishop admitted that more of his own time had been devoted to the work of education and the intellectual training of the young, than would have been justifiable under other circumstances: "but in this I feel I am preparing some who may be hereafter employed in the ministry of the Word: and to others I am imparting a tone of mind which may be of use in improving the general character and aspect of the country." His objective was quite clear: "My hope has been throughout that, by training several in the acquaintance in the grammars of many different languages, they may at some future day be able to analyse more clearly the framework and structure of the Indian tongues from a deeper insight into the principles of comparative grammar."

In the same year, 1850, to encourage pupils the Bishop instituted scholarships that provided free tuition, £10 sterling as pocket money, and the privilege of sitting at the teachers' tables at meals. The first two such scholars went on to Peterhouse, Cambridge—the first of a long procession of students going to the English universities from St. John's. The senior, Colin Campbell McKenzie, later became the first Superintendent of Education in the Province of British Columbia; the other, Roderick Ross, entered the service of the Honourable Company. Bishop Anderson had already succeeded in obtaining support from two of the other English missionary societies for the expansion of this work.

[10]David Anderson, *Charges to the Clergy of Rupert's Land* (London, 1851), 42. Bishop David Anderson delivered five Charges to his clergy during his episcopate, which were issued and printed separately, only later being brought together in one bound volume.

In 1849 the Society for the Promotion of Christian Knowledge made a grant of £700 sterling to the Bishop of which £300 was spent in completing the purchase of the Red River Academy property from the Macallum estate, £300 in extending and improving the buildings, and £100 on books and library.

From 1854 to 1859 the Society for the Propagation of the Gospel paid the stipend of the Reverend Thomas Cochrane,[11] son of the Archdeacon, as being in charge of the "Collegiate School for the training, among others, of candidates for the Ministry." In 1855 also he organized the first Collegiate Board, with a distinguished company of members: the Bishop, Archdeacons Cockran and Hunter, Colonel Caldwell (then Governor of the Settlement), Judge F. G. Johnston (the Recorder), Mr. J. S. Clouston (H.B.C. Accountant), and Revs. Abraham Cowley (Indian Settlement), W. H. Taylor (St. James) and C. Hillyer.[12] The Board held its first and only meeting on May 22, 1855. After 1856 the bright hopes for the institution seem to have faded, due perhaps to the Bishop's absence in England, and the heavier burden he was called upon to bear owing to the expansion of the work in the Diocese, particularly in the northwest in subsequent years.[13] From this time until 1866 the school remained closed, and higher education lapsed for the time being in the Red River Settlement.

The Upper Church becomes St. John's Cathedral

A Bishop must necessarily have a seat, even if the church he selects is only temporarily used as such, under the name of Pro-Cathedral. For several years after his arrival in his Diocese the Bishop of Rupert's Land was without one. He consecrated the Lower Church as St. Andrew's on December 19, 1849, and here his first ordinations took place (John Chapman, December 23, 1849; Henry Budd, deacon, John Chapman and William H. Taylor, priests, December 22, 1850; Thomas Cochrane, June 6, 1852), but he lived fifteen miles away and his interests seem more and more to have centred around the Upper Church and the school close to it. The consecration of either the Upper Church or the Middle Church was a matter attended with some difficulty, as they seem to have been looked upon as community churches rather than as specifically Church of England ones. The Presbyterian element in the Settlement claimed proprietary rights in both churches,

[11]*Two Hundred Years of the S.P.G., 1701-1900* (London, ca. 1901). The Appendix lists missionaries supported during this period. Thomas Cochrane was educated at the C.M.S. school in England for sons of missionaries, and graduated from University College in the University of Durham in 1845. He always suffered from ill-health, never held a specific pastoral charge in Rupert's Land, and spent most of his ministerial life teaching, either at St. John's Collegiate School, Parish school or at Portage la Prairie. He died in Toronto in 1868.

[12]R.L.A., *St. John's College, Winnipeg, Papers.*

[13]A. C. Garrioch, *The Correction Line* (Winnipeg, 1933), 101.

and in the burial ground at the Upper Church. These rights were, to some extent, acknowledged, and the Hudson's Bay officials, both in London and in the Northern Department, were unwilling to yield to either side.

In the summer of 1850 Eden Colville became Governor of Rupert's Land and a settlement was reached on the basis: (1) that the Upper Church should be valued and a proportionate amount be paid to each seceder from the congregation: (2) that the right to burial in the existing churchyard be reserved: (3) that a grant of land on Frog Plain should be made to the trustees of the Presbyterian community: (4) that the Company would make a grant of £150 towards building a new church there.[14] And so, after thirty years of being ministered to by the Church of England, the Presbyterians finally secured a minister and church of their own. The Reverend John Black arrived from Montreal on September 19, 1851, and thereupon three hundred people left the Church of England to form his congregation. Twenty-eight seats were vacated in the Upper Church and their proprietors were paid £84 by the Bishop.

When the Bishop consecrated the Middle Church as St. Paul's on January 6, 1853, there was a protest that it was an interference with their proprietary rights by two of the residents, and the circumstance gave a good deal of pain to him. The Upper Church was consecrated on October 28, in the same year, as the Church of St. John the Evangelist. The Bishop announced in his second Charge on December 27, 1853, "of consecrations we have had two, though not of new Churches, St. Paul's and St. John's, with the churchyard of the former. The local difficulties, which for a time prevented the consecration of the latter Church, having at length been obviated, the Church, in which we are met, now bears the name of that Apostle and Evangelist, to whom this day of our anniversary is more especially dedicated. St. John's would thus be in effect, though not in name, our Cathedral Church, set apart for purposes of more solemn assembly, until at some future day a more suitable structure can be raised."

Although it had survived the great flood of 1852, the stone Upper Church built by the Reverend David Jones in 1833 had so deteriorated that its walls had had to be buttressed with timbers, and it was generally acknowledged that it would have to be replaced. To the task of raising funds for rebuilding St. John's, the Bishop applied himself when he visited England in 1856, and he secured plans there from an architect friend in Derby. These, however, had to be much modified,

[14]E. E. Rich and A. M. Johnson, ed., *London Correspondence Inward from Eden Colvile* (London, Hudson's Bay Record Society, 1956). W. L. Morton, Introduction: pp. xcix, civ, cv; Letters: pp. 83-96, 121, 197-199, 250-254. Garrioch, *op. cit.*, 162, 169-175. C.M.S.A., Letters of Rev. W. Cockran, December 12, 1851.

and it was not until the summer of 1861 that a new building was begun, towards which the Hudson's Bay Company and the Society for the Promotion of Christian Knowledge each contributed £500. The last service in the old building was held on Whitsunday, May 19, 1861. By the following year sufficient funds were available to add a tower to the new church and the opportunity was taken to lay the corner-stone on June 4, 1862.

Part of the account printed in the *Nor'Wester* of June 11, 1862, is worth quoting:

On last Wednesday the 4th inst., the ceremony of laying the corner stone of St. John's Cathedral was performed. All the Clergy of the Settlement were present. . . . The following, moreover, who might not have been expected were present; Rev. William Stagg of Fairford, Rev. James Settee of Fort Pelly and Rev. R. McDonald of Islington. Among laymen there were—His Excellency A. G. Dallas, Esq., Governor in Chief of Rupert's Land, William McTavish, Esq., local Governor of Red River Settlement, John Black, Esq., [William Caldwell] Editor of the *Nor'Wester*, John Inkster, Esq., Councillor of Assiniboia, and a great many others, not a few Presbyterians being among the number. The main building being already completed, the south corner of the tower was honoured with the bottled memorial deposits. . . .

The Rev. John Chapman having offered up Prayer, the Bishop invited Governor Dallas to lay the Corner-Stone, explaining that it was not strictly the commencing of a new work. Twenty-nine years before the foundation of the previous Church had been laid by Mr. H. H. Berens, the present Governor of the Company in London, and it was a happy coincidence that the name of the Governor in Chief in Rupert's Land should be joined with that of Mr. Berens that day. The building now being erected was only a modest and unpretending Church to which he hoped the tower to be founded today would give something of character and appearance, making it a landmark to the traveller on the plains. . . .

The Rev. W. H. Taylor, as Registrar of the Diocese, enumerated the documents to be deposited under the Corner-Stone. . . . This done the Lord Bishop led the way out of the Church to the corner of the tower . . . and Governor Dallas then took a Mason's hammer, and gently tapping the corner stone said, — "In the name of the Father and of the Son and of the Holy Spirit, I now lay the corner stone of this Cathedral."

The vote of thanks to the Governor was moved by Archdeacon Hunter and seconded by Recorder John Black. Mr. Black expressed his great satisfaction as an old member of the church in seeing there friends from different Protestant denominations, and felt it implied the spirit of charity and love in the Settlement, which he trusted would be strengthened and would foster a spirit of harmonious co-operation in every good work. "The Doxology was then sung and the Lord Bishop of Rupert's Land offered up prayer and pronounced the Bene-diction. The laying of the corner stone of St. John's Cathedral is the first public act performed by Governor Dallas in this country—not an unsuitable inauguration of any Governor's career."

Within two years this sixty-foot tower was the cause of much anxiety, and even of alarm on one occasion, when an over-large flag in heavy wind wrapped itself around one of the pinnacles and dropped the latter with a bang on the roof during morning prayer. Letters appeared in the *Nor'Wester*, daily measurements were made of the decline of the perpendicularity by the Reverend T. T. Smith, who was temporarily in charge of the church, and the public was reassured by Archdeacon Hunter, the senior cleric. On April 6, 1872, the tower was reported to be twenty-six inches out of perpendicular and leaning heavily against the main building. It was taken down in 1875 and the west wall rebuilt. Finally, in 1913, the whole building was declared unsafe and the last service in it was conducted on November 2, 1913, by Canon (later Dean) J. W. Matheson. In 1926, the old building was pulled down and its stones incorporated in the foundation and north wall of the present Cathedral.[15]

In his second Charge on December 27, 1853, Bishop Anderson announced that the Diocese had in a manner divided itself into three portions, for practical purposes sufficiently distinct.

This is a beginning, and has naturally led to that organization of the two parts of the Diocese (the third being not yet ripe for it) which I announced officially today, the creation of the two Archdeaconries, the one of Assiniboia, the other of Cumberland and York. To the one Archdeaconry I have appointed, and admitted in your presence, the senior clergyman among us, [the Reverend W. Cockran] as a small token of approval of the labours of more than a quarter of a century in this Settlement, which in no little measure he has contributed to found. . . . To the other Archdeaconry an absent brother will be appointed, and in his case (for the gifts of all are different) it is energy in carrying out translations into the native tongue, as well as practical wisdom in planting and conducting subordinate stations on the Saskatchewan, that I would wish to distinguish and reward. [The Reverend James Hunter of Christ Church, Cumberland] . . . and now, if anything in the providence of God should happen to myself; I leave the work in the hands of those who would not suffer harm or injury to accrue to it.

Moose Factory: "The Net in the Bay"

The third district to which Bishop Anderson referred in his Charge on December 27, 1853, was the area that centred around Moose Factory at the south end of James Bay. It was not until 1850 that the Church

[15]*C.M.S. Proceedings 1859-60.* Bishop Anderson visited Stanley on the Churchill River in the summer of 1859, and was greatly impressed with the beautiful Holy Trinity Church there, then recently completed by Rev. Robert Hunt. The Bishop felt that it would make an admirable cathedral church, but for the fact that it was constructed of wood. Holy Trinity Church survives as the oldest Anglican church in the diocese and in the civil Province of Saskatchewan. Bishop Anderson's St. John's Cathedral, Red River, built of stone in 1862, has been only a memory for more than forty years.

of England became interested in the Moose Factory district, and a further move was made towards the east when in the summer of 1851 the Reverend Robert James made his way up the Winnipeg River to a point where the Lac Seul or English River joins it, and prepared the way for a mission station at a place called White Dog (for many years better known as Islington).[16]

The story of Christian work at Moose Factory goes back to 1840 when the English Wesleyan Methodist Missionary Society established a mission there under the direction of the Reverend George Barnley. The invitation to do this came from the Hudson's Bay Company, which had been impressed by the work being done by this Society in western Ontario, where Governor Simpson had personally had contact with it. William Cockran and John Smithurst were then the only C.M.S. and Church of England missionaries in Rupert's Land, their efforts being largely confined to the area of the Red River, and there probably seemed little prospect of adding to their number.

And so in the early spring of 1840 four Wesleyan Methodist missionaries made their way into Rupert's Land. The Reverend James Evans, who was born at Kingston-on-Hull, England, in 1801, had been in eastern Canada since 1820. He was made superintendent of the mission, and established himself at Norway House, then the nerve-centre of the Hudson's Bay Company's activities.[17] A cairn and tablet outside the little church at Rossville commemorates his service there, but a more enduring and living monument remains in the syllabic characters by which he taught the Crees of Rupert's Land to read.

[16]C.M.S.A., Diary of Rev. Robert James. His journey was begun on May 14, 1851; White Dog was reached on June 3. The return was begun on June 10, and James arrived back at Grand Rapids on June 18. There is a marginal note: "Absolute fact . . . (but it would be imprudent to give it publicity) it is but too probable that the agents of the Hon. Hudson's Bay Co., will endeavour to strangle the infant settlement" [at White Dog].

[17]J. H. Riddell, Methodism in the Middle West (Toronto, 1946). Methodist Missionary Society Archives, London, England (hereafter M.M.S.A.), Papers related to the Wesleyan Missions, No. LXXIX (March, 1840), p. 27, on the departure of missionaries: "The Rev. Messrs. G. Barnley, W. Mason and R. T. Rundle embarked at Liverpool by the 'Sheridan' for New York on 10th March on their way to the Territory of the Hudson's Bay Company, to commence Missionary Operations amongst the settlers and tribes of that vast region of North America, under the protection and chiefly at the expense of the Company whose proposals to the Society have been of the most liberal and honourable character." Wesleyan Missionary Notices, No. 18119, New Series, June and July 1840, p. 27. (Postscript, Arrival of Missionaries.) "The Revs. Barnley, Mason and Rundle arrived in New York on their way to the Territory of the Honourable the Hudson's Bay Company on the 12th of April." Wesleyan Missionary Notices, Vol. 10, No. 46, New Series, October 1842: Letter from James Evans, July 7, 1842. Wesleyan Missionary Notices, Vol. 10, No. 49, New Series, January 1843, pp. 225-235: R. T. Rundle reached Norway House on June 5, 1840, having travelled with the H.B.C. brigade that left Lachine on April 2. James Evans arrived in early August. He commenced clearing the ground for the new mission station at Norway House on August 25, 1840.

The Reverend Robert T. Rundle went as far as Edmonton and for eight years laboured among the Indians of the foothills.

The Reverend William Mason went first to Rainy Lake, about where Fort Frances now is, but as the work was not prospering particularly, in 1843 he went to Norway House and three years later succeeded Evans as superintendent. On June 29, 1854, Mr. Mason was ordained by Bishop Anderson in the Upper Church (St. John's), priested on July 25, and sent to York Factory, where he remained until he returned to England about 1870. Of him, Bishop Machray said to his Synod in 1873: "He leaves behind with us a noble monument to his service. A district which he found heathen is left Christian. The Indian converts are able to read in their own tongue the Bible which he translated."

The fourth of these Wesleyan Methodist missionaries was the Reverend George Barnley who made his way to Moose Factory direct from Montreal by way of the Ottawa River, Lakes Temiskaming and Abitibi. He spent eight years in the district before returning to the active Methodist ministry in England. Dr. J. H. Riddell, in *Methodism in the Middle West*, describes him as being "cast in a thoughtful, gentle, introspective mold." While he was at Moose, a youth named John Alexander MacKay came under his influence and had his thoughts turned to the work of the Church. More than seventy years later, at the Centenary Proceedings of the Diocese of Rupert's Land in 1920, that same youth, now become the Venerable (in title and age) Archdeacon of Saskatchewan, said: "I think of George Barnley as my spiritual father."

Mr. Barnley was not replaced when he left Moose Factory and for a time Christian work there lapsed. The appeal of the Hudson's Bay Company officers to the new Bishop of Rupert's Land for ministrations, was passed on by Bishop Anderson to the Church Missionary Society. The appeal received the warm approval of the newly-formed Corresponding Committee of the C.M.S. in Rupert's Land, which held its first meeting on October 30, 1850. (It consisted of the Bishop, Major Caldwell, the Reverend William Cockran and the Reverend R. James.) The Committee "hailed with joy the news of the appointment of another missionary from England and suggested Moose as the suitable station, having been given up by the Hon. Hudson's Bay Company with its Church for this purpose." It seems likely that Chief Factor Robert Miles, who was then in charge of Moose Factory, may have had a good deal of influence in this matter. He and his wife were sincere Christian people who devoted much of their own time to the welfare of the Indians among whom they lived.

Bishop Anderson, in his Charge in 1850, announced "two others,

Moose Fort, James Bay, and Swan River were offered to him by the Hon. Company; from the former the Wesleyans have latterly withdrawn and I hope it may be occupied this summer by a clergyman from the Church Missionary Society, who will gradually open up communications and intercourse with the Indians at Albany, Rupert's Land and the East Main."

The Bishop's letter to the Society reached its destination in the early spring of 1851. The Reverend Henry Venn, the Secretary, replied in a letter dated April 3, "the Committee are making every exertion to find a suitable person for Moose Factory. The Company have promised a passage. If a clergyman cannot be procured they will send out a Schoolmaster to act as a Catechist." The Committee had to take action in May, if it was not to be too late, and so on May 10 a young man named John Horden of Exeter received a letter from Mr. Venn asking whether he were prepared to undertake work at Moose Factory immediately, at the same time suggesting that the Committee felt it would be expedient and advantageous if he went as a married man.[18]

John Horden goes to Moose Factory

John Horden was a native of Exeter, born there in 1828, the eldest son of William Horden, a printer by trade, and his wife Sarah. The boy was educated at St. John's School, and at an early age expressed the desire to become a missionary, but it was not until 1850 that he felt able to offer himself to the C.M.S., and then he hoped to be accepted for work in India. When he left school he was apprenticed to a blacksmith, but having served his time he took up teaching, in which profession he proved himself very capable and he is said to have taught himself, during this period, both Latin and Greek. On May 24, 1851, Horden relinquished the teaching post he was then occupying; on May 25, Miss Elizabeth Oke and he were married; on May 28 they left Exeter for London; on June 8 they sailed for James Bay from Gravesend. The voyage was attended by the usual delays in the ice, but Moose was reached on August 26, 1851.

Horden has written his own description of the scene that greeted him when they landed: "On reaching the Fort, which stands on a rather large island, . . . on the same side of the river, stood a neat little church with a suitable tower, while still farther on were a few Indian tents. . . ."[19]

[18]*Canadian Church Magazine and Missionary News*, Toronto, Domestic and Foreign Missionary Society (March, 1887), 212. Address given by Mrs. Gregory at Hamilton, Ontario. *London Correspondence Inward from Eden Colvile*, 81-82. C.M.S.A., *Minutes of the Committee of Correspondence*, March 10, 1851. Letter from T. D. Anderson, Everton to Henry Venn, May 23, 1851.

[19]C.M.S.A., Letter and Diary of John Horden, August 26, 1851.

Within a few hours of his arrival he visited the whole community, and then began to work systematically on the Cree language the day after he reached Moose. With the aid of an Indian interpreter he even composed a short address that he read to his congregation that same evening. So hard did he work that in a few months he was able to preach in the language without aid, though he found learning Cree more trying than learning either Greek or Latin.[20] He made his first long missionary journey when he visited Albany in January, 1852.

In the summer of 1852 Bishop Anderson made the long journey to Moose by canoe and left his own account of it in *The Net in the Bay*, one of the most charming of all books written on missionary adventure in Canada. The journey of twelve hundred miles took twenty-six and a half days. The Bishop upon his arrival was very impressed with his first view of the place ("very pleasant, more so than any other part of Rupert's Land I have yet visited"), and with the fact that Mr. Horden was at the time engaged with a service and so found at his work, "as a bishop might wish to find all connected with him."

Horden had prepared books by hand in Cree syllabics containing the Ten Commandments, a few leading texts, embodying the essence of the Gospel, and a few short hymns; these he encouraged his people to copy for themselves. The Bishop looked at them and was astonished at what he had accomplished in so short a time. At service, the Indians were given fifteen minutes of instruction in syllabics at the beginning, which the Bishop felt paved the way for the further instruction they received. A couple of days after his arrival, the Bishop examined Horden in the Greek Testament and arranged to read with him the two Epistles to Timothy. He noted: "Being satisfied, from the journals I had before received, and what I now saw of his work, as to his fitness, I resolved, if possible, to ordain him during my stay here, and thus save a large outlay and a great loss of time."

August 22 is described by the Bishop as a remarkable Sunday, his last on this visitation; to the Reverend E. A. and Mrs. Watkins, it was their first in their new field; to Mr. Horden, that of his ordination; to many of the congregation that of their reappearance at the Table of the Lord, from which they had long been debarred; to the Indians who had been confirmed the previous Sunday, that of their first Communion. On August 24, Horden was ordained priest, and the sermon was preached by the Reverend E. A. Watkins. The Bishop left Moose on August 25 and arrived back at the Red River Settlement on October 15, after a somewhat hazardous journey.

Two years after he came to Moose, the ship, in 1853, brought

[20]A. R. Buckland, *John Horden, Missionary Bishop* (Toronto, undated), 38-39.

Horden every requisite for a small printing office. The story is that when his translations in the syllabic characters were sent home to England for printing, it was determined that it would be easier and quicker to cast the type, send the press and let him do his own printing on the spot. The first of these books was issued in 1855, and there is in the Rupert's Land Provincial Archives a copy of a *Bible Catechism in Moose Speech,* dated that year, as printed at Moose Factory.[21] John Horden knew nothing of the printing trade, but he taught himself and also a small boy who helped him. It was slow work, and so different from the hand methods they had seen him use before, that some of his faithful Indians feared this new task had turned his brain. But when the first eight pages were printed off, their delight was almost as great as his own; 1,600 copies of St. Matthew's Gospel in three dialects were issued from this press in the winter of 1854. Before he left with Mrs. Horden for his first holiday in England in 1865, it was estimated that 1,800 Indians in the district had either been baptized or were ready for baptism.

Fort George

The Reverend E. A. and Mrs. Watkins were actually the missionaries promised by the C.M.S. for Moose Factory, but Bishop Anderson, having determined to retain the Hordens at Moose Factory, arranged for the Watkins to go to Fort George,[22] one of the older posts of the Hudson's Bay Company, some distance north on the east coast of James Bay. There they remained until the summer of 1857. Watkins and his wife then travelled first to the Red River Settlement, where for the winter he took charge of C.M.S. work in Sugar Point (since 1860 the parish of St. Clement's Mapleton), and again in the spring of 1858 to The Pas, where they remained until they returned to England in 1863. Like Horden, Watkins gained considerable skill in the Cree language, translating parts of the New Testament, and to him the Church is indebted for the first Cree dictionary.[23]

This work of translation and instruction right on the ground was one of the most valuable contributions made by the early missionaries, who were in direct contact with the Indian people. The Reverend John Smithurst made a small beginning at the Indian Settlement; Archdeacon James and Mrs. Hunter made the first major contribution in this direction when they were at The Pas, using the ordinary

[21]T. C. B. Boon, "Use of Catechisms and Syllabics by the Early Missionaries of Rupert's Land," *The Bulletin,* No. 13 (Toronto, United Church Publishing House, 1960). This gives a fuller account of John Horden's work and his printing press than can be given here.

[22]C.M.S.A., Diary of Rev. E. A. Watkins, August 19, 1853.

[23]Watkins' *Cree Dictionary* was published by the S.P.C.K. in 1865. It has since been revised, but is the basis of the present standard dictionary.

English alphabet, and their translations, since revised, are still in use. But tremendous progress was made when Horden adopted the syllabic system invented by Evans, and as this was concurrently used by the Reverend William and Mrs. Mason at York Factory, the people of the area became familiar with it, and are still using it, one hundred years later. Mr. Mason and his wife, Sophia, daughter of Thomas Thomas of the Hudson's Bay Company, were responsible for the production of the first complete Bible in Cree syllabics, and Mason spent four years in England (1858-1862) in order to see it through the press.[24]

The Reverend Robert and Mrs. Hunt at Lac la Ronge improved on Horden's method of writing out the material and getting the Indians to copy it, by themselves, using a zincograph, apparently an early type of duplicator, to multiply the copies of scriptural material they prepared for their Indians.

Bishop Anderson, when he found syllabics were being used from York Factory down to Norway House, was not impressed; in fact, he was concerned about the matter. Writing to the C.M.S. from York Factory on August 22, 1849, about conditions in the country at the time of his arrival, after commending the Wesleyans as being "instruments of good," and praising their efforts to keep the natives from spirits, he added: "they have, very unfortunately as far as I can see, adopted a new character, the invention of the late Mr. Evans. . . . A few of the Indians can read by these syllabic characters. But if they had only been taught to read their own language in our letters, it would have been one step towards the acquirement of the English tongue."

After seeing the work done at Moose, he modified his opinion, and in his second Charge of December 27, 1853, after commenting that it was "surely an era in the history of our country, that we now have the first Gospel in the Cree tongue, printed in clear and bold type, so as to be capable of use in our schools," he said:

I was sorry to find, that an impression had been conveyed by my previous Charge, that I had wholly condemned the use of these symbols, and that I would not lend my sanction to any translations made in them. . . . As a matter of taste and scholarship, I still prefer

[24]T. C. B. Boon, *op. cit.* The title page to the first Cree Bible, published in 1862 by the British and Foreign Bible Society, bears only the name of William Mason, as translator, and this has been a matter of criticism, particularly by J. H. Riddell in *Methodism in the Middle West.* How this happened is now unexplainable. Bishop Anderson appreciated the work of the Wesleyan Methodist missionaries, regarded some of them as good Cree scholars, and in a letter to the C.M.S. stated that one of his objects in visiting England in 1856 was to propose to the Bible Society the production of a Cree Bible for the use of the C.M.S. *and* the Canadian Wesleyan Missionary Society. R.L.A., Letter from B. and F. B. S., W. J. Bradnock to T. C. B. Boon, July 7, 1961: "The Record says that it [the Cree Bible] was translated by W. Mason, assisted by his wife, Sophia Mason, H. Steinhauer [an Indian pastor], J. Sinclair [a half-breed] and other natives."

the other for the eye, and would recommend it to any clergyman wishing to understand and speak the language. . . . but the ease with which the Indian can both read and write in the Syllabic character, . . . the rapidity with which he can acquire it, . . . the little compass into which he can throw a few hymns and leading texts, these practical advantages recommend it to me for the Indian.

Rapid progress indeed was made in the spread of the Gospel during the first decade of Bishop Anderson's episcopate, progress that has been summed up in two verses that were added to Bishop Heber's well-known missionary hymn, "From Greenland's icy mountains"[25]:

> Now Greenland's icy mountains
> Have caught the joyous sound,
> Glad tidings of salvation
> Are gathering all around;
> Red River, Moose and Fairford
> Peel forth the Sabbath bell,
> The Saviour's Name is honoured,
> Of Christ e'en babes can tell.

> From Indian in his wigwam,
> From Hunter in his lair,
> From swift canoe, from snowy tent,
> Sounds sweet the voice of prayer,
> Uplifted is the Indian's hand,
> Uprais'd the wild man's heart,
> In our Great Father, Three in One
> He, too, now has his part.

Mackenzie River

The second great piece of missionary endeavour begun during Bishop Anderson's episcopate was the evangelization of the Mackenzie River valley.

About 1778 a young Scotsman named Alexander Mackenzie came to Fort Chipewyan on Lake Athabasca. He spent the winter with the veteran Peter Pond, and they very quietly proceeded to explore the river to the north. When they set up a camp on an island off the Arctic coast[26] on July 12, 1789, a new era was opened in the history of Canada, and a new era in the work of the Church. Mackenzie was also the first to penetrate the Peace River country. For more than twenty-five years a fierce conflict between the English and the Montreal companies continued in the Mackenzie River basin, but it came to an end in 1820.

In 1821 George Simpson was appointed by Nicholas Garry as

[25]David Anderson, *The Net in the Bay* (2nd ed., London, 1873), 310.
[26]Douglas MacKay, *The Honourable Company*, 94-95. A. S. Morton, *A History of the Canadian West to 1870-1871*, 412.

Governor of the Northern Department of Rupert's Land, and it is to Simpson that Edmonton owes the early date of its importance, for after 1825 he tried to abandon the old Methye Portage trail into the Athabasca Valley, and began instead to freight goods by roads between Edmonton and Fort Assiniboine.[27] During the next twenty-five years, the explorations of Robert Campbell opened up the western side of the Mackenzie area, and in 1847 Fort Yukon was established by Alexander Hunter Murray. Thus was the ground surveyed and prepared which later was to become a fertile field for the work of the Church.

As early as 1848 Archdeacon Hunter, when at The Pas, had received a message from a Chief named Tripe de Roche (Rockweed) in the Athabascan country, asking that a teacher be sent to his people. To do this was quite impossible at the time for the work at Lac la Ronge was still awaiting consolidation. The Archdeacon, however, never allowed the request to escape his mind, and ten years later, in the summer of 1858, he obtained leave of absence from St. Andrew's in order to carry out this mission in the Northwest. He left rather hurriedly, owing to instructions from Governor Simpson being late in arriving.[28] He wrote an interesting letter to the C.M.S., dated July 31, 1858, from Portage la Loche (Lat. 56 N. Long. 109 W.):

I am writing to you now from the long Portage, about 1500 miles on my way to the Mackenzie River. We arrived here on the 26th instant, making the journey about fifty days from Red River to this place. During the latter part of our journey we had very wet weather . . . thus we sat sixteen and eighteen hours daily in an open boat, and sometimes in very heavy rain. The number of portages we have crossed is about forty-eight; in English River we made three and four daily. . . .

On leaving here we shall go down the current rapidly; five days will take us to Athabasca Lake, another five days to Great Slave Lake, and about five days more to Fort Simpson, on the banks of the mighty Mackenzie River. I shall, however, next spring, God willing, when the ice breaks up in the Mackenzie River, proceed down about 500 miles, visiting Fort Norman and Fort Good Hope, and return in time to Fort Simpson to proceed out to Portage la Loche with the Mackenzie River brigades. . . .

The gentlemen in this district recommend that two married Missionaries be sent out; young men, with good health and active habits, and having an aptitude for acquiring languages. If they come, I can promise them one of the most interesting and enterprizing fields of labour in the whole country. . . .

[27]*Ibid.*, 701. E. E. Rich, *Hudson's Bay Company 1670-1870*, II, 489.
[28]R.L.A., *Minutes of the Corresponding Committee of the Church Missionary Society at Red River*, May 26, 1858. *Church Missionary Society Intelligencer—* 1859 (December), contains Archdeacon Hunter's own account of this, and his report of November 8, 1858.

I had previously recommended single men to be sent out, but, in consultation with gentlemen here from the district, they say young married men would be the best, and, if possible, two should be sent at once. I leave it now for our friends to say whether this effort shall be made in vain.

Hunter reached Fort Simpson on August 16, and from there carried out the plans he had indicated in this letter to the Church Missionary Society. He returned to the Red River in the autumn of 1859. It is recorded that in the same year, on June 10, the Reverend William West Kirkby proceeded to Fort Simpson, where he established a permanent mission station and built the first St. David's Church. Mr. Kirkby had come from England in 1852 to take charge of the Model School at St. Andrew's. He was ordained deacon by Bishop Anderson on December 24, 1854, and priest on January 1, 1856, in St. John's Pro-Cathedral, but continued his work in the Settlement until he left with his wife and family for Fort Simpson.

Kirkby was a great traveller, and in 1861 he made a journey memorable in missionary annals. That summer he descended the Mackenzie to Peel River, ascended the latter to Fort McPherson, and crossed the Rocky Mountains to La Pierre's House. Here he was received by the Tukudh or Loucheux Indians with a warmth that was unexpected, for their reputation was not good. The chief medicine man renounced his "curious arts" in the presence of all, and murder, infanticide, and polygamy were publicly confessed and solemnly abandoned. From La Pierre's House, Mr. Kirkby continued his journey by the West Rat and Porcupine Rivers, and passed Rampart House to Fort Yukon within the Alaskan Border. He repeated this journey the following year and on his return to Fort Simpson early in September, 1862, was met by the Reverend Robert McDonald, and so discovered that the appeal of Archdeacon Hunter for a second missionary for the Athabascan District had been answered.[29]

McDonald resumed his journey to the north and succeeded in reaching Fort Yukon before winter set in. Thus began the forty-two years of missionary service he was to give to the Loucheux people. Mr. Kirkby continued his missionary work at Fort Simpson until 1868, when he returned to England on furlough.

[29] In printing Mr. Kirkby's journals in condensed form in the Church Missionary Society's publications, and in "M.E.J.," *The Dayspring in the West* (London, 1875), the two journeys became confused. His own letter to the Church Missionary Society, November 9, 1862, makes it clear that there was a second journey, and that it was made that year. On May 29, 1861 he left Fort Simpson, reached Fort Youcon on July 5, and got back to Fort Simpson on August 29, (letter of November 30, 1861). In 1862 he left Fort Simpson on May 26, and arrived at Fort Youcon on June 27.

The First Ordinands and Their Work

During his episcopate, Bishop Anderson ordained twenty candidates for Holy Orders. Four of these were Cree Indians, four were country-born, that is of Scots and Indian ancestry, and twelve came from England. In addition he priested the Reverend W. H. Taylor, who was a deacon, having been ordained in Newfoundland, when he came to the diocese.

The Bishop's first ordinand was John Chapman who came out with him. Mr. Chapman had worked under the Bishop as lay reader at All Saints', Derby, and he was the first to be sent to western Canada by the Colonial and Continental Church Society. The ordination took place on December 23, 1849, the first in the diocese after its erection, and a year later, together with the Reverend W. H. Taylor, Mr. Chapman was ordained priest; both services took place in St. Andrew's Church, then the only consecrated church in the diocese. Chapman was appointed to the Middle Church, where he remained until 1864, when he removed to High Bluff, in 1867 returning to England. Archbishop Matheson said of him, "he was an ideal pastor . . . guiding and teaching the settlers not merely in spiritual concerns, but showing them how to live and prosper as tillers of the soil."

When Bishop Anderson returned from The Pas in the summer of 1850 he brought with him Henry Budd and the two young men, Henry Budd the younger and James R. Settee. The ordination of the elder Henry Budd on December 22, 1850, in St. Andrew's Church was a notable occasion, for it marked the beginning of a native ministry (not only in Rupert's Land but on the North American continent) and so realized one of the main aims and desires of the Church Missionary Society.

The Reverend Thomas Cochrane, who was ordained on June 6, 1852, was the only son of the Venerable Archdeacon Cockran. (The alteration in spelling was a family arrangement.) Most of his ministry was devoted to teaching in St. John's Collegiate School and assisting his father in the new work on the Portage Plains. He died in Toronto in the summer of 1868.

On December 19, 1852, the ordinands were, first, Griffith Owen Corbett, the second man sent out by the Colonial and Continental Church Society, who was placed in charge of Holy Trinity, Headingley, then a new field to the west of the present city of Winnipeg. The other candidate was Robert McDonald, who has already been mentioned in connection with the Yukon. He was born in Point Douglas (not far from the present Canadian Pacific Railway station in Winnipeg), in 1829. His first charge after ordination was the mission

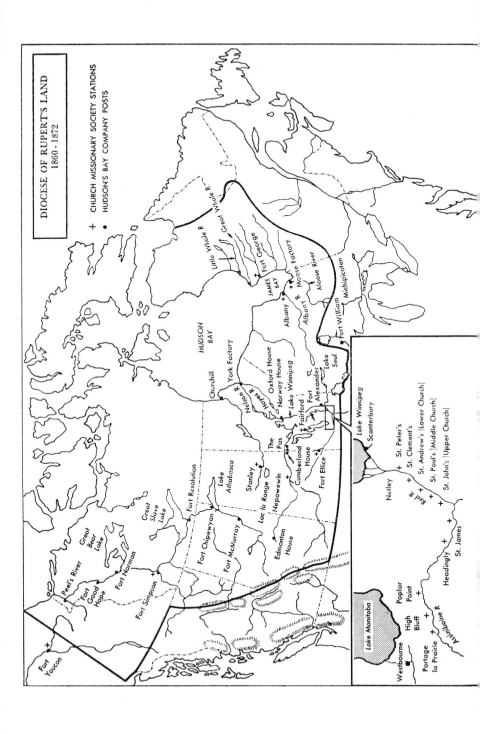

DIOCESE OF RUPERT'S LAND
1860 - 1872

+ CHURCH MISSIONARY SOCIETY STATIONS
• HUDSON'S BAY COMPANY POSTS

at White Dog (Islington) where he spent most of the next ten years, before going to his life's work in the Mackenzie River area.

The ordination, which took place on Christmas Day, 1853, is memorable for two reasons; it was the first held in the old Upper Church, newly consecrated as St. John's Church, and the ordinand was the Reverend James Settee, the second native Indian to become a Church of England clergyman.. James Settee the elder might well be described as "the great itinerant," for after he was ordained he spent the best part of his active life spreading the Gospel through the country between the Saskatchewan and Qu'Appelle Rivers.

June 29, 1854, saw the ordination of William Mason and William Stagg. The work of the former has already been mentioned. Mr. Stagg was an Englishman sent out by the Church Missionary Society. He succeeded Mr. Cowley at the difficult mission among the Saulteaux at Fairford, where he ministered for over eleven years. Fairford, during his ministry, became the centre from which missionary expeditions were sent out on the western plains, with the result that permanent stations were opened in the Touchwood Hills and at Fort Ellice, the latter close to the junction of the Qu'Appelle and Assiniboine Rivers.

The Reverend Henry George spent his first year in the country, teaching school at Fort Alexander, and at the same time preparing for Holy Orders. He was ordained deacon on January 1, 1856. The son of an army surgeon, he had been educated at King's College, London, with a view to entering the medical profession, but decided to give himself to the work of the Church. Mr. George's attitude to his work is plainly indicated in a note left by the Reverend John Ryerson: "Mr. George's station is not yet determined, but he says, although a young man, he has come out with the intention of not returning, having consecrated his life to missionary work in the Hudson's Bay territory; and he had not been in York a day before he began learning the Cree language."[30] Henry George was ordained priest on June 1, 1856, and for the next three years was in charge of the Cumberland Mission at The Pas. From 1859 to 1865 he was incumbent of Westbourne, then a new agricultural settlement southwest of Lake Manitoba in the White Mud River valley. In 1865 George succeeded his father-in-law, Archdeacon Cockran, at St. Mary's, Portage la Prairie. He died in 1881.

Thomas Hamilton Fleming was ordained by Bishop Anderson on May 17, 1857, in All Saints' Church, Derby, England, and was priested

[30]John Ryerson, *Hudson's Bay, or a Missionary Tour of the Territories of the Hudson's Bay Company* (Toronto, 1855), 112.

at Moose Factory in 1860. (More will be said of him in connection with Moosonee.) There was again a double ordination on August 1, 1858, the candidates being Joseph Phelps Gardiner and Henry Cochrane. Mr. Gardiner became the first resident missionary at Churchill, but was only there briefly, spending more of his time on the shores of the Bay at York Factory. In 1865 he succeeded Archdeacon Hunter at St. Andrew's, where he spent some years. His name appears in the secular history of the Red River, as he met the Wolseley Expedition of 1869 at Rat Portage in boats that had been provided privately by himself, Archdeacon McLean and Bishop Machray, and so assisted in guiding that expedition to Winnipeg.

Henry Cochrane was the third native to be ordained. Born at the Indian Settlement and sponsored as a candidate for Holy Orders by the local Church Missionary Society Committee, his ministry was spent almost as much with the white settlers as among his own people. The perfection of his diction and the beauty of his sermons were long remembered in Winnipeg. The full details of his life have never been gathered together, but there was much tragedy in it. His ministry ranged from The Pas to Fort Frances. He died in loneliness at the Jackhead mission on Lake Winnipeg in 1898.

Thomas Thistlewaite Smith was ordained on May 17, 1860, but spent only a few years in Canada, mostly at Stanley and The Pas. His intense interest in nature made a great impression on the Indians. His diaries show him to have been an earnest missionary, deeply interested in the welfare of the people among whom he worked.

The story of Thomas Vincent is one of the early epics of the Church, but except to note that he was ordained at Moose Factory on July 11, 1860, it is best left to its proper setting in the history of the Diocese of Moosonee. On July 21, 1861, the Bishop ordained Henry Budd the younger, and Thomas Cook. Henry Budd had been sent to the Islington Institute of the Church Missionary Society in London, England, where he made an excellent impression, and took up the work at Nepowewin (which had been begun by his father some years before), a station situated near Fort à la Corne, a little east of the forks of the North and South Saskatchewan Rivers. Shortly after he was priested in 1863, he fell a victim to tuberculosis, and died in 1865. The Reverend Thomas Cook was the son of Joseph Cook, for long the catechist and schoolmaster at the Indian Settlement, [St. Peter's, Dynevor]. Thomas Cook's earlier associations had been with Archdeacon Cockran, but after his ordination he worked for a year at The Pas under the Reverend E. A. Watkins, and then became the first permanent missionary at Fort Ellice in 1862, where he was supported by the S.P.G.[31] He went to Westbourne in 1877, and was there until he died in 1891.

Like Thomas Vincent, John Alexander MacKay was of Hudson's Bay Company stock, and his earliest years were also associated with the Moose Factory district. He was trained as a catechist by Horden and Watkins. His ordination took place on May 29, 1862, the service being held in St. Paul's, Middlechurch.

Beginning his ministry at York Factory (1862-1864), he was successively at The Pas (1864-1866), Stanley (1866-1874), and other points in the Saskatchewan area. He spent over sixty years in the ministry, and at his death in 1923 was sincerely mourned by the Indians, who had known him as a wise friend, and the Church, as a gifted scholar and sound advisor.

Two other names must be mentioned. The Reverend W. H. Taylor, came to the Diocese of Rupert's Land in September, 1850, and a month later was appointed to organize a church in what was then called the District of Assiniboia, but has always been better known as St. James. The work was supported for many years by the Society for the Propagation of the Gospel, the first it gave to any parish in western Canada. Mr. Taylor built the first (now old) St. James' Church in 1853, the first rectory in the summer of 1851. The Hudson's Bay Company gave a handsome grant of land, part of which is still held as the cemetery, and most of the rest was later disposed of to form a considerable endowment for the parish. The first services were held in a schoolhouse, which seems to have been on the west side of Omand's Creek. Taylor was also the first registrar of the Diocese. He retired in 1867, returned to England and lived in Clifton, Bristol, until he died on January 19, 1873.

On March 25, 1864, Bishop Anderson ordained a young Englishman, Robert Phair, who had been trained by the C.M.S. at its Islington Institute and was appointed to the Islington mission. This was the beginning of a long ministry to the Indians in that part of Rupert's Land, which since 1899 has been the Diocese of Keewatin. In fact, it lasted for fifty-three years, for he did not retire until 1915, having been Archdeacon of Islington for twenty-seven years.

Conclusion of the First Episcopate in Rupert's Land

After remarking upon the departure of Governor Dallas from the Settlement, Mr. Joseph Hargrave, in his book *Red River,* says: "On the 31st of May (1864) another departure occurred, which, in the minds of a great many in the settlement, left a blank very decidedly

[31]R.L.A., *Fort Ellice Papers,* David Anderson to Ernest Hawkins, April 7, 1862; Ernest Hawkins to David Anderson, August 19, 1862. (S.P.G. Correspondence.)

felt and regretted." Thus he tells of Bishop Anderson leaving the Diocese of Rupert's Land for England, and adds, "although it was by no means certain that His Lordship would not return to the country, the belief that such was the case was general and strong." The demands made upon the Bishop, both in the Settlement and outside, for some time had been the cause of considerable strain, and there is little doubt that he felt it would be unwise to try to carry on, as both his health and the work would suffer.

Dr. Anderson did not actually resign as Bishop of Rupert's Land until later in the year, when he had been in England for several months and had taken the opportunity to consult both the ecclesiastical and secular authorities there. On September 7 it was announced that he had accepted the living of St. Andrew's, the Parish Church of Clifton, Bristol. So came to an end the episcopate of the First Bishop of Rupert's Land, but he never ceased to interest himself in the welfare of the Church in western Canada and was the regular correspondent, often the adviser and always the supporter, of his successor, Bishop Machray. His support was indeed valuable in the councils of the great missionary societies. For sixteen years he remained vicar of Clifton, but was forced to retire in 1881 owing to ill health. He died on November 5, 1885, and is buried in the Parish Churchyard of Clifton.[32]

Bishop Anderson's resignation marks the end of the first era in the life of the Church of England in Rupert's Land. When he came in 1849 there were only five clergy in the country; when he left there were twenty-two. He found a "cathedral," the sides of which were propped up with timbers; he left one that is still remembered with affection, although now but part of its successor. Of his ordinands, John Horden became a great Bishop, and five not only attained the dignity of Archdeacon but lived lives of singular usefulness, each making an outstanding contribution to the work of the Church in general and his own diocese in particular. Dr. Anderson was not a great preacher but his sermons, even if long at times, were quite in line with the evangelical preaching of his day, and some of the passages in them are very appealing.[33] The Reverend Benjamin McKenzie, who was one of his pupils, in his memoirs describes him as "a truly loving and lovable man." He made a lasting impression upon the mind of another small boy when he visited the parish school

[32]R.L.A., *David Anderson Papers*, *The Clifton Chronicle*, Bristol, England, deals with the filling of the incumbency of Clifton Parish Church: April 27, May 18, August 10, August 31, September 7, October 5, October 26, and November 16, 1864. *The Western Daily Press*, Bristol, November 6, 1885, contained an appropriate memorial of Bishop Anderson's life and work.

[33]John Ryerson, *op. cit.*, 64-65. The Earl of Southesk, *Saskatchewan and the Rocky Mountains* (Edinburgh, 1875), 32-33, 362-363.

at Middle Church in 1860; in his centenary sermon in 1920, Archbishop Matheson said, "I can remember the saintly and scholarly Bishop Anderson, not only a Bishop but a visiting pastor who went about doing good and praying in the homes of the settlers."

Looking back over David Anderson's episcopate and surveying how much he accomplished with few resources, one cannot help but feel that he was not only a great man and a great bishop, but primarily a great Christian.

CHAPTER SIX

Robert Machray: Scholar and Statesman

✦✦❬❙❳❧✦✦✦❬❙❳❧✦✦✦❬❙❳❧✦✦✦❬❙❳❧✦✦✦❬❙❳❧✦✦✦❬❙❳❧✦✦✦❬❙❳❧✦✦✦❬❙❳❧✦✦

He fed them with a faithful and true heart, and ruled them prudently with all his power. Psalm LXXVIII, 73.

INSCRIPTION ON THE MACHRAY MONUMENT IN
ST. JOHN'S CATHEDRAL CHURCHYARD, WINNIPEG.

✦✦❬❙❳❧✦✦✦❬❙❳❧✦✦✦❬❙❳❧✦✦✦❬❙❳❧✦✦✦❬❙❳❧✦✦✦❬❙❳❧✦✦✦❬❙❳❧✦✦✦❬❙❳❧✦✦

Bishop Anderson's resignation took effect on October 4, 1864. Very shortly afterwards the Bishopric was informally offered to the Reverend Robert Machray, M.A., Dean of Sidney Sussex College, Cambridge, who consented to undertake the work.[1] The formal offer of the Bishopric by command of Queen Victoria was made in the beginning of January, 1865, but the offer and Robert Machray's acceptance of it were not publicly announced for some months, and the Royal Mandate for the consecration was not issued until May 19, 1865.[2] Bishop Machray was consecrated in the chapel of Lambeth Palace on June 24, 1865, by the Archbishop of Canterbury (Longley).[3]

Robert Machray was born in Aberdeen on May 17, 1831, the son of Robert Machray, who was a member of the Society of Advocates of Aberdeen, an ancient and important legal organization in the north of Scotland. His mother, Christian Macallum, was early left a widow.

[1]Robert Machray, *Life of Robert Machray . . . Archbishop of Rupert's Land* (Toronto, 1909), has been used as source material in this chapter, except where otherwise indicated. The late Archbishop S. P. Matheson told the writer that all of Archbishop Machray's papers were sent to his nephew, Robert Machray, then residing in Aberdeen, and that after the *Life* had been completed these papers were ruined by the flooding of a basement in which they had been stored, pending their return to Winnipeg. Some few things have survived that are now in the Archives of the Ecclesiastical Province of Rupert's Land, notably the two volumes of Synod Journals and pamphlets he had collected and bound for his own use. Some letters and memoranda are to be found amongst the State Papers in the Provincial Archives of Manitoba, and in the letter files of the English Missionary Societies.

[2]*Ibid*, 93 states that the delay was due to the Colenso case, which involved the right of the Crown to present to Colonial Bishoprics. C.M.S.A., Letters of James Hunter. Archdeacon Hunter received a letter from Bishop David Anderson, dated October 21, 1864, which confirms the early approach to Machray. Hunter wrote indignantly to the Church Missionary Society on December 1, pointing out that public opinion at Red River was in favour of himself as second Bishop of the Diocese of Rupert's Land, and that he had fully expected to be nominated.

[3]*Ibid.*, 98. C. H. Mockridge, *The Bishops of the Church of England in Canada and Newfoundland* (Toronto, 1896), 210. O. R. Rowley, *The Anglican Episcopate of Canada and Newfoundland* (London, 1928), 44-47, omits Suther.

and so the education of young Robert was largely acquired through an uncle, Theodore Allan.

Robert entered the old King's College of Aberdeen in 1847. His education up to this point had been purely classical, but at King's College he commenced the study of mathematics; when he graduated in 1851 it was as the outstanding man of his year in academic achievement. In October of that year he entered Sidney Sussex College, Cambridge; he worked so hard that he was placed first in the First Class in Mathematics for his year in the college Christmas examinations, and was elected a Foundation Scholar; at the end of the year he was elected to a Taylor Exhibition of £60 a year.[4]

He did not take the very high place that was expected of him in the Mathematical Tripos in January, 1855, but later in the year he entered a competitive examination for a Foundation Fellowship at Sidney; this he won, and held for the rest of his life. At this time, when there was a much closer association between teaching posts and the Church, a Fellowship was regarded as a title for Orders, and the Bishop of Ely agreed to accept Mr. Machray as a candidate. He prepared himself for Deacon's Orders, and was ordained on Sunday, November 11, 1855 in Ely Cathedral. The same Bishop ordained him priest on November 9, 1856.

In 1857, he became acquainted with Dr. Forbes, the incumbent of St. George's, Douglas, Isle of Man, and spent a year on the island in charge of one of the church districts in Douglas. It was here that Mr. Machray first became interested in the work of the Church Missionary Society. In 1858 he proceeded to the degree of M.A. at Cambridge, resumed connection with his old college, and was invited to return there as Dean, which post he took up at the end of that year. One of the conditions of his acceptance of the office was that he should be at liberty to take up parish or other church work while in residence. In 1859 he found such work first in the small Parish of Newton, about seven miles southwest of Cambridge; in 1862 in the Parish of Madingley. During his residence at Cambridge he was a very active member of the local branch of the Church Missionary Society and became well known to its leading members in London.

In the early part of 1865 he had the opportunity to confer with the committees of the great missionary societies. He also had many long and intimate conversations with Bishop Anderson, with whom he formed a close and lasting friendship, and met Archdeacon Hunter,

[4]*Ibid.*, 11 and 74. Although brought up as a Presbyterian and in Presbyterian surroundings, from the time he was a boy Robert Machray desired to become a member of the Anglican Church. He was confirmed by the Bishop of Ely early in 1853.

who was then in England, taking his last furlough before retiring from the service of the C.M.S.

When he left England Bishop Machray had three objectives in mind: to encourage a native Church; to induce each congregation to aim persistently at self-support; and to secure the ground for the Church of England.[5] His last two months before sailing he spent in raising funds and organizing an English Committee to maintain public interest in the work. The first episcopal act carried out by the new Bishop was on June 25, 1865, when, at the request of the Bishop of London, he ordained to the priesthood, in St. Paul's, Covent Garden, the Reverend William Carpenter Bompas, whose subsequent life was to be dedicated to missionary service in the Yukon and along the Mackenzie River.

Rupert's Land in 1865

It seems necessary here to take up briefly the conditions of the Hudson's Bay Company territory. Fifteen years before there had been little question about the supremacy and powers of the Company in Rupert's Land. During those years a variety of events occurred that had a disintegrating influence within the territory itself; in addition there were pressures from outside. The removal of a number of settlers from the Middle Church district to the neighbourhood of Portage la Prairie during the years 1851-1853, where they were outside the recognized area of the Settlement, greatly disturbed Sir George Simpson, Governor of the Company, and the efforts of the Church to assist them under the leadership of Archdeacon Cockran put rather a strain upon the Company's relationship with the Archdeacon and the Bishop. Members of the community around Fort Garry itself had openly questioned the exclusive rights of the Company to trade in furs, and the Company had found it impossible to suppress free trading effectively. In London, pressure brought upon the Imperial government to inquire into the validity of the Company's famous charter resulted in the appointment of a Select Committee by the British Parliament in 1857, to consider the administration of the Company in general, the possibility of settlement on a large scale in Rupert's Land, and the future of Vancouver Island.

About this time, on the American side of the border, the railways were being pushed farther westward, and as they got nearer to St. Paul, Minnesota, there arose the problems of settlers coming into Canada from the United States, threats of invasion from Sioux Indians, and questions of trade, especially of fur trading across the border. Canada in 1849 was beginning to take an increasing interest in the

[5]*Ibid.*, 96-97.

western prairies and public opinion was gathering which was adverse to the trade and interests of the Honourable Company. Leading Canadians took the matter up and proposed that Rupert's Land should be taken over by Canada but there was no suggestion that the Company should be in any way compensated, and no guarantee that the deeds it had issued, conveying land-holding rights to the settlers, would be respected. It was this attitude towards the land on the part of both government and people in Canada, that had a disturbing influence upon residents in the Red River Settlement.

Both the Imperial and the Canadian governments took steps to acquire a more certain knowledge of the country: the Palliser Expedition made its investigations in 1857-1858; S. J. Dawson surveyed possible routes from the Great Lakes to the Red River, and about the same time Prof. H. Y. Hind of the University of Toronto investigated conditions on the prairies themselves. The British government, through its Colonial Secretary, the Duke of Newcastle, began quietly to consider setting up the Red River Settlement as a Crown Colony. In 1862 the Government of Canada decided to open up steamboat communications with Fort William, and in July of the same year Edward Watkins, President of the Grand Trunk Railway, brought forward proposals for passenger traffic and telegraphic communications to the west coast. This proposal was blocked by the Company's refusal to grant the land required, and Watkins only achieved his object by forming a new company that, at the end of June, 1863, took over the property and charter rights of the Company of Adventurers Trading into Hudson's Bay. This brought a new crisis in Rupert's Land. The connection of the London Committee of the Hudson's Bay Company with its "wintering partners" (chief traders and factors who did the fur trading in the field and shared in the profits), had deteriorated after the death of Sir George Simpson in 1860. When rumours of the sale of the Company were abroad these wintering partners asked to be consulted, but they were not, and this caused great resentment among them and the residents of the Colony, in which, incidentally, the new Company showed no interest. Confederation, which brought the Dominion of Canada into being on July 1, 1867, opened the way for the final negotiations with the Company for the surrender of its charter. What is known as the Deed of Surrender was executed on December 19, 1869, but once again the residents in the Red River Settlement were ignored.

Something must also be said about the state of the Church in Rupert's Land at this time. In 1862 two of the most capable missionaries in the diocese returned to England with their families, the Reverends Robert Hunt of Stanley and E. A. Watkins of Cumberland.

The Missions at Fairford, in the Cumberland District, and the Lac la Ronge District all suffered considerably during these years from the inroads of free traders who had no compunction about exchanging the Indians' furs for liquor; for a time this traffic seriously interfered with the work of the Church. In the summer of 1865 Archdeacon Hunter, then incumbent of St. Andrew's, went back to England ostensibly on furlough, but he never returned to Canada. He was a strong vigorous man, equally eloquent in English and Cree, and he had travelled farther over the diocese than even Bishop Anderson himself. The Archdeacon became vicar of St. Matthew's Church, Bayswater, London. He died in 1882, but he and his wife, Jean Ross of Norway House, continued their translation work for many years after settling in England, and their tombstone in Highgate Cemetery bears the inscription: "By their joint labours they gave the Bible and the Prayer Book in their native tongues to the Cree Indians of Northwest America."

Two weeks before Bishop Machray arrived at the Red River Settlement, the other stalwart from the early days, Archdeacon Cockran, died. These and other changes presented a new field of problems to the new bishop; in their solution he had to rely upon his own judgment.

Bishop Machray arrives in the Diocese

Bishop Machray at the time was only thirty-four, the youngest bishop of the Church of England. His arrival in western Canada marked the beginning of a new era in the history of the Church; it was quite fitting that he should have arrived by a new route. He went from England by way of New York, through Chicago to St. Paul, Minnesota, where he was met by Colin Inkster, later Sheriff. They travelled by train to St. Cloud, and from there had a rather hazardous journey to the Red River Settlement, where they arrived on October 13, 1865.

Bishop Machray commenced his work with vigour. He took personal charge of the Parish of St. John, instituted regular monthly Communions throughout the Diocese, and proceeded to organize parishes wherever possible. Gently but firmly he encouraged offertories to be taken at the services. He made preparations for a conference for May 30, 1866, in which, in addition to the clergy, each parish would be represented by two vestrymen. He also preached in every church in the immediate neighbourhood, then left St. John's on January 11, 1866, for a visitation that entailed a thousand miles of winter travelling, during which he visited and held Confirmations at twelve mission stations, going as far to the northwest as Nepowewin. His outward route took him through Fairford and The Pas, and he returned by way of Qu'Appelle Lakes and Fort Ellice. The determination to revive St. John's College, to train men and provide higher education in the country, became firmly rooted in his mind, and it was towards this goal that he bent his efforts immediately after returning to the Red River Settlement.

The Revival of St. John's College

It is customary to think of Robert Machray as a great administrator. Many think of him as a great educationist who revived St. John's College and School in Winnipeg. A now decreasing number remember his as a true Father in God, who fostered the expanding work of his own Diocese with consummate devotion.

It is difficult to separate aspects of his life, but probably Machray as educationist, would be given precedence; an educational institution was the foundation of his work, his aim from the beginning. On November 10, 1865, hardly a month after his arrival in the Red River Settlement, he wrote to Prebendary Bullock of the S.P.G.: 'I believe that the whole success of my effort here will depend, under God, upon the success of what I purpose—to establish a College." The college that he outlined was to consist of a theological school and a higher school for the Red River Settlement.

There was little left of Bishop Anderson's College in 1865, except some dilapidated buildings. At the last meeting of its governing board, the two surviving members, the Reverends A. Cowley and W. H. Taylor, stated "that the Board, feeling that they never had the college practically put into their hands, and having little or no knowledge of its circumstances, resign whatever was committed to them into the hands of the Bishop that arrangements may be made for beginning the College 'de novo.' "[6] And yet something had endured: the tradition of high academic achievement, plain living, and loyal service that had come from the days of John Macallum.

At the first conference of clergy and laity of the Diocese of Rupert's Land on May 30, 1866, the Bishop deplored the low state of education in the Settlement and laid before it plans to re-establish St. John's College. The English missionary societies had given him great encouragement, and the Reverend John McLean, a distinguished graduate of Aberdeen, had accepted his invitation to come as Warden; the C.M.S. had co-operated by placing Mr. McLean on its staff as theological tutor.

McLean arrived in the Settlement at the beginning of October and

[6]This entry is in the oldest of the Minute Books of St. John's College, Winnipeg, Minutes of the College Board, May 29, 1866. These minutes incorporate those of the meeting on May 22, 1855.

became not only Warden of St. John's College, but also Archdeacon of Assiniboia and incumbent of the Cathedral. The College began its work on November 1, 1866. Some of the dilapidated buildings had been restored, and Archdeacon McLean moved into a house adjacent to Bishop's Court, known as St. Cross. It had been built by Archdeacon Cockran, and was the home in the 1850's of a girls' school conducted by Mrs. Mills, who was brought out from England in 1851 to take charge of it. Under the new management, the Reverend S. Pritchard brought his school in from Middle Church to make it an integral part of the College, and himself became English Master.[7]

About a year later, May 29, 1867, a second Conference was held, and in the course of his address Bishop Machray made a clarion call to the Church to go into action: "Next to the Ministry of the Word and Sacraments comes the Office of educating the young, so that they may receive a sound and religious education." After explaining the government of the college, he said there were three senior theological students and twenty-six pupils in the College School, of whom seven attended a junior theological class; seven out of the ten were preparing for missionary work among the pagan Indians.

The College was incorporated at the first session of the new Manitoba Legislature by an Act dated May 3, 1871. Regularly endowed Professorships in Systematic and Exegetical Theology, Ecclesiastical History and Music were established in the latter part of 1874; each by statute, in 1876, was attached to a residentiary Canonry of St. John's Cathedral. On June 12, 1876, when Bishop Machray handed the College over to the care of the Synod of the Diocese of Rupert's Land, he said: "When we look to the future a further question is pressed upon us—namely, Education. I feel increasingly the importance of our being able to raise up a Ministry of our own. . . . The building up of this College has been my great effort."[8]

While higher education was in this way being provided by the Church, the obligation of providing elementary education was now removed. By an Act passed in 1871 at the first meeting of the Legislature, the Province of Manitoba assumed responsibility for a minimum requirement of education; regular public schools were being built in Winnipeg and other places. The privilege of religious instruction was

[7]This school was founded by John Pritchard, the agent of Lord Selkirk in the earliest days of the Red River Settlement, who conducted it in a house known as "The Elms" on the east side of the Red River. The Council of the Northern Department from time to time expressed its appreciation of Mr. Pritchard's work by giving his school financial support, and tradition is that it derived a number of its pupils from the families of fur traders in the States. About 1862 the school was moved to a site just north of St. Paul's, Middle Church, by his son, Samuel Pritchard (who was ordained by Bishop Machray in 1866). The Middle Church house survived until about 1940.

[8]*Journal of the Synod of the Diocese of Rupert's Land, 1876*, p. 18.

accepted in some parts of the country, but not in others, and no definite policy was ever established by the Church. In Manitoba, the Reverend W. C. Pinkham, later Archdeacon, of St. James' became Superintendent of Schools in 1872, and the Bishop was Chairman of the Education Council from its inception.

While great progress in educational efficiency was made under the Archdeacon's guidance, even the Bishop himself could not stem the current of public opinion in the direction of secularism, though he tried hard to hold the ground. Speaking to the Synod of 1877, he said:

There is nothing to prevent in our schools the daily recognition of the necessity of divine blessing, and of the Word of God as the source of all wisdom and knowledge, in the opening and closing of the school by a simple form of prayer and the reading of God's Word. Further there is nothing that should prevent the learning of the Apostles' Creed and the Ten Commandments and the Lord's Prayer, and the use of a Catechism explaining these that would bring before the minds of the young the leading facts of revealed religion and the Christian Faith. . . . We must endeavour to work with the system that is established by the State, and, as far as we can, supply its deficiences. . . .[9]

An additional burden was assumed by the Bishop in 1877 when, in order to provide for the better education of girls, St. John's Ladies' College was established on a site on Redwood Avenue. This foundation was the result of Archdeacon Cowley's visit to England, where he enlisted the sympathy of the Reverend Henry Wright, then Honorary Secretary of the C.M.S., who generously provided £1,500, later increased to £2,000, to make it possible.

Advancement in the Work of the Church

As a missionary diocese, the size of Rupert's Land was almost beyond comprehension; as a place of residence, the Red River Settlement was still extremely isolated.

The affairs of the Church needed alteration and amendment. Robert Machray was always regarded as an evangelical, but he was a very strong Churchman who loved the Church and, in his own words, "saw no way of doing things better than that which she has directed." He was disturbed by the lack of churchmanship he found in the Settlement. This was an inheritance from the days when the Selkirk Settlers had attended the Red River churches. Besides the institution of monthly Communion Services and more systematic parochial organization, he sought to improve the musical side of the services and to educate the people in the direction of self-support by making the offertory a feature of the weekly services.

The first Conference of the Diocese met on May 30, 1866. There

[9]*Ibid.*, 1877, p. 4.

were only ten clergy present, of whom three came from outside points (the others were too far away), and there were eighteen lay representatives, but there was nothing informal about the proceedings. There was a full morning service with Holy Communion in the Cathedral; the sermon was preached by the Reverend J. P. Gardiner of St. Andrew's. In the afternoon, the Bishop addressed the Conference, which assembled in St. John's parish schoolhouse, and began by expressing his hope that their meeting was the first step towards a Synod. He emphasized that the laity should have a large place in the affairs of the Church, and said that he was anxious that the congregations should become self-supporting, underlining the principle that self-support involved self-government within the Church. The Bishop also looked forward to starting endowment funds to provide an income for various church purposes.

A year later, May 29, 1867, a second Conference was held. This time only eight clergy responded when the roll was called, but there were nineteen laymen present, representing ten parishes. The Bishop remarked that their numbers were small, and that in comparison with other dioceses, the field of work might seem small too, "yet the field, if small, is our field. That should be enough to lend it every attraction, and to demand from us all we can do for it in Christ."[10] He spoke of the difficulties in the way of self-government, but recommended that the Conference decide to form itself into a Synod; "For myself, I have no hope for a young struggling Church like ours which has no endowments, but in the free interchange of the thoughts and views of its members." The Bishop discussed at length the supply and support of clergy, the formation of various necessary funds, and spent considerable time upon the subject of education, in relation to what were then termed the common schools of the parishes. Another considerable portion of the address was devoted to the review of the Church's work among the Indians and prospective white settlers, this latter topic being stimulated by the fact that Confederation was in the air, and the railways in the United States were getting nearer to the border almost every day. He pleaded that the English missionary societies should delay enforcing their policy of decreasing grants to old stations in view of the different circumstances of the diocese, compared with other colonial dioceses.

The first Synod of the Diocese of Rupert's Land met on February 24, 1869. Twenty-four names of clergy now appear on the roll, of whom fourteen were present. The Bishop delivered his Primary Charge, a lively and interesting address of more than 20,000 words,

[10]*Report of the Second Conference of Clergy and Lay Delegates in the Diocese of Rupert's Land*, May 29, 1867, p. 6.

immediately after the Nicene Creed at the opening service. After giving an account of his recent visitation to the mission at Moose, to the Provincial Synod of Canada, and to the Triennial Convention of the Episcopal Church in New York, the Bishop turned his attention to the changes in the Settlement and the future of the country. He felt that the country was different from what it had been, and that the dangerous and disadvantageous isolation of the past would soon be at an end. Out of every £100 given to relieve the famine of 1868, caused by grasshoppers, £70 had been spent on freighting the grain. But there was no cause for despondency in the future: said the Bishop, "nothing is wanting to make this a great and prosperous country, but a sufficient population and easy access to the outer world." There was the usual review of the schools, the finances, and the episcopal work, which brought out the pressing need of Bishops in the Moose and Mackenzie River districts. He discussed the difficulties that had to be met with respect to Indian Missions, and the social problems arising in Indian life. In closing, he urged the laity to acquaint themselves with the doctrine of the church, and said "I would to God you all knew the learning, the piety, the humble reverence for truth, the child-like submission to what was most probably the belief and practice of the first and purest ages of Christianity, that met together to determine and hand down that greatest treasure in the English language, after the Bible, our Book of Common Prayer."[11]

No further Synod was held until January 8, 1873, because of the unsettled conditions caused by the first Riel Rebellion, and a necessary visit of the Bishop to England in connection with the division of the Diocese. By 1873 the time was ripe for this expansion of the work. The affairs of the Red River Settlement from this point are largely only of local interest, and henceforth the growth of the Ecclesiastical Province of Rupert's Land becomes the main theme.

The Birth of the Ecclesiastical Province of Rupert's Land

For more than fifty years after the arrival of the Selkirk Settlers in western Canada, its rivers and streams were the highways of the country; the Hudson's Bay Company posts were located on their banks, and the packets of the fur traders followed their courses. The missionary followed the trader, and the station of the former was often not far from that of the latter. In the early seventies of the last century the time became ripe for the unwieldy Diocese of Rupert's Land to be divided; the pattern of the division closely followed that established by the first missionaries twenty or thirty years before.

In 1840 Henry Budd was sent as a catechist to the Cumberland

<hr>

[11]*Journal of the Synod of the Diocese of Rupert's Land, 1869,* p. 49.

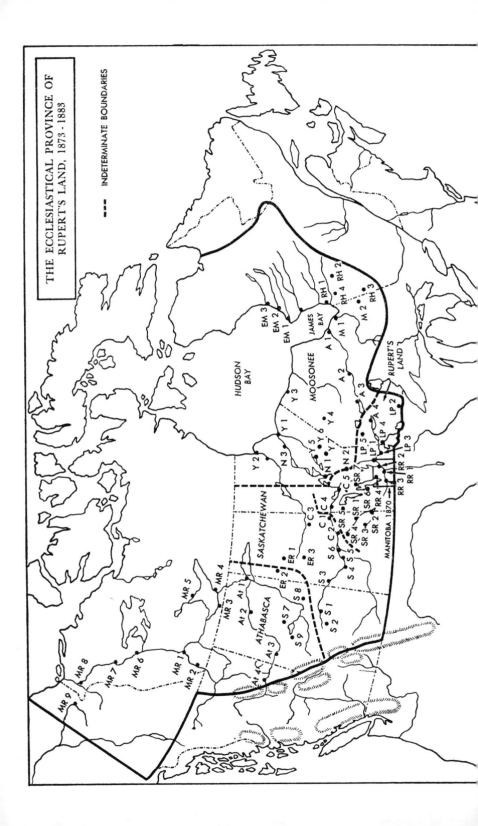

THE ECCLESIASTICAL PROVINCE OF
RUPERT'S LAND, 1873 - 1883

■ ■ ■ INDETERMINATE BOUNDARIES

HUDSON
BAY

JAMES
BAY

MOOSONEE

RUPERT'S
LAND

SASKATCHEWAN

ATHABASCA

MANITOBA 1870

The Ecclesiastical Province of Rupert's Land, 1873-1883, as set up by the Synod of the Diocese of Rupert's Land on January 8, 1873, in terms of Hudson's Bay Company districts and sub-districts, the mapped boundaries of which were indeterminate. They sufficed for organizational purposes until 1883.

KEY TO DISTRICTS AND POSTS

ALBANY
A 1 Albany Factory
A 2 Martin's Falls
A 3 Osnaburgh House
A 4 Lac Seul

ATHABASCA
At 1 Fort Chipewyan
At 2 Fort Vermilion
At 3 Fort Dunvegan
At 4 Fort St. John

CUMBERLAND
C 1 Cumberland House
C 2 Fort à la Corne
C 3 Pelican Lake
C 4 The Pas
C 5 Grand Rapid Portage

EAST MAIN
EM 1 Fort George
EM 2 Great Whale River
EM 3 Little Whale River

ENGLISH RIVER
ER 1 Isle à la Crosse
ER 2 Portage la Loche
ER 3 Green Lake

LAC LA PLUIE
LP 1 Fort Alexander
LP 2 Fort Frances
LP 3 Lac du Bonnet
LP 4 Rat Portage
LP 5 Trout Lake

MACKENZIE RIVER
MR 1 Fort Simpson
MR 2 Fort Liard
MR 3 Hay River
MR 4 Fort Resolution
MR 5 Fort Rae
MR 6 Fort Norman
MR 7 Fort Good Hope
MR 8 Peel's River
MR 9 La Pierre's House

MOOSE
M 1 Moose Factory
M 2 Abitibi

NORWAY HOUSE
N 1 Norway House
N 2 Beren's River
N 3 Nelson's River

RED RIVER
RR 1 Upper Fort Garry
RR 2 Lower Fort Garry
RR 3 White Horse Plains

RUPERT'S HOUSE
RH 1 Rupert's House
RH 2 Mistassini
RH 3 Teniskamay
RH 4 Woswonaby

SASKATCHEWAN
S 1 Edmonton House
S 2 Rocky Mountain House
S 3 Fort Pitt
S 4 Battle River
S 5 Carlton House
S 6 Fort Albert
S 7 Whitefish Lake
S 8 Lac la Biche
S 9 Lesser Slave Lake

SWAN RIVER
SR 1 Fort Pelly
SR 2 Fort Ellice
SR 3 Qu'Appelle Lakes
SR 4 Touchwood Hills
SR 5 Shoal River
SR 6 Manitobah
SR 7 Fairford

YORK
Y 1 York Factory
Y 2 Churchill
Y 3 Severn
Y 4 Trout Lake
Y 5 Oxford House
Y 6 God's Lake
Y 7 Island Lake

House District, where he founded the Devon Mission at the place now known as The Pas. In 1846 James Settee was sent to the Churchill River District in what is now northern Saskatchewan, where he began a mission at Lac la Ronge, which later was transferred to Stanley. The mission at Moose Factory on James Bay, which was begun by the Wesleyan Methodists in 1840 and conducted by them for eight years, after their withdrawal was taken over by the Church Missionary Society and re-established in 1851 by John Horden. The journey of the Venerable James Hunter to the Mackenzie River in 1858 resulted in the opening up of the basins of the Mackenzie and the Yukon to missionaries. The C.M.S. began its long connection with this part of the country when the Reverend William West Kirkby went to Fort Simpson in 1859, to be followed in 1862 by the Reverend Robert MacDonald, who went as far as Fort Yukon, and in 1865 by the Reverend William Carpenter Bompas. In each case the work had expanded and the mission stations in the area multiplied.

For one bishop to attempt to exercise episcopal functions over such an area was an impossibility, owing to the limitations of travel. Bishop Machray visited Moose on his way to eastern Canada and the United States in 1868. It was a difficult journey, and he was confronted with the problem of an increasing number of settlers, besides growing responsibilities attached to St. John's College and School. The division of the Diocese became imperative.

After delays caused by the Riel Rebellion in 1869, Bishop Machray went to England in the summer of 1871, where the whole matter was laid before the Archbishop of Canterbury and the two great missionary societies. He met the C.M.S. on October 24, and his proposals were received with sympathy. In the months that followed he was strongly supported by his Archdeacons, McLean and Cowley—who wrote to the C.M.S. independently, outlining an almost identical scheme—and by Horden and Bompas. As well, Bishop Anderson and the Reverend James Hunter vigorously favoured the proposal. On June 10, 1872, the C.M.S. agreed to provide the funds necessary to establish the Dioceses of the Hudson Bay, now Moosonee, and Athabasca, the original area of which included the present Diocese of the Yukon and much of the present Diocese of The Arctic. There never was any question as to who should be the Bishops: John Horden was consecrated in Westminster Abbey on the fifteenth of December, 1872, and William Carpenter Bompas on May 3, 1874, in St. Mary's Church, Lambeth.

Both these new Dioceses were easily recognized as specifically missionary Dioceses, but the case of Saskatchewan was held to be different. The broad prairie lands, through which the Saskatchewan River flows, were foreseen to be areas of future agricultural development, lands to be farmed by settlers of perhaps many nationalities, but certainly not to any extent by native Indians. The appeal in this case, therefore, was made to the S.P.G., which promised generous co-operation. In addition, in June, 1873, Archdeacon McLean left for England in order to raise an endowment for the Diocese of which he was the prospective Bishop. He was consecrated in St. Mary's Church, Lambeth, at the same service as William Carpenter Bompas was consecrated Bishop of Athabasca, on May 3, 1874.

The first Provincial Synod in eastern Canada came into being by an Act of the Crown exercising Royal prerogatives, but the formation of the Provincial Synod of Rupert's Land was an Act of the Church. By 1873 the first step in the formation of the new Ecclesiastical Province was an accomplished fact, and Bishop Horden already had been consecrated for the James Bay area. A Synod of the Diocese of Rupert's Land was held on January 8, 1873, to which Bishop Machray gave an account of his negotiations with the missionary societies in England, and the Synod passed a Canon provisionally defining the limits of the new Dioceses. The second clause in this Canon provided "that the Dioceses thus formed be an Ecclesiastical Province to be called the Province of Rupert's Land," while the third clause said "that as soon as the new Dioceses or at least two of them have been organized by the appointment of Bishops, a Provincial Synod to represent the whole Church in Rupert's Land be convened by the Bishop of Rupert's Land."[12]

The Bishop pointed out that the formation of these Bishoprics would enable them, by means of the Bishops and clerical and lay delegates from each Diocese, to obtain a thorough and effective representation of the whole Church in Rupert's Land, and would put it in a position to proceed practically toward self-government. The new Bishops would hold the same position in relation to himself as Suffragan Bishops did to the Bishops in England. In the Letters Patent founding the See of Rupert's Land, the Crown had reserved power to divide the Diocese with the consent of the Archbishop of Canterbury and the Bishop of Rupert's Land, for the time being, but this reference was to a time when there was no legislature in the country. The position had now changed and the Crown would not issue new Letters Patent. The new Bishops, therefore, would have their authority from the Church alone. The Bishop further stated that he had been advised by two eminent counsel in England that at present it was not desirable for him to resign by deed his rights, as Bishop of Rupert's Land, over the new Sees. These rights, however, would lie dormant, and the

[12]*Ibid.*, *1873*, pp. 4-5.

Church in Rupert's Land would provide an organization for the new Dioceses and a Constitution under which the Bishops would have due authority. He pointed out that the temporary procedure would be to consult those who supplied the funds for the Bishoprics and sent out the missionaries; the assent of the Archbishop of Canterbury and himself would also be required, and the consent of the Crown would effect the issuance of Royal Licence for the consecrations in England.[13]

In 1875 a Synod of the Diocese of Rupert's Land met on June 10, and was informed by Bishop Machray that it met under new circumstances. The meeting of the Provincial Synod was to be held in Winnipeg in August, and the chief business of this Synod was to elect clerical and lay delegates to it. Seven clerical and seven lay delegates were then elected, and this closed the business of the Synod.

The first Provincial Synod of Rupert's Land met on August 3, 1875. In his Charge, Bishop Machray said that the delegates had met together to determine the form of their future organization. The Bishop of Athabasca had found it impossible to be with them, but would be a consenting party to the draft of a Constitution made by the other Bishops. Owing to the late introduction of clergy into the new dioceses, two of the dioceses would not be represented in the House of Delegates. The representatives of the Diocese of Rupert's Land would, therefore, have to study the more carefully the interests of the whole Province. He discussed the origin of the Provincial Synod and said that the Archbishop of Canterbury, Dr. Tait, while he had been instrumental in bringing the formation to a successful conclusion, had also given his express consent to its formation. Bishop Machray questioned whether it would ever be desirable for the western dioceses to be incorporated in one provincial system, with either eastern Canada or British Columbia, though they might have at some time a council or assembly for the whole Dominion.

The interests of their dioceses were bound up with each other, politically as well as religiously, and above all it was absolutely necessary that the great societies, upon which they mainly depended at the time, should have the fullest confidence that any provincial action would be suited to the circumstances and exigencies of the work. It should be borne in mind that the objective of the Provincial Synod was not to legislate for local matters, but for questions affecting the whole Province, and the Bishop reminded them that dioceses far distant from Winnipeg were interested in this matter. It did not seem equitable to put all dioceses on the same basis of representation, and there might be times when it would be impossible for a particular diocese to be represented. He suggested that these difficulties might

[13]*Ibid.*, 11.

be overcome through voting by dioceses, or by the Acts of Synod being made provisional only until the Diocesan Synods had consented. Another important and difficult question was going to be that of the appointment of Bishops. Peculiar care had to be exercised in the case of the Bishopric of Rupert's Land because the trusteeship of the endowment was not in their own hands; ultimately there might be no objection to the Diocesan Synod having the appointment, but they had to make sure that the arrangements could be approved by the Archbishop of Canterbury and the Leith trustees.

The first act of the House of Delegates was to elect the Venerable Abraham Cowley, Archdeacon of Cumberland, as Prolocutor. Archdeacon Cowley had served for thirty-four years as a missionary in western Canada and was the senior clergyman in the Province.

The minutes of the first Provincial Synod of Rupert's Land are still interesting reading. There was no lack of formality in the proceedings, and an obvious sense of responsibility, and yet there are still a few touches that reveal the intimacy of the times; for example, the announcement of Archdeacon Cowley as Prolocutor "was received with great satisfaction" by the House of Bishops. The Reverend Canon Grisdale was elected as first secretary, and the following persons attended: Clerical Delegates for the Diocese of Rupert's Land: Ven. Archdeacon Cowley, Rev. Canon O'Meara, Rev. W. C. Pinkham, Rev. H. George, Rev. Dr. Clarke, Rev. R. Young, Rev. T. N. Wilson, Rev. S. Pritchard. Lay Delegates for the Diocese of Rupert's Land: Hon. Chief Justice Wood; Hon. Colin Inkster, President of the Executive Council in Manitoba; Hon. J. Norquay, Provincial Secretary; Hon. E. H. G. G. Hay; S. L. Bedson, Esq.; Captain W. Kennedy, and H. R. O'Rielly, Esq. Clerical Delegate for the Diocese of Athabasca: Rev. Canon Grisdale. Lay Delegate for the Diocese of Athabasca: W. G. Fonseca, Esq. The Dioceses of Moosonee and Saskatchewan were not represented by delegates. Amongst these are great names in the history of the West. Cyprian Pinkham and Richard Young later became Bishops. The Honourable Colin Inkster lived to become known to the present generation of Winnipeg residents, serving for many years as Sheriff and for still longer as Warden of St. John's Cathedral. The Honourable John Norquay, from St. Andrew's was once Premier of Manitoba. The family of Mr. Hay has been noted for its public service and support of the Church. Mr. Bedson was Governor of the Penitentiary at Stony Mountain. Captain Kennedy, who was an old H.B.C. official, was buried just outside the east window of St. Andrew's Church. Mr. O'Rielly was connected with the parish of St. James, and Mr. Fonseca was a founder of the parish of Holy Trinity, Winnipeg.

The first business submitted to the House of Delegates by the House of Bishops was a draft of the Constitution of the Provincial Synod, and as this had already been circulated, it was taken as read and the House resolved itself into a committee of the whole under the chairmanship of the Honourable Chief Justice to consider it clause by clause. Most of the draft was readily accepted, but there was a good deal of discussion over the clause dealing with subdivisions of the dioceses, and concerning the appointment of new bishops. But it was finally decided that before a bishop could be elected by a synod, the diocese must contain at least twelve clergy who were supported either by endowments or their congregations. This number has since been reached, but it was many years before any bishop was elected by a synod in western Canada.

The fourth clause of Section IV, which dealt with the number of clerical and lay delegates to be elected to the Provincial Synod by each Diocesan Synod, seems to have caused considerable debate, for the minutes record that "an animated discussion took place on this motion." However, after consideration in committee, it was resolved that each diocese should be represented by not more than seven of each order, a number that stood until 1933, when, owing to the multiplication of dioceses and the expense of carrying a synod of such an unwieldy size, the number was reduced to four of each order.[14] The original representation was only arranged after a conference with the House of Bishops in which the delegates were represented by a committee of six.

The House of Delegates made its earliest movement towards the unity of the Church when it passed a resolution, moved by the Reverend W. C. Pinkham and seconded by Captain Kennedy, "that the Upper House are hereby respectfully requested to communicate through the Metropolitan with the Bishop of British Columbia, inviting his Diocese to take such action as may lead to its union with the Ecclesiastical Province of Rupert's Land." Surely this was a wonderful launching out into the future; the only means of reaching British Columbia in those days was by an arduous trip, mostly by canoe.

This first Provincial Synod had a distinguished visitor in the person of the Right Reverend H. B. Whipple, D.D., Bishop of Minnesota, who preached at the service held in St. John's Cathedral on Wednesday morning, August fourth. Some of the things he said still have freshness and point: "These are no days for timid councils or for doubting

[14]*Journal of the Provincial Synod of Rupert's Land, 1933*, p. 35. *Ibid.*, 1939, p. 25.

faith. . . . To your infant Church is committed the work of laying the foundations of schools, hospitals, Churches. . . . In these new fields a Bishop's life is one of deferred hopes. . . ." Speaking particularly of Indian work, pointing out the effect of immigration upon the natives, he said: "Unless you give the Indian a home for the wigwam, implements of husbandry for the chase and schools and Churches for his heathen dances and grand medicine; unless you give him something to live for, there may come to you, as there has often come to us, a time when the wail of massacre shall be heard throughout your desolated country. The problem is yours to solve. . . ." No official group in western Canada in the years that have passed since that sermon was preached has taken a more sincere, helpful or sustained interest in the welfare of the Indian than the Provincial Synod of Rupert's Land.

The first Provincial Synod of Rupert's Land has a fine record of positive achievements, reflecting at every stage the progressive attitude of the Canadian West and the far-seeing outlook of the members of the Church of England. The second Provincial Synod, which met in 1879, only held a short session, chiefly to ratify the work of the first. The Metropolitan announced that the Archbishop of Canterbury, Dr. Tait, as Primate of the Province, had given his full approval to the Acts of the first Provincial Synod. Notice of the formation of the Ecclesiastical Province had been sent to all the Archbishops, the Primus of Scotland, all Metropolitans in the colonies, and the Presiding Bishop of the American Church. The Province of Rupert's Land had now been recognized throughout the whole Church, and Bishop Machray said that he had been placed beside the other Metropolitans at the Lambeth Conference (1878) by the Archbishop of Canterbury. This recognition of the Province as such by the whole Church still stands and is a matter of importance. Actually, a Province is of more importance in the view of the whole Church than a General Synod, and it is worth noting that General Synod of the Anglican Church of Canada really exercises its powers with the consent of our Provincial Synods, which have suspended some of their rights and privileges so that General Synod may use them for the benefit of the whole Church.

The Synod of 1883 rearranged the boundaries of the dioceses, both old and new, to correspond with the lines ruled on the map of Canada by the civil authorities earlier in the year.[15] It was about this time that the idea was first canvassed of making provincial ecclesiastical boundaries correspond with provincial civil boundaries. With the formation of General Synod, however, the idea faded away, though

[15]*Ibid.*, *1883*, pp. 12-13. The map that was published by the Department of the Interior is dated March 15, 1883. It can be consulted in P.A.C. A photostat is in R.L.A.

at a much later date (1912) the greater part of Ontario was formed into a Provincial Synod on its own account. In 1883, however, this issue was avoided. The Diocese of Qu'Appelle was successfully formed, and agreement upon the division of the Diocese of Athabasca was reached.

The Provincial Synod of 1887 was notable, in part, because nine Bishops were in Winnipeg, including five out of six Bishops of the Province; Bishop Thorold of Rochester, England; Bishop Baldwin of Huron; Bishop Whipple of Minnesota and Bishop Walker of North Dakota; and the Reverend F. E. Wigram, Honorary Secretary of the C.M.S., who preached the sermon at the opening service of Synod. It saw the launching of two great movements: agreement regarding the formation of the Diocese of Calgary, and the first discussions in the west on the unifying of the Church of England in Canada by means of a General Synod. The second of these was the subject of a special meeting of the Provincial Synod in August, 1890, immediately previous to the meeting of the well-known Winnipeg Conference on the fifteenth and sixteenth of that month.

The Provincial Synod of Rupert's Land was always whole-heartedly in favour of the formation of a General Synod, but, nevertheless, was determined that it should suffer no dissolution itself in the process. The only dissenting voice in 1890 was that of Bishop Anson of Qu'Appelle, who argued that if the proposed General Synod were endowed with real power, there would be nothing worthwhile left for any Provincial Synod, while if the Provincial Synods retained their power, nothing would be gained by creating the extra machinery of a General Synod. Subsequent events have from time to time emphasized much of Bishop Anson's point of view.

Throughout its history, the Provincial Synod of Rupert's Land has constantly proved its usefulness in forming a meeting place for the discussion of problems essentially belonging to the Church in western Canada, and such pronouncements as it has made have always carried weight. It has a great tradition in its zeal for missions, both amongst white settlers and Indians; it has shown no less zeal in its attitude to the social, educational and moral problems of the day. The general principle of its deliberations is stated in words taken from the sermon preached by the late Bishop Grisdale before the Provincial Synod of 1899: "We should be men of our own day, busy in the tasks of our own times. We should be careful not to live in the ideal past, still less in an ideal present. We should understand the requirements of our own times and be in touch with the age and country in which we live."

The Changing Scene

Before proceeding to trace the story of the Church in the newly constituted dioceses that now formed the Ecclesiastical Province of Rupert's Land, it is important that some account should be given of the Church within the confines of what was left of the original Diocese of Rupert's Land itself, for the settlement that grew up at The Forks, as the junction of the Assiniboine with the Red River was commonly known, developed with a rapidity that was surprising, into the City of Winnipeg.

More than ten years before 1865, something in the nature of a small settlement had begun to arise at the junction of the Portage la Prairie trail with the Red River trail, running up to Fort Garry. Here, in due time, the community began to assume the shape of a village. By 1870 a tri-weekly stage was running to Fort Abercrombie in Minnesota, and shallow-draft stern-wheelers were navigating the twisting channel of the upper reaches of the Red River. The Church kept abreast of this development. In 1867 Archdeacon McLean began to hold services in the Court House, just outside the enclosure of Fort Garry. A congregation was organized on April 8, by which time £115 had already been subscribed with a view to building a church, and a building committee was appointed, consisting of the Archdeacon, Andrew McDermot, William Dreever and W. G. Fonseca. However, for the time being, services were held in the Red River Hall, over a store almost opposite the corner where Portage Avenue now meets Main Street.

The first Holy Trinity Church was opened on Wednesday, November 4, 1868. It stood on a piece of land given by the Hudson's Bay Company on the southwest corner of Garry Street and Portage Avenue. When Archdeacon McLean left for England in 1873, the Reverend J. D. O'Meara, later Dean of Rupert's Land, took charge of the parish until the spring of 1875 when he was succeeded by Canon Grisdale, under whose able management a new church was erected on the same site. The furnishings for this church came from the second St. Paul's Church, Middle Church, then being demolished to make way for the present St. Paul's. The new Holy Trinity Church was ready by the time the first permanent incumbent of the parish arrived in Winnipeg, and the induction of the Rev. Octave Fortin took place on November 11, 1875. This church had consisted only of a chancel and transept, but the congregation grew so rapidly during the next five years that a nave sixty feet long was added.

By 1883 the expansion of both congregation and city was so advanced that plans were made to proceed with the present beautiful and well-known church, the corner-stone of which was laid by Bishop Machray on August 13, 1883; this church was formally opened on August 4, 1884. It cost $59,800, and its erection was a great act of practical faith in the future of Winnipeg; the parish borrowed $75,000 from the bank in order to cover the cost of the new building and other liabilities. Archdeacon Fortin (as he became in 1887) exercised an outstanding ministry in the city for forty-two years; his forceful preaching, acumen, and lovable personality will long be remembered. Thus was founded the Mother Church of Winnipeg.[16]

St. John's Cathedral and Chapter

The division of the Diocese made possible and necessary some reorganization of the affairs of the Church in Rupert's Land itself. In 1874 Bishop Machray established St. John's as a "Real Cathedral," and this term meant something definite in the mind of the Bishop. The Church had no endowments bringing in revenue, but it did possess a glebe of several hundred acres.[17] It was largely on the potential value of this glebe that the Bishop established the Dean and Chapter of St. John's Cathedral. At the first session of the Manitoba Legislature in 1871, both the Bishop of Rupert's Land (as a "Corporation Sole") and St. John's College had been incorporated. (The Act incorporating the Synod of the Diocese of Rupert's Land is dated April 19, 1886.) An Act to incorporate the Dean and Chapter of St. John's Cathedral Church gained assent on July 22, 1874, by which it was able to hold lands or other endowments and deal with financial matters like any other corporation.

To the Dean and Chapter the Bishop transferred the Cathedral Glebe with certain reservations, and in effect the Dean and Chapter became incumbents of the Cathedral parish. The Bishop, however, had a wider view of the duties of the Dean and Chapter, which he made public on the occasion of the installation of the newly appointed

[16]Dawson Richardson, ed., *Sixty Years and After* (Winnipeg, 1928).

[17]As with all titles relating to land in western Canada that was occupied by the Anglican Church in the time of the Hudson's Bay Company's regime, or before the days of provincial organization, there is difficulty in getting satisfactory evidence about surveys and adjustments, original deeds and subsequent transfers, or of satisfactory legal titles at all in some cases. Many details regarding the "Glebe" of St. John's Cathedral, Winnipeg, have yet to be cleared up, and to trace the way in which about 800 acres of land came into the possession of Bishop Machray as a "Corporation Sole" is not yet possible. The *Journal of the Synod of the Diocese of Rupert's Land, 1886,* has appended to it a report of the Glebe of the Cathedral, but it has never appeared satisfactory to the writer, and its accuracy cannot be guaranteed. The Dominion Survey of Parishes in the Red River Settlement, made in 1877, established the Anglican Church property in this neighbourhood as being all, or part, of Lots 43/44, St. John's. When these were subdivided a tripartite division of the smaller lots was made between the Episcopal Endowment Fund, the Dean and Chapter of St. John's Cathedral and St. John's College, but the proportion to each corporation is not apparent.

Dean, the Reverend Canon John Grisdale, and two Canons, the Reverend J. D. O'Meara and Archdeacon W. C. Pinkham, on April 12, 1882, which made the Cathedral a missionary centre of the Diocese.[18]

For fifty years the Dean and Chapter was a strength and stay to the work of the Church in the Diocese of Rupert's Land, and formed a training ground for subsequent service in the Ecclesiastical Province and elsewhere. Since 1874 six of the Canons have been consecrated Bishops: Grisdale of Qu'Appelle, Pinkham of Calgary, Stephenson of Nelson, New Zealand, Pierce of Athabasca, Matheson of Rupert's Land, and Barfoot of Edmonton and Rupert's Land. The latter two also were Primates of the Church of England in Canada.

University and College

The year 1877 brought an event that was to have far-reaching consequences for the Church and St. John's College. This was the founding of the University of Manitoba by a statute of the Provincial Legislature, dated February 20. Higher education in the Province of Manitoba at this time was being provided by three separate institutions: St. Boniface College on the east side of the Red River; St. John's College and Manitoba College, each an independent corporation fostered by its own particular branch of the Church. The Honourable Joseph Royal, in introducing the measure in the legislature, said that the government felt that the foundation of a provincial university might be somewhat premature, but that it had been urged upon the government for two years. It has always been assumed that the Honourable Alexander Morris, then Lieutenant-Governor of Manitoba, was the inspiration at the source, and speculation continues as to how he achieved his goal; in any event it made Manitoba unique in that its university was provided for so early in the province's history. Bishop Machray, who was appointed first Chancellor, a position he held until his death, devoted part of his Charge to the subject when he met the Synod of Rupert's Land on May 23:

I have to congratulate you on the passing of an Act last session creating the University of Manitoba. . . . It unites all the Denominations and Colleges in the examinations for Degrees in Arts, Sciences, Medicine and Law. By its recognition of denominational colleges with their own internal government secured to them, it satisfies those who feel the first importance of a religious character and control while it does not prevent the future affiliation of colleges independent of such direction. It also at the same time secures for the different denominations, with

[18]R.L.A., *Sundry Rupert's Land Papers, Sermon* by Bishop Machray preached at the Installation of Canon John Grisdale, November 2, 1874 (Winnipeg, Diocese of Rupert's Land, 1874), *Special Services at St. John's Cathedral, Manitoba,* on "Wednesday, April 12th, '82", at the installation and induction of the Dean and two Canons.

the consent of their governing bodies, the power to establish in their Colleges a Faculty for conferring Theological Degrees. I feel very much gratified with the result. All is gained that I desired.

The colleges were affiliated with the university, their students were registered by it, their teaching staffs were recognized by the university as satisfactory instructors and examiners, but it was an entity in itself, not a federation of the colleges. At the time of its founding the university had neither site nor staff; its officers consisted of the chancellor and a registrar; its governing body was a council; the colleges provided the instruction, and from their staffs were appointed the examiners.[19]

For nearly twenty-five years this system continued; the council of the university, to which the colleges sent delegates, working out a common scheme of studies, holding examinations and conferring degrees. It was not until the endowment of Dominion land became effective, about 1900, that schemes were definitely undertaken for joint instruction, which resulted in the university's taking over the teaching of science in 1902, while receiving considerable financial support from the provincial government. This year marked a change in the policy and circumstances of the university.

During the years 1880 to 1900 the Bishop used his efforts to improve the financial condition of St. John's College and strengthen its staff. The first step forward was made in 1883 when one wing of the new building was erected on four acres of land on the west side of Main Street.

Academically, the years 1880 to 1900 were ones of brilliance, in both staff and students. The Bishop himself occupied the chair of Church History and Liturgiology until 1883, when he appointed his young nephew and namesake, who had just returned from Cambridge, to the post. The eloquent and much loved Irish-Canadian, Canon J. D. O'Meara, was Professor of Systematic Theology; Canon S. P. Matheson held the chair of Exegetical Theology; Canon G. F. Coombes was Professor of Music, Precentor of the Cathedral and lecturer in Classics. Towards the end of the period the Reverend W. A. Burman joined the staff as steward, bursar and lecturer in Botany. The Reverend J. F. Cross became Machray Fellow in Mathematics when he returned from Cambridge in 1898.

In spite of academic prosperity, accommodation was always a problem. In 1891 the old buildings on the river bank were abandoned and the work of the College School coalesced with that of the College in the new building, a rather uncomfortable arrangement, with which Bishop Machray himself was not at all pleased, but which was to continue for more than fifty years.

[19]*Journal of the Synod of the Diocese of Rupert's Land, 1887,* p. 15.

The Beginning of the Struggle to Maintain the Missions

Writing to his Commissary, the Reverend C. A. Jones, in February of 1881, the Bishop himself said "an Act has just been passed by the Dominion Parliament by which the construction of the Canadian Pacific Railway has been committed to a great financial company. There are 280 miles of railway branching out from Winnipeg in my diocese, on which trains now regularly run. By July 1882, Winnipeg is to be connected with Lake Superior. By July 1884, Winnipeg is to have a line for 1,000 miles west . . . this will open up the largest extent of wheat lands in America. There has never been such an opening to immigration. There is no doubt of the issue of the future." The government surveys through the West opened up lands for homesteading; the railways brought the homesteaders, and the importance of missions to the Indians began to decline rapidly. The importance of trying to bring the Church and its ministrations to the incoming settlers, scattered far and wide on each side of the railways as they advanced westward, became the major problem of the Bishop, and continued to be the problem of the Church for the next fifty years.

With the consent of the Archbishop of Canterbury, Bishop Machray addressed a strong appeal to the Society for the Propagation of the Gospel, the Colonial and Continental Church Society and the Society for Promoting Christian Knowledge, for assistance. But many of the new settlers were coming from eastern Canada, and the Bishop went to Montreal early in 1881 to address a committee of the Church in the east on the situation. He said that a contribution of $4,000 a year would meet the most pressing wants at the moment, and the committee decided to assess the dioceses of eastern Canada for that amount; actually, that year the Bishop received $860 from these dioceses. He wanted the Church in eastern Canada to follow the example of the Presbyterian Church in sending to the West both men and money, but this was never done. In 1883 the Presbyterians appointed thirteen new missionaries, supported by $16,000, for their work in western Canada, bringing the number of their men up to forty. The response made by this body may be partly accounted for by the fact that many of the settlers who came from Ontario had church affiliations there and had no hesitation in writing back home, putting their plight before their friends. In 1882 the Methodist Board of Missions appointed the Reverend George Young as its Superintendent of Missions in the Northwest. Thirty-six Methodist ministers were already in the field and able to attend, in 1885, the second conference of that church when it was held in Winnipeg.[20]

[20]J. H. Riddell, *Methodism in the Middle West* (Toronto, 1946), 116.

To the Synod of 1883 Bishop Machray reported that fifty municipalities had been organized in Manitoba alone, but only fifteen of them were being served by clergy, and seven hundred other townships were surveyed but unorganized and without ministrations. He asked for the appointment of a general missionary whose business it would be to organize the work of the Church in these rural areas.

The Church of England in eastern Canada, beset with problems of its own, seems to have been at that time under some wrong impressions with regard to the western prairies. One of these was, as the Secretary of the Diocese of Montreal wrote to the Bishop, "that the spiritual needs of the Northwest were exaggerated," though the writer disassociated himself personally from this point of view. A second impression was that the Church in Rupert's Land was well provided for financially because it had a Cathedral and Dean and Chapter and College in Winnipeg, which were endowed; furthermore, the West was abundantly prosperous and well able to look after its own church extension. Bishop Machray said in 1882 that one of the Canadian Bishops had written, remonstrating with him for having spent so large a sum of money in building a splendid Cathedral instead of giving it to the missions; one of the missionaries of the Diocese of Algoma had thought to strengthen his own appeal for funds by remarking that the Diocese in which he worked had no Cathedral. Bishop Machray found such misconceptions very painful, more so because he was convinced that they had originated through gossip within the Diocese itself. He affirmed that education was the root of all true progress and asserted soundly: "I believe the Cathedral and College system of St. John's have been the salvation of the country. . . ."

The immediate problem in the eighties was not confined to Manitoba. As the C.P.R. pushed westward, southern Saskatchewan was opened to settlement. Between Brandon and Regina only one priest of the Church was in the field, the Reverend J. P. Sargeant, and towards the end of 1882 Bishop Machray, in a private letter to the S.P.G., urged that the new territory, then called Assiniboia, which centred on Regina, ought to have a bishop for itself as it was impossible for him to look after it properly. His appeal interested the Honourable and Reverend A. J. R. Anson, then rector of Woolwich, who decided to devote himself to missionary work in western Canada.

A meeting of the Provincial Synod, held on August 9, 1883, passed the following resolution:

First.—Whereas the Bishops of Rupert's Land and Saskatchewan have consented to the separation from their Dioceses of such portions of their respective Dioceses as lie within the District of Assiniboia in the northwest territory as defined by the Dominion Parliament and set forth in the map, under date 15th March, 1883. Therefore the Provincial Synod hereby forms the said District of Assiniboia into a Diocese to be known at present as the Diocese of Assiniboia. Second.— The Provincial Synod hereby authorizes the Metropolitan to inform the Lord Archbishop of Canterbury, Primate of this Province, of the formation of the Diocese of Assiniboia, and to request the Primate to appoint a Bishop for the said Diocese of Assiniboia as soon as His Grace is satisfied with respect to the provision for the support of the said Bishop.

Canon Anson was appointed to the new Diocese by the Archbishop of Canterbury on May 23, 1884, and was consecrated in Lambeth Parish Church on June 24. Among the Bishops taking part was Bishop McLean of Saskatchewan.

The Diocese of Rupert's Land in the Eighties and Nineties

So much has been said about Bishop Machray's work in connection with education, the organization of the Provincial Synod and the general expansion of the work in the Church, that it may seem as if the nearer field has been overlooked. This criticism was even advanced in the Bishop's own day more than once, and strongly denied by him. His educational objective was to train and equip men who would go out into the mission field. His organization of the Dean and Chapter of St. John's Cathedral was in a large part to provide ministrations within the immediate and accessible area of Manitoba where the pressure for extended work by the Church was first felt. Following the establishment of Holy Trinity, Winnipeg, to which reference has already been made, and the arrival of the Reverend O. Fortin in 1875, Canon Grisdale turned his attention to the older settlement of Point Douglas and began a Sunday School in the home of W. G. Fonseca. In 1876, with the help of the Church Missionary Society, a small church was erected on the corner of Princess and Henry Streets, and to this, known as Christ Church, the Reverend H. T. Leslie was appointed as curate. In 1882, when Canon Grisdale became Dean of Rupert's Land, the Reverend Edwyn S. W. Pentreath came from Moncton, New Brunswick, as first rector of the parish. A selfless, good-hearted, energetic man, Mr. Pentreath proved himself a tower of strength to the Church in the Diocese. Under his leadership Christ Church became noted for the tremendous work it did amongst the immigrants, especially after the Canadian Pacific Railway reached Winnipeg. Pentreath's wisdom was acknowledged by his colleagues, who sent him as a delegate to Provincial and General Synods, and his work in Winnipeg was recognized in his appointment as the first Honorary Canon of St. John's Cathedral, February 3, 1891.

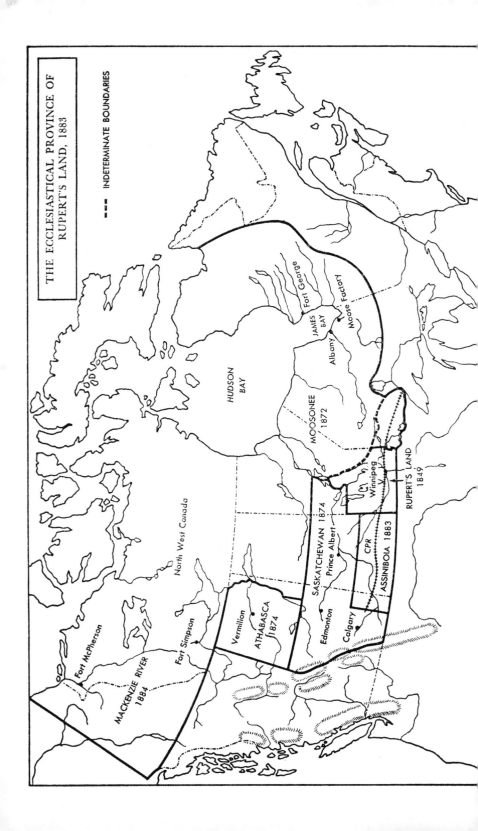

THE ECCLESIASTICAL PROVINCE OF
RUPERT'S LAND, 1883

■ ■ ■ INDETERMINATE BOUNDARIES

Fort George

JAMES
BAY

Moose Factory

Albany

HUDSON
BAY

MOOSONEE
1872

Winnipeg

RUPERT'S LAND
1849

North West Canada

SASKATCHEWAN 1874

Prince Albert

CPR

ASSINIBOIA 1883

Edmonton

Calgary

Vermilion

ATHABASCA
1874

Fort McPherson

MACKENZIE RIVER
1884

Fort Simpson

The Bishop was always urging upon his people the necessity of self-help, and in 1881 the Parish of Holy Trinity, Winnipeg, guaranteed $800 a year to the Home Mission Fund, and expressed a wish for another new district to be more directly connected with itself. The parish took under its care what was described as "the promising new town of Brandon," with which was associated Millford and Roundthwaite. The same year the Church got as far west as La Riviere and Whitewater in the Turtle Mountain. Farther north services were being held in Rapid City by the Reverend G. Turnbull, and also in the Presbyterian Church at Selkirk by the incumbent of St. Clement's, young Mr. A. E. Cowley, and had for several years been held by Canon S. P. Matheson in Victoria near Stonewall, but in 1883 a new church was built in the latter town. Emerson, which seems to have been opened as a mission point about 1872, five years later was in charge of the Reverend M. Jukes, and by 1881 services that had been started at Morris by Canon J. D. O'Meara were in charge of the Reverend H. D. Cooper, a resident missionary. In the Boyne District (now Carman) and at the now defunct Nelsonville (later the town moved *en bloc* to Morden), then become a place of importance, the work was in charge of the Reverend T. N. Wilson. To the west of Lake Winnipeg, the Gladstone country was becoming so settled that there was urgent need for a missionary, but there were no funds available, and the Minnedosa country still farther west had to be served from Rapid City.

In his Charge to his Synod of November 24, 1880, the Bishop said:

Our missionaries at Nelsonville and Rapid City are simply lost in the vast tracts of settled country that their ministrations touch. In southwest Manitoba, in which Nelsonville lies, there is a settled district 42 miles by 72 miles containing 84 townships, of which at least 66 townships are fully settled. So, again, if we turn to that part of the country where Rapid City is, we find a similar enormous region, being the northwest of Manitoba and the Little Saskatchewan country. And both these districts extended westward indefinitely.

After considering in detail the settlers' problems and difficulties, he went on:

It is clear, then, to anyone knowing the circumstances of the country— I think it should be clear to everyone simply hearing of them—that every denomination must for a time give assistance, if their people are

The Ecclesiastical Province of Rupert's Land, 1883. The publication of a general map of the North West Territories, including Manitoba, on March 15, 1883, enabled the Provincial Synod of that year not only to set up the new Diocese of Assiniboia (Qu'Appelle), but also to redefine the boundaries of Saskatchewan with respect to Rupert's Land and Athabasca, dividing the latter with the creation of the Diocese of Mackenzie River. (*Journal of the Provincial Synod of Rupert's Land, 1883*, pp. 11, 12, 14.)

to have a missionary amongst them. If our people do not receive from us the ministrations of a missionary, they will, in a majority of cases, go to the body from which they receive them. New accessions of numbers to our Church from year to year will not add to our strength, for the older settlers will have ceased to acknowledge us. History will repeat itself. It will be the old story. The large country districts will be lost to us. We shall more and more become a Church of town congregations.

By 1881 it was considered expedient, for its better organization, to divide the Diocese into five Rural Deaneries. During these years the work of the Indian Missions was still largely dependent upon the support of the Church Missionary Society, but new fields were still being opened or strengthened, even in the now contracted Diocese of Rupert's Land. The Reverend R. Phair opened a mission at Fort Frances and other points nearby were placed in the care of catechists. Work was begun again in the Touchwood Hills, on the Fort Ellice-Birtle side, by the Reverend Joseph Reader. Grand Rapids at the mouth of the Saskatchewan River was reopened and steps were begun to establish a mission for the Sioux Indians, who had taken refuge in Manitoba and settled on the Assiniboine twenty-five miles west of Brandon. This mission was opened in 1879 by the Reverend W. A. and Mrs. Burman. The formation of the Dioceses of Moosonee and Saskatchewan had removed the larger part of the Indian work from Rupert's Land, and after the Cumberland District was transferred to Saskatchewan by the Provincial Synod in 1883, St. Peter's, Dynevor, and Fairford were the only large missions left in Manitoba itself. In the part of Rupert's Land that lay in Ontario, Islington (White Dog) and Lac Seul were the chief points, though with the coming of the railway Rat Portage (later Kenora) was gaining importance.

One other event in the work amongs the Indians of the Diocese of Rupert's Land at this time was the establishment in 1889 of the Indian Industrial School at Middle Church with the co-operation of the Dominion Government. This was one of the first experiments on the part of both church and government in the way of a residential school, and one that endeavoured to turn the Indian into a craftsman; it was co-educational. Under the direction of the Reverend W. A. Burman, it was organized on sound lines and proved very successful.[21]

An earlier section of this chapter has been entitled, "The beginning

[21]Three "Industrial Schools" are associated with the Anglican Church in Rupert's Land. Battleford (Rev. Tomas Clarke), 1883, and Calgary (Rev. G. H. Hogbin), 1897, are the other two. The Minutes of the Church Missionary Society Finance Committee at Red River (or Rupert's Land) of November 2, and December 9, 1897, indicate the policy of both the Indian Department and the Church with respect to this type of school at that time. Archbishop Machray's considered opinion on the matter, and on the difficulties that faced the Church regarding it, is stated.

of the struggle to maintain the Missions." It was a struggle for men to man them, for funds to maintain them, for buildings to house them. The demands of a constantly expanding population and the continual opening of new municipalities to settlement created unceasing strain. The Diocese of Rupert's Land itself responded generously to the appeals of its Bishop for increased funds to meet the changing situation. An inspection of the published accounts of both the Home Mission Fund, as it eventually was called, and the Native Pastorate Fund during these years is an interesting study and reveals an interminable list of special collections and individual donations, the latter in their parochial aspect indicating the names of the majority of the church members of the time. It is impossible to go into detail but the figures seem to show that at least sixty per cent of this fund was raised locally. The amount, however, raised by the Home Mission Fund was only about one-third of the total cost of sustaining the missions among the white settlers, and the rest of the necessary funds were derived from the S.P.G. and other English missionary societies.

CHAPTER SEVEN

Moosonee: Diocese of the Hudson's Bay

His whole ministerial life, covering some forty-two years, was spent in
and for Moosonee. . . . He was wonderfully equipped by natural gifts
for the duties of a missionary in an isolated post and country. . . .
Marvellously quick in the acquisition of a new language, he was further
endowed by God's grace with disposition and energy for proclaiming at
all times and in all ways with delight the blessed Gospel of the grace
with which was all his own joy and trust.

ARCHBISHOP MACHRAY'S CHARGE
TO THE PROVINCIAL SYNOD, *1893*

The Diocese of Moosonee did not actually come into being until the
Reverend John Horden was consecrated in Westminster Abbey on
December 15, 1872, as its first Bishop. There is a personal aspect
about these forty-two years which is not to be found in the story of
any other Dioceses of the Ecclesiastical Province of Rupert's Land.
Only the travels of his contemporary, William Carpenter Bompas, in
the Mackenzie River Valley Dioceses, are in any way comparable to
those of John Horden the missionary or John Horden the Bishop.

When Bishop Anderson left Moose Factory in September, 1852,
there were only two clergymen in the district, the Reverend John
Horden at Moose Factory and the Reverend E. A. Watkins at Fort
George, more than two hundred miles up the east coast. That winter
Horden gave himself up to his little school, to his translation work,
and later to such building operations as in the course of time became
necessary. Horden's diary records summer journeys to Albany, 100
miles north of Moose; to Hannah Bay, 50 miles still farther east, as
well as Kevoogoonisse, 430 miles to the south. In addition, he had
to visit occasionally Martin's Falls, 300 miles up the Albany River;
Osnaburgh House, 200 miles farther west; Flying Post, 100 miles from
Kevoogoonisse; and New Brunswick, 100 miles from Flying Post. The
work, however, prospered in spite of these long distances and much of
its success must be ascribed to the fact that wherever he went Horden
taught the natives to read. This instruction in reading their own
language in syllabic symbols he always regarded as the most important
and the most productive part of his work, for he found that natives
whom he had taught to read, whether Indian or Eskimo, invariably

120

taught other natives to read also, and the little books printed on the hand-press at Moose Factory were eagerly bought, carried to far-off places and used to the best advantage. It is little wonder, therefore, that Horden spent all the time he could upon translation. But the capacity of this press was not enough, and so in 1858 when the Reverend William Mason of York Factory took the Cree Bible to England to be printed, he also took Horden's translation of the Prayer Book into Moosonee syllabics and a hymn book that Horden had prepared in the same characters, to get these printed in larger quantities.

Thomas Vincent

Thomas Vincent was born on March 1, 1835, at Osnaburgh House where his father John Vincent was a fur trader for the Hudson's Bay Company. The Vincents left the service of the Hudson's Bay Company in 1840 and made their home at Middle Church, where their son attended the parish school. Later he entered St. John's Collegiate School, and in 1855 Bishop Anderson took him to Moose Factory to work under Mr. Horden as a catechist. At Moose Factory he not only taught school but also studied systematically under Horden's direction. Here, too, he met, another young man whose people were associated with the Honourable Company—John Alexander Mackay.[1] These were the first of several young men prepared by John Horden for the ministry. It was no life of ease. The early hours of the morning were devoted to manual work, then came three hours of teaching in the school. The first two hours after lunch were devoted to systematic study under Mr. Horden's tutorship, and the next two hours might be spent helping in the printing room or studying the language; the evenings were occupied in further study.

The Bishop again visited Moose Factory early in the summer of 1860, and Thomas Vincent was ordained. Bishop Anderson has left a personal note about this in the 1873 edition of *The Net in the Bay*:

Mr. Thomas Vincent was admitted to Deacon's Orders—a service of no little interest to Mr. Horden and myself. . . . Mr. Vincent had been carefully prepared for ordination by Mr. Horden, and had given proof of steadiness and zeal. He had been for a time at Rupert's House, and was now to be sent to Albany to take Mr. Fleming's place. It was a pleasure to me to set him apart for the ministry, having known him almost from boyhood.

[1] About 1857 the Mackay family left Moose Factory and went to the Red River, taking up land in the neighbourhood of Lower Fort Garry. J. A. Mackay continued to work under the direction of Rev. J. Horden until the summer of 1860, when he joined his parents there. This gave him the opportunity to keep on with his preparation for the ministry under the supervision of Bishop Anderson himself, and possibly with help from Archdeacon Hunter at St. Andrew's.

After his ordination Thomas Vincent was sent to Albany, a point 100 miles from Moose Factory and one that Mr. Horden had been able to visit only occasionally; the work, however, had prospered. Here Vincent first had to build a house in which to live and then a church to meet the needs of his growing congregation. The work was difficult, for many of the Indians were still in their primitive state. Honesty was uncommon, polygamy fairly customary, and life was cheap. However, by the quality of his own character and teaching, Horden was able to report of him that "a better appointment could not have been made."

Bishop Anderson, who had visited England in 1856, says in the note already quoted, "I had held an ordination in the summer of 1863, in some of its features the most interesting I had ever had. It was the largest in number, and the four ordained were all of them born in the country, and immediately after ordination they separated to spots far removed from each other. Mr. Thomas Vincent, who had been summoned from Albany for the purpose, was one of those ordained priests." This ordination took place on Whit Tuesday, May 26, 1863, which necessitated Mr. Vincent's travelling in winter. He left Albany in February on snowshoes in company with the half-breed mail-carriers, and as the party had to travel light they depended on their guns for game during the journey of 1,300 miles—probably the only case of a man walking that distance for purposes of ordination. At the Red River Vincent found Mackay, whom he had not seen for some years. They received priests' orders in St. John's Cathedral; Henry Budd, Jr., who went to Nepowewin; and Thomas Cook the son of Joseph Cook of the Indian Settlement, who went to Fort Ellice, were ordained priests at the same time. Vincent returned to Albany by canoe, travelling by the same route he had originally taken there, preaching to the Indians and administering the Sacraments as he went. Almost the whole of Thomas Vincent's ministry was concerned with the area drained by the great Albany River and its tributaries. He was made Archdeacon of Moose in 1883 by Bishop Horden in recognition of his faithfulness and experience.[2]

Realizing the great opening for the preaching of the Gospel around James Bay and the manifold difficulties Horden had in trying to cover so large a territory by himself, Bishop Anderson had always endeavoured to procure additional help. When he was in England the winter

[2]R. L. A., *The Northam Papers*. Rev. P. A. Northam was himself a missionary along the Albany River, 1921-1931, and collected much material for a Life of Thomas Vincent, which he always hoped to write. Northam died early in 1960, and through the courtesy of his brothers, Pierrepont Arthur Northam's Moosonee Papers became the property of the Rupert's Land Archives.

of 1856, the matter was constantly in his mind. In his notes to the 1873 edition of *The Net in the Bay* the Bishop said:

Nor was the appeal made in vain; it was determined that another labourer should be sent to Moose, and that I should ordain him before again quitting England. I ventured to propose that it should be in All Saints', Derby, the church which I had left on going abroad, and by commission from the Bishop of Lichfield, and through the kindness of Rev. E. W. Foley I was able to accomplish this. Shortly after his ordination Mr. Thomas Hamilton Fleming proceeded to James' Bay by the summer ship.[3]

After his arrival at Moose Factory, Mr. Fleming took up his work with very great vigour but with too little care, with the result that by 1860 he was quite worn out and the state of his health caused the Bishop great anxiety:

Mr. Fleming, whom I had ordained in England, met me here. It was very delightful to find the high degree of respect and affection in which Mr. Horden and he were held by all at Moose. . . .Mr. Fleming had in his short ministry, gained the good-will of all, but the pain was finding him in weakened health, and that great exposure to weather had brought on serious illness. [Mr. Fleming went to Great Whale River in March 1859, a distance of 500 miles, on snowshoes,—sleeping in the open with temperatures varying from −18° F. to −37° F.]. . . . We still fondly hoped, that with youth on his side, he might rally and return to the work. . . . Under these circumstances, I could not hesitate in carrying out my original plan of admitting him to full orders. He was accordingly ordained priest. . . . Soon after this Mr. Fleming went home, and for a time seemed to improve in health, but was never able for ministerial work again, and died eventually under his father's roof in Ireland.[4]

Floods at Moose Factory

One of the drawbacks to life at Moose Factory was the susceptibility of the district to heavy floods when the ice broke up in the spring, a situation difficult to contend with because the land is said to have no hills within seventy miles of the river. The flood of 1857 was fairly high, but that of 1860 was worse. At that time Horden was occupied in building his new church, the present St. Thomas' Church, the framework of which was already set up on the foundations. One Sunday morning it floated off and was carried about a quarter of a mile away by the water, but was rescued and dragged back to its right position. Mr. Horden observed: "The ice made much more havoc than it did in '57. A few days after the water had subsided, I found my garden thickly planted with ice blocks of a considerable size; but our gardening operations were not impeded, we were able to raise a

[3]David Anderson, *The Net in the Bay* (London, 1873), 311.
[4]*Ibid.*, 318-319.

large quantity of potatoes of very good quality."[5] A similar threat
came in May, 1861: "On return from Church one Sunday evening,
the river presented an awful appearance. . . . We abandoned our house,
having first taken every precaution to guard against the fury of the
waters, but, although the threat was so formidable we experienced no
flood, and having spent a few pleasant days at the establishment of the
Hudson's Bay Company [it was on higher ground] we returned and
at once begun our gardening. The children look upon a flood as a
rare treat. To them it is something of a pleasant, exciting nature,
after the dull monotony of a seven or eight months winter."[6]

Travel South and North

In the 1850's and 1860's travel in this part of northern Ontario was
an arduous matter. Writing in 1861, Horden says, "Last autumn I
took a journey to Kevoogoonisse; it is about 430 miles distant, and
during the whole way I saw no tent or house, nor even a human being,
until I arrived within a short distance of the Post. I appeared to be
passing through a forgotten land; I saw trees by tens of thousands,
living, decaying, and dead; I saw majestic waterfalls, and passed
through fearful rapids; I walked over long and difficult places, and day
after day struck my little tent, and felt grieved at seeing no new faces,
nor any to whom I might impart some spiritual blessing."[7]

In 1862 Horden paid a visit to Whale River, the most southerly point
to which the Eskimos came to do their trading. This time he was able
to remain with the Eskimos eight days, and his account relates:

The Eskimo appear to me to be kind, cheerful, docile, persevering,
and honest. Nothing could exceed the desire they professed for instruction, nothing the exertions they made to learn to read, nothing the
attention with which they listened to the Word of God. I was fortunate (but should I not use another word?) in obtaining the services of a
young Eskimo as my interpreter, who had received instruction from
missionaries (Moravians) while living on the coast of Labrador. He
spoke English but imperfectly; but knew some hymns and texts
exceedingly well, and showed himself most willing to assist me to the
fullest extent of his power. . . . Soon after six we had a service with
the Eskimo; about twenty-five were present.
     The service was commenced by singing a hymn; reading followed,
then prayer, the Lord's Prayer being repeated aloud by all; singing
again; then a long lesson on the "Syllabarium", i.e. the system of reading by syllables, without the labour of spelling. They were then

[5]Beatrice Batty, *Forty Years among the Indians and Eskimo* (London, 1893),
28.   Beatrice Batty was the editor of *The Coral Magazine*, published by the
Church Missionary Society for younger readers, through whose interest a good
deal of money was raised for the Diocese of Moosonee. In writing about Bishop
Horden she used his diaries and personal letters to her.
[6]*Ibid.*, 29.
[7]*Ibid.*, 30-31.

instructed in Watt's First Catechism, and another hymn completed the service. After having taken my breakfast, I assembled the Indians, who were nearly twice the number of the Eskimo, but not half as painstaking.

I then took a lesson from my Eskimo interpreter, writing questions and obtaining his assistance in translating a portion of the baptismal and marriage services; I then went to the Eskimo tents until dinner-time. . . . My next visit was to a tent where younger people were assembled. I asked a few questions, which they readily answered. I was pleased at this, as showing that they could understand me. I then dined, and took a short stroll along the river towards the sea, to see what prospect there was for the whale fishermen. The fishers were there, waiting patiently, but with the look of disappointment on their countenances. . . . Leaving them, I went to hold a second service with my Eskimo, then another with my Indians. It was then tea-time. I spent an hour with my Eskimo interpreter, after which I held an English service with the master and mistress, the only English-speaking woman for hundreds of miles, and the European servants of the company.

I was so deeply impressed with the conduct of the Eskimo, their anxiety to learn, and their love for the truths of Christianity, that I could not forbid water that some of them should be baptized.[8]

St. Thomas' Church, Moose Factory

The original church at Moose Factory, which was there when the Hordens arrived in 1851, was built by the Reverend George Barnley. It was replaced by a larger one in 1860. This second church was built by workmen of the Hudson's Bay Company and its estimated cost in those days was £1,000; it was opened on Whitsunday, May 15, 1864. The Chancel was not built until twenty years later, and was opened on Whitsunday, June 4, 1885. "The Holy Table, Prayer Desks and Choir Stalls were made by local workmen; . . ." the Lectern by the Reverend T. B. Holland [rector, 1900-1907]; the Sanctuary Chairs and stone Font came from England; the original organ was damaged on several occasions by the flood waters and had to be replaced by a smaller one, given by the Toronto Woman's Auxiliary. The east window was sent from the old country, and its framework was made at Moose Factory.

St. Thomas' had some remarkable experiences with floods. In 1894 the water rose so rapidly that it was a foot up the Altar and the church filled with mud; again in 1917 ice thirty feet high was piled up against it with such force that much damage was done.

From 1872 to 1903, St. Thomas' was the Pro-Cathedral of the Diocese of Moosonee, but Bishop Holmes (third Bishop of Moosonee), desirous of having better contact with the southern portion of the Diocese and

[8]*Ibid.*, 44-47.

the "outside world," decided to live at Chapleau; his successor, Bishop J. G. Anderson, removed north again to Cochrane. The centre of population having shifted farther south by 1943, Bishop R. J. Renison took up his residence at Schumacher, Ontario, and established St. Matthew's Church at Timmins as the Pro-Cathedral. With the appointment of the Right Reverend Neville R. Clarke (1951) as Suffragan Bishop of Moosonee residing at Moose Factory, St. Thomas' would seem to have reverted to something of its original stature.[9]

The Hordens' First Return to England

The Hordens had planned to take a furlough in England in 1864, but when the summer of 1864 arrived no ship came. The shallow waters in the vicinity never permitted the Hudson's Bay Company's ship to come within some miles of Moose Factory, so goods and passengers always had to be transported to land by a shallow-draft schooner. This schooner stood "outside" until October 7, an unusually late date, and that night, in the middle of a heavy storm, reports of signal guns were heard at sea. They were not those, however, of the expected ship but of a sister schooner from York Factory, sent to tell the people of Moose that their ship had been wrecked on Mansfield Island. Mr. and Mrs. Horden were thus delayed until 1865.

While they were away, Mr. Vincent took charge of Moose Factory and found his work very encouraging. He visited an outpost in the Rupert's River district that summer and before leaving had forty-eight Baptisms, half the number being adults; the Abitibi River, which seldom saw a missionary at that time, was also visited with good results.[10]

Bishop Machray visits Moose in 1868

When John Horden returned he began a series of his long journeys, first going south to Brunswick House where he spent about nine days. He then went up the east coast to Rupert's House, where he found between three and four hundred Indians assembled to meet him under the guidance of their teacher, Matamashkum. At Fort George he met a good body of Christian Indians with their teacher William Keshkumash. After a few days there he sailed farther north for Great Whale River but the schooner was stopped by ice, and having successively journeyed in a small boat and a canoe, he ended up on foot. The ice having moved out, the schooner was able to finish her journey and once more he started out, this time for Little Whale River, where

[9]*Ibid.*, 55. "St. Thomas' Church, Moose Factory," *Canadian Churchman*, Toronto (August 25, 1932).

[10]Beatrice Batty, *Forty Years among the Indians and Eskimo* (London, 1893), 58.

he met the Eskimos and admitted four families into the Christian Church. He returned to Moose on August 30.[11]

On part of this trip to the north Horden was accompanied by Bishop Machray, for that summer the Bishop made a long trip through the United States to Faribault, North Dakota, Milwaukee and Nashota in Wisconsin, where there were church colleges, training men for the ministry. He returned by way of Sault Ste. Marie to Michipicoten; from there he made his way to Moose Factory, arriving on June 28. He then visited Rupert's House and Albany, and returned to Michipicoten by way of New Brunswick House. At each place the Bishop had Confirmations after holding classes for instruction. At these services he read his special part in Indian, Horden having translated the words and taught him how to pronounce them. This was probably the only time in his life that Bishop Machray used in his episcopal work any language other than English.[12]

The Movement towards a Diocese

The chief result of this visitation seems to have been a strengthening of the conviction in Bishop Machray's mind that the area needed a bishop of its own. He discussed the question with John Horden, whose first suggestion was the formation of the Hudson's Bay Company territory missions into an Archdeaconry, but the Bishop thought that this would not meet the circumstances, and in the end Horden agreed with him. Before leaving Moose Factory, the Bishop promised to bring the matter to the notice of the C.M.S. with a view to the speedy appointment of a bishop for Hudson's Bay. In September of that year Horden himself wrote to the Society, urging the consecration of a bishop for these missions to which he gave the general name of Moosonee, the name finally selected for the diocese eventually formed.

The troubles of the Riel Rebellion (1869-1870) prevented any definite local action on the Bishop's part, and the principal arrangements made with the Church Missionary Society to provide for two new bishops seem to have been promoted by correspondence and were finally settled during his visit to England in 1871. The decision that guaranteed the provision was actually not made by the C.M.S. till June 10, 1872, but in the meantime Horden had been communicated with and had agreed to accept the nomination of the Archbishop of Canterbury to be Bishop Designate.[13]

Bishop Horden was consecrated as Bishop of Moosonee on Sunday, December 15, 1872, at Westminster Abbey by the Archbishop of

[11]*Ibid.*, 60-65.
[12]Robert Machray, *Life of Robert Machray . . . Archbishop of Rupert's Land*, 150-153.
[13]*Ibid.*, 225-228.

Canterbury (Dr. Tait). He returned to Moose Factory via New York and Michipicoten. Upon his arrival at Moose, he wrote: "I got my work of translation forward by devoting to it a few extra hours daily. . . . This is what I have accomplished since I returned in July: I have revised our Indian Hymn Book, adding to it a large number of new hymns. I have translated all the First Lessons between the Tenth Sunday after Trinity and the First Sunday in Lent, as well as some for many of the Holy Days. What I wish to accomplish is the Psalter, the First Lessons, and the New Testament to be bound up in one volume."[14]

On September 9, 1873, Bishop Horden wrote about his Diocese to the Church Missionary Society:

1st. *The Eskimos:* God has seen fit in His loving wisdom once more to try that infant church. Sometime since, I appointed Leutolft, an Eskimo trained by the Moravians, to be their teacher. He was soon after drowned. Then John Horden became the teacher of his countrymen. He was cut off suddenly. Lastly, Timothy Komuk, a very energetic man, and apparently as strong as man could possibly be, was appointed, and I have just heard that he too has passed away. 2nd. *The Sotos:* [sic] These occupy a large portion of the diocese, and many of them are still heathen, although the Gospel is making progress among them. *Osnaburgh* and *Martin's Falls* will be visited by Mr. Vincent next year; and if a suitable man can be found at either of these places, he will be brought down to be placed under training. From *Matawakumma* too I hope to get down a man and his wife next summer. 3rd. *The Crees:* These are the best cared-for portion of the Indian family in the diocese, and among them the greatest spiritual results have been obtained. Almost all of them, scattered over an immense area, are nominally, at least, Christian.[15]

In 1874, he wrote, "Each year finds me busier than its predecessor. . . . I have before me for next summer a most extensive journey; I go to Red River to attend the First Meeting of our Provincial Synod, and then to York Factory, travelling over 4,000 miles."

The school at Moose Factory, under the Bishop's own superintendency, was going on well at this time. One boy who had been educated there, Edward Richards, was already assisting as a teacher. Later, in 1887, he was to be ordained deacon by the Bishop, and for ten years after he was priested, in 1888, to be stationed at Rupert's House, from there going to Fort Hope.[16]

The journey by the Bishop to Winnipeg was made in due course,

[14]Beatrice Batty, *op. cit.*, 78.
[15]*Church Missionary Society Intelligencer, 1873-1874*, p. 216. John Horden to the Church Missionary Society, September 9, 1873. The spelling "Soto" is euphonic, but was common a hundred years ago for the word now written "Salteaux." Original spellings in documents have been retained.
[16]Beatrice Batty, *op. cit.*, 65, 87.

but he proceeded no farther, confining his episcopal visits to the southern parts of his Diocese. The limits of the Diocese of Moosonee at that time were governed by Clause III of a Canon of the Diocese of Rupert's Land passed at its Synod in 1873: "The Diocese of the Hudson's Bay to consist of the Moose or Southern Department of the Hudson's Bay, with the districts of Churchill, York, Oxford, and Severn."

New Help for the Growing Work

The appeals the Bishop made in England for men and money were not without success. In 1875 there came to Moose Factory the Reverend John Henry Keen, a graduate of the C.M.S. College at Islington, who was ordained in that year by the Bishop of London for service overseas. At Christmas Mr. Keen went to Rupert's House and there exercised his ministry until 1882, when he returned to England.[17]

Mr. Keen was replaced in the Diocese of Moosonee in 1882 by the Reverend Henry Nevitt, who for three years had been curate at Heigham in the Diocese of Norwich. Mr. Nevitt held various charges in the Diocese of Moosonee until he returned to England in 1891.

Enough has been said already to indicate the very keen interest Bishop Horden had in the Eskimo people on the east side of Hudson Bay, and his appeal for a man to undertake work among them found its response in the person of Edmund James Peck, who arrived at Moose Factory on September 7, 1876. Edmund James Peck was born on April 15, 1850, at Rusholm near Manchester. He was left an orphan by the death of his father when he was only thirteen years old, and entered the navy in which he remained until 1875, when he took his discharge in order to become scripture reader in the Parish of Newmarket under the Reverend T. Romaine Gorett.[18] While at Newmarket he felt the call to be a missionary and so entered the Church Missionary Society's Preparatory Institute at Reading in the latter part of the year. This same institution in Reading gave another great practical missionary to northern Canada, the Reverend John Hines of Saskatchewan, and it was the training ground for two others, Archdeacon J. W. Tims and Canon H. W. G. Stocken, pioneer missionaries to the Blackfoot Indians in the Diocese of Calgary.

Mr. Peck had been only a few months at Reading when he was asked if he would go to the Diocese of Moosonee to preach the Gospel to the Eskimos. He readily assented. His chief treasure on the voyage was a

[17]Rev. J. H. Keen held curacies in north London, England, from 1882 to 1890, and then returned to the Canadian mission field, but to the Diocese of Caledonia; in 1899 he went to Metlakatla, B.C., where he did much work in the translation of the Haida language.

[18]Arthur Lewis, *The Life and Work of E. J. Peck amongst the Eskimo* (London, 1904).

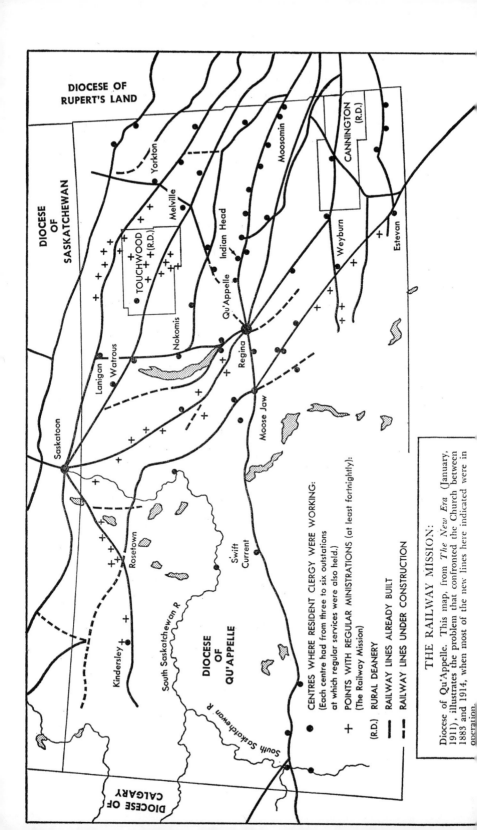

THE RAILWAY MISSION:

Diocese of Qu'Appelle. This map, from *The New Era* (January, 1911), illustrates the problem that confronted the Church between 1883 and 1914, when most of the new lines here indicated were in operation.

● CENTRES WHERE RESIDENT CLERGY WERE WORKING:
(Each centre had from three to six outstations at which regular services were also held.)

+ POINTS WITH REGULAR MINISTRATIONS (at least fortnightly):
(The Railway Mission)

(R.D.) RURAL DEANERY

—— RAILWAY LINES ALREADY BUILT

- - - RAILWAY LINES UNDER CONSTRUCTION

DIOCESE OF RUPERT'S LAND

DIOCESE OF SASKATCHEWAN

DIOCESE OF QU'APPELLE

DIOCESE OF CALGARY

CANNINGTON (R.D.)

TOUCHWOOD (R.D.)

Yorkton

Melville

Moosomin

Indian Head

Weyburn

Estevan

Qu'Appelle

Regina

Nokomis

Watrous

Lanigan

Saskatoon

Moose Jaw

Swift Current

Rosetown

Kindersley

South Saskatchewan R.

South Saskatchewan R.

copy of the New Testament in Eskimo, translated by the Moravians working on the coast of Labrador, and by carefully studying it and comparing it with the English version, he acquired the meaning of many words. Owing to the lateness of the season he only spent a week at Moose Factory before proceeding to Little Whale River. A Christian Eskimo from Labrador, Adam Lucy, accompanied him as interpreter. A log house had been built for him there, its double walls packed with oakum between as insulation, and in this house Peck settled down to work. He found that the previous labours of the Reverend E. A. Watkins (twenty years before), and of Bishop Horden, had prepared the way. One of the baptized converts, John Mulocto, became a tower of strength to both missionary and mission.

Early in 1878, Peck returned to Moose and was ordained deacon by the Bishop on February third. The Bishop made him write a sermon in Cree, as part of his ordination examinations. At Moose, too, Peck found his new church awaiting him, but was not able to get it to Little Whale River until the following year. On December 20 he wrote to the Reverend Henry Wright of the C.M.S.:

You will be delighted to hear that God has enabled me to erect the iron church. It is a nice, neat little building, measuring (exlusive of chancel) forty feet long by twenty wide. I was about eight weeks erecting it, the Eskimos being employed by the Hudson's Bay Company; I was, therefore, only able to have their help for eight days.

The building was opened on Sunday, October 26 (1879). I preached in Eskimo, Indian, and English to my small flock. . . . I shall now be able to speak to the people with some comfort, whereas formerly I was forced to pack them in my little house, or go into the open air, or have them in the Hudson's Bay Company's quarters.

In 1891, when the Hudson's Bay Company decided to abandon its trading station at Little Whale River and concentrate on Great Whale River sixty miles to the south, it was considered expedient to move this church back to Fort George, where at that time Mr. Peck was making his headquarters.[19] In the summer of 1879 Peck was joined by Edward Richards, who for some years travelled around the country as an itinerant missionary to the Indians.

Mr. Peck was priested in 1879, and in 1884 returned to England for a short time, and there married Miss Coleman. The following year

[19]*Ibid.*, 96. In 1876, immediately after Mr. Peck's arrival at Little Whale River, Bishop Horden wrote to the Church Missionary Society urging that an "iron church" be sent out to him, as wood for building was lacking at the northern post. Through the kindness of private friends of the Society's officers, the building was procured at a cost of £300, and sent out to Moose Factory in 1877. Such buildings were common in England in Victorian days; they were framed with wood and covered with sheets of corrugated, galvanized iron, the woodwork being pre-cut, fitted and numbered ready for re-assembly according to plan, needing only the most simple tools and little expert labour. They did useful temporary service.

Mr. and Mrs. Peck moved south to Fort George where they remained until 1893, much of the work being accomplished with the aid of a steam launch provided for the mission.

In the meantime, the work in the south had been stabilized by the appointment of the Reverend John Saunders to Matawakumma. Mr. Saunders was an Ojibway who had been ordained to the diaconate by Bishop Horden in 1876.[20] His station was in the country through which the Canadian National Railway now passes from Folyet to Gogama. In the winter of 1878-1879, Saunders joined the Bishop at Moose Factory and with his co-operation the Moosonee Hymn Book, Service of Morning Prayer and one of the Gospels were translated into the Ojibway tongue. The fact that four different languages were spoken in the Diocese did not make the work any easier.

York Factory and Fort Churchill

In June, 1879, having left the Reverend J. H. Keen in charge of Moose Factory, the Bishop started on his long contemplated journey to York Factory. From Moose, on June 30, he went to Michipicoten, where a steamer took him to Sault Ste. Marie, as there was no direct communication apparently between Michipicoten and Fort William. From there he crossed Lake Superior to Duluth and finally reached Winnipeg by steamer down the Red River. In Winnipeg he attended the Provincial Synod. From Winnipeg he travelled to York Factory by the old Hudson's Bay Company route.[21]

York Factory was without the regular ministrations of the Church until the Reverend William Mason was appointed there. Mr. Mason retired in 1870 and left for England; at the same time the Reverend William West Kirkby returned from his furlough in England, but arrived too late to have any hope of reaching Fort Simpson that year. He therefore took temporary charge of York Factory, but actually remained there for nine years.

Kirkby was by nature a traveller and he extended the work of the Church to Fort Severn on the coast and inland to Trout Lake. He had worked among the Chipewyan Indians of the Mackenzie River district, and finding Chipewyan Indians at Fort Churchill, 190 miles north of York Factory, he was able to minister to them in their own language. "In the course of his term of service in Hudson's Bay, he translated the New Testament, the Prayer Book, Hymns and a Manual of Family Prayers into the Chipewyan Language, and he also compiled a Hymnal for the Cree Indians of the York Mission." Amongst other things, he trained a young Indian, William Dick of

---

[20]John Saunders sent an autobiography of himself to the Church Missionary Society on July 18, 1876, which is preserved in the correspondence files. His name in the records is at times spelled "Sanders."

[21]Beatrice Batty, op. cit., 106.

Trout Lake, with a view to making him a catechist. William himself had been baptized by Mr. Mason and proved himself an excellent and spiritually-minded Christian leader of his people for many years. On August 11, 1889, William Dick was ordained deacon by Bishop Horden at York Factory. He was ordained priest by Bishop Newnham in 1895.[22]

Mr. Kirkby became the first Archdeacon of the Diocese of Moosonee in 1876. He left the diocese in 1879 to take a parish in New Jersey, U.S.A., where he died in the eighty-first year of his age on September 7, 1907.

Bishop Horden did not arrive at York Factory till September 19, and deeply regretted missing Archdeacon Kirkby, who had sailed for England a week before. The Bishop had never met him personally. Before the Archdeacon left, however, his successor, the Reverend George Smith Winter, had reached York Factory.[23] Mr. Winter, who had trained at the C.M.S. Islington College, was ordained by the Bishop of London in 1879 for overseas service, and to the priesthood at York Factory in 1880 by Bishop Horden. Winter was appointed Archdeacon of York in 1886 and remained there until 1894, when he removed to the Diocese of Saskatchewan and took charge of the Sturgeon Lake Mission. In 1898 he translated *The Peep of Day* into Cree, which story was quite popular among the Indians for a while, but being only a story it eventually lost their interest. He returned to England in 1899.

Until January, Bishop Horden conducted an English school at York Factory daily. He also instructed Winter in Cree, and twice a week gave lessons to the Europeans and native servants of the Company. On February second, he started out for Churchill. The journey proved to be most difficult as it had to be performed largely on snowshoes. The winds were bitter, the temperatures low, going to forty-six below zero, and their destination was not reached until February 11.[24]

The Bishop spent some months at Churchill working among the Eskimos and Chipewyans. This place had long been one of interest to the Church; Bishop Anderson had tried to establish a mission there and the Reverend Joseph Gardiner,[25] who was ordained by him in

[22]*Church Missionary Society Intelligencer, 1890*, p. 67.
[23]Batty, *op. cit.*, 107.
[24]A. R. Buckland, *John Horden, Missionary Bishop* (Toronto, n.d.), 78, 81-88. Buckland was associate secretary for the C.M.S. in the Diocese of York 1884-1887, secretary of the Religious Tract Society 1902-1917, and editor of *The Record*, an evangelical Anglican weekly, 1887-1908.
[25]Joseph Phelps Gardiner has been mentioned as one of Bishop David Anderson's ordinands. He returned to England in 1872, but retained his association with the Church Missionary Society by becoming associate organizer of their work in the dioceses of Chester, Manchester and Carlisle, and then for twenty-five years was incumbent of Bishop Ryder's Church in Birmingham.

1857, made more than one attempt to work there during the six years that he spent as an itinerating missionary in the Diocese.

Bishop Horden sailed directly from York Factory to England in the summer of 1880 and did not return to Moose Factory until 1882.[26]

Bishop Horden's Primary Charge

In 1879 Bishop Horden made his first official visitation of his diocese; he delivered his Primary Charge at Moose Factory. The Church Missionary Society published considerable portions of it, from which the following are extracts:[27]

As long as there is such an abundance of land, of surprising richness, in the boundless prairies of Manitoba and Saskatchewan, no one will seek to make a home in the secluded forests of Moosonee. . . . With the exception of the fur trade, there is nothing whatever to attract capital to the diocese. We know, then, what we have to provide for, and need not in the least disquiet ourselves about the contingencies of the future. . . .

In the organization of the diocese I have divided it into six districts; York, Albany, Moose, Matawakumma, Rupert's River, and East Main. In each of these, with the exception of Rupert's River, we have a resident missionary. . . . As to churches, we have them at Churchill, York, Severn, Trout Lake, Albany, Moose (where there is likewise an excellent schoolhouse), Rupert's House, and Matawakumma; one for Little Whale River is now lying here, which, I trust, will be forwarded to the place of its destination, and erected next summer; while I hope that in a few years we shall hear of one being at Osnaburgh, Flying Post, Misenabe, Mistasimee, and Fort George. For several of those already in existence, we are indebted to the liberality of the Hudson's Bay Company.

Bishop Horden's Last Ten Years

Bishop Horden's appeal to the church people of England in 1882 begins: "The Diocese of Moosonee is of recent formation, having been severed from the original gigantic Diocese of Rupert's Land in 1872, and like all such infant dioceses stands urgently in need of pecuniary support."[28] The Church Missionary Society was not able to more than pay the salaries of its agents and the Bishop desired to relieve it of additional responsibility. He had therefore instituted three funds: The Moosonee Church Extension Fund for general purposes, for which he hoped to raise £5,000 or £6,000; a Fund for the Education of the children of Native Clergy, which would require about £3,000; and a Church Building Fund, which he hoped would reach the same amount.

[26]A. R. Buckland, *Joseph Horden, Missionary Bishop*, 96-97.
[27]*Church Missionary Society Intelligencer and Record*, 1879, Vol. 4, New Series, p. 654 ff. R.L.A., *The Northam Papers*. According to Bishop Newnham there were three clergy present on this occasion, but he does not name them. There were only four in the diocese then, Vincent, Keen, Peck and Saunders.
[28]R. L. A. A copy of this appeal is among the Moosonee Papers.

Charters had been granted for the construction of railways from Manitoba and Saskatchewan to Fort Churchill and York Factory. Both of these would run for the greater part through the Diocese, and they must be ready to provide for the spiritual wants of new settlers along these lines. Even at present he had four stations requiring resident missionaries—Churchill, Trout Lake, Rupert's House and Osnaburgh. The second fund was needed because the stipends of native catechists were quite insufficient to meet the expense of educating their children. His appeal was sympathetically received, and by the time the copy now in the Rupert's Land Archives was printed, £7,190 had been subscribed towards these objects.

The Bishop returned to Canada by himself in the summer of 1882. This time he travelled up the Ottawa River, spending a Sunday at Mattawa, centre of the lumber trade of the Upper Ottawa Valley. Crossing Lake Abitibi to the Moose River, he reached Moose Factory in time to welcome the Reverend Henry Nevitt and Mr. Joseph Lofthouse. The former remained at Moose Factory, conducting services and school, but the latter went with Mr. Peck to spend his first winter at Little Whale River, and get acquainted with the Eskimos and their language. Joseph Lofthouse, a graduate of the C.M.S. College at Islington, was ordained deacon, July first, and priest July eighth, by the Bishop in 1884, and then proceeded to York Factory for the winter to take the place of the Reverend G. S. Winter. In 1886 he went to Churchill, where he remained until 1898.

In the summer of 1884 the Bishop made a long trip up the Albany River, visiting Martin's Falls, where he found the Indians more deeply heathen than in any other part of the Diocese, and then on to Osnaburgh House where he appointed a trusty native catechist, named James Umbasi.

During that winter of 1884 Bishop Horden spent some time revising the Cree translation of *The Pilgrim's Progress,* that had been made by Mr. Vincent. In March, 1886, it was possible to release Mr. Nevitt from Moose Factory in order to establish a permanent mission station at Rupert's House. "For many years I had longed," says the Bishop, "with a most earnest longing, to see a missionary established there."

On May 31, 1888, Bishop Horden left Moose Factory for his fourth trip to England, where he attended the Lambeth Conference and presided over the C.M.S. evening meeting at Exeter Hall in 1889. Upon his return to Canada in the summer of that year, he went straight through to Winnipeg from the east coast and then on to York Factory. He wrote to the C.M.S. on August 11, 1889:

Returning to York, I spent some time there, doing my best to strengthen the hands of the Archdeacon and Mrs. Winter, who have faithfully laboured amid great difficulties. . . . They had a large number of persons present for confirmation, and, what was even better still, they had a fine Indian—Mr. Dick, already alluded to—to present for ordination. . . . I have now eight clergy—two at work among the Eskimo; both Europeans, and six among the Indians, of whom no less than four are Natives of the diocese, while a fifth is an archdeacon in the neighbouring Diocese of Saskatchewan (Archdeacon J. A. Mackay). After about a fortnight's stay, a vessel arrived from Moose factory for the first time for twenty years, and this enabled me to come to the Moose district. I arrived safely at Moose, and, finding everything going on well, I determined on coming on to Rupert's House for the winter, with the hope of being able to materially assist the excellent Native Clergyman, the Rev. E. Richards. . . .[29]

In the summer of 1890, he visited the East Main River, where he was much gratified by the progress Christianity had made amongst the Eskimos. At the beginning of 1891 he announced with much joy, "I have now ready for the press The Pentateuch, Isaiah, Jeremiah, The Lamentations, Ezekiel and Daniel: The Psalms and New Testament have been in print for some years."[30] Incidentally, in order to do this work Bishop Horden had acquired a knowledge of Hebrew. He says, "I generally read a Chapter of the Hebrew Bible every morning. I was never taught to read it. I never heard a word of it read, except what is contained in the English Bible; yet I have read the Hebrew Bible right through, carefully and grammatically."[31]

The summer of 1891 was made particularly difficult by an influenza epidemic. Further, the Nevitts had to return to England as Mr. Nevitt's health had failed, but in August there was an event destined to be of much importance to the Diocese. This was the arrival at Moose Factory of the Reverend Jervois A. Newnham. When Bishop Horden realized that his own health was failing somewhat, and his ability to withstand long journeys was rapidly diminishing, he felt that his resignation of the Diocese could not long be delayed, and he sought for one who might succeed him; he found Jervois Newnham, then rector of St. Matthias' Church, Montreal. Mr. Newnham took up the work with great energy, and according to the *Canadian Church Magazine and Mission News,* by Christmas was able to conduct all the

[29]*Church Missionary Society Intelligencer and Record, 1890,* John Horden to the Church Missionary Society, August 11, 1889.
[30]Batty, *op. cit.,* 199. R. L. A., British and Foreign Bible Society File. W. J. Bradnock (Translations Secretary, British and Foreign Bible Society, London), to T. C. B. Boon, July 7, 1961, regarding Horden's translations: "The B. F. B. S. published his New Testament in 1876, and this was reprinted in an edition of 1,000 copies in 1909. Before his death in 1893, it is recorded that he completed his version of the whole Old Testament and presented the manuscript to the B. F. B. S. Our Society, however, was obliged to decline to publish it owing to the fact that the dialect, Moose Cree, was spoken by only a 1,000 Indians." The unprinted manuscript is still in the Bible House, London, England (1961).
[31]Batty, *op. cit.,* 184.

Indian services, preach and administer the Holy Communion in the Cree tongue, within four months of beginning to learn to read it.[32]

Towards the close of 1891 Mrs. Vincent died at Albany and was brought to Moose for burial by the Archdeacon. The Bishop returned to Albany with his old friend and colleague and spent Christmas and New Year's Day with him. It was his last trip to Albany. Upon his return to Moose he turned again to his translation work, and rejoiced that he was able to finish his translation of the Cree Bible on May 6, 1892. In June he visited Rupert's House for a short time.[33]

He returned north to visit Fort George and Whale River in July, and at the end of the summer he had the pleasure of welcoming W. G. Walton, whom he ordained and sent to Fort George to replace Peck, who was obliged to take his wife and family to England. Walton had actually been destined for the distant post of Ungava, but arrangements could not be made for him to go there. While in charge of Fort George, he also devoted himself to the Eskimos on the east side of the Hudson Bay for the following thirty-two years. Peck had reached Ungava in 1885, after being driven back three times before he succeeded in crossing the eight hundred miles of the Labrador Peninsula, but he had been repaid by meeting at Ungava many Eskimos anxious to hear about Christianity. It was not until the turn of the century that the Ungava Mission was opened by the Reverend S. M. Stewart of the Colonial and Continental Church Society.

William Walton's ordination to the diaconate is said to have been Bishop Horden's last episcopal act. One other name must be associated with him—that of young Richard Faries, who had spent seven years under his tutorship and then entered Montreal Diocesan Theological College in the fall of 1892. Archdeacon Faries (as he has been for many years) says, "I shall never forget the emotional grip of the Bishop's hand and his last words, as I stepped into the canoe. 'Be a credit to your teacher, my boy, and be a faithful servant to your Master, the Lord Jesus.' "

On November 21, 1892, after apparently being in very good health, the Bishop was suddenly afflicted with a violent attack of rheumatism, but continued to do as much work as he could with the help of Mr. Richards, who was then at Moose Factory, and his general progress seemed to be satisfactory. He died rather unexpectedly at the home

[32]*Canadian Church Magazine and Mission News* (Toronto, October, 1893), 217. If this achievement sounds unusual, it must be remembered that Mr. Newnham was under the expert tuition of Bishop Horden. The sermons he used were his own, but they were translated into Cree for him by the Bishop, and then read from this manuscript by Mr. Newnham. F. P. Shearwood, *By Water and the Word* (Toronto, 1943), 35.

[33]A. R. Buckland, *John Horden, Missionary Bishop*, 130-133.

of his daughter on the morning of January 12, 1893.[34] The funeral was delayed until January 21 in order that Archdeacon Vincent might come from Albany to conduct it, and he was buried in what is known as the Fort Graveyard at Moose.

The present John Horden School is his chief memorial at Moose Factory. There is one to him in the Cathedral at Exeter, England, and another on the wall of the school in that city under whose roof he first resolved to be a missionary. His work is well summed up in the words of the late Archbishop Machray to the Provincial Synod of 1893, which are at the head of this chapter. The Bishop was a strong Churchman with deep evangelical convictions, but widely read in contemporary affairs and tolerant of the views of others. He had an ever present sense that God had given him a special work to do, and he had a passion for work.

Bishop J. A. Newnham

Bishop Horden's wishes with respect to his successor met with the warm approval of the Church Missionary Society and the House of Bishops of the Provincial Synod of Rupert's Land, which elected the Reverend Jervois Arthur Newnham as Bishop of the Diocese of Moosonee on April 15, 1893. He was consecrated in Holy Trinity Church, Winnipeg, on Sunday, August 6. Bishop Newnham left immediately after for Moose Factory so that he might arrive there and take up his work before winter set in, feeling that his presence in his Diocese would be of more value to it than his attendance at the first meeting of General Synod, which took place in September of that year.

Bishop Newnham was a native of Somerset, England, having been born at Coombe Down vicarage on October 15, 1852. He was educated at Bath College, came to Canada when he was twenty-one, and studied theology at Montreal Diocesan College. He graduated from McGill University in 1878 and was ordained deacon by Bishop Oxenden on Sunday, May 5, of that year in St. George's Church, Montreal. He was priested by Bishop Bond in St. Paul's Church, Shawville, P.Q., on August 11, 1880. In 1886 he was made rector of St. Matthias' Church, Westmount. In the summer of 1890 he resigned this charge to work in the Diocese of Moosonee under Bishop Horden.[35]

For ten years Bishop Newnham shepherded the growing missionary work in his Diocese before he was translated to the Diocese of Saskatchewan. The outstanding features of his episcopate in Moosonee were the establishing of a new centre of work among the Eskimos on

[34]*Ibid.*, 134-140.
[35]C. H. Mockridge, *The Bishops of the Church of England in Canada and Newfoundland* (Toronto, 1896), 275-276. O. R. Rowley, *The Anglican Episcopate of Canada and Newfoundland* (London, 1928), 106-107. "Historical Sketches," *Canadian Church Magazine and Mission News*, no. 88 (October, 1893), 217.

the north side of Hudson Bay, and the uniting of the western part of the diocese with that part of the civil Province of Ontario that was in Rupert's Land, and an area of the eastern part of the Province of Manitoba (also in Rupert's Land), to form the new Diocese of Keewatin.

The Reverend E. J. Peck Goes to Baffin Land

In the summer of 1891 Mr. Peck was obliged to return to England because of the serious illness of his wife. Upon his arrival there he had an interesting interview with the Committee of the C.M.S.; to quote from its summary, "he had searched out the Eskimos to the utmost of his power; 140 adults were now under instruction, of whom eighty are baptized. He had trained five Eskimo teachers, of whom three have died, and two are now at work. He had translated many portions of the New Testament into the local Eskimo dialect. . . . He urged on the Committee the spiritual needs of the Eskimos north of Hudson's Bay; and expressed his willingness to go amongst them in whaling vessels if a younger man would take his present work." Thus he laid before the Committee a proposal that had been in his mind for some time. One of the Secretaries of the C.M.S., the Reverend David Fenn, advised him to write to the Reverend Sholto Douglas, incumbent of St. Silas', Glasgow, a man likely able to put him in touch with merchants who had dealings with the more distant Eskimos, and through Mr. Douglas he secured introductions whereby he became acquainted with Crawford Noble. This gentleman had only the week before completed the purchase of a whaling station on Blacklead Island in Cumberland Sound, and was happy to offer Peck a passage free of charge for himself and his goods and allow him to take up residence there.

The Church Missionary Society thereupon sanctioned this new departure, but on condition that a colleague could be found to join him. It so happened that Peck was one of the speakers at the C.M.S. Anniversary Meeting in Exeter Hall that year, and the appeal he made brought a response from a young man named J. C. Parker, a former student of the Society's institution at Clapham, who had also received some medical training.

The two missionaries left London on June 27, 1894, and travelled to Aberdeen, but the sailing of their ship was delayed until Monday, July 9, when they signed articles at the customs house and so became members of the ship's company; Peck signed on as chaplain and Parker as surgeon. The vessel in which they sailed was the *Alert*. They sighted Cape Mercy on August 18 and anchored off Blacklead Island on August 21. After landing Peck and Parker and their property, the

Alert left for Kikkerton, another station belonging to Mr. Noble on the other side of Cumberland Sound.

Mr. Peck found no difficulty in talking to the Eskimos as there was little difference in dialect between the ones he met there and those he had known at Whale River and Fort George. Their first work, however, was to put into repair the two-roomed shack Noble had lent them. They found at Blacklead Island about forty tents of Eskimos and the population numbered 171. They spent much of the mornings on the Eskimo language and conducted a school for the children in the afternoons. The Eskimos themselves built the church in the form of a large tent of skins, about twenty feet long and ten feet wide, and here on Sunday, October 7, services were commenced.[36]

Blacklead Island

The Eskimos were quite kind to them and brought them seal meat on a number of occasions. Food, however, was often scarce among the natives, and the missionaries devised a plan of inviting one family to tea every day, after which, says Mr. Peck, "I take our large English Bible and explain to them that this is the book which God has given to teach men the way to heaven. A suitable portion is then translated and explained. Before we part they kneel down and we have prayer together."[37]

In April Mr. Peck made his way to Kikkerton over the ice and received a good deal of encouragement in his work. He had one of the strangest churches on record: "Having no house in which the people could assemble, I requested some Eskimos to build a large circular wall of snow about six feet high to keep out the piercing wind. . . . This was our Arctic Church. Our Services consisted of Hymns and Prayer, and I then delivered them some simple scriptural truths."[38]

The missionaries did not confine themselves to the two stations, but moved around on the ice visiting Eskimo encampments, at times actually living with them. In the spring of 1896, for example, Peck wrote that he was staying at an Eskimo village consisting of fourteen snow houses, which had in all fifty-five inhabitants and was situated on the frozen sea some four miles from the mainland.

The Death of Mr. Parker

In the meantime Parker had made such progress in the language that he was able to take meetings and instruct the people. His medical skill

[36]E. J. Peck, *The History and Present Status of the Work amongst the Eskimo*, an Address given at the Centenary of the Arrival of John West at the Red River in 1820. (Winnipeg, 1922). This was published separately, and also included in W. B. Heeney, ed., *The Centenary Celebration in 1920* (Winnipeg, 1922).
[37]Arthur Lewis, *The Life and Work of E. J. Peck amongst the Eskimo*, 224.
[38]*Ibid.*, 236.

and sympathetic manner made him something of a favourite with them and the native children were quite attached to him. Somewhat short in stature, he became known as "Luktakuluk," which is "the kind little doctor." In August, 1896, Parker and seven companions unfortunately lost their lives by drowning, owing to the capsizing of the boat in which they were sailing.

Parker's death was a very severe blow to Peck; he felt his loss intensely. "He was so strong and reliant a companion, so useful with the people, so ever willing to do anything."[39]

The *Alert* arrived on August 22 and brought Charles George Sampson, a layman trained at the C.M.S. Islington institution, whose purpose in coming was to permit Peck to return to England and see his Gospels in Eskimo through the press. Peck hesitated at leaving him, but after three weeks Sampson was on such good terms with the Eskimos and was making such good progress with the language, that it seemed possible and right to go. His Four Gospels were printed by the Bible Society and Peck brought a stock of them with him when he returned to Blacklead Island by the *Alert* in the summer of 1897. He also brought back with him a prefabricated house, which he and Sampson fitted together when they had managed to find a site for it among the rough rocks. There were so many Eskimos in the neighbourhood at the time that the missionaries decided to live in the old house and use the new one for the church.

First Converts in 1901

The difficulties with which the missionaries had to contend were not only those of the weather and isolation. From time to time many of the Eskimos took part in their own old heathen ceremonies, but there were always some who held fast to the Christian teaching.

Of their work during these years, speaking of the effect of the printed books, Peck says that when he returned to Blacklead Island several of the people learned to read these precious pages. "Following our usual plan of work, Services were held night after night in our little Church, and each Gospel was expounded from beginning to end."

On August 28, 1898, the work was reinforced by the arrival of Julian William Bilby. By 1900 about seventy children were under instruction in the school and most of them were making very good progress. The Eskimo standards of life in many respects seemed also to have improved but it was not until December, 1900, that any marked change was noticeable, and then some of the men began to come to two services instead of one. On January 8, 1901, Peck was

[39]*Ibid.*, 238.

greatly cheered when one of the women came to him of her own accord to say that her heart had been moved by the Word of God. On January fourteenth and fifteenth, after a special address on the subject of Baptism, two men and twenty-four women came to him wishing to be enrolled as candidates for Baptism, and were consequently brought under special instruction. Three were baptized on Whitsunday, May 26, 1901, the first fruits of seven years work at Blacklead Island.

The Reverend E. W. T. Greenshield

Mr. Sampson had returned to England when Mr. Bilby came, and in 1901 Bilby was replaced by E. W. T. Greenshield, who was ordained deacon and priest by the Bishop of London when he was in England in 1904.

The mission was greatly helped and strengthened by Greenshield's strong personality and his remarkable linguistic powers. On February 9, 1902, two men and five women were baptized and others confessed their faith. That summer the missionaries had the joy of seeing one of the converts become, after due preparation, a catechist in the Church; Peter Tooluakjuak was for many years a witness for Christ in Cumberland Sound. During the summer a visit was paid to an American Whaling Station near Frobisher Bay, and later by a whaling ship to a place called Kivetok on Davies Strait, some eighty miles within the Arctic Circle. There Peck found a woman named Pudlo who had previously lived at Blacklead Island, where she had learned to read the Gospels; at Kivetok she had told others of the Gospel and taught some to read.

About 1907 a Dundee firm established a mining station at Lake Harbour; some Eskimos from Blacklead Island had already travelled there and preached the Gospel. The C.M.S. when it heard of this took up the work. On July 30, 1909, a sailing vessel called the *Lorna Doone* chartered from the Grenfell Mission, sailed from St. John's Newfoundland, carrying supplies of provisions and coal for two years and a prefabricated mission house, for Lake Harbour, which was reached on August 27. The names associated with this station are the Reverends J. W. Bilby and A. L. Fleming, later to be the first Bishop of The Arctic.

After 1915 the work was carried on by two paid Eskimo catechists and four voluntary teachers, but Mr. Peck continued to make visits there whenever he could. The situation of the missionaries eased somewhat after the Hudson's Bay Company established a post at Lake Harbour in 1911, and it became possible for them to obtain transportation on the Company's supply ship. In his account of the work among the Eskimos, published in the *Rupert's Land Centenary Volume* in 1920, Peck said of Lake Harbour: "1918 was a year of years in the history of the mission, for Dr. Anderson [the Bishop of Moosonee] was able to visit this year some of the northern stations in his extensive Diocese. . . . Sunday, August 11th, was a memorable day, when thirty-eight Eskimos were confirmed by the Bishop and many were baptized."

Formation of the Diocese of Keewatin

The western side of Hudson Bay lay in the Diocese of Moosonee, but was only accessible, to a Bishop who lived at Moose Factory, by a long journey. Bishop Newnham, while he found travelling conditions improved, discovered the same difficulty in making episcopal visitations in the Archdeaconry of York,[40] and hence consideration began to be given to the formation of a new diocese that would take in the western side of the Bay. In his Charge to the Provincial Synod of Rupert's Land on August 9, 1899, Archbishop Machray brought the matter forward: "There is a proposal before you from the Bishop of Moosonee. . . . The visitation of the Western part of his Diocese from Moose Factory has turned out very arduous and unsatisfactory, and the time is evidently near when from various causes, the administration of the Eastern half of my Diocese, lying in the Province of Ontario, as the Church will need it, will be quite out of my power. . . . I believe arrangements can be made by the Bishop of Moosonee which will give every reason to hope for an early appointment of a Bishop."

It took three years before the final arrangements for the endowment fund of the new diocese were completed. Bishop Newnham was willing that $25,000 from the endowment of the Diocese of Moosonee

[40]*The Northam Papers*, Bishop Newnham's manuscript notes on his work around Hudson Bay: "1895 . . . After visiting York and Churchill the Bp. went along the coast to Severn Post. He had taken all necessary steps *a year beforehand* to have a canoe and Indians to take him thence to Albany & so to Moose Ft. This was something of a venture, Bp. Horden had returned from York Ft. to Moose Ft. via Winnipeg & Minnabie. By going this way the bishop would have the whole journey within the diocese & among his own Indians & would meet some who had never seen their bishop, & perhaps not seen a missionary. The two young Indians who formed the bishop's crew only knew a little of it, but depended upon meeting others who would give them information. It was a 'Cross-country' route, changing from one system of river and lake to another, & it took 7 weeks from York to Moose Ft. Most of this country had never been traversed by a missionary, & perhaps not by a white man since the early days of the H. B. C." "1899 . . . He [Bishop Newnham] stayed at Churchill from October to January, 1900, meeting there Crees, Chipewyan & Eskimos—Then accompanied by Rev. R. Faries of York Ft., he walked on snowshoes to York Ft. & stayed there till May. *1900* May-June he visited Trout Lake . . . Thence the Bp. went by God's Lake & Oxford House to Norway House, & on to Winnipeg. The journey from Trout Lake to Winnipeg took 5 weeks, & much of the road was only known to two of the crew, & not well by those. Hardly any rations could be obtained at Trout Lake but pounded dried fish [fish pemmican]." These notes were dated September 3, 1929, just after they had been compiled; Bishop Newnham was then seventy-seven.

should be transferred to the endowment of the new diocese, but legal difficulties arose that could only be settled by an Act of Parliament, and consequently he had to travel 400 miles on snowshoes in March of 1901, to the railway, in order to appear before a parliamentary committee in Ottawa and justify his proposals. The Provincial Synod of Rupert's Land in 1902 approved of what had been done, ratified the situation by resolution, and thus the Diocese Keewatin came into being in 1902, though quite constitutionally founded in 1899.[41] The formal announcement that the Standing Committee on the Election of Bishops had met on April ninth and elected the Venerable Joseph Lofthouse, Archdeacon of Moose, as Bishop of Keewatin, was not made until after this resolution was passed, though the new Bishop had been consecrated the Sunday before the Synod commenced and delegates from the new diocese were present as members of the Synod.[42]

Moosonee Again

When I came to Moosonee more than forty years ago, I entered a land of yesterday. The twilight of the Romance of Hudson's Bay Company still hovered like a haze over Ontario's back door.
The Dominion Government sent down occasional surveyors. The Indians were left alone. . . . There were only two outside interests, the Old Company that came for fur, and the Missionaries who remembered that Indians had souls.[43]

These words are a retrospective glance by Bishop R. J. Renison of Moosonee at the days around the turn of the century, when he was associated with the Diocese as missionary at Albany (1899-1909), and Archdeacon of Moose (1907-1912). For the sake of the Indian, Bishop Newnham fought valiantly the hazards of travel, the vagaries of weather, and the difficulties of isolation. Whether he actually covered 17,000 miles in ten years, as one of his biographers suggested, may be a generous estimate.[44] The division of the Diocese, for which he was largely responsible, was a practical advance; yet although he was able to meet the Eskimo, the foundation of missions to these people in Baffin Land must be attributed to the Reverend E. J. Peck and the Church Missionary Society.
In the primitive surroundings of Moose Factory, her husband often

[41]*Journal of the Provincial Synod of Rupert's Land, 1899*, pp. 33-34. Message "B" from the House of Bishops to the House of Delegates. *Journal of the Provincial Synod of Rupert's Land, 1902*, pp. 36-37. Message "U" from the House of Bishops to the House of Delegates.
[42]O. R. Rowley, *The Anglican Episcopate of Canada and Newfoundland* (London, 1928), 126-127. Bishop Lofthouse was consecrated on August 17; the Provincial Synod of Rupert's Land met on August 20, 1902.
[43]R. J. Renison, "New Life in Moosonee," *M. S. C. C. Quarterly Bulletin, VII* (Toronto, December, 1946), 2.
[44]F. P. Shearwood, *By Water and the Word* [n.d.]. The appendix lists Bishop Newnham's journeys during his episcopate in Moosonee.

away, Mrs. Newnham kept a gracious and hospitable home, established the first hospital services there, in a simple form to which she gave much time herself, and secured the first trained nurse and deaconess in the area—Miss M. A. Johnson. The departure of Bishop and Mrs. Newnham from Moose Factory in May, 1904, for Prince Albert, Saskatchewan, marked the end of an era in the history of the Diocese of Moosonee.

In a history of this kind it is difficult to make more than a passing reference to many of the Church's most faithful servants. The Proceedings of the Church Missionary Society in 1902 reports the death of the Reverend John Saunders of Biscotasing on February 23. The first native ordinand of the Diocese, he had given more than thirty years of devoted service among the Ojibways in its southern part; in this he was greatly aided by his wife, who was one of the girls trained by Bishop Horden in the school at Moose Factory.

Bishop and Mrs. Newnham paid a visit to England in 1902 and brought back with them the Reverend J. E. Woodall. A graduate of the London College of Divinity, Mr. Woodall had been ordained deacon and priest in the Diocese of Lichfield, but his work had been confined to curacies in London. His association with Moosonee was to last for more than forty years, for many of which he was Archdeacon.

In 1899, after forty-two years in the Diocese, Archdeacon Vincent retired to the Victoria district, near Stonewall, Manitoba, but he gladly seized the opportunity, when it was offered by the government, to take the census in James Bay in 1901, and so renew the ties that bound him to the people there. In 1906 he returned again at the call of Bishop Holmes "to fill a vacancy for a while," but after a few months of great happiness he died there on January 16, 1907. His body was taken on a dog sleigh over a hundred miles of ice and snow to be buried by that of his wife in the old churchyard at Moose Factory. The quality of the Archdeacon's work, and his resourcefulness, can hardly be shown better than by quoting the last report he sent to the Church Missionary Society before resigning in 1899. (He had been working on the church at Albany):

I built this church many years ago. It is a wooden building, strongly spiked together with long iron nails. Our timber, however, is not very durable. . . . I had no one to help me but one young lad. . . . We raised this heavy building by means of wedges, to the height I wanted, removed all the decayed timber and replaced it with good solid lumber. I spent the greater part of two months over it. It was hard, hard work for me, but I have the satisfaction of knowing that my church is good for another twenty years, should no accident happen to it. While engaged in this heavy work we still conducted our daily services and other meetings. At the usual time day-school opened and we kept all our mission work moving. I wish often that we were nearer than we are to the four churches I am trying to get built. I am 210 miles from the nearest one and 550 miles from the furthest.

Actually the church lasted for another sixty years, when, owing to decay and changed circumstances at Albany in site and population, it became necessary to pull it down.

Bishop George Holmes

In 1903 the endowment for the Diocese of Calgary was completed. Bishop Pinkham, on September 30, resigned the See of Saskatchewan. The House of Bishops of the Ecclesiastical Province of Rupert's Land, in Session at Winnipeg, translated Bishop Newnham of Moosonee to the See of Saskatchewan.

For more than a year the Diocese of Moosonee was without a bishop, but on November 26, 1904, the House of Bishops elected as Bishop of Moosonee the Venerable George Holmes, then Archdeacon of Athabasca.

Bishop Holmes was born on November 23, 1858, at Holme in Westmorland, England, was educated in Reading and trained at the Church Missionary Society's College at Islington. Coming to Canada in 1885, his journey west was delayed by the circumstances of the Riel Rebellion and he spent a year in missionary work at Fort Frances, Ontario. He was ordained deacon on Trinity Sunday, June 5, 1887, by Bishop Young of Athabasca in St. Saviour's Church, Dunvegan,[45] and priest on July 8, 1888, in St. Luke's Church, Fort Vermilion. The whole of his ministry in the Diocese of Athabasca centred in St. Peter's Mission and School on Lesser Slave Lake, which he established under the direction of Bishop Young. Holmes became Archdeacon in 1901. He was consecrated in St. Paul's Church, Regina, on January 25, 1905, by Bishop Pinkham of Calgary, the senior Bishop in the Province of Rupert's Land, as it was then without a Metropolitan.[46]

There can be little doubt that Bishop Holmes was elected to the Diocese of Moosonee because of his previous success among the Indians. He could "think in Indian" and use those figures and forms of speech that most directly moved and touched an Indian heart. That his primary acquaintance and familiarity in this respect was with the Chipewyan dialect and Western Cree of the Athabasca country was not of great help to him in reading and speaking the Eastern Cree of Moosonee, which he found difficult. At the time of his election he had a sturdy and strong physique, was inured to the

---

[45]*Crockford's Clerical Directory, 1898*, p. 2018.
[46]O. R. Rowley, *op. cit.*, 142-143.

hardships to be met in travelling, and was always prepared to share the life of the Indian. Of the course of diocesan affairs during his episcopate little can be said, because there seem to be few records of the period. No report on Indian Missions was presented to the Provincial Synod of Rupert's Land between its meetings of 1902 and 1923.[47] In April, 1907, it was reported that a new Indian boarding school was being built at Chapleau at a cost of $2,500, that the town had raised $1,700 towards a new church, and that a new church had been built at Biscostasing, about eighty miles east of Chapleau on the C.P.R. Actually Bishop Holmes only lived at Moose Factory for a short time after his consecration, and then moved to Chapleau, a divisional point on the railway, just within the boundary of the Diocese. That Bishop Holmes had some considerable interest in the Chapleau School is indicated by the fact that when the school was rebuilt by the Indian Department about 1920, Canon Prewer, the Principal, was engaged in raising $5,000 to provide a chapel in memory of him.

Bishop Holmes remained with the Diocese of Moosonee little more than four years. On April 15, 1909, he was translated by the House of Bishops to the Diocese of Athabasca, which had been entirely without episcopal oversight since Bishop Reeve of Mackenzie River had resigned his position as Commissary on August 31, 1907.

Bishop John George Anderson

At the same meeting of the House of Bishops at which arrangements were made for Bishop Holmes to go to Athabasca, the Reverend John George Anderson, incumbent of St. Peter's, Dynevor, near Selkirk, Manitoba, the church of the old Indian Settlement on Red River, was elected as Bishop of Moosonee.[48] Bishop Anderson came of the H.B.C. "House People" ancestry and was brought up in the St. Andrew's district of Red River. Here he attended school as a boy, passing on to St. John's College, Winnipeg, where in 1880 he was put on the "preparendi list" of students supported by the C.M.S., and placed in the Honours Class of the University of Manitoba when he took his B.A. in 1886. He completed his B.D. in 1888. He was ordained deacon by Bishop Machray on August 18, 1889, in St. Mary's

[47]*Journal of the Provincial Synod of Rupert's Land, 1923*, pp. 69-72. Appendix 4: Memorandum re Indian Missions.

[48]R. L. A., *The Northam Papers*, Bishop John George Anderson: P. A. Northam to T. C. B. Boon (n.d., but ca. 1958). "He was somewhat diffident about accepting his election, but it was pointed out to him that a great opportunity was offered for putting his talents to good use; his complete command of the language of the Cree nation, his training under the eye of the great Archbishop [Machray] and, as well, there was to his credit some twenty years' experience in Indian missionary work. So he accepted his election."

Church, Portage la Prairie, and priest on June 29, 1890, in Holy Trinity Church, Winnipeg. As a deacon he worked for a year as C.M.S. missionary at Lac Seul, Ontario, then still in the Diocese of Rupert's Land, but the following year he was appointed to St. Peter's where he remained until he was elected Bishop of Moosonee. Bishop Anderson was consecrated on Whitsunday, May 16, 1909, in St. Andrew's Church, the spiritual home of his boyhood, by Archbishop Matheson of Rupert's Land.[49] Bishop Anderson came to the Diocese of Moosonee at a time when the work was rapidly changing its nature. The railways mentioned by Bishop Horden in his Charge of thirty years before had not materialized, but railways that had not been foreseen were being constructed. The Transcontinental was being built through what is now known as the clay belt from Quebec to Winnipeg, as part of the expansion of the Grand Trunk Railway. Bishop Horden had remarked that no minerals had been found, but the turn of the century saw nickel mining begun in a big way at Sudbury. The railway began to push north from North Bay through the Cobalt district to meet the Grand Trunk Railway at Cochrane. In the area between Lakes Timiskaming and Abitibi were discovered the rich gold fields of Ontario and Quebec, which lie partly in the Diocese of Moosonee. The demand for paper intensified the activities of the pulpwood industry. Gold and pulpwood brought about the development of electricity by water-power; thus, Bishop Anderson found himself no longer the Bishop of an Indian diocese, sparsely settled by the native hunter and trapper. He made his home at Cochrane, Ontario, where the railways met and where one branch of the Abitibi River was not far away.

Cochrane in 1909 was still a shanty town with a very mixed population of about nine hundred, mostly railway men. Through the efforts of H. V. Fricker of the Colonial and Continental Church Society, and the Reverend A. D. Renshall, a church, forty feet by twenty-two feet, was built in 1909 by local help. This church, and its successor, became the Pro-Cathedral of the Diocese during the episcopate of Bishop Anderson. During his time, too, the work among the Indians was largely extended, new missions being opened up along the Albany River, and at new points on the transcontinental railway. The Bishop himself was active, and experienced in the ways of a canoe. It is said that he was always met at one mission station by two men with a canoe from the next station he intended to visit, and that during the ensuing voyage, with their help, he brushed up his knowledge of the particular dialect used at his destination.

The episcopate of John George Anderson lasted thirty-four years,

⁴⁹O. R. Rowley, op. cit., 152-153.

and may with some fairness be divided into three periods: 1909-1920, 1920-1933, 1933-1943. The progress of work among the Eskimo Missions has been mentioned. The building of the new transcontinental railway, the Algoma Central Railway, and their linkage with what is now the Canadian National main line from Sioux Lookout to Capreol, produced the Western Moosonee Mission centred in Hearst, and largely supported by the Colonial and Continental Church Society. This mission was organized by the Reverend J. N. Blodgett, who was appointed to Chapleau in 1917. What is now known as the Ontario Northland Railway had reached Cochrane in 1908, and by 1920 some of the newer places along the latter line had progressed to such an extent that immediate grants of $500 to Matheson and $300 to Porquis Junction were urged. The need for churches at these places and at Monteith, Iroquois Falls, South Porcupine, as well as Smooth Rock, Foleyet and Cochrane itself, was advanced for consideration. At the 1920 Synod the Bishop commended the Diocese for having subscribed $43,000 to the Anglican Forward Movement, when it had only been asked for $25,000. He suggested that the portion returnable to the Diocese under the scheme should be set up as a clergy endowment fund.

The Synod had been preceded and prepared for by two Conferences of clergy and laity in 1917 and 1919, and at the latter the formal motion constituting the Synod had been moved by the Reverend E. J. Peck, senior clergyman of the diocese. Consequently it was possible in 1920 to present to this Synod a draft of Constitution and Canons, with Rules of Procedure, and these were approved after some discussion. This first Synod was held at Timmins.

The second Synod of the Diocese was held at Chapleau in 1921. The Bishop called attention to the fact that the inability of the Missionary Society of the Church in Canada to take over the Indian and Eskimo work in 1921 had caused considerable financial difficulty, and that the announcement that it would do so had led the Moosonee and Keewatin Association in England to end its existence and to amalgamate with the Colonial and Continental Church Society.

At the fourth Synod, held at Cochrane in 1926, the emphasis was on the Indian and Eskimo work of the Church, stimulated perhaps by the presence of two missionaries from the actual field: the Reverends H. Cartlidge of Waswanipie, and P. A. Northam of Albany, whose work in those missions the Bishop outlined and warmly commended. He also referred to the death of the Reverend E. J. Peck in Ottawa on September 10, 1924, and said that the English-Eskimo Dictionary Dr. Peck had spent so long in preparing had, with the help of the late Reverend R. H. Archer and Mrs. Archer of Ottawa, been finished just before he died, and was published as a memorial to him by the Church of the Ascension Thank-Offering Fund, of Hamilton.[50] Dr. Peck's successor at Fort George, the Reverend W. G. Walton, had resigned in 1924 after thirty-two years of service in that mission. The Bishop said that a deep debt of gratitude was owing to Mr. Walton, for, almost single-handed, he had revised, prepared and seen through the press the Peck Memorial Eskimo Dictionary. There had been a great deal of difficulty in replacing Walton at Fort George, and after several disappointments he had decided to ordain a local catechist of long experience for the work, and so had ordained Fred Mark to the diaconate at Moose in July, 1925.

The Reverend W. G. Walton, in 1924, was one of the last few links of the Diocese of Moosonee with the old C.M.S. days and the time of Bishop Horden. His influence extended from Fort George to Fort Chimo in Ungava, a distance of perhaps a thousand miles. He had spent much time on translation work, and was particularly interested in getting his people to read and sing. He and Mrs. Walton had experienced the hardships of the early days. One of their daughters, Mrs. Violet Holmes, contributed some of her recollections of Fort George to the September, 1952, number of the *Arctic News*:

I was born at Fort George one cold day in January. My mother had a half-breed woman for a nurse and she was not used to handling little babies dressed as we dress them. Accordingly my mother put me in a moss bag as the Indian women do their children. So began the life I lived in this part of the Arctic for seventeen years and I saw something of what early missionary life there was like. . . . I remember the great excitement when our yearly supply boat came in the autumn. The fun of opening the cases, seeing our new clothes and having the larder re-stocked with new supplies of food. The early summer always saw the shelves depleted. . . .

I learned to say the Lord's Prayer like any other child in a Christian home. But mine was the added privilege to hear and know the brotherhood of people speaking a different language—yet one in Christ Jesus—as my "Our Father Who art in heaven" joined with the Indians saying "Noo Tawwinan chi chee chi shee coots ah tiyan."

The H. B. store did not cater extensively to Missionaries' wives who wanted to give their husbands a Christmas or birthday gift. My mother solved her problem by giving it to God. I will ever remember the expression on my father's face the time he opened an envelope laid on his breakfast plate one Christmas Day. Inside was the hymn "Love lifted me," translated into Cree, perfect in metre and rhythm.

To this Synod of 1926 Bishop Anderson gave some account of his visitations. In 1923 he had gone to Osnaburgh, Fort Hope, Ogoki

[50]Robert John Renison, formerly of Albany himself (1899-1909), and later Bishop of Moosonee (1943-1954), was rector of The Church of the Ascension, Hamilton, at this time.

River, Albany and Pagwa. He had confirmed one hundred and thirty-four persons, and the offerings amounted to $522. In 1925 he had gone to Moose Factory for the ordination of the Reverend Fred Mark; Charlton, Albany, where he had ordained another native catechist, the Reverend Andrew Wesley; Rupert's House, Fort George and Whale River. The total disance travelled was about 1,500 miles, compared with 1,700 miles in 1923. The Reverend B. Atkinson, in addition, had visited missions in Hudson Strait and gone as far north as Pangnirtung and Pond's Inlet. The H.B.C. had taken over the old buildings on Blacklead Island, and was paying half the cost of the new ones at Pangnirtung. The B.C.M.S. of England had undertaken the support of missionaries at these new stations, as the M.S.C.C. could only provide for the one at Lake Harbour. Two noteworthy resolutions by Northam and Cartlidge were: (a) to establish catechists' schools—which was approved, but thirty years elapsed before they were really organized; and (b) a suggestion of conferences of missionaries in the James Bay area, to take place three months before each Synod, so that recommendations regarding Indian work could be forwarded to it. This was amended to a request for the division of the diocese into three rural deaneries. It was announced at the next Synod that this had been done; the Deaneries of Chapleau, Cochrane and Moose were formed, with the Reverends H. Hesketh, R. S. Cushing and P. A. Northam as Rural Deans. A third resolution at the 1926 Synod, reiterating the demand of 1923, asked that all the work of the Canadian Church among Indians and Eskimos be put under one episcopal control and directive. This was forwarded to the Provincial Synod, and became another step towards the formation of the Diocese of The Arctic.

The Synod of 1928, which met at Timmins, devoted itself to routine business. The only Indian representatives were two chiefs, Alex. Pekoday from Elsas and S. Luke from Metagama, both missions near Chapleau. Rural Dean Northam was congratulated upon the excellent new school he had built at Albany and the new church at Attawapiscat. The Bishop reported that his travels in 1926 had extended on the east coast of James Bay as far as Whale River, and inland as far east as Mistassini; in 1927, on the western side as far as Fort Hope and Ogoki River. He mentioned that the Indians there had carefully pulled down the church at Martin's Falls (no longer needed), floated the material down the river, and rebuilt it at Ogoki. The proposed Vincent Memorial Hospital at Albany had not materialized, and he asked the approval of the Synod for the erection of a memorial tablet there as an interim token, and this was approved. The Bishop also surveyed at length the affairs of the Arctic missions and the negotiations that had resulted in the appointment of an Arctic Committee by agreement with the four dioceses concerned in the work—Moosonee, Keewatin, Mackenzie River and Yukon—in which the pooling of resources aimed at reaching all the Eskimos was an essential part. As the Bishop of the senior diocese concerned he had had the privilege of appointing the Reverend A. L. Fleming as the first Archdeacon of The Arctic. This point marks the beginning of the movement towards the second division of the Diocese.

The second period, 1920-1933, was one of accelerated growth and change that also saw thorny problems arising from the impact of the white man on the Indian way of life. Probably no other Bishop of the Canadian Church has seen this problem with clearer eyes or been more sympathetic in dealing with it. A brilliant scholar, capable administrator and a cultivated man, it was sometimes charged that in Bishop Anderson's long association with the Indians he became too much like them himself in the way in which he looked upon life. Perhaps it was a good fault.

Separation from the Ecclesiastical Province of Rupert's Land

The financial disaster of the Province of Rupert's Land in 1932, of which more will be said later, dealt a heavy blow to the Diocese of Moosonee, which lost its episcopal endowment. Recovery, as in the case of other dioceses affected, was not achieved for several years, in fact not until the Restoration Fund had been made effective. In the interval changes took place in the outlook of the Church, and the opportunity was taken to reorganize some provincial boundaries. At the twenty-second meeting of the Provincial Synod of Rupert's Land on September 13, 1933, the recommendation that the Diocese of Moosonee be transferred to the Ecclesiastical Province of Ontario received unanimous concurrence, and so the diocese ceased to be part of the Province of Rupert's Land. From that time its history belongs to the Province of Ontario.[51]

[51]*Journal of the Provincial Synod of Rupert's Land, 1933*, pp. 43, 107. Appendix VI: Report of the Boundaries Committee.

CHAPTER EIGHT

The Dioceses of the Saskatchewan Valley

SASKATCHEWAN–CALGARY–EDMONTON

The characteristics of the times and country in which God has placed us are worthy of our reverent study. We ought to have a lively and intelligent perception of the spiritual dangers and needs which are peculiar to the particular period. . . . We must be in touch with the spirit of the age, and alive to its special tendencies and difficulties.

BISHOP GRISDALE'S SERMON, PROVINCIAL SYNOD, *1899*

John McLean was born in Portsoy, Scotland, on November 17, 1828. He eventually became a student at King's College in Aberdeen, where he met Robert Machray in 1847. Even at that time John McLean was an able scholar, and a High Bursar of the College in Latin and Greek. They both graduated as Masters of Arts in 1851. John McLean joined a large manufacturing firm in London, and having acquired French, German and Spanish, was placed in charge of the foreign correspondence of his firm.

In the summer of 1858 Robert Machray received a letter from John McLean intimating the latter's intentions of taking Holy Orders. While living in London, McLean had become an active member of The Church of England Young Men's Society, and had been accepted as a candidate by the Bishop of Ripon.

Dr. Hellmuth (later to be Bishop of Huron), then General Superintendent of the Canadian work of the Colonial and Continental Church Society, was in England that summer and proposed that John McLean should come to Canada. This he accepted, and being ordained deacon by Bishop Cronyn of Huron on August 1, 1858, was appointed curate of St. Paul's Cathedral in London, Ontario, a position he held for seven years. McLean was priested on December 15, 1858, and had the unusual experience of preaching his own ordination sermon.

When the necessity of refounding St. John's College arose in the mind of Bishop Machray in 1865, he invited his old friend the Reverend John McLean to become its first Warden. The late Archbishop Matheson, who was one of McLean's pupils, said that he was "the

153

best and most inspiring teacher I ever sat under." He took a prominent part in the synods and conferences of the diocese, and established and built the first church in the present city of Winnipeg, Holy Trinity.

The Society for the Propagation of the Gospel had promised its assistance to a bishop for Saskatchewan, but it was necessary to raise considerable money before the consecration of such a bishop could take place. In 1873 Dr. McLean went to England where he was singularly successful in appealing for funds, his efforts raising £6,200 (approximately $31,000). His brief biography in Mockridge's *The Bishops of the Church of England in Canada and Newfoundland* states that "he boldly encountered men in their homes and offices, and preached to them the necessity of giving to the support of the Gospel." Further visits to England increased the endowment, first to $50,000 in 1878, and then to $75,000 in 1884.

Bishop McLean was consecrated at the same time as Bishop Bompas, May 3, 1874, in St. Mary's Parish Church, Lambeth, by the Archbishop of Canterbury, Dr. Tait.[1]

Bishop McLean Goes to his Diocese

Bishop McLean did not come back to Canada until the autumn of the year. On January 28, 1875, he set out from the Red River. "He held a series of confirmations and services all along the route. Thus he journeyed for more than a thousand miles over trackless wastes of snow, on the lakes, along the rivers, and through the woods. In this primary tour the Bishop visited Nepowewin Mission, a field occupied some years previously by the Church Missionary Society, and served by a native missionary, the Reverend Luke Caldwell, who died shortly after; Prince Albert, having a population of about 500, but no church building; and White Fish Lake, afterwards Asisippe, sixty miles north of Carlton House, in charge of John Hines, a catechist, assisted by George McKay, "a native of the country."[2]

He reached Prince Albert about the middle of February, when the old Church of St. Mary's was under construction. At first the settlement of Prince Albert followed the Red River pattern and homes were scattered along three or four miles of river frontage. But gradually the city has become consolidated, and now old St. Mary's stands in quiet isolation by the riverside, some distance from the town. A plain

[1]P. A. C., *Privy Council File*, Letter No. 97, April 10, 1874. The nominations of Bishop McLean to the Diocese of Saskatchewan, and Bishop Bompas to the Diocese of Athabasca, were each approved by Orders in Council of the Government of Canada before Patents were issued by the Crown for their consecration by the Archbishop of Canterbury. C. H. Mockridge, *The Bishops of the Church of England in Canada and Newfoundland* (Toronto, 1896), 275-282. O. R. Rowley, *The Episcopate of Canada and Newfoundland* (London, 1928), 60 61.
[2]C. H. Mockridge, *op. cit.*, 277-278.

and simple little building, in a beautifully kept churchyard, St. Mary's still preserves its own inspiring dignity. It was here on January 9, 1876, that Bishop McLean conducted his first ordination, John Hines of the C.M.S. being made deacon.

When the Bishop first arrived in his Diocese there was only one fully-ordained clergyman, the Reverend John Alexander Mackay, who was stationed at Stanley, and a native deacon, the Reverend Luke Caldwell who was at Fort à la Corne. Mr. Hines had come out to the country north of the Saskatchewan at the suggestion of Bishop Bompas in the spring of 1874 and had travelled with the Bishop's party to Winnipeg, from which point he made his way west with his own outfit. As far as the Touchwood Hills he was accompanied by Archdeacon Cowley and the Reverend J. and Mrs. Reader, who had also come from England with him. Hines was an experienced farmer and had been appointed by the Church Missionary Society to open up a new mission station at some suitable place where the Indians of the Plains might not only receive Christian teaching but also be induced to settle down to a regular agricultural life. Mr. Hines has told his own story in a simple, unvarnished style in his book *The Red Indians of the Plains*, in itself something of a history of the Diocese of Saskatchewan. His own account of his ordination has some interest: "I was ordained deacon by the Right Reverend John McLean, D.C.L., the first Bishop of Saskatchewan, in the first English Church built in the Saskatchewan [valley], and I was the first one he had ordained since his consecration."[3]

In the winter of 1876 Bishop McLean paid his first visit to Edmonton, where he made arrangements for the site and buildings of the original All Saints' Church. To Edmonton, in September, 1875, had come Dr. William Newton, the first missionary in the Diocese of Saskatchewan to be supported by the S.P.G. With his arrival the number of clergy had been doubled, and a new point of great importance became a centre of work. At that time Fort Edmonton was the great supply depot for the north. For heavier goods the old route from Cumberland House to the Churchill River and over Portage la Loche, or Methy Portage, had been abandoned in favour of York Boats on the Saskatchewan and a road to Fort Assiniboine.[4]

The Saskatchewan Country

When Bishop McLean entered upon the work of his Diocese in 1875, its centre of population lay north of the South Saskatchewan

[3]John Hines, *The Red Indians of the Plains* (London, 1915), 131-132.
[4]The road from Edmonton to Athabasca Landing was not cut until 1883. The S.S. *Northcote* was running on the Saskatchewan River in 1874, and the telegraph reached Edmonton in 1879.

River. The white settlers who had arrived there had mainly come from the banks of the Red River in Manitoba, not a few of them from the parts now called Old Kildonan and Middlechurch. The Indian work was among the Swampy Crees who spoke a similar language to those of Manitoba and northern Ontario. But the centre of balance was rapidly changing. In 1874 the newly-organized North West Mounted Police went on the march and established one of their stations that year at old Fort Macleod, which then lay about two and a half miles east of its later location. On September 22, 1877, a treaty was made with the Plains Indians. They were signs of the times: shortly after the settlement of southern Alberta was underway, the Indians, who had roamed at will, were being gathered into various Reserves. The struggling Church was trying to keep up and serve both movements of population.

In August, 1882, the Bishop was able to tell his first Synod that there were sixteen clergy in the Diocese besides himself, ten catechists and schoolmasters, and twenty-nine mission stations. Bishop McLean had limitless confidence in the future of the resources and possibilities of western Canada, and pictured them in glowing terms for the audiences he addressed in eastern Canada, at a time when many of the leading statesmen were pouring ridicule upon the idea of building a railway across the country. In spite of the great extent of his territory, Bishop McLean made it his business to visit all mission stations at certain intervals, from Lake Winnipeg in the northeast to Fort Macleod and the foothills of the Rockies in the southwest.

Previous to 1874 work among the Indians had followed two well-travelled routes, along which one or more mission stations had successively been established. The northern route was that of the canoe, up the Saskatchewan River as far as Cumberland House; and then it turned northwest to Lac la Ronge and Stanley on the Churchill River. This area was at the time in charge of John Alexander Mackay, who had been sent there by Bishop Anderson immediately after he had received priest's orders in 1864. The point of contact in the southern part of the diocese was the Touchwood Hills, which lay a little to the northwest of Fort Ellice and within reach of the Qu'Appelle Valley; this station seems to have been on the direct trail to Fort Carlton. The work of the Church in this part of the country, however, had not prospered to the extent it had in the north, partly because the Plains Indians were of a more independent nature; partly because they had not had the same long contact with the white man, as the Crees to the north had through the Hudson's Bay Company; partly because they roamed over a much wider area and were less accessible to the approaches of the missionary than Indians who gained their livelihood by fishing or trapping.[5]

The Reverend Thomas Cook has already been mentioned as having gone to Fort Ellice in 1862, but ten years before that the Reverend Charles Hillyer, accompanied by a native catechist named Charles Pratt,[6] had spent some months in the Qu'Appelle country, and so, earlier still, had the Reverend James Settee, whose exact movements are hard to trace. Actually, Cook and Reader[7] were regarded as belonging to the Diocese of Rupert's Land, and within the jurisdiction of Bishop Machray. Diocesan boundaries at that time were defined more in terms of Hudson's Bay Company districts than geographical surveys, and consequently were somewhat indeterminate.[8]

In 1865 Charles Pratt taught school on the prairies in the vicinity of Fort Qu'Appelle, at a place called Lakesend, near the eastern shore of Echo Lake. The schoolhouse was a crude log cabin, and he carved letters of the alphabet on wooden blocks for the instruction of his pupils.

North of the North Saskatchewan

A new field, in more senses than one, was broken when John Hines crossed the North Saskatchewan with his outfit of oxen, horses and wagons, accompanied by young David Stranger, a native of St. Peter's,

[5]C. M. S. A., Diary of Rev. James Settee, March 20, 1867. James Settee opened a school, supported by the C. M. S., at one of the Qu'Appelle Lakes (or it may have been Beaver Creek, as the name Qu'Appelle seems to have been used rather indefinitely at this time). The work prospered there for about a year, but the attitude of the Indians became unfriendly and the school was closed. Settee went to The Pas. In 1846 James Hunter sent him to Lac la Ronge; James Settee is regarded as the founder of this mission.

[6]Minutes of the Church Missionary Society Corresponding Committee at Red River, June 7, 1852. Permission was accorded Rev. Charles Hillyer to go to Fort Pelly and work with Charles Pratt, the catechist there, among the Plain Crees. Charles Pratt is listed as a boy attending the Church Missionary Society's school at Red River (George Harbidge report, July 1, 1824), described as an Assiniboine, aged 8. An interesting boy, "upon the whole he may be called a good boy," he was "of French extraction." Charles was among the last group of boys baptized by John West on June 8, 1823. He worked for the Hudson's Bay Company after leaving school, was sent to Fort Pelly, and there began catechetical work on his own initiative. In 1848 he was back at Red River taking some training under Rev. W. Cockran at the house called St. Cross. The rest of his long life was spent as a catechist and school-teacher in the Fort Pelly-Touchwood Hills-Qu'Appelle area, and he is buried in St. Luke's churchyard, Raymore, Saskatchewan.

[7]Rev. Joseph Reader was at the Touchwood Hills as a lay catechist in 1874, he and Mrs. Reader having come out with the same party as John Hines, under Bishop Bompas. Ordained by Bishop Machray, Reader went to the Devon Mission at The Pas in 1884, where he spent three years, during which he became attracted by the tenets of the Plymouth Brethren. About 1888 he left the Anglican Church. He spent the rest of his life, however, in this part of the country, and with the aid of a printing press he imported, continued to spread the faith in the way he had come to understand it, a matter that caused no little embarrassment to the Anglican Church.

[8]Journal of the Provincial Synod of Rupert's Land, 1873, p. 4.

Red River, and young George McKay. Hines headed along the trail towards Green Lake. The Green Lake country, however, was found quite unsuitable for farming, and the party returned south and built winter quarters near White Fish Lake. Here, early in October, they were visited by two Indians, and, Hines observed, "they proved to be father and son and I thought I never saw a finer built man than the elder of the two."[9]

This Indian, whose name was Chief Star Blanket, had a long and revealing conversation with the missionary in which he expressed the desire that he and his people should be instructed in the Christian religion, and also taught to settle down to an agricultural life, for the Chief already foresaw the coming shortage of buffalo. It was at the Chief's suggestion that the new mission was established at Sandy Lake in the Shell River valley in the spring of 1875.[10] Later in the same year Chief Big Child and his fifteen tents came to Sandy Lake, but eventually settled at Snake Plain, about twenty miles south, "but our work did not end even here. Another Chief and his followers, living seventy-five miles north of Sandy Lake, had also heard of our doings and had paid us several visits, and pressed me to visit them occasionally at Stony Lake, the place where they resided."[11] This group of Indians, in due time, embraced Christianity and did not spare themselves in learning to farm and helping to build their own church. A notable convert of the time was Peter Ka-Ka-Soo, who became so efficient in reading and writing that the winter after he was baptized he volunteered to teach the syllabic characters to his fellow countrymen. No one has ever been able to estimate the number of converts he made to Christianity in this way, but certainly his work had a wide influence.[12]

The first building erected at Sandy Lake was a single-roomed house, eighteen feet by sixteen feet. This building, said Hines, served the fourfold purpose of school, kitchen, dining-room, and bedroom for the missionary and his man for nearly two years. The first Church Council held in the Diocese of Saskatchewan was held in this room. Three were present: Bishop McLean, the Reverend J. A. Mackay, who had come from the Stanley Mission on the English River, and Mr. Hines. It was at this meeting in a log hut in the wilderness that the formation of a training school for young Indians, to fit them for the dual capacity of teachers and catechists, was first discussed and plans formed to bring it into effect. This school for catechists came into being in 1879 and was the nucleus of the present Emmanuel College.[13]

[9]John Hines, *The Red Indians of the Plains* (London, 1915), 78.
[10]*Ibid.*, 81-83.
[11]*Ibid.*, 164.
[12]*Ibid.*, 153-154.
[13]*Ibid.*, 91-92.

The second building at Sandy Lake was built by the voluntary labour of the Indians themselves. For five days of the week it was used as a school. Church was held there on Sundays, and in its spare time the sod-roofed structure became a carpenter's shop. Hines purposely deferred building a permanent church until government surveys had settled the limits of the Reserves, and when one was built it was on the exact spot where the Indians had been accustomed to assemble for their heathen religious ceremonies. This church was completed about 1879, but not dedicated until May 8, 1881, owing to the inability of the Bishop to get there earlier. It was given the name of St. Mark.[14]

Mr. Hines continued his work in this district until 1888 when he became incumbent at The Pas and Superintendent of Indian Missions in the eastern part of the Diocese. He was priested in 1880.

The Effect of the Indian Treaties

It took considerable time after Confederation for the Government of Canada to bring the affairs of the old Hudson's Bay Company Territory in the west into order, and provide a proper organization to maintain the order established. The first step forward was the organization of the Province of Manitoba, which became effective on May 12, 1870. But this new province only extended a little farther west than Portage la Prairie (its western boundary passing through the Cypress Hills and Gladstone); its northern boundary (parallel fifty degrees and thirty minutes north) was a little south of the present town of Gimli. It took another three years to provide a legislative body for the rest of the territory, and it was not until March 8, 1873, that the Northwest Council held its first meeting at Government House, Fort Garry. One of its duties was to suggest measures and conditions under which treaties could be made with the various Indian bands for their proper settlement. It is interesting to note that the first act of this council was one to prevent the sale of spirituous liquors in the Northwest Territories.

Hines, who was contemporary with the events of this time, and also a warm and understanding friend of the Plains Indians, said that the measures of prohibition taken by the government were instigated by the Indians themselves, and named his friends Star Blanket and Big Child as two of those who appealed to the government to protect their people against the liquor traffic.[15]

In due course treaties with the Indians were made, those that concerned the Plain and Wood Crees of Northern Saskatchewan being concluded at Fort Carlton on August 23, 1876. The interpreter on

[14]*Ibid.*, 151, 175.
[15]*Ibid.*, 150-152.

this occasion was Charles Pratt, one of the Reverend John West's C.M.S. boys. The Indians were given the right to choose any part of the country to settle, the amount of land to be reserved depending upon the number in the band, on the basis of 640 acres for every five persons. Each band was to be provided with oxen, cows, farm implements, seed grain and provisions for a limited number of years. The promise was also made that as soon as the people desired to have their children taught, and the number of children was such as to justify a school on the Reserve, the government would make a grant of £60 a year towards the teacher's salary; the choice of teacher would lie with the church whose agents were doing missionary work on any particular Reserve.

The settlement of the Indians on Reserves under these treaties gave new opportunities to the Church, of which Bishop McLean was quick to take advantage. In 1877 the Reverend John Alexander Mackay left Stanley and went to Battleford, where he opened missions on several Reserves during the two years he spent there. In the same year he was joined at Battleford by John Hope, the younger son of Withewacapo of York Factory, who had been trained in the C.M.S. School at the Red River Settlement, was an employee of the Hudson's Bay Company for eleven years, and is known to have established on his own account a mission and school at Great Bear Lake for the "Dog-Rib" Chipewyan Indians. For seventeen years John Hope was the faithful catechist on the Battleford Reserve, where he was long remembered as "The Teacher." With tarpaper for a blackboard, and well-thumbed primers, John Hope taught the "Three R's" and a new way of life to the Indians of the Moosomin, Thunderchild, Sweet Grass and Red Pheasant Reserves. In all of these he served for a time before his death on August 13, 1894, at the age of seventy-seven.[16]

Owing largely to the work of Robert Terrill Rundle, 1840-1848, the Reverend George McDougall and his son, the Reverend John McDougall, the Indians of the Foothills (now the western part of Alberta, extending from the U.S.A. boundary to a little north of Edmonton) had come under the influence of the Methodist Church some years before the Diocese of Saskatchewan was constituted. But for such work as Dr. Newton was able to do in the immediate neighbourhood of Edmonton, the Church of England had no contact with the Foothill tribes. In 1878, however, a mission was opened among the Peigan Indians, whose Reserve was in the ranching country close to the international border, and to this mission came the Reverend

<hr/>

[16]C. Wetton, *Saskatoon Star-Phoenix* (n.d.; *ca.* 1947). This is based on a memorial tribute to John Hope, that appeared in the *Saskatoon Herald* after his death in 1894, written by P. C. Pembrum, well known for his long service with the Hudson's Bay Company in the Mackenzie River country.

George McKay. Subsequent to the opening of the Sandy Lake Mission, McKay went to Sidney Sussex College, Cambridge, and was ordained deacon and priest by Bishop McLean in 1878, receiving deacon's orders on June 22, 1878, in St. Saviour's Church, Brixton Rise in London. He made his way from London to his new charge through New York and Montana, at a time when this journey was quite an adventure and seldom without incident. McKay continued his work in this part of Alberta very successfully until the Riel Rebellion of 1885. He had been brought up among the Indians of the plains, spoke their language, understood their outlook and way of life. Progress was made among the Peigans, Bloods and Sarcees during these seven years.

The Beginning of Emmanuel College

It was not until 1879 that Bishop McLean was able to carry out the plans made in 1874, and commence in Prince Albert the school designed to train native catechists and teachers. The project was a cherished one, for the Bishop keenly felt the need in the Diocese for trained interpreters, schoolmasters, and catechists.

Emmanuel College began in a very small way indeed in log buildings, with the Bishop himself as Warden and chief instructor in most subjects, but the Reverend John Alexander Mackay was brought from Battleford to be tutor in Cree, at the same time exercising pastoral care over Indian Missions within accessible distance of Prince Albert. The Reverend J. A. Mackay was made Canon of the Diocese in 1881 and became its first Archdeacon in 1884.

Among those who entered as students was Edward K. Matheson, whose name must be joined to those of John Alexander Mackay, John Hines, George McKay and Thomas Clarke as pioneers in the Indian missionary work of the Diocese. Edward K. Matheson was born in Kildonan, Red River, on April 21, 1855, and came west under the leadership of the Reverend J. A. Mackay with the Reverend Thomas Clarke in the summer of 1877. For two years he taught school at Snake Plain and Sandy Lake, and so got his earliest training under the Reverend John Hines. Matheson was ordained deacon on May 2, 1880, priested on April 10, 1881, and became the first divinity graduate of Emmanuel College in 1882. In August, 1886, Edward Matheson went to Lethbridge. The first church was built there during his incumbency, and the first women's church organization in the Diocese of Saskatchewan commenced under the name of the Guild of St. Monica. In 1888 he returned to the Saskatchewan valley and took charge of St. George's, Battleford; the little settlement of Saskatoon was an outlying point of his district. After being in Prince Albert again from 1893 to 1895, he returned to Battleford in the latter year to become Principal of the Industrial School, a position he held for nearly twenty years. During his principalship the school was self-supporting and received no aid from the Church. After 1914 he became Superintendent of Indian Missions, a post he held until he became an invalid about ten years before his death in 1931.[17]

Other students at Emmanuel College in these early years were Robert Inkster (1880), J. F. Pritchard (1885), J. Badger (1886), J. R. Settee (1886), D. D. Macdonald (1887), and James Taylor (1887), the years being those of graduation.

The Prince Albert district did not go unaffected by the optimism of the early eighties, and the promise of expansion and future prosperity found outlet in a meeting held there in 1882, at which it was decided to establish a Saskatchewan University, which, unlike the University of Manitoba, was definitely to be linked with the Church. The rest cannot better be told than in the words of the 1927 calendar of Emmanuel College: "In May, 1883, the Governor-General in Council sanctioned an Act [46 Vict. Cap. 47] to establish and incorporate the University of Saskatchewan, and to authorize the establishment of Colleges within the limits of the Diocese of Saskatchewan." The Bishop of the Diocese was constituted, by the charter, Chancellor of the University. A senate was elected, statutes and by-laws were passed, and confirmed by the Governor-General. Power was given by the charter to confer degrees in all faculties provided by the statutes, after a prescribed course of study, and upon examinations held in accordance with the regulations. The Bishop also secured certain property and funds for the endowment of the college. At the close of that year, Bishop McLean reported thirty-four pupils, of whom four were preparing to pass the entrance examination to the University of Saskatchewan. The course included the various branches of Theology, Moral Philosophy, Logic, Agricultural Chemistry, Classics, Mathematics, Indian Languages, and English Literature, under the Bishop and two professors.[18]

The Riel Rebellion of 1885, the death of Bishop McLean in 1886, and the sudden expansion of population in the southern part of what is now Alberta, which caused Bishop Pinkham to live in Calgary, deflected interest from the work of the college as a training ground

[17]Campbell Innes, "Canon E. K. Matheson," *Canadian North-West Historical Society Publications*, I (1927), 16-28.
[18]*Ibid.*, 58-60. *Canadian Churchman* (June 13, 1929), 375-387. J. E. Murray, "Early History of Emmanuel College," *Saskatchewan History*, IX (Autumn, 1956). John Hines, *op. cit.*, 91-92.

for catechists, and for some years it seemed to be more a high school, until a new influx of white settlers in the Saskatchewan valley at the beginning of the century brought about its revival and reorganization.

The Death of Bishop McLean

At his Synod in 1886, Bishop McLean reported that the Diocese had twenty-two clergy, eleven of whom were C.M.S. men; seven supported by the S.P.G.; and seven catechists. New churches had been erected at Fort Macleod, Pincher Creek, Calgary and Battleford, several of which were nearly self-supporting. Almost immediately after the Synod the Bishop left on a visitation to the western missions, as far as Calgary. According to the late Archdeacon Tims, Bishop McLean then went to Edmonton by democrat, intending to return the same way. The remainder of that story has been told by the late Canon E. K. Matheson:

As he and those with him in the "democrat" wagon were going down the steep hill at Edmonton, the horses became unmanageable, plunging about until they overturned the vehicle. The Bishop was thrown out violently, sustaining very severe internal injuries. He was taken back into the Fort, where he received all possible care and treatment. It became apparent after some days that the injuries were of a nature that might terminate fatally. The Bishop, knowing this, determined to make a final effort to reach his home in Prince Albert, where his family resided. To drive overland was out of the question. . . . Only one possible way remained, and that was to float down the North Saskatchewan River. In company of one of his sons and two hired men, the Bishop embarked and started on his five-hundred mile voyage down the river on his last journey. It was the month of October. The days were not very warm and the nights were cold. The Bishop suffered considerable discomfort on the voyage. In due time they arrived at the landing place at Prince Albert. All was done for him that human love and kindness could do, and although he appeared to rally somewhat at first, he gradually became weaker until at length God called him to his long home and that valiant soldier and servant of Christ laid aside his armour on Sunday morning, the 7th of November, 1886, at the early age of fifty-eight years.[19]

Bishop McLean has been described by those who knew him well not only as an apostle of hard work, but of work well and thoroughly done. He energized and inspired others with his own enthusiasm. "He was a broad Churchman—broad ecclesiastically, mentally, sympathetically and physically."[20] His character was firm and decisive. Canon E. K. Matheson says: "He was your friend or your opponent, and you knew it," but also adds, "he was a man of large ideas; he attempted great things for God; he expected great things from God, and he was not disappointed."[21]

[19]E. K. Matheson, "John McLean," in W. B. Heeney, ed., *Leaders of the Canadian Church*, Second Series (Toronto, 1920).
[20]*Ibid.*, 246-247.
[21]*Ibid.*, 240.

William Cyprian Pinkham, Second Bishop of Saskatchewan and First Bishop of Calgary

Bishop Pinkham was consecrated in Holy Trinity Church, Winnipeg, on Sunday, August 7, 1887. It was on the eve of a meeting of a Provincial Synod and there were more than the usual number of Bishops present, for assisting the Metropolitan of Rupert's Land (Machray) were the Bishops of Moosonee (Horden), Qu'Appelle (Anson), Athabasca (Young), Huron (Baldwin), and three from beyond Canada, the Bishops of Minnesota (Whipple), Rochester (Thorold), and North Dakota (Walker).

William Cyprian Pinkham was born in St. John's, Newfoundland, in 1844, and was educated at the Church of England Academy there. In 1865, when he was twenty-one, he proceeded to St. Augustine's College in Canterbury, England, to study theology, completing his course in 1868. After his final examination, Prebendary Bullock, Secretary of the S.P.G., offered him the curacy of St. James' Church in Rupert's Land. When he arrived at Montreal he learned that Bishop Machray was expected to be in London, Ontario, so he proceeded to London and was allowed to sit for ordination examinations. Pinkham was ordained deacon on August 16 by Bishop Cronyn. In due course he arrived in Winnipeg and undertook the work at St. James', then an isolated settlement on the Assiniboine River between Winnipeg and Portage la Prairie. He was priested on February 21, 1869, by Bishop Machray.

When the Province of Manitoba passed its First Educational Act in 1871, Pinkham was appointed a member of the Council of Education, and in the following year he became Superintendent of Education in Manitoba, a post he held during twelve of the most formative years of that province's educational system.

In 1881 Pinkham resigned the parish of St. James because of the pressure of his educational work. An article written in February, 1887, when it had just become known that he had accepted the nomination of the Archbishop of Canterbury (Benson) to become Bishop of Saskatchewan, remarks that "to his practical suggestions is largely due the efficiency of the present educational machinery in the Province; in particular we may mention the Collegiate Department in our Public Schools." In 1879 the Archbishop of Canterbury (Dr. Tait) conferred upon him the degree of Bachelor of Divinity, "on account of his services to the Church and especially in the cause of education."[22] In 1881, also, Mr. Pinkham was elected Secretary of the Synod of Rupert's Land and appointed Archdeacon of Manitoba.

[22]C. H. Mockridge, op. cit., 356-357. O. R. Rowley, *The Anglican Episcopate of Canada and Newfoundland*, 91-92. *St. John's College Magazine* (Winnipeg, March, 1887), substantiates this statement.

The Diocese of Calgary: "Preview"

By the time Bishop Pinkham became Bishop of Saskatchewan in 1887, that diocese had already developed a "triangular problem" of its own, one that did not grow less acute as the years passed. The focal points of this problem were in the districts of Prince Albert, Edmonton and Calgary. To the north of Prince Albert lay the great Indian mission field of northern Saskatchewan, and in Prince Albert itself was Emmanuel College, of which Bishop McLean had hoped so much. In the southern part of the present Province of Alberta there was an urgent call for work among an entirely different type of Indian from the northern Cree, also among a different type of white settler.

The Bishop-designate made a tour of as much of the Diocese as he could reach in order to meet the clergy and become acquainted with conditions. Whether the subsequent event was a consequence of this, it is hard to say, but on August 12, 1887, the Provincial Synod of Rupert's Land formally agreed to constitute the Civil Territory of Alberta as the Diocese of Calgary, subject to the consent of the Archbishop of Canterbury and the Bishop of Saskatchewan. The motion made it clear that Bishop Pinkham was to be Bishop of both dioceses until a sufficient endowment could be provided for the new one, and that then he was to have his choice of diocese. As Bishop of Saskatchewan, Bishop Pinkham gave his formal consent under his seal on February 25, 1888, and on March 27, Archbishop Benson appointed him as Bishop of Calgary.

In the summer of 1888 the new Bishop had to make another choice, this time whether he would attend the Lambeth Conference and address meetings of the great missionary societies in England, or make a visitation of the Diocese of Saskatchewan, which could only be done in the summer. He determined that his duty lay in England, and while there he succeeded in raising $6,000 for his work in Canada, which was apportioned among funds for the See House, Calgary schools, the mission funds of both dioceses and the Saskatchewan Clergy Endowment Fund.

In southern Alberta, Indian work was proceeding amongst the Blackfoot, Bloods, Sarcees and Peigans, and amongst early missionaries were the Reverend George McKay, the Reverend Robert Inkster, the Reverend S. Trivett and J. W. Tims, who came out from England and began the work among the Blackfoot on the Reserve near Gleichen.

Of the Reverend George McKay something has already been said. The Reverend Robert Inkster was one of the early students of Emmanuel College who was ordained in 1880 and spent six years as S.P.G. missionary to the Indians at Saddle Lake. In the spring of that year he went to the Sarcee Reserve near Fish Creek (better known now as Midnapore), but, although fluent in Cree, he had much difficulty with the Sarcee language and so in 1888 returned north to take charge of the Red Pheasant Reserve near Battleford, where he remained until his retirement in 1906.

The Reverend Samuel Trivett was trained at the C.M.S. College, Islington, ordained deacon and priest in 1878 by Bishop McLean, and for three years was in charge of the mission at Stanley. In 1881 he moved to the Blood Reserve near Fort Macleod, where his pioneer work seems to have been both exciting and adventurous. "The Rev. S. Trivett not only travelled over the large Indian Reserve which was under his care [the largest in Canada]: he paid frequent visits to Pincher Creek and held services for the few scattered settlers in that district. It was looked upon as the 'garden' of the West, and amongst the few families to be found there was that of the late Col. Macleod, who led the North West Mounted Police into Southern Alberta. Mr. Trivett also crossed the Old Man River [there were no bridges or even ferries in those days] and visited scattered ranchers on Willow Creek and the Little Bow River."[23] In this district he worked for ten years and in 1891 left to become incumbent of Clearwater in Manitoba. Subsequently he spent many years in the Diocese of Nova Scotia and lived to an advanced age.

The Reverend J. W. Tims was the eldest son of John Tims the well-known boat-builder of Staines. After receiving his training at Islington, he was ordained by the Bishop of London and left on June 9, 1883, for New York. He says in his reminiscences, "The C.M.S. could not tell me how to travel after reaching New York, but I was instructed to ask my way. . . . I was told to proceed to a place called Blackfoot Crossing. . . . I inquired my way at New York. . . . I was informed that Helena, in Montana, then the end of the track of the Northern Pacific Railway, was the nearest point to Blackfoot Crossing. . . ." The eight-day journey to Fort Macleod was completed in the I. G. Baker Express, an open wagon drawn by four mules, and it was with relief that Mr. Tims crossed the Milk River ridge, marking the boundary of Canada. At Fort Macleod he was met by Mr. Trivett, who took him to the Blood Reserve where he had his first experience of mission work with the Indians, and of Indian hospitality. After a week-end spent around Fort Macleod, Tims and Trivett made the three-day journey to Blackfoot Crossing by buckboard.

Our first visit was to the great Chief Crowfoot. . . . Through an interpreter we made known the object of our visit. . . . Crowfoot said that they had too many teachers already . . . but that there was no

[23]*Calgary Diocesan Gazette* (Trinity, 1928), 21.

one at the north camp where Old Sun was chief. If we would go and see Old Sun and get his sanction to start a mission near him, we were at liberty to do so and he would raise no objection. We went at once to Old Sun, who received us warmly and said he would be glad to have me live near him and teach his people.

Mr. Tims was licenced to do the work of a missionary on the Blackfoot Reserve and, until provisions were made, to minister to the settlers in the adjacent territory. . . . With 2,000 wild and uncivilized heathen Indians speaking a language not reduced to writing as his primary work, the possibility of caring for the spiritual needs of the scattered settlers over so wide a territory was very small. Until he had so far mastered the Blackfoot language as to be able to teach the Indians, he gave his time every Sunday to the white people in the vicinity. There was never a Sunday that he failed to hold religious Services somewhere.[24]

In the government cookhouse, in his own house after it was built, in the carpenters' tent when the C.P.R. began to erect buildings at Gleichen, in the station-house when it was up, later in the waiting room when the ticket office was used as a vestry, the services continued until St. Andrew's Church, Gleichen, was erected in 1886.

Eventually the mission house was built on the Blackfoot Reserve, "a good log building twenty by thirty feet with shingled roof and wooden floor. . . . Here, with a homemade table and bedstead and an empty nail keg for a seat, Mr. Tims settled down to his work. . . . The missionary took every opportunity to learn new words in the Indian language and each day added to his vocabulary. When winter came he occupied the long evenings by placing the new words in their proper places in his vocabulary, and in grinding them off so that he would ever remember them."[25]

Tims was a member of the last Synod of the then Diocese of Saskatchewan held by Bishop McLean, and relates that in order to get to Prince Albert he went by train from Gleichen to Qu'Appelle and then 260 miles by stage, which took him a week. He preached the ordination sermon in Prince Albert at this time when the Reverend R. Hilton was made deacon and the Reverend J. R. Settee, son of the well-known Reverend James Settee, was priested. He returned south with the Reverend E. K. Matheson, who was on his way to organize St. Augustine's, Lethbridge, which in 1891 was to become the second self-supporting parish in the Diocese of Calgary.[26]

Mr. Tims' recollections of the founding of the Church in Calgary are important. He says that in October, 1883, seven churchmen, including G. E. King and R. Fletcher, met together in an informal

[24]*Ibid.*, 21.
[25]*Ibid.*, 24-25.
[26]*Calgary Diocesan Gazette* (Christmas, 1928), 29-30. *Calgary Diocesan Gazette* (Trinity, 1929), 26.

manner around the stove in King's General Store, then in east Calgary, and drew up a letter that was signed by each of them and addressed to Tims at the Blackfoot Reserve, with the request that they might have the benefit of the Church's services occasionally in Calgary.

The letter was sent on to Bishop McLean, who had sailed again to England, and in the meantime Tims undertook to visit Calgary once a fortnight. The first regular service was held in the orderly room at the old barracks of the North West Mounted Police, in November. A number of civilians attended this service and the members of the Mounted Police came in force under command of the late General Steele, at that time "Captain."

The services continued until Easter, 1884. On Easter morning there were over eighty persons present. In the afternoon of that day a business meeting was held. A committee of seven was appointed to take the place of those appointed when Bishop McLean first visited Calgary in 1883, and who had done nothing. The new committee consisted of J. G. Fitzgerald, secretary; G. E. King, treasurer; and Messrs. Geddes, Pettit, Thomas, Dr. Lindsay and Sergeant-Major Lake. These were to look out for a suitable building site, solicit subscriptions, and report to another meeting ten days hence. At this next meeting the committee reported such success that Mr. McCroskie, an architect, was asked to prepare plans for a church, which was, a few weeks after, erected on the site of the present Pro-Cathedral.[27]

At the Easter meeting, Tims read a letter from Bishop McLean, who was still in England, stating that he had arranged for the Reverend E. Paske Smith to come out to Calgary and that he was expected to arrive in time for Whitsunday.

By this time building was going ahead on the new townsite that the C.P.R. had surveyed in Section 15. A large hall called Boyton Hall had been erected on Eighth Avenue East, and this was engaged by the committee for the Sunday Services until such time as the church buildings could be completed.

The site chosen for the church was thought by some to be too far west of the barracks. During the month of June the Reverend E. Paske Smith visited the construction camps along the line of the railway west, held services for the men, and made collections for the new church.

The Calgary church, called the Church of the Redeemer, was opened for service on August 2, 1884.

"On Sunday, October 12th, the first Ordination Service took place in Calgary when the Reverend J. W. Tims was admitted to the priest-

[27]*Calgary Diocesan Gazette* (Trinity, 1928), 25-26. B. F. L. Clarke, *Cathedrals outside the British Isles* (London, 1958): "The Cathedral of The Redeemer, Calgary" confirms Archdeacon Tims' statement.

hood, the assisting clergy being the Reverend E. Paske Smith and the Reverend S. Trivett." The parish of the Church of the Redeemer became self-supporting in the fall of 1887.

"From Calgary, the Bishop and Mrs. McLean went to Gleichen and the Blackfoot Reserve. He decided to recommend the C.M.S. to erect three school buildings and guaranteed forty pounds a year for the salary of one teacher to supplement the $300 government grant."[28]

First Synod of the Diocese of Calgary

Bishop Pinkham, as first Bishop of Calgary, called a Synod of the new Diocese for February 21, 1889. Bishop Machray preached the opening sermon and urged the members not be too optimistic about the future of their part of the country, but to be content to develop along sound lines. There were eleven clergy and nine lay delegates present, two of whom were later destined to take Holy Orders and assume great responsibilities in the Diocese of Edmonton: they were Henry Allen Gray, then working as a lay reader amongst the Sarcees (First Bishop of Edmonton), and (Archdeacon) F. C. Cornish. Among the clergy was Dr. Newton, incumbent of All Saints', Edmonton, a parish then being maintained by the S.P.G.[29]

Calgary—The Riel Rebellion—the Reverend George McKay

The first news of the Riel Rebellion of 1885 reached Calgary on March 24 and caused great excitement. Some years previously (1881) Major General Strange had retired from the army and taken up land on the north bank of the Bow River just west of the Blackfoot Reserve.[30] When the Riel Rebellion came to a head the majority of the North West Mounted Police at Calgary were hurried east, leaving only one officer and five men on duty there. On March 29 Major General Strange received a telegram from Ottawa asking him to raise a corps to take part, and this he consented to do. On April 20 this column left for Edmonton. The Reverend George McKay went with it as a scout and interpreter, and so useful were his services that he was mentioned in despatches.

Canon McKay did not return to southern Alberta after peace was restored. He became Archdeacon and for the next two years was general missionary in the Prince Albert neighbourhood, after which he became incumbent of St. Alban's, Prince Albert (now the Pro-Cathedral). He retained the title of Archdeacon of Alberta until the early 1900's. He left the Diocese of Saskatchewan for the U.S.A.

[28]*Calgary Diocesan Gazette* (Trinity, 1928), 27-28.
[29]*Proceedings of the Synod of the Diocese of Calgary, 1889.*
[30]*Calgary Diocesan Gazette* (Trinity, 1928). It was known as The Military Colonization Ranch. Fortnightly services were held there by Mr. Tims.

in 1900, where he spent the rest of his long life in the service of the Protestant Episcopal Church in South Dakota and Wyoming. Between 1897 and 1900, during the time of the Klondike Gold Rush, he worked in the Yukon. He was ninety-five years of age when he died on December 12, 1949.[31]

Progress in Indian and Educational Work

No account of the early work among the Blackfoot and Sarcee Indians would be complete without mentioning the Reverend Harry William Gibbon Stocken and his brother the Reverend Stanley John Stocken. The former was a friend and contemporary of Archdeacon Tims at the C.M.S. College, Islington; in 1887 he came as the Archdeacon's assistant on the Blackfoot Reserve and was ordained by Bishop Pinkham the same year. After he was priested in 1888 he took charge of the Sarcee Reserve, where he was stationed until 1895. During his last two years there he also had charge of St. Paul's, Fish Creek (Midnapore).

In 1895 an exchange was made: the Archdeacon went to the Sarcee Reserve and Stocken to the Blackfoot Reserve, an arrangement that appears to have turned out most happily. Canon Stocken (as he later became) served this mission for thirty-eight years, retiring in 1933, but frequently visited it again.

The Reverend S. J. Stocken came to the Diocese of Calgary in 1894, when he was ordained deacon, and as such worked for six years on the Sarcee Reserve. In 1900 he was priested, and in 1901 joined his brother on the Blackfoot Reserve by becoming principal of the residential school there.

In the early years of each of the western dioceses the question of education in one form or another always came up. Bishop Pinkham, in the early days of his episcopate, had in mind the establishing of such an institution in Calgary, although he could not see his way to continue the already existing Emmanuel College in Prince Albert. The scheme fell through, but he did succeed in founding, in 1889, St. Hilda's School for Girls, which for more than forty years was to render good service.[32]

In 1889, too, the Bishop made an agreement with the parish that the Church of the Redeemer be constituted as a Pro-Cathedral, and the Bishop was given the right to preach or appoint the preacher at one service on twenty Sundays of the year, including the great festivals.[33]

In 1890 an adjustment of the northern boundary of the Diocese was

[31]R. L. A., The George McKay Papers (Saskatchewan).
[32]Proceedings of the Synod of the Diocese of Calgary, 1892, pp. 16-18.
[33]Ibid., 1889, pp. 30-31.

made by the Provincial Synod, which brought part of it fifteen miles south of its original location; this was made so that Bishop Young of Athabasca might live at Athabasca Landing, which was more accessible to railway communications in the south and equally convenient for reaching northerly mission stations in his Diocese.[34]

At the end of 1890 it was found that the Methodist Church, which had more or less withdrawn from the Blood Reserve, was willing to do so completely when its missionary there, the Reverend John McLean, retired. Mr. Tims was empowered to negotiate the transfer of the property to the Anglican Church. The Reverend J. McDougal represented the Methodist Church on this occasion and the sum agreed upon was $1,000, which amount was chiefly provided by the kindness of the Toronto Diocesan Woman's Auxiliary.[35]

The Reverend Frank Swainson was missionary on the Blood Reserve from 1892 to 1897, and the work he commenced has since resolved itself into the finest of the Church's Indian residential schools, whose pupils now regularly acquire a full high school education.

The Diocese of Calgary Secures its Independency

As time went on it became increasingly apparent that the Diocese of Calgary must be separated from the Diocese of Saskatchewan. Difficulties arose, however, over the division of the endowment, and the S.P.G. was not in agreement with the first proposals. In 1899 the Diocese of Saskatchewan agreed to transfer $16,200 of its endowment to the Diocese of Calgary,[36] but it was not until 1903 that the Calgary endowment was completed; thereupon, Bishop Pinkham resigned the See of Saskatchewan on September 30 and continued as Bishop of Calgary. In the years 1888 to 1903 settlement between Calgary and Edmonton had been growing. A Rural Deanery of Edmonton was formed in 1894 and the Reverend A. Stunden, then rector of All Saints', Edmonton, became the first Rural Dean. Another step in diocesan organization was taken in 1895 when two Archdeaconries were constituted. The Reverend A. W. F. Cooper, then rector of the Church of the Redeemer in Calgary, became first Archdeacon of Calgary and Mr. Tims first Archdeacon of Macleod, the latter position having attached to it the superintendency of all the Indian mission work.[37]

The Reverend Arthur William Francis Cooper had a very dis-

[34]*Ibid.*, 1892, pp. 20-21.
[35]*Ibid.*, 14-16. R. L. A. The Archdeacon J. W. Tims' papers have his commission from Bishop Pinkham to carry out this business.
[36]*Journal of the Provincial Synod of Rupert's Land*, 1899, p. 45. *Proceedings of the Synod of the Diocese of Calgary, 1900*, pp. 10-12.
[37]*Calgary Diocesan Gazette* (Michaelmas, 1929), 24. *Proceedings of the Synod of the Diocese of Calgary, 1896*, p. 8.

tinguished career at Trinity College, Dublin. In 1873 he was ordained by the Bishop of Cashel, and he held various charges in Ireland until 1885 when Cooper came to the Diocese of Montreal, where he spent two years before becoming the rector of the Church of the Redeemer in Calgary. He returned to Ireland in 1898.[38]

The Early Days of Edmonton

Bishop McLean of Saskatchewan returned to Canada after his consecration in 1874, by way of Montreal. There he met with the Provincial Synod of Canada, then in session, and appealed for two clergymen to go to his Diocese of Saskatchewan as missionaries. One of those who answered his appeal was the Reverend William Newton, who had been a missionary in the Muskoka District while it was still in the Diocese of Toronto. He had established the Rousseau Mission and built a church. It was finally arranged that he should go to Edmonton as a missionary supported by the S.P.G.[39]

Fort Edmonton was originally established about 1795, being one of the forts built by William Tomison, the "Inland Chief" of the Hudson's Bay Company. In time this fort grew to be more than a trading post. York boats were built there, and for years it flourished under the colourful personality of John Rowand. It always seems curious that the Anglican Church should have disregarded Edmonton as a centre until so late as 1875; for more than fifteen years previously it had extended its work down the Mackenzie River as far as Fort McPherson and the Yukon.[40]

Towards Edmonton, in the spring of 1875, Mr. Newton turned with resolution and fortitude. In a little book entitled *Twenty Years on*

[38]*Crockford's Clerical Directory, 1898.*
[39]*Ibid.* The Directory states that Dr. Newton was incumbent of Rousseau, 1870-1874, but he was not on the clergy list of the Diocese of Algoma when Bishop Fauquier was consecrated on October 28, 1873, and the Bishop reported to the Provincial Synod of Canada in September, 1874, that Rousseau was vacant. A letter from Bishop McLean to the S. P. G., dated October 22, 1874, refers to Dr. Newton as missionary at Hastings, Ontario, but the Diocese of Toronto does not seem to have any record of this appointment. Bishop McLean writes, "I have the most unqualified testimony as to Dr. Newton's piety, scholarship and missionary zeal and experience from three clergymen who are my personal friends and in whose judgment I have confidence."
[40]*Minutes of the Corresponding Committee of the Church Missionary Society at Red River,* July 28, 1854. It is stated that Rev. William Mason (then about to leave to take up work at York Factory, who had fourteen years' experience as a Wesleyan Methodist missionary) suggested the suitability of Edmonton as a mission centre. "Much conversation was had on the subject but there seemed to be no disposition to urge it on the Parent Committee at present." The Roman missions of St. Anne (1843), Isle à la Crosse and Red Deer Lake (1845), were in Cree country, but when they were commenced the Church Missionary Society could only afford to maintain the work at the Red River, and that at The Pas. It assisted in the extension of the latter to Lac la Ronge. The peripatetic efforts of Rev. R. T. Rundle in the foothills of the Rockies were not so successful as to encourage the Society (or Bishop Anderson, after 1849) to consider Edmonton. The country south of Edmonton was not fur country, and it is hardly likely that the Hudson's Bay Company would have accepted responsibility for the safety and supply of mission stations.

the Saskatchewan, published in England in 1897, he has left a most interesting record of his journey there and of later experiences. It is a remarkable book for three reasons: the little he says about himself personally, his outspoken comments on the life of the country, and his fearless criticism of the Hudson's Bay Company, particularly respecting its final settlement with the Dominion government. Newton spent a large part of the winter of 1874 trying to get information on how to reach Edmonton, but received little help. Nevertheless he set out, convinced that while the way was by no means plain, it was a way of faith; he arrived at Collingwood, Ontario. From Port Arthur, Newton started out on the Dawson Trail, which he had been told in Ontario was a very convenient and expeditious road. But this did not prove to be the case; there were endless delays.

Eventually he reached the prairies and Winnipeg. Newton was favourably impressed with the Manitoba prairie, but not with Winnipeg. At last, in the first week of July, he was able to take up his tent, which he had pitched outside old Fort Garry, and start for the West.

South of Fort Pitt, Mr. Newton had his first experience with the Indians, then beginning to be perturbed over the advancement of settlement. Messengers from a band of Crees investigated the camp with a view to opposing his passage through their country. They held a conference and agreed that it was not reasonable to ask Newton to return east, accepted him as a friend and brother, and gave him all the help they could. This good feeling was maintained throughout the vicissitudes of twenty years.

After three weeks at Fort Carlton, Newton journeyed west to Battle River, north to Buffalo Lake, and then hit the trail leading from the Bow River to Edmonton, which he reached on September 28, 1875, after a strenuous five months' journey.

Edmonton Prospects in 1875

In 1875 nearly all the residents at Edmonton were servants of the Hudson's Bay Company. Mr. Newton writes, "I had at hand a tent, a surplice, a Prayer Book and a Bible. There was no parsonage, no church, nor any means for building either. I had been sent as a missionary to the settlers, but where were they?" For a few days he received kindly hospitality at the Fort, and then moved into a log building, only partly finished, which he used as both residence and church; from the first, a few persons attended the services. Hudson's Bay Company officers were glad to renew old Church associations as they passed to other forts. Surveyors and Mounted Police were offered frequent services, children were collected for instruction, the Indian tents were visited, and the banner of the Church was unfurled over a new, vast and hitherto unoccupied region. Twenty years later

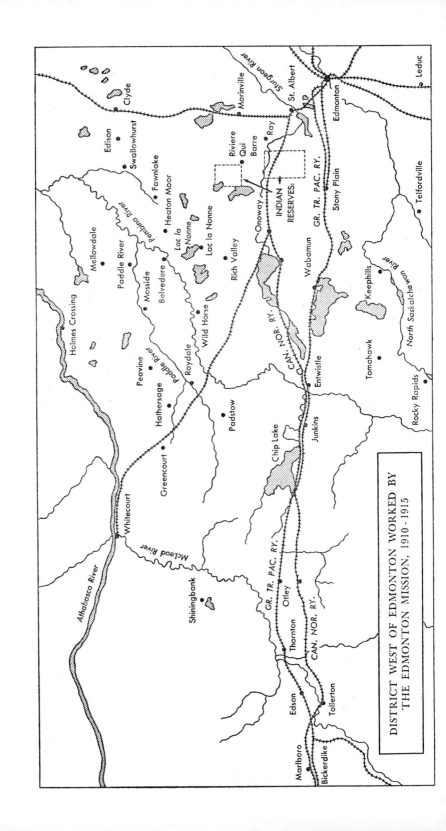

DISTRICT WEST OF EDMONTON WORKED BY
THE EDMONTON MISSION, 1910 - 1915

Newton was able to write, "I am thankful that the honour fell on me of being the pioneer missionary of what is now an extensive diocese." He lost no time in settling down to his work in the Edmonton District. On October 22, 1875, he wrote to Bishop McLean, asking for supplies of hymn books and Prayer Books in both English and Cree, adding, "My present Sunday Services are a Sunday School in the Mission House at 9 o'clock, Divine Service at 10, partly English and partly Cree. At 12 o'clock the horses are harnessed and I drive fast to Fort Saskatchewan . . . and hold Service as near 3 o'clock as I can manage it, the distance being about 30 miles."

On December 20, 1876, a report was sent to the S.P.G. The mission covered about twenty-five miles of the country, including Fort Saskatchewan, the Upper Settlement, Fort Edmonton and Long Lake, though sometimes the work was carried farther. The mission had about twenty-five families and a varying number of Her Majesty's Mounted Police force, but comprised about half the Protestant population. There was an average attendance at church of twenty. There were seven communicants, often increased by men on the Canadian Pacific Railway survey, and by others passing to the forts of the Hudson's Bay Company. Five candidates were prepared for Confirmation. During a recent visit by the Bishop, a most influential committee had been formed for the purpose of erecting a small church near the Fort of Edmonton; of the members, Colonel Jarvis of the N.W.M.P. and Chief Factor Hardisty seem to have been the most prominent. Sunday Schools were being conducted at Edmonton and the Upper Settlement, besides which there often were week-day classes for religious and general instruction.

The First All Saints' Church at Edmonton

Mr. Newton reported to the S.P.G. on June 25, 1878:

Notwithstanding sickness and other drawbacks, our people have met their own incidental expenses and in addition, have given, chiefly in labour, about 150 dollars towards the Church now building at Edmonton. The frame of the Church is erected, and the roof completed, and I did hope to begin to hold Services in it at Whitsuntide; but the man who contracted for the door and windows failed in his engagement and they are being made at Victoria, 90 miles off. With every care, the cost of the building is frightful. . . . The Church, when finished, will be a pretty building, —it is picturesquely situated on the banks of the Saskatchewan. Several circumstances have occurred greatly to encourage the friends of Church of England missions in this part of the world, notably one at Victoria, an Indian and Half-Breed Settlement. At that place there is a Hudson's Bay fort and from sixty to a hundred families. Some years ago, most or all of these people were connected with our missions in or around Manitoba, but moving westward after the buffalo they were lost to us. For hundreds of miles there is no Church of England mission. . . . Ever since I came to Edmonton, they have been urging me to visit them occasionally, and although it is 90 miles off, and several rivers have to be crossed, without bridges, I have gone several times and always found a warm welcome and good congregations, indeed it is usual for every family to be present at all the Services. They have sent a petition to our excellent and energetic Bishop begging that a clergyman might be sent to them; and that petition represents every family belonging to that settlement.

It is always a matter of regret that we know so little about Dr. Newton's early years. He was born in England in 1828. Old friends have a vivid recollection of the really remarkable collection of books in the library at the Hermitage. Newton entered the Anglican ministry in 1870, when he was ordained deacon by the Bishop of Toronto (Bethune), and he was priested in 1871. His first and only mission in that diocese was Rousseau.

Dr. Newton describes his work around Edmonton as being of three varieties: the Indian work, the town work, and that of a travelling missionary. A proposal made by Bishop McLean in 1881, that Dr. Newton should take charge of the Indian Mission at Fort Macleod and be replaced by a younger man in Edmonton, was never carried farther, though after the appointment of the Reverend Charles Cunningham to All Saints', Edmonton, in 1891, "The Little Doctor" dropped the town work and gave himself almost entirely to that of travelling missionary, ministering to a territory that extended as far as Beaver Lake to the east, Sturgeon River to the north, and occasionally as far south as Red Deer. His main centres, however, were Belmont, Clover Bar and Fort Saskatchewan. The quality of his work and his long service in the old and undivided Diocese of Saskatchewan had received recognition years before, when in 1883 he was appointed one of its first two Canons.

After twenty years of service in the Edmonton District, an endeavour was made to arrange terms with the Society for the Propagation of the Gospel on which he could retire, but negotiations fell through and Newton continued his work for another three years. Later he moved to Victoria, B.C., where he lived for more than ten years; he died there at his home "The Glen," at Cadboro Bay, and was buried in St. Luke's Cemetery, Cedar Hill, on February 11, 1910. The tablet that marks his grave was erected by the Diocese he served so faithfully and so long.[41]

[41]T. C. B. Boon, "Newton of Edmonton," *Canadian Churchman* (August 17, 1950). L. G. Thomas, "Canon William Newton," *The Edmonton Churchman* (September, 1950). F. A. Peake, "William Newton, Anglican Beginnings in and about Edmonton," *Canadian Church Historical Society*, Off-print No. 7 (March, 1961). This is an extension of an M.A. thesis, University of Alberta, 1952.

CHAPTER NINE

Assiniboia: Diocese of Qu'Appelle

••◄⊰⫷⊱►•••◄⊰⫷⊱►•••◄⊰⫷⊱►•••◄⊰⫷⊱►•••◄⊰⫷⊱►•••◄⊰⫷⊱►•••◄⊰⫷⊱►•••◄⊰⫷⊱►••

This great country . . . only really began to be opened for settlement some nineteen years ago, when railways entered. . . . Our Missions from this condition of settlement have so small a number of families scattered over a vast area, that . . . it is, at present an utter impossibility to establish and maintain the services of the Church without extensive outside help. This process . . . will be going on for many more years in the further west.

ARCHBISHOP MACHRAY'S CHARGE TO THE
PROVINCIAL SYNOD OF RUPERT'S LAND, 1889.

••◄⊰⫷⊱►•••◄⊰⫷⊱►•••◄⊰⫷⊱►•••◄⊰⫷⊱►•••◄⊰⫷⊱►•••◄⊰⫷⊱►•••◄⊰⫷⊱►•••◄⊰⫷⊱►••

Early Days: Qu'Appelle

The first excursion of the Church onto the Great Plains took place in January, 1821, when the Reverend John West visited Beaver Creek. He was impressed by the air of independence shown by the Indians he happened to meet there, but also witnessed the degrading effect of alcohol on them.

In the 1850's some effort was made to reach this part of the country from Fairford, and also through the Swan River valley. The Reverend James Settee has left an interesting note in his journal, dated March 20, 1867:

Cannacisse, a Qu'Appelle Indian, who came as a deputy from the Cree camp . . . made an appeal in behalf of his tribe to the Church Missionary Society to send them a teacher, he asked me to take the Qu'Appelle Lakes again, assuring me that no ill-treatment should be shown to me, as it was once done by them. The Qu'Appelle Lakes belong to the Church Missionary Society: I opened that Mission as early as 1842. Charles Pratt followed it up in about 1848, and Rev. C. Hillyer in 1850, and Mr. Stagg and myself entered it in 1854: so there is a great amount of work done there in the way of spiritual doings.

The Reverend W. Stagg was in charge of Fairford from 1854 to 1866.

The usual date given for the commencement of work at the Qu'Appelle Lakes is 1857. Mr. Settee was there at the earlier time he mentioned, but in 1846 was sent to Lac la Ronge, where he remained for seven or eight years as a catechist. After his ordination in 1853 he went to the Swan River District, working under the general direction of the Reverend W. Stagg of Fairford. Mr. Stagg, in a letter dated August 25 of that year, wrote: "We have been able to travel over a large tract of the country, and preach the Gospel to its scattered inhabitants. I might say that nearly all the Salteaux north of Red River have heard the Gospel from us, myself seeing in winter Shoal River, Fort Pelly, Duck Bay and Touchwood Hills and the Salteaux." The district of Swan River was the old Hudson's Bay Company's district, which took in a considerable amount of the western plains. The Venerable J. A. Mackay, who was well acquainted with Mr. Settee, writing of him in *Leaders of the Canadian Church* said that the Plains Indians were, at that time, the wildest and most savage people in the country, and that Settee established no permanent mission there. This was to be the work of Charles Pratt, who established a school in 1865 in the vicinity of Fort Qu'Appelle.

After some years at Fort Qu'Appelle, Pratt moved to a Reserve farther north in the neighbourhood of the South Saskatchewan. At the time of the 1885 Rebellion he is said to have led his people away from the trouble. When Charles Pratt died does not seem to be known, but his grave is in the churchyard of St. Luke's Church at Raymore, Saskatchewan, a parish close to Gordon's Indian Reserve. Mrs. Thomas Cook, the wife of the missionary at Fort Ellice, summed up his work by saying, "Charles is not a missionary of words, but of deeds."

How long this work continued at Qu'Appelle is uncertain, but it was reinforced in 1862 by the appointment of the Reverend Thomas Cook as missionary at Fort Ellice. Cook probably had fifteen or twenty years' experience in Indian Mission work before his ordination. Fort Ellice was situated about four miles away from the junction of the Qu'Appelle River with the Assiniboine; it replaced the old Beaver Creek House from 1831, and for more than forty years was one of the chief gateways for the Company's trade with the west. In the seventies it was one of the first posts occupied by a detachment of the newly-formed North West Mounted Police. The missionary at Fort Ellice was supported by the S.P.G., though the Society did not ordinarily interest itself in Indian Missions.[1]

The Church and the New Settlers on the Plains

The Church in Rupert's Land was altered by the building of the railways. The first line to reach Winnipeg was built from the south and completed in 1879, by which time the population of the city

[1]S.P.G.A., Bishop of Rupert's Land to Secretary of the S.P.G.: Letters dated August 10, 1959; October 12, 1860; May 30, 1861; April 7, 1862. These indicate that the S.P.G. had supported Rev. Thomas Cochrane while he was at St. John's Collegiate Institute, but that when this was closed the Society refused to transfer the grant to Rev. John Chapman at Middlechurch. It was finally agreed to give the grant to Rev. Thomas Cook at Fort Ellice.

had increased to the comparatively large number of 10,000. Bishop Machray found his work becoming arduous. Writing to the Secretary of the Colonial and Continental Church Society in October, 1880, he apologized for delay in sending reports to the Society, "but I can only say that I am doing the work of two or three men. . . ." At the same time he wrote to the Archbishop of Canterbury explaining the inability of the Diocese to cope with this influx of settlers, unless there were further assistance from England in men and money. A pamphlet was issued in November, 1882, by the Society for the Propagation of the Gospel, which set out the whole problem and asked for a liberal and prompt response to the special appeal being made for northwest Canada by the Archbishop of Canterbury.

In the summer of 1883, the Reverend W. Henry Cooper, an S.P.G. missionary formerly in Australia and New Zealand, came to Winnipeg and travelled through southern Manitoba to Virden, then went to Broadview where a few services had been held by the Reverend John Paine Sargent, who had recently been appointed travelling missionary and had made his headquarters at Brandon. From Broadview Mr. Cooper returned to Virden and Winnipeg, then went back to Moose Jaw, where a small church was later opened in 1884 by Mr. Sargent. The same summer (1883) the Reverend Alfred Osborn was sent out by the Society to take up work in the new diocese. Osborn settled in Regina, where a church dedicated to St. Paul was erected on the site of the present Pro-Cathedral.[2]

Diocese of Qu'Appelle

The Diocese of Qu'Appelle, or Assiniboia as it was first known, might be said to have begun with the consecration of the Honourable and Reverend Adelbert John Robert Anson in Lambeth Parish Church on June 24, 1884, by Archbishop Benson of Canterbury.[3]

Bishop Anson, the third son of the first Earl of Lichfield, was born in 1840, educated at Eton and Christ Church, Oxford. He received his training for Holy Orders at the Theological College, Lichfield, and was ordained by Bishop Lonsdale of that Diocese in 1864. His immediate experiences were in the highly industrial area of South Staffordshire, successively at Wolverhampton, Bilston, Handsworth and Sedgley. He became rector of Woolwich in 1875. When Canon Anson announced to his congregation at Woolwich that he was leaving to go to Canada, he said that he felt the call was one he could not

[2]G. N. Dobie, "A J. R. Anson," in W. B. Heeney, ed., *Leaders of the Canadian Church*, Second Series (Toronto, 1920). C. H. Mockridge, *The Bishops of the Church of England in Canada and Newfoundland*, 339-345.
[3]*Ibid.*, 341. O. R. Rowley, *The Anglican Episcopate of Canada and Newfoundland*, 80-81.

resist; it seemed to him an emergency of the Church, "which those clergy, who like myself have no special home ties . . . might do something to help to alleviate by volunteering for the work. . . . I do not in the least consider it as of necessity a lifelong work. In a few years, say ten, the pressure will probably have passed away."[4]

In the autumn of the same year (1883), Canon Anson paid a visit to northwest Canada to meet the Bishop of Rupert's Land, and to gain some personal knowledge of the district in which his new work was to lie, and of its inhabitants. The Bishop of Rupert's Land appointed him as his Commissary "in organizing Missions, and in the general superintendence of the Diocese of Assiniboia," and not long after his return to England Canon Anson issued a paper; the following extracts will show the lines upon which he proposed to carry out that work.

The Province of Assiniboia extends west of Manitoba for 450 miles, and northward from the frontier of the United States for about 200 miles. It is now under the jurisdiction of the Bishop of Rupert's Land, but was made a separate diocese by an Act of the Provincial Synod this spring. . . . In this Province are situated the favourite settlements of the Qu'Appelle Valley and the Moose Mountains. The Canadian Pacific Railway passes through the whole length of this Province, east to west, about midway between the north and south. Along the line of this railway . . . there is already a considerable population, rapidly increasing—Moosomin, Whitewood, Broadview, Indian Head, Qu'Appelle, Regina, Moose Jaw, Swift Current and Medicine Hat. Regina is the Capital of the civil Province, and the headquarters of the Provincial Government and of the Mounted Police. *It is the only place where there is now a resident clergyman.* The following are among the general principles on which it is hoped to carry on the Church work in this province:—"*To* bring the privileges of the Church, and the means of Grace, within the reach of *all* persons resident within the area . . . by means of an itinerating ministry. Largely to supplement the regular ministrations of the clergy by lay helpers. Wherever services are held, those who attend them will be expected to contribute towards the general work of the Church in the province. No regular stipends will be paid out of the general fund, but only the necessary expenses of the workers. . . . An association will be formed in England for prayer and work on behalf of this province.[5]

Canon Anson then set to work to establish an organization in England in support of the new Diocese, and before he left England again Canon Curteis, who had been Principal of the Lichfield Theological College when Canon Anson was a student there, had consented to act as his Commissary; diocesan or county secretaries had been appointed, and the services of between twenty and thirty lay

[4]*Canadian Church Magazine and Mission News*, 1888, p. 24.
[5]*Ibid.*, 63.

correspondents secured, while a large number of associates had been enlisted.

Canon Anson also laboured vigorously to obtain men and raise funds to carry on the work needed. He met with success in his efforts, raising a little over £2,500, and promises of subscriptions to the amount of £400 a year for five years, in addition. Canon Anson had consented to appeal for funds in England on the express condition that the appeal should not be to provide a stipend for himself, but solely to support additional clergy in Assiniboia. It had now, however, been decided that Assiniboia should have a bishop of its own, which was clearly desirable. But no bishop could be consecrated in England for overseas until some provision was guaranteed to the See, either by endowment, or by an annual grant from a society. There was no hope of a guarantee, except from England. Canon Anson therefore consented to hand over £2,000 of the amount he had raised to the S.P.G. to be used by them for the benefit of the Diocese. The Society then offered to give £400 a year for the income of the Bishop, until an endowment of £10,000 could be raised, and at the same time promised £1,000 towards the endowment fund, voted £800 for the maintenance of the clergy for 1885, and a lump sum of £500 for the erection of buildings. The Colonial Bishoprics Fund and the S.P.C.K. also gave £2,000 each towards the endowment of the Bishopric. So the question of provision for a bishop was settled; then, just as Canon Anson was about to sail on his return voyage to Canada, the Archbishop of Canterbury offered him the Bishopric, and urged on him the duty of accepting it. Canon Anson shrank from accepting the offer under the circumstances, yet he felt that it was plainly his duty to place himself at the head of the work. He had already agreed to take several priests and laymen with him, for no remuneration beyond the necessary expenses of livelihood, and of carrying on the work. But it appeared as if an income were to be forced upon him. He adopted at once the only solution that presented itself to his honest, self-sacrificing mind. "In accepting the Bishopric," Anson stated in his address to his first Diocesan Synod, "I felt that I could regard this income, as I certainly shall do, as simply so much more added by the Society to the Common Fund."

The Bishop left London on July second and sailed from Liverpool the following day, accompanied by one priest [un-named], and three laymen, W. Shafto Agassiz, Paul Lyon and Leslie Hoskins, the first two subsequently becoming priests. Reaching Quebec on a Sunday, he proceeded to Montreal, Toronto, via Lake Huron and Superior, thence through Winnipeg to his new Diocese.

The Bishop arrived in Regina at 4:30 a.m. on Friday, July 25.

At that early hour he was met at the station by four clergy, three laymen on the staff, and the churchwardens of St. Paul's, Regina. At 8:00 a.m. there was a celebration of the Holy Communion, the Bishop being celebrant.

At a subsequent conference with the clergy, Bishop Anson announced that there would be six districts, each with its centre and at least four outstations.

1. The Rev. W. W. Bolton was to have charge of the Moose Mountain district with Mr. Agassiz as his assistant, and his centre would be Moosomin.

2. The Rev. J. W. Gregory, with Mr. Paul Lyon as his assistant, would have his centre at Qu'Appelle Station, and would take Wolseley, Grenfell and Broadview as his outstations.

3. The Rev. J. P. Sargent would make Moose Jaw his centre and take all the territory along the line of the C.P.R. as far as Medicine Hat.

4. Regina would be the Bishop's centre with the Rev. H. Havelock Smith as assistant, taking the district north as far as Long Lake, including Craven.

5. The Touchwood Hills under the Rev. Gilbert Cook included the work on Gordon's Indian Reserve, Day Star's I.R., and Poorman's I.R. Charles Pratt was the Indian catechist.

6. Fort Qu'Appelle would be the centre for the Rev. Dan Lewis, with four outstations, including the Bell Farm, now Indian Head.[6]

First Synod of Qu'Appelle Diocese

The first Synod was held in St. Paul's Church, Regina, on Wednesday, September 17, 1884, at which Bishop Anson presided. The clergy were: Rev. J. P. Sargent, Moose Jaw; Rev. Gilbert Cook, Touchwood; Rev. Daniel Lewis, Ft. Qu'Appelle; Rev. W. W. Bolton, Moosomin; Rev. J. W. Gregory, Qu'Appelle; Rev. H. H. Smith, Regina. The lay delegates were: G. T. Marsh, and W. Cayley Hamilton, Regina; Leslie Gordon, Qu'Appelle; S. Cruthers, Ft. Qu'Appelle; R. E. Sherlock, Grenfell; E. D. Kirby, Moose Jaw; Chas. Marshallsay, Whitewood; S. S. Simpson, Pense; J. A. Cavannagh, Medicine Hat; and W. W. Young, Moosomin. The principal acts of the Synod were the Charge of the Bishop; the preparation of the Act of Incorporation of the Synod, which was assented to by the Federal Parliament on May 1, 1885, and provision for the drafting of the Constitution and Canons of the Diocese, which were passed at the second session of the Synod that met in St. Paul's, Regina, on June 5, 1885.

[6]R.L.A. and The Synod Office, Regina, Saskatchewan. E. H. Knowles, *A Record of Bishop Anson*, f. 2 (an unpublished MS compiled with introduction by Bishop Knowles of Qu'Appelle, 1935-1950).

In October a disaster befell the mission. The Bishop's house at Regina was destroyed by fire while he was absent at Medicine Hat in the most westerly part of his Diocese. Not only was the house destroyed, but everything that he had brought out from England was burned, with the exception of books that were on the ground floor; all his papers and manuscripts, and even the communion plate, were lost. The disaster, however, excited much sympathy among his friends in England, and the mission did not suffer in the end.[7]

The new diocese was at first known by the name of the political district with which it was coterminous, Assiniboia. The Bishop, however, felt that this was not in accordance with ecclesiastical usage, and that a diocese should not take its name from a vast territory. He had himself moved from Regina to Qu'Appelle as the most advantageous centre for his work. With the sanction, therefore, of the Metropolitan and of the Prolocutor of the House of Delegates of the Provincial Synod of Rupert's Land, he wrote to every member of his Diocesan Synod, placing before them the three names of Assiniboia, Regina and Qu'Appelle, and asking them in their answers to draw their pens through the two names they thought undesirable. The result was that out of eighteen members (eight clergy and ten laymen) fifteen recorded their votes for Qu'Appelle as the name of the See, and thus the important question was decided, and the Bishop became for the future the Bishop of Qu'Appelle, a designation confirmed by the Provincial Synod of Rupert's Land at its meeting in 1887.

The object of the Bishop's appointment was the ministrations to new settlers from overseas. It was estimated that 5,500 people, widely scattered as they were, would be within reach of the Church. He found, however, that he had in addition about 5,000 Plains Indians in his care, occupying six Reserves, forty per cent of whom where still pagan. Bishop Anson brought with him to the Diocese (according to Canon Legge), a staff of eight priests, one deacon and six laymen; there were approximately three hundred communicants of the Church of England in that part of the country at the time. Services were commenced during the next two or three years at fifty-one different points.

St. John's College, Qu'Appelle

With the new Bishop came also a new idea respecting church organization, that of a clergy community centre. To carry out this plan St. John's College, Qu'Appelle, was opened on October 28, 1885, as a centre for the training of both theological and agricultural students. It was erected at a cost of £2,800, derived mainly from two generous contributors. It was organized in three sections: some of the men were

---

[7]*Canadian Church Magazine and Mission News*, 1888, p. 54.

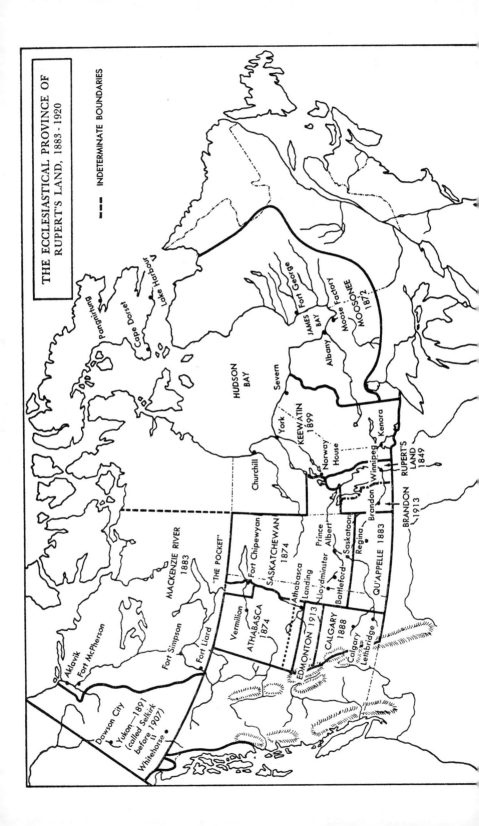

THE ECCLESIASTICAL PROVINCE OF
RUPERT'S LAND, 1883 - 1920

- - - INDETERMINATE BOUNDARIES

to be prepared for Holy Orders, others to receive training in agriculture with a view to settlement in the country, and a third group, in the nature of a "Brotherhood," was instituted to look after the work needed to maintain the institution. This St. John's College stood in 640 acres of its own. The agricultural students were required to pay £60 a year for their instruction and maintenance. Archdeacon Dobie, writing in *Leaders of the Canadian Church* about Bishop Anson, says, "That the scheme did not fulfill its anticipations in no way detracts from the vision of the man. He was determined, above all things, that the Church over which he presided should be as far as possible a self-supporting Church, free from dependence upon England for the money necessary to carry on that work." Lack of experience in a new country and lack of rain, which produced a series of crop failures, finally proved too much and the institution was closed.[8]

Bishop Anson also tried to establish a school for about forty boys on the same site. This was built in 1886, but the clergyman appointed as principal was taken ill and had to return to England, and it was two years before he was replaced. The Bishop was very concerned about education. Public schools in the Diocese in the 1880's were few and far apart. In his Charge to his Synod in 1890 he said: "Education in the truths of our holy religion is no exception to other education.

The Ecclesiastical Province of Rupert's Land, 1883-1920. Changes that have taken place in the Province between these dates are indicated; the boundaries are those of 1920. The Diocese of Brandon, set up in 1913, was not organized on an independent basis until 1924.

Athabasca South Boundary

The 1883 boundary between the civil districts of Athabasca and Alberta is approximately Lat. 55°N, almost coincident with the line between Townships 69 and 70 on contemporary maps. The boundary between the Dioceses of Athabasca and Edmonton appears never to have been defined by any synod, but is taken to be the line between Townships 63 and 64, which is 42 miles south. Bishop Pinkham and Bishop Young seem to have agreed to this line so that the latter might live at Athabasca Landing, a much better location for road and mail connections with the outside than Fort Vermilion on the Peace River. The Diocese of Edmonton in 1933 tried to get the boundary restored to the north between Townships 68 and 69, but its memorial was tabled without action. (*Journal of the Provincial Synod of Rupert's Land, 1933*, pp. 108-109.)

"The Pocket"

When Archdeacon J. R. Lucas was made Bishop of Mackenzie River in 1913, he felt it necessary to reside at a place with more mails than Fort Simpson, where he had spent thirteen years. He came to an arrangement with Bishop Robins (which was approved by the Provincial Synod) to have an area around Fort Chipewyan taken into the Diocese of Mackenzie River, which in later years became known as "The Pocket." (*Journal of the Provincial Synod of Rupert's Land, 1913*, p. 46.)

[8]G. N. Dobie, *op. cit.*, 290, 291. L. N. Murray, "St. John's College, Qu'Appelle, 1885-1894," *Saskatchewan History*, XI (Winter, 1958).

If it is to have any effects on the mind of the young, it must be clear, definite, dogmatic." The establishing of the North West Territories as a unit of state organization, after the signing of the treaties with the Indians in the early seventies, had resulted in the enactment of a separate school system, such as was common in the regularly organized provinces at the time. The Bishop felt very strongly that it was wrong for one religious body to have special privileges while all other religious bodies should be grouped together. Archdeacon Dobie observed: "He maintained that the Catholic Faith of Churchmen was something more than a mere negation, and it was a real grief to him that Churchmen should be content to acquiesce without a protest against anomalies existing. . . . To educate the intellect only was to leave untouched the great moral forces upon which the nation should be built. He was a voice crying in the wilderness."[9]

The Church made definite progress in its early years in Qu'Appelle. Churches had been built before 1888 at Whitewood, Moose Mountain, Qu'Appelle, Moosomin, Grenfell, Medicine Hat, Fort Qu'Appelle and two other points. Two schools had been established for Indian children, one at Fort Pelly and the other in the Touchwood Hills; the latter is still continued as Gordon's Reserve School, Punnichy.

Bishop Anson's Nine Years in Qu'Appelle

Bishop Anson resigned the Diocese of Qu'Appelle on August 30, 1892, and his resignation became effective on October 27. Upon his return to England he was appointed Warden of St. John's Hospital in Lichfield, a position he held until 1898 when he was made a Residentiary Canon of that Diocese and Assistant Bishop. He died on May 27, 1909, and was buried at Colwich, Staffordshire.

In many respects Bishop Anson was far in advance of his times. From the first he organized a Synod that met regularly each year, beginning with 1884, and his Charges on these occasions were able addresses that often dealt with burning questions of the day. His views on some of these were considered a little extraordinary. He thought it absurd to call the Church in Canada The Church of England, "as if it were possible that the Church of England could be in Canada," and he opposed the sending of missionary contributions away from the country to the support of the strong societies in England, for example, which was then customary. He endeavoured to identify himself with Canada and evidently longed to see a national Church built up for the Dominion, of course in strict communion with the Mother Church, but quite independent of her.[10] Although

[9]G. N. Dobie, op. cit., 293.
[10]C. H. Mockridge, op. cit., 345.

Bishop Anson established a parochial system in his Diocese, he also tried to establish a strong central fund to which all parishes would contribute and from which all the parish clergy would be paid.

Bishop Anson was not only a sound scholar but has been described as a man of great personal holiness and a preacher of great earnestness. He was not easily understood, but he laid the foundations of the Church in Qu'Appelle true and deep, and the debt of that Diocese to him has always been recognized, for clergy and people appreciated his great sympathy, singleness of heart, simplicity of life, and forgetfulness of self, while intent upon helping and encouraging others.

The Right Reverend W. J. Burn, M.A., D.D.
Second Bishop of Qu'Appelle

By 1892 it was quite obvious that the Church of England in Canada was beginning to feel the stirring of a general movement in the direction of constitutional development. The discussions in the 1890 Winnipeg Conference, looking to the formation of a General Synod and the autonomy of the Church in Canada, are one indication of this feeling. Another is to be found in the fact that the House of Bishops of the Ecclesiastical Province of Rupert's Land was beginning to feel that bishops should be men of genuine Canadian experience, well acquainted with the country and its problems.[11]

Archbishop Benson nominated as second Bishop of Qu'Appelle the Reverend William John Burn, Vicar of Coniscliffe, Darlington, in the Diocese of Durham. Mr. Burn was born at Southmoor, Sunderland, on October 28, 1851, and educated at Richmond Grammar School in Yorkshire and St. John's College, Cambridge. He was ordained deacon by Bishop Woodford of Ely on Sunday, December 28, 1874, and priested later by the same Bishop. For a couple of years he acted as curate of St. Andrew's Church, Chesterton, near Cambridge, but in 1876 he returned to his native county and diocese, first as curate of St. Paul's, Jarrow-on-Tyne (1876-1881), and then as vicar of St. Peter's in the same place (1881-1890). In 1890 he moved to the rural vicarage of Coniscliffe.

Bishop Burn was consecrated in Westminster Abbey on March 25, 1893, by Archbishop Benson of Canterbury.[12] He was enthroned in

---

[11]*Ibid.*, 371. O. R. Rowley, *op. cit.*, 104-105. *Note:* Archdeacon E. S. W. Pentreath has left a note in the register of old Christ Church, Winnipeg, of which he was rector at the time, that in 1892 the names of the Dean of Rupert's Land (Grisdale) and himself were submitted by the Metropolitan of Rupert's Land (Machray) to the Archbishop of Canterbury (Benson) for the vacant Diocese of Qu'Appelle. He says, "the influence, however, of the English Committee and friends was too strong, and the result was the ignoring of the Metropolitan's recommendation of a man at work in the Canadian Church field."

[12]C. H. Mockridge, *op. cit.*, 371. O. R. Rowley, *op. cit.*, 104, 105.

St. Peter's Pro-Cathedral, Qu'Appelle, on May 20, 1893. The Synod met on July 5, 1893, under the Commissary, the Reverend J. P. Sargent. Bishop Burn himself presided over the one held on May 30, 1894; his Charge was concise and businesslike. Actually, in spite of the completion of the endowment, the financial position of the Diocese at the time was not good. The property at Qu'Appelle, including the College and See House, was burdened with debt and had to be relinquished. The Bishop removed to Indian Head as a consequence where Lord Brassey, who had acquired extensive holdings in that part of the country, built a house for him, also a church and a home for girls, the latter coming under the direction of Mrs. Burn.

Bishop Burn sincerely desired to strengthen the spiritual side of the work of the Church in his Diocese and had planned to have synods only biennially so that he might meet his clergy in the alternate years for devotional purposes. Of his Diocese he remarked that life was one continual struggle and the isolation very trying, calling for the heroism of loneliness.[13] During his short episcopate there was a momentary pause in the rate of immigration, perhaps caused by some dry years. When, shortly after presiding over his Synod, he died suddenly of heart-failure on June 16, 1896, at the early age of forty-five, he was greatly lamented. He had singular beauty of character, great devotion, and was an able administrator.

The Provincial Synod of Rupert's Land has already arranged for its meeting to be held at Regina on August 12, 1896, and preaching at the opening service in St. Paul's Church, Bishop Young of Athabasca said that only the pastors and congregations of the Diocese themselves could really understand the greatness of their loss. Archbishop Machray, in opening his Charge, said the Synod met under a heavy cloud, when it had been hoped to have been cheered by the bright presence and hearty welcome of the genial prelate who, for so short a time, had presided over the Diocese.

Election of Bishop John Grisdale

Having expressed his sympathy with the Diocese of Qu'Appelle, Archbishop Machray observed:

The weightiest business before this Synod is the election of a Bishop to fill the See that has been so unexpectedly vacated. The responsibility has been placed on the Bishops, and they consider that it is right and necessary that they should assume that responsibility. The Bishops have, however, given the most careful consideration to the memorial of the Executive Committee suggesting, that in the present position of the fund by which the work of the diocese is supported, it would be desirable to elect some clergyman well-known in England. The Bishops

[13]Mockridge, *op. cit.*, 372.

sympathize very deeply with the Committee in its anxiety respecting the continuance of the funds from England, but they are convinced that the present critical condition of the finances affords only a stronger reason for adhering to the opinion which they have each and all come to, that the wisest course is to elect as Bishop a clergyman accustomed to the circumstances of the country and its people, who has secured in the past the goodwill of the laity, and has had large experience in mission organization and work.

This statement by the Metropolitan indicated that since 1892 a major constitutional change in the affairs of the Province had taken place. It is advisable, therefore, to give in detail the circumstances of Bishop Grisdale's election, it being the first time the Provincial Synod elected a Bishop. Previous to this, such appointments were made by the Archbishop of Canterbury as Primate.

The original Canon Six of the Constitution of the Ecclesiastical Province of Rupert's Land had left the selection of a new Bishop (apart from Rupert's Land itself) with the Archbishop of Canterbury, unless there were at least twelve clergymen in the Diocese either supported by endowment or by their own congregations. In the latter case the Bishop would be elected by a Diocesan Synod, subject to the confirmation of the election by the House of Bishops. The only exception was to be the case of a missionary diocese where the Bishop was supported by the Church Missionary Society, in which case the Society was given the right of nomination. In 1893 the Provincial Synod of Rupert's Land met in August. The first meeting of the new General Synod was appointed for September, but the Provincial Synod of Canada, having expressed its general approval of the Winnipeg Scheme of 1890, the Ecclesiastical Province of Rupert's Land at this meeting adjusted its Constitution in several particulars so that it would be in line with the Constitution proposed for the General Synod. This was an act of faith at the time, but subsequent events justified it. In the amended Constitution of 1893 it was provided: (1) That a Diocese with six self-supporting parishes could elect its own Bishop, subject to confirmation of the election by the House of Bishops; (2) That in Missionary Dioceses, which had not six self-supporting parishes, the Society that provided the Bishop's stipend would still have the right of nomination, but in consultation with the Metropolitan and at least two other Bishops of the Province; (3) That in all other cases the selection should be made by the House of Bishops, convened for the purpose by the Metropolitan, subject to the assent (a) of the House of Delegates, if the vacancy occurred within three calendar months of the date of the next meeting of the Provincial Synod, or (b) if the vacancy did not occur within three months of an arranged meeting of the Synod, the Bishop was elected by a majority of the Bishops with the assent of a standing committee of the House of Delegates, set up for that purpose at each meeting of the Provincial Synod; the Diocese concerned would have four members on this committee, compared with two members from each of the other Dioceses. This removed the appointment of Bishops from the hands of the Archbishop of Canterbury. Bishop Machray made this quite clear in his Charge to the Provincial Synod in 1893, and added that he could not pass over this subject "without stating that we would be very ungrateful and ungracious if we did not recognize the great courtesy to us of both the present and the late Archbishops [of Canterbury, Benson and Tait] and their unhesitating readiness to help us in this and every other matter to the utmost of their power; and I express my own deep sense of their anxiety, in the appointment of our Bishops to do what was best for us and most acceptable to us."

On the afternoon of Wednesday, August 12, 1896, the second message ("B") received by the House of Delegates from the House of Bishops, was as follows: "The House of Bishops has unanimously selected the Very Reverend Dean Grisdale, D.D., D.C.L., Dean of Rupert's Land and Prolocutor of the House of Delegates, to fill the vacancy of Qu'Appelle and asks the assent of the House of Delegates." Dean Grisdale left the chair and called upon the Deputy Prolocutor, Archdeacon Cooper of Calgary, to preside over the session. The House adjourned for five minutes and then proceeded to set up the necessary machinery to discover whether it was willing to assent to message "B" or not. When the ballot was taken, the scrutineers declared it to be twenty-eight assent and nineteen non-assent. On the motion of delegates from Qu'Appelle the ballot was taken by Orders with the following result: clergy—assent 13, non-assent 10; laity—assent 15, non-assent 9. The vote was now ordered to be taken by Dioceses, with the interesting result that Qu'Appelle itself was the only one that voted almost solidly non-assent. The House of Delegates then concurred in message "B." The following morning it was announced that Dr. Grisdale had accepted the nomination.[14]

It may be conveniently noted here as a point in the constitutional development of the Church's organization that the circumstances of this election under the Constitution of 1893 seem to have had a disturbing effect on the minds of some of the delegates of the western Dioceses. At the Provincial Synod of Rupert's Land held in Winnipeg on August 9, 1899, memorials on the subject of the election of Bishops were received from both the Diocese of Qu'Appelle and the Diocese of Calgary, complaining that the rights of the Diocese under Subsection three of Section seven of the Constitution were not sufficiently

[14] *Journal of the Provincial Synod of Rupert's Land, 1896*, pp. 27-29.

protected. The Diocese of Qu'Appelle thought the rights of the Diocese were "manifestly ignored" and "the liberty of the Church set aside." It asked for the right of election by the Diocese if there were twenty *licensed* clergy in it, and if not, until that time the House of Bishops should be required to have the assent of the clerical and lay delegates of the Diocese concerned. The Diocese of Calgary agreed that the rights of the Dioceses were insufficiently protected, suggesting as its remedy that the Synod of the Diocese concerned should, by votes of each Order voting separately, nominate three names to the House of Bishops, from which the latter should make a selection and appointment. If the first three names submitted were not acceptable to the House of Bishops, the Synod should recommend a second list of three names.

The House of Bishops did not see its way to recommend any change at the time because the Constitutional arrangement of 1893 was a unanimously accepted compromise, and at this 1899 Synod there was only a bare majority of the Bishops present. The Constitution had been set up with the Church's best interests in view. "The House of Bishops feels, too, that with the progress of the country it cannot be long before the Dioceses that have sent up their memorials will have six clergymen qualified as required, and if there is a strong desire for the privilege this may be an incitement to self-support that is so desirable."

The House of Delegates in its reply asserted that there was a strong feeling of dissatisfaction concerning the method of electing a bishop under the circumstances noted, and this it was trying to remove. It asked the Upper House to confer with a committee that it named, which would report to the next Synod. The House of Bishops agreed to this, but there does not seem to be any evidence of such a meeting taking place. The House of Bishops, however, was right in its prophecy that the situation would never arise again. The fourth Bishop of Qu'Appelle and the second Bishop of Calgary were duly elected by Diocesan Synods.[15]

[15]*Ibid., 1899*, p. 38. Memorial from the Diocese of Qu'Appelle; p. 29 Memorial from the Diocese of Calgary; p. 52 Message "M" from the House of Bishops to the House of Delegates; pp. 54-55 Message 12 from the House of Delegates to the House of Bishops. *Note:* Canon VII of the Constitution and Canons of the Ecclesiastical Province of Rupert's Land published in 1913, became Canon VI in the 1929 edition, due to the dropping of the original Canon IV of 1893, which had become obsolete on the enactment of Act 6 of the Provincial Synod of Rupert's Land in 1923 (Journal of that Synod, p. 59). The wording of Canon VI of 1929 does not differ from that of Canon VII of 1913. At the Provincial Synod of 1960 proposals were made to give the clause a more explicit title, and to provide that a bishop could only be elected by a synod if the diocese concerned had eight self-supporting parishes (the term was very closely defined) and eighteen clergy holding the bishop's licence. This was carried in the House of Bishops, but received one dissenting vote in the House of Delegates. (*Journal of the Provincial Synod of Rupert's Land, 1960*, pp. 28 and 77.)

The consecration of the new Bishop of Qu'Appelle did not take place in Regina but in Holy Trinity Church, Winnipeg. The service was held on Sunday, August 30, immediately preceding the second meeting of General Synod, which opened in Winnipeg on September 2, 1896.[16] The new Bishop was enthroned on September 23 at St. Peter's Pro-Cathedral, Qu'Appelle, and thus was begun a fruitful and happy episcopate lasting fifteen years.

The Right Reverend John Grisdale, D.D.

John Grisdale was born on June 25, 1845, at Bolton, Lancashire, England. From early boyhood he was keenly interested in the work of the church and resolved to become a missionary. He was encouraged in his ambition by the Reverend Canon Powell, then vicar of Bolton, and received his early training from the Reverend Edmund Warbreck who was curate at that time. Mr. Grisdale entered the C.M.S. College at Islington in 1865, graduated as senior student in 1870, was ordained deacon on June 12 of that year by Bishop Jackson of London, then sailed for India. Here he spent a short time as curate at the Old Church in Calcutta and then was appointed as master in St. John's College, Agra. Unfortunately, Grisdale experienced a severe attack of sunstroke that forced his return to England in 1871. For a time he was curate to the Reverend J. B. Whiting at Broomfield in Essex. In 1872 the C.M.S. was anxious to send him to Jerusalem; the medical board refused to pass him, however, suggesting that Canada might offer a more suitable climate, and so arrangements were made for him to meet Bishop Machray who was then in England.

John Grisdale was priested on December 22, 1872, by the Bishop of London, and in the spring of 1873 sailed for Canada, where his first appointment was that of incumbent of St. Andrew's, Manitoba. In 1874 Bishop Machray established the Dean and Chapter of St. John's Cathedral, and Grisdale became Professor of Systematic Theology in St. John's College and Canon of the Cathedral. In 1875 the Archbishop of Canterbury (Tait) conferred on him the Lambeth B.D. In 1882 he was instituted as Dean of Rupert's Land and took the chair of Pastoral Theology in the College. From 1875 to 1883 he was Secretary of the Provincial Synod of Rupert's Land, and from 1890 to 1896 Prolocutor of the Synod.

Upon his return from India in 1871, Grisdale married Annie Chaplin. In Canada she took a keen interest in the work of the Woman's Auxiliary, becoming the first President of the Rupert's Land Board (1887 to 1894).[17]

[16]Rowley, *op. cit.*, 112-113.
[17]Historical Sketch No. 112, *Canadian Church Magazine and Mission News* (October, 1895). R.L.A., The Bishop John Grisdale Papers.

In 1897 Bishop Grisdale visited England in the interests of the diocese, and thus his first Synod did not meet until June 15, 1898. In his Charge he drew attention to the S.P.G. policy of gradually lessening grants, the most serious problem to be met. He said that apart from the Qu'Appelle Association there were only two sources from which the deficiency they faced could be made up: the Church in eastern Canada and the Diocese itself. He hoped that with the General Synod fully organized a greater missionary spirit would be stirred up throughout the whole Church, but the situation still called for greater self-denial and greater liberality upon their own part.

The Close of the Century

During the next six years settlement in the Diocese continued and the Church made valiant efforts to serve its people, scattered at many different points in this area of southern Saskatchewan. The work was hampered by lack of men and money. Bishops and Synods pleaded in vain with the Society for the Propagation of the Gospel to alter its policy of reducing grants; Prebendary Tucker, the Secretary, was sympathetic but the Society itself seemed adamant. The Diocese of Qu'Appelle received generous assistance through these years from the Qu'Appelle Association, but most disappointing was the attitude of eastern Canada, which seemed as stony as that of the S.P.G. It had been hoped that with the formation of General Synod the missionary work of the Church of England in Canada would be reorganized and its objectives unified, but time dragged on and no progress in this direction appeared to be made.

In the meantime the story of earlier years was repeated. "Other bodies," as Archbishop Machray used to call them (though other bishops were more direct in their references), poured both men and money into the mission fields of the prairies. Both the Presbyterian and Methodist Churches made commendable efforts to evangelize the prairie settlers, a considerable proportion of whom (especially from Ontario) were of their own persuasion, and their people down east in both cases gave generously to ensure that their Churches ministered to their people in the West. Some Anglican people were lost because the Church could not get to them, and rather than be without religion at all they attached themselves to the nearest Presbyterian or Methodist church. The Boer War drew a considerable enlistment of young Englishmen who were members of the Church of England, and these were often amongst the most loyal in support of their local church. The beginning of the new century brought with it a fresh expansion of railway building and a new government policy on European immigration, which increased the population of the Diocese of Qu'Appelle particularly without increasing the strength of her church membership.

The Reverend M. T. M. Harding: General Missionary

In the year 1903 a step forward was taken in the appointment of the Reverend M. T. M. Harding as Archdeacon and General Missionary. Archdeacon Harding travelled 20,000 miles in some years, doing his work as general missionary. Branch lines were being extended rapidly, this being the only way to make the main lines pay. In 1903 the main feeder was the Soo Line from the United States, which met the Canadian Pacific Railway at Moose Jaw; but a new line was already under construction from Regina to Prince Albert, and an extension from Dunmore had been laid in the direction of the Crow's Nest Pass. The Manitoba and Northwest Railway was crossing the northeast corner of the diocese, while an extension of the C.P.R. from Manitoba had reached Arcola. The Bishop appealed for men and money for the Josephburg district to the south of Medicine Hat; for the Swift Current district where the new little church at Swift Current itself was the only one in a distance of 112 miles; for the Arcola district; and for the country west of Yorkton where there was needed "an active, tactful, unmarried clergyman to gather the flock together, and start centres of work as the new settlers come in."[18]

About 1906 the situation began to improve. An anonymous donation of $1,000 made possible the appointment of the Reverend W. A. White as special organizing missionary in the northeast part of the diocese, and a renewal of this gift the following year enabled the work to be extended to the Strassburg district, then to the Lanigan and Last Mountain areas. A further step forward was made in 1908 when the Prairie Brotherhood was formed. The S.P.G. made itself responsible for this undertaking for a number of years, and 12,000 square miles were set apart in the southern part of the diocese, where the members carried on under the direction of the Reverend W. H. McLean.

Dean John Payne Sargent

In 1903 the Venerable John Payne Sargent was made first Dean of the Diocese; the Pro-Cathedral was still St Peter's at Qu'Appelle where he had been rector for ten years. Dean Sargent was a graduate of King's College, Windsor, Nova Scotia, in which diocese he had served with distinction from the time of his ordination in 1864 until

[18]*The New Era* (Toronto, M.S.C.C., 1904-1914). Reports from Qu'Appelle Diocese and sundry articles on the work of the Church there.

he moved to Manitoba in 1880. Here he was the first travelling missionary on the newly-constructed C.P.R. line going west; in 1884 he made Moose Jaw his headquarters and founded St. John's Church there. In 1887 he moved back east to Moosomin and in 1890 to Fort Qu'Appelle. He had been made Archdeacon of Assiniboia in 1897.[19]

St. Chad's College

It is not surprising that in 1907 the Diocese determined to start training its own men for the ministry. Suitable candidates were available and there was always the possibility of obtaining more, if the requirement of a university degree were overlooked. Bishop Machray of Rupert's Land and Bishop McLean of Saskatchewan had done this successfully in the past, and the practice was being revived on a considerable scale by Bishop Newnham and Archdeacon Lloyd at Prince Albert. In the background was the precedent set by Bishop Anson himself in the now defunct St. John's College, Qu'Appelle. The project received the warm support of the Qu'Appelle Association and the Shropshire Mission to North-Western Canada, the latter guaranteeing £4,000 a year for five years.

Theological training was in the hands of the Bishop, the Dean and the Archdeacon; the first Warden was the Reverend Charles Littler who had been educated at St. John's College, Winnipeg, where he took his B.D. in 1887. Mr. Littler had had a wide experience of prairie life, and before returning to England in 1902 he was rector of Selkirk, Manitoba. In England he had been Organizing Secretary for the S.P.G. in the Diocese of Lichfield for three years, and spent an equal length of time at St. Chad's, Shrewsbury. The College now founded at Regina derived its name from the most famous of the Saxon Bishops of the Diocese of Lichfield. By 1910 the Hostel of St. Chad's, as it was known, had already prepared seven men for Holy Orders.

St. Chad's owes much to Dean G. Nelson Dobie, Warden from 1903 to 1933, and Canon R. J. Morrice who was associated with him in the College's work for many years. The College has supplied about two-thirds of the clergy in the Diocese.[20]

The Archbishops' Western Canada Fund

The construction of the Grand Trunk Pacific Railway and the extension of the Canadian Northern system, each offering new opportunities to the settler by opening up new districts, continued to increase the problems of the Church, but at the same time a new spirit of understanding and co-operation arose in England. Perhaps

[19]*Crockford's Clerical Directory, 1908.*
[20]*Canadian Churchman* (September 21, 1950).

this was in some measure due to the influence of Bishop Henry Hutchinson Montgomery who had held the See of Tasmania (1889-1901) previous to his appointment as Secretary of the S.P.G., and therefore brought a fresh approach to the problem, which appears to have had the effect of stimulating the S.P.G. into raising a special Northwest Canada Fund. Part of the Pan-Anglican Thank-Offering was received for special educational objects; the Church of Ireland also sent a handsome contribution for general purposes. Archdeacon Lloyd stirred the Colonial and Continental Church Society, though its efforts were directed principally toward the southern part of the Diocese of Saskatchewan.

The other effort, which benefitted all the prairie Dioceses of Rupert's Land, was the institution of a special appeal by the Archbishops of Canterbury and York on February 26, 1909. Archbishops Randall Davidson and Cosmo Gordon Lang said: "We appeal for four things—for interest and prayer, for men and money. We want the clergy to see that the Church of England ought to be sending out fifty men for each of the next ten years. We want all to see that this boundless opportunity . . . if not used, must soon be lost. . . ." The attitude of the Church in England in this effort is admirably expressed in a letter from the Archbishop of Canterbury that Archbishop Matheson read into his Charge to the Provincial Synod of Rupert's Land in 1910: "Our one wish is to act in full co-operation with the authorities in Canada. . . . We desire to help you to lay strong foundations for the upbuilding of the Church in the great nation that is to be, when your plains are peopled and your cities built."

This appeal touched the imagination of the Church in England and met with an immediate and hearty response. Young clergymen and young laymen volunteered for the Canadian field; funds came in in a gratifying way. The Colonial and Continental Church Society took over the district of Carson and Herbert in the central part of the Diocese of Qu'Appelle. A Railway Mission was centred in Regina, from which its missionaries travelled from point to point along the lines. Churches were built and many beautiful furnishings were sent out for them. The five years from 1909 to 1914 were years of great progress.[21]

The Episcopate of Bishop M. T. M. Harding

In 1909 Bishop Grisdale asked his Synod to provide the growing Diocese with a Coadjutor Bishop, and the Synod responded by electing at its June third meeting, the Venerable Malcolm Taylor McAdam

[21]*Occasional Papers of the Qu'Appelle Association; The Archbishops' Western Canada Fund (Occasional Papers)*; Reports and Pamphlets issued by the Colonial and Continental Church Society; *The New Era*, 1904-1914.

Harding to the office; he was consecrated on St. Matthew's Day, September 21, 1909, in St. Paul's Church, Regina.

Bishop Harding was born at Barkway in Hertfordshire, England, on January 20, 1864, and educated at the City of London College and King's College, London. At the age of twenty-four he came to Canada and was ordained deacon by the Bishop of Ontario (Lewis) on May 13, 1888, at Trinity Church, Brockville, Ontario, where he served as curate for a year. Harding was priested on June 16, 1889, in St. George's Cathedral, Kingston, where he held a curacy for three years. In 1893 Mr. Harding came west to take charge of St. Matthew's Church in Brandon, Manitoba.

Bishop Grisdale resigned the See of Qu'Appelle on June 30, 1911, after an episcopate of fifteen years, and retired to Winnipeg, where he was a well-known figure until his death on January 27, 1922.[22]

Bishop Harding assumed full jurisdiction over the Diocese of Qu'Appelle at a time when everything was at a peak of prosperity. An advance in organization was made by the setting up of a synod office in Regina with a full-time secretary, the object being to relieve the Bishop of unnecessary routine work. To this post was appointed the Reverend Edwin H. Knowles, LL.B., who thus began the thirty-eight years of administrative service he gave to the Diocese as Secretary-Treasurer, Archdeacon and Bishop.

In 1912, too, a new opportunity was seized to consolidate the Cathedral, College, Bishop's residence and subsidiary houses for missioners on one site in Regina.[23] The growing necessity of more accommodation in St. Chad's Hostel was the problem that initiated the new movement. A committee of the executive met the government and arranged to purchase a site of fifteen acres with one hundred and fifty yards fronting on Lake Wascana and facing the Legislative Building, on condition that buildings costing at least $80,000 would be erected within three years. The City of Regina generously granted $15,000 towards the project.

Buildings of which corner-stones were laid on August 6, 1913, were the college, together with a chapel in the form of a chancel, to serve not only the students but also the parishioners in that part of the city. This chapel was a memorial to Bishop Burn and its corner-stone was laid by Mrs. Burn. Later a Bishop's residence, Synod Office, Community House for the workers of the Railway Mission, and a

[22]O. R. Rowley, "Bishops, Priests and Kings: The Most Reverend Malcolm Taylor McAdam Harding, D.D.," *Canadian Churchman* (May 5, 1938). O. R. Rowley, *The Anglican Episcopate of Canada and Newfoundland*, 154-155.

[23]*Qu'Appelle Occasional Papers*, No. 114, 1914. St. Paul's Church, Regina, was not constituted the Pro-Cathedral of the Diocese until 1944. Only the Bishop's pastoral staff was removed to St. Paul's from St. Peter's, Qu'Appelle, the original Pro-Cathedral.

larger house for members of the Fellowship of the Maple Leaf, were built upon the same site.

The outbreak of war in 1914 greatly affected the work of the Church in the Diocese of Qu'Appelle, owing to the very large number of young male members who enlisted in either the Canadian or the British Army. St. Chad's differed in no way from the other theological colleges; the majority of its students felt it their duty to enlist. When the college was reopened in 1919 the number of students was small. In the meantime the college building had become the home of the Qu'Appelle Diocesan Girls' School, founded in 1918 under the direction of the Sisters of St. John the Divine, and so the college work was moved into St. Cuthbert's House.

Archdeacon Burgett

A noteworthy addition to the staff of the Diocese was made upon Bishop Harding's return from England in the spring of 1913, when the Reverend Arthur E. Burgett, M.A., then rector of St. Paul's Church in Quebec, became general missionary. Mr. Burgett had had an interesting career, for after completing his courses at Cambridge he had spent some years in the army before entering Cuddeston Theological College in 1896. In 1905 he came to Canada and after some time as assistant at the Cathedral in Quebec City, Burgett was made rector of St. Paul's, but he also undertook duties of a missionary nature and became well acquainted with the inhospitable coasts of Quebec and Labrador. He was made Archdeacon of Assiniboia in 1918, and during the whole of his ten years' association with the Diocese of Qu'Appelle he worked unremittingly, building up the Church in every part of the territory under his supervision. Feeling that the needs farther west were imperative, in 1924 at the request of Bishop Gray he assumed the work of general missionary in the Diocese of Edmonton.[24]

The progress and problems of the Diocese of Qu'Appelle after 1920 were much the same as those experienced by neighbouring dioceses largely dependent upon agriculture. The era of railway building was practically over; a few new branch lines were completed, and some that had been planned were never laid. In the first part of the 1920's there was little new immigration, but some returned soldiers settled under the Government Land Scheme for the assistance of veterans of the first war. There were a large number of vacant parishes, for which condition circumstances of the theological colleges during the war years were blamed.

In 1920 Bishop Harding suffered a breakdown in health that entailed

[24]*Crockford's Clerical Directory, 1936.*

some months of rest, and as a result the Synod of the Diocese of Qu'Appelle applied to the Provincial Synod when it met at Winnipeg in October for an Assistant Bishop. Much as the Provincial Synod sympathized with the Bishop of Qu'Appelle, it was found that there were difficulties in the way of allowing such an appointment, not the least of which was the constitutional requirement of a guaranteed income. After much discussion and a variety of resolutions, the matter was turned over to a committee. It was finally agreed and confirmed by the Provincial Synod in 1923 that circumstances other than age and infirmity might permit the appointment of an Assistant Bishop, provided that he could occupy some position, office or dignity in the Diocese that should have an income or salary which, in the opinion of the Metropolitan, would be permanent, sufficient and suitable for his maintenance.[25] This incident is an interesting point in the constitutional development of the Church, but it brought no relief to the Bishop of Qu'Appelle.

During the 1920's some enterprising changes in methods of church work took place. One was the new van work, now associated with the Sunday School by Post, by which thousands of children have been reached weekly through the mails. This work of the caravans was begun by Miss F. A. Eva Hasell in 1920.[26] These caravans and their workers reached many out-of-the-way homes during the summer season, making contacts with children known to the Sunday School by Post, finding new pupils, discovering candidates for Baptism, and Confirmation, and holding services where opportunity offered. Three such vans worked steadily each summer in the Diocese of Qu'Appelle. The work of the Mothers' Union began in Qu'Appelle in 1910, but it was not until the spring of 1925 that affiliation was completed with the Central Council in England and the Diocesan M.U. became federated with the Dominion Mothers' Union The appeal of Bishop Harding to the Mothers' Union in England in 1926 resulted in a new motor caravan to undertake the ministrations of the Church in an area of three thousand square miles in the southern part of the diocese.

In 1924 the Diocese of Brandon came into being through the division of the Diocese of Rupert's Land. In order to deal with certain

[25] *Journals of the Provincial Synod of Rupert's Land*, 1920 and 1923.
[26] R.L.A., Qu'Appelle Papers: Letters, Miss Evelyn Gwynne to Rev. A. Harding Priest of the G.B.R.E., Toronto, August 26, 1953. The work of the Sunday School by Post was begun in a small way in 1905 by Mrs. Gwynne and Rev. T. G. Beal of Grenfell, Saskatchewan, to meet the needs of from ten to sixteen children in the neighbourhood who were unable to attend Sunday School regularly. The work grew and about a year later Archdeacon Lloyd of the Diocese of Saskatchewan adopted the plan, centring the work for that Diocese in Saskatoon. Miss Eva Hasell's caravan work greatly extended the project by adding effective personal contact with the children and their homes, which had not previously been possible.

parts of his Diocese for which he could not find men, Bishop Thomas organized a community of women which became known as the Bishop's Messengers. Eventually, by arrangement between the two Bishops, a house of this community was established at Fort Pelly in the northeast corner of the Diocese of Qu'Appelle.

Towards the end of 1934, having passed his seventieth year and reached the twenty-fifth of his episcopate, Bishop Harding determined that the time had come for him to retire and leave the Diocese of Qu'Appelle to younger and more active hands; but he did not contemplate a retirement from the ministry and was planning to take up parochial or lighter episcopal work in England. A call of duty caused him to change his plans. On October 30, 1934, Archbishop Stringer, the Metropolitan of the Province, died suddenly in Winnipeg and Bishop Harding as the senior Bishop in the Province had to assume the responsibility of summoning the Provincial Committee to elect a Metropolitan. The Committee met on December 12 and on the sixth ballot elected Bishop Harding as the new Metropolitan. He accepted what was then an extremely difficult position, obviously because he felt it his duty.

Bishop Edwin H. Knowles

The Diocese of Qu'Appelle elected Archdeacon Edwin Herbert Knowles as the fifth Bishop of the Diocese. He had graduated as a student of St. John's College, Winnipeg, at the University of Manitoba in Law in 1902, and after completing his theological training was ordained deacon in 1905 and priest in 1906 by Bishop Grisdale. His parochial experience began with his appointment as curate of Buffalo Lake, Saskatchewan, in 1905, where he was rector from 1906 to 1909, and continued when he went on to Kamsack, where he remained two years. The Diocese early recognized his administrative ability by electing him Clerical Secretary of its Synod in 1911, and he held this office until he became Bishop. He was appointed Archdeacon in 1918.

Bishop Knowles was consecrated in St. Paul's Pro-Cathedral, Regina, on June 24, 1935, by the Metropolitan of Rupert's Land (Harding),[27] and entered on his episcopate at a time when the economic situation of the Diocese, owing to drought, was at its lowest fortune. The ruin caused by dust storms and want of water was making farming impossible and large numbers from the southern communities were either on government relief, moving on their own account, or being moved by the government to other locations. The M.S.C.C. issued a special appeal for a fund to assist the clergy in the stricken areas, pleading

[27]A. R. Kelley and D. B. Rogers, *The Anglican Episcopate of Canada*, II (Toronto, Department of Religious Education, 1961), 56-57.

vigorously for enough money to raise their stipends to sixty dollars a month, of which it was frankly admitted that half would go toward travelling expenses.

The Years of Drought and Dust

In his Charge to the Synod of 1939, Bishop Knowles remarked: "In the Synod of 1937 we looked back on five most difficult years in which continued drought and crop failures had created heavy problems for us all. Another two years have passed, and our difficulties have been intensified by a total crop failure throughout the whole Diocese in 1937 and with but little improvement in the financial situation last year, through rusted crops. . . . The period of adversity through which we have passed has been a very real test of faith but we are here to thank God for the health and strength to carry on."

During these years the income of the parishes showed the slow but certain effect of the reduction in the incomes of the people, but the fact that it was slow indicated that the members of the Church were making a very real effort to support their clergy and parishes. The central funds of the Diocese were also affected by the situation and it became necessary during these years either to reduce grants made to the clergy or to group parishes together under one clergyman in order to maintain them. This latter action brought little relief owing to the greatly increased expense of travelling over much larger areas. A further change made to ease financing was to have the Diocese pay stipendiary grants on a monthly instead of quarterly basis, but the third month's payment was dependent upon the Diocese's having first received the missionary apportionment for the quarter in full from the parishes. In spite of these handicaps the Church moved with its people and in areas where land was opened up for new settlements new churches were erected. A stone church was built at Langbank near Wawota entirely by voluntary labour, another at Maryfield, and still another at Eston.

The story of the depression years, which affected the Diocese of Qu'Appelle to a greater extent than any of the other Dioceses in the Ecclesiastical Province of Rupert's Land, is one that cannot be related in any more detail than has been done so far. An admirable overall picture was presented to the Synod of the Diocese held on June 3, 1942, by the Committee on Statistics and State of the Church under the signature of its Chairman, Archdeacon J. K. Irwin, at that time Secretary of the Synod. Where, in 1929, there had been 92 clergy in the Diocese, in 1939 there were 75; 8,995 families had become 8,972 families; the total amount raised in the parishes had dropped from $240,551 to $118,081; the amount paid in stipends from $112,844 to

$55,929; and the apportionments paid by the parishes for mission funds had decreased from $26,168 to $15,510. But the real work of the Church was being carried on effectively, as indicated by the fact that the number of communicants in this same period increased from 11,125 to 12,651. In his Charge to the Synod of 1942, Bishop Knowles spoke of the improved position of the trust funds since the Synod of 1939. At that time he had noted that the See Endowment Fund was about $1,800 less than the $75,000 minimum required under the regulations of the Provincial Synod for a diocese to elect its own bishop. He had also mentioned that a very generous offer had been received from the Archbishops' Western Canada Fund to provide £2,447 for the See Endowment Fund on the basis of pound for pound being raised by the Diocese, which offer they had accepted. Through bequests, gifts and the assistance of the Qu'Appelle Association they had then been able to claim £900. Subsequently they had received further assistance from the Qu'Appelle Association and two ladies in England had provided the balance of £1,197 required to meet the offer in full. The See Endowment Fund then stood at $96,388. Their anxiety about the Clergy Sustentation Fund had been relieved to some extent by a gift of £1,000 from Mrs. Salusbury of Winchester, England, who had previously provided the money to build the church at Eston. A gift of $500 had also been received from Canon Guy P. Terry who had commenced his ministry in the Diocese in 1892 at Oxbow and Estevan.

St. Chad's College had its troubled times, too, but survived as far as staff was concerned through the co-operation of the local clergy. Its worst problem, apart from the shortage of candidates for the ministry, was the deterioration of the premises themselves.

In the latter part of the episcopate of Bishop Knowles, changes took place in the work of the Diocese that relieved it of some financial obligations and promised to increase its efficiency. The first of these was the reorganization of the Synod Office staff in the early part of 1950. The Reverend F. E. B. Badham, who had been Secretary of the Synod for six years, returned to parish work as rector of Weyburn, of which district he was to become Archdeacon in 1952. At the same time the Reverend Canon W. H. B. Scharpe laid down the office of treasurer of the Diocese, which he had held since 1921 when it was first instituted. Previous to 1921 Canon Scharpe had served as accountant for two years, and before that he was missionary at the Day Star Indian Reserve for a short time. A man of remarkable character, he was held in high regard by the whole Diocese. He died on November 8, 1953, in Victoria, B.C., on the verge of ninety years of age. The two diocesan positions were consolidated in 1950 and G. W. Pickett was appointed to the office.

The residential school at Gordon's Reserve, Punnichy, had always been something of a problem to the Diocese, which was responsible for its founding and maintenance. In 1946 the Synod of Qu'Appelle asked the Indian Schools Commission to assume the responsibility, and the Commission agreed. Unfortunately difficulties arose, because of the condition of the buildings and the inadequacy of the water supply, which it took the Commission and the Department of Indian Affairs a long time to overcome. Meanwhile, for a time, the school was closed, then reopened for day classes only for several years, but finally, in 1953, once more began its full time work as a residential school. The work of the Church, however, suffered considerably during these six years.

Archbishop Harding died on April 30, 1949, and the Diocese of Qu'Appelle instituted in 1950 the Harding Memorial Fund to restore the diocesan buildings in Regina which, after more than thirty years, were beginning to show the deterioration of age. In the course of a couple of years about $17,000 was received from nearly 2,000 subscribers, and the most pressing repairs were completed at a cost of about $15,600; in addition a bronze memorial plaque to the Archbishop's memory was placed in St. Chad's Chapel.

Bishop Michael E. Coleman

Bishop Knowles resigned in the spring of 1950, and the Synod met on May 31 under the Administrator of the Diocese, the Very Reverend Dean Cole, to elect a successor. The Synod elected the Reverend Canon Michael Edward Coleman, Canon Lecturer and Diocesan Missioner of the Diocese of British Columbia, as sixth Bishop of Qu'Appelle. He was consecrated on August 24, in St. Paul's Pro-Cathedral, Regina, by the Metropolitan (Sherman).[28]

Bishop Coleman was born at Sutton Bridge, Lincolnshire, England, on April third, 1902, and educated at Bradfield College, and the Bishop's Hostel, Lincoln. He was ordained deacon by Bishop Haywood of Southwell at Trinity, 1927, and priested by the same Bishop, Trinity, 1928. From 1927 to 1930 he was curate of the Parish Church, Hucknall, and then spent five years as chaplain to Toc H in Lancashire and two years as commissioner to Toc H in Canada. From 1937 to 1942 he was curate and acting vicar of All Hallows, Barking by the Tower, London, England.

[28]*Ibid.*, 120-121.

CHAPTER TEN

The Farther Northwest
Athabasca – Mackenzie River – Yukon

To the missionary of the North, who in his travels oft has occasion to make use of the great Mackenzie River or one or other of its main tributaries, there was always at hand a striking metaphor, for they presented in their never-ceasing flow an apt figure of the passing of time, which, so far as the temporal life of the individual man extends, so soon merges into the fathomless ocean of eternity; but for the more practical purposes of life the finest metaphor lies up-stream, for he who is paddling his canoe in that direction against the opposing force that is ever threatening to drag him backwards, soon has the lesson driven home that, if there is to be good progress and a perfect end, there must be constant watchfulness and unflagging effort.

THE FAR AND FURRY NORTH
by Rev. A. C. Garrioch

Archdeacon Robert McDonald

In the middle of the nineteenth century the Mackenzie River basin was still the land of the fur trader, and no Church of England missionary travelled its waters until Archdeacon Hunter went to Fort Simpson in 1858. His report caused the Reverend William West Kirkby to be sent there in 1859, and it was the account of the further travels of this energetic and enthusiastic man that arrested the attention of the Church. There is evidence, however, that the Gospel was first carried into the Mackenzie River basin by two of the first pupils of the C.M.S. School (James and John Hope)[1] established in the Red River Settlement by the Reverend John West.

The news of Kirkby's journey to Fort Yukon reached the Red River Settlement in 1862, and so stirred the people of the Parish of St. Andrew's that they determined to send another missionary north at their own expense; in Robert McDonald they found one ready and willing to go.

Robert McDonald[2] was born in Point Douglas in 1829. His father,

[1]*John Rae's Correspondence with the Hudson's Bay Company on Arctic Exploration, 1844-1855* (London, The Hudson's Bay Record Society, 1953), 359-360.
[2]A. C. Garrioch and I. O. Stringer, "Robert McDonald," in W. B. Heeney, ed., *Leaders of the Canadian Church*, Second Series (Toronto, 1920), 111-132; H. A. Cody, *The Apostle of the North* (Toronto, 1908); *Crockford's Clerical Directory, 1908*. McDonald's own diaries and letters are in the Rupert's Land Archives, but the process of reducing them to order was incomplete at the time of writing (1961).

Neil McDonald, was for a time an employee of the Hudson's Bay Company, but later took up land in the Red River valley. His mother was Ann Logan, a daughter of William Logan, a retired officer of the Company. Robert McDonald was educated in St. John's Parish School, and under the Reverend John Macallum at the Red River Academy, where he proved himself a good scholar. It may be noted that he and R. Caldwell, Master of Corpus Christi College, Cambridge, were the only two students of Bishop Anderson's time to be elected as Fellows of St. John's College, Winnipeg. Robert McDonald took his theological training from Bishop Anderson and was ordained by him on December 19, 1852; he was priested on June 5, 1853. McDonald was first appointed to the mission at The White Dog, the first to be established among the Ojibway Indians. Here he ministered until he left for the Mackenzie River valley, with the exception of a brief period at St. James, just west of Winnipeg.

Robert McDonald arrived at Fort Simpson in September, 1862. There he met Mr. Kirkby and proceeded with all speed to Fort Yukon, which he reached in October. His work there amongst the Loucheux or Tukudh Indians was most successful and at the end of two years he was able to baptize the first converts to Christianity in that region. The permanency of the work he did may be judged by the fact that in 1906 an archdeacon of the Protestant Episcopal Church of the United States, which was then beginning to show its first interest in mission work in the Alaska territory, found a remote tribe of these Indians using McDonald's translations of the Bible and Prayer Book, and still praying fervently day by day for "our Most Gracious Sovereign Lady Queen Victoria." It is said to have taken a considerable time to persuade them that they ought to be praying for the President of the United States.

McDonald continued his work in this northern district for more than two years, when a report that he was in failing health reached Bishop Anderson, then in England, shortly before he preached the sermon at the Anniversary Service of the Church Missionary Society in St. Bride's Church, London, England, on May first, 1865. In the course of this sermon Bishop Anderson told of the lonely post at Fort Yukon, and of the failing health of the missionary who was trying bravely to hold on to his work until he could be replaced. Lifting his voice the Bishop uttered those words, which have become so memorable, "Shall no one come forward to take up the standard of the Lord as it falls from his hands, and to occupy the ground?" The appeal was answered; after the service a young Lincolnshire curate walked into the vestry and offered himself for the work.

McDonald, however, recovered his health sufficiently to remain at

Fort Yukon until 1871, when, owing to Russia's sale of Alaska to the United States in 1867, he removed to Fort McPherson on the Peel River, a post to which Eskimos and Loucheux Indians both came to trade with the Hudson's Bay Company. Archdeacon McDonald remained at Fort McPherson until his retirement in 1904, but during those years he was twice in England to see editions of his translations through the press. The District of Mackenzie River was created the Diocese of Athabasca in 1874; Robert McDonald became its first Archdeacon a year later and was the vigorous representative of that diocese and the later Diocese of Mackenzie River at more than one Provincial Synod. He was indefatigable in his journeys to preach the Gospel to small and scattered groups of the Indian people, and on two occasions reached the shores of the Arctic Ocean. He was the first to discover gold in the Yukon, in 1863, a fact recalled by the *London Times* when the Klondike became front page news in 1898, but no claims were ever staked on behalf of the Church.[3]

Archdeacon McDonald married in 1877 one of his converts, Julia Smith, who was the greatest help to him, accompanying him on his journeys and assisting him in his translations of the Bible, Prayer Book, and the preparation of a hymn book in Tukudh. He made himself the master of this language and used Roman letters in making his translations because he claimed the sounds of the language were too many and too complicated to be reproduced in the syllabics. He devoted the years of his retirement, which began in 1904, to compiling a Tukudh Grammar, which came off the press in 1911 and was his last published work. During the last years of his life he lived unobtrusively in a small house in Point Douglas, Winnipeg, situated on what was part of the farm where he had spent his boyhood. He died at the age of eighty-four, August 29, 1913, honoured sincerely by the men of his own generation as the most singularly successful missionary of his time. Archdeacon McDonald was buried in St. John's Cathedral churchyard.

William Carpenter Bompas

The young Lincolnshire curate, who responded so readily to the appeal made by Bishop Anderson for a man to replace Robert McDonald, was William Carpenter Bompas, well described by his biographer, the late Archdeacon H. A. Cody, as "The Apostle of the North."[4]

[3]"Forty-five Years in the Yukon," *Winnipeg Free Press* (August 14, 1909), 4. Golden Jubilee Booklet of St. Paul's, Dawson City, Y.T., 1947, p. 3.

[4]H. A. Cody, *op. cit.*, is the basis of what is now written about William Carpenter Bompas, except as otherwise noted. A. C. Garrioch, *The Far and Furry North* (Winnipeg, 1925), in semi-fictional style gives a contemporary background picture of life in the Mackenzie River area at this time. Mr. Bompas appears in this as "Rev. Charles Snow."

Mr. Bompas, the fourth son of Charles Carpenter Bompas, Sergeant-at-Law, was born in London on January 20, 1834. He was expected to take up the profession of the Law, but a severe illness in 1858 gave him the opportunity to give more thought to a cherished project of entering the ministry; on December 18, 1859, he was ordained deacon by Bishop Jackson of Lincoln. For two years he was curate of Sutton-on-the-Marsh in Lincolnshire, a difficult parish with a scattered population. His next experience was in an overcrowded industrial centre, New Radford in Nottinghamshire, where he also spent two years, then returned to Alford in Lincolnshire. About that time he offered himself to the Church Missionary Society for work in the East, but, being over thirty years of age, the committee thought him too old to cope with the language. His offer to go Canada's North-west, however, was very willingly accepted and he began his preparations at once.

Journey to Fort Simpson, N.W.T.

One of Mr. Bompas' characteristics was a firm determination to overcome all obstacles, and he aimed to arrive at Fort Simpson before Christmas in 1865. On June 25 he was ordained priest by Bishop Machray in St. Paul's, Covent Garden, this being the first episcopal act by the Bishop who himself had been consecrated the day before. Mr. Bompas left London on June 30, reached New York on July 12, and travelled by rail through Chicago to La Crosse, where he took the steamer for St. Paul.

The Settlement was reached early in August, but Bompas did not stay there long, leaving as soon as he could for the north. There are two interesting references to his journey to be found in the *Church Missionary Record* of 1867. The first is in a letter from the Reverend Abraham Cowley, dated August 10, 1865:[5] "Mr. Bompas left at about seven o'clock this morning in Mr. Mowat's boat. He will go to Norway House to meet, if possible, the Isle à la Crosse brigade." The second is an entry in the journal of the Reverend Thomas Thistlewaite Smith,[6] then stationed at the Devon Mission at The Pas, and dated August 28, 1865: "In the evening the Isle à la Crosse brigade, under Mr. Samuel McKenzie, arrived, when I had the pleasure of welcoming Rev. W. C. Bompas as a fellow-worker in this part of the vine-yard. . . . He is most zealous, for he has come on without his luggage, and without the necessary clothing to defend him from the cold, which he will experience before reaching Isle à la Crosse. This can be

[5]C.M.S.A., Archdeacon Abraham Cowley Papers.
[6]C.M.S.A., The Diary of Rev. Thomas Thistlewaite Smith.

remedied now, and as he is anxious to proceed, we must do all we can to further his object. Spent the evening in cheering conversation with Brother Bompas, and was glad to be able to communicate to him good accounts of Mr. Kirkby." *August 29th* "Commended Mr. Bompas to the care of Mr. McKenzie, who said that he would do all he could to forward him on his way, and if it was a late fall, he would probably reach the Long Portage before the setting in of the ice, and perhaps even Athabasca. *The Fact was, they had picked up Brother Bompas alone on a point in Lake Winnipeg, where the boats which had brought him from Red River had landed him, telling him that boats would be passing soon to pick him up,* so that he was a perfect stranger to them."

Portage la Loche was reached on October 12, the journey taking sixty-three days, but at first it did not seem possible to go farther. Mr. Bompas, however, secured a canoe and two French half-breeds, and in eight days made the difficult journey to Fort Chipewyan. Here a pressing invitation to remain for the winter was declined and Bompas set off to the north in a big canoe with three Indian boys, but conditions were such that the water route had to be abandoned and the journey to Fort Resolution, on the south side of Great Slave Lake, was made tortuously through the bush. Here they had to spend a month, owing to the weather, then made their way by snowshoe and dog-sleigh to Big Island, where they met the dog-mail from the north. Leaving with this outfit when it returned on the seventeenth of December, Bompas reached Fort Simpson early Christmas morning, where he was warmly welcomed by a surprised but extremely joyful Mr. Kirkby.

The Travelling Missionary

Mr. Bompas stayed at Fort Simpson, studying the native languages and assisting Mr. Kirkby with his work until Easter, 1866, when he made his way down the Mackenzie River to Fort Norman. There the Hudson's Bay Company built a house for him and supplied a teacher named Murdo McLeod. The school was provided essentially for orphans left by a scarlet fever epidemic in the district in 1865; it was closed as such in 1868. Bompas occupied his time in visiting the separate tents, trying to convey the simple truths of the Gospel to the natives. He did not find it hard to live with them; they were quiet, inoffensive and usually occupied in some useful way. At a conference between McDonald, Kirkby and himself at Fort Simpson in August of that year, it was decided that Bompas should undertake a "roving commission" rather than a settled station. Consequently he left Fort

Norman on January 10, 1867, and made his way by Fort Rae and Fort Resolution (both on Great Slave Lake) to Fort Chipewyan near the west end of Lake Athabasca, a point at which he strongly advocated a permanent station, which would form a connecting link with Fort Simpson.

Spending nearly a year at Fort Chipewyan, Mr. Bompas left in January, 1868, and made his way up the Peace River to Fort Vermilion, where he found himself among the Beaver Indians, whose condition he described as very pitiable. As to physical surroundings, his keen observation noted how suitable the country was for farming and stock raising. In the summer he returned to Fort Simpson to permit Kirkby to take his first furlough after sixteen years absence from England. On this furlough, Kirkby saw through the press the Chipewyan translations he had made of the Gospels of St. Mark and St. John. In the summer of 1869 the Reverend W. D. Reeve, later to become Archdeacon and second Bishop of Mackenzie River (1891), arrived to take over, and Mr. Bompas left for the first of his journeys to the farther north.

First Contact with Western Eskimos

This time his destination was Fort Yukon and so he reached, in July, 1869, the point for which he had set out from England. But on his way through Fort McPherson he met a number of Eskimos who invited him to go down to the coast wtih them. This Bompas could not do at the time, but in the spring of 1870 he made his way back over the mountains to Fort McPherson and from there to the coast. On his way he was smitten with snow blindness and had to be led by the hand of his guide, yet they made twenty-five miles a day. He visited several camps and the Eskimos were considerably excited by his presence, as he was the first white man they had met in this way. Bompas returned to Fort McPherson when the ice went out of the river, travelling with a band of Eskimos, but much ice remained and progress was unusually slow. The blame for this condition was laid on him and the situation became most critical. But while Bompas slept in peace with a good conscience, an old Eskimo named Shipataitook, who had taken a great fancy to him, told the others of an hypothetical dream in which he envisioned dreadful things happening to them if they should arrive at Fort McPherson without the missionary. From this time he was treated with attentive care and arrived safely at the Fort on June 18, to enjoy the hospitality of Andrew Flett, then in charge of it, and the assistance of Mrs. Flett in his study of the Loucheux language. Bompas arrived back again at Fort Vermilion in October, having travelled 4,700 miles by canoe.

The Peace River Country

Archdeacon Cody has described Bompas as a "detached cruiser" speeding from place to place that he might bring in the Gospel dawn to widely scattered bands of Indians. Certainly he covered a tremendous amount of territory in 1871 in the upper part of the Peace River country. From Fort Vermilion to Fort Chipewyan and Fond du Lac on Lake Athabasca, then back up to Rocky Mountain Portage where he noted that gold had been found in the district south, evidently the Cariboo. He also prophesied the construction of roads from the Peace River country into British Columbia, which materialized when the Hart Highway was completed. In writing to his sister that spring he remarked that he must have vaccinated about 500 Indians. The previous year smallpox had been a scourge and more than 2,000 of the natives had died at one of the Hudson's Bay Company Posts.

That fall he was instructed by the C.M.S. Committee at the Red River to go to Fort Yukon in order to relieve McDonald, who had been given leave of absence after ten years of service. Bompas made his way north from Fort Vermilion to Great Slave Lake by the Hay River and saw for the first time the Alexandra Fall, as he named it, which he thought one of the wonders of the world: "It is a perpendicular fall of about 150 feet high by 500 feet wide, and of surpassing beauty."

Mr. Bompas was perturbed at having to leave his work in the southern country; he was afraid the Indians would lose confidence in the permanence and reliability of their instruction. He spent the winter among the camps of the Loucheux Indians and remarked that they treated him like Christian brethren all the winter. He estimated that he walked one thousand miles that winter, but did not think it was as much as he used to walk in a winter in the streets of London.

Early realizing that it was impossible to cover adequately the whole of his huge episcopate, Bishop Machray had begun to make plans for its division. On June 10, 1872, the General Committee of the C.M.S. agreed to these plans and undertook to provide the stipend of the new Bishops. But while it was known that Horden was willing to accept nomination, distance prevented any easy communication with Bompas. In fact he was still at Fort Yukon when the news reached him in the early summer of 1873. He shrank from the thought of becoming a bishop, and that July he started for England with the express purpose of turning the Church Missionary Society from the idea.

Leaving Fort Yukon with a couple of Indian boys, Bompas travelled up the Porcupine River till he reached the Rocky Mountains, where the boys left him to return to the Fort. Alone and on foot he made his way across the Rockies in the face of furious snow storms, taking just three days. With the aid of two other Indian lads, he made the 800 miles from Fort McPherson to Fort Simpson by September 2, "after three weeks of fatiguing towing," then contended with more snow storms till Portage la Loche was reached on October 8. He had covered 2,600 miles. Bompas was held there for ten days by the weather; then, accompanied by two Hudson's Bay Company servants, he walked to Buffalo Lake and was guided by a band of Indians to Isle à la Crosse. Again delayed for ten days, he travelled with three Company men to Green Lake by dogs and sledge, but the weather became milder and they had to walk from there to Fort Carlton, which took five days. From Carlton House, Touchwood Hills was reached with a horse and sledge, and through the kindness of the postmaster there, Bompas was furnished with a cariole and dogs, and so covered about four hundred miles to the Red River, which he reached on December 31. Nor did his adventures cease here; there was a terrible journey to Moorhead by stagecoach; his train was stuck in a snowdrift; a second stagecoach overturned; the train to Montreal was derailed; and finally the *Scandinavian* had a rough voyage across the Atlantic. After these experiences Bompas commented: "On the whole, the dogs may be counted to hold their own in competing with horseflesh or steam, whether on land or water."

Upon arriving in England on February 3, 1874, he spent some effort trying to persuade the Church Missionary Society to change its plans for him, but he was unsuccessful and on May third was consecrated in St. Mary's, the Parish Church of Lambeth in London, as first Bishop of Athabasca, by Archbishop Tait of Canterbury.[7]

The Call to the North

Very fittingly the sermon was preached by Bishop David Anderson, who had resigned but ten years before from the Diocese of Rupert's Land, which, by the consecrations taking place that day, would be

---

[7]No difficulty seems to have arisen respecting the consecration of John Horden as Bishop of Moosonee in 1872 (Robert Machray, *Life of Robert Machray . . . Archbishop of Rupert's Land*, 226-227), but when the Archbishop of Canterbury sent on to the Colonial Secretary the request of the Church Missionary Society for the issuance of a mandate for the consecration of Bishop Bompas, Lord Kimberley felt that it should be referred to the Canadian Government as Canada had "annexed" the territory of the proposed diocese. A committee of the Cabinet consulted with the Minister of Justice and reported that "no objection can be raised by the Government of Canada." This decision was transmitted by Lord Dufferin to the Colonial Secretary on April 30, 1874. The same situation appears to have arisen with regard to Bishop McLean's consecration for Saskatchewan, but this was settled by a telegram sent on April 10, 1874. P.A.C., Privy Council Papers: Order in Council No. 561-C, of 1874.

divided into four dioceses. Addressing some words to Bishop Bompas, Bishop Anderson observed:

In leaving for the distant sphere of Athabasca, brother, it is to no untried work that you proceed. . . . You have been there for more than eight years, in labours abundant, and your love has not lessened nor your zeal slackened. You have brought home, as the fruit of your labour, portions of Scripture, prayers and hymns, in seven different dialects or tongues. You are ready to take the precious treasure out with you—the translations printed and prepared by the Society for Promoting Christian Knowledge. You have also one complete Gospel, that of St. Mark, which the British and Foreign Bible Society has enabled you to carry through the Press. But you left good treasure behind, in souls warmed with love of Christ and softened by the spirit of Grace. You have the hearts of the Indians and the Esquimaux.

Mrs. Bompas

The week that began with this Consecration was to be the last that Bishop Bompas ever spent in England. On May 7, he was married to Miss Charlotte Selina Cox, by Bishop David Anderson. Mrs. Bompas was the daughter of Dr. Joseph Cox of Montague Square and had a brother who was vicar of Bishops Tawton in Devonshire. Part of her life had been spent in Italy where she acquired such a knowledge and love of the Italian language that a copy of Dante was her constant companion. They sailed from Liverpool on the old Cunard steamship *China*, after what the Bishop declared was the hardest week he had ever experienced. Mrs. R. J. Bowen, the wife of the first missionary to the Klondike miners at Forty Mile, and later first rector of St. Paul's, Dawson, knew Mrs. Bompas quite intimately twenty years later, and noted that she "was a very spirited lady, very energetic and capable of many things. One wonders how such a frail little lady kept up so long." The few remaining portraits of her reveal something of her courage, patience, dignity and charm.[8]

Journey to the West

The Bishop and Mrs. Bompas did not sail alone. Their party included the Bishop's sister, returning to Lennoxville, Quebec; the Reverend Robert and Mrs. Phair, who were going back to their work among the Indians at Fort Frances; two other men destined for the ministry, and their brides (Mr. and Mrs. Arthur Shaw who were being placed by the Bishop at Fort Chipewyan, and Mr. and Mrs. J. Reader who were to begin their work in the Touchwood Hills and be long associated with The Pas); Miss Emma M. Moore, whose brother was already a clergyman in the Diocese of Rupert's Land; and John Hines, who left an

[8]Reminiscences of Mrs. R. J. Bowen, *Northern Lights*, XXX (August, 1941), 7. Mrs. Bowen, née Miss Mellett, was the first teacher to work in the Diocese of Selkirk (Yukon), to which she went in 1893.

interesting account of the voyage. He recalled: "The trip was by far the roughest I ever experienced; we were twelve days in reaching New Jersey from Liverpool . . . and in order to pass the time profitably, the Bishop undertook to instruct us in the language of the people we were going to work amongst . . . in addition to being able to read a little, we committed to memory The Lord's Prayer—Mrs. Bompas in the language of the Beaver Indians, and I in the language of the Cree Indians. New York was reached on Whitsunday, May 24th, in time to attend the Service at St. Mark's Church, where the Bishop preached in the evening."

It may be remarked that like other voyages, this one was not without its romance, for Miss Moore became Mrs. John Hines on June 22, 1876; the wedding took place in St. John's Cathedral, Winnipeg. The Reverend John Hines has also left an account of the journey from New York to Winnipeg. They could only get an "accommodation train," which seemed to travel as it pleased. The second part of the journey was by stern-wheeler down the Red River from Fargo, which took another week.

Fort Simpson

The Bishop's party was too late to join the regular Portage la Loche Brigade when it left from Lower Fort Garry, but seems to have over-taken it later and proceeded by the usual route to Portage la Loche on the height of land that separates the waters draining to the Arctic Sea from those going into Hudson Bay. Here they joined the Mackenzie River Brigade, and so to Fort Chipewyan and on to Great Slave Lake; at Fort Providence they found the Reverend W. D. and Mrs. Reeve who joined them, and Fort Simpson was reached on September 24. The shadow of starvation was hanging over the Fort as only a week's supply of food was left. On November 28 the Bishop ordained Mr. Reeve priest, the first ordination held in the Diocese. Reeve had first come to Fort Simpson in 1869, having previously graduated from the C.M.S. College at Islington, and been ordained deacon by Bishop Machray of Rupert's Land.

Bishop Bompas assembled the first Synod of his Diocese at Fort Simpson on September 4, 1876. Three clergy were there: Robert McDonald of Fort McPherson on the Peel River, who had been appointed Archdeacon the previous year; the Reverend W. D. Reeve, who had been in charge of Fort Simpson for several years; and the Reverend Alfred C. Garrioch, quite recently ordained, who had been pioneering at Fort Vermilion on the Peace River. Besides, there were three laymen: Allen Hardisty and William Norn, catechists, and George Sandison, a servant of the Hudson's Bay Company.

Mission Farm First in Peace River

One of the problems that constantly beset Bishop Bompas during the first ten years of his experience in the Mackenzie River valley was famine caused by the failure of game, or the impossibility of getting in the supplies from outside. When he returned to the Peace River country in the spring of 1878 from his long and arduous trip to Metlakatla, near Port Essington, B.C., he found conditions so acute that he determined to effect a plan that had long been forming in his mind. "A mission-farm in connection with the mission," he wrote, "seems almost a necessity, for . . . the wild animals of the woods are ceasing to yield even a precarious subsistence."

Accordingly, a new mission was commenced at Dunvegan in 1879 as this point at the time seemed likely to become a place of importance, "being a convenient door of ingress and egress to and from the north," as it was for a good many years after. Thomas Bunn, who had done successful school work at Chipewyan, was placed in charge, with George Garrioch, previously at Fort Vermilion, in control of the farm. Later, additional farming was undertaken at Smoky River, while at Fort Vermilion Mr. Lawrence took over, and in 1880 the farm there had to be enlarged. The name of his son, Sheridan Lawrence, has become famous in Peace River agricultural circles.

First Steamboats on the Mackenzie

Production always entails the problem of distribution, and Bishop Bompas was the first to promote the idea of a steamboat on the Mackenzie River. The plans of the Bishop, however, were never carried out as the Hudson's Bay Company, thinking that such a boat would cause the Company to lose prestige with the natives, took action on its own account. In 1882 it built the little steamer *Graham* (135 feet long, with a speed of $5\frac{1}{2}$ miles per hour) at Fort Chipewyan, in 1885 the *Wrigley* at Fort Smith, and a few years later the stern-wheeler *Athabasca* at Athabasca Landing, for use on the Upper Athabasca River.

Eskimos and Yukon

For some years Bishop Bompas had been concerned about work among the Eskimos and Indians of the Upper Yukon valley. Archdeacon McDonald had been at Fort Yukon as far back as 1862 and had made considerable progress there, but had withdrawn to Fort McPherson on the Peel River after the territory was purchased by the United States.[9] The American Church had done nothing. Bishop Bompas

[9]The purchase of Alaska took place in 1867. The U.S.A. took formal possession of Fort Yukon in 1869, Bishop Bompas being present at the ceremony. (H. A. Cody, *op. cit.*, 107.) The Hudson's Bay Company did not discontinue business at Fort Yukon immediately, and consequently Robert McDonald, who lived at the Fort, did not withdraw to Fort McPherson on the Peel River until 1871 (*Crockford's Clerical Directory*, 1908).

had no inhibitions concerning international boundaries, and from time to time made strong appeals for men and money to man this part of the field. The Indians themselves pleaded for missionaries. Finally the appeal was answered. An anonymous gift of one thousand pounds was placed with the Church Missionary Society to forward the work and the Reverend T. H. Canham, a young C.M.S. missionary who had spent the winter of 1881 in charge of the Parish of St. Mary's, Portage la Prairie, made his way by boat and canoe to Fort McPherson, where he stayed the next few years doing missionary work and acquiring competence in the Eskimo and Tukudh languages. Mr. Canham was made Archdeacon in 1893 after six years of work on the lower Yukon. He served thirty-five years in that part of the Diocese of Athabasca, later to become the Diocese of Yukon, and lived to the age of ninety-five. The anonymous donor was the Bishop's brother, George Bompas.

Diocese of Mackenzie River

After spending the winter of 1881 at Fort Norman, Bishop Bompas left for Fort McPherson, intending to visit Archdeacon McDonald who had been in poor health. But hearing better reports of him when he arrived at Fort Good Hope, he turned back to Fort Norman and took Mrs. Bompas to Fort Resolution on the south side of Great Slave Lake. He went on to Fort Chipewyan, from there to Fort Vermilion and other points on the Peace River, returned to Vermilion and spent three months there teaching school. Then, becoming anxious about the southern work, he walked the two hundred miles from this post to Fort Chipewyan, which he reached on March first. Here he heard that Mrs. Bompas was ill so he hurried north, but finding her in "tolerable health" he spent only two weeks there, then pushed north to Fort McPherson again.

This incessant travelling, however, was beginning to tell upon the Bishop's health; but, he wrote, "if the zeal and affection of friends at home would provide an additional Bishop for Peace River, then I think the whole diocese, as large as half of Europe, might be viewed as an end worth an effort to accomplish. If the diocese remains undivided, my [itinerancies] will be inconsistent with domestic life, and I have asked Mrs. Bompas to revisit England next year."

The result of his appeal was that the C.M.S. invited the Reverend Richard Young, then incumbent of St. Andrew's, Red River, and the local assistant secretary of their mission, to visit the Peace River area and report to them. This he did in the summer of 1884. The Provincial Synod of Rupert's Land, at the instance of Archdeacon McDonald, had already consented to the division of the Diocese of Athabasca at its meeting in August, 1883, and the C.M.S. seems to have found the money willingly. When Mr. Young returned to the Red River in the fall he was consecrated in St. John's Cathedral, Winnipeg, as Bishop of Athabasca on October 18, 1884, by Bishop Machray as Metropolitan, the first Bishop to be so consecrated in the Canadian Northwest.

The new Diocese in the Northwest duly received the name of Mackenzie River[10] when it came into being in the latter part of 1884, and Bishop Bompas took charge of it with great satisfaction. Still far away from the restraints of civilization, he felt he would be able to accomplish more definite work, and give more time to his beloved translations. The southern area retained the name of Athabasca.

The Largest Area and Smallest Population

Even with two hundred thousand square miles set up as the Diocese of Athabasca under Bishop Young, the new diocese to the north was still of excessive size, possibly at least eight hundred thousand square miles; its population of scattered Indian bands may have averaged one to every hundred square miles. It has always been a difficult area with which to deal. Twice it has been divided. In 1891 its northwest part was erected into the Diocese of Yukon (Selkirk originally was the name) and in 1933 its northern portion was absorbed into the new Diocese of The Arctic. The large central portion has been a problem amongst the dioceses of the Church. Without a bishop from 1907 to 1913 and 1926 to 1929, it never really was adequately endowed and suffered a staggering blow from the loss of the Church's funds in 1932. The detailed story of this Diocese is something of a tragedy in ecclesiastical history. Yet there are many bright spots, though names once well known are fading in the twilight of time.

Pioneer Clergy

Rampart House is on the Porcupine River at the boundary of Alaska, about three hundred miles west of Fort McPherson, and to this post in 1881 came the Reverend V. C. Sim, a young man of great earnestness who worked unceasingly for four years among the Tukudh Indians.

[10]The northern boundary of the Diocese of Athabasca was defined by the Provincial Synod of Rupert's Land in 1883 as "the sixtieth parallel of latitude from the western boundary of the present Diocese of Athabasca up to the one hundredth and eighteenth meridian of longitude; then along it northerly to the sixty-third parallel of latitude; then easterly along this parallel of latitude to the eastern boundary of the present Diocese." (*Journal of the Provincial Synod of Rupert's Land, 1883*, p. 14.) However, except for the period 1933-1947, when the Deanery of Mackenzie River was incorporated in Athabasca, the northern boundary of the Diocese of Athabasca was 60° latitude.

In the fall of 1884 at a point on the Porcupine River, he was met with active opposition by the local medicine man who made the nights hideous with his noise so that Mr. Sim could not sleep. Returning to Rampart House he had a hard winter nursing sick Indians. In the spring his health gave way. The Reverend T. H. Canham was brought from Peel River, and gave what help he could. Sim was eagerly looking for the annual mail, so Canham made the return trip to Peel River (over 450 miles) to get it; but when he arrived back the sick man was too weak to hear his letters read, and he died on May 11, 1885.

Among the late Archdeacon Tims' (of Calgary) papers was found a faded newspaper clipping recording the death of the Reverend William Spendlove on June 22, 1931. Mr. Spendlove was ordained by Bishop Bompas in 1881, priested in 1883, and in charge of Fort Simpson from 1881 to 1887. In 1888 he went to Fort Rae, where he stayed until 1895. From 1899 to 1905 he was at Fort Norman. Upon his return to England he became rector of Drayton in the Diocese of Oxford, and during his ministry there was a great awakening of interest in that district of missionary work overseas. The year he came to Canada Spendlove married Rose Gadsby, who so endeared herself to the natives that she was known to them as "the woman with the big good heart." She died at Banbury in 1911.

Bishop Bompas held a Synod of the Diocese of Mackenzie River at Fort Simpson in August, 1886, at which steps were taken to organize a school for Indian children, and toward further division of the diocese. On August 29 he ordained John W. Ellington and David N. Kirkby to the diaconate. Mr. Ellington was sent to the junction of the Porcupine River and Forty Mile Creek in the Dawson district of the Yukon. Mining was being done here even in the eighties, though the Klondike rush was not to come for ten years. At Forty Mile, Ellington laboured earnestly, but the miners played so many pranks upon him, and made his life such a burden, that mind and body both gave way and he had to be taken back to England, where he died in 1892. David N. Kirkby was born at Fort Simpson, where his father, the Reverend W. W. Kirkby, had been first missionary in 1859.

Fort Rae in 1886

The lot of the missionary is always harder than that of the trader or explorer, for he has to contend with more difficult situations with less resources to fall back on, yet is expected to show greater courage, kindness and generosity. Still harder has been the lot of the missionary's wife, who in the majority of cases seems to have come to a primitive, isolated log shack straight from England, to spend months at a time without any contacts with the outside world.

One of the prized possessions of the writer is a copy of Humphry's work on the *Book of Common Prayer*, which bears on its fly-leaf the inscription: "W. Jno. Garton, C.M.S., 1881." In that year Mr. Garton graduated from the Islington Training College and proceeded to Fort Rae, now not far from Yellowknife, where he spent two years as a lay worker before being ordained in 1883. Here in 1876 the Reverend W. D. Reeve and his wife had opened a boarding school for Indian children in a log shack fourteen feet square. Garton had planned to return to England in 1885 to be married, but Bishop Bompas persuaded him otherwise and arranged for the bride to come out. She arrived in Winnipeg in May, 1885, to find the Northwest Rebellion in full progress; it also delayed the arrival of the bridegroom, who had difficulty in getting out of the north. Nevertheless, the wedding took place in old St. Andrew's on September second. Garton then took charge of the parish of Gladstone, Manitoba, until things settled down. On April 20, 1886, the Gartons, after going by C.P.R. to Calgary, spent two weeks getting from there to Edmonton, and another week in reaching Athabasca Landing. The river trip to Fort Resolution was exciting. It took them seven days to row across Great Slave Lake to Fort Rae, with some assistance from a blanket used as a sail. Mrs. Garton recalled that "it rained for three days. My husband had tried to build a house ready for me, but he had very poor materials. The roof leaked everywhere. I spent that first night under an umbrella. The next night we put up the tent—yes, in the house." Owing to the rebellion supplies did not get through. Mr. Garton got the Indians to make and put out nets, three thousand whitefish were caught. That winter they ate fish "straight" and drank tea "straight," without milk or sugar.

Missionary Life

Mrs. Garton has given a vivid picture of the life at this outpost.

My missionary was an itinerant and supposed to travel around the lake to Providence, Hay River, Resolution and anywhere else he could, but that year he could not go. There was no dried meat for food for man or boy, and the dogs' food inadequate. The Company absolutely refused to outfit him as usual. So he had to stay home. There was school to keep later on . . . he had to spend the morning cutting and hauling the half-cord of wood we burnt each day, and some of the afternoon cutting it up and doing some of the other chores. I kept morning school by the light of the open fire. . . . Candles were scarce. . . . We had taken some in, and we had a few John had made. . . . One day I begged him to let me have one or two to fry some fish for a change. I was so tired of baked fish morning and evening, and boiled midday. . . . Our house was very cold . . . we had to sleep with the blanket over our heads. . . . But it was not all gloomy and sad. We were young and healthy, and in many ways comfortable and thankful. We enjoyed our flourishing school, and we had a little portable organ. . . . The next year we moved to Fort Simpson, where it seemed like Heaven.

1886 was a bad year for everybody owing to the scarcity of meat; even dinner at Synod at Fort Simpson one day consisted only of barley and a few potatoes.

First Synod of Mackenzie River

The first Synod of the Diocese of Mackenzie River, which met at Fort Simpson in August, 1886, passed motions pressing the Church Missionary Society to send more men, and urging a further division of the diocese upon the Provincial Synod of Rupert's Land. In 1887 it sent the Reverend W. Spendlove to support the case. The Society responded that year by sending John Hawksley to open up new work farther up the Liard River, where Bishop Bompas spent some time with him. The Bishop was alone again as Mrs. Bompas had gone to England. The Indians all missed her and asked continually about her return. "I tell the Indians and everyone else that I sent you home against your will," the Bishop wrote to her; "I told them yesterday that Christ died for them long ago, and that was enough. There was no occasion for you to die for them as well, however willing you might be."

With the removal of Mr. Ellington the Indians were without a teacher along the Yukon. The Bishop longed to go there, so urged the Church Missionary Society either to accept his resignation or relieve him of half of the diocese so that he might go to the Yukon country himself. He had no inclination to leave the country; he wrote, "I find the needle points west rather than east, and north rather than south." He was urged to return to England for a time but felt that "he had been so long dead and buried that a short visit, as if from the grave, would not be of much use."

Fort Norman in 1890

The winter of 1890 found Bishop Bompas living by himself in the church at Fort Norman. Work was begun there in 1866 when he had stayed for nearly a year. It was rather a grim point, subject to wild storms or dead calms of intense cold, shut in by dense forests and difficult mountains. Yet the Bishop was perfectly happy: he said, "It is only this winter that I find life worth living and I think God has paid me handsomely for twenty-five years' mission service in

Mackenzie River." He was a very self-contained man, and had lived so much alone in tent or cabin that he had learned to be wholly independent of external aid. His wants were simple. An iron cup, plate and knife with one or two kettles were his culinary equipment. A hole in the snow, a corner in a boat, wigwam or log hut, provided space six feet by two feet for sleeping accommodation. "Imagine him," wrote the Reverend W. Spendlove from the same Fort Norman nearly ten years later, "seated on a box in a twelve foot room without furniture, and there cooking, teaching, studying, early and late, always at work never at ease, never known to take a holiday."

In August, 1891, Bishop Bompas packed up and left for the further northwest. His successor to the Diocese of Mackenzie River had been chosen, and he passed over the Rocky Mountains to undertake the oversight of the Diocese, at first called Selkirk, but now known as Yukon.

Bishop William Day Reeve[11]

At the time of his appointment as Bishop of Mackenzie River, William Day Reeve had already had more than twenty years experience as a missionary in the Diocese. He was born in 1844 at Harmton in Lincolnshire, England, where he was educated, and spent two years at farm work, followed by a period of business training. Experiencing a call to be a missionary, he offered himself to the Church Missionary Society and was sent to its Islington College for training, but he was still in his junior theological year when, on the recommendation of the Reverend W. W. Kirkby, he was approved for service in the Diocese of Athabasca. He had barely a month to secure a year's supplies, get married and procure the necessary outfit for himself and his bride. The Reeves sailed for New York four days after their wedding in April, 1869, and reached Winnipeg by way of St. Cloud and the prairie trails. He was ordained deacon on June 6 by Bishop Machray. Then came the three months' journey by canoe to Fort Simpson; for ten years this post was to be the centre of his work.

In 1879 Reeve moved to Fort Chipewyan, and a year later took a furlough in England, during which he saw through the press Bishop Bompas' translation of the Gospels into Tenni or Slavi for the Mackenzie Indians. In 1883 he was made Archdeacon, but a year later found himself separated from his old associates by the division

[11]The Provincial Synod of Rupert's Land in 1890 formally agreed to the division of the Diocese of Mackenzie River, the new Diocese to be west of the Rocky Mountains. Bishop Reeve was appointed jointly by the Archbishop of Canterbury and the Church Missionary Society. (*Journal of the Provincial Synod of Rupert's Land, 1893*, pp. 22-24.) C. H. Mockridge, *The Bishops of the Church of England in Canada and Newfoundland*, 364-368. O. R. Rowley, *The Anglican Episcopate of Canada and Newfoundland*, 98-99.

of the Diocese.[12] In 1889 he again returned to England and guided more translations by Bishop Bompas and Archdeacon McDonald through the press. Ever since 1885 Bishop Bompas had urged Archdeacon Reeve to allow himself to be appointed Bishop, but he did not consent until 1891. He was consecrated in Holy Trinity Church, Winnipeg, November 29, by Bishop Machray, Metropolitan. Bishop Reeve made Fort Simpson his "See City" and commenced his work with a staff of seven.

Diocese of Selkirk

With the arrangements for the division of the Mackenzie River Diocese completed, Bishop Bompas withdrew himself to Forty Mile on the Yukon River at the end of August, 1891, but later moved on and spent the winter at the most remote of his mission stations, Rampart House. The year 1892 saw the return of Mrs. Bompas, who had been in England since 1887 owing to ill health. In the same party were the Reverend T. H. (later Archdeacon) and Mrs. Canham, the Reverend G. C. and Mrs. Wallis, and Mr. B. Totty. The Bishop stationed the Canhams at Selkirk, where the Lewes joins the Pelly River; Mr. and Mrs. Wallis at Rampart House; and Mr. Totty at Forty Mile. Unfortunately, Mrs. Wallis' health necessitated their returning to England within a year. The Canhams remained in the Diocese until 1924, and Mr. Totty (afterwards Canon) was destined to give his life's work to the Yukon.

The Klondike Gold Rush

Gold was found in the Yukon River valley by Archdeacon Robert McDonald in 1863, but the discovery did not attract attention until the early nineties when miners, experienced in the United States, worked their way through British Columbia and Alaska, settling at the junction of Forty Mile Creek and the Yukon River. Bishop Bompas did what he could for them and they greatly respected him, but he found this "white" work quite a problem. It became a much bigger one after the discovery of gold in the Klondike. All sorts and conditions of men made their way to the Yukon by every route, the most famous being that over the Whitehorse Pass, the "Trail of 98." In due time, however, the Bishop's problem was solved. On August 4, 1895, R. J. Bowen arrived at Forty Mile. Mr. Bowen relates that when he landed at Forty Mile, Bishop Bompas greeted him and

[12]Reeve continued the duties of Archdeacon of Chipewyan, for Bishop Young appears to have maintained him in this appointment in the continuing Diocese of Athabasca. He is listed as "Archdeacon Reeve, a delegate from Athabasca" in the *Journal of the Provincial Synod of Rupert's Land* in 1887.

then added: "This steamer is late and as soon as our outfits are landed on the bank of the river opposite the mission house, I am going to Selkirk to visit the most southerly point now being occupied in the Diocese."[13] So for ten days Bowen found himself in full charge of the Indian Mission at Forty Mile, without knowing a word of the people's language.

In the spring of 1896 there was a general stampede to a new find of gold at Circle City, Alaska, and Bowen was "loaned" by Bishop Bompas to Bishop Rowe of Alaska to follow the missing congregation as best he could to its new location. He was recalled in 1897, however, to begin work at Dawson City, where he built a small log church at the north end of the old police reserve and near the site of the present St. Paul's Church. The first services were held there on October 4, 1897.

In 1896 the Reverend H. A. and Mrs. Naylor and F. F. Flewelling arrived. Previously, in 1893, Miss Mellet, who had come out from Ireland and was the first unmarried white woman to enter the Diocese, said that the Bishop met her at St. Michael and must have been disappointed when only one meek little person arrived; he had been expecting several recruits. "He held Services, baptized children, taught the people, listened patiently to their talk and evidently advised them as to health and other matters. He seemed able to understand their dialect, as he knew their chief language, for they always looked happy, smiled and nodded their agreement with him."

Development of Schools

The influx of miners brought a growing number of half-breed children and presented Bishop Bompas with a problem that gave him great anxiety. To solve it he opened his home to eleven Indian and half-breed children and thus organized the first residential school in the Yukon. Miss Mellet became the teacher of this school, and she noted: "The school at Forty Mile was a great mixture, all sorts and sizes and ages came to learn to read—men, women and children. . . . We had nothing in the way of equipment . . . no pictures, no maps, no globes, but the people themselves were so willing to help and be helped. It was their first school and they loved it."[14]

In addition to her teaching Miss Mellet did some very practical nursing, undoubtedly saving the life of Bishop Bompas on one occasion when he was very ill. She became the wife of the Reverend R. J. Bowen, and her services to the pioneer community were outstanding.

[13]Reminiscences of Rev. R. J. Bowen, *Northern Lights*, XXX (August, 1941), 2-5. (This was the quarterly journal of the Diocese of Yukon.)
[14]Reminiscences of Mrs. R. J. Bowen, *op. cit.*, 6.

Later, the Indian school work was transferred by the Bishop to Cariboo Crossing (now known as Carcross) at the southern end of the Diocese. Hostels were subsequently provided in Dawson City for boys and girls to enable them to continue their education at the public school there.

Expansion to the South Yukon

Illness was a constant problem, as the Reverend R. J. Bowen recorded: With so many people congregated, without any care for sanitation, disease and sickness developed very rapidly. . . . I contracted Typhoid Malarial Fever in May, 1899, which forced my removal, broken in health. Mrs. Bowen accompanied me on furlough to England, where, after recovery, deputation work was undertaken for the Colonial and Continental Church Society. . . . While in England I received a letter from Bishop Bompas, to the effect that development was taking place in the southern end of the diocese and that Whitehorse, only 110 miles from the coast, would probably suit me, as I was forbidden to return to Dawson. I accepted the mission at Whitehorse. August 1st, 1900, I was again pioneering. The first services held in Whitehorse were in a small tent. . . . October saw the Church built. The chancel was partitioned off and we lived in it during the winter. . . . The work at Whitehorse was like all places I had occupied both mechanical, educational and ministerial. In addition to parochial work there was the work of holding services in the railway camps of the White Pass and Yukon Railway. In May 1903 I was forced to leave the Yukon for good on account of another severe illness.

The Venerable H. A. Cody, the biographer of Bishop Bompas, writes:

In response to an appeal made in 1904 by the Rev. I. O. Stringer, rector of Christ Church, Whitehorse, I went to the Yukon as travelling missionary. Bishop Bompas, who was living at Caribou Crossing, which he later named Carcross, needed a man to visit the new mining district at Alsek and other places in southern Yukon. That year I travelled by pack-horse over the trail to the Alsek region, and in the fall by canoe, the "Skookum" from Caribou Crossing to McClintick, Tagish, etc., with an Indian, Billy Johnson. During the winter and spring of 1905 visits were made by dog-team with Capt. Jimmy Jackson as guide along the Dawson trail to Tantalus, then up the Yukon to Little and Big Salmon, Hootalinqua, Livingstone Creek, and other places. That spring we went to Champagne Landing, and from there into Dalton Post.[15]

The death of Archbishop Machray on March 9, 1904, made Bishop Bompas the senior Bishop of the Province. At the call of duty he hurried to Winnipeg, which he reached on April 3, to preside over a meeting of the Provincial House of Bishops. Nearly thirty years had lapsed since he was last there. Advantage of his presence was taken

[15]Reminiscences of Archdeacon H. A. Cody, *Northern Lights*, XXX (August, 1941), 8-9.

to hold a big missionary rally in the city, and the late Archbishop Matheson commented upon the life of hardship and adventure to which the Bishop had been exposed. Bishop Bompas replied: "It is you men at the centre, with your telephones and your telegrams, who have the hardships. We have a soft time in the north, nobody ever worries us." The fact is that he delighted in the simple life and had little regard for outward things. He seldom wore his episcopal robes, being quite content with an old-fashioned surplice and black stole, but he had a very high regard for the episcopal office, and used to be quite annoyed when the Epiphany Appeals were sent direct to his clergy by the Mission Board in Toronto. "No Bishop has any other authority than over his own See, and all requests should come through the Bishop." After his retirement he continued to live at Carcross, where the Church of St. Saviour's had been built in 1904 through the assistance of the Toronto Woman's Auxiliary. His quiet life, spent largely among his books and with the Indian children, came suddenly to an end on June 9, 1906, and he was buried in the Indian cemetery.

The Reverend Isaac O. Stringer

The story of the Reverend Isaac O. Stringer is an epic on its own. The circumstances of his call to the mission field under Bishop Reeve, the years that he and Mrs. Stringer spent on Herschel Island with the Eskimos and American whalers, and their labours in reducing the native language to writing have often been told, but belong rather to the story of the Diocese of Mackenzie River in which he spent the earlier years of his ministry. While on a long furlough in 1902, Mr. Stringer was warned that he had developed eye trouble and must not return to the Arctic. At the invitation of Bishop Bompas he left the Diocese of Mackenzie River and succeeded the Reverend R. J. Bowen at Whitehorse. Here his outstanding qualities became so apparent that when Bishop Bompas, feeling the burdens of age and infirmity, decided he must retire, the Bishops and Electoral Committee of the Province of Rupert's Land elected Mr. Stringer to succeed him on November 15, 1905. He was consecrated on December 17, in St. John's Cathedral, Winnipeg, by Archbishop Matheson of Rupert's Land.[16]

The Bishop Who Ate His Boots

Bishop Stringer set himself the task of laying the foundation of an organized diocese, and so held a Synod at Whitehorse, September 10, 1907; four clergy and three laymen attended. Archdeacon Cody claims that nine were present at this Synod and names them as being the

[16]O. R. Rowley, *op. cit.*, 144-145.

Bishop, the Reverends A. E. O'Meara, J. Hawksley, J. M. Comyn-Ching, and himself, with Major Snyder, Isaac Taylor, F. R. Peele and W. D. Young. Dawson was chosen as the "See City" and became the home of Bishop and Mrs. Stringer until 1931. Much of the Bishop's time was spent in raising funds for the operation of the diocese and its endowment, and while Bishop Stringer was not an orator, Bishop Sovereign has written: "He held congregations and audiences by his manifest sincerity, his enthusiasm and devotion." The description the Bishop loved to give of himself was one by an English reporter: "The Bishop of the Snows stood beside the big centre table in a London drawing-room, with the forehead of a Doctor of Divinity, the physique and jaw of a prize-fighter and mild blue eyes of a child."

Bishop Stringer was equally active in the Diocese itself, and the danger and hardships of his journeys have become almost legendary. The event that caused him to be known as "the Bishop who ate his boots" took place in the autumn of 1909, when, having visited the Eskimos on the Arctic coast with Archdeacon Whittaker, he tried to return to Dawson by a shortcut over the Rockies from Peel River, in company with C. F. Johnston. Unfortunately the weather broke, food ran short, game customarily found had already migrated, the trail was uncertain. The Bishop's diary records: *"Thursday, October 21st: Breakfast off sealskin boot, soles and tops boiled and toasted. Soles better than tops."* Shortly after children's voices were heard and houses seen. "We stopped and thanked God for bringing us in sight of human habitation."

Upon the resignation of Archbishop Matheson, Bishop Stringer was elected Metropolitan of Rupert's Land on April 15, 1931, and enthroned in St. John's Cathedral, Winnipeg, on September first.

A Helpful Helper

Lay workers in the northern missions of the Church have come and gone, their time often short, their service seldom recorded or even remembered. Archdeacon C. E. Whittaker, of the Diocese of Mackenzie River, has left us an admirable account of one such servant of God[17]:

When Mr. Stringer came north after his first furlough and brought his wife with him, they were accompanied by Mr. W. D. Young, the bride's maternal uncle. . . . Mr. Young had been a farmer and was a general handyman, being equally at ease in duties indoors or out, and there are many duties about a self-helpful mission. After one year at McPherson, Bishop Reeve sent the Stringers to Herschel and Mr. Young continued with them during the four years of their residence

[17]C. E. Whittaker, "A Helpful Helper," *Canadian Churchman* (July 7, 1938).

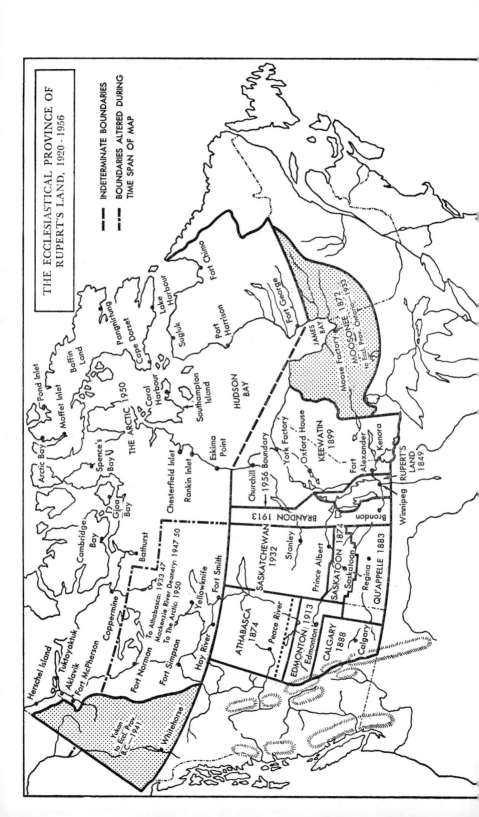

THE ECCLESIASTICAL PROVINCE OF RUPERT'S LAND, 1920 - 1956

▬ ▪ ▬ INDETERMINATE BOUNDARIES
▬ ▪ ▪ BOUNDARIES ALTERED DURING
      TIME SPAN OF MAP

Herschel Island
Tuktoyaktuk
Aklavik
Fort McPherson
Coppermine
Cambridge Bay
Gjoa Bay
Spence's Bay
Baffin Land
Moffet Inlet
Pond Inlet
Arctic Bay
Bathurst
Panghirung
Cape Dorset
Coral Harbour
THE ARCTIC 1950
Lake Harbour
Fort Chimo
Port Harrison
Sugluk
Southampton Island
Chesterfield Inlet
Rankin Inlet
Eskimo Point
HUDSON BAY
Fort George
JAMES BAY
MOOSONEE 1872 - 1933
(to Eccl. Prov. Ontario)
Moose Factory
York Factory
Oxford House
KEEWATIN 1899
Fort Alexander
Kenora
RUPERT'S LAND 1849
Winnipeg
Brandon
BRANDON 1913
Churchill
1956 Boundary
SASKATCHEWAN 1932
Stanley
Prince Albert
SASKATOON 1874
Saskatoon
Regina
QU'APPELLE 1883
Calgary
CALGARY 1888
EDMONTON 1913
Edmonton
Peace River
ATHABASCA 1874
To Athabasca: 1933 47
Mackenzie River Deanery: 1947 50
To The Arctic: 1950
Yellowknife
Fort Smith
Hay River
Fort Simpson
Fort Norman
Whitehorse
to Yukon, Eccl. Prov. B.C. — 1941

there. . . . His work was varied. Care of the dogs and their feed, securing wood for fuel, managing trade with the natives, when trading ships were absent. Travelling into the mountains for fresh meat, attending fish nets in summer, cutting and hauling ice for the water supply in winter.

In 1905, Mr. Stringer succeded Bishop Bompas as Bishop of Selkirk, and soon called Mr. Young to his aid again. There he served in Dawson, Moosehide, and Carcross, or wherever he could fill a need. In 1909, Mr. Henry Fry, my helper in Mackenzie Delta, had need of someone to erect mission buildings at Kitigazuit, and Mr. Young was sent to him from Dawson, travelling about a thousand miles. He remained for five years, often in charge of a station, exerting a steadying influence on the natives and a very effective helpfulness to the young missionaries with whom he lived. . . . After the Armistice, when Bishop Stringer returned from overseas, he brought a new recruit for the Eskimo work. Rev. W. A. Geddes to begin a new mission at Shingle Point. Mr. Young was chosen to accompany and assist him. They crossed the mountains in 1920 on a toilsome journey of several weeks and on reaching their destination, gathered drift logs, which they hewed on one side, and built a residence and a small church, which buildings have been the base of our work there, including the Eskimo School, until the new residential school was built at Aklavik. . . . For loyalty, hard commonsense, wise dealing with both Indians and Eskimo, cheerful disposition, steadfast faith, . . . no other lay helper in the northern work can compare with him.

The Ecclesiastical Province of Rupert's Land, 1920-1956. The Provincial Synod of Rupert's Land, on September 13, 1933, agreed to transfer the Yukon and Moosonee Dioceses to other Provinces with which it felt they had closer and more natural associations. The Synod authorized changes in other diocesan boundaries to erect the new Diocese of Saskatchewan, and adjust the boundary between Saskatoon and Qu'Appelle. The map indicates the result of changes from 1920 to 1956. It also shows mission stations of the enlarged Diocese of The Arctic.

Adjustments in Boundaries: 1920-1956

Edmonton and Saskatchewan: *Journal of the Provincial Synod of Rupert's Land,* [hereafter *J*], *1926,* pp. 46-47.

Saskatchewan and Athabasca: *J, 1926,* p. 46.

Saskatoon and Saskatchewan: *J, 1933,* p. 107, section B5.

Saskatoon and Qu'Appelle: *J, 1933,* pp. 107-108, section B6.

Saskatchewan and Brandon: *J, 1933,* p. 107, section B5, part 1.

Yukon to British Columbia: *J, 1933,* p. 107, section A1.

Moosonee to Ontario: *J, 1933,* p. 107, section A2.

Boundaries of The Arctic: *J, 1933,* pp. 42-43.

Mackenzie River (South) and Athabasca: *J, 1933,* p. 33, Message "*T*".

Mackenzie River Deanery separated from Athabasca: *J, 1947,* p. 32.

Mackenzie River Deanery to The Arctic: *J, 1950,* p. 32.

Keewatin and Brandon: *J, 1956,* pp. 64-65.

Synods of the Diocese of Yukon

Synod journals are valuable because they provide reliable contemporary evidence of decisions and policy; the Bishop's Charges reflect the trend of events and opinion as well as his own considered outlook. Synods of the Diocese of Yukon never seem to have been hurried; they were more in the nature of "missionary conferences."

Bishop Stringer's first Charge in 1907 dealt specifically with the position of the native people in the Yukon, which at the time was quite undetermined in law. He urged that the government should make treaties with the Indians, or otherwise compensate them for the invasion of the natural resources of the country by the white man; their natural right to hunt should be established, their trapping and fishing rights preserved; selected lands should be reserved for the headquarters of the tribes and good titles to such properties assured to them; they should be assisted in building proper houses; medicine and medical attendance should be provided for them. With these principles the members were in cordial agreement.

At the second Synod (1911) discussion ranged about amendment to the Dominion Land Titles Act, which it was considered did not give sufficient protection to the natives. Education also came up for review, and though its importance was realized it was pointed out that it was not yet a government concern. That the Church was intensely interested in the economic welfare of the Indian was shown by the decision to petition the government to introduce reindeer into the country as compensation for the decrease in deer. The first Synod had been held at Whitehorse, but it was then decided to make Dawson city the "See City" of the Diocese and all subsequent Synods were held there. The diminishing importance of Dawson after World War II caused the "See City" to be changed back again to Whitehorse during the episcopate of Archbishop Adams (1947-1952).

Little of historic importance emerged from the Synod of 1915, except the fact that the Reverend J. Hawksley[18] had been appointed as the first Government Indian Agent in the Yukon, but at the Synod of 1920 it was announced that the endowment of the Diocese had been completed, and that the government was now supporting the Indian day schools. In 1923 Bishop Stringer made a touching reference to the death of the Reverend Amos Njootla, whom he had ordained in

[18]John Hawksley went to the Mackenzie River Diocese in 1887, and was stationed at the Liard River. Ordained deacon in 1891, priest in 1894, he served at Fort Norman, Fort Yukon, Moosehide, Carcross, Selkirk (Y.T.), and as general missionary at Dawson City. In 1914 he was appointed as first Government Indian Agent in the Yukon Territory. He had the reputation of being second only to Robert McDonald as a Tukudh or Loucheux language expert.

1911, and who had spent his ministry at Rampart House; his wife was a daughter of the Reverend John Ttssiettla, the first Loucheux Indian admitted to Holy Orders (by Bishop Reeve of Mackenzie River in 1893), of whom little is known except that he spent his ministry at Peel River. It was also announced at this Synod that the M.S.C.C. had taken over full responsibility for the Choutla School at Carcross. A Hostel had been opened at Dawson City on September 21, 1920, under the superintendency of Miss E. J. Naftel, once head of the Deaconess Home in Toronto, and for five years on the staff of the Choutla School. This system proved so successful that it was later extended widely over the northern territories.

Much of the Bishop's Charge to the 1928 Synod was devoted to new opportunities in the mission field made possible by the consolidation of Eskimo work under Archdeacon Fleming. He appealed for the avoidance of sectionalism, apparently of a geographical nature, as he warned against the development of an eastern and a western point of view, and called for unity in outlook and endeavour in the work of the Arctic. Bishop Stringer met the Synod of the Diocese of Yukon for the last time at its seventh meeting, July fifth, 1931, two months after he had been elected Metropolitan of the Province. The staff of the Diocese, during his twenty-five years, from its original size of five clergy, two lay catechists, three lay readers and three women workers, had been expanded to fifteen clergy, three native catechists and thirteen women workers, all but one of the latter being engaged in work at the Choutla and Shingle Point Schools, or St. Paul's Hostel at Dawson City. The Diocese parted from Bishop and Mrs. Stringer and their family with mingled feelings of pride and regret, for Mrs. Stringer's unselfish service had won her great affection among the people, and their sons had done service as lay readers. Within the Diocese the Bishop had done much to carry out the ideal of the Church Missionary Society of a native ministry, and in addition to men already mentioned he had ordained the Reverends Julius Kendi in 1918 (for the Mayo mission), Richard Martin in 1926 (for Peel River), Thomas Umaok in 1927, and added John Martin (Mackenzie River, 1924) to the diocesan staff for Ross River.

Old Crow Reserve

The Old Crow Indian village lies about fifty miles east of Rampart House. The people who lived there were originally called the Rat Lake tribe, and among these people both Robert McDonald and Bishop Bompas did early work. One of their first converts was John Tizya, who learned to read the Bible, Prayer Book and hymn book in the Tukudh language, and then taught the boys and girls around him to read their own language. His teaching was done in skin houses by open firelight, and at the end of forty years of this work he became blind. After John Tizya saw log cabins for the first time he decided to build one for himself at the mouth of the Crow River. Thus he laid the foundations of the settlement where the people live today. Writing for the M.S.C.C. *Quarterly Bulletin* of March, 1948, Mrs. Clara Tizya, a daughter-in-law, reported: "Here John Tizya used his own cabin for Church and called the people to Service by beating a frying-pan with a stick. He used up a good many frying-pans before he was given a bell by Bishop Stringer. Later the people built their own Church, mission house and small schoolhouse. When John died, he was laid to rest by the people he loved and whom he had tried to show how to be good Christians."

Later, in Bishop Geddes' time, the Reverend Julius Kendi, a native priest, and Mrs. Kendi were sent to Old Crow from Mayo, where they had spent ten years among the white people. "Mrs. Kendi organized the first W.A. branch in the village. Every woman and girl took part in the work and in two years, through their efforts, the Church had been completely decorated, new pews and stoves bought and many pretty beaded frontals made for the altar." It was from this small village of generous-minded and devoted Christian people that the first contribution to the Restoration Fund was received in 1933, according to Bishop Sovereign's Charge to the Synod of the Diocese in Athabasca in 1936. (He was Bishop of the Yukon in 1932.) They also sent, early in the Second World War, a gift of $393 for the relief of homeless and orphaned children in England.

Yukon—Since 1932

Bishop Stringer's successor, the Right Reverend A. H. Sovereign, only had brief tenure of the Diocese.[19] The financial disaster to the Church in 1932 caused rearrangements to be made in the Missionary Dioceses of the north, and he was translated to the Diocese of Athabasca in September of that year. Bishop Geddes of Mackenzie River was given the oversight of the Yukon. The consecration of the Venerable A. L. Fleming on December 21, 1933, as the first Bishop of The Arctic caused further changes: the northern half of the Diocese of Mackenzie River became part of the Diocese of The Arctic; the southern part was placed under the jurisdiction of the Bishop of Athabasca. Subsequent to the Provincial Synod of 1939, when the matter

[19]A. R. Kelley and D. B. Rogers, *The Anglican Episcopate of Canada and Newfoundland, II* (Toronto, 1961), 32-34.

was left in the hands of the Metropolitan, the Diocese of The Yukon became part of the Province of British Columbia, and thus was ended almost eighty years of direct connection with the Red River.[20]

The Diocese of Mackenzie River from 1891

It is now necessary to return to that part of the Diocese of Mackenzie River which retained that name, and to trace its story through the episcopates of its three Bishops, William Day Reeve, 1891-1907; James Richard Lucas, 1913-1926; William Archibald Geddes, 1929-1933. Between the episcopates of Bishop Reeve and Bishop Lucas, the northern and larger part of the Diocese was placed under the supervision of Bishop Stringer of the Yukon, and the southern part under Bishop Holmes of Athabasca. From 1933 to 1947 the part of the Diocese south of the Arctic Circle was added to the Diocese of Athabasca, the part to the north becoming part of the newly-formed Diocese of The Arctic. In 1947 the Provincial Synod of Rupert's Land designated this part of Athabasca as the Mackenzie River Deanery, and asked the Metropolitan to supervise the work with a view to discovering the best method of dealing with the district. The Provincial Synod of 1950 added the whole of it to the Diocese of The Arctic.

Bishop Reeve, upon his return to the Mackenzie River in the summer of 1892, located himself at Fort Simpson as the most suitable place for his centre of work. Before returning to the north, however, Bishop Reeve visited eastern Canada in order to stimulate fresh interest in the Diocese, and while there was fortunate in finding two young men who, each in his own field, were to give outstanding service in spreading the Gospel. The best known of them was Isaac O. Stringer, part of whose subsequent career has already been traced in connection with the Diocese of Yukon. The other was the Reverend Thomas Jabez Marsh who founded and carried on the mission station at Hay River on the south side of Great Slave Lake from 1893 to 1907. Both these missionaries were supported largely by funds raised in Ontario.

Mr. Stringer was ordained by Bishop Reeve in the Church of the Redeemer in Toronto on May 15, 1892, and the next day set out with him on the long journey to the north, which did not end until July 14 when they reached Fort McPherson. The Bishop then decided that it would be best for Stringer to proceed to the coast at once, so he went on his way and reached the first Eskimo village on August

[20]The Diocese of Yukon was formally transferred to the Province of British Columbia by letter from Archbishop Harding (Metropolitan of Rupert's Land), dated December 8, 1941. The Province of British Columbia had, on November 16, passed a Canon providing for election of Bishops of The Yukon by the Executive Committee of the Province. [*Acts of the Bishops of Rupert's Land* (Winnipeg, Diocesan Registrar's Office), 40.]

fourth, where he was cordially and hospitably received by the natives.[21] During the winter the missionary made his way to La Pierre's House, westward over the divide, then northward to Herschel Island, returning in the summer of 1894 to Fort McPherson where Bishop Reeve ordained him priest on July fifteenth in St. Matthew's Church.

In 1895 Bishop Reeve brought with him to Fort McPherson Charles Edward Whittaker, whom he ordained the following year, and who was later to become Archdeacon. Whittaker and the Bishop accompanied Stringer to Herschel Island that summer and Whittaker remained there. Stringer left Herschel Island to go on furlough to eastern Canada, the first stage of the journey being made by American whaling ship to San Francisco. While home on furlough he was married on March tenth, 1896, to Sadie Alexander. They settled on Herschel Island, and it was 1901 before they saw eastern Canada again. During these five years the Stringers acquired the language of the Eskimo, committed it to writing, and translated parts of the New Testament, Prayer Book, and some hymns. Their home was a centre of Christian influence for the two or three hundred sailors who customarily wintered on the island; both services and school were provided for them. Mrs. Stringer, in addition to her family cares, did much nursing among both the sailors and the natives. In 1901 the Stringers went on furlough, but in Ontario Mr. Stringer was told that the condition of his eyes would not permit him to return to the Arctic. As a consequence he accepted the invitation of Bishop Bompas to go to Whitehorse, and thus began his service to God in the Diocese of Yukon, which was to extend over twenty-nine years, as related elsewhere in this book.

The Hay River Mission

The Reverend Thomas Jabez Marsh[22] also went north in the summer of 1892 and was stationed at Fort Liard. After spending a year there, it was decided that he should move farther south, and a new location was chosen near the mouth of the Hay River on the southern shore of Great Slave Lake. An Indian encampment was already there. Marsh went to work with such energy that by June, 1894, a large mission house was practically completed; it became a boarding school for forty children. About ten years later a church was added and eventually a hospital. This mission station had contacts with seven distinct Indian tribes: the Chipewyans, Slaves, Dog Ribs, Yellow Knifes, Beavers, Mountain Indians and Tukudhs, whose languages seemed to be derived from a common source. Miss Anna B. Marsh joined her

[21]A. H. Sovereign, "Archbishop I. O. Stringer," in W. B. Heeney, ed., *Leaders of the Canadian Church*, Third Series (Toronto, 1943).
[22]*The New Era* (February, 1903).

brother in the autumn of 1895, the first of a considerable number of faithful women who served this mission. The school at Fort Resolution was closed in the same year and the children transferred to Hay River. Mr. Marsh remained at Hay River until 1907 when he went to the Diocese of Caledonia. He was succeeded by the Reverend Alfred James Vale, who remained at this post for some years[23], and the work progressed in a very encouraging way. By 1920 there were more than fifty Indian and Eskimo children being trained at this school, and the hospital was proving increasingly useful. This latter work had been begun as far back as 1895 when young Dr. Henry LeRoy Reazin went there from Toronto to assist Marsh. Like Stringer, Marsh and Whittaker, Dr. Reazin was supported by the Canadian Church Missionary Society. This Society was a development of the "Wycliffe Missions," an association of alumni of Wycliffe College, Toronto.

About 1920 Miss Neville went there as matron and nurse. She was still there in 1941 when Archbishop Harding of Rupert's Land made a pastoral visit to the missions of the Mackenzie River, but at that time the school had been abandoned and its work transferred to Aklavik in the Mackenzie River delta, though a day school was still in operation under the Reverend S. E. Richards, whom the Archbishop described as "school teacher, postmaster, lamplighter of two lighthouses, government weather recorder and missionary." Archdeacon Marsh passed by two years later on his way to Aklavik, and in a brief tribute to Miss Neville in *The Canadian Churchman* voiced his regret that no other missionaries were at this post, as the work was much in excess of what one woman could be expected to do alone. The hospital only had eight beds, but at times it was hard pressed.

Mackenzie River and Athabasca: Insufficient Endowments

The resignation of Bishop Young of Athabasca at the end of 1903 laid the administration of that Diocese temporarily upon Bishop Reeve. The endowment of Athabasca did not permit the immediate election of a new bishop, and actually Bishop Reeve administered the diocese up to the time of his own resignation of the Diocese of Mackenzie River on August 31, 1907. In the minutes of the Provincial Synod of 1905 (August ninth), message "K" from the Upper House stated: "The Bishop of Mackenzie River had expressed his wish to resign that See, and be Bishop of Athabasca only, thereby surrendering his episcopal allowance from the C.M.S. for Mackenzie River, and being temporarily dependent for his support upon the assured gifts of certain friends." After discussion and conference, the Lower House concurred

[23]Rev. A. J. Vale was at Hay River from 1907 to 1928, and then became Principal of the Chapleau School in Ontario, where he spent more than twenty years.

in this and also in the rest of message "K", which called attention to the unsatisfactory administration of the two Dioceses and urged the completion of the Episcopal Endowment Fund of Athabasca without delay. Nothing further seems to have happened, but in the minutes of the meeting of the Provincial Synod in 1907 (August fourteenth), the Lower House passed a resolution, which read in part: "Whereas it is understood that the Endowment for the Diocese of Athabasca has been completed and whereas it is a practical certainty that in the near future the tide of immigration will set into the Diocese of Athabasca . . . in the opinion of this House of Delegates it is highly desirable that a Bishop for the Diocese of Athabasca should be at once appointed. . . ." It was not, however, until April 15, 1909, that the See of Athabasca was filled by the translation to it of Bishop Holmes of Moosonee.

The resignation of Bishop Reeve was received with regret and it left the Diocese of Mackenzie River in exactly the same position as the Diocese of Athabasca had been four years previously, without sufficient endowment to warrant the appointment of a successor. Archbishop Matheson, in his Charge to the Provincial Synod of 1909 (August tenth), commented: "The See of Mackenzie River remains vacant, as the Episcopal Endowment has not yet been completed. . . . At my request the Diocese has been administered under a commission from me by the Bishops of Athabasca and Yukon."

This situation continued until 1913 when Archbishop Matheson again referred to it:

I am glad to be able to inform the Synod that the Episcopal Endowment [of the Diocese of Mackenzie River] is now completed, and that a Bishop has been elected by the House of Bishops and the Standing Committee of the House of Delegates, in the person of Dr. Lucas. . . . His long experience with the conditions of the country, his devoted and successful work, his capacity as a man of affairs, together with his spiritual qualities, have marked him out clearly as the man of God's choice for the high office in the Church. The formation, as well as the completion of the Endowment Fund, we owe to the efforts of the former Bishop of Mackenzie River, Dr. Reeve, now of Toronto. The Church and the Province is under deep and abiding obligation to Bishop Reeve for what he has thus done in not only giving a large portion of his life to the work in the far north, but also for making permanent provision for the placing of a Chief Shepherd of the Church in the former sphere of his labours.

Dr. Reeve became Assistant Bishop of Toronto on September 3, 1907, a position he held until the end of December, 1924, when he was obliged to resign because of ill health. He died on May 12, 1925, in the eighty-second year of his age, the fifty-sixth of his ministry, and the thirty-fourth of his episcopate.

Bishop James Richard Lucas

James Richard Lucas was born at Brighton, England, on August 20, 1867, and after being trained at the Church Missionary College at Islington, took up work in the Diocese of Athabasca under Bishop Young. Much of his subsequent life seemed to centre around St. Paul's Church, Fort Chipewyan, for he was ordained deacon there on June 12, 1892, priest in the same church on July 5, 1893, and was in charge of that mission until the end of 1899. From 1900 to 1907 he was at St. David's Church, Fort Simpson; he became Archdeacon of Mackenzie River in 1906 and in 1908 the Secretary-Treasurer of the Diocese. He was consecrated as Bishop of Mackenzie River in Holy Trinity Church, Winnipeg, on August 31, 1913, by the Metropolitan (Matheson).[24]

Bishop Lucas, during his latter years as Archdeacon, had become increasingly aware of the inconvenience of Fort Simpson as a centre from which to administer the affairs of the Diocese. When reporting upon a visitation Bishop Stringer had made to the Diocese, he recalled, "the Bishop proceeded to Fort Smith, where he selected a site for a new mission house and Church to be built there as a headquarters of this Diocese. Both he and Bishop Holmes of Athabasca considered it absolutely necessary that the headquarters should be transferred from Simpson, with but three mails a year, to Fort Smith which now enjoys at least eight per annum.[25]

Fort Smith, however, was not destined to be the location. In 1913 Bishop Lucas came to an arrangement with the Bishop of Athabasca whereby the area around Fort Chipewyan was transferred from Athabasca to Mackenzie River, and this alteration in boundaries was confirmed at the Provincial Synod of that year. This area became known as "The Pocket," and at Fort Chipewyan Bishop Lucas made his headquarters throughout his episcopate. In 1920 he repaired and enlarged St. Paul's Church, which had been built sometime during the eighties when Bishop Reeve was incumbent. In this church "there was no imported material other than glass and nails used in its construction. . . . Every timber had to be made by hand labour [whipsaw], transported from forest to building site, floated down the stream and placed in its proper position in this House of Prayer. . . . The inside was sealed with handsawn lumber and the roof covered with handmade shingles split and shaved to the required thickness. Great credit is due these faithful workmen for today, even in the severest weather, this church can easily be heated. . . . This original building

[24]O. R. Rowley, op. cit., 178-179.
[25]The New Era (October, 1910).

stood unchanged until the time of Bishop Lucas."[26] When the church was reopened in 1921 a bishop's chair and prayer desk were given by the Bishop and Mrs. Lucas as a thank-offering to mark the occasion of their twenty-fifth wedding anniversary and the safe return of two sons from World War I. The Reverend A. J. Warwick was there from 1899 to 1905; the Reverend O. J. Roberts from 1905 until 1912; after a lapse of two years the Reverend C. H. Quarterman was in charge for a couple of years; then from 1918 to 1926 it was the Reverend W. Gibson. After Bishop Lucas' retirement in 1927 the mission was unoccupied for a few months, for the first time in its long history, but in 1928 the Gibsons, feeling the call to the north, returned for a couple of years. "The Pocket" remained as part of the Mackenzie River Diocese until 1933, when, owing to changing circumstances, the Provincial Synod approved "that the area of the Diocese of Mackenzie River lying southward of the Arctic Circle be added to the Diocese of Athabasca."

Mission Work on the Arctic Coast

During the episcopate of Bishop Lucas there was a notable advance in the Eskimo work. In 1914 the Bishop ordained a graduate of Emmanuel College named Henry Girling, and sent him in 1915 with two lay readers to Coronation Gulf, where the missionaries eventually took over the house at Bernard Harbour that had been occupied by the Canadian Arctic Expedition. This was not the first effort of the Church to reach the Blonde Eskimos whom Vilhjalmur Stefansson, the Arctic explorer, had first discovered in 1910 in the neighbourhood of Coppermine River. In that same year W. H. Fry,[27] who had already been working for three years along the coast, attempted to reach these people but failed because he lacked a suitable vessel.

Aklavik

The second point of advance was a place at the mouth of the Mackenzie River, now well known by the name of Aklavik. Archdeacon Whittaker noted that when he "first saw the location, in 1895, it was called Okpik's place, because an Eskimo Okpik once built a cabin there . . . there was no Eskimo within 100 miles, nor an Indian much nearer." About 1916 the fur traders began to build posts at this place in order to be nearer to the Eskimos, and to gather in their peltries as soon as caught, rather than wait for them to be brought to Fort McPherson or Arctic Red River. In 1919 the Church of England established a residential mission at Aklavik, and the first

[26]G. A. Crawley, "Diamond Jubilee, St. Paul's Church, Fort Chipewyan, N.W.T.," *Canadian Churchman* (March 14, 1940).
[27]*Crockford's Clerical Directory, 1916.* Mr. Fry was ordained in 1912.

All Saints' Hospital was opened in 1926 by Archdeacon Whittaker as Bishop's Commissary for the Diocese.

According to the late Bishop Fleming, in an address on July third, 1929, when still Archdeacon of The Arctic, "In 1927, a mission house was built at Cambridge Bay, Victoria Island. . . . Another missionary who first went north fourteen years ago . . . will take charge of the mission in the summer of 1929. . . . The first residential school in Canada for Eskimo children only will be opened at Shingle Point in August 1929." The work at Shingle Point had begun in 1922 with the erection of a mission house and church.

Archdeaconry of the Arctic

The resignation of Bishop Lucas, on March 31, 1926, brought more acutely to members of the M.S.C.C. and the Provincial Synod the question as to whether the time had arrived when the work of the Church in the Arctic should be consolidated under a Bishop of its own. By 1929 the M.S.C.C. had taken the initiative on its own account and the Arctic work in the Dioceses of Moosonee and Keewatin had been unified by the appointment of the Venerable A. L. Fleming, with the title of Archdeacon of The Arctic under a commission of the Bishop of Moosonee, and operating also in the Diocese of Keewatin under sanction of the Bishop of that Diocese.[28]

Bishop W. A. Geddes, 1928-1933

On September 27, 1928, the Provincial House of Bishops and the Standing Committee on the Election of Bishops met in Winnipeg for the purpose of electing a successor to Bishop Lucas. The Metropolitan took the opportunity to explain the situation at some length. That they were able to meet was largely due to the fact that the Bishop of Athabasca (Dr. Robins) had volunteered to devote two portions of his annual vacations to supplementing the episcopal endowment of Mackenzie River and Athabasca. He had first visited California and raised a considerable sum there; subsequently he had gone to the eastern states and added to this. The Bishop of the Yukon had approached Colonel R. W. Leonard on the subject, with the result that the Metropolitan received a cheque for $15,000. The result was that the Episcopal Endowment of Mackenzie River had

[28]Message No. 9 from the House of Delegates to the House of Bishops, *Journal of the Provincial Synod of Rupert's Land, 1923,* p. 37. Message "I" from the House of Bishops to the House of Delegates, *ibid.,* pp. 37-38. Resolution sent to the Boundaries Committee by the House of Delegates, *ibid., 1926,* p. 41. The Synod of the Diocese of Moosonee was responsible in both cases (the latter in modified form) for proposing that the entire Indian and Eskimo work should be under one episcopate.

been augmented from about $50,000 to over $70,000, and this had warranted their election of a bishop.

The Committee elected the Venerable William Archibald Geddes, already Archdeacon of the Diocese of Mackenzie River and experienced in Eskimo work along the coast. He was consecrated on February 3, 1929, in St. John's Cathedral, Winnipeg, by the Metropolitan (Matheson).

Born in the Magdalen Islands in 1894, Bishop Geddes was a graduate of Dalhousie University, Halifax, and Wycliffe College, Toronto. After his ordination, he became missionary at Herschel Island, his chief station until he was elected Bishop.[29]

Bishop Geddes began his work by making a careful survey of the whole diocese, during which he spent several months at each point, partly with a view to determining the best place to live in order to make his supervision most effective. He spent the winter of 1930 at Fort Simpson; that of 1931 at Fort Chipewyan; 1932 at Hay River; and 1933 at Fort Smith, which, because of its growing importance, was the centre of government administration for the territory. Bishop Geddes, however, by this time was on his way out from Mackenzie River, his ultimate destination being Dawson City in the Yukon, of which See he was to remain in charge until his death on April 16, 1947, at the early age of fifty-four.

Revision of Diocesan Boundaries — 1933

The translation of Bishop Geddes to the Diocese of Yukon was caused in the first place by the financial disaster that overtook the Ecclesiastical Province of Rupert's Land in 1932, in which the endowments of the Missionary Bishoprics of Athabasca, Moosonee, Mackenzie River and Yukon vanished. On August 31, 1931, the Reverend Arthur Henry Sovereign had been elected third Bishop of Yukon in place of Bishop Stringer who, the previous April, had been elected Metropolitan of Rupert's Land. At the same time the Very Reverend Robert John Renison of Vancouver had been elected fifth Bishop of Athabasca in succession to Bishop Robins. In the summer of 1932 Bishop Renison resigned on accepting the rectorship of St. Paul's Church, Toronto, but when the time came, on September 22, to elect a new Bishop of Athabasca, it was decided after much deliberation to translate Bishop Sovereign from Yukon to Athabasca and to ask Bishop Geddes, for the time being, to undertake the charge of the Diocese of Yukon as well as his own; a year later his connection with Mackenzie River ended.

When the Synod of the Province met in full session in 1933

[29]A. R. Kelley and D. B. Rogers, *op. cit.*, 26-27.

(September thirteenth) it decided to consent to the formation of the Diocese of The Arctic in accordance with the recommendations of the Arctic Mission Fund Committee, which had sponsored the Archdeaconry of The Arctic, and of the Anglican National Commission. The formation of this new Diocese removed from the Diocese of Mackenzie River the portion north of the Arctic Circle, and by a further resolution the part to the south of the Arctic Circle was added to the Diocese of Athabasca. This laid a very heavy burden upon the Bishop of Athabasca, which he contended with for some ten years; then the executive of his Diocese petitioned the Primate of All Canada and the Metropolitan of Rupert's Land that he be relieved of it.

Mackenzie River under Bishop Sovereign

In spite of these troubles in its constitution, organization and finances, determined and valiant efforts were made by those temporarily in authority to maintain the real work of the Church in the Mackenzie River itself. In 1939, through the efforts of Bishop Sovereign of Athabasca, the new Bompas Memorial Hospital was erected at Fort Norman; the first sod was turned by Archbishop Owen, then Primate of All Canada, on June 19. The Archbishop was making a personal survey of the whole of the Diocese of Athabasca.

The discovery of gold at Yellowknife in 1934, followed by other richer strikes, attracted an increasing number of miners and mechanics into this neighbourhood, within comparatively short distance of the old mission post Fort Rae. At Christmas, 1938, the first Church of England ministrations were held here when the Reverend S. E. Richards, missionary at Hay River on the other side of Great Slave Lake, flew in to marry a young couple and to baptize the first white baby (a girl) born there. The first permanent worker, the Reverend Cecil Randell, went to Yellowknife in June, 1939. Services were held at two centres and two Sunday School classes began. Tent services were held during the rest of the summer, then a small church was erected. On January 25, 1940, a Church Ladies' Aid was organized that raised the funds for the building of Holy Trinity Church, which was consecrated in July, 1941. The congregation has steadily continued to progress with the growth of the town, and in 1953 realized the proud achievement of being the first self-supporting parish in the Diocese of The Arctic. The Reverend Tom Greenwood was rector at Yellowknife from 1949 to 1952, during which time he was also Rural Dean of the Mackenzie River Deanery. He was elected Bishop of Yukon in 1953. It was also in the years following World War II that the Reverend S. J. and Mrs. Bell spent five years at Fort Simpson.

Athabasca — The Diocese of the Peace River Country

We must now return to the southern part of the original Diocese, which retained the name of Athabasca. The Consecration of the Right Reverend Richard Young on October 18, 1884, has already been mentioned at an earlier point in this chapter. He spent most of the year 1885 in England working for the Church Missionary Society and in the interests of his Diocese. Bishop Young returned to Canada in the fall of the year, and when he arrived in Winnipeg he persuaded the Reverend Malcolm and Mrs. Scott to undertake work in Athabasca. The Scotts were both members of his former parish, St. Andrew's, Red River. The Bishop spent the winter at Fort Vermilion, which he made his headquarters, and there he held the first Synod of his reorganized Diocese on July 6, 1888. Present were Archdeacon Reeve of Chipewyan; the Reverend A. C. Garrioch, who had recently been stationed at Dunvegan; the Reverend George Holmes, then at St. Peter's Mission on Lesser Slave Lake (not far from the site of the present town of Grouard); and the Reverend Malcolm Scott of Fort Vermilion. Four laymen were present. The Reverend J. G. Brick was absent. Mr. Garrioch has left an account of his adventures in reaching this Synod[30]:

We travelled on a raft, and left at 7 a.m., Saturday, June 30th. In constructing the raft I studied to make it large enough to be safe, yet small enough to be manageable. . . . Our little craft acted well, always keeping midstream, and we reached the Peace River Landing at 7 p.m. [Saturday] where we found Mr. Holmes[31] standing ready to help us land. . . . On Monday morning Mr. Holmes and I enlarged our raft . . . and we resumed our journey. To lose no time we divided our nights into two watches, and thus we travelled on, stopping only for a few minutes each day to replenish our stock of fuel. . . . On the evening of July 5th we sighted Fort Vermilion. . . . We landed here and went on to the Mission. . . . Vermilion, which has always been an important trading-post begins to assume the appearance of a farming settlement. . . . Among the new features that arrested my attention in the Unjaga Mission group of houses, was the Bishop's Palace, standing between Mr. Scott's place and the cathedral. It is a neat but unpretentious building.

The Cathedral Service preceded actual business, and was in this instance so arranged that each ordained missionary should do his share in officiating. . . . On Sunday, at morning service, Mr. Holmes was admitted to priest's orders. An excellent sermon was preached to us by the Ven. Archdeacon Reeve, who proved conclusively from scripture that there were originally three orders of clergy; but I think he forgot to inform us as to when it was first found necessary to have Archdeacons.

[30]*Canadian Church Magazine and Mission News* (February, 1889).
[31]Rev. George Holmes, later to be third Bishop of Moosonee and third Bishop of Athabasca. O. R. Rowley, *op. cit.*, 142-143.

Of all our sayings and doings at Vermilion, the best to my mind, took place on Sunday afternoon, when we all met in the Cathedral for a genuine missionary meeting. There, in simple language, we related our experiences in the mission field. There we united in invoking the blessings of God upon our future efforts in the work of the Gospel.

We commenced our homeward journey on Wednesday, July 11th. . . . We travelled in two dug-outs, propelled by means of paddle, pole or towline.

Early Indian Work in Athabasca

The Peace River country in the eighties of last century was still Indian country, and the chief work of Bishop Young and his clergy was directed towards the conversion and improvement of the natives. The Beaver Indians, who inhabited this territory, had been a powerful tribe but the inroads of disease was causing their numbers to diminish quite rapidly. The Reverend George Holmes began the mission at St. Peter's, Lesser Slave Lake, in 1886 when he went there as school-master and catechist. Heathen customs were still being practised; these people, however, did have a firm belief in the Great Spirit. The following year, when Holmes was ordained deacon, the Bishop established St. Peter's as a permanent mission, and the first mission house, a building twenty-six by eighteen feet with a small lean-to kitchen, was completed in 1888. Half of it served as dining-room, sitting-room and bedroom for the missionary, while the other half was used as a church and schoolhouse. In this building work was carried on for three years. At first only a day school was conducted, but in 1892 eight girls were taken as boarders into the mission house and twelve boys were placed in an Indian home nearby. Two years later a new home was built and Miss Dartness, whose salary was paid by the Woman's Auxiliary, became matron. By 1900 new buildings had to be erected owing to the demand for accommodation, and the farm attached to the mission was producing the necessary supplies of beef and milk, grain and vegetables.

From St. Peter's as a centre, other mission points were opened up at Stony Point, Whitefish Lake and Wapuscow (now spelled Wabasca). Both these latter points were a considerable distance away. Whitefish Lake was about sixty miles north of St. Peter's; St. Andrew's Mission there was opened in 1891 by the Reverend H. Robinson. In 1894 the Reverend William Grove White became the missionary and the church was built. In 1906 a home for 17 Indian children was added. This mission continued to grow for some years under the care of Mr. White. He was the first of three brothers to serve in the Diocese of Athabasca; the work of seven members of the family in the Diocese is commemorated on a plaque in All Saints' Church, Athabasca. Together they contributed one hundred ninety-four years of service to the Diocese. In 1912 Mr. White took charge of All Saints', Athabasca Landing, then in 1917 removed to St. Mary's, High Prairie, where he remained until his resignation in 1933. In 1924 he was made Canon; he died in Edmonton on June 4, 1939. The second brother, Alfred Speechly White, joined the Wabasca School staff in 1895, two years later entered Wycliffe College, Toronto, and was ordained in 1899. For fifteen years he was in charge of St. Luke's Mission, Fort Vermilion. He then became Archdeacon of Indian Missions and went to the school at Wabasca, where he carried on until his return to England in 1926. He died in April, 1950, and in his Charge to the Synod that summer Bishop Sovereign referred to him as "a courageous and devoted pioneer, a man of God, a humble Christian." The third brother, the Reverend Charles Dewe White, became principal of the school at Whitefish Lake in 1897 and devoted practically the whole of his life to the work there. He remained a layman until 1921, when he was ordained on July 27 by Bishop Robins at the time of the Synod. He died at High Prairie on May 13, 1938, shortly after retiring from his work. A sister, Mary Sinclair White, served as a matron at St. Luke's, Fort Vermilion, from 1900 to 1908; another sister, Edith White, taught at the same school from 1903 to 1908.

The mission at Wapuscow was opened in 1894 by the Reverend C. R. Weaver, and in 1950 a fine new residential school was erected at the expense of the Department of Indian Affairs. This mission, in spite of its remoteness, perhaps because of it, has continued throughout the years to do successful work. The first building was burned down in 1904, but replaced in 1906.

Mr. Holmes, who became Archdeacon of Athabasca in 1901 and was elected Bishop of Moosonee in 1905, was succeeded at St. Peter's Mission by the Reverend Malcolm Scott. After being missionary at Fort Vermilion from 1886 to 1900, Scott had spent five years as incumbment of the parish of Westbourne, Rupert's Land. Upon returning to the Diocese of Athabasca, he became Archdeacon and held that position till 1910 when he once more returned to Manitoba owing to ill health; but for the last four years of his active service, 1914 to 1918, Scott was incumbent of St. Peter's, Dynevor. He died in 1918. His successor, Archdeacon Robins, wrote of him upon his retirement that he had spent the best years of his life in the Diocese of Athabasca and had given so generously of his means that he was now a poor man; "but he is one of the noblest and most heroic men that I have ever met in the Church of England."

Changing conditions after World War I finally caused the mission at St. Peter's, Lesser Slave Lake, to be closed. The buildings were reported dismantled and the land sold at the 1944 meeting of the Synod.

When the Diocese of Athabasca celebrated its seventy-fifth anniversary in 1949 a brief history of its work was published under the editorship of the Reverend Roland Hill. It was observed that "as long as our Indian mission work was financed and manned by Britain it prospered. But gradually the responsibility was drifting from England to the Canadian Church. British missionaries were still the backbone of the work when the Indian Schools were taken over by the M.S.C.C. in 1923. . . . As the white population moved in, the Indians retreated and school attendance declined. Finally . . . only Wabasca and Whitefish were left and these have been maintained only by a real struggle."

The Reverend John Gough Brick

The Reverend John Gough Brick was the first missionary to the Beaver Indians at Dunvegan, then a Hudson's Bay Company post of some importance.[32] In 1886 he removed to Smoky River, a location later known as Shaftesbury, where he reported to Bishop Young that fertile prairies were "ready to receive a colonial population." Mr. Brick toured eastern Canada and worked up a large subscription list to support this mission, not only for missionary work but also to purchase all the necessary machinery for successful farming in the most improved manner of the time. For several years he had a good deal of success, but by 1894 frosts had done much to damage his schemes and he retired owing to broken health. He died in 1897.

The Church pioneered farming in the Peace River country under the guidance of Bishop Bompas, and in connection with its mission stations and schools continued to lead in this agricultural experiment for many years. Farming, however, as a church project, was finally abandoned at the time of the seventh Synod of Athabasca in 1910. Bishop Holmes remarked in his Charge: "After twenty-four years experience, I do not hesitate to say that mission farms, in the hands of missionaries, have proved to militate against rather than help the spiritual interests of the work."

Fort Vermilion and Athabasca Landing: Bishop Young

Bishop Young first established his headquarters at Fort Vermilion, at that time the most important Hudson's Bay Company post in the Diocese and the most convenient point from which to journey to its

---

[32]C. H. Mockridge, *op. cit.*, 349. J. G. MacGregor, *The Land of Twelve Foot Davis* (Edmonton, Applied Arts Products Limited, 1952), 253-255, 259-260.

various parts. This mission was opened in 1876 by the Reverend A. C. Garrioch, and during his incumbency, which lasted for nine years, St. Luke's Church and parsonage were built, mainly by his own labours. It was here, too, that he translated the Gospel of St. Mark, a catechism, a hymnal and parts of the Prayer Book into the Beaver language. At Fort Vermilion, in 1879, the Irene Training School and Industrial Farm were established. This was one of the points in the Peace River country where grain was first grown on a large scale. In 1891 the training school was placed under the care of the Reverend A. J. Warwick, who was there for six years before going north to Fort Chipewyan.

About the time that the southern part of the Diocese of Athabasca was first divided from the Mackenzie River area (1883), the Hudson's Bay Company abandoned the old canoe routes from the east. Instead, a trail was cut from Edmonton to a point on the Athabasca River that became known as Athabasca Landing. The trail from Edmonton to Calgary assumed a great importance, especially when the railway reached the latter place. The result was that Bishop Young left Fort Vermilion and settled at Athabasca Landing.[33]

The Church began its work here on June first, 1894, and a school was opened in the mission house with Miss Wooster as teacher. Within a few months the Bishop had taken up residence and the first St. Matthew's Church was built. The same year Bishop Young had a printing press set up in his study, upon which small books containing Bible passages, hymns and prayers were produced in syllabics for the natives.

At the end of 1903 Bishop Young resigned owing to ill health and retired to Liverpool, England. He died at Southborough in Kent on July 12, 1905, at the age of sixty-two, and was buried in St. James's churchyard there.

At the meeting of the Provincial Synod later that year, Archbishop Matheson remarked that Bishop Young was a man greatly esteemed, first of all for his work; he had sacrificed his life in the service of God and the Church. A man of kindly disposition combined with strong character, he had been beloved by a large circle of friends for his excellent qualities of head and heart.

During Bishop Young's episcopate the work of the Diocese remained largely that of evangelizing the Indians, educating and caring for their children. Towards the end of the century an infiltration of white people began, not a few of whom were miners, coming through the mountain passes from Prince George into the western end of the

[33]The exact date of Bishop Young's removal to Athabasca Landing has not been established.

valley. The gold rush of the Klondike brought many new men into the country, seeking the Yukon by way of the Mackenzie River, or the still more hazardous route that in 1942 became the Alaska Highway. Of those who failed, many never survived, but a few either returned to or remained in the Peace River country and became pioneer settlers there.[34] Treaties with the Indians in this part of Canada were not begun until 1899, but when they had been completed, surveyors came in to plot out the country; the usual settlement by enterprising farmers was soon on its way. Settlement between Edmonton and Athabasca Landing received a considerable impetus from the great fire of 1894, which, starting from a campfire, spread south and east until it had cleared the entire bush down to the Red Water River. The devastation was tremendous, but it cleared the land for settlement.

The Right Reverend George Holmes, Third Bishop of Athabasca

For the next three years the Diocese had as its Bishop the Right Reverend W. D. Reeve of Mackenzie River, acting as Commissary. Bishop Reeve moved from Fort Simpson to Athabasca Landing, and while he was there the Memorial Church of All Saints was built. On April 15, 1909, Bishop George Holmes of Moosonee was translated to the Diocese of Athabasca. The Diocese was well known to him for the major part of his life's work had been devoted to it, but changes were taking place as new settlers came, seeking land. By 1909 railway communications between Edmonton and the East had been greatly increased and improved; settlers were beginning to push farther to the northwest over bush and prairie trails, some crossing the height of land between the Athabasca valley and Little Smoky River, and so getting into the Grande Prairie country towards the west end of the Peace River valley A few years later it was the old Edson trail along which these people passed. The Church was there before the settlers, the Bishop and Archdeacon Scott having paid a visit to the Grande Prairie country in 1909. The Reverend F. W. Moxhay was the first permanent missionary, and the centre was at Lake Saskatoon, where he had acquired a homestead. Another clergyman, Canon Smith, also homesteaded seven miles west of Grande Prairie, where on Sunday afternoons the homesteaders for miles around assembled for service, and through the efforts of this "congregation" the Church of St. George came into being in 1912. The most westerly parish of the Diocese of Athabasca, Beaver Lodge, was not organized until 1915.

[34]J. G. MacGregor, *op. cit.*, 310-321.

Like every Bishop before him, Bishop Holmes found it necessary to appeal to England for men and money to carry on the work. Shortly after he became Bishop of Athabasca, he gained a notable recruit in the person of the Reverend Edwin Frederick Robins who took charge of Athabasca Landing, and in 1910 succeeded the Venerable Malcolm Scott as Archdeacon. Mr. Robins was a Londoner, trained at the C.M.S. College at Islington, but after ordination by Bishop Temple of London, May 20, 1894, he had gone as a missionary to the Lahore District of the Punjab in India for three years. In 1902 he became vicar of Thorpe-le-Soken in the Essex part of the Diocese of St. Albans. He left this parish, "because there is work to do out there in Athabasca which it seems to me that, in the providence of God, we are called to try and do." In the *New Era* of September, 1910, Archdeacon Robins wrote extensively of the opportunity opening up in the Diocese. "The march of the settlers through Athabasca Landing was an extraordinary sight. There was no other gateway to the north." There were two main streams of these settlers, one from eastern Canada, the other from the northern part of the United States, and they were very mixed in nationality. They had received Bishop Holmes and himself very cordially, but "their first concern is to get the ground opened up, to see the harvest, and to guarantee the future; and God is not their first thought."

In the late autumn of 1911, Bishop Holmes went to England in the interests of his Diocese. He had just completed a journey to the Arctic, and on his way overseas addressed many meetings in eastern Canada. He had not been in good health for some time, but it came as a shock to those who knew him to learn that he had died in London on February 3, 1912. Except for a brief three years as Bishop of Moosonee, he had devoted twenty-six years of his life largely to the Peace River country, and he died at the age of fifty-four. The *Canadian Churchman* of February 8, 1912, said that "few who heard him could be deaf to his appeals, either for workers or for money . . . the downright goodness, the sincerity, the earnestness, the obvious common sense of the man won his hearers' hearts and pockets. . . . He never shrank from expressing his conscientious convictions on any subject. Of him, it may fittingly be said: 'He was a good man and full of the Holy Ghost and of Faith.' "

The Right Reverend Edwin Frederick Robins, Fourth Bishop of Athabasca

On October 24, 1912, the Venerable Edwin Frederick Robins was elected Bishop of Athabasca, and he was consecrated in St. John's

Cathedral, Winnipeg, on Sunday, November 24, by the Metropolitan (Matheson).[35]

During the next twenty years the Indian work of the Diocese retreated before the growing importance of the white work. The census of 1911 shows the population of the country to have been less than 2,000, including settlers, traders, missionaries and Indians. The census of 1921 gave the figure as 20,000, and in the next eight years the population is said to have trebled. The fact that Peace River wheat won the world's championship four years in succession gave a great impetus to further settlement. During the early thirties people were leaving the dried-out areas of the southern prairies; for years they lived a marginal existence, but won out in the end through persistence and faith.

For a time during this long period, Athabasca Landing continued to be a place of importance, particularly after it was connected by railway with Edmonton in 1916. This importance diminished after the Alberta Great Waterways Railway was completed to Waterways, near Fort McMurray, in 1924.

The Reverend Robert Little went to Athabasca Landing in 1928, and was appointed Archdeacon. He had joined the staff of the Diocese in 1913 and ministered in three different areas of it, the eastern district of Athabasca, the eastern district of western Peace River, and the eastern district of Grande Prairie, which he was obliged to resign in 1925. To the efforts of Archdeacon and Mrs. Little is to be credited the establishment of the boys' and girls' hostels at Athabasca Landing, begun so that children of those in outlying districts might continue their higher education in a Christian atmosphere. The countryside had changed in the course of years; the bush trails of 1913 had been replaced by settlement, and until he resigned in 1950 Archdeacon Little was reputed to be serving the largest parish in the Canadian Church. There were fourteen different points at which services were conducted.

The construction of the Edmonton, Dunvegan and British Columbia Railway, which skirted the south shore of Lesser Slave Lake before turning north again at McLennan, reached Peace River Crossing (under the name of the Central Alberta Railway) in 1916, and the sparsely populated area on the north side of the Peace River took on a new importance. Previously, this area could only be reached by the old ninety mile long trail that crossed the river at Dunvegan. The school and farm at the Shaftesbury Mission was about twelve miles south of the Crossing; when settlement began in earnest about 1910, the Reverend Robert Holmes, a brother of the Bishop, took complete charge. Holmes had worked there from 1907 to 1910 while still a deacon. During these years the importance of Shaftesbury diminished and that of Peace River Crossing increased, so that in 1910 the first log church was built there and opened for services. The Shaftesbury Mission was finally closed in 1914, the children being transferred to St. Peter's School on Lesser Slave Lake. The centre of work became Peach River Crossing. In 1915 the call for a senior man in the country to the west of Grande Prairie was so imperative that in July Mr. and Mrs. Holmes moved to Lake Saskatoon, where their work achieved great success. Holmes died very suddenly a year later; his death was deeply felt, for he was sincerely interested in the people and the country.

With the changing centre of population, the Bishop of Athabasca finally took up his residence at Peace River Crossing in 1915, and in 1916 the railway reached that far.

Caravans, Bishop's Messengers and the
Sunday School by Post

In 1928 Eva Hasell and Iris Sayle extended their carvan work at Athabasca. Their primary object was to gather together children at remote farms and arrange for them to receive Christian instruction through the Sunday School by Post. The "vanners," however, were welcome, not only for this service but because they were so helpful to the many isolated families they visited. The work had to be suspended for a time during World War II but eventually five vans were working in the Diocese of Athabasca and gradually parishes came to be organized as districts were better populated.

The Fellowship of the Maple Leaf has also been of assistance to the Diocese in establishing the Bishop's Messengers, who have done pioneer work at many points where it was not possible to provide a clergyman. Malvern House in Peace River was built, with contributions from Malvern, England, as a centre to which the workers could from time to time return, and by fellowship and study be renewed in spirit for further work.

Bishop Robert John Renison Succeeds Bishop Robins in 1931

Bishop Robins resigned the Diocese of Athabasca at the end of 1930, returned to England and was appointed Assistant Bishop of Norwich; he died in March, 1953. Bishop Pierce, in his Charge to the twenty-fifth Synod of the Diocese of Athabasca (June 6, 1951) said Bishop Robins was a "great and a good man. His were the difficult pioneer years, when there was little comfort anywhere in the north. . . . He laboured constantly to lay the foundations of the Church in this country, and he laid them strongly, for he was one of the statesmen of the Church in the West." The Diocese of Athabasca was incorporated under his guidance on October 3, 1914, by an Act of the Provincial Legislature.

Bishop Robins was succeeded by the Very Reverend Robert J. Renison, then Dean of the Diocese of New Westminster, who was consecrated in Christ Church Cathedral, Vancouver, on January 6, 1932, by the Metropolitan (Stringer).[36] Bishop Renison, however, resigned the See later that summer to accept the rectorship of St. Paul's Church in Toronto, a position he held until August 25, 1943, when he was elected to the See of Moosonee. He became Metropolitan of Ontario in January, 1952.

The Episcopate of the
Right Reverend Arthur Henry Sovereign

The circumstances that caused the Right Reverend Arthur Henry Sovereign to be translated from the Diocese of Yukon to that of Athabasca in September, 1932, have already been dealt with in connection with the history of the former Diocese; his episcopate lasted until 1950. Bishop Sovereign was called upon first of all to supervise a much larger area than his immediate predecessors, owing to the inclusion of the southern half of Mackenzie River Diocese in that of Athabasca, a situation that made the work of the Bishop much more difficult. Between 1929 and 1949, thirty-two new churches were built in the enlarged diocese; seven were moved to new sites, twelve new parish halls were erected and eighteen new rectories built, besides the hostels at Athabasca Landing and the hospitals at Keg River and Fort Norman.

O. R. Rowley, biographer of the Bishops of Canada, said of Bishop Sovereign: "His endless energy and unquenchable zeal have inspired his clergy and workers to unbelievable accomplishments. Thus in less than two decades the Church of the 'last great frontier' has, under the leadership of the Bishop, been transformed from a struggling child, to a strong, healthy and vigorous youth."[37]

Bishop Sovereign was the first Canadian-born Bishop of Athabasca. A native of Woodstock, Ontario, as a boy he came under the influence of the Reverend J. C. Farthing, later Bishop of Montreal, who suggested his training for the ministry. Bishop Sovereign graduated from the University of Toronto in 1905; later, he took post-graduate work

[36]Kelley and Rogers, op cit., 36-38. R. J. Renison, One Day at a Time (Toronto, Kingswood House, 1957), 130-149.
[37]O. R. Rowley, "Bishop, Priests and Kings, VII—The Bishop of Athabasca," Canadian Churchman (October 28, 1937).

at Oxford, also the General Synod B.D. He began his ministry as assistant at Christ Church, Vancouver, and in 1909 became rector of St. Mark's in the Kitsilano district of that city.

One of the great events of the episcopate of Bishop Sovereign was the building of the new St. James' Cathedral and parish hall at Peace River in 1936. This was a gift to the diocese by "the anonymous donor," and was the last she made; her only reservation was that the organ must be financed by the parish. The hangings that belonged to the old log church of 1910 were placed in the chapel of the new Cathedral. This church was consecrated as the Cathedral of the Diocese on April 20, 1949, and the Reverend Roland Hill was appointed as its first Dean, the agreement between the Bishop and the parish having been drawn up and approved by the Synod of 1948. In 1946, through another generous gift from England, the Synod Hall was erected in the Cathedral grounds.

The Right Reverend Reginald James Pierce

Bishop Sovereign resigned the Diocese of Athabasca on August 31, 1950, and on September 12, the Reverend Canon Reginald James Pierce, Warden of St. John's College, Winnipeg, was elected as Bishop to succeed him. Born in Plymouth, England, educated at the Universities of Saskatchewan and London, England, and a graduate in theology of Emmanuel College, Saskatoon, he was ordained deacon by Bishop Renison on May 22, 1932. He had spent six years in the Diocese of Athabasca at Slave Lake, Colinton, and Grande Prairie. From 1938 to 1941 he was rector of South Saanich, B.C., and then for two years rector of St. Barnabas' Church, Calgary, before becoming Warden of St. John's College in 1943. Bishop Pierce was consecrated in St. James' Cathedral, Peace River, on St. Luke's Day, October 18, 1950, by the Metropolitan (Sherman).[38]

The story of Athabasca, over three-quarters of a century, has been one of Christian endeavour, courage and achievement.

[38]Kelley and Rogers, *op. cit.*, 122-123.

CHAPTER ELEVEN

Sixty Years of the Diocese of Rupert's Land

And, now, Reverend Brethren and Brethren of the Laity, I cannot conclude this address without a word of caution. The unbounded prosperity and hopefulness of the present is not without its risk. Many of us cannot have yet forgotten the cruel reverses and ruinous reaction of the 1882 period. Again, I think, we are faced today, by two imminent dangers, one of over-speculation leading to exaggerated values and by and by to disastrous losses—the other of extravagant living and an unhealthy pursuit of gain, which must prove most demoralizing and injurious to the Christian Life.

Let us pray that, as our people in this fair land grow in material means, they may still more richly abound in those heavenly treasures which moth and rust cannot consume, laid up where thieves cannot break through and steal.

FROM THE LAST CHARGE OF ARCHBISHOP MACHRAY TO THE SYNOD OF THE DIOCESE OF RUPERT'S LAND, JULY 8, 1903.

The year 1890 is a momentous one in the history of the Church of England in Canada, for in it was taken the first practical step towards the formation of the General Synod of the Church. Here we can only indicate a few of the events and decisions that led to the holding of what is generally known as the Winnipeg Conference on August fifteenth of that year.

The idea of a Church that would include all the dioceses in Canada pre-dated Confederation, for in its Declaration of Principles, the Provincial Synod of Canada at its first meeting in 1861 stated that one of its objects was "to promote further consolidation and united action of the whole of the Dioceses of British North America." In the West, at the first meeting of the Provincial Synod of Rupert's Land in 1875, Bishop Machray remarked that he doubted whether it would ever be desirable for the western dioceses to be incorporated into one Provincial system for the whole country, though at some time there might be a Council or Assembly for the whole Dominion. The question did not come up again in Rupert's Land until 1888.

In 1886, the Synod of the Diocese of Huron, at the instigation of Charles Jenkins of Petrolia, Ontario, sent up a resolution to the Provincial Synod of Canada urging the formation of a General Synod, which was given favourable consideration by that body when it met in October. But this acceptance took the form of a suggestion that the

Provincial body implement its own powers so that it would be able to legislate for the whole Church. In 1888 the Synod of Toronto on its own account produced a somewhat complicated scheme, a copy of which was sent to all the Bishops and thus was brought to the attention of the Synod of the Diocese of Rupert's Land by Bishop Machray when it met in that year. The proposal was welcomed as a principle, but the matter was left to the Executive Committee and no further action can be traced.

The Provincial Synod of Canada met again in 1889 and decided to call a Conference of the whole Church to meet in Winnipeg in 1890.[1] This Conference was called by communicating with individual Bishops, and after some correspondence it was arranged that the Conference should meet on August 15, 1890, and the Provincial Synod of Rupert's Land on August 13, so that the latter might be able to discuss what part it would take in the deliberations.

The sermon at the opening service of this Provincial Synod was preached by Bishop Sweatman of Toronto, who spoke of the need for unity in the Church as an inward necessity for its own welfare as the Body of Christ, and an outward necessity so that it might better impress Christian principles upon the life of the community. In the afternoon the Synod received a message from the House of Bishops that expressed sympathy with the idea of uniting the Church in British North America, but stated its conviction that Provincial Synods were needed for the discussion of local wants and feelings; it was essential that they should be recognized, though in subordination to the General Synod. Consideration of this message was postponed until the next day. The session of Thursday, August 14, was one of the most lively in the history of the Synod. The propriety of having a General Synod was agreed upon by all, but the matter of retaining the Provincial Synods was the point of contention. The delegates finally accepted the resolution from the House of Bishops and appointed themselves as a body to meet the delegates from the East the following day.

The Conference met in St. John's College and its first session was called to order on August 15 by Bishop Machray, who subsequently was elected to preside. Canon S. P. Matheson of Winnipeg and Dr. L. H. Davidson, Q.C., of Montreal were appointed secretaries. The Bishop of Toronto (Sweatman), as Chairman of the Committee of the Provincial Synod of Canada, reviewed the circumstances that had led to this calling of the Conference. Canon Matheson read the resolution

[1] J. G. Hodgins, ed., *Anglican Church Consolidation*, Record of the Proceedings of the Conference at Winnipeg of Representatives of the Provincial Synods of Canada and Rupert's Land . . . ; August 15 and 16, 1890 (Toronto, 1891). T. C. B. Boon, *The Winnipeg Conference of 1890*, Toronto, Canadian Church Historical Society, Occasional Papers No. 4, 1960.

passed by the Synod of the Province of Rupert's Land. Bishop Machray then associated himself with all that had been said by Bishop Sweatman and outlined his own ideas regarding the work and limits of a General Synod.

The motion of Bishop Baldwin of Huron, seconded by Mr. Wrigley of Winnipeg, that a committee be appointed to consider a form or draft of union and report in an hour, was withdrawn. The case against the retention of the Provincial Synods, to which it was supposed some of the eastern delegates were committed, was admirably pleaded by Bishop Anson of Qu'Appelle, who expressed great regret that in this matter he would differ from his Metropolitan. Mr. Jenkins and Mr. Imlach then brought in a six-point scheme for the formation of a General Synod, which was laid on one side while the Conference settled two other points: the first, that it was expedient to form a General Synod, the second affirming the necessity of retaining the provinces. The Jenkins-Imlach scheme was then sent to a committee, whose report was received and adopted on the Saturday morning, and has since become known as the Winnipeg Scheme. The Synod of the Province of Rupert's Land met again on the Monday and affirmed its acceptance of all that had been done.

The Winnipeg Scheme contained three clauses: the first set out the expediency of consolidating the various branches of the Church of England in British North America; the second affirmed the necessity of retaining the Ecclesiastical Provinces; the third, in five sections, outlined the membership, constitution, presidency and powers of a General Synod. It further suggested that the following objects should come within its jurisdiction: (a) matters of doctrine, worship and discipline, (b) all agencies employed in the carrying on of the Church's work, (c) the missionary and educational work of the Church, and such technical matters as the provision of superannuation funds, regulation of the education and training of candidates for Holy Orders, the transference of clergy from one diocese to another, adjustment of provincial boundaries, and the constitution and powers of an appellate tribunal.

For three years little was heard of the scheme, much to the concern and disappointment of the western dioceses. When the Synod of the Diocese of Rupert's Land met in 1891, Bishop Machray was only able to report that the Diocese of Toronto alone had accepted the scheme, though various Synods had appointed committees to consider it. The Diocese of Montreal had gone on record as opposed to the retention of Provincial Synods and the Diocese of Huron had favoured their gradual extinction. When the Diocesan Synod met again in 1892, Bishop Machray could only add that the Provincial Synod of Canada had referred the scheme back to the dioceses again, and even when the Provincial Synod of Rupert's Land met on August 10, 1893, the situation was still uncertain.

The delegates to what proved to be the first General Synod met in Toronto on September thirteenth, 1893. Those from Rupert's Land were committed to the Synod's formation; those from the eastern dioceses were ready to debate the matter. Three declarations were accepted the following morning. They had been prepared by a committee consisting of the Bishops of Rupert's Land, Toronto and New Westminster, together with twelve clerical and twelve lay delegates. These affirmed (1) that the Church of England in Canada desired to continue as an integral part of the Anglican Communion; (2) that the General Synod, when formed, should not take away from or interfere with any existing rights, powers, or jurisdiction of any Diocesan Synod within its own territorial limits; (3) that the constitution of a General Synod involved no change in the existing system of Provincial Synods. Bishop Machray, who presented this report (seconded by Dr. L. H. Davidson of Montreal), moved its adoption: "We, the Bishops of the the Church of England in the Dominion of Canada, together with the clerical and lay delegates present, do hereby declare that we do now constitute a General Synod of the Church of England in the Dominion of Canada." This was carried unanimously, and in the end the constitution drafted by the Winnipeg Conference was passed without substantial change. The title of Primate of All Canada was ordered conferred upon the President of General Synod, and that of Archbishop upon him and the Metropolitans of the Provinces. The election of Bishop Machray as first Primate gave general satisfaction, particularly so in western Canada.[2]

It has been necessary to deal with the formation of General Synod at some length, not only because of its importance in the development of the Church as a whole, but because of the steady support given to the principle of a unified Church of England in Canada by the Province of Rupert's Land.

Threatened Withdrawal of English Grants

Early in the summer of 1896, the Diocese of Rupert's Land received a heavy blow when it heard that on May 13 the Standing Committee of the S.P.G. had passed a resolution, sent up by its Applications Sub-Committee, as follows:

The Sub-Committee have had their attention called to the large sum annually paid by the Society to the Canadian Dioceses, at the present time nearly £9,000 per annum. The Sub-Committee feel that in view

[2]Robert Machray, *Life of Robert Machray . . . Archbishop of Rupert's Land,* 381-392.

of the fact that all the Canadian Dioceses, excepting Caledonia, now form one consolidated Church, the poorer Dioceses have a claim on the richer far stronger than was the case before the Consolidation of the Ecclesiastical Provinces, and much more urgent than they have on the Society. To mark this their opinion the Sub-Committee have reduced those Canadian annual grants, which are not appropriated to "privileged" clergy, by ten percent, for 1897, and have further reductions in view in the following years. In some exceptional cases a portion of the reduction has been restored by a distinct vote, but the principle of which they approve has been asserted.

Meanwhile the Sub-Committee recommend that the Canadian Bishops be informed that after the year 1900 the Society will look to the Canadian Church to relieve it of all its pecuniary responsibilities in the Dominion.[3]

When Archbishop Machray addressed the Provincial Synod of Rupert's Land at Regina on August 12, 1896, he alluded to this resolution when he commented on the request of the Diocese of Qu'Appelle that the Bishop about to be elected in place of Bishop Burn should be a clergyman well known in England: "With respect to the grant from the S.P.G. the Bishops could not bring themselves to believe that the Society will, on full inquiry and consideration, carry out their Resolution as far as the Northwest Dioceses are concerned, for they feel that this would be disastrous to the Church, but they did not consider that the circumstance of the Bishop being from England could in the least influence the action of the Society—an action which affects equally all the Dioceses having new settlements. . . . Besides they hope that larger help may shortly be received from Eastern Canada" [and, with reference to the newly-formed General Synod], "undoubtedly, what is at present most pressing for the life and growth of the Church is the adoption of a wise policy in its mission work. The Church suffers most from want of single and united effort."

The First Attempt to form the M.S.C.C.

The General Synod met in Winnipeg in September of 1896, but, to the disappointment of Archbishop Machray, did little except iron out a number of technical matters. The chief point of deliberation was the Court of Final Appeal for the Church in Canada. A Board of Missions was also proposed for all Canada, to take the place of the Domestic and Foreign Mission Society of the Ecclesiastical Province of Canada. To the chagrin of the West, the new board never came into operation, its formation being impeded by the persistence of the very organization it was supposed to replace, to which some of the eastern dioceses continued firmly to cling. The Diocese of Montreal refused to appoint representatives on the Mission Committee of General

[3]*Ibid.*, 406.

Synod, claiming that it was contrary to the basic principles on which it was founded, and protested against any interference with the Mission Society. In spite of the fact that its monthly paper, *The Canadian Church Magazine and Mission News,* under the editorship of the Society's secretary, Dr. C. H. Mockridge, had given much space and excellent publicity to the needs of the West, a spirit of parochialism seems to have been prevalent in eastern Canada about this time, and it was becoming increasingly difficult to get deputations from the West welcomed by either the dioceses or larger parishes in the East. In the meantime the action of the S.P.G. made the situation critical; the strongest representations continued to be made for some years, urging that its policy be changed. The Venerable Society, however, stood by the principle it had enunciated and only alleviated its policy to the extent of a series of special grants to meet specific situations. Not until the General Synod of 1902 was the missionary work of the Church of England in Canada reorganized on a satisfactory basis and set to face the future.

In 1896 another matter that greatly affected the Diocese of Rupert's Land became apparent. Thirty years of extremely strenuous life had begun to tell on the health of Archbishop Machray. When he was in England in 1896 he was seriously ill for some months, but managed to carry on his appeals to the missionary societies, who sent deputations to his bedside instead of requiring him personally to meet their committees. The lightening of his work became an obvious necessity, and in 1898 he was relieved of the mathematical teaching in St. John's College by the foundation of the Machray Fellowships and the appointment of the Reverend James Frost Cross as the first Machray Fellow, a position he retained for more than forty years. In 1899 further relief was promised when the Provincial Synod of Rupert's Land agreed to the formation of the Diocese of Keewatin.

Founding of the Diocese of Keewatin

The original Diocese of Rupert's Land, as set up by the Provincial Synod of 1875, consisted of the Province of Manitoba (the old "postage-stamp" Province) and the original Hudson's Bay Company Districts of Cumberland (except the Sub-District of Fort la Corne), Swan River, Norway House and Lac la Pluie. The western boundary, except to the north, was fairly well defined, but the eastern area took in much of Ontario, including the present country around Fort Frances, and to the north that around Lac Seul and the present Sioux Lookout. In 1899 the eastern boundary of Rupert's Land, under the new arrangement, was defined as "the line between ranges 8 and 9 east of the Principal Meridian in the Province of Manitoba to the point where the said line would strike the shore of Lake Winnipeg; thence along the eastern shore of the said lake," which made the eastern boundary of the Diocese only about 35 miles from the City of Winnipeg. The Bishop of Moosonee agreed to find $25,000 for the episcopal endowment of the new diocese, and the S.P.G. and the S.P.C.K. were each asked to contribute £100 for each £900 raised by the diocese for the completion of the endowment. It was left to the two Bishops to decide when the endowment was sufficient to warrant the appointment of a bishop. How the rest of the money was provided seems obscure,[4] but when the Provincial Synod of Rupert's Land met again on August 20, 1902, the Diocese of Keewatin was already in existence and the new Bishop (the Right Reverend Joseph Lofthouse, Sr.) was welcomed to its sittings; he had been consecrated the previous Sunday, August 17.

Unhappily, owing to illness, Archbishop Machray was not present at this Synod, and Bishop Young of Athabasca acted for the Metropolitan at the Consecration. He also presided at the Synod and read Archbishop Machray's Charge, in which he expressed appreciation of the establishment of the Diocese of Keewatin and the completion of the endowment for the Diocese of Calgary. As Bishop Pinkham wished to retain the latter, the election of a new Bishop of Saskatchewan could be held at an early date. A considerable portion of the Charge was taken up with a discussion of mission work, and the effect of the rapidly increasing number of small towns at the numerous railway stations. "And as they grow they will decline to be satisfied with the fortnightly service, but will demand a weekly service, then two services on Sunday, then the whole time of their clergymen. . . . There must be new missions, otherwise we shall drift gradually into the position of a large part of the American Church, ministering only to towns, and letting the country go; and to let the country go is to lose hold of large classes in the towns, for it is the country that gradually feeds the towns. Evidently there will be a demand for a large increase of missions which will necessitate an increase of means for the support of missionaries." The Charge went on to discuss first the attitude of the English missionary societies, then what was happening with regard to the General Synod missionary efforts, and the effect that the expected passing of the new Canon (which the Archbishop had prepared) at the meeting of General Synod at Montreal in 1902 would have upon the West. He pointed out that under this Canon it would no longer be

[4]It is assumed that the Rupert's Land Episcopal Endowment Fund contributed a share to this Episcopal Endowment Fund for Keewatin, but no information about the Rupert's Land Fund has ever been published, except the amount of its losses in 1932 which had to be replaced through the Restoration Fund of 1933. The S.P.C.K. gave £1,000 to the Keewatin Fund in 1901, and £200 in 1907, according to its Grants Book.

possible to make appeals for specific dioceses, only for the general missionary work of the Church, and all offerings would go to the general fund, from which the western dioceses might hope to get some benefit: "In my own Diocese the effort for the Home Mission Fund is so vigorously worked that it is hard to see what can be expected for the fund of the General Synod. Still I hope we shall do what we can, and not be behind others in loyalty to the arrangements of the Church."

Archbishop Machray also brought to the attention of the Synod the question of the supply of men, and raised the matter of the relationship of St. John's College to the Provincial Synod, something he had never done before. This support was urged because of new developments in the University of Manitoba. St. John's was the only theological college in the West actually training men for the Anglican ministry. The Synod was also warned that the C.M.S. schemes for reduction of grants were in operation and block grants would cease in twelve and a half years. While the Archbishop sympathized with the object of the Society, he thought its action premature, but as the Church and the country owed a debt to the Society beyond any acknowledgment, he did not propose to challenge its action.

The Archbishop was not able to preside at the General Synod of 1902, but the Canon he drafted respecting missionary work of the Church was accepted unanimously in both Houses. Before the Synod closed, the Mission Board was formed and the Reverend L. N. Tucker of Vancouver was appointed Organizing Secretary. Thus came into being the great Society to which every member of the Church of England in Canada belongs, now familiarly known as the M.S.C.C.— The Missionary Society of the Church in Canada.

Archbishop Machray had gone to England in May, 1902, on important business for the Church and, as Prelate of the Order of St. Michael and St. George, to attend the Coronation of King Edward VII in Westminster Abbey. He was not at all well when he left Winnipeg and became worse after his arrival in England, where he spent eleven months in hospital under special treatment. His condition was somewhat improved when he returned to Canada in May, 1903, and he was able to hold an Ordination on June 14. When he met the Diocesan Synod on July eighth, he said that he required a Suffragan. The Provincial Synod met on October first, and the House of Bishops unanimously elected the Very Reverend Samuel Pritchard Matheson, Dean of Rupert's Land, as Assistant Bishop. At the same Synod the Right Reverend Jervois Arthur Newnham was translated from the Diocese of Moosonee to the Diocese of Saskatchewan. Both these appointments, but particularly the first, gave Archbishop Machray great satisfaction. Writing to his old friend, the Reverend C. A. Jones, on November 23, he said: "My dear friend and pupil Dean Matheson was consecrated on the 15th, this is a great relief—he can take all outside work." The Archbishop was then able to take up the question with the S.P.G. of more financial help for St. John's College, especially needed because of the new situation in the University of Manitoba, which had just built its own first permanent unit on what was known as "the Broadway Site." He also pressed the necessity of a warden for the college, and one of his last letters pleaded with the Church Missionary Society to make a grant to the endowment of the Bishopric of Selkirk (now Yukon), then still held by Bishop Bompas.

The spring of 1904 brought a rapid deterioration in the Archbishop's health and he died in his sleep on the evening of March ninth in the seventy-third year of his age, the forty-ninth of his ministry and the thirty-ninth of his episcopate: "Mourning was universal. The Archbishop had felt a great pride in the North-West, and the North-West was not less proud of him. He had been identified with it from the beginning—in a true sense he was the North-West, its leader in the things that were best, the greatest of its pioneers. It had come to know him, to trust him, to honour him, to love him. It was not only the members of his own Church who mourned him—they, indeed, sorrowed as for a father lost—but of all the Churches of the land."[5] No more fitting words were ever placed on a memorial than those that mark the grave of Robert Machray in the shadow of St. John's Cathedral, Winnipeg. "He fed them with a faithful and true heart, and ruled them prudently with all his power."

Samuel Pritchard Matheson—Second Metropolitan and Third Bishop of Rupert's Land

The original Canons of the Ecclesiastical Province of Rupert's Land contained no special provision for the election of a Metropolitan, but only affirmed, under Canon VII[6]: "The present Bishop of Rupert's Land is hereby appointed Metropolitan, and the Diocese of Rupert's Land is hereby constituted the Metropolitical See during the tenure of office of the present Bishop, and as long as the Bishop of Rupert's Land shall be appointed by the Archbishop of Canterbury, provided that the question of the appointment of the Metropolitan and Metropolitical See shall be subject to revision by the Provincial Synod, as

[5]Robert Machray, op. cit., 456.
[6]Reports of the Synod of the Diocese of Rupert's Land, June 10, 1875, and January 12, 1876, with an appendix: "The Constitution of the Church of England in Rupert's Land"; VII, Appointment of the Metropolitan, p. 26.

soon as the Diocese of Rupert's Land obtains the right of electing its Bishops." There the matter stood until 1893 when, owing to the formation of General Synod, the appointment of the Bishop of Rupert's Land no longer came within the powers of the Archbishop of Canterbury, hence some action had to be taken. The new Canon VII reaffirmed that the Bishop of Rupert's Land is Metropolitan and the Diocese of Rupert's Land is the Metropolitical See, but provided that on the vacancy of the See it should be filled as follows: "Two names shall be chosen by the Synod of the Diocese of Rupert's Land, of whom the House of Bishops shall select one, who shall be Bishop of Rupert's Land and Metropolitan." The provision subject to Sub-Section I of Section VI appears to indicate that the election or selection of two names was to be governed by the rules that normally applied to the election of any Bishop in the Province.

The Synod of the Diocese of Rupert's Land met on April 20, 1904, to carry out its duty under this Canon, and the first ballot was taken before the close of the first session. The voting was reported by Orders when the Synod met in the afternoon, and as far as the first name was concerned, there was no question; Bishop Matheson received a majority of votes from each Order. The choice of the second man proved a much more difficult problem, but after fourteen ballots it was announced that Bishop George Rodney Eden of Wakefield, England, had been elected as the other name. Synod adjourned until June 14, when it was informed that Bishop Eden had declined to allow his name to go forward; the Synod was again adjourned, but resumed on January 10, 1905. On the fourth ballot it was declared that Archdeacon E. S. W. Pentreath of Columbia had been chosen, and he allowed his name to stand. The House of Bishops of the Province met on March first and elected Bishop Matheson as Metropolitan, an office he was to hold until the end of 1931, a period of nearly twenty-six years.

Samuel Pritchard Matheson was born on September 20, 1852, in West Kildonan (Winnipeg). His father, John Matheson, was the son of one of the Selkirk Settlers, and his mother was the daughter of John Pritchard. She died when the boy was quite young and he was brought up by an aunt who lived at Middlechurch. When his uncle, the Reverend Samuel Pritchard, moved his school from Middlechurch to St. John's to form part of the new St. John's College School of 1866, young Matheson entered that school and thus began the connection with St. John's College and St. John's Cathedral that lasted for the rest of his life. He graduated from the College in 1874, but did not receive the degree of B.D. from the University of Manitoba until

1887.[7] He was ordained deacon by Bishop Machray on September 26, 1875. From 1874 to 1882 he was a master in St. John's College School, being also Deputy Headmaster from 1879 to 1903, when he became Assistant Bishop. During these years he gained parochial experience, first as priest-in-charge of the Township of Victoria (Stonewall, Manitoba) from 1875 to 1878, and then as incumbent of St. Paul's Church, Middlechurch, from 1881 to 1886. In 1882 Matheson was appointed Professor of Exegetical Theology in St. John's College and Canon of St. John's Cathedral. He held the Canonry until 1902 when he became Dean, and the professorship until 1906. He followed in the steps of his predecessor when he became Chairman of the Advisory Board of Education in Manitoba in 1905, and Chancellor of the University in 1908. He was elected fourth Primate of All Canada on April 26, 1909, in succession to Archbishop Sweatman.

Archbishop Matheson met his first Synod of the Diocese of Rupert's Land on June 20, 1905, and some idea of the size and importance to which the Diocese had grown may be gathered from the fact that sixty-eight clergy and seventy-seven laymen answered the roll. In the past two years twenty-six churches had been built and opened, and from Easter, 1904, until Easter, 1905, eight hundred and thirty-nine persons had been confirmed, the largest number of Confirmations in one year in the history of the Diocese. Seven parishes had become independent rectories, and the Clergy Endowment Fund had been increased by £1,000 through the generosity of the S.P.G., the S.P.C.K.[8] and the Diocesan Woman's Auxiliary. The M.S.C.C. had also given generous support, providing $8,593; the Archbishop remarked upon the difference it would have made to the work of the Church had this Society existed twenty years earlier. He pleaded for better stipends for the clergy. "The expense of living has increased very appreciably in this country, yet I know devoted men in this Diocese who have been endeavouring to maintain a wife and family, keep a horse, and in some cases, two horses, on a salary under $700.00 per annum, and that irregularly paid. These things ought not to be. . . . The minimum salary of a clergyman should, I think, be not less than $800.00 per

[7]This is the date given in a list of Graduates published about 1936, which list was checked with the University Registrar's records before it was issued by St. John's College; this, however, is not decisive as the Univerity lost all its early records when the McIntyre Building was destroyed in the fire of 1898. *Crockford's Clerical Directory*, 1898, dates S. P. Matheson's B.D. as 1879; St. John's College Council Minutes as April 17, 1880; O. R. Rowley, *The Anglican Episcopate of Canada and Newfoundland*, p. 129, as 1882. W. L. Morton, *One University* (Toronto, 1957), states that the affiliated Colleges of Manitoba University could not award degrees in Divinity before 1895, when the University of Manitoba Act was amended to give them the power to do so. However, the College lists twenty-one B.D.'s that pre-date 1895.

[8]The S.P.C.K. Grant Book lists: £2,000 in 1882, £500 in 1888, and £250 in 1901, but no later contributions to this Fund.

annum, with a free house, and this salary should be paid quarterly."
The Archbishop also referred to St. John's College, the debt on
which had been reduced to about $25,000; the General Endowment
Fund, however, had been increased by the same amount, chiefly
through a gift of $10,000 from Lord Strathcona and a legacy of £2,000
from the late Miss Fowler, which had enabled them to claim a further
£1,000 from the S.P.G. The Reverend W. J. Garton had succeeded
in collecting $29,000 for the new building fund. It was also most
necessary to have an adequate endowment for a Warden:

He must be no mediocre man. The success of our College and the
character of the students who will go out from its walls will depend
largely upon the calibre of the man who will be at the head of the
College. The time has gone by in this Diocese when one and the same
man can be Bishop and Warden of the College as well. The Church
has outgrown this. When I became Bishop I at once saw that I had
to choose between the Diocese and the College. It was a severe wrench
. . . but I chose the Diocese. Now, if our Church people wish this
to continue . . . they must so equip their College as to make it possible
for it to do without the Bishop, except as a visitor.

This meant a new building, an endowment for a Warden's Chair, an
additional lecturer in Higher English, and the provision of a salary
for a Headmaster of the College School; these were minimum requirements if St. John's was to hold its place with the other affiliated colleges
of the University, and would not be accomplished merely by placing
sympathetic resolutions on the minute books. With the exception of
the two brief years when the Reverend J. J. Robinson (formerly Dean
of Belfast) was Warden, from 1905 to 1921 the affairs of St. John's
College were without adequate leadership. Temporary expedients
were used to meet pressing needs of the moment, but none of the
suggested minimum requirements was ever met, and it is to the want
of adequate leadership during this period that many of the subsequent
troubles of the College can be traced.

A survey of the reports of the rural deans to this Synod confirms the
story about the expanding work of the Diocese. Holy Trinity in
Winnipeg was flourishing under the leadership of Archdeacon Fortin,
and a branch of the Brotherhood of St. Andrew was in active working
order, owing considerably to the efforts of the Reverend C. W. McKim,
the curate. Christ Church was the rallying point for many young
people from the old country and its offshoot, St. Mark's, Point Douglas,
was growing; old St. George's had cleared itself of debt and had six
hundred and twenty-five pupils in its Sunday School; St. Luke's, Fort
Rouge, under the Reverend T. W. Savary, had built a beautiful
new church costing $20,000; St. Peter's, on Selkirk Avenue (the Rev-
erend S. Fea) was talking of building a new church, and St. Matthew's

"on the west side of the city" was making progress; St. James' had a new Sunday School building, while St. Philip's, Norwood, and St. Cuthbert's, Elmwood, were getting away to a good start.

In southern Manitoba the movement of population towards the city was already beginning in the Morden district, but farther west churches had been built at Manitou and New Haven. At Glenboro, the new church was a commodious brick building with a stone basement for Sunday School. "It has been erected largely through the efforts of Mr. Wells, a promising student of St. John's College." (George Anderson Wells became Warden of St. John's College in 1921, and Bishop of Cariboo in 1934.)

In the northern part of the Diocese new centres had been formed in the neighbourhood of Stonewall and Foxton; new churches were built at Cloverdale and Little Britain (Lockport), and the church at Beausejour was being completed. The southwestern part of the Diocese had suffered from the weather, congregations being "winter-killed," and they were handicapped by a lack of men. Yet progress was being made; a new church had been completed at Elgin, another was being prepared for at Ninga. Brandon was beginning to look towards the formation of other parishes in the town where the Reverend A. U. De Pencier, later to become Archbishop of New Westminster, had just taken up his work.

In 1909 the Archbishop reported to his Synod that fourteen new churches had been built at various points, including St. Matthew's, St. Margaret's, St. Barnabas' in Winnipeg, and St. Mary's in Brandon. In two years he had consecrated nine churches as free of debt. This Synod took up some matters of wider than diocesan interest. At the request of General Synod, it appointed a Standing Committee on Moral and Social Reform, which appears to have been the first step toward what is now known as the Council for Social Service. It surveyed in considerable detail the temperance situation in the Province of Manitoba and outlined a scheme of reform that it pledged to support. The question of whether the Diocese of Rupert's Land should continue to be the Metropolitical See was postponed. The Canon of the Provincial Synod, which governed the election of the Metropolitan, was regarded with disfavour by several of the dioceses in the Province of Rupert's Land and the subject had been debated at length at the Provincial Synod in 1907. After several complicated motions had been discussed and rejected, a joint session of the two Houses was held, and agreement was reached on one point: "That no settlement of this much vexed question is possible without the Diocese of Rupert's Land relinquishing the right either of electing its own Diocesan Bishop or of its own Metropolitan supremacy."

Archbishop Matheson, in his Charge to this Diocesan Synod of 1909, expressed himself strongly in favour of retaining the Metropolitical See: "I believe it to be in the interests of the peace and harmony of the Church in the Province that our Diocese should relinquish more of its share and voice in the election of its own Bishop in return for being allowed the privilege of retaining the Metropolitanship."

Home Mission Fund

It had always been the cherished ambition of Archbishop Machray to have a self-supporting diocese. He had looked upon the assistance of the English missionary societies as but a temporary expedient that would enable the Church to become firmly established. The promotion of endowment funds was only one phase in the fulfilment of the aim. The Church Endowment Fund and the Diocesan Fund seem to have been started in 1867 when the Harvest Thanksgiving offertories were given for that purpose, also grants by the parishes of St. John's and St. Andrew's. The Diocesan Fund was first mentioned in the Bishop's Charge to the Synod in 1869, and the Native Pastorate Fund appears then as already in existence. In the Synod Report for 1881 the terms "Church Endowment Fund" and "Diocesan Fund" disappeared from the records and were replaced by the title "Home Mission Fund." There is no specific reference to this change to be found in the 1881 Synod Report, but due regulations were set up by that Synod for carrying on the work of the diocesan missions, and a Canon was adopted by it for the formation of Rural Deaneries, expected to knit the work much more closely together in the rural districts. The Home Mission Fund has continued to be the financial backbone of the Church in the Diocese of Rupert's Land ever since.

After the formation of the M.S.C.C. in 1902, Rupert's Land received much greater support from this organization than it had previously obtained through its direct appeals and deputations to eastern Canada. For example, in 1903, a time of transition, about $1,700 was received through the old Domestic and Foreign Mission Society; in 1905, through the Missionary Society of the Church in Canada, this sum had grown to $8,593. Naturally the Diocese had to raise its share for the general fund of the M.S.C.C., and it was quite an effort to raise the additional amount for what was regarded as "outside work." In 1905 Archbishop Matheson expressed his appreciation of the generosity of the M.S.C.C., but said that as time went on the Diocese must reduce its demands upon the Society; thus it asked for a much smaller grant, something of an act of faith. "Last year our apportionment was $3,000, which we did not quite reach. We must try to do better next year. While we are still a missionary Diocese and have many calls upon us, yet we are no longer very young. Our people are becoming better off, and it behoves us to take our place as a giving as well as a receiving Diocese."

By 1909 the M.S.C.C. grant to Rupert's Land had been reduced to $7,000, and the amount for which the latter was asked rose to $8,400. At the beginning of January, 1911, the Diocese of Rupert's Land ceased to be one of the missionary dioceses of the Canadian Church, an advance of great satisfaction to Archbishop Matheson; he warned his Synod, however, "our Home Mission Fund must, under all circumstances be not only kept up but be increased in its amount as the years go on." Assistance was needed in fostering missions in new places in the country, commencing new parishes in Winnipeg; a large quantity of land had been opened for homesteading on both sides of Lake Manitoba, and the railways were extending in the inter-lake country.

When the Synod met in 1914 there was some change in the situation. The country had hardly been as prosperous for the last year or two, and while the Archbishop could not complain about the support given to the Home Mission Fund (nearly $19,000), he was grieved by the deficit of over $2,000 in the contribution to the M.S.C.C. This, however, was only the beginning of thirty years when, due to economic and other circumstances, the Diocese of Rupert's Land found it extremely difficult to raise what was considered its proper share of the general mission funds of the Church in Canada.

St. John's Cathedral

In his Charge to the Synod of 1911, Archbishop Matheson drew the attention of the members to the fact that St. John's Cathedral was inadequate both from the diocesan and the parish point of view. Rupert's Land had the best organized cathedral system in the Dominion of Canada, but the old Cathedral was now only a very modest parish church. Archbishop Machray had felt that there were more necessary and practical things to be attended to than the building of a grand cathedral. Archbishop Matheson placed before the Synod plans for a new cathedral that would cost about $300,000. It would take a number of years to complete it: "The idea is to finish the Nave within two years and be ready for opening in 1913, one of the centenary anniversary years of the arrival of the first settlers to what is now St. John's, and to have the whole structure finished in 1920, the One Hundredth Anniversary of the starting of the first Church of England Services in St. John's on the arrival of the Rev. John West in 1820." The Archbishop then dealt with the somewhat vexed question of site, for even at that time there were people who thought the location of a new cathedral should be in the centre of Winnipeg. The Archbishop commented: "I am convinced that St. John's is historically the proper place for the Cathedral. That spot is unique in the history of church development in the whole of Canada. . . . St. John's is the birth spot not only of the church in Manitoba but of the church throughout the whole of North West Canada, including Hudson Bay, James Bay and whole of the East Main coast. From the work begun there in 1820 . . . the nine dioceses comprising the Ecclesiastical Province of Rupert's Land have grown."

The Synod, however, met this proposal with a lack of enthusiasm and ended by setting up a committee to confer with the Dean and Chapter and the Vestry of the Cathedral Parish, and the Council of St. John's College, with regard to the Cathedral problem, and report to the next Synod. The question of the proper celebration of the centenary, and the coming of the Reverend John West, came up again at the Synod of 1914, when the Archbishop intimated that he still hoped to have a new Cathedral built by 1920, though nothing had yet been done. No further action appears to have been taken by the Synod.

Early in 1913 the old Cathedral of 1862 had been declared unsafe, and the last service ever to be held in it was conducted on November 2, 1913, by Canon J. W. Matheson. For the next thirteen years the services were held in the Pro-Cathedral at the corner of Main and Church Streets. This building had originally been erected as a parish hall in 1887, and a basement was put under it in 1905. During the summer of 1913 the building was enlarged and remodelled. It was not until 1922 that plans again began to move. The parish had not been idle during these years in spite of the war, and had kept its building fund alive. Actually, the parish had had a new church in mind since December, 1883, when it had donated the Christmas Day offering as a nucleus for a building fund. It had supported the Archbishop's proposals in 1913 and received promises of over $35,000, about half of which had actually been paid in cash. In the intervening years, however, the parish had contributed substantial amounts of money to the establishment of St. Peter's, St. Martin's, St. Stephen's, St. Anne's and St. Chrysostom's, all of which were its daughter parishes. In 1910 it had met the architect's bill of $2,500 for the plans of a cathedral that was never to be built.

By 1922 the Pro-Cathedral was becoming overcrowded and the lack of accommodation for church organizations had become a problem. The vestry of the cathedral, therefore, sent a delegation to the Archbishop to discuss the matter of financing and constructing a new church, felt to be a necessity for the parish, which might also be suitable for a cathedral. The parish thought the limit it could raise was $40,000, and that the cost of a cathedral in excess of this amount should be borne by the Diocese at large. Archbishop Matheson, when he met the Synod on June 27, 1923, made a stirring appeal for the co-operation of the Diocese in the building of a cathedral as a memorial to Archbishop Machray: "As time goes on and my own term of office must at no distant date come to a close, I am naturally anxious that something really worthy of that great man's memory should be set up during the lifetime of his immediate successor." The parish itself made strenuous efforts, having so much success that on February 12, 1924, a permanent building committee was set up. The country, however, was passing through what has since become known as the "little depression," and the Archbishop met with some discouragement, both as to the raising of funds and the project itself. He told a parish meeting on January 19, 1925, that he had not been idle, but that he had never met so many obstacles and difficulties. Harry Shave, in *Our Heritage,* his story of St. John's Cathedral, writes: "The . . . indomitable spirit of the Archbishop now asserted itself in full measure. Besides writing hundreds of letters to personal friends and interviewing a great many, he arranged with the clergy of the Diocese to institute a drive in the various parishes for funds with which to build the proposed memorial to his beloved friend and predecessor."

Shortly after the signing of the contract by the Dean and Chapter in March, 1926, the old Cathedral was demolished and part of the stone was used in the inner north wall of the new building. A clause in the contract had provided that unless sufficient money were in sight for the completion of the building, only the nave would be erected. By the end of June there was only approximately $70,000 in sight, of the $95,000 needed. But at this juncture the Dean and Chapter and the Cemetery Board each loaned $10,000 from their own funds, and so it was possible to complete the building. The first services were held in the new Cathedral on Sunday, December 5, 1926.

First Proposals for a Brandon Diocese

The end of the first decade of the twentieth century saw a new wave of prosperity in western Canada, reflected in the cities by an upward swing in the real estate market, in the rural areas by a sturdy determination to assert the rights of the farmer. Winnipeg was already the gateway of commerce, the seat of government and university, and the home of the grain trade, which the farmers viewed with considerable suspicion. In the western part of the Province of Manitoba, the city of Brandon began to show signs of a growing importance and became the centre of a Farmers' Movement that was to have a marked effect upon the life of the province for the next thirty years. There was every indication that Brandon was becoming the agricultural metropolis, as Winnipeg had become the commercial and administrative one. Among the notices of motion sent out with the announcement of the forthcoming Synod to be held on June 28, 1911, was one to be moved by the Reverend W. P. Reeve, rector and rural dean of Brandon, seconded by the Reverend J. E. Lindsay of Carberry, "that in consideration of the important duties entailed upon the Archbishop in addition to the care of the Diocese, and in view of recent legislation for the maintenance of Rupert's Land as the fixed Metropolitical See, a division of this Diocese is advisable and necessary." Behind this motion, however, was the desire of the western part of the Diocese for independence; there, a considerable number of the clergy were younger men, both vigorous and vocal. When the matter came to the House on the afternoon of August 10, the Archbishop intervened to say that he was very much opposed to any step that would lead to the division of the Diocese. He felt that neither the number of clergy nor the extent of the episcopal duties involved warranted the division. At this critical point their main efforts ought to be directed toward increasing the Home Mission Fund, for its enlargement was imperative; assistance from the M.S.C.C. had been relinquished. He suggested that the best solution, for the moment, would be the appointment of a full-time archdeacon.

At the Synod of 1912 it was agreed to make application to the Provincial Synod for the division of the Diocese, and when the Provincial Synod met on August 27, 1913, the first message from the House of Bishops set off as the Diocese of Brandon the part of Manitoba west of the line between ranges nine and ten west of the principal meridian, and west of Lakes Manitoba and Winnipegosis, placing the territory under the jurisdiction and administration of the Bishop of Rupert's Land until such time as he, as Metropolitan, could be satisfied that funds were sufficient to support a Bishop.

When Archbishop Matheson met the diocesan Synod in June, 1914, he said he hoped that the new Diocese would be established within three years at the most. Two months later the outbreak of World War I changed the whole situation. The Venerable Wilfrid W. H. Thomas, as Archdeacon and general missionary, a post to which he had been temporarily appointed in 1912, assumed more and more supervision of the new diocesan area.

St. John's College and College School

Little has been said so far about St. John's College and College School. Since their re-founding by Bishop Machray in 1866, the fortunes of these institutions had closely followed the pattern of the fortune of the country. Increasing population and prosperity brought to the College and School increasing enrolment, greater opportunity and greater usefulness. Particularly was this the case after the formation of the University of Manitoba in 1877, of which St. John's was one of the three foundation colleges, but the very circumstances that caused it to prosper as an educational institution often brought financial anxieties.

It is beyond the scope of this work to write the history of the College in any detail, but there is a curious rhythm in the story of its affairs which may be noted. It has been served by a succession of brilliant professors; it has produced many gifted graduates who have taken high and responsible positions in the Church and State; it has fought its way out of financial anxieties more than once. The Diocesan and Provincial Synods of Rupert's Land have passed pious resolutions promising help and support, which for the most part have been promptly forgotten, and yet the College survives and carries on.

It would be doing an injustice to a number of the best known and most honoured names in the history of the Church of England in western Canada not to mention some of the staff whose devotion was largely to the College and the local mission field. Of the members of the staff of the College at the time it became part of the University, Canon J. D. O'Meara was Professor of Systematic Theology, a chair that has always been associated with the teaching of Philosophy. He became Dean of the Cathedral when Dr. John Grisdale was elected Bishop of Qu'Appelle in 1896. Dr. O'Meara, an eloquent preacher and sound scholar, was responsible for the foundation of the original, but now defunct, St. George's Parish in the centre of Winnipeg.[9] The Reverend George Frederick Coombes joined the staff of St. John's College as Professor of Music and Precentor of the Cathedral in the eighties, and his skill in this field was much appreciated in Winnipeg. He was an excellent classical scholar, and after the death of Archbishop Machray was appointed to the chair of Church History; when Bishop Matheson was elected Metropolitan, Canon Coombes became Dean of Rupert's Land. He was Prolocutor of the Provincial Synod of Rupert's Land from 1909 to 1920. When the University organized

[9] "Old" St. George's Church, to which reference is here made, was at the corner of Isabel and Bannatyne. Services were first held in this neighbourhood in 1881-1882, and Canon J. D. O'Meara took charge in 1883. Rev. Josias Jesse Roy was incumbent of the parish, 1886-1919. During World War I this area of the city changed as a residential neighbourhood, and in 1917 the diocesan executive committee reported that a loan had been made on the property that would enable a new St. George's Church to be erected at Grosvenor and Wilton, in the new Crescentwood district in the southwest part of the city. To this church Rev. Henry D. Martin, curate of Holy Trinity, was appointed in 1918. Old St. George's was sold in 1927, and subsequently pulled down.

in 1914 a separate department of Classics under its scheme of teaching Arts, Dean Coombes became its first professor of Greek.

Almost the last appointments to the college and cathedral staff made by Archbishop Machray were those of the Reverend J. O. Murray as Professor of Systematic Theology, and the Reverend E. E. M. Phair as Professor of Pastoral Theology. Canon Murray's association with the college was a long one. From 1902 to 1918, and again from 1926 to 1943, his agile mind, sound scholarship and warm-hearted interest in people, caused him to be indefatigable in his pastoral duties in the Cathedral parish, and in the councils of the Church. He was a doughty fighter on behalf of any principle he felt should be upheld. Canon Phair was a graduate of the College and University in 1889, who completed his theological training at Ridley Hall, Cambridge, and then for about ten years engaged in parish work in England. His loss in the sinking of the *Lusitania* in 1916 brought widespread regret. In 1905 the Reverend John William Matheson joined the staff of the College as lecturer in Exegetical Theology; he, too, had been an outstanding scholar of St. John's, where he was a contemporary of Canon Phair. He succeeded Canon Richard Talbot in the full professorship in 1912 and followed the Very Reverend G. F. Coombes as Dean in 1922. He resigned this position in 1934, but continued to lecture at the College for another ten years. Regarded as one of the best scholars in the Church in western Canada, a man of forceful personality, Matheson left an impression on his students and associates that will not easily be forgotten. Canon E. A. W. Gill spent twenty years at Minnedosa, Manitoba, as rector and rural dean before resuming scholastic work in 1910. He came to Winnipeg as incumbent of St. Martin's, and lecturer in Moderns at the College. Canon Gill was promoted to the chair of Pastoral Theology in 1918 and continued on the College staff for nearly twenty-five years. His wide reading was shared with his students, rather than imparted to them. Reference has already been made to the Reverend J. F. Cross. Machray Fellow in Mathematics from 1899, he became Dean of the College in 1916, but his contribution to its life was made as much outside the classroom as in it. He had a remarkable power of simplification in teaching his own subjects. His genial and understanding outlook brought him a place of singular affection in the hearts of successive generations of students.

Academic distinctions and brilliant staff notwithstanding, the College no sooner got over one difficulty than it ran into others. It never seemed to command the whole-hearted support of the Church. This may have been partly due to its endowments, which seem to have given the impression that St. John's College was a wealthy institution;

it may have been partly because of the fact that clerical members of the college staff, as part of the mission staff of the Cathedral, were so busy fostering the work of the Church in new parishes in Winnipeg, as well as out in the country, that they had no time to make appeals for the College and its work, a characteristic annual feature of other colleges affiliated with the University. In the last decade of the nineteenth century the general change in University curricula, which brought greater emphasis upon the teaching of scientific subjects, presented an academic and financial problem to the colleges associated in the University of Manitoba. At first the colleges endeavoured to teach a certain amount of this work themselves, and in St. John's, Professor E. B. Kenrick and the Reverend W. A. Burman were the first lecturers in Chemistry and Botany.

An amendment to its charter, made in 1889, enabled the university to undertake instruction; but it did nothing until 1897, when negotiations were begun for it to teach natural science and to provide a permanent building for the purpose, completed in January, 1901. In 1904 five professorships were established and the colleges ceased to take any further interest in natural science. This new building was located on part of the old Hudson's Bay Company's property on Broadway. This was very convenient for Manitoba and Wesley Colleges, only a few minutes' walk away, but extremely inconvenient for students from St. John's, which was three miles distant. Upon the assurance of the University that the Broadway site was to be a permanent location, St. John's College acquired a considerable piece of property on the west side of Osborne Street,[10] and with Canon W. J. Garton as its agent pressed forward with its new building fund, in spite of a debt of $25,000 on its buildings in St. John's.

In 1910, however, the University entered an agreement for a permanent site in Tuxedo, a suburb to the southwest of Winnipeg. The government of Manitoba showed no enthusiasm in providing the necessary funds to proceed with this scheme, and a further complication arose in 1913 when the government itself set aside a large tract of land adjacent to the new Agricultural College property in St. Vital and offered to erect certain buildings for the University. This site, now the permanent home of the University of Manitoba, is commonly known as the Fort Garry site. It is only fair to the government of Manitoba to say that it had before it the findings of a Royal Commission, which it had set up in 1907 under the chairmanship of Sir J. A. M.

[10]Opposite the Legislative Building, and now occupied by the head office of The Great West Life Assurance Company. The property cost about $11,400 (Archbishop Matheson once told the writer that he obtained a gift of $10,000 from Lord Strathcona towards this), and during the twenty-eight years it was held the College paid the city of Winnipeg approximately $33,000 in taxes.

Aikens. This was a very comprehensive document, and upon reading it after more than forty years, one would say that the majority of its recommendations have since been incorporated into the university fabric; the only recommendation with regard to a university site was a suggestion of proximity to the Agricultural College.

In the meantime the pressure on St. John's was so great, both in the college and school, that in 1912 a new temporary building was erected on the north side of Church Avenue (long known as "The Annex") and the main building was extended, providing for a chapel, domestic staff quarters, and a gymnasium. During World War I there were few students, because of enlistments in the armed forces, and the work was carried on by a skeleton staff. The school, however, grew to such an extent that the addition known as Hamber Hall was added in 1920. In 1921 the college entered on a new lease of life with the appointment of the Reverend G. A. Wells as Warden. The teaching of a full Arts course was resumed, the new Warden secured considerable funds for the training of men in Theology, raising rather more than dollar for dollar with what the Diocese itself provided. There was a further increase in the student body in 1929 when the University transferred its senior division work to Fort Garry, the Agricultural College having been determined the permanent university site. This latter move had been strongly recommended by a second Royal Commission, the one of 1923 under the chairmanship of Dr. Walter Murray, President of the University of Saskatchewan. Presented as part of this latter report, issued in 1924, was one by Dr. W. S. Learned of the Carnegie Foundation for the Advancement of Teaching, which dealt specially with the fellowship between the University and the affiliated colleges. It was intimated that when the Carnegie Foundation had completed the work of establishing King's College, Nova Scotia, on the campus of Dalhousie University in Halifax, it would give favourable consideration to assisting a scheme whereby the affiliated colleges of the University of Manitoba might be housed in their own quarters on the campus at Fort Garry. It was not the fault of St. John's College that this scheme was never brought to a successful conclusion. Nearly thirty-five years were to pass, and the Learned Report of 1924 was forgotten, before St. John's College was built on the university campus at Fort Garry at the cost of nearly a million dollars.

The years between the two World Wars were singularly productive. The appointment of the Reverend W. C. de Pauley, a brilliant young Irishman, to the chair of Systematic Theology in 1920 brought a new emphasis to an old subject; his return to parochial work in Ireland in 1926 was regretted. The appointment of Canon J. W. Matheson as

Dean of Rupert's Land in 1922 caused him to vacate the chair of Exegetical Theology for the lighter duties of the chair of Ecclesiastical History and Liturgiology. The Church Missionary Society, which still had the right of appointment to the professorship of Exegesis at the time, replaced him with the Reverend P. W. Stephenson, a scholar of considerable experience in educational work in India, who threw himself into the work of College, Cathedral and Diocese with great enthusiasm and drive for the next four years, but then returned to his homeland of Australia. The Church Missionary Society then appointed to the professorship a young graduate of Trinity Hall, Cambridge, with distinguished academic standing, the Reverend H. G. G. Herklots, whose lively disposition, evangelical missionary outlook, skilful pen and wide interest in life generally, did great service to the College and Church during the next six years. The re-admission of women students in 1929 increased the number of the student body, and women were added to the staff on the Arts side. The first Dean of Women was Miss Marion W. Smith, whose excellent scholarship and good sense did much to make the time of integration a happy one.

The Closing Years of Archbishop Matheson

On September 30, 1930, Archbishop Matheson resigned as Primate of All Canada, and on January 31, 1931, resigned the See of Rupert's Land. He felt that having passed his seventy-eighth year, the burden of office was getting too great for him. The news of his retirement was received with great regret, not only in the Diocese to which he had given much of his life, but in the Church generally, which recognized his great qualities of sound leadership and good judgment. The twenty-one years of his primacy had seen not only the consolidation of the three great departments of the General Synod, but a great expansion of their work. Under the energetic direction of Canon Sidney Gould the work of the M.S.C.C. had been greatly extended in China, Japan and India. The consecration of Bishop W. C. White as first Bishop of Honan in 1909, and Bishop H. J. Hamilton as first Bishop of Mid-Japan in 1912, had been notable advances in the foreign field. In Canada, though there had been difficulties in the missionary dioceses, the success of the Anglican Forward Movement after World War I had promoted wide interest, and gradually the foundations for the new Diocese of The Arctic had been laid. Under the leadership of Dr. R. A. Hiltz, with the very able assistance of Dr. D. B. Rogers as editorial secretary after 1920, the General Board of Religious Education had revised the Sunday School system of the Church and entered the field of youth education. The special gifts and organizing ability of Canon C. W. Vernon, who became secretary of the Council for

Christian Social Service in 1919, brought the Church to a better understanding of its place in the social developments of the time. The consecration of Bishop Thomas in 1924 to the Diocese of Brandon brought some relief to the Archbishop himself, but the growth of suburban parishes around Winnipeg, and difficulties arising in some of the older ones in the central part of the city, gave him concern. Industrial development had almost isolated Christ Church, but about 1930 it became the centre of an outburst of social service activity. In the two years of the depression, before there was government action, a thousand men a month were being fed and helped on their way to employment. The influx of a new Canadian population was rapidly diminishing the necessity of St. Peter's on Selkirk Avenue (it was closed in 1934), and there were serious misgivings about the future of Holy Trinity. The parish of St. Luke's was seriously affected by the financial depression of the early thirties. Archdeacon R. B. McElheran continued to fill St. Matthew's by his effective pastoral ministry, until he was called to the Principalship of Wycliffe College, Toronto, in 1930. A new and very beautiful All Saints' Church was built at the corner of Broadway and Osborne in 1926 under the Reverend H. R. Ragg; the city had acquired the old site under a scheme of street improvements. On the east side of Red River St. Phillip's, which had grown considerably under the ministry of the Reverend W. Cowans in the new suburb south of St. Boniface after the war, made more rapid progress under the care of the Reverend F. W. Goodeve from 1924. To the south in St. Vital, St. Mark's and St. Mary Magdalene were moving towards parochial independence through the efforts of devoted laymen. On the north side of the city the Cathedral missions of St. Anne's in West Kildonan and St. Martin's were gaining strength under the Reverends H. McCartney and Percy Heywood, the latter building a new church in the early twenties. In East Kildonan, similar progress had been made at St. Stephen's under the Reverends J. A. Shirley and H. Sherstone. The Reverend F. Glover went to St. Margaret's, in the residential district south of Portage Avenue, in 1921 and, at the time this is written, is entering on his thirty-ninth year as rector, a record only exceeded in the diocese by Archdeacon Fortin's forty-two years at Holy Trinity. St. Jude's, close to the Winnipeg General Hospital, under the Reverend G. Horrobin, had effectively replaced Old St. George's; St. Patrick's on Valour Road was bridging the gap between St. Matthew's and St. James'; St. Paul's in Fort Garry had begun its independence as a parish under the Reverend A. R. Hall; and in River Heights, to the west of the new St. George's that was gaining importance with the Reverend H. D. Martin as rector, the newer parish of St. Aidan's had built a basement church under the guidance of Dr. R. C. Johnstone. St. Thomas', Weston, and St. George's, Transcona, were experiencing the usual struggles of districts largely populated by railway workers on shifts.

In the rural parts of the Diocese it was a time of problems. Portage la Prairie continued a strong parish under Canon D. T. Parker, but elsewhere deterioration in farm prosperity, changing population, and a constantly moving ministry hindered effective progress in the Church; with these conditions the Archbishop could no longer contend. Warden Wells, as unofficial general missionary, and the students of St. John's College, however, gave a great deal of help during these years.

Archbishop Matheson lived in retirement until May 19, 1942, when he died in the eighty-ninth year of his age. Although his public appearances were rare during the eleven years of his retirement, he maintained a keen interest in the affairs of the Church. His life was woven into the history of the Church in Canada; there were few important events after 1875 with which he was not connected, and the whole community looked on him with affection and respect. The death in 1934 of his old friend Sheriff Colin Inkster, who had been a member of Synod for fifty-two years and rector's warden of St. John's Cathedral for sixty-three years, saddened him. The Honourable John Bracken said of the Archbishop: "His was a life of effort and achievement and one in which it was his lot to see the prospering of his work from the foundation he helped to lay."

Election of Archbishop Stringer

The Electoral Committee of the Province of Rupert's Land met on April 15, 1931, under the presidency of Bishop Stringer of the Yukon, as senior Bishop. Eight names appeared on the first ballot, of whom six were bishops; on the fourth ballot it was announced that Bishop I. O. Stringer had been elected, and he was enthroned in St. John's Cathedral on September first. His simple dignity, friendly disposition and obvious earnestness to do what was right for the Diocese brought sincere reciprocity on the part of the church people. The laymen of the Diocese seemed to acquire new enthusiasm under his leadership, and in the spring of 1932 a survey was conducted on the needs of the Diocese. It was a model report, but unhappily circumstances arose that caused it to be laid aside, and the implementation of its recommendations was never carried out.

Financial Disaster: The Machray Defalcations

Towards the end of August, 1932, the city of Winnipeg was astounded and the Anglican Church dismayed to learn that defalcations had occurred in the affairs of Machray and Sharpe of Winnipeg. This long established and much respected firm had, for more than fifty years, been the finanical agent of both the Land Board of the University of Manitoba, for which it had also handled other trust funds, and of the Church of England in the Province of Rupert's Land. The senior member of the firm, John A. Machray, was the first Chancellor of the Diocese of Rupert's Land, Chairman of the University Board of Governors, Bursar of both the University and St. John's College. This combination of positions brought unusual powers under his sole direction. Defective administrative practices in the affairs of Machray and Sharpe had been known and recognized for some years by those who had professional contact with the firm, but the reputation of Machray, and his managing clerk R. H. Shanks, stood high in the city; criticism and comment never came into the open and the real state of affairs was not even suspected. The first approximate estimates of the losses indicated that the university and the Church had lost about $800,000 each.

A Synod of the Diocese was held on October 19, and the whole matter can best be understood by reference to the report presented by the newly appointed Chancellor, Jules Preudhomme, to this Synod; the figures follow.

(1) Archbishop of Rupert's Land	$116,991.10	
Chafyn Grove Trust	4,190.79	
Tukudh Trust	10,556.31	
		$131,238.20
(2) Clergy Widows' and Orphans' Fund	85,504.21	
Clergy Superannuation Fund	34,000.00	
		119,504.21
(3) Episcopal Endowment Fund,		
Diocese of Athabasca	77,630.61	
Bishop of Keewatin	84,548.73	
Bishop of Moosonee	83,646.48	
Bishop of Mackenzie River	59,254.00	
Diocese of Yukon	54,672.60	
		359,752.42
(4) Dean and Chapter of St. John's Cathedral	28,586.29	
St. John's College; Sundry Trusts	119,560.42	
		148,146.71
		$758,146.71

These figures are rather less in amount, and of a later date, than those released by *The Canadian Churchman* on October 6, 1932, but accuracy was impossible at that time.[11] (The Preudhomme Report is included as an appendix to this chapter.)

The Chancellor then summarized the adjustments being made in the Province and in the Diocese for the curtailment of current expenditures to meet the situation that had arisen, and discussed the steps being taken to restore the capital of the funds in full. The M.S.C.C. was undertaking a campaign for the restoration of the endowment funds of the five dioceses concerned, and he pleaded that the restoration of the other funds should be made part of an overall appeal to the Church in Canada. A three-year campaign was commenced under the direction of Canon Sydney Gould, secretary of the M.S.C.C., which was successful, largely because of his consummate skill in handling situations and people, and his relentless energy. When the situation was fully understood across Canada, church members responded generously. That response was made not only to the need, but also out of sympathy with Archbishop Stringer, who addressed meeting after meeting in eastern Canada. He saw the defalcations not simply as a matter of restoring missing funds, but as an opportunity to advance the work of the Church. In his closing address to this Synod (certainly the shortest and probably the most important in the long history of the Diocese), the Archbishop said: "The eyes of men are on the Church and either she is going to move forward in the power of Christ or she will become a dying Church. The time is ripe and over ripe for us to move forward. We must not count the cost. . . . Let us go back to our parishes and our homes renewed in spirit and with fresh determination to carry out the great work of the Master. God helping us we shall move forward in His strength and by His power. Let us remember that Christ will be with us all along the way."

As a temporary measure, while the Restoration Fund was being completed, the stipends of the missionary Bishops and the current requirements of the beneficiary funds were provided by a levy of seven per cent placed upon the stipends of the officials and missionaries in Canada and overseas (including those paid by the Woman's Auxiliary) of the Missionary Society, and from voluntary contributions by the general body of Bishops and clergy. In the Diocese of Rupert's Land, which was not included in this scheme as it was not regarded as a missionary diocese, those immediately affected by the financial situation were the Archbishop himself, the members of the Dean and Chapter of St. John's Cathedral, and the staffs of St. John's College and College School. Drastic steps were taken without delay to make it

[11]Machray and Sharpe's affairs were found to be in an indescribable state of confusion when examined, and it is doubtful whether more than approximations were ever possible; certainly not at the time, and no comprehensive figures have been published since.

possible to carry on the work of the educational institutions. The property known as Bishop's Court, which had been acquired by Bishop Anderson as an episcopal residence, with the house that had been built by Archdeacon Matheson to replace the old log building, was sold; the old deanery, close by the Cathedral, was used instead. The cost of making further repairs to the house was considered an unjustifiable expenditure, and the annual taxes were thought to be excessive.

The College and School found themselves almost inextricably tangled up with the University, and therefore with the provincial government, over a mortgage that technically left them homeless; moreover, the effects of the great financial recession in the United States were being seriously felt in western Canada. The situation was overcome by the entire college staff agreeing to accept one hundred dollars a month in cash (if it could be provided), together with a free house and fuel; an equivalent system was worked out for the school staff; and an arrangement was made with the Winnipeg creditors to accept payment of past debts on a *pro rata* basis as collections could be made, and to do business in future on a strictly cash basis. About two years later an arrangement was made with General Synod, as trustees of the Restoration Fund, whereby $25,000 was placed at the disposal of the College; it became possible to arrange a final settlement with the University and outstanding creditors. The campaign for the Restoration Fund was brought to a successful conclusion, but the restored capital could only be reinvested at about three per cent owing to conditions in the economic market of the 1930's, causing current income to be seriously diminished.

The Death of Archbishop Stringer

The sudden death of Archbishop Stringer on the afternoon of October 30, 1934, was a great loss, not only to the Diocese but to the Church as a whole. As the *Winnipeg Tribune* noted: "An Archbishop is dead and a City mourns!" During his brief episcopate in Rupert's Land he had endeared himself to many outside the Church, as well as to its members, by his kindliness and sympathetic nature. Archbishop Owen expressed the feelings of the Church of England in Canada when he described him as truly an Israelite without guile: "He leaves a noble record behind him, a record of selfless, heroic work for Christ, the Church of England, to which he was devoted, and for Canada. A great leader has gone from us."

The Election of Archbishop Harding

The Electoral Committee of the Province of Rupert's Land met on December 12, 1934, under the chairmanship of the Bishop of

Qu'Appelle (Harding), as senior Bishop, to elect a new Metropolitan. On the sixth ballot the Right Reverend Malcolm Taylor McAdam Harding was declared elected. He was enthroned as Metropolitan on February 2, 1935, in St. John's Cathedral. He brought to the tangled affairs of the Church in the Diocese of Rupert's Land the wisdom derived from twenty-five years of administrative work as a bishop. His unusually wide knowledge of ecclesiastical business, shrewd judgment, firmness of disposition, and capacity for decisive action made an important contribution to both Diocese and Province at a critical time. His episcopate may be looked upon as a period of re-consolidation. The early part of it was necessarily devoted to straightening out the financial affairs of the Diocese and College, but his wise counsel to the clergy, his emphasis at all times upon the requirements of the *Book of Common Prayer,* his revival of the work in the rural deaneries, encouragement of lay readers, expansion of the Church in the Interlake area, and his straightforward addresses all helped to re-establish the work of the Church after its cataclysmic disaster.

In the educational field of the Diocese there were two outstanding events: the reorganization of the Diocesan Board of Religious Education in 1938, which made it a more effective committee by increasing its membership and broadening the scope of its activities, and the emergence of St. John's College from some of its more harassing troubles. The election of the Reverend G. A. Wells, who had been Warden of St. John's College for the past thirteen years, as Bishop of Cariboo in September, 1934, left a vacancy that was not filled until May, 1935, when Canon Walter Foster Barfoot, formerly professor of New Testament in Emmanuel College, Saskatoon, but at the time professor of Church History in the College, was appointed Warden. The next three years saw an increase in the student body and the addition of new members to the staff, despite the depression. In 1937 Canon Barfoot went to England to re-establish the connection between the College and the great missionary societies. He remained there for the first six months of 1938 and achieved some success in securing new support. Efforts were made in western Canada at the same time to resuscitate interest in the College. Unfortunately the outbreak of war in 1939 caused the collapse of both these efforts, and in 1940 the College temporarily abandoned instruction in all subjects in the Junior Division of Arts of the University, continuing only such senior work as could be taught by the theological staff.

Canon Barfoot was elected Bishop of Edmonton on January 29, 1941, but his consecration was delayed till the end of the academic session, taking place on April 25. He was succeeded as Warden by

Canon R. S. K. Seeley, then Professor of Exegetical Theology at St. John's.

Archbishop Harding resigned at the end of 1942, spending the rest of his life in retirement in Victoria, British Columbia, until his death on April 30, 1949, in the eighty-sixth year of his life, the sixty-first of his ministry and the fortieth of his episcopate.

The Right Reverend Louis Ralph Sherman
Becomes Metropolitan

The committee to elect a Metropolitan in place of Archbishop Harding met on February 11, 1943, with the senior Bishop of the Province, the Right Reverend W. W. H. Thomas of Brandon, presiding. On the third ballot it was announced that the Right Reverend Louis Ralph Sherman, Bishop of Calgary, had been elected. Bishop Sherman was then in the fifty-sixth year of his life, the thirty-first of his ministry, and had been Bishop of Calgary for sixteen years.

With his vigorous personality, impressive intellectual gifts and capacity for leadership, he brought to the Diocese a new outlook, and in a number of directions stirred it into what might be described as enthusiastic action. Nowhere was this better or more continuously shown than in the increased amount of missionary giving reported from year to year. The apportionments received for the Home Mission Fund in 1937 were $13,528, of which approximately $3,500 went to the central funds of the Church. While there had been some improvement during the intervening years, the plan for gradually increasing such apportionments, put forward by the Archbishop in 1946, met with an excellent response; in 1947 the amount received was nearly $30,500, and in 1948 almost $35,000. By 1953 the amount contributed was over $62,000, of which over $16,500 was devoted to the central missionary funds of the Church. The success of this endeavour was due to voluntary acceptance by the parishes of greatly increased objectives, when they became aware of the real needs of the church, and consequent gradual adoption of a system of every member canvass in the parishes.[12]

Approximately two-thirds of the diocesan budget was for the Home Mission Fund. Archbishop Sherman consistently pleaded for increased stipends for all missionary clergy and it gave him great satisfaction when, at the end of 1952, the executive committee of the Diocese agreed to raise the minimum stipend of incumbents in its

---

[12]The success of this effort to increase diocesan giving was largely due to the indefatigable work of Richard H. Pook, Secretary-Treasurer of the Diocese, 1933-1958. Mr. Pook achieved over the years a deservedly high reputation in the service of the Diocesan, Provincial and General Synods of the Anglican Church in Canada. His skilful, business-like approach, and unbiased judgment on any matter submitted to him, made him a valued adviser on the business of the Church.

missionary parishes to $2,400 a year, though for several years previously much assistance had been given them through a system of cost-of-living bonuses. At the same time, the self-supporting parishes agreed to meet this new minimum.

The last financial campaign in which the Archbishop showed his exceptional powers of leadership was one of church extension in order to meet the demand for churches in new areas of Winnipeg. The canvass for this in the summer of 1953 reached $603,000 in cash and pledges, while the high spiritual level upon which it was conducted was productive of new life in the parishes taking part.

In 1945 a drastic change took place in the circumstances of St. John's College when the "Annex" of 1912 on Church Avenue was sold and the College moved into premises at the corner of Broadway and Hargrave. The College benefited from a very considerably increased grant from the Diocese and the generosity of private subscribers. The scope of its work, however, was still limited in spite of additions to its staff, and the fact that the university itself was now conducted entirely on the Fort Garry site was a detriment to increased enrolment. The Reverend Reginald J. Pierce became Warden of the College in 1943 in succession to Canon Seeley, who had been appointed Dean of St. George's Cathedral, Kingston, Ontario. Under Canon Pierce the theological studies of the College were emphasized, and the general arts work began to recover from the effects of the war. Upon his election as Bishop of Athabasca in September, 1950, an old student of the College, who had had wide ministerial and educational experience, the Reverend L. F. Wilmot, was appointed Warden.

At the Synod of the Diocese in 1949, it was reported that the transfer of properties of the Dean and Chapter of St. John's Cathedral to the Synod had been successfully completed, and this marks the end of the Dean and Chapter of the Cathedral as constituted in 1874. For a good many years there had been some dissatisfaction in the Cathedral parish over the fact that it had what might be termed "a collective ministry" instead of a rector of its own. An attempt had been made by the Synod of 1938 to placate this feeling by amending Section XII of the Cathedral Statutes so as to set up a sixth canonry, which could be filled without endowment when the parish consented to provide an adequate stipend. The holder of this canonry was to be responsible for the cure of souls, visiting in the parish, and carrying out the duties of an ordinary rector.[13] Provision was made, however, for the retention of the rights and privileges of other members of the Chapter; this arrangement worked satisfactorily for several years. On the financial

[13]Canon W. E. Jackson (1938-1941) was the only appointee to this "Sixth Canonry" under the amended statute.

side, while the loss of capital of the Dean and Chapter was replaced through the Restoration Fund, no attempt was ever made to increase it so as to provide proportionately the previous standard of stipend for the canonries. The funds were considerably decreased about 1941 when it was found necessary for the Dean and Chapter to undertake most of the expense of reinforcing the foundations under the chancel of the Cathedral. During World War II only two new Canons were appointed,[14] both members of the College staff, and finally in 1947 the Cathedral parish was reconstituted as the Parish of St. John the Evangelist, with its own rector. The Reverend J. O. Anderson, who became rector in October, 1949, was also appointed Dean of Rupert's Land. Since the resignation of the Very Reverend J. W. Matheson in 1934, there had been no Dean of Rupert's Land, the senior Canon assuming charge of the Cathedral.

Archbishop Sherman was always greatly concerned over the scattered communities of church people in the country, many of whom were without regular ministrations of the Church because of vacancies in rural parishes, partly due to the difficulty of obtaining men and, in some parishes, adequate stipends. The Archbishop, therefore, revived in 1946 the position of general missionary, whose work it was to minister to all the isolated points in the diocese.[15] The area between Lakes Winnipeg and Manitoba, which had been opened up for settlement about 1912, was one that from about 1925 caused grave concern because of its economic difficulties. The Reverend H. J. Tomkins, when he was rector of St. Andrew's Parish, Red River, (1931-1939) made a personal visitation through a large part of this area, and for several years the work of the Church was carried on there by a small

[14]Canon W. J. Merrick (1940-1953) became professor of Church History, and Canon R. J. Pierce (1943-1950) professor of Exegetical Theology, as well as Warden of the College. Canon R. S. K. Seeley held this professorship from 1938-1943. By Statute, residentiary canonries were attached to the professorial chairs of Exegetical and Systematic Theology and Church History. The "Sixth Canonry" was originally designated to a chair of Church Music, to be held by the Precentor of St. John' Cathedral (if and when such an appointment might be possible; Canon G. F. Coombes held it from 1883 to 1905, when he became Dean and transferred to the Professorship of Church History). The two Archdeacons of the Diocese held the first two canonries, which were deemed non-residential. The Dean of the Cathedral *might* be Professor of Pastoral Theology if he so desired, but not necessarily vice versa. Dean Grisdale (1882-1896) was the only holder of both positions simultaneously.

[15]After the establishment of the Diocese of Brandon in 1924, it was erroneously thought that a general missionary was unnecessary in the Diocese of Rupert's Land. This mistake was finally rectified under pressure of circumstances by the appointment of the Reverend A. R. Hall (1923-1933). The lapse of fifteen years before the position was again filled was caused by lack of funds in the Diocese, and by World War II. Then Archdeacon R. N. R. Holmes (1947-1950) and Rev. R. F. Dawson (1950-1956) held the position. In this latter period it entailed serving sixteen parishes, with forty-one churches, and travelling about 2.500 miles a month by car. The situation was eased after 1955 by a scheme that linked city curates with country parishes, and later by an increase in the number of clergy in the diocese.

community of clergy and lay workers whose permanent home was St. Andrew's rectory. To support this, the Interlake Fellowship was organized. After the community was disbanded, the work was taken over by Bishop's Messengers located at Eriksdale, and then continued to receive the generous support of members of the Fellowship.

On July 31, 1953, Archbishop Sherman died suddenly while on holiday at Clear Lake, Manitoba. He will be remembered for his business ability, forceful personality, and his power as a speaker. By his forthrightness in the councils of the Church he made a permanent contribution to the expansion of its work in the Diocese of Rupert's Land and in Canada as a whole.

The Election of Archbishop Barfoot

On October 7, 1953, the committee of the Provincial Synod met in Winnipeg and elected as Metropolitan the Most Reverend Walter Foster Barfoot, Archbishop of Edmonton and Primate of All Canada. Archbishop Barfoot had been elected Primate on September 7, 1951, and was enthroned in St. John's Cathedral as Bishop and Metropolitan of Rupert's Land on January 4, 1954. Thus, for the third time, the Primacy of the Church of England in Canada became associated with the Diocese and Province of Rupert's Land.[16]

APPENDIX A
St. John's College School and St. John's Ladies' School

Just as the Red River Academy (1833-1859) was an effort on the part of the Church to meet the requirements of boys and girls for higher education in the days of the fur trade, so St. John's College School and St. John's Ladies' School were the pioneer schools of higher education during the years of expansion in western Canada. Provincial systems of communication and education were in process of organization. The influence of the Church's schools was wide, their work greatly appreciated, but the superior financial position of the publicly supported institution brought insoluble problems to all private institutions in the western provinces. St. John's College School closed in 1950.

The College School was an integral part of the College from 1866 to 1912, after which gradual separation took place, to be completed in 1945. School teaching has generally been regarded as a transient trade in this country of opportunity, but there were a number of masters who stayed sufficiently long on the staff of the College School to have a permanent influence upon the lives of those they taught, and their names are now recorded: in the earlier days, R. C. Bourne, Thomas Warburton, E. W. Hamber, and Arthur T. Cowley; in later years Lestock H. Adams, E. J. Lewis, J. C. Iliffe, A. M. Headlam and Arthur Wilbraham. The name of Walter Burman is in an exceptional category. He entered the school as a small boy about 1890, passed on through the College, joined the staff in 1902, and ended his career when he resigned in 1946 as Headmaster, after serving in that position for thirty-three years. A man of strong personality, marked Christian character and great ability as a teacher, he exercised a beneficent and lasting influence on all

[16]A. R. Kelley and D. B. Rogers, *The Anglican Episcopate of Canada and Newfoundland*, II (Toronto, 1961), 88-89.

those who came under his care and guidance.* During his leadership the School reached its highest reputation, greatest success, and survived the hazards of depression and war.

The St. John's College Ladies' School was founded on October 23, 1876, by the Committee of the Church Missionary Society in Rupert's Land, with the consent and co-operation of the College Council; this was made possible by a gift of £1,500 from the Reverend Henry Wright, then connected with the C.M.S. in London, England. The board of governors established six representatives on it from the Council and Committee. The first premises were on Redwood Avenue at the corner of Main Street, and members of the College staff taught some of the classes; the first Principal was Miss Hart Davies (Mrs. A. E. Cowley). About 1918 St. John's College acquired Havergal College in Winnipeg (a branch of the Toronto institution) and the two schools were united under the name of Rupert's Land Ladies' College, with which are associated the names of Miss E. L. Jones, Miss Gladys Millard and Miss E. M. Bartlett as Principals. After World War II enrolment in such private schools in the west dropped. Rupert's Land Ladies' College was amalgamated with the United Church's Riverbend School on equitable terms, and the reorganized school has since been carried on under the name of Balmoral Hall.

APPENDIX B

Part of Chancellor Jules Preudhomme's Report to the Synod of the Diocese of Rupert's Land on October 19, 1932:

The enclosed statement shows the amounts reported by the auditors as missing from the different trust funds which were managed by Machray and Sharpe. These amounts are taken from the statement submitted to the creditors under the bankruptcy proceedings, although different figures were previously furnished by the auditors, the difference being due to interest having been added in the earlier statement and not in the figures submitted to the creditors, and to the production of certain documents which were first listed as missing. The auditors point out, however, that the statements do not in all cases agree with the books, and they do not therefore guarantee the statements. They also point out that the amounts shown as missing are arrived at by checking over the securities found in the vault of Machray and Sharpe against statements also found in the vault parcelled up with the remaining securities, and in some cases in empty pockets, showing the list of securities which should be in the pockets. The auditors took special care to point out, however, that they do not guarantee the validity or value of the securities left. Most of these are in the form of mortgages, and they have not been able to verify the balances due under the mortgages by reference to the mortgagors, nor have they been able to satisfy themselves that the mortgages have not been paid up or nearly paid up. The Trustee in Bankruptcy is taking steps to have this done. No search has been made of the lands to ascertain whether there are any other mortgages in existence prior or subsequent to the mortgages shown, nor has any investigation been made as to the value of the lands shown in the mortgages. This is being done by the Trustee, and this work of the Trustee will be made available to the Church and will be supplemented by representatives of the Church organizations. The total loss is shown as $758,641.54. If, however, the balances assumed to be in existence substantially disappear in the vanishing of the value of the securities, then of course this amount will be increased accordingly. . . .

Under a deed authorized by the relevant statutes of the constitution, the Dean and Chapter and of St. John's College have been handed over to the authority of the Diocese of Rupert's Land, subject to the consent of His Grace the Archbishop, but this did not impose any financial obligations upon the

*T. C. B. Boon, "Walter Burman of St. John's, Winnipeg," *Canadian Churchman* (January 10, 1948), 17.

Diocese of Rupert's Land because of the endowments out of which the expenses of the Dean and Chapter were provided, and the fact that St. John's College as a separate corporation managed its own affairs, and paid its way by means of the endowments and fees from students, as well as some revenue from lands now forming part of the St. John's Cemetery. The disappearance of the endowment funds will now make very material difference.

With respect to the Clergy Widows' and Orphans' Fund and Clergy Superannuation Fund, these were managed by committees which made direct contact with Machray and Sharpe. Only a part of the funds receivable by the beneficiaries of these funds came from this Ecclesiastical Province. The balance is still obtainable from the Pensions Committee of the Church with Headquarters in Toronto.

With respect to the funds of the Missionary Dioceses, each endowment was managed separately, a committee of local Winnipeg men being appointed in each case, and in each case the committee was in direct contact with Machray and Sharpe. It was obvious that such funds as those appertaining to the Trusts of Athabasca, Yukon, Mackenzie River, Moosonee, and Keewatin could not be invested in those different Dioceses, and it was not illogical for the investments to be made from a centre such as Winnipeg under the management of local committees. That was the machinery employed. The disappearance of these funds now places upon all churchmen throughout Canada the responsibility of restoring the episcopal endowments in question. The Missionary Society of the Canadian Church has made definite temporary provision for the stipends of these Bishops. The Chafyn Grove Trusts and the Tukudh Trusts were also managed by committees appointed for the purpose.

Bankruptcy proceedings have been taken against Machray and Sharpe with a view to rendering their assets available for distribution among the creditors, and the Royal Trust Company has been appointed the Trustee. The inspectors have been appointed in the bankruptcy proceedings, of whom Mr. J. Preudhomme represents the Church.

An action was brought by a creditor named Smith to have a Receiver appointed for the trust property, naming W. S. Newton & Company as the Receiver. This was refused by the Court, due to the opposition of the University, the Church concurring in this opposition.

On a motion made to the Court on behalf of the Archbishop of Rupert's Land, the Dean and Chapter of St. John's Cathedral, and St. John's College, The Royal Trust Company was appointed Receiver of such portions of the trust estate as it is impossible to segregate, the reason being that so far it has been impossible to segregate the property appertaining to each individual trust or private creditor, the one from the other, or from the estate of the firm. The auditors have done some work with this end in view and have made a preliminary report, but it will take some considerable time for a conclusive report to be made. Assuming the monies shown as missing from the funds produced interest at 5%, the sum of $37,932.08 would be required to replace the lost income. For some time it will be impossible to obtain any income from any balance in hand, so it will be necessary to make full provision for meeting the expenses of the different Dioceses and organizations depending upon the income from the funds which were held by Machray and Sharpe. Perhaps a readjustment of the activities of these bodies might bring about a reduction in the expenses and in the money required to meet them. Steps to this end have already been taken.

. . . So far as these various corporations and trusts are concerned, the system seems to have grown up of allowing Mr. Machray, as Agent or Bursar, or as an individual, to handle the funds and properties, and it has been stated in evidence before the Commission that some of these funds were invested in his own name. The bonds would appear to have been, in most cases, bearer bonds. If the mortgages or securities of each of these various funds had been taken in the name of the Corporations or the Trustees, the securities should not have disappeared without the concurrence of the Corporations or Trustees by their executing Deeds or Discharges of Mortgages.

This explanation, of course, does not and cannot take into account whether any losses occurred by unprofitable investments or the payment of income out of principal. It will be readily seen that if the losses did occur in that way in the past years, and income and taxes were continued to be paid, the principal must be used up. . . .

CHAPTER TWELVE

The Saskatchewan Valley Since the 1890's
Saskatchewan–Saskatoon–A New Saskatchewan

⋯❖⋘⪼❖⋯❖⋘⪼❖⋯❖⋘⪼❖⋯❖⋘⪼❖⋯❖⋘⪼❖⋯❖⋘⪼❖⋯❖⋘⪼❖⋯

The first Synod of this diocese over which I presided was held July 23rd to 26th, 1905. We initiated then the plan which we have kept up, of beginning with Synod Sunday, the only diocese, I think which does this. There was on that Sunday, as now, an ordination in the morning, and the Synod sermon in the evening. . . . At that Synod, there were 19 clergy and 27 lay delegates present. Last year there were 47 clergy and 40 lay delegates present. In 1905 there were in the diocese 25 clergy only, representing 66 congregations, not one parish being self-supporting. In 1920 the numbers had increased to 64 clergy, 322 congregations, and 26 self-supporting parishes. You had in 1905 been five years without a Synod. . . .

It was in the 1905 Synod that the first steps were taken towards closing Emmanuel College as an Indian Boarding School, and restoring it to the status and purpose of its foundation, viz.: a University and Theological College for the training of Clergy, Lay Readers and Teachers. To that Synod also I was able to report the formation of the six first parish branches of the Woman's Auxiliary. Those six have now become one hundred and five!

BISHOP NEWNHAM'S CHARGE
TO THE SYNOD OF *1921*

⋯❖⋘⪼❖⋯❖⋘⪼❖⋯❖⋘⪼❖⋯❖⋘⪼❖⋯❖⋘⪼❖⋯❖⋘⪼❖⋯❖⋘⪼❖⋯

One again we come back to the Saskatchewan valley. At the end of the nineteenth century the river itself had ceased to be important, and the governing factor in the development of the country was the railway, which brought the immigrants. It has already been shown how the construction of the Canadian Pacific Railway caused the formation of the Dioceses of Qu'Appelle and Calgary. North of the Touchwood Hills, however, between the western boundary of Manitoba and the Edmonton country, was a large section of prairie land where settlement was not to develop to any extent until after the turn of the century. A valiant attempt was made about 1883 to open up the countryside in the immediate neighbourhood of the present city of Saskatoon as a Temperance Colony, but the project failed. The Church did not exactly neglect the Diocese of Saskatchewan for the sixteen years between 1887 and 1903, but it did not show any conspicuous enthusiasm with respect to this area. During this period the work of the church in the Diocese of Saskatchewan continued to be chiefly among the Indians. Of the clergy who met at the Synod held in Prince Albert

287

on August 8, 1891, eleven were supported by the Church Missionary Society; one was in charge of the Battleford Industrial School; four were incumbents respectively of the two churches in Prince Albert, of Battleford (then the centre of administration of the North West Territories), and of Halcrow.

The Bishop's Charge on this occasion reflects the condition of the country. His chief concern was with the Indian work, and the increase in interest shown in it "by the various Woman's Auxiliaries which have been formed in Eastern Canada in recent years. The zeal, energy, and ability of these auxiliaries appear likely to do more to make the Church of England in Canada a missionary church than any other effort yet put forth."

Emmanuel College, responsible for the training of several of the clergy then at work in the diocese, appeared to be passing under a cloud and to have reached the status of an Indian school dependent upon government grants, at which level it was to remain for the next thirteen years.

One topic came up for discussion, to reappear time and time again, and that was the question of opening and closing the day schools with a Bible reading and prayer in all Protestant public schools, in the North West Territory. The Synod added provision for learning and reciting the Apostles' Creed, the Lord's Prayer and the Ten Commandments at stated times during school hours. Another very interesting resolution was one introduced by Chief Atahkakoop (Star Blanket), seconded by Chief James Smith: "That this Synod having reason to fear, that the importance of family worship is too often lost sight of, desires earnestly to press its observance on all heads of families, throughout the Diocese."

When the Synod met on August 22, 1894, there was little change in the general situation. Archdeacon George McKay had resigned the incumbency of St. Alban's, Prince Albert, owing to ill health.[1] Canon James Flett had resigned parochial duty to become public school inspector under the territorial government. The Reverend G. S. Winter, formerly Archdeacon of York, had taken charge of the mission at Sandy Lake, founded by the Reverend John Hines.

At this Synod the Bishop announced terms of the agreement with the parish of St. Alban's, Prince Albert (the only self-supporting parish in the diocese), whereby it became the pro-cathedral. He reported that

[1]George McKay went to British Columbia (*Crockford's Clerical Directory, 1898,* gives his address as Fort Donald, B.C.), and tradition has it that he was in the Klondike. In 1902 he moved to South Dakota, U.S.A., and in 1917 into Wyoming, where he spent ten years before retiring from active service with the Protestant Episcopal Church. He was ninety-five when he died at Hot Springs, S.D., on December 12, 1949, the last survivor of the Winnipeg Conference of 1890.

there were twenty clergy in the Diocese of Saskatchewan, and the number in the Diocese of Calgary would shortly be increased to eighteen. Each diocese really ought to have its own Bishop, and he had done everything in his power to bring this about. Much of the Bishop's Charge was of course directed to the subject of Indian missions. The grant from the Church Missionary Society was apparently being decreased at the rate of one-twentieth a year. This decrease was to have gone into effect three years previously, but the Bishop's representations had caused the C.M.S. to stay its hand. The Bishop said, "I am well aware of two things, first, that our Indians are much poorer now, and therefore far less able to support church work than they were twenty years ago; and secondly, that we are obliged to spend more on Indian education than was formerly the case. The Indian Department does, indeed, allow $300 per annum salary to the teacher of any ordinary Indian day school and whose existence it approves . . . but it provides no residence for the teacher. . . . Then there are one or two schools which we have felt obliged to maintain and for whose maintenance the Department does not give a dollar."[2] He was, however, grateful to the Indian Department for its continuance of the Battleford Industrial School.

Bishop Jervois A. Newnham takes Charge

The completion of the episcopal endowment of the Diocese of Calgary, which diocese Bishop Pinkham decided to retain, necessitated a new appointment for the Diocese of Saskatchewan, and on October first, 1903, the House of Bishops translated Bishop Jervois Arthur Newnham from the Diocese of Moosonee to the Diocese of Saskatchewan. He was singularly well equipped by education and experience to be Bishop of the Diocese of Saskatchewan during its period of expansion and change.

Bishop Newnham met the Synod of the Diocese of Saskatchewan for the first time on July 23, 1905, and some indication of the circumstance is found in the quotation at the head of this chapter. The Bishop said that during the twelve months he had been in residence in the Diocese he had visited all the organized missions and some districts where work was just beginning; he had travelled at least 4,000 miles. From what he had seen, he had become painfully aware that the Church of England had fallen behind other churches, for it had not nearly enough workers. The work had to be directed over such a large area that the clergy could not get into that personal touch with their people. The shortcomings were summarized by the Bishop: "Churches closed, missions vacant, the support of your clergy promised

[2]*Journal of the Proceedings of the Synod of the Diocese of Saskatchewan,* 1894.

by the people, yet withheld; congregations far smaller than they should be, while our own people go to other Churches; drunkenness is common while no effort is made to stem the tide; Churches closed from Sunday evening to the following Sunday morning, no wonder if the Church has gone backwards instead of forwards." He pleaded first of all for a spiritual revival of God's grace within themselves; for better methods of work; wiser organization; a closer confidence and sympathy between clergy and laity; a more ready and liberal giving for the support of the clergy and the spread of the Church. Some of these things had been urged by his predecessor: Bishop Pinkham in his Charge had told them, "I feel that no one rightly appreciates the religion that costs him nothing, and that no one can give of his substance for the Lord's work, in a true spirit without feeling his heart enlarged."

The Synod had already put on record a resolution with regard to Indian converts, "that the duty of almsgiving be constantly explained and earnestly impressed upon all our Indian converts . . . because they can in this way please God and promote the interests of the Church." The Bishop hoped that this would be a principle of action throughout the Diocese. He asked for a more active interest on the part of the laity, for there was a sad lack of lay workers.

From this time the Diocese of Saskatchewan took a permanent interest in the social welfare of the whole countryside. The Bishop called attention to the fact that there was not a single church temperance society in the Diocese, and hoped that steps would be taken to form one. The Synod responded by setting up committees to organize and carry on work along the lines of the Church of England Temperance Society, to encourage the formation of Sunday Schools, and to study the question of Sunday observance.

The organization of the rural deaneries was revised so that in future the rural deans would be nominated to the Bishop by the clergy in the deanery. The necessity of ruri-decanal meetings was emphasized, to lessen that spirit of selfishness that considers each parish exists by and for itself. Thus at this Synod principles were established upon which the work of the Church was to be promoted in the Diocese of Saskatchewan for the next fifteen years.

The Barr Colony

A noteworthy addition to the list of clergy published in the Proceedings of the Synod of the Diocese of Saskatchewan held in June, 1905, is the name of the Reverend G. E. Lloyd, M.A., of Lloydminster. His name, with the title of Venerable Archdeacon, and those of six other clergy and four catechists in the similar list of 1906, is prefixed with a note that they were "emigration" clergy and catechists. The Bishop made no comment on the Archdeacon's appointment in his Charge, except to remark that there was an increase of sixteen workers in the Diocese, which did not mean sixteen new missions but some forty-five or more new mission centres. During the last year they had been able to build "11 new churches, 1 church hall, 3 parsonages and 2 'shacks' facetiously called 'Lambeth Palaces,' and others were in the course of building or meditated." The fact is that there was a flood of new settlers coming into the Diocese, particularly its southern part. The most notable group has since become known as the Barr Colonists, though originally the name Britannia was associated with the settlement.

The Reverend George Exton Lloyd was a Londoner, born on January 6, 1861. He came to Canada in 1881 and attended Wycliffe College, Toronto. He was ordained deacon in old St. George's Church, Winnipeg, on July 12, 1885, by Bishop Machray, acting for Bishop Sweatman of Toronto. Mr. Lloyd came west in 1885 with Colonel Otter's troops at the time of the Riel Rebellion. In 1890 he became rector of Rothesay in New Brunswick and there established a residential school for boys (now known as Rothesay Collegiate School), of which he acted as principal. He returned to England to undertake permanent deputation work for the Colonial and Continental Church Society. At the close of the Boer War in 1902, certain difficulties arose respecting the returning troops. Work was not plentiful and men who had seen the wide open spaces of South Africa became restless upon their return to Great Britain. This turned Lloyd's thoughts to the matter of emigration, and as a consequence he wrote a letter to the *London Times* to say that he would be delighted to advise any who might consider going to Canada, of which country he had had twenty years experience. He was astonished when he received thousands of replies.

Some days later (according to Mrs. A. N. Wetton of North Battleford, who, in her book *The Promised Land*, has given us the fullest account of the Barr Colony), Mr. Lloyd was visited by the Reverend Isaac M. Barr, who had fifteen years farming experience in western Canada.[3] Barr explained that he had already made plans to take out

[3]C. R. Forster Bliss, ed., *The Clerical Guide and Churchman's Directory,* 1879: "BARR, Isaac. Born in Canada. Undergraduate University of Toronto. Studied Theology at the Hellmuth College, London, Ontario. Ordained Deacon 1871, by the Right Rev. Dr. Cronyn; Priest the same year by the Right Rev. Dr. Hellmuth. Appointed 1) Curate, Woodstock; 2) Exeter; 3) Examining Chaplain to Bishop of Saskatchewan; 4) Incumbent of Point Edward cum Perche. Now Rector, Newport." E. K. Matheson, "The Church of England amongst English-speaking Settlers," *Canadian North-West Historical Society Publications,* I (1927), 40. Canon Matheson states that Bishop McLean brought Mr. Barr from eastern Canada in 1875, and that he served the missions of St. Mary and St. Catherine, Prince Albert, for more than a year before returning east.

a party of settlers the following year, and Lloyd turned over to him the enquiries he had received. These, apparently, were followed by many others, and the scheme of settlement included plans for co-operative stores, medical care and other welfare projects for which money was forwarded by the applicants.[4] Many of the enquirers also wanted to know what provision was being made for Church and Sunday School. The only Church of England clergyman anywhere near the proposed districts of settlement was the Reverend J. F. Dyke Parker who was at Battleford, a hundred miles away. Mr. Lloyd took up this problem with the Colonial and Continental Church Society and an effort was made to find a suitable chaplain to accompany the party. Although a number of applications were considered, none was from a clergyman with Canadian experience. Finally Lloyd determined to go himself.

On March 31, 1903, Mr. and Mrs. Lloyd were on board the S.S. *Lake Manitoba* along with 2,684 men, women and children, ready to sail from Liverpool. They arrived at Saint John, New Brunswick, on Friday, April 10. As a leader and manager, Isaac Barr was a failure; he lost the confidence of his people and Lloyd was elected to take his place. He demurred at first because he had been engaged by the Colonial and Continental Church Society as their chaplain, but he finally consented on condition that a committee of twelve be appointed to assist in the management until settlement on the land could be completed. Lloyd informed the C. and C.C.S. of this move in a letter dated June 24, 1903, written from the N.W.M.P. Barracks at North Battleford.

In July Lloyd was able to acquire an old log school on the Onion Lake Indian Reserve from the Reverend J. R. Matheson. A house, twenty-two feet by twenty-six was built. Services were held there on Sundays when the weather no longer permitted them to be held in a large tent outside. There was room in the building for only 100 people at a time. The congregation sang from khaki-covered hymn books made for the soldiers in South Africa. The type was small and hard to read when the only light came from two stable lanterns, one at the front door and the other at the back, but they had wonderful services.

In 1905 the "Minster" was built, a log building forty-two feet by twenty, with a chancel twelve feet square. For the privilege of carving their names on the logs, the congregation paid $3 for the larger ones, $2 for those across the front, and $1 for the short ones between the windows. This was the cost of cutting, hauling and spiking them.

[4] J. H. McCormick, *Lloydminster* (London, 1920), contains a reprint of the pamphlet "British Settlements in North Western Canada on Free Grant Lands," issued in 1902 by Rev. I. M. Barr, curate-in-charge, St. Saviour's Church, Tollington Park, London, N., and an appendix summarizing the land regulations.

Before the Indians left for Onion Lake again, after completing the log work, a service of dedication was held on July 10. The foundation log had carved on it, "St. John's Minster, laid July 10th, 1904," and it was placed in position by the wardens, Nathaniel Jones and R. N. Blackburn. The church was officially opened by Bishop Newnham on August twelfth, amid great rejoicings.

While Lloyd was the leader, organizer and mentor of the colonists, Mrs. Lloyd took a large part in helping to establish the settlement; her patience, kindliness and steadfast faith not only enabled her to surmount her own particular trials and difficulties, but made her of much help to others.

Emmanuel College

Three factors brought Emmanuel College before the Synod of 1906: the first was the dissatisfaction felt with the attitude of the Department of Indian Affairs, which was not thought to be giving sufficient financial backing to it as an Indian school; the institution was to be closed, unless further financial support were forthcoming. The second issue was that the civil Province of Saskatchewan was beginning to talk about a provincial university that would be established in Saskatoon; the third and most critical issue arose from the rush of new settlers and the necessity of providing ministrations for them. On the motion of Archdeacon Lloyd, seconded by the Reverend D. D. McDonald, a long resolution was passed, consolidating several previous ones. It may be summarized briefly as stating the necessity of impressing upon the Board of the M.S.C.C. the new needs of the Diocese, and welcoming the proposed visit of Bishop Montgomery, Secretary of the S.P.G., and of the Reverend J. D. Mullins, Secretary of the C. and C.C.S. to the Diocese. A second motion by Archdeacon Lloyd, seconded by James McKay, K.C., recalled that at the Synod of 1905 it had been decided "that the present status and work of Emmanuel College be considered with a view to the reversion of the College (as far as possible) to the original purpose of its foundation by— (a) the formation of winter training classes in Divinity; [January 15th to April 15th] for Candidates for the office of: 1. Teachers and Parochial Lay Readers, 2. Diocesan Readers and Catechists, 3. Deacons." A Resolution by Archdeacon Lloyd and seconded by the Reverend T. Clarke instructed the executive committee to take the whole subject of the University of Saskatchewan, for which the Diocese held the Charter, into consideration with a view to making definite proposals at the next session of Synod, and in the meantime to take steps to revive the Charter already granted.

The events that followed can best be pictured by quoting, first of all, from Bishop Newnham's Charge to the 1907 Synod (June ninth):

Nor must we forget that this wonderful advance is due, under God's blessing, largely to the enterprise, self-denying labours, far-sightedness, organizing skill and enthusiasm of Archdeacon Lloyd. . . . But I may say that his enthusiasm and optimism have proved contagious, affecting first myself and the Sec. and Board of the M.S.C.C. Then . . . Bishop Montgomery and the Sec. of the C. & C.C.S., as they passed through the diocese, so they invited him to England. . . .

And secondly from an article by Archdeacon Lloyd himself, written originally for the *Greater Britain Messenger*, but reproduced in the March, 1910, number of *The New Era*:

When I came over to the Old Country in 1906 for men to open new missions, fifty-five catechists responded and went out to work in the Diocese of Saskatchewan. It then became necessary to provide for the education and Divinity training of these men. . . .
I moved down 250 miles from my first home in the original British Colony to Prince Albert, and with the assistance of the Bishop, Rural Dean Dewdney, the Rev. D. T. Davies, and the Rev. C. L. Malaher formed classes of about twenty-five men each.
This plan did not continue for very long. The Bishop was too busy to give lectures, and I myself was too often away from home to deal with the college work efficiently, so we had to get down to solid permanent college training in a larger way. Eventually I gave up travelling round the diocese and lectured regularly on Systematic Theology instead. The Rev. John Tuckey, M.A., Trinity College, Dublin, came on to the staff, and the Rev. H. S. Broadbent, M.A., Oxford, resigned his rectory in Saskatoon to come up to Prince Albert and make lecturing his chief work.[5]

The clergy list of 1907 exhibits the change, for the twenty-six clergy of 1906 had increased to thirty-two in 1907, and the nine licensed catechists of 1906 to eighty-one by 1907. There are some interesting names in those 1907 lists. The Reverends A. D. A. Dewdney, first rector of St. Alban's, Prince Albert, and C. Carruthers, rector of Lloydminster. Among the deacons was the Reverend J. Harrison Hill, who became associated with the Manitoba and Saskatchewan Bible Societies. Fifteen of the catechists were engaged exclusively in Indian work; Edward Ahenakew, Alexander Ahenakew and W. Tomalin, were all students of Wycliffe College. Included in the other sixty-six are the names of several who gave outstanding service to the Church in western Canada: J. B. Gibson, A. E. Greenhalgh, C. W. Morris (who later devoted himself to Indian work in the Saskatchewan Valley), and E. Pierce-Goulding.

[5] *The New Era* (March, 1910). The full account of the first buildings and primitive conditions of work is interesting, but too long for reproduction here.

Thirteenth Meeting of the Synod: The First
to be held at Saskatoon

In 1908, for the first time, the Synod of the Diocese of Saskatchewan met away from Prince Albert. Bishop Newnham justified the Synod's being called at Saskatoon by the fact that the city already had four Anglican churches with full congregations, two of them self-supporting, that it was the locality of the catechists' camp, had within its limits the headquarters of the Saskatchewan deaconesses, and was also the railway centre of the diocese. He emphasized, however, that it was only an experiment because he felt there was an advantage in continuity and historic sentiment; also he feared that meeting away from Prince Albert might almost disenfranchise the Indian missionaries in the north and on the Lower Saskatchewan. He added, almost in the nature of a prophecy, "I realize that perhaps before many years Saskatoon may be the Cathedral City of a Sister (or Daughter) Diocese; and our only chance of coming here to a Synod may be when the Provincial or General Synod is held here." The Diocese of Saskatoon did come into being, but not until 1932, long after Bishop Newnham's time, and then it was the Mother Diocese which changed its name to that of the new See City and left its daughter to continue under the old title.

The Bishop's Charge on this occasion dealt directly and indirectly with the progress of the new missions. The scheme of theological training had been a success; already some sixty men had had their three months training and a college course, and their work in the field bore testimony to the value of this education. He announced: "The Saskatchewan Theological College is now an established fact, it is the first Faculty of the University in active work."

A new step in advance had been made in another direction, the Bishop continued: "The diocese also now possesses here in Saskatoon a Deaconesses' Home adopted to the simple wants of the earnest ladies who live there, which serves as a centre from which are reached by correspondence the remotest missions, and by personal contact the wives and daughters who disembark here before proceeding to their widely scattered homes." This house was provided and maintained by the four deaconesses themselves, and their friends in England, free of expense to the diocese.

The work of the Indian missions, particularly that of the schools, had been hampered, the Bishop declared, by "the uncertain, hesitating and uneconomical policy (if they have a policy) of the Indian Department of the Canadian government," but the Diocese had managed to keep all the day schools open, and the Diocesan Board of Missions had taken its stand along with the representatives of other dioceses in repelling criticism of the efficiency with which this work had been met.

In reporting upon the Board of the M.S.C.C., which he had attended the previous October, the Bishop said that it was distinguished chiefly

(1) By an unfair and ill-judged attack on the work of our Indian Missions in the West, led by a few with more zeal than knowledge of the facts, and incorporated in the Report of the Board, in spite of an understanding that it should not appear: (2) By a decided expression on the part of nearly all the Eastern representatives that they felt the burden of the Church's work among our new settlers was too heavy for them to bear, and that if the total amount asked for by the Board for all apportionments was so largely increased, that increase must be raised mostly from the Western Dioceses themselves. This sentiment was carried out in the final lists of amounts to be asked for from each Diocese, and we thus found the contribution asked for from Saskatchewan suddenly doubled, i.e. from $7,000 to $14,000. It is not for me to judge of the capacity of the Church in the East to meet the claims made on it by the West. But I wish to say this, that the West, as far as I can remember, though feeling that an undue proportion of the increase had been asked for from us, yet did not hesitate to accept the assessment, and to urge upon the Western Church (each Bishop in his own Diocese) that every effort should be made to meet this call.

There is a happier note towards the end of this Charge when the Bishop turned again to an educational matter: "I have a strong hope that before another Synod meets the Provincial University will be located here somewhere in the Diocese, either here or at Prince Albert, and that we shall no longer have to maintain a small unaided Church University in opposition to that of the Province, but that on honourable terms we shall be able to merge ours in theirs, and thus to establish our Theological College more firmly as a faculty of the Provincial University, and so carry out the spirit of the farsighted policy of our honoured first Bishop, the Right Reverend John McLean. I also hope that before that time we shall have in good working order a Girls' Boarding School under Church auspices. . . ." This school was St. Alban's, Prince Albert.

An interesting item in the report of the executive committee to the 1908 Synod comes under the heading of "Clergy and Catechists Homesteading etc.", which stated: "The Bishop was requested to send out a circular to all Catechists and new Clergy, pointing out that in no case are they allowed to take up homesteads and that no secular work shall be taken up, without first obtaining the consent of the Bishop, and warning the Catechists against the idea of marriage before ordination; and that every man having a Diocesan pony should be warned against lending his pony or other Church property."

The Synod met again in Prince Albert in 1909 (June 13). In the Diocese, with the arrival of sixteen students from Montreal and Toronto, it had been possible to open several new missions, but what could be done with these missions when the men returned to college in the fall remained a problem. Since the last Synod five clergymen, fifteen catechists and one lay worker had been received. The immediate problem was financial: the M.S.C.C. Board had hitherto generously encouraged the expansion of work in the Diocese; in 1908 it had received $14,000 out of the $17,500 promised, and had been encouraged to expect the same in 1909. Consequently it had planned the work on this basis; however, at the end of three months the Diocese had been suddenly notified that the grant would only be one-half, or $8,500, of which they would probably only get $7,000. "And when we naturally protested, the final answer was that they had no more to give us." The Bishop told the Synod that the only solution was economy on the part of the executive, and every effort on the part of the laity to increase their contribution. The report of the executive committee contains an item revealing that the executive had refused to accept liability for a parochial overdraft at a bank in one case, and for a parochial contract with a builder, which happened to be unpaid, in another. "The Synod is not in any way responsible for the debts of the different parishes or missions, without written authority from the Executive Committee of the Synod."

This Synod of 1909 received, for the first time in four years, a very full report on the Indian missions, written and presented by its veteran Superintendent, the Venerable J. A. Mackay. In his preliminary survey, Archdeacon Mackay pointed out that the Indians were by no means a vanishing race; in the previous ten years their number had increased by 10,000. His next observation is worth recording:

Formerly they roamed the prairies, lived in leather teepees, with plenty of ventilation and pure air, and had an abundant supply of fresh meat for their subsistence. From this they changed to the Reserve life, living in wretched and often overcrowded shacks, and carrying into their habitations all the habits of camp life. And then the change of food. From abundance of fresh buffalo meat they had to subsist on a dole of flour and salt bacon. . . . Anyone who knows the conditions through which these Indians have passed must realize the fact that a race that can pass through such an experience without more loss is not likely to die out.

They were disturbed and disappointed over the little that had been done by the Church of England across Canada for the Indians. In eastern Canada, out of 32,125 Indians only 5,301 were Anglicans, and even this proportion was largely due to the work of the English Society called The New England Company. In British Columbia, out of 24,964 Indians there were 4,334 Anglicans, and this work had been done entirely by the Church Misionary Society. In the Ecclesiastical Province of Rupert's Land there were 53,116 Indians, of whom 17,000 were Anglicans. This was the largest of the church groups and its existence was also due to the Church Missionary Society. He added, "It must be confessed, therefore, that our Canadian Church has a showing in this branch of work that, to say the least, is humiliating; and when we attempt to present the claims of our Indian Mission work to the officers and representatives of our M.S.C.C. in the east, we have to take into account this apathy in the past." The financial position was becoming more and more serious. The C.M.S. was steadily carrying out its scheme of withdrawal; its support would terminate at the end of seven years. It seemed strange that the C.M.S. had not arranged with the M.S.C.C. to take over this work, but such a course had never been attempted. Strictly speaking the Indian work was still a diocesan matter. The C.M.S. announced, "We are not going to support you anymore, the Canadian Church ought to do it"; the M.S.C.C. practically asserted, "We can't do it." The Church owed a debt of gratitude, however, to the British and Foreign Bible Society and the S.P.C.K. for their assistance in publishing the Holy Scriptures and Bishop Oxenden's *The Pathway to Safety* in the Cree language; and the Woman's Auxiliary for its never failing help, especially with regard to the schools.

Emmanuel College moves to Saskatoon

The great event of the latter part of 1909 was the removal of Emmanuel College and its students from Prince Albert to Saskatoon. The Provincial Government had finally decided to establish the new University at Saskatoon, and the Diocesan authorities had satisfied themselves that it was legally within the powers of the Synod of the Diocese of Saskatchewan to remove the College to another site. The University site not being actually ready, lots were bought close to it upon which temporary buildings were erected. We cannot do better, however, than quote what Archdeacon Lloyd wrote at the time, as published in the 1910 Report of the Colonial and Continental Church Society:

One term's work closed in Prince Albert about September 15, 1909, and a new term had to begin in Saskatoon with thirty-five men in residence within ten days or so afterwards.

On Friday evening at 6 p.m. the examination papers were finished in Prince Albert, and by eight o'clock on Saturday morning twenty-five students and three lecturers had their coats off, and tables, chairs, books, boards, lamps and desks, tents and kitchen utensils were being loaded on to a wagon and then on to a freight-cart for transportation to Saskatoon.

By Monday morning we were at Saskatoon with fifteen students and two lecturers. . . . Under the superintendence of a carpenter we went to work to put up the buildings for the new term of thirty-five men who would be coming in for lectures on September 25.

First a good shack . . . for the cook and his wife and helper. . . . Then a similar shack . . . was begun for the Dean in residence, Mr. Tuckey. When we had finished it . . . we were quite proud of our handiwork.

Mr. Broadbent did not need a shack. He had already bought three lots of land in the same block, and had had a very nice house built on his own property by the carpenters. . . . A small 'Lambeth Palace' (the popular name for a catechist's shack) . . . brought by road from Warman . . . was the Archdeacon's bedroom and office.

But what about sleeping quarters? . . . Constructing a sixty-five feet building . . . was too much even for prairie clergy and catechists. So we gave all our attention to the other work . . . leaving the dormitory building to the carpenters.

The Reverend J. T. Tuckey, who was acting Principal of the College, wrote at the time, "Our little Chapel is a very unpretentious building, and contains just a Communion Table, Lectern, and home-made Prayer Desk, and a small organ. But, small and plain as it is, we find it a great comfort and help to have it."

To the Synod of 1910 (June 12) the Bishop spoke very appreciatively of the work that had been done by the catechists under the direction of Archdeacon Lloyd. "The first band to come numbered 57; 42 have joined since; 19 have dropped out, leaving 80 at date. Of these, 27 have proceeded step by step to the senior class, and in all probability all, or nearly all of these will pass out next September, and be eligible for ordination as deacons. Thus 99 catechists . . . have been doing . . . missionary work, which would have been left undone but for them, for we neither could get clergymen to fill these positions, nor could we have paid clerical stipends." Turning to Emmanuel College, he said, "Here is a valuable asset, provided so far almost without any expense to the Diocese, men and money furnished generously by Church people from elsewhere. . . . The C. and C.C.S. have generously provided the salaries of Principal and Assistants for five years, and along with other societies will help towards the permanent endowment required."

Principal Lloyd, in the course of his report to this Synod, said, when speaking of the ordination of deacons that was to take place, "I would invite the attention of the Synod to the fact that no matter what has happened in the West during the last few years in the way of imperfect training and hasty ordinations, the Diocese of Saskatchewan has not been guilty of lowering the standard of the ministry. These men will have then served a full five years, and will have justified themselves in character, practical ability and Divinity education."

The report of 1911 states that Sunday, September 25, 1910, was the red letter day for the Diocese. The twenty-seven candidates were on that day ordained by Bishop Newnham in St. Alban's Pro-Cathedral.

The contract had been let for the larger half of the proposed permanent buildings, which had been designed by the architects responsible for the university buildings and so would be in a style harmonious with them; the estimated cost was $52,000. A number of gifts were reported at this time, the C. and C.C.S. was collecting a large sum for the building fund, the town of Rugby in England was providing $25,000, the estimated cost of lecture rooms, and Rugby School had built the College chapel. The new College building was officially opened on June 8, 1912.

The Synod of 1913 (June 8) considered a letter from the C. and C.C.S. dated May 22, 1913, the substance of which was that the Society was willing to take over the College and relieve the Diocese of financial responsibility for running it for a period of ten years. This offer stipulated that the Society would not pledge itself to the enlargement of the College, but only to the maintenance of the fabric in a state of fair repair. The local management of the College would be in the hands of a Board, nominated by the Society, with the Bishop of the Diocese as chairman. At the end of the period the College would revert to the Diocese entirely, unless a new agreement were to be made.

Principal Lloyd continued to guide the affairs of the College until the summer of 1916 when he was asked by the C. and C.C.S. to return to England to do deputation work. He was succeeded as Principal of Emmanuel College by the Reverend J. N. Carpenter, D.D. The effect of World War I was, of course, to reduce the number of students (twenty-four out of thirty-nine enlisted in the Armed Forces in 1914), and the College was temporarily closed at the end of the academic year in 1917. Dr. Carpenter returned to India to undertake educational work there.

General Progress, 1910 to 1920

In his Charge to the Synod of 1910, Bishop Newnham reviewed the general work of the Diocese, and complained of the pressure under which they all seemed to be labouring. What they really needed was an Archdeacon for the work among the new settlers who would do for them what Archdeacon Mackay was doing for the Indian work. The Bishop had been trying to accomplish more than he could perform: "I have not left the diocese for two years now . . . to join the other Bishops in council, whether at the Board of Missions or in committee. . . . I am not sure whether I was right . . . in leaving this diocese unrepresented, but I could not find it in my heart to stop my work here for the fortnight required." He quoted figures showing an increase of twenty-five per cent in the number of clerical and lay workers, and said that the diocese contained five rectories, eighty-five parishes and missions with two hundred and twenty-eight centres; twenty-four new churches had been opened since January, 1909, eight more were in the course of erection, and there were from twenty-five to thirty-five new districts needing to be opened up.

The synodical committee on the state of the Church, which considered the Bishop's Charge, suggested that application should be made to the Archbishops' Western Canada Fund for a grant to meet the stipend of the proposed Archdeacon, the need for whose help was fully realized. The only missionary society at the time that was increasing its support was the C. and C.C.S., and the Synod was disturbed over the difficulty in finding funds to meet the necessities of areas of its work among both Indians and white citizens.

A year later the Bishop reported that the Council of Archbishops' Western Canada Fund had voted about $6,000 to Saskatchewan for the support of three or four missions. This was not to be drawn all at once, nor all in two or three years, nor was it necessarily to be repeated when exhausted, but the Bishop thought the amount would support three men for five or six years. The Bishop added, "Owing to the exaggerated and optimistic statements published about our harvests and prospects, and the way in which the drawbacks and losses are kept out of sight, English people and congregations had the idea that we were already a fairly rich people." This grant from the A.W.C.F. was used in fostering the work along the Melfort branch on the Canadian Northern Railway east of Prince Albert, from Barrows Junction to Fenton.

An Archdeacon was provided for the Bishop by the appointment of the Venerable Alfred Daniel Alexander Dewdney, whose vigorous personality impressed itself upon all parts of the work of the Diocese for the next eleven years. Bishop Newnham, in his last Charge to the Synod in 1921, said, "I cannot begin to tell you all the lines of work in the Diocese he carries on; but perhaps you already know them. He can run a magazine, a printing press, a Bishop, a young parson, or an old Ford car with equal facility. There is only one thing he seems unable to do—to take a holiday." Archdeacon

Dewdney had been ordained deacon on June 27, 1886, in St. George's Church, Woodstock, Ontario, by Bishop Baldwin of Huron. In 1886 he came to the Diocese of Saskatchewan as rector of St. Alban's Pro-Cathedral, Prince Albert. He took an active part in reviving Emmanuel College, lecturing there on Apologetics from 1906 to 1921, and from 1918 to 1921 on Dogmatics also. His reports to the Synod of the Diocese are a contribution to its history, second only to the Charges of the Bishop, and as an organizer, counsellor, adjustor, few dioceses have had his equal as Archdeacon. On October 19, 1921, he was elected second Bishop of Keewatin.

In 1914 Bishop Newnham completed ten years as Bishop of Saskatchewan. When the Synod met in June he rejoiced in all that had been accomplished and was able to look back on a great deal of progress, but at the moment, owing to poor crops, the story of the year was rather one of retreat than advance, and the business depression had not helped. Yet he felt there was a hopeful side because the Diocese had raised as a whole $100,000 towards all objects during the year. The greater part of this had been contributed towards the building of churches, parsonages and the stipends of rectors. He was thankful that members of older and richer parishes had showed such willingness, zeal and liberality; "But I wish to point out that most of this was for their own Parish, and I would appeal to them to remember their "poor relations," the country parishes, and the infant missions. . . ."

It is noteworthy that the Diocese of Saskatchewan in 1913, for the first time, paid its M.S.C.C. apportionment in full, and also that in October, 1913, the Executive of the Board of the M.S.C.C. met in Saskatoon for the first time. Quite a number of delegates visited city and country parishes on this occasion. The Bishop called attention to this and said, "They will more fully sympathize with our difficulties and wants, but they also noted that we have some strong parishes and some liberal supporters, and they will probably expect us to give more to the M.S.C.C. and to ask less from it."

Because of the war there was no meeting of the Synod until 1916 (June 11) at Prince Albert, and the Bishop's Charge, necessarily, had much to say about the war. "The Diocese had given 11 Clergymen to the military call . . . and 24 of our students and two catechists as combatants or to hospital and ambulance corps; besides all three sons of Principal Lloyd."

1918 Synod: Appointment of New Canons

It had been planned to hold the Synod at North Battleford in 1918, but that year was the twenty-fifth anniversary of the Bishop's Consecration, and by his special wish the meeting was held at Prince Albert instead, so that he might welcome its members to the See City of his Diocese.

In his Charge to the Synod, Bishop Newnham mentioned that the Reverend J. R. Matheson had died in August, 1916, and the Reverend Robert Inkster, at the advanced age of eighty-two, in June, 1918. Attention has already been drawn to Mr. Inkster's ministry. John R. Matheson was a brother of Canon Edward K. Matheson. He was over forty when he entered the ministry and had already made a reputation in the West by his prowess as a runner, athlete, guide, horse trader, poker player, in fact anything but what he was to become in later life when sincere conversion made him a man of God. In 1892 he began work among the Indians at Onion Lake, and finding that he could make no progress with the tumble-down day school, he ended by establishing a boarding school there, which for many years he conducted at his own expense with some help from a government grant. He was ordained deacon in 1894 and priest in 1897. In his work he was greatly assisted by his wife, who had been educated at Queen's University, and on deciding to become a missionary had spent some time in India. They were married in 1891; she returned to study medicine at the Women's Medical College in Toronto, from which she graduated in 1898 with a degree from Trinity College, and came back to Onion Lake to establish a hospital there in connection with the mission. A few years later the Indian Department recognized her services and appointed her officially as a doctor to the Indians at a salary of $300 a year. When Mr. Matheson's health failed, Dr. Matheson took over the conduct of the school, and after his death she remained at Onion Lake until the spring of 1918 when she was appointed Medical Inspector of the Winnipeg Public Schools, from which position she retired in 1941, at the age of seventy-five. In June, 1948, the University of Toronto conferred upon her an Honorary Degree in Medicine, this being the fiftieth year of her graduation. The Reverend J. R. and Mrs. Matheson had nine children of their own, two of whom died in early childhood, and they legally adopted five orphans as well. Their great work in the north was conducted practically without cost to the Church, for the largest stipend they ever received was $600 a year. Mrs. Matheson died on January 15, 1958, and is buried at Onion Lake.[6]

Honorary Canons

There were few honorary canons of the Diocese of Saskatchewan in its early years, and apparently no attempt to organize a Cathedral Chapter, but there is also a problem of the reliability of information,

[6]Alexander Sutherland, "The Mathesons of the Red River," *Canadian North-West Historical Society Publications*, I (1927), 7-15. R. M. Buck, "Dr. Elizabeth Matheson," *Toronto Saturday Night* (October 23, 1948), 32-33.

as the various sources differ, especially in dates. Only two of the first six of these dignitaries (apart from the Archdeacons) were diocesan clergy: Canon James Flett (1880-1892), and Canon William Newton of Edmonton (1883).[7] Canon E. St. J. B. Smith of St. John's, Saskatoon was appointed in 1907, and Canon E. K. Matheson of Battleford in 1912. Bishop Newnham told the 1918 Synod that canonries had no duties attached to them, and that they were "often the only way in which a bishop can show his appreciation of faithful work." He was therefore appointing four: the Reverends T. Clarke, R. R. McLennan, W. E. J. Paul and J. I. Strong. Canons Clarke and Paul were rural deans.

The Reverend Thomas Clarke had graduated from the C.M.S. Islington College in 1877, been ordained deacon in 1879, priest in 1883 by Bishop McLean, and from 1879 to 1901 had been missionary at Battleford, where he had established the Industrial School, and was its Principal until 1895. Mrs. Clarke had then moved to the northeast part of the diocese, and made Melfort the centre of his mission work.

The Reverend Roderick Richard McLennan was born in St. Andrew's Parish, Red River, and educated at St. John's College, Winnipeg, where he graduated with first class classical honours in 1881, taking his B.D. degree in 1888. He was ordained deacon in 1883 and priest in 1884 by Bishop Machray of Rupert's Land, but his life was spent in Indian work in the Diocese of Saskatchewan. He was at Cumberland House, 1883-1888, Stanley, 1888-1906, and then moved to the parish of Glen Mary and Coxby, which included Fort à la Corne where he conducted his work among the Indians until his sudden death on June 17, 1926.

The Reverend John Irwin Strong graduated from Montreal Diocesan College in 1890 and was ordained deacon by the Bishop of Huron in 1893, and priest in 1894 by the Bishop of Montreal. His early experience had been in the Province of Quebec. He had been appointed rector of the Pro-Cathedral of St. Alban's, Prince Albert, in 1911, and had become much beloved in the community.

The Reverend William Edmund Jeffrey Paul was educated at Trinity College, Cambridge, England, graduating L.L.B. in 1907 and B.A. in 1908. He was ordained deacon in 1908, and priest in 1909 in the Diocese of Cashel, Ireland. He had come to the Diocese of

[7]The other Honorary Canons of this period were: Rev. William Bannington Curran (1878-1896), rector of St. Thomas, Hamilton, Ontario; Rev. John Hawksley of Brixton, London, England, Commissary to Bishops McLean and Pinkham, 1874-1896 (Canon 1883-   ); Rev. William Henry Cooper, closely associated with S.P.G. work in Australia and New Zealand, in Canada 1887-1889 (Canon 1883-   ); Rev. John Banning Richardson of St. Paul's, London, Ontario (Canon 1885-1906).

Saskatchewan in 1911, and served as a "driving clergyman" in the Lloydminster and Meota belts. In 1921 he offered himself for Indian work, to which the rest of his life has been devoted. He was appointed Archdeacon of Saskatchewan in 1927 and Superintendent of Indian Missions.

The Devon Mission and Christ Church, The Pas

The problem of dealing with the settlement of the Barr Colony and the general opening up of the western part of the Diocese hardly had been met when the arrival of the Canadian Northern Railway at The Pas, and the consequent alteration in the Devon Mission, produced another problem that took some years to settle. A railway from the prairies to Hudson Bay finally took a route to the west of Lake Manitoba, and eventually reached The Pas in 1909. On September 6, 1910, the first sod was turned at The Pas to begin construction of the government railway to the Hudson Bay, and in the winter of 1910 work was begun on the piers of the bridge across the river. This bridge was completed in 1913 and the railway extended about fifty-six miles north, opening up that country to the lumber industry.

The problem this presented to the Church was due to the fact that the railway crossed the Reserve and Mission Island. The Indian Reserve was sold and the people moved to the north side of the river to a new Reserve where there were no churches. Mission Island itself was included in the town survey.

When the Diocese of Saskatchewan was constituted its entire territory was outside any province; it now found that it had mission properties within both Provinces of Manitoba and Saskatchewan for which it had no title, and it was reported to the 1911 Synod that Archdeacon Mackay had been sent to Ottawa with documents to establish the claims of the Church to mission lands, particularly those of The Pas. Nothing could be done about The Pas as the survey was incomplete, but the government gave the Diocese the patent for its land at Grand Rapids and asked for statutory declarations that the other lands had been occupied by the Church before the Reserve Treaties were made.

In 1913 James McKay, M.P., was asked to try and obtain compensation for the right of way across Mission Island, and for damage to property caused by the railway's crossing it. At that time it would seem that the Diocese had been granted title by the government to fifty-nine acres, but thought that it should be granted one hundred and sixty acres, the customary amount the government was giving to squatters who had settled on land in the early days, and so pressed for title to another one hundred and one acres. Late in 1913 the government appears to have made an offer to compensate the Diocese, but this was considered inadequate. On October first, 1914, however, the government said that it could not find any authority under which the applications for the additional acreage could be granted, and presumably because of alterations due to the war, the Diocese, in 1915, accepted the government's payment on October 29 of $2,000 for the land taken for the railway, with $300 in interest covering three years.

The Pas was now a town, and Mission Island within its limits, but up to this time the taxes payable had been quite reasonable; the executive committee therefore was more than astonished in the fall of 1915 to receive a notice assessing the Diocese's property at over $80,000, and coupled with it a demand for taxes for the current year of $1,648. However, on negotiation, the assessment was reduced to $18,000; the taxes to $630, and the question was considered as to whether the diocesan lands should ever have been included in the townsite at all. In 1916 it was discovered that adjustment could only be made by legislative action, and negotiations were therefore opened up with the town of The Pas whereby Mission Island was transferred to the town as a public park in perpetuity for $1,200, but care was taken to enter a caveat on the part of the Diocese to ensure that the agreement would be kept in the future.

The Christ Church congregation bought the historic church from the Indians in 1916 for $1,750, and in October, 1918, the Caroline Green Memorial Church was built on the Reserve by the Woman's Auxiliary of the Ottawa Diocese as a memorial to a former president, and dedicated to St. Michael and All Angels. According to Archdeacon Mackay this was, at the time, the only church in the Diocese built of stone. In 1921 the Indians themselves built a second church on the Reserve, and although it was done without official sanction, they were granted $500 towards it by the Diocese out of proceeds from the sale of Christ Church, being held as a diocesan trust.

After a number of years of negotiation with the Indian Department, the Church at last succeeded in getting the latter to erect a new residential school (The Mackay School) on the Devon Reserve, which was opened in the fall of 1914 and was the best constructed and most up-to-date of the three residential schools in the Diocese. The first principal was the Reverend Louis Laronde, an ex-pupil of the Battleford Industrial School and a graduate of St. John's College, Winnipeg; he remained in charge until 1917, when he felt it his duty to enlist in the army, and Archdeacon Mackay temporarily took over. This school, for the next fifteen years, was under the direction of the

Reverend Albert Fraser. Unfortunately, it was burned down in 1933 and not replaced.[8]

Work on the Hudson Bay Railway was suspended until 1923, when construction began again, but Churchill was not actually reached until March 29, 1929. This railway opened up new mines and other resources, bringing more problems to the missionary work of the Church, but from 1929 these belonged to the Diocese of Brandon, which at the request of Bishop Lloyd had taken over for administration the area of the Diocese of Saskatchewan that lay in the northern part of the Province of Manitoba.

Resignation of Bishop Newnham

Bishop Newnham announced his resignation of the See of Saskatchewan on February 2, 1921, to take effect upon October 15, and so presided over his last meeting of the Synod when it met on June twelfth that year. His last Charge seems to have been equally divided between two matters. He reviewed the work of the Diocese, in which, "The Bishop often gets credit for the success and welfare of his Diocese, when that credit is due to his colleagues and advisors. . . . The only credit due to me is for gathering around me such a capable cabinet and for having the faith and courage to sanction their enterprise." Secondly, the state of the Church as a whole was reviewed as he had learned it by his attendance at the Lambeth Conference in 1920 and the World Conference on Faith and Order at Geneva. The substance of what he had to say about his own Diocese forms the introduction to this chapter.

Bishop and Mrs. Newnham returned to England, where, until 1925, he was rector of All Saints' Church, Clifton, Bedfordshire, but in the latter year they came back to Canada and made their home in Hamilton, Ontario, where the Bishop died in 1941, in the eighty-ninth year of his age, the sixty-third of his ministry, and the forty-eighth of his episcopate.

The report of the Venerable John A. Mackay called attention to the death of the Reverend J. R. Settee, which had occurred during the year. Mr. Settee was a son of the Reverend James Settee (second Indian ordinand in Rupert's Land) and had spent a good many years as a catechist amongst the Indians before he was ordained in 1885. The Archdeacon said of him,

His title to Holy Orders was the efficient work that he did, especially at Moose Lake. . . . fifty-eight years ago, the Moose Lake Indians seemed absolutely hopeless. . . . It was about twenty years afterwards

[8]The Department of Indian Affairs did not replace the Mackay School until 1957, when one of the same name was opened at Dauphin, Manitoba, 265 miles to the south of The Pas by number ten highway.

that Mr. Settee was sent to open a permanent mission at Moose Lake. He started from Prince Albert in a small flat boat of his own building, and made his way with his family to Moose Lake. In the way of tools he had an axe and an auger. He went into the bush and built himself a log shanty. In January 1885 I was travelling in the Lower Saskatchewan and I visited Moose Lake. I baptized over thirty Indians. It was a most impressive Service. . . in a log shanty that was both church and mission house: there were no ecclesiastical surroundings, but possibly there was joy in the presence of the Angels of God. Bishop Pinkham ordained J. R. Settee for the proofs of his ministry at Moose Lake; he was afterwards in charge of Sandy Lake mission for a time, and later was at Cumberland, where he passed away last autumn.

For the first time for many years the Synod of the Diocese was without the services of the Reverend James Taylor, who had officially retired as Secretary-Treasurer, May first. His name first appears as Honorary Clerical Secretary of the Synod in 1905, and he was appointed Secretary-Treasurer in 1909. Mr. Taylor was born at Moose Factory on James Bay, April second, 1850. His parents moved to St. Andrew's parish on the Red River; he completed his education there and for some time was school teacher in the parish school. He moved to Saskatchewan in 1890 and was ordained deacon by Bishop Pinkham in 1896 and priest in 1898. His first charge was the Assissippi Mission at Sandy Lake. He was appointed Principal of Emmanuel College in October, 1899, and bore the burden of conducting it for seven years as an Indian school, with negligible help from the Diocese, until it was closed as such in 1906. James Taylor spent the remaining years of his life with members of his family at Portland, Oregon, and died there at the end of May, 1924.[9]

As Secretary-Treasurer he was succeeded by the Reverend H. Wallace, and the Reverend H. Sherstone was appointed to a new position as General and Financial Missionary of the Diocese. Mr. Sherstone was one of Archdeacon Lloyd's catechists at Emmanuel College; he had been ordained deacon in 1913 and priest in 1914. He had been Clerical Secretary to the Synod of 1920 and Diocesan Organizer of the Anglican Forward Movement.

The Election of the Reverend George Exton Lloyd, D.D., as Fourth Bishop of Saskatchewan

A special meeting of the Synod of the Diocese of Saskatchewan, under the presidency of the Venerable J. A. Mackay, met in Prince Albert on November 30, 1921, for the purpose of electing a successor to Bishop Newnham. Having arranged that the delegates from the Indian missions might vote in Cree, the Synod proceeded to ballot, and on the

[9]"Emmanuel College, Prince Albert," *The New Era* (October, 1903), 1-3.

second ballot the Reverend George Exton Lloyd, D.D., was declared elected. While awaiting a reply from Dr. Lloyd, who was in England, the Synod decided that as it had not received a visit from the Archbishop and Metropolitan for many years, it would request that the consecration should take place in St. John's, Saskatoon.

Bishop Lloyd was consecrated in St. John's Church, Saskatoon, on Sunday, March 12, 1922, by the Metropolitan of Rupert's Land (Matheson). He was enthroned in St. Alban's Pro-Cathedral, Prince Albert, on Sunday, October 20, 1922.[10]

The Synod of the Diocese met again in regular session on June 18, 1922, for the twenty-fifth time. Bishop Lloyd first of all told the members of the work he had done during his five years in England in connection with the Fellowship of the Maple Leaf, and of the success the teachers sent out by the Fellowship were having in unifying the diverse nationalities in the school districts in which they were placed. He had decided not to occupy Bishopsthorpe (in Prince Albert) unless the Diocese insisted on it, as the expense and upkeep were too high; he had taken over instead the house that used to be the Archdeaconry. He suggested that Bishopsthorpe should be used as a hostel for young men attending the Collegiate Institute, thus extending the plan they were already using in connection with young women at St. Alban's.

The Bishop dealt at length with the position of women workers in the Church, with particular reference to the revival of the Order of Deaconess, which had been recommended by the Lambeth Conference in 1920, about which the General Synod had passed a new Canon at its last meeting. He then explained the circumstance under which he had ordained Deaconess Mabel Jones; he wanted it understood that she came to the Diocese as a ministerial worker, not as a social helper. He added, "In my Judgment, the Canon of the General Synod; the Service Form used, and the Letters of Orders, and licences issued to Deaconess Mabel Jones, constitutes her 'Clergy,' in section I of the Constitution and Canons of the Diocese of Saskatchewan; and as such, she will be called to take her seat on the floor of this Synod next year."

With regard to Emmanuel College, he paid a tribute to the work of the Reverend L. H. C. Hopkins, who almost single-handed had been carrying on the work of the College for the past year. The Diocese had a vital interest in the College, although through the agreement with the C. and C.C.S. it was managed by an independent statutory council. At the last meeting of this board it had been announced that the Reverend Professor W. T. T. Hallam of Wycliffe College had accepted the Principalship of Emmanuel College and would begin his work in September.

[10]O. R. Rowley, *The Anglican Episcopate of Canada and Newfoundland*, 192-193.

The Diocese was $25,000 in debt, and it was evident that it could not afford an archdeacon for work among white citizens until it was out of debt and the vacant missions staffed with more men. He was asking the rural deans to take over all those parts of the archdeacon's work that it was possible for them to do. The Bishop said that he was studying the question of cars versus horses carefully as he travelled around the country. In many cases he was inclined to think that cars were making for absolute inefficiency during the almost seven months of winter and bad roads, and there was a marked tendency to look upon country points as summer stations only. "I want to say at once that clergy who slack down on their winter congregations will find a very stern opposition from the Bishop."

This Synod marked the sixtieth year of the ministry of Archdeacon J. A. Mackay, and his fortieth as Archdeacon. In his report, which was presented immediately following a resolution of congratulation, the Archdeacon placed before the Synod what he termed the work as a whole. They were working on twenty-nine out of the forty-two Indian Reserves in the Diocese, and on thirteen of them all the Indians were Anglican members; on sixteen other Reserves the people were divided between the Church of England and the Church of Rome. The Diocese had eighteen churches, three school chapels, and the prospect of erecting four more churches. The question of maintaining missions was still the most serious question. The matter of financial withdrawal of the C.M.S. in 1920 had been discussed by the General Synod in 1918, and it had been hoped that through the Anglican Forward Movement the work would be entirely undertaken by the M.S.C.C., for part of the A.F.M. had been the raising of an endowment of half a million dollars for the Indian and Eskimo work. They had been disappointed in this, for the Board of Management of the M.S.C.C. had adopted a resolution that as a matter of procedure responsibility for the Indian boarding schools should first be assumed, and the question of Indian missions left for further careful examination. The M.S.C.C., in the meantime, was to make such provision for them as its resources would allow. He called attention to the fact that the agreement between the Board of Management and the Diocese in February, 1921, stipulated that, "Upon the acceptance and execution of this document, the Board of Missions shall assume responsibility to the full extent of its financial ability for the Indian Missions and Schools of the Diocese." The Board of Missions had seen fit to assume responsibility for the three residential schools only. He showed that of the three schools, the one at Onion Lake was the only one requiring financial assistance. There was, therefore, no urgent reason why the Board should assume control of the residential schools, but very urgent reasons why they should assist the mission work. They must not imagine that the eastern members of the Board had any other idea than to do what to them seemed best, but they needed a better knowledge of the real condition of things, and it was for the members of the Synod to try to clarify the position for them. "The present misapplication of the Indian and Eskimo Fund does not concern us only, but it concerns every diocese that has Indian Missions, and I think we may depend on the support of those Dioceses, if we can present our case before the Board of Management."

This was the last report the Archdeacon made to the Synod of Saskatchewan, for he died at Battleford on November 26, 1923, and was buried in St. Mary's Cemetery, Prince Albert. He had served the Church under six Bishops, and thought of nothing but the welfare of his Indian friends. With his passing was broken the last link that bound the Church of the old Hudson's Bay Company days with the Church of the twentieth century.[11]

The Diocese of Saskatchewan celebrated its jubilee on the occasion of the Synod held in Prince Albert, June 15 to 19, 1924. The Bishop reviewed the state of the Church over several past years, besides enumerating the benefactions received from the English Missionary Societies. The Indian work had been reorganized and was now divided into three areas, eastern, western and central, under the care of the Reverends Rural Dean Fraser, Edward Ahenakew and Canon Paul as general missionaries.

For the first time church camps had been established and eight of them were being held during July and August for the benefit of church boys. A new hostel for boys, St. George's College, was full to the doors and seven of the boys were being confirmed. On June 14 the Bishop had signed a contract for the immediate erection of a teachers' hostel on behalf of the C. and C.C.S. committee, which was to be built close to the new Normal School in Saskatoon. He drew the attention of the Synod to the building of two new churches that were somewhat out of the ordinary: the first was a fine log school with an added chancel, erected on Thunderchild's Reserve through the efforts of Mr. Ahenakew; the second was the log church that had just been completed and opened in the Soldiers' Settlement at Porcupine, south of Prairie River.

The Bishop referred to the fact that it was proposed to sub-divide the Diocese of Qu'Appelle; the boundary between the Dioceses of

[11]"Archdeacon J. A. Mackay, D.D.," *The New Era* (July, 1912), 263-266. John Alexander Mackay was ordained in 1862, appointed Canon of the Diocese of Saskatchewan in 1881, and Archdeacon in 1884. He was the only fully ordained clergyman working in the Diocese when it was formed in 1874.

Saskatchewan and Qu'Appelle at the time, between townships thirty-four and thirty-five, was a drawback to their missionary work. He felt that setting the boundary line farther south, to that between townships thirty and thirty-one[12] would not do Qu'Appelle any real harm and would be a great benefit to the Saskatoon area.

The Diocesan Woman's Auxiliary had been supporting the Reverend Edward Ahenakew as their own missionary at a cost of $1,000 a year, but the Bishop had been able to get Mr. Ahenakew put on the list in the Bible Churchman's Missionary Society. At his suggestion, the W.A. was undertaking the whole cost of the "Student's Summer Services," about $2,500; he felt that this was a great step forward. Bishop Lloyd concluded his Charge by discussing the question of British immigration and the part that the Church in the Diocese should be taking with regard to it. The Synod responded by requesting a small committee to make known the opportunities for securing bona fide land settlers through the scheme of the British government, and recommended that a welcoming and welfare committee be appointed in each parish.

The Emmanuel College report noted that a library fund of $1,000 had been given by Sir John and Lady Aird of Toronto, and a gift of $1,000 from Mr. and Mrs. Owen of Halifax. For the first time in some years the College had a graduating class, and there was growing interest in the work it was doing. The July commemoration ceremonies included a service in St. Alban's Pro-Cathedral, at which the preacher was the Metropolitan and Primate, Archbishop S. P. Matheson. Six notable Indian chiefs attended an open air convocation of Emmanuel College: Chiefs Robert of Onion Lake; Star Blanket; Poundmaker; Blackman from the Cumberland House District; and John Smith, then a centenarian, who had been a member of all the Synods since its inception, and who is said to have given the Diocese its name of Saskatchewan, "the River which flows swiftly and forever." A memorial service was also held in St. Mary's cemetery at the graves of Bishop McLean and Archdeacon Mackay.

By 1926 the reorganization of the Diocese was under consideration. The western part of it lay in Alberta, the eastern part of it in Manitoba, and in the part within the limits of Saskatchewan it was becoming obvious that there was a natural division between the north and the south, accentuated by the growing importance of Saskatoon. The suggestion of a separate See in the Saskatoon belt had been discussed shortly after Emmanuel College was moved there, and had received considerable support. Nothing had come of the proposal because it had involved the transfer of part of the Diocese of Qu'Appelle, and

[12]This would have made it twenty-four miles farther south.

that Diocese had been unwilling to part with what was asked for.[13] It was decided by the Synod that the Provincial Synod should be asked to give a kind of general consent and blessing to the division of the Diocese, which would permit negotiations to be opened up with other Dioceses, and also permit an interior rearrangement when the time was ripe. This blessing was duly received and a preliminary step was taken in the Diocese of Saskatchewan through a decision to create two archdeaconries as an experiment, one for the north and one for the south, and at the same time it was agreed that the executive committee should meet alternately in Prince Albert and Saskatoon, for all practical purposes dividing itself into two executives to handle the affairs of each area. No immediate appointments to the archdeaconries were made, however, and it is not until 1929 that the Venerable R. H. A. Haslam, M.A., D.D., was noted as the first Archdeacon of Saskatoon, and the Venerable W. Burd, D.C.M., as Archdeacon of Prince Albert.

Agricultural settlement was becoming extensive in the western part of the northern section of the Diocese, and Emmanuel College found itself unable, by reason of its association with the University of Saskatchewan, to provide either enough men as catechists, or men who could stay long enough in the field during the year to do worth-while work. Bishop Lloyd, therefore, proposed to reopen part of the St. Alban's School building in Prince Albert as a catechists' school, along the same lines as the one he had created in the old Emmanuel College buildings in 1906. The proposal was not favourably received by Emmanuel College and its supporters, who, though not able to provide the needed catechists themselves, raised the objection that the men to be trained under the new scheme would be insufficiently prepared for Holy Orders, and after ordination would lower the standard of the clergy.

The Synod of 1926 had warmly supported the proposal to set up this Catechists' School, or Bishop's College, and the Bishop himself stood manfully by the plans, for he felt deeply his responsibility to maintain the mission work in the Diocese. Later, when the men had been

---

[13]*Journal of the Provincial Synod of Rupert's Land, 1926,* pp. 60-64. This Synod received memorials from the Dioceses of Qu'Appelle, Edmonton and Saskatchewan, each propounding a scheme of boundary rearrangement. Only the proposal to make the Edmonton-Athabasca eastern boundary coincident with that between the civil Provinces of Alberta and Saskatchewan received sanction. Act 19 of this Synod reads, "Resolution approving generally of setting apart two new Dioceses to be carved out of those of Saskatchewan and Qu'Appelle." This was message "M" from the House of Bishops, which received concurrence in the House of Delegates (*Ibid.,* 39-40). The last paragraph of message "Y" from the House of Bishops recommended that no action be taken to extend the Diocese of Saskatchewan to the south, in view of the attitude of the Bishops concerned (*Ibid.,* 45-46).

trained, some ordained, and most useful work had been done, the scheme lapsed.

The transfer of the Alberta section of the Diocese to Edmonton was accomplished, and dates from May first, 1927. The Diocese of Edmonton took over all the assets, liabilities and obligations of this part of the Diocese on the understanding that it was also to receive all M.S.C.C. or Dominion Woman's Auxiliary grants being used in the district at the date of transfer, but not any of the grants received from any of the English missionary societies.

The borderline parishes, particularly Lloydminster, Northminster and Onion Lake, were to have the right to retain their congregations and parochial areas, regardless of the civil boundaries, and equitable arrangements were made respecting the transfer of clergy and catechists.

The long continued interest of Bishop Lloyd in British immigration, and the urgency with which he pleaded for the Church's interests in its encouragement resulted in the acceptance in 1927 of H. G. Dawson's offer (he was later well known in the grain trade in Winnipeg), of his house in Melfort for a hostel, chiefly for immigrant boys. It formed a clearing station where they were received from England and placed on farms. In the course of its first two years, one hundred and twenty-three boys and forty-seven men were so placed. The hostel was under obligation to look after the boys for three years, and there was government inspection.

The Sunday School by Post celebrated its twenty-first birthday in the Diocese of Saskatchewan in 1929. This, too, was originally one of Bishop Lloyd's schemes that came to maturity under the able organization of Miss J. L. Bolton.[14] The first papers were sent out in March, 1907, and in 1929 there were 7,500 pupils on the roll. This work was started by the Ladies' Association of the C. and C.C.S., and later aided by the Dominion Board of the Woman's Auxiliary.

Bishop Lloyd retired in 1931. Through his vigour, forthrightness and capacity as a leader, the Diocese made real progress during his episcopate. Fearless and outspoken, he disliked compromise and had that gift of greatness of always being able to look beyond the person to the policy. After some years of retirement in British Columbia, he died on December 8, 1940, in the seventy-ninth year of his age, the fifty-fifth of his ministry, and the nineteenth of his episcopate.

Bishop William Thomas Thompson Hallam

The Diocese of Saskatchewan elected as its fifth Bishop the Reverend William Thomas Thompson Hallam (the Principal of Emmanuel

[14]The dates refer only to the Diocese of Saskatchewan. Sunday School by Post work originated in the Diocese of Qu'Appelle in 1905 (see n. 26, chap. xii).

College from 1922 to 1927), then rector of The Church of the Ascension, Hamilton, Ontario. The election was made on July 28, and he was consecrated on October 28, 1931, in St. John's Cathedral, Saskatoon. He was enthroned in St. Alban's Pro-Cathedral, Prince Albert. on November first.[15]

Bishop Hallam was born in Derby, England, in 1878, came to Canada in 1887, and received his early education in London, Ontario. He graduated at Dalhousie University in 1901. After his ordination in 1903 Bishop Hallam had a few years experience in parish work, then was Professor of New Testament Literature at Wycliffe College, Toronto, from 1908 to 1922, after which he went to Emmanuel College, Saskatoon. During his time there as principal, the academic standards of the college were raised and the staff strengthened by a number of notable appointments: the Reverends F. H. Wilkinson (now Bishop of Toronto) as Professor of Old Testament; W. F. Barfoot (since Bishop of Edmonton, Primate of All Canada, and Metropolitan of Rupert's land) as Professor of New Testament; W. S. Wickendon as Professor of Church History and Liturgics; and R. M. Millman, who had spent nineteen years of his ministry in Japan.

Division of the Originial Diocese of Saskatchewan

Act 19 of the Provincial Synod of Rupert's Land (1926), approving generally of setting apart two new dioceses to be "carved out" of Saskatchewan and Qu'Appelle, appears to have been regarded by Bishop Lloyd and his Diocese as a permission to go ahead with the plan as far as they were able; setting up the north and south archdeaconries in 1929 seemed a practical experiment to test administration possibilities. No reference is to be found in the Journal of the Provincial Synod of 1929 to the Diocese of Saskatchewan, although the efforts being made in the Diocese of Qu'Appelle to achieve its own division were noted with appreciation. Bishop Lloyd, however, was a man of great determination, and if he could not gain his objective by one method was never deterred from trying another. When the Provincial Synod met again in September, 1933, the sermon at the opening service was preached by the Right Reverend William Thompson Hallam, now Bishop of Saskatoon, and in addition to those from the Diocese of that name there were delegates from the new Diocese of Saskatchewan.

A contemporary report states: "The next step was taken at the Synod held in Prince Albert in June 1931,[16] when the boundaries of

---

[15]A. R. Kelley and D. B. Rogers, *The Anglican Episcopate of Canada and Newfoundland*, 28-30. H. J. Cody, "The Right Rev. W. T. T. Hallam . . . Bishop of Saskatoon," *Canadian Churchman* (June 16, 1949), 196.
[16]"Gift of $80,000 Makes Possible Desired Change," *Saskatoon Star-Phoenix* (November 9, 1932), pp. 3 and 11.

the two dioceses were defined and names agreed upon, the division to become effective immediately the new bishopric endowment fund was provided. The approval[17] of the whole church in Canada was given when the General Synod in Toronto, in September, 1931, endorsed the proposed appeal for raising an episcopal endowment fund for the new diocese in northern Saskatchewan sanctioned by the Provincial Synod of Rupert's Land." According to this paper the decision to divide the original Diocese of Saskatchewan was made at a meeting of the executive held on November 7, 1932, following the announcement that a gift of $80,000 for the endowment of the new Bishopric had made it possible. The date of Bishop Hallam's assumption of the title Bishop of Saskatoon is usually given as November 9, 1932.

This gift of $80,000 came from "the anonymous donor," and it was to be known as "The Bishop Lloyd Memorial Bishopric Endowment Fund." Bishop Lloyd knew the giver personally, but she desired that her name should be withheld, and it was never divulged. When Bishop Lloyd was touring England before World War I, seeking men and money to promote the work of the Church on the western prairies, the son of the anonymous donor decided to enter this work, in response to his appeal to a group of students at Cambridge University. War broke out before he was able to do so; he immediately volunteered and was killed in action. His mother, desiring to carry out her son's wishes, instructed her solicitor to assist the work of the Church in western Canada by means of anonymous gifts, after making careful investigation as to where such help was most needed. After making several visits, the solicitor, Stanley J. Attenborough, became thoroughly conversant with the situation in Rupert's Land, and upon his recommendation generous gifts were made to several dioceses. It was Mr. Attenborough's conviction of the necessity of dividing the Diocese of Saskatchewan that brought about the provision of the new endowment.

The southern boundary of the Diocese of Saskatoon was not adjusted until after the diocese had come into being. The Provincial Synod held in 1933 had a busy time dealing with the problems of four of the older dioceses, and setting up the new one of the Arctic, and this in the face of financial difficulty. The division of the Diocese of Saskatchewan was an accomplished fact, and this is probably the reason why details of the approval of the formation of the Dioceses

[17]The word "approval" here is without any legal significance; it is beyond the power of General Synod to set up any diocese, or alter the boundaries of any diocese in the ecclesiastical Province of Rupert's Land. Nor does the word "endorsed" indicate anything more than the general sympathy of the members of General Synod towards the idea of a new diocese in central Saskatchewan.

of Saskatoon and Saskatchewan are concealed in the pages of the report of the boundaries committee. Also in this report are details of the adjustment between the Dioceses of Saskatoon and Qu'Appelle on their common boundary. Both dioceses ceded territory to each other, but the actual line established was almost impossible to follow without a township map of Saskatchewan. Saskatoon secured most of the territory it wanted south of the city, and to the west, and Qu'Appelle got some to the northeast along the Manitoba border, to the north of the 34-35 township line. Message "E" made these changes effective on July first, 1934.[18]

The local contemporary report, to which reference already has been made, also announced: "By the action of the Executive Committee the Diocese of Saskatoon becomes the continuing and senior diocese, and the Diocese of Saskatchewan, with Prince Albert as its See City, becomes the new diocese."[19] In a news sheet issued by the Diocese of Saskatoon in January, 1933, this aspect of continuity was made the basis of a statement that everything would continue unchanged; no new executive would be elected. Only those members no longer living within the limits of the Diocese would retire; even the Indian work was to be under the direction of Archdeacon Paul and the Reverend E. Ahenakew, though they would be serving both Dioceses. Presumably the necessary legal adjustments were made through the local provincial legislature.

City and Diocese of Saskatoon: 1932

The Diocese of Saskatoon in 1932 was estimated to cover slightly less than 25,000 square miles. It had twenty-one rectories and parishes and thirty-two missions. There were two Indian missions. There were thirty-seven clergy and seventeen lay readers. These figures do not seem to have changed over several years; in fact by 1937 the number of clergy had only increased to forty-one.[20]

[18]Message "E" from the House of Bishops to the House of Delegates, *Journal of the Provincial Synod of Rupert's Land*, 1933, p. 36; Message 24 from the House of Delegates to the House of Bishops, *ibid.*, p. 45; Message "T" from the House of Bishops to the House of Delegates, *ibid.*, p. 49; Appendix VI, Report of Committee on Diocesan Boundaries, *ibid.*, pp. 106-109.

[19]"Gift of $80,000 Makes Possible Desired Change," *Saskatoon Star-Phoenix* (November 9, 1932), pp. 3 and 11. *Diocese of Saskatoon News Sheet* (January, 1933), 2.

[20]*Year Book of the Church of England in Canada, 1933*, and *ibid.*, 1938. Most of the information about the Diocese of Saskatoon (1932-1947) had to be derived from such unofficial sources as reports found in the *Canadian Churchman* or the local press during these years. In this respect the collection of private papers owned by Mrs. A. N. Wetton of North Battleford, which was kindly placed at the writer's disposal by her, has been invaluable. The Diocese of Saskatoon does not appear to have printed Synod Journals or Bishop's Charges during these years.

The main source of wealth in this central part of Saskatchewan was farming, not at that time mechanized as it has become over the past twenty years, though there were signs of this development before 1930. This part of the province was covered with a network of railways, serving small towns and producing divisional points with larger populations. There were, perhaps, between fifteen and twenty of these larger towns in the Diocese. Of these, Lloydminster was probably the best known, and North Battleford the largest and most important. Saskatoon, which claimed to be the chief distributing point over 47,000 square miles of the province, with an industrial output worth more than ten million dollars a year, and the university, towered over them all. It had long been the unofficial centre of the work of the Church in the undivided Diocese. Bishop Lloyd always seems to have regarded it as the centre of his most effective work. The life of the Anglican Church there was undoubtedly strong. The first services were held there in 1887 and for seven years were conducted in the old stone schoolhouse by lay readers. For the next three years they were supplied by the missionary from Duck Lake. Then they lapsed for six years, but were revived in 1902 under the Reverend W. E. Edmonds, a young graduate of St. John's College, Winnipeg, who had just been ordained in the Diocese of Saskatchewan. In 1903 the original chancel of the old St. John's Church was built.[21] The congregation grew larger as time went on; in 1907 it became self-supporting and secured its first rector, the Reverend E. B. Smith. In 1911 Saskatoon, in common with the rest of western Canada, was experiencing growth and prosperity. The present site on Spadina Crescent was secured, and the new church, which faces the river, was begun. It was an ambitious effort, with seating accommodation for eleven hundred, and it cost $118,000. In 1924, the year the Diocese of Saskatchewan celebrated its jubilee, Bishop Lloyd raised the status of the church to that of St. John's Cathedral, stating at the time that the purpose of a Cathedral in these days was "to form a rallying centre for every spiritual activity throughout the diocese," and in the first number of *The Cathedral Monthly*[22] he gave details of the new constitution:

(1) Following the example of a number of modern cathedrals the Bishop is his own Dean. (2) The Chapter consists of the Bishop, Sub-Dean, Precentor, Chancellor and Canon Residentiary, together with

[21]*Saskatoon Phoenix* (December 14, 1912). Rev. W. E. Edmonds returned to Manitoba in 1905, and later went to Edmonton, where he was in charge of St. John's Church for seventeen years, and then assistant at Holy Trinity.

[22]*The Cathedral Monthly*, Saskatoon, St. John's Cathedral Parish (January, 1924).

five Prebendaries. (3) The Great Chapter includes the Chapter, together with a Vice-Chancellor, Treasurer, Lay Treasurer, Legal Assessor, Recorder and two Bishop's Wardens. (4) Then we have the Corporation, consisting of the Chapter, the Great Chapter and eighteen representative laymen from the congregation or diocese. Thus the lay element is probably stronger in St. John's Cathedral than any other in the world.

The Canon Residentiary, the Reverend E. C. Earp, continued to exercise the functions of rector; the other appointments were honorary.

Christ Church was begun in 1906 through the efforts of a layman, John Ashworth, who wished to see another Anglican church in the city to the west and north of the C.P.R. tracks, and gave the site for it. A basement church was begun soon after, in which the first service was held on April 19, 1907. From 1926 to 1937 this church was served by the Reverend Roy Melville; economic and political circumstances prevented the church being completed until after World War II.[23]

St. George's Church was established about the same time (1906) and so developed under the ministry of the Reverend H. Assister that it became self-supporting in 1912. St. James' Church owed much in its early days to the efforts of the Reverend H. R. Broadbent, a member of the staff of Emmanuel College. By 1912 it, too, had a membership of about 200 families. These were the oldest churches in the city;[24] others have grown up as development proceeded: St. Mark's, St. Luke's, All Saints' and Holy Trinity.

Saskatoon Faces Problems

By 1934 the Diocese of Saskatoon was lying within the dried-out area of the Province of Saskatchewan, and troubles were ahead. Bishop Hallam wrote an article for the *Canadian Churchman* that appeared on September 13. The result of the continued drought was that community efforts, such as church, lodge, or Grain Growers' Association, no longer interested people who were thoroughly discouraged; 'isms and 'asms were gaining popularity because of the loneliness of the people; community or combined Sunday Schools were damaging the Church because they did not lead to Confirmation classes. Actually the Church had not recovered from its setback of 1914 to 1918 when, owing to the war, many of the missions had to be closed; later, the resumption of services was not always welcomed and often resented. The meagre grants from the M.S.C.C. and the slender diocesan resources were hard on the clergy who had to suffer reduced stipends.

[23]*Canadian Churchman* (December 20, 1945), 7.
[24]*Saskatoon Phoenix* (December 14, 1912).

New settlers coming in from dried-out areas farther south had nothing; they came in debt and poverty. The diocesan endowments were not lost, but were becoming "moth-eaten." Changes took place about this time in the staff of the Emmanuel College. Bishop Hallam had been replaced in 1927 by the Reverend R. H. A. Haslam, who had had fifteen years missionary experience in India before coming to St. James' Church in Saskatoon in 1923; Archdeacon Haslam carried on as Principal for ten years. The Reverend F. H. Wilkinson had gone to St. Stephen's, Calgary in 1928, and his place was taken by the Reverend E. H. Maddocks. The Reverend W. F. Barfoot went to St. John's College, Winnipeg in 1934, and his work was placed under the Reverend P. W. Downer. The Reverend W. S. Wickendon left in 1935 to take charge of a parish in England. In 1937 Archdeacon Haslam was followed as principal by the Reverend W. A. Ferguson, who after four years in Saskatoon became principal of Montreal Diocesan Theological College. The Reverend S. C. Steer, a former student of Emmanuel, an excellent scholar with experience in the educational field, relinquished the position of vice-principal of the London College of Divinity, and returned to Saskatoon as Principal in 1941.

It was reported to the Synod of the Diocese held on March 7, 1935, that the southern boundary question had at last been settled. The missions of Wynyard, Watrous, Viscount, Delisle and Kerrobert were now in the Diocese of Saskatoon.[25] Qu'Appelle had gained eighteen townships on the Manitoba border. The Synod also heard that the Sunday School by Post was serving 7,700 children from 3,000 families; the cost of supplies, $2,893, was being paid by the C. and C.C.S. The van workers in 1934 had travelled 5,012 miles (of which 878 miles had been done on foot, partly because of bad roads, but also to save gasoline), and they had visited 1,126 families.[26]

In the spring of 1936 Bishop Hallam went to England and addressed the annual meeting of the Colonial and Continental Church Society, which for the last thirty years had been the mainstay of the work of the Church in the area of the Diocese of Saskatoon and of Emmanuel College. While in England he secured grants towards building four prairie churches, organized a "Friends of Saskatoon Cathedral" association, which produced $1,500 towards the removal of its debts, and another fund had given him $600 towards a See House. The S.P.C.K. was giving $2,500 through the M.S.C.C. for the relief of the clergy in the western part of the Diocese. This was welcome news, for the

Diocese that year went $22,000 in debt, and only succeeded in gathering in fifty-seven per cent of its apportionment.[27]

The situation in 1937 was even gloomier. It was the driest year of the "dry thirties." Sloughs and creeks had disappeared; their location could hardly be remembered, and there was no moisture in the subsoil. The old familiar cry of "next year" had ceased to have any significance, and it was reported that the dry weather had moved farther north, and was afflicting the Diocese of Saskatchewan. The following year seems to have been no better. In December Bishop Hallam issued a bulletin proclaiming a state of emergency in the Diocese; the M.S.C.C. was unable to pay expected grants, and their own receipts were short because of continued bad crops. There were further hardships for the men in the field, an experience common to all the prairie dioceses. But Qu'Appelle and Saskatoon were the two most seriously affected, though the eastern parts of Edmonton and Calgary were nearly as badly off. In 1939 World War II broke out in September, and new problems were caused by the movement of population towards war work and urbanization, besides that of enlistment in the armed forces.

Indian Work in the Diocese of Saskatoon

The Diocese of Saskatoon was necessitated by an increased population of white people, due to the flood of immigration in the first ten years of the twentieth century, and the subsequent settlement of returned men after World War I. The Diocese is not usually associated with Indian work; nevertheless it contains within its borders what are generally known as the Battleford Reserves: Little Pine's, Poundmaker's, Sweetgrass, Red Pheasant, Stoney, Moosomin's and Saulteaux Reserves. These Reserves always appear to have been troublesome to the government departments, and the Church has had its own difficulties in working on them; the co-operative effort of both government and Church in the Battleford Industrial School seems to have been the most satisfactory achievement, and it is hard to understand why the school should have been closed, or why similar institutions elsewhere should have been discontinued.

When these missions became the responsibility of the Diocese of Saskatoon they continued under the general supervision of Archdeacon Paul, by mutual arrangement with the Diocese of Saskatchewan. The Reverend William Thomas Sheasby was then at the Red Pheasant Reserve, where he was to continue until 1949; his services were recognized by his appointment to a canonry in 1933, when he had completed ten years in the Battleford district.

[27]*Ibid.* (February 6 and June 11, 1936).

The closing of the Industrial School at Battleford in 1914 resulted in the provision of what were called "Improved Day Schools" on the Reserves. Day schools had existed on some of the Reserves for eight to ten years before 1885, but their operation had been difficult. The new improved ones were designed to set more satisfactory standards, and attract better qualified teachers; for some years the scheme progressed with fair success.

Some progress appeared to have been made by 1933, when it was reported that the heathen Reserves, Chagoness and Nut Lake (north of Humbolt), were being visited regularly by the general missioner and Archdeacon Paul, but six years later it was stated that nothing further could be done with the Saulteaux at Chagoness. A school had been built there in 1938; it was undenominational, but would probably be better described as secular. There was an agreement with the government that no religious teaching should be given until it was desired. The prospect of erecting a small mission at Nut Lake had been vetoed by the Indian Department in Ottawa. In 1942 it was mentioned that Canon Sheasby was visiting Moosomin's and the Saulteaux Reserve, as well as looking after Red Pheasant and Stoney. The Reverend L. W. Howarth of Paynton was in charge of Little Pine's, and the catechist, B. Pooyak,[28] was doing good work at Sweetgrass. Little Pine's had had an Indian clergyman there in 1938 for a year, the Reverend Arthur Wesley Moses, a graduate of Emmanuel College in Theology. The schoolmaster at the time was Adam Cuthand, who later was also ordained, but both eventually moved into the Diocese of Saskatchewan. From that Diocese, however, in 1943 the Reverend Ahab Spence went to Little Pine's from Stanley, and took charge of Paynton and Bressaylor as well in 1946. A native Cree, well educated and with a great personality, he has done admirable work for the Church. In 1950 Canon H. E. Hives (later to become Bishop of Keewatin) was appointed Bishop's Commissary of Indian Work in the Diocese of Saskatoon.[29]

After World War II

Little emerges from the period of the war itself. There was a Synod on June 19, 1945, and the Bishop warned the delegates that the Church did not live in a vacuum: "She would have no mission if she were not

[28]C. Wetton, "Baptiste Pooyak of Sweet Grass—Devout Christian, Well-read," *Saskatoon Star-Phoenix* (February 28, 1951), 13.

[29]Reports of the Committee on Indian Work, *Journal of the Provincial Synod of Rupert's Land*, 1926, pp. 25-28; *ibid.*, 1929, pp. 35-39 (apparently duplicates the report of 1926); Appendix III, *ibid.*, 1933, pp. 89-99; Appendix VIII, *ibid.*, 1939, pp. 75-81; Appendix IV, *ibid.*, 1942, pp. 45-48; Appendix IV, *ibid.*, 1947, pp. 73-77; Appendix V, *ibid.*, 1950, pp. 67-73.

inextricably and vitally involved in her environment." There had been an increase in prosperity during the war years, and for the third year in succession they had paid their apportionment in full, besides reducing the diocesan debt by more than $4,000. A See House had been obtained and named Bishopscourt after the original home of Bishop McLean. The staff of Emmanuel College had been strengthened by the addition of the Reverend J. D. F. Beattie, B.A., D.D., who had been in the diocese for ten years. The Bishop reviewed some of the progress of the Diocese: In 1931 the area included in the Diocese had had twenty-two clergy, nineteen students. Of the clergy, eleven were serving in rectories and eleven in parishes [missions?]. The Diocese in 1945 was served by nine clergy in rectories, twenty in missions, two stipendiary lay readers and seven students. Four missions had been closed, five had been without students for three years, but four had an ordained ministry. The Bishop welcomed the Reverend Ralph Kenneth Sampson as Archdeacon of Saskatoon, as well as the new honorary canons, the Reverends H. Bowles, rector of Christ Church, Saskatoon and J. W. Bulleyment of Biggar. "To mark the gift of more than forty years of service in Saskatchewan from the inauguration of the Barr Colony to the present day, the former years spent as Lay Reader and farmer and the latter years as a Clergyman, I have appointed Rev. Lucian Freeman as a minor Canon of the Cathedral. . . ."[30]

By 1949 the situation of the Church with respect to the Indian schools had definitely improved as the government had assumed the cost of upkeep, repairs and equipment, as well as salaries of teachers. The Diocese only had two schools, but the one at Little Pine's Reserve had achieved an enviable record under Miss Cunningham, and it was being sustained under Mrs. Sprague so that Ottawa regarded it as a model day school. Canon Hives was giving a lift to the work through his knowledge of Cree and understanding of the Indian people, as well as receiving congratulations on the publication of his new Cree Grammar, on which he had worked for ten years. In another rural field, the "white work," the retirement of pioneers, and flow of young people to urban areas, which had begun during the war, were becoming difficult problems for the prairie dioceses to solve.

In the educational field Emmanuel College was ceasing to be a merely diocesan institution and was training men for all dioceses in the west, thus carrying out the expressed wish of the C. and C.C.S. The summer schools, which had been held there in alternate years since 1933, had assisted in relating Christianity to the life of the day.

[30]*Proceedings of the Synod of the Diocese of Saskatoon, 1945.*

In 1949, too, at North Battleford, through the local ministerial association, religious instruction on an agreed syllabus was being given by clergy in the public schools. The number of Anglican children writing the G.B.R.E. Sunday School examinations, however, was declining to such an extent that some alarm was being felt.[31] In 1949 Bishop Hallam announced his approaching resignation to the Synod, due to take place on the anniversary of his consecration, July 28. "For myself, I have everything to thank you for, your friendship, your loyalty, your help, your patience, and especially for your prayers in time of need." After paying tribute to the work of his archdeacons and the secretary-treasurer, the Bishop concluded: "The Christian must not lapse into a respectable worldliness in the comfortable belief that he can rest assured in his possession of Grace. The costly Grace of God is turned into cheap grace without discipleship." He urged the clergy to the constant ministry of pastoral visitation, warned the laity that there was no place for spectators, and that gifts of money did not exhaust either possibilities or duties.

Bishop Wilfred Eastland Fuller

The Synod of the Diocese of Saskatoon met on August 23, 1949, and elected the Very Reverend Wilfred Eastland Fuller, Dean of St. John's Cathedral, Saskatoon, as successor to Bishop Hallam. He was consecrated on October 18 in the Cathedral in Saskatoon, and enthroned there the same day as the second Bishop of Saskatoon and sixth Bishop of the continuing diocese.

Bishop Fuller was a native of Peterborough, Ontario, where he received his early education, and a graduate of the University of Toronto in Arts and of Wycliffe College in Theology. He was ordained deacon by Bishop J. A. Richardson of Fredericton on February 24, 1925. He became rector of the Cathedral Church of St. John the Evangelist in Saskatoon in 1942, and Dean of the Diocese at the same time.

In February, 1950, while on his way east to attend a conference, he was taken ill on the train at Rivers, Manitoba, and died in Brandon Hospital, February 22. With his passing, the Diocese of Saskatoon lost a vigorous and forceful leader who had hoped to strengthen its work in many directions, and had already shouldered a large part of his episcopal responsibilities. Saskatoon had come to regard him as a great citizen who took a deep interest in its affairs.[32]

[31]*Ibid.*, 1949.
[32]*Crockford's Clerical Directory*, 1947. Kelley and Rogers, *op. cit.*, 112-113. *The Year Book of the Anglican Church of Canada*, 1960. *The Saskatoon Star-Phoenix* (February 23, 1953).

The Election of Bishop Sidney Charles Steer

The Synod met again on Tuesday, May 11, 1950, and elected Principal Sidney Charles Steer, M.A., D.D., of Emmanuel College as Bishop in succession to Bishop Fuller. He was consecrated in the Cathedral at Saskatoon on July 25 as third Bishop of the Diocese and seventh in the continuity.

A native of the Guildford district of Surrey, England, Bishop Steer was educated at Margate and Guildford Grammar Schools; he graduated from Emmanuel College in 1928, taking his L.Th. in 1929, the year of his ordination both as deacon and priest. From 1933 to 1941 he was on the staff of St. John's Hall, Highbury, an Anglican Theological College associated with the University of London, as tutor and Vice-Principal. He then returned to Saskatoon.[33]

Saskatchewan: New Diocese under the Old Name

Each time the original diocese has been divided the part retaining the name "Saskatchewan" has always been the pioneer area. . . . when the diocese of Saskatoon was set up, we started with the proverbial "shoe lace." We took our share of the existing diocesan debts, most of the large Indian work and 90,000 square miles of territory, comprising bush lands, mineral land, forests and waterways. Twenty thousand settlers had come up from the dried-out areas of the province and had to be cared for. . . .[34]

This was the situation when Bishop Hallam became Bishop of Saskatoon and the Diocese of Saskatchewan came into being on November ninth, 1932. The Synod of the new Diocese met in Prince Albert and elected the Venerable Walter Burd as Bishop, and he was consecrated in St. Alban's Cathedral there on March 12, 1933.[35] He was then forty-five years of age; he had studied analytical chemistry at the University of Sheffield and was working in this profession when he felt the call to the mission field. He entered Wycliffe College in Toronto in 1913, but war interrupted his studies. After another year at Wycliffe, and two years as General Secretary of the Brotherhood of St. Andrew, the call to the ministry could no longer be denied; he was ordained deacon and priest by Bishop Lloyd in 1922. After four years at Tisdale, he became Canon Residentiary and Precentor of St. Alban's in Prince Albert, and when the experimental division of the original Diocese into two archdeaconries was made in 1929, he was appointed to the northern part. His zeal, experience and personality made his election as Bishop quite logical.

[33]*Crockford's Clerical Directory, 1957-1958.* Kelley and Rogers, *op. cit.*, 118-119.
[34]"A Message from the Bishop," *Canadian Churchman* (May 12, 1938), 296.
[35]Kelley and Rogers, *op. cit.*, 46-47.

Prince Albert was the oldest, and by far the largest, most wealthy and most important place in the Diocese. Melfort and Tisdale on the eastern side and Shellbrook, a little to the west, were the only other towns of any size, though some developed later. Melfort, Tisdale, Leask, and Medstead are just within the Diocese. Little consideration is needed to see that economic prosperity here was entirely dependent upon agriculture and the exploitation of natural resources, for the towns themselves were only administration and distribution points. The work of the Church depended upon grants from the M.S.C.C. and other church societies.

Within two years Bishop Burd was pleading for support, or at least protesting against diminished support. In 1934 he issued a strong appeal against the reduction of the diocesan grant from General Synod sources, which appeal was sent to all delegates attending the meeting of General Synod in Montreal. Such reduction would leave the Diocese $7,000 short of its needs. Saskatchewan was not eligible for any special grants as it was not considered to be in a dried-out area, though it had to minister to people coming from such areas. The Diocese was now $12,547 in debt, its clergy were getting an average of $55 a month and paying their own travelling expenses, but it had paid eighty per cent of its General Synod apportionments. The appeal failed. In the *Canadian Churchman* of October 23 there appeared a letter from the Bishop saying that the Diocese was only getting $12,225 in grants. He appealed for subscriptions to the amount of $3,000, as he did not feel that General Synod represented the will of the Church regarding Saskatchewan.[36] In January, 1935, it was noted that the diocesan missionary apportionment had been paid up to within $100 of its assessment, and so the General Synod assessment had been paid in full.

Apparently it was about this time that an infection arising from a war wound in his foot was beginning to affect the Bishop's leg, causing him to spend much time in Winnipeg General Hospital. The work of the Church, however, was carried on with vigour by Archdeacons Paul and G. H. Holmes. Two events early in 1935 seem worth recording. The district of Nipawin in the Carrot River country was growing as new settlers came in, and when a new school was built at Mossy Lake ("away up north in the bush"), the Reverend H. Parrott was asked to conduct a service of thanksgiving at its opening. In April Archbishop Owen preached at an interdenominational service of witness in Prince Albert. Bishop Burd worked hard to promote better interdenominational relationship and co-operation. At an early date he had approached the United Church with a definite scheme in

[36]*Canadian Churchman* (September 13 and October 23, 1934).

which the membership of both churches was safeguarded, and in 1938 he was able to say that it had worked well; eighteen out of twenty-two churches that had been built in his time served all non-Roman denominations in their districts.[37]

A Synod was held in June, 1935, at which Bishop Burd was able to preside. For the first time three women sat as lay delegates. The Diocese was carrying on, but only by the help of the outside societies, and there was a deficit in the stipend fund of $7,843. One new church had been built in 1933, however, five in 1934, and ten were planned for the current year to serve new settlements. There were fifty-six churches in thirty-four congregations, but forty-six congregations were without any church. Indian work was progressing; 3,000 out of 5,800 in the Diocese were Anglicans, and they had three Indian students studying for the ministry. On the western side of the Diocese a new stone church was opened at Deer Creek, near Fort Pitt. It was said at the time that it was the only such church in the Diocese, built by voluntary labour but with funds from the old country. At the end of the year St. Alban's Hostel for boys in Prince Albert was closed, due to insufficient enrolment; the boys were transferred to Nesbitt House, the United Church institution.

The Bishop's health was showing signs of improvement, but it was felt expedient that he should be allowed a long period of rest. In October the Diocese gave him a year's leave of absence and he went to California, Archdeacon Paul being appointed commissary in his absence. A policy of decentralization seems to have been instituted for a time, designed to keep interest and work very much alive; this was the holding of "Deanery Synods" at Melfort, Prince Albert and Turtleford, at which free discussion of the affairs of the district and diocese was promoted and encouraged, and a diocesan branch of the Canadian Laymen's Association was organized in the See City.[38] Five new churches were built on the western side of the Diocese in 1936, and a new one was built at Fort à la Corne by the Indians themselves, as a memorial to Canon R. R. McLennan.

Bishop Burd returned to the Diocese late in 1937 much improved in health, but early in December disaster struck. As he and Mrs. Burd were returning from a conference in Saskatoon, driving by car through a very heavy blizzard in which visibility was almost zero, they suffered a head-on collision with another vehicle a mile north of Duck Lake. Shortly after, Mrs. Burd died from injuries, and the Bishop began once more a series of periods in hospital. But he was well enough to spend six weeks in the Diocese in the spring, presided over the

Synod held in June, and on November first took the service of Holy Communion in a parish church north of Prince Albert. His improved condition was not maintained, however, and he resigned on March 31, 1939. Shortly afterward he retired to Victoria, B.C., where he died on August second. He was buried in St. Mary's Churchyard in Prince Albert on August seventh.

In 1938 two other events took place. The city of Prince Albert took leave of Canon F. J. Stevens, who had been there for ten years. He had spent five years at St. George's Hostel and then been Canon Residentiary at St. Alban's. This was at the end of the year, but in August there was a conference on Indian work at which thirty-two workers and five government officials were present. The occasion seems noteworthy as a new approach to a common problem. On May 12, 1938, a special number of the *Canadian Churchman* was issued commemorating the progress made in the Diocese's first five years. Respecting matters not already mentioned, it may be noted that the Sunday School by Post had increased in membership in the previous two years by twenty-five per cent, and had enrolled 4,940 pupils. The Woman's Auxiliary had doubled its number of branches and members in five years, and had increased its junior membership as well. The Diocese now had four caravans working in the summer months. The Indian work in the Diocese had been well maintained, though the field was wide and much of it beyond the reach of roads and railways. The two residential schools (Onion Lake and Lac la Ronge), each with a capacity of about one hundred pupils, were under the management of the M.S.C.C. There were six clergy in missions and nine lay missionaries, of whom five were also teaching school. Day schools on the Reserves were having a profound influence for good, as the teaching in the school was carried directly into the home by the children.[39]

The Election of Bishop Henry D. Martin

The Diocese of Saskatchewan naturally expected to elect a new Bishop to take Bishop Burd's place, but it did not have the number of self-supporting parishes required by the Canon of the Province of Rupert's Land. The matter came before the Synod of the Province, which met on June 14, 1939. In his Charge, Archbishop Harding said:

It was the sincere hope of many influential friends in both Canada and England, that, at least for a time, the Dioceses of Saskatoon and Saskatchewan could be amalgamated and some agreement reached whereby the hard-pressed Missionary Clergy of both Dioceses might profit financially. After considerable correspondence and many inter-

[39]W. E. J. Paul, "Indian Missions in Saskatchewan," *Canadian Churchman* (May 12, 1938), 298-299.

views between responsible parties, this arrangement has been deemed impracticable and a call issued to the House of Bishops to elect a Bishop of Saskatchewan, with the consent of the House of Delegates.

On Thursday morning, June 15, the House of Bishops sent a message saying that by a majority vote the Reverend Henry David Martin had been selected for the vacant See of Saskatchewan. After a general ballot in the House of Delegates, ballots by Orders and Dioceses were demanded and taken; each showed a majority in favour of concurrence with the House of Bishops, which was so notified.[40] The Venerable G. H. Holmes assured the Bishop-elect that he would be received gladly when the time came for the Diocese to greet its new Bishop.

Bishop Martin was consecrated in St. Alban's Cathedral, Prince Albert, on August 24, 1939, and enthroned the same evening, entering on an episcopate that was to last for twenty-one years.[41] A native of London, England, he was educated at St. Paul's School there, and then at Wycliffe College, Toronto. Ordained in the Diocese of Fredericton in 1915, he served in St. John, N.B., before going to Holy Trinity, Winnipeg, in October of 1916. When St. George's Church was re-established in 1918 in Crescentwood, he was appointed rector; during his twenty-one year incumbency this church became one of the strongest in the city of Winnipeg, notable for its interest in missionary work.

In 1941 Archdeacon Holmes undertook parochial work in the Diocese of British Columbia.[42] Originally a graduate of Emmanuel College, he had come back to the Diocese in 1919, to St. George's Church, Saskatoon, where he was rector for ten years, and then became Canon Residentiary of St. Alban's Cathedral from 1929 to 1933, when he was appointed Archdeacon. This archdeaconry was not filled until 1956, when Canon W. F. Payton was appointed. Canon Payton came to Saskatchewan from the Diocese of Niagara in 1942 to be Canon Missioner and Secretary-Treasurer of the Diocese, in which posts he still remains.

Indian Work After 1940

During the long series of dry years the Indian population of northern Saskatchewan had had its troubles because of shortage of fur-bearing animals and unfair competition from white trappers and fishing com-

[40]*Journal of the Provincial Synod of Rupert's Land, 1939*, pp. 26-27. The House of Bishops and the House of Delegates met separately at this time. Under Canon VI (1953 amendment) the Houses now meet together, but still vote separately.
[41]Kelley and Rogers, *op. cit.*, II, 76-77. "Canon Henry D. Martin accepts Bishopric," *Winnipeg Tribune* (June 16, 1939), 2.
[42]*Crockford's Clerical Directory, 1957-1958*, p. 551.

panies. The Indian was the primary concern of the Dominion government, but outside the actual Reserves the natural resources of forests, lakes and animals were under the control of the province, and it took quite a time for the province to realize that a hungry Indian was also one of its hungry citizens. From the time the western prairie provinces took over their own natural resources there has been trouble between their governments and the Indians on the matter of licences, and the infringement of what the Indian considers his inherent right—to live off the country. The economic conditions on the Indian Reserves, all through the history of the Anglican Church in western Canada, both before and after the treaty years, have been a great concern to the missionaries engaged in this work, and the Church has put up a hard fight to improve them. The reports submitted to the provincial Synod of Rupert's Land document and emphasize the attitude of the Church. Compiled from 1939 to 1947 by Archdeacon Paul, they reflect particularly the situation in Saskatchewan. Among topics discussed were the efforts being made to increase manual and technical training for those children not going on to residential schools, the betterment of medical services, efforts to encourage community farms and gardens on the Reserves, and the encouragement of dam construction to conserve muskrats. In 1947 a carefully worded report was introduced which spoke of a new approach to Indian work by both church and government, and the necessity of proper training for those entering the field, whether "workers" or teachers.

In 1949 the attention of General Synod was focused for a time on the Indian work of the Church, but the impression made seems to have been slight and its resolution futile: (1) It was agreed that a survey of Indian work was desirable. (2) It refused to recommend that a field secretary be appointed to make this survey. (3) It suggested that bishops having Indian work should confer and select one of their members, or some person thoroughly conversant with the work among the Indians, to devote several months to making a survey and report with recommendations. This was not only an exhibition of want of understanding and sympathy with the Indian problem as such, but also of the situation facing all western bishops in their own dioceses at the time, the complementary difficulties of maintaining their rural parishes and meeting the imperative demands of urban expansion. The ineptitude of General Synod's attitude has since been reflected in the unsatisfactory Indian Act of 1951.

It is only right that a note should be added regarding the actual men in the field. Archdeacon Paul was a worthy successor to Archdeacon John Alexander Mackay, and handled very ably the Indian work in the Diocese of Saskatchewan during twenty-five years of fast transition through drought and famine, war years and post-war years of readjustment. Canon Albert Fraser spent most of his ministry in the eastern part of the original diocese; Canon Edward Ahenakew devoted the larger part of his time to the central Reserves; Canon G. J. Waite divided his between John Smith's Reserve and Montreal Lake; the Reverend C. J. Parker has been at Cumberland House ever since his ordination; and the Reverend Henry Ellis has done his entire work at Onion Lake residential school.[43] These men have enjoyed the respect and confidence of their contemporaries, and Canon Ahenakew has long been regarded with affection and admiration in Provincial and General Synods, where he has spoken eloquently and effectively for his people. Since 1874 the Diocese of Saskatchewan has led, in the traditional policy of the Province of Rupert's Land, in encouraging and using a native ministry. Over the last twenty-five years Ahab Spence, Stanley and Adam Cuthand, Arthur Wesley Moses and Smith Atimoyoo have shown the tradition to be active and effective. The loss of both the residential schools at Onion Lake and Lac la Ronge by fire proved in time not quite the disaster it then appeared, for the schools have been re-established in Prince Albert. The improved communications of the post-war period have made them accessible to the districts in which they originated, educational standards have improved, administration difficulties have been lessened, and the way to economic and social integration widened.

"White work" in the southern part of the Diocese has shown variable prosperity. The importance of Prince Albert itself has grown; there was some increase in industry during the war, and through new roads, new settlement and its airfield, the city became something of a gateway to the north. Generally, however, conditions seem to have been against a settled ministry; constant changes in the local parsonage invariably produce an unsettled condition in local parochial life. Perhaps a short survey will indicate this better. In 1947 there were twenty-six clergy in the Diocese: thirteen had been ordained before 1940, and thirteen by Bishop Martin; eighteen were engaged in "white work," eight in Indian work. Eight years later (1955) only two of the pre-1940 group and one of the post-1940 group were still engaged in "white work," but from the Indian work only one of each group had gone. Of the seventeen who had left the diocese in those years, eleven had been ordained by Bishop Martin between 1940 and 1947. No doubt each had a good reason for leaving, but to the Diocese it seemed something of a wastage. Of those remaining in "white work" Canon H. E. Ashmore had spent most of his ministry in the extreme western part

[43]*Ibid.:* Canon Edward Ahenakew, p. 8; Rev. H. Ellis, p. 355; Canon Albert Fraser, p. 465 (died 1960); Rev. C. J. Parker, p. 887; Canon G. J. Waite, p. 1206.

of the Diocese, and Canon S. H. F. Jarvis had served entirely at Tisdale. Both had been trained in Bishop's College at Prince Albert. The Reverend W. B. Harper had been at Spiritwood since 1941. In 1945 steps were taken to preserve old St. Mary's Church in Prince Albert, which Bishop McLean had found under construction when he first arrived there seventy years before. On September ninth there was a pilgrimage to this historic little church and a memorial service was held there. Both church and cemetery have been beautifully kept. In 1949 a new church was opened at Nipawin. In October, 1949, the clergy of the Diocese presented to Bishop Martin a Pastoral Staff to mark the completion of ten years of his episcopate; it was not only an expression of the affection in which he was held, but a tribute to his leadership and administration of the Diocese through ten difficult years.

CHAPTER THIRTEEN

The Upper Saskatchewan Valley
Since the 1890's: The Diocese of Calgary

Your Bishop, while one of my clergy, was early called to fill a most responsible position for the young Province—that of Superintendent of Education. . . .Later on he became more closely connected with me, when he succeeded Bishop McLean as Archdeacon and Canon of my Cathedral. . . . He proved an able, effective and acceptable worker for us and he acquired an experience that cannot but be of essential service in his new position.

I think the Bishop has done well in urging on the division of his diocese. The work of the church here must before many years be carried on by itself. . . . And the very first step for this is giving a voice and responsibility to the Laity.

ARCHBISHOP MACHRAY'S SERMON TO THE
FIRST SYNOD OF CALGARY

When Bishop Pinkham met the eighth Synod of the Diocese of Calgary in 1904, he was able to announce that the Episcopal Endowment Fund was completed, and that he had resigned the See of Saskatchewan. It had taken him ten years to bring the fund up to the then minimum requirement of $60,000.[1]

During the first ten years of the twentieth century there was a new rush of settlement in the West due to the offer of free land, which had been made known in central Europe; more immigrants came in this period than during the previous thirty years. In 1905 Alberta was constituted a Province, the railways rapidly extended their branch lines, and new settlements seemed to spring up overnight. In order to try and meet this contingency the Reverend W. F. Webb, Secretary of the Synod, was sent to the east to make known the needs of the west, and plead for financial support for the Diocese. As a result, new missions were opened at Frank on the Crow's Nest line and at High River. A large number of clergy came from England and other parts during this period, but with few exceptions only stayed a few months. One of these exceptions was the Reverend S. Cubitt,[2] who came as an hon-

[1]*Proceedings of the Synod of the Diocese of Calgary, 1898*, pp. 17-18. *Ibid., 1900*, pp. 10-12. *Journal of the Provincial Synod of Rupert's Land, 1899*, p. 45. *Ibid., 1902*, pp. 18 and 29.
[2]*Crockford's Clerical Directory, 1925*, p. 353. Curate of Ludlow, 1895-1898, and 1901-1907.

orary worker and remained for two and half years. The Reverend
E. C. Paget[3] came in 1900, after twenty-five years experience in educational and parochial work in England and the United States, as rector
of the Pro-Cathedral, in 1901 becoming the first Dean of Calgary. The
Reverend G. E. Gale joined the staff of the Diocese at the same time
and, like Dean Paget, gave the rest of his life in its service.

Financial difficulty was a persistent problem. In 1901, $14,000 was
raised by the people of the Diocese for church work. Grants from
outside sources were by no means great: the S.P.G. was giving £483,
but £100 of this went to Canon Newton of Edmonton, who had been
superannuated; the C. and C.C.S. was making a grant of £225; the
S.P.C.K. up to that time had been giving one-fifth of the cost of church
buildings up to $2,500. In 1904 this Society notified the Bishop that
the diocese would receive no more block grants; said its secretary, "The
time has come to let the Canadian Church fall in line with the rest of
the world. . . . If Newfoundland and the West Indies can manage, I
do not see why the N.W.T. should not likewise succeed in building
Churches without debt." At the time this was received, thirty-seven
out of seventy-one congregations were worshipping in private houses
and schools.[4] The C.M.S., which had been supporting the Blood,
Blackfoot, Peigan and Sarcee Missions, also announced that it proposed
reducing its grants by one-twelfth annually, commencing January 1,
1904, in the hope that the newly-formed M.S.C.C. would in future
take over responsibility for the Indian Missions; the only exception
was that the salary of Archdeacon Tims would be continued as long as
he was on the list of Northwest Canadian Missionaries.

In 1904 the Reverend W. F. Webb was appointed Archdeacon of
Calgary, a position vacant since Archdeacon Cooper had returned to
Ireland in 1898; C. F. P. Conybeare, K.C., was appointed Chancellor.
The three canonries of St. Peter, St. Paul and St. John had already been
created in 1899 and were held by the Reverends R. Hilton, H. W. G.
Stocken and H. Havelock Smith. Holders of these canonries were
expected to promote the study of Church History, Foreign Missions and
the Prayer Book, each delivering a sermon in the Cathedral once a year
on his particular subject. Two other canonries were established in
1907, those of St. Augustine (for the promotion of Indian education)

[3]*Ibid.*, p. 1150. Keble College, Oxford, First Class in Modern History, 1874.
Deacon 1875, Priest 1876, Gloucester and Bristol. Principal of Dorchester Missionary College, 1878-1884; Assistant at Devonport Cathedral, Iowa, U.S.A., 1886-
1887; Rector, Holy Trinity, Muscatine, U.S.A., 1887-1899; Rector, Revelstoke,
B.C., 1899-1900; Dean of Calgary, 1901.

[4]After 1904 the Grants Book of the S.P.C.K. shows payment of small grants
to many individual churches, but only three of £1,000 each: to "church building"
in 1907, Bishop Pinkham's School in 1909, and towards the endowment of the
Diocese of Edmonton in 1911.

and St. Aidan. The first holder of the former was the Reverend G. H. Hogbin, then Principal of the Indian Industrial School, and of the latter, the Reverend G. H. Webb, then general missionary of the Diocese. The sixth Canonry of St. George was created in 1911, and to it the Reverend A. J. B. Dewdney was appointed.

There were few self-supporting parishes in the diocese when it became independent of Saskatchewan in 1903: Edmonton and Strathcona in the north; Calgary, Red Deer, Macleod and Lethbridge within the southern area; but in 1904 Pincher Creek[5] in the south and Wetaskiwin in the north became rectories. In 1908 High River, and in 1910 St. Cyprian's, Lethbridge,[6] Taber, Nanton, Claresholme, Gleichen, Okotoks, Innisfail, St. John's and St. Stephen's (Calgary) and Christ Church (Edmonton) reached self-support, making a total of eighteen rectories in the diocese. Archdeacon Tims remarked, "It was not so difficult in those days for a parish to attain that distinction as it is today. The total salary required for a priest was $700 and in one or two cases the clergy were so desirous of having their parishes declared Rectories that they voluntarily did without any Diocesan grants and lived on $500, the most their Parish could provide."[7] One of the difficulties of the clergy was the enormous territory they were expected to cover, many of them holding services in six centres, and more often in eight or ten, people being gathered together in schoolhouses, farm dwellings or log shacks, but between 1903 and 1913 fifty-two churches were built.

In 1904 the Synod of the Diocese met for the first and only time outside Calgary; Edmonton, which had just become a city, was the place honoured, an indication of the events that led to the formation of the Diocese of Edmonton in 1913.

In 1905 an attempt was made to extend the organizational work of the Church by the appointment of the Reverend G. H. Webb as general missionary. Most of his work at first was devoted to ministrations in vacant parishes. In his first seven months he conducted one hundred and one services for thirty-six different congregations, held thirteen parochial meetings, attended three rural deanery conferences, took a parochial mission lasting eight days, and travelled 1,240 miles per month at a time when travelling was mostly done on horseback or by

[5]*Proceedings of the Synod of the Diocese of Calgary, 1900,* Bishop Pinkham's Charge. The fact that there were six such parishes in the Diocese brought the addition of a Canon governing the election of the Bishop of the Diocese, to its Constitution.

[6]*Crockford's Clerical Directory, 1916-1917,* p. 2056. Here are listed three Lethbridge churches: St. Augustine's, St. Mary the Virgin and St. Cyprian's, as "rectories." St. Cyprian's had no rector in 1925, and thereafter disappeared from Crockford's listings.

[7]*Calgary Diocesan Gazette* (Easter, 1930), 31.

buggy. In the autumn of 1909 Canon Webb resigned this post to become assistant rector of All Saints', Edmonton (he was later the first Archdeacon of that Diocese), and the financial difficulties of the Diocese of Calgary prevented the appointment of any successor to him at that time.

The suggestion that the Edmonton area should be constituted as a Diocese was first brought forward by the Bishop himself in 1908, but the Synod did not feel the time had yet come; however, it was suggested that a Bishop who had been for a time a Suffragan Bishop in England should be placed at Edmonton. To this the Bishop objected on the grounds that "the day has long gone by for bringing Bishops from England for Canadian Sees, and in this way appointing leaders who have everything to learn in regard to local conditions as to the country, its people and so on." A second objection was that the proposed new diocesan area did not contain the required number of clergymen within it to give it power to elect its own Bishop.

About this time some further assistance was received from England through three missionaries who were employed in construction camps and supported by the Navvy Missionary Society. In 1910 the pressure was considerably relieved in the northern part of the Diocese by the arrival of the Reverend W. G. Boyd to establish St. Faith's Mission, sponsored by the Archbishops' Western Canada Fund. A similar mission house was set up at Lethbridge, where in 1913 there were ten clergy with four lay readers under Canon W. H. Mowatt as their head,[8] who were responsible for the whole of the district south of the Crow's Nest Railway line, with the exception of Fishburn and the Blood Reserve. Churches were built at Coutts and Warner in 1911; at Sunnydale, Hazelmere and Cardston in 1912; at Ewelme and Burdett in 1913; and St. Saviour's at Foremost in 1914. "Except that the Clergy and Lay-Readers sent out from England received the Bishop's License, the work was carried on as though the Mission was a separate diocese within the Diocese. The placing of men, the organization of buildings and in fact the whole management of the work was done without any reference to the Executive Committee of the Diocese or the Bishop."[9]

One hundred and forty-three workers, clerical and lay, came to western Canada during the ten years or so that the missions were active; the majority of them spent their time in the original Diocese of Calgary. How many more would have come, and how much more

[8]*Crockford's Clerical Directory, 1916-1917*, p. 2056.
[9]*Calgary Diocesan Gazette* (Michaelmas, 1930), 32-33. What follows in the text of this book is based upon Archdeacon Tims' summary of the work of The Archbishops' Western Canada Fund in the Diocese of Calgary.

would have been accomplished in laying the foundations of the Anglican Church in western Canada, had not the First World War intervened, is impossible to say.

Canon Mowatt returned to England in 1916 and gradually the missioners withdrew, but a great endeavour was made in England to raise enough money as a capital fund, the interest on which would be used in maintaining the work the missions had started. A closing service in connection with the fund was held in Westminster Abbey in June, 1920, and the amount of the fund, then solemnly presented, was £37,095. A voucher for this sum, accompanied by the deeds of trust governing its disposition, was placed by the Archbishop of Rupert's Land on the offertory plate at the opening service of the John West centenary celebration held in Holy Trinity Church, Winnipeg, in October of the same year, and the money was later handed over to the Dioceses concerned. The Diocese of Calgary received about $42,000. The trust deed required that clergy belonging to the mission could only be used for pioneer work, that there should be a central mission house, and that members of the mission should meet together for conferences and meditation.

The Calgary Indian Missions

The Diocese of Calgary, from its earliest days, always has been concerned with missions to the Indians. It has within its boundaries three of the largest Indian Reserves in Canada, and it has been incessant in its efforts to promote the welfare and education of these people, and in endeavours to persuade the Canadian government to carry out the treaties made with them in every particular. The work was greatly assisted by the English societies, particularly the C.M.S., but the Diocese pioneered in the erection of residential schools. "The Victoria Home" for Peigan children near Brockett, Alberta, was erected with funds solicited chiefly by a rancher in the district in commemoration of the Golden Jubilee of Queen Victoria.[10] The mission was for many years in charge of the Reverend W. R. Haynes, who had come out to the Blackfoot Mission in 1899, and also been a teacher on the Blood Reserve. His knowledge of the language enabled him to get in close touch with the people.[11] The church was built on the Reserve in 1901, the Indians themselves hauling all the materials and providing funds for the organ. Grants from the C.M.S., the S.P.C.K., the W.A. in eastern Canada and the Diocesan Mission Fund met the cost of

[10]*Proceedings of the Synod of the Diocese of Calgary, 1898*, pp. 15, 22, 123. *Calgary Diocesan Gazette* (Christmas, 1929), 25.
[11]Rev. W. R. Haynes was ordained in 1904 and took charge of this mission, but illness in 1910 brought his resignation as Principal of Victoria House. He continued as missionary on the Reserve. *Ibid.* (Trinity, 1930), 27, 30.

material and labour. The success of the residential schools gradually drew increasing support and interest from the Indian Department of the federal government, which in 1910 agreed to increase its grants to all schools within easy distance of the railway to $100 per head, and to schools more than one hundred miles from the railway to $125. About 1900 the missionary on the Blood Reserve, who also had charge of St. Paul's School, was the Reverend A. de B. Owen; he never learned the language, but in his time the school was brought to a high standard of efficiency. He had as a teacher of exceptional qualifications, Miss Wells, who practically spent herself upon the children, and who, when she gave up teaching, continued to live on the Reserve and mother the girls who graduated from the school. The Reverend G. E. Gale took charge of the mission in 1904 at a time when it extended for seventy miles along the banks of the Belly and St. Mary Rivers, but having mastered the language he was able to go about without an interpreter, and managed to visit every home on the Reserve. He was joined in 1909 by S. H. Middleton who showed a remarkable aptitude as a linguist. Mr. Middleton was ordained in 1911, received priest's Orders in 1913, and for more than forty years devoted himself entirely to the interests of the people on the Blood Reserve.[12]

The Blackfoot Reserve north of Gleichen was one of the earliest missionary efforts among the Indians of the Plains, and the people have always been noted for their courage, superior powers of organization, and independency. The mission owed its foundation in 1883 to Archdeacon Tims, who translated much of the Prayer Book and the New Testament into the tribal dialect. It owed more, perhaps, to the long, careful and persistent efforts of the Reverend H. W. Gibbon Stocken and his brother, the Reverend Stanley J. Stocken, who for many years were the missionaries and teachers on the Reserve. Schools were established on the Reserve, at the North Camp for girls and at the South Camp for boys. A hospital was erected about 1897, to which Dr. Turner gave his services as honorary physician for the first three years, and his two daughters, who were supported by the Toronto W.A., were respectively matron and nurse.

By 1901 the government was sufficiently interested in the education of the Indians to agree to take over a considerable part of school costs; as a consequence the South Camp School was closed and the whole work concentrated on a location about a mile north of the North Camp School building. The new school unit became known as "Old Sun's School" after the head chief of the South Blackfoot, and the building was used until 1909, when it was condemned. For about

[12]*Crockford's Clerical Directory, 1957-1958,* p. 791. *Calgary Diocesan Gazette* (Trinity, 1930), 26-27.

two years day schools were substituted, and then in 1911 the government erected a new building that was used until 1928, when it was destroyed by fire. During these years missionaries were greatly assisted by two native catechists, Paul Pokapinni and David Summakend.

The Reverend H. W. Gibbon Stocken retired from the Blackfoot work at the end of 1923 after thirty-seven years service as a missionary, of which twenty-five had been spent on this Reserve. He was succeeded by the Reverend F. M. R. Gibney, who made a favourable impression among the Indians both as a missionary and as the Principal of the Old Sun School. He was in charge of the work until 1930 when, upon his resignation, the Reverend J. W. House became Principal. Mr. Gibney, in turn, took over the work on the Sarcee Reserve, following Archdeacon Tims, who had resigned his connection with the Church Missionary Society after forty-seven years of service. Mrs. S. J. Stocken died on October 29, 1915, and her husband, the Reverend S. J. Stocken, only survived her by a few weeks, passing away on January 16, 1916. His wife, as Miss Symonds, had come to the Blackfoot Mission in 1891 as a teacher, and married Stanley Stocken a few years later; both were highly regarded for their saintly characters and influence with the natives.

As time went on the work among the Blackfoot prospered, and two more mission halls were built on the Reserve. On the occasion of Bishop Sherman's first visit to the Reserve in June, 1927, three lay readers were formally licensed, Paul Littlewalker, Silas Wolfcollar and Earl Calfchild, the latter a former pupil of the Old Sun School.[13]

The Sarcee Reserve near Calgary is the smallest of the four in the Diocese; its people originally were Beaver Indians from the Peace River country, who left it because of famine conditions and finally became integrated with, or at least accepted by, the Blackfoot. Work was begun among them in 1887 by the Reverend Robert Inkster, but he found the language difficult, and it was taken over by Canon Stocken a little before 1888. In 1895, as it was considered expedient that Archdeacon Tims should leave the Blackfoot Reserve, an exchange was made, and the Archdeacon continued to work among the Sarcees until he retired in September, 1930. He was the last survivor of the missionaries sent directly to the Indians by the Church Missionary Society. In his report to the Diocesan Synod in February, 1931, the Archdeacon mentioned that a new Old Sun School had been opened the previous December first, and had cost the government $200,000. It marked another stage in the history of that Reserve; when he had begun work there in 1883 it was estimated there were two

[13]*Ibid.*, 24-26.

thousand heathen Indians on the Reserve, but the government return in 1929 showed there were only thirty-one left.

The work on the Sarcee Reserve was supported by the Diocese with some help from the eastern W.A.'s. The children were gradually gathered into a succession of small residential schools, and there was a small log church, the latter being re-erected as the Church of St. Barnabas in 1909, dedicated by Bishop Holmes of Athabasca. A new boarding school was completed there in January of 1914, but with the withdrawal of the Church Missionary Society's support, even though there was increased government support, this proved a heavy burden upon the Diocese; however in 1916 it was reported that ninety out of one hundred ninety-three people on the Reserve were members of the Church, and that twenty boys and fourteen girls were in the school. The other schools were able to contribute to their own support by agricultural activities. The Blood School in 1918 had thirty-five acres under crop, and the Blackfoot about fifty acres, with the prospect of breaking about sixty more. The Peigans had prospered both in crops and cattle, but there was very little possibility of prosperity on the Sarcee Reserve, because it only had about five acres under cultivation, and the children were too young to be able to do very much.

In his Charge to the Synod, which met on June tenth, 1919, the Bishop said that he was happy to announce that on March 15 the Reverend Canon Gould, Secretary of the M.S.C.C., had informed him that the executive committee had formally assumed full responsibility for the diocesan Indian boarding schools and missions as from the first of the year, including the financial deficit at the end of 1918, and in the future would control, support and administer them with the reservation only of his canonical rights to the Bishop. This relieved the diocese of a debt of $20,500. The work was temporarily placed in the hands of a local commission consisting of Chancellor Savary, Archdeacon Tims and Sidney Houlton, Secretary-Treasurer of the Diocese, which was primarily responsible to the executive of the M.S.C.C. The Synod approved these proposals, pledged its warm support to the Anglican Forward Movement, and no doubt was as glad as the Bishop to have the load lifted. It had been an anxiety, for thirty-two years.

The missions, however, continued to be organized as parishes and bore the usual responsibilities as to apportionments. In 1922 the four Reserves were reported to have a population of 2,395 people; the number of church families was 156, the number of baptized members 866, of which 283 were communicants, over half of them belonging to the Peigan Reserve. They had contributed, during 1920 and 1921, $1,249 to the funds of the Diocese, nearly half of which had come from the Blood Reserve; the Sarcee Mission had raised $424, the Blackfoot $145, and the Peigans $125.

Urban Expansion in Calgary

Until 1905 the Pro-Cathedral of the Redeemer was the only Anglican church in the city of Calgary, but by that time the population had increased to well over 4,000, the city was growing towards the west, and it was decided that this part should be left in the care of the original church. St. John's was opened on January 6, 1905. Its site was to the east of the junction between the Elbow and Bow Rivers. In 1907 St. John's became self-supporting and for three years had as its rector the Reverend G. A. Ray. The Reverend G. E. Gale took charge on September 4, 1910, and a new church was under construction in 1911 in the 1400 block on Eighth Avenue East. Canon Gale ministered to this parish for twenty-five years.

Some account has already been given of the founding of St. Stephen's Church in the southwestern part of the city. The first rector was Archdeacon W. F. Webb. The original church was extended more than once by the addition of aisles and chancel, but plans made in 1912 for the erection of a permanent building did not materialize until 1950 when Archdeacon Maddocks was rector.

Work in the parish of St. Barnabas on the northwestern side of the Bow River was begun in the same year, 1906. That part of the city was then regarded as being out in the country. There were only "some ten places built and a total population of some 50 souls." The first church was used until 1912, when E. H. Riley offered to erect a new building as a memorial to members of his family. The parish was self-supporting in 1910 and had a fine record. (Shortly after it celebrated its fiftieth anniversary as a parish in 1956, the church was destroyed by fire, but it was rebuilt.)

In 1909 a second church was begun on the north side of the river, considerably to the north of St. Barnabas', and its earliest records indicate that it was in charge of a lay reader, M. C. F. Reade. The first recorded meeting of the parishioners took place on January 9, 1911. The present St. Michael's and All Angels was completed in the latter part of 1928.

By 1911 the population of the city had risen to more than 43,000, and two new parishes were established that year, All Saints' in the northeastern part and St. George's in what is known as the Parkview district.[14] In 1910 the Bishop received a promise of a site from F. C. Lowers for a church in Elbow Park, but nothing further materialized until June, 1912, when a parish was organized under the name of Christ Church. The first services were held on January 5, 1913; the church itself was not actually in use until 1926. St. Mark's and St.

[14]*The New Era* (May, 1912), 187. Map of the City of Calgary, showing churches and possible missions.

Martin's churches were the result of the vestry of St. Stephen's seeing the necessity of expanding its work in the south and western parts of the city. St. Martin's was formed as a parish in 1914. St. Mark's, in Glengarry, was completed in 1913.[15]

The Anglican Forward Movement and Calgary

The Anglican Forward Movement, which did much to relieve the financial anxieties of the Calgary Diocese, during its campaign had received admirable and enthusiastic support in the Diocese itself.[16] The idea that the Church should make a special effort to preserve and carry on its missionary work seems to have arisen from the spirit of self-sacrifice that was apparent during the years of World War I, and found expression in a report of the assessment committee to the M.S.C.C. Board of Management in 1916, which resulted in proposals being made in 1918 that the General Synod should become responsible for all the Indian and Eskimo work after 1920, in which year the C.M.S. was expected to withdraw its assistance. One of the speakers at the General Synod was the Bishop of Mackenzie River (Lucas). The Bishop told the Synod that he had to leave the next day in order to catch the last scow, going down the river to his home at Fort Chipewyan, and he appealed for assistance in paying the freight charges on necessary supplies for his clergy who were ministering to the Eskimos on the shores of the Arctic Sea. The M.S.C.C., however, did not have the fifteen hundred dollars he requested. The Synod was greatly moved; one layman said the money must be forthcoming, and that if necessary he would go out and collect it himself, or pay it out of his own pocket. As a consequence, a resolution was moved by G. B. Nicholson, seconded by T. Mortimer, which asked that the Primate appoint a special committee to work out a plan in co-operation with the executive committee by which an appeal might be made to the whole Canadian Church. A committee of laymen was formed with representatives from every Diocese, Chancellor Savary and E. J. Fream representing Calgary. The Anglican Forward Movement was finally launched with an objective of $2,500,000. Of this, $300,000 was designated as "A War Memorial Endowment Fund" for work among the Indians and Eskimos; $750,000 as a beneficiary fund, the current interest of which was to provide old age pensions for the clergy and their widows; and $600,000 for a diocesan local needs fund, to be distributed among the Dioceses in order to meet exceptional needs. Under the direction of Archdeacon Hayes and Miss M. E. Cox, Diocesan President of the W.A., $38,000

[15]*Calgary Diocesan Gazette* (Christmas, 1933), 8-19, records this urban progress.
[16]*Ibid.* (Michaelmas, 1931), 29-31.

was raised in the Diocese of Calgary, of which the Diocese received back over $10,000, which was added to its Clergy, Mission and Sustentation Fund.

St. Hilda's College and Bishop Pinkham's School

Bishop Pinkham, like Bishops Machray and McLean, was always keenly interested in education. It is not surprising, therefore, that he brought the matter of education in the North West Territories to the attention of his first Synod in the Diocese of Calgary. Owing to the difficulty of gathering the children together, Sunday Schools, although very desirable, were almost impossible to organize, and as far as the day schools were concerned it seemed impossible to reach any common denominational formula of religious teaching, that could be pressed upon the government or trustees for adoption. He was anxious for the establishment of church schools, at least higher schools for boys and girls, under diocesan control, which might offer a more complete system of education than the state schools found possible.

Calgary's position as a central and distributing point is being more and more recognized; and its location seems to mark it out for its becoming an educational as well as an ecclesiastical centre. Bishop McLean recognized this shortly before his death, and selected an excellent site in this town. This site I have purchased from the government with part of the money I raised in England; and since my return I have written a strong appeal in one of the leading Church papers in England, for funds for building and furnishing a Girls' School, and for teachers. . . . In the meantime this Parish has under consideration a scheme which might result in the establishment of a Girls' School on a small scale, at an early date.

This seems to be the first reference in the diocesan records to the school, that later became known as St. Hilda's College, which offered an all-round education to girls in the southern part of the Territories and the southern part of Alberta for nearly fifty years.[17] It appears to have been conducted as a private foundation without any direct diocesan responsibility, though reports of its affairs were submitted regularly to the Synod. In 1916 it was reported that in spite of the effects of the First World War, the school had had an average attendance of ten boarders and twenty-five day pupils. In 1921 there was no regular Synod but a conference of clergy and laity was held at which the affairs of the Diocese were discussed with considerable freedom. Sidney Houlton reported extensively upon its financial matters, announcing that "the Bishop Pinkham College and St. Hilda's College have not cost the diocese one dollar." Nevertheless, the financial condition of St. Hilda's College appears to have been unsatisfactory, and

[17]*Proceedings of the Synod of the Diocese of Calgary, 1892*, pp. 16-19.

a deputation of parents approached the Synod in 1924 to discuss its continuance.[18] At the same time the Synod heard a special report on St. Hilda's prepared by J. C. Brokovski, and by its Resolution No. 72 said that without prejudice to its legal position the Synod recognized the moral responsibility of the Diocese with respect to the mortgage debt on St. Hilda's College, and appointed a small committee to co-operate with the board of governors in providing the money necessary to discharge the mortgage, either by the sale of the property or otherwise. After this, there is no further mention of St. Hilda's College in the published records.

Bishop Pinkham's School was a much later foundation. The Bishop laid the corner-stone on May 31, 1911, and it opened on September 21 of that year with eight boarders and seventeen day boys under Principal A. P. Hayes, F.I.G.C.M. By 1913 the school had thirty-four boarders and thirteen day boys. Some consideration was being given to the enlargement of the buildings with a view to housing in them a divinity college or hostel as well. Bishop Pinkham called attention to this latter project in his Charge to his Synod in June, 1914, remarking, "Since the beginning of the present year I have been making full representations to S.P.G. to give us substantial assistance in starting as soon as possible our Hostel or Divinity College, and Archdeacon Hogbin has done all in his power to back these representations up." The Archdeacon, who was in England in the spring of 1914, met with the American Sub-Committee of the S.P.G. in April and gained its support. The Bishop added in his Charge, "We shall never get the men we need for our Missions until we train them here . . . so we must get our Hostel in operation as soon as possible. . . ."

Unfortunately, the World War I intervened, and the plan for the Diocese of Calgary to train its own men for the ministry seems to have been abandoned. The school itself suffered severely; the report presented to the Synod in February, 1916, showed that the boarders had dropped to thirteen, though day boys remained at eighteen. The majority of the staff seem to have enlisted, as well as a considerable number of former pupils, but Canon Murrell Wright had collected donations amounting to $1,777. The solvency of the school seems to have been sustained from it; in fact it had a balance of $55,447 of assets over liabilities at the end of 1915, but the prospects were not good, and to the regret of the Bishop the school was closed in 1916.

Bishop's Court

One of the problems that every Diocese in the Province of Rupert's Land had had to face, sooner or later, was that of trying to provide a

[18]*Ibid.*, 1921, Resolutions Nos. 31 and 33.

suitable residence for its Bishop. Bishop Pinkham became Bishop of Saskatchewan in 1887, but less than a year later the Diocese was divided and he became in addition Bishop of Calgary. Largely due to the fact that Prince Albert was in a part of the country where there seemed no immediate prospect of development, the Bishop determined to live in Calgary, which was more accessible because of the C.P.R. It was a good many years before the Bishop had anything but a rented house,[19] which he paid for out of his own income, and periodically he complained about this to the Synod. In 1894 he said that "rent and taxes amount now to nearly $700 per annum," and he had to pay this large proportion at a time when the income from invested funds of the Saskatchewan Bishopric was only bringing in about $2,400 a year. It was not until the year before the Diocese of Calgary became independent (1903) that the Synod was in a position to authorize the purchase of a See House for the sum of $4,300, situated on the north side of the Bow River. The purchase was made possible by a grant from the Colonial Bishopric's Fund of £500 and a gift of £200 from a personal friend of the Bishop.[20]

Assistant Bishop

In 1916 Bishop Pinkham asked the Synod, which met on February 15, to give him an assistant: "Being now in my seventy-second year and in my twenty-ninth year as a Bishop, after forty-seven and a half years in the ministry of the Church of God in North-West Canada, even though my health at the present time is excellent, and I am so far, thank God, physically equal to my work, I have felt that the time has come, to take the first step, looking to the appointment of an assistant." He had asked the executive of the Diocese, and it in turn had requested the Chancellor, to bring before the Synod the necessary changes in Diocesan Canon XV to enable the Synod to elect such an assistant. He proposed to apply to the Provincial Synod for the power to do so when that Synod met in August. The necessary changes were introduced in the report of the committee, and the Canons and Rules of Order were amended accordingly. When the Provincial Synod of Rupert's Land met in Edmonton on August 9, 1916, message "A" from the House of Bishops read: "The House of Bishops begs to inform the House of Delegates that it has considered the application of the Right Reverend the Bishop of Calgary for the appointment of an Assistant Bishop, and has unanimously decided that such application should be

[19]Jean A. Pinkham, "Reminiscences of an Oldtimer," *Calgary Herald* (November 8, 1924), 5. This was contributed by Mrs. Pinkham herself.
[20]In 1913 this house was sold for $15,000 and the C. W. Paterson property purchased for $32,000. The latter was sold in 1923 for $21,000, and 1818 First Street East was purchased, which was cleared of debt and back taxes by 1926.

346

granted and asks the concurrence of the House of Delegates therein."
At this point trouble began. Mr. Kirkpatrick of Edmonton, seconded
by the Reverend W. B. Heeney of Winnipeg, moved concurrence, but
Archdeacon Tims of Calgary, seconded by the Reverend C. W.
McKim of Edmonton, offered as an amendment the addition—"Provided the
salary of an Assistant Bishop is guaranteed to the satisfaction of the
Metropolitan before the election of the Assistant Bishop takes place."
On a point of order, the Prolocutor (Dean Coombes) ruled that the
amendment was in order, but his ruling was not sustained by the
House. The motion of concurrence was then withdrawn by its sponsors,
and two lay delegates from Calgary, Judge Jackson and W. A. Geddes,
brought in a motion of non-concurrence that was carried unanimously.

When the Provincial Synod met on October 10, 1920, the whole
question of the appointment of Assistant Bishops came up for review,
and the Bishops outlined their proposed amendments to Section IX
of the Provincial Constitution. The difficulties in the way of acceptance were first the possibilities of appointing an Assistant Bishop in
the Diocese of Rupert's Land, which was the fixed Metropolitical See,
and secondly the Bishops' request of an endowment of $75,000 for
an Assistant Bishop before such could be elected, though some discre-
tion was left with the Metropolitan, if he were satisfied that a salary
of $4,500 per annum was guaranteed by a recognized missionary
society. Upon receiving this latter message the Lower House promptly
deleted the reference to Assistant Bishops. Later, before anything
had been settled, a message came from the Bishops approving an
application from the Diocese of Qu'Appelle for the appointment of an
Assistant Bishop as soon as the Metropolitan was satisfied that the
income was provided in accordance with the resolution passed by the
Synod. The main difficulty at this point seems to have been the right
of succession to the diocese, the Bishops holding out very strongly for
it and refusing to accept any diocesan expression of opinion made
previous to the application.

The Lower House asked for a joint session; the Bishops preferred to
receive a delegation. This resulted in Chancellor Machray's rewriting
the whole of Section IX,[21] and adding to it a sub-section A, specifying

[21] *Journal of the Provincial Synod of Rupert's Land, 1916*, pp. 32-33: Message
"A" from the House of Bishops to the House of Delegates, and discussion thereon.
Ibid., 32: Request for reconsideration and deputation. *Ibid., 1920*: Message "H"
from the House of Bishops to the House of Delegates, and discussion thereon,
pp. 32-33 and 33-36. *Ibid.*, p. 37: Message "K" from the House of Bishops to
the House of Delegates, and amendment eliminating the application to Assistant
Bishops. *Ibid.*: Message "O" from the House of Bishops to the House of Delegates regarding Qu'Appelle. *Ibid.*, 40-41, 44-50: General discussion on Canon IX
of the Constitution. Page 64, appendix, gives text of new Canon IX; p. 53, Act I
of this Synod. *Ibid., 1923*, 34-36. The new Canon was renumbered as Canon
VIII in the revised Constitution published in 1929.

that the office of Assistant Bishop might be attached to some position, office or dignity in the diocese that had a permanent, sufficient suitable salary. This was accepted after it had been amended to keep the right of approving applications for Assistant Bishops with the Provincial Synod as a whole, not merely with the House of Bishops, and after a settlement of the situation in Rupert's Land that gave the Diocesan Synod the right to have an Assistant Bishop under the customary rules, but without giving him the right of succession. The amended Canon IX came under discussion again in 1923, and having been passed in two successive Synods by the necessary majorities, the new rule came into force at once, and has been effective ever since.

When Bishop Pinkham again met the Synod of Calgary on February 19 and 20, 1924, he said in his Charge that the matter had at last been straightened out in the Provincial Synod, and he was applying for an Assistant. At the second session the formal application from the Bishop was read and a motion was made that it be approved. This was referred to a committee of the whole House, and after discussion Resolution 15 was brought in, "That this House and Committee assembled regrets that it cannot see its way to concur at the present time, in the Bishop's request for an Assistant Bishop, owing to financial difficulties which may arise in the Diocese, and that in view of his advanced age, the Bishop be asked to save his strength, so far as possible, for his episcopal work in the Diocese."

The Closing Years of Bishop Pinkham's Episcopate

The Synod of 1924 (his twentieth in the Diocese of Calgary) was the last over which Bishop Pinkham presided, then in his eightieth year. He commented upon the fact that the number of clergy in the Diocese had dropped to forty, but there were six students in attendance at St. John's College, Winnipeg; during the year there had been 451 confirmations, considerably more than usual. He had been more than delighted with the meetings of the General Synod boards at Calgary in September of 1923, the first time the boards had met at any place west of Winnipeg. The Bishop felt that both the Diocese and members of the boards had profited greatly.

Without the help of the Assistant Bishop he hoped for, and in spite of the able assistance of Archdeacon Hayes as Organizing Clerical Secretary for the Diocese, of Archdeacon Tims as the indefatigable Superintendent of the Indian Missions, and of Archdeacon A. J. B. Dewdney, who had devoted himself to the Church's welfare in the Diocese since 1909, the aged Bishop found it increasingly difficult to carry on. Two years later, on February 17, 1926, he tendered his resignation to the executive of the Diocese, to become effective on

August 7, which would be the thirty-ninth anniversary of his consecration. After his resignation his health gradually failed. He died on July 18th, 1928, in the eighty-third year of his age, the sixtieth of his ministry and the forty-first of his episcopate.

Of his earlier life much has been told in connection with the Diocese of Rupert's Land, where his work began, and of his appointment as Bishop of Saskatchewan. The Diocese of Calgary reached its peak of strength in 1913 when there were 94 clergy and 54 lay workers, 110 organized parishes, and 147 unorganized districts. The First World War, and subsequent years of economic stress, diminished this number considerably. In the memorial article (which appeared under the signature of Canon S. H. Middleton in the Michaelmas Number of the *Calgary Diocesan Gazette* in 1928), it was observed that very few Bishops had been called upon to summon such executive ability as Dr. Pinkham. "He was truly a great pioneer, a veritable land-mark. He loved the city in which he lived as well as it loved him. No wonder Calgary was proud of its first Bishop. . . . That wisdom which so many especially associate with him rested on his honesty of thought and his unfailing faith and consciousness of the presence of God."

Louis Ralph Sherman,
Second Bishop of Calgary

The twenty-first meeting of the Synod of the Diocese of Calgary was held on October 5, 1926, under the presidency of Dean Paget, to elect a successor to Bishop Pinkham. On the first ballot after the nominating one, the Very Reverend Louis Ralph Sherman, Dean of Quebec, was declared elected by a majority of both Orders.

The new Bishop was born in Fredericton, N.B., on August 26, 1886. Educated in the public schools, he graduated from the University of New Brunswick in 1907, took the L.S.T. at Bishop's University, Lennoxville, P.Q., in 1909. In the same year he was elected a Rhodes Scholar, and went to Christ Church, Oxford. After a year at Cuddesdon, he was ordained by Bishop Winnington Ingram of London in 1912. In 1914 he came back to Canada as curate of Trinity Church, St. John, N.B. In 1917 he became rector of Trinity Church, Toronto, and in 1925 rector of Holy Trinity Cathedral in Quebec and Dean of the Diocese. Bishop Sherman was consecrated on February 24, 1927, in the Pro-Cathedral Church of the Redeemer, Calgary, by the Metropolitan of Rupert's Land (Matheson).[22]

In its new Bishop, the Diocese of Calgary secured a leader who not only had a brilliant and scholarly mind, but a forthright and vigorous personality, energetic and outspoken, at times regardless of where the

[22]O. R. Rowley, *The Anglican Episcopate of Canada and Newfoundland*, 208-209.

chips fell. With him the Diocese began a new era of expansion. The Synod of the Diocese of Calgary met for the first time under his presidency on November 9, 1927, and he opened his Charge by saying that the previous eight months had been the happiest in his life, but he had to record the death of three faithful servants of the Church. Edward Clarence Paget, Dean of Calgary, had died March 27. Paget Hall, in which the Synod was meeting, was a monument to his devotion and industry. "But far greater than any made by hands is the spiritual temple that he helped to build in the hearts and lives of his people." Their second loss was that of Charles Frederick Pringle Conybeare, K.C., D.C.L., who had played an honourable part in the growing life of western Canada, particularly at Lethbridge, and in connection with St. Augustine's Church. Mr. Conybeare had been solicitor for the diocese from 1900 and Chancellor from 1904, holding these offices until 1918. They had also lost his successor, Henry Phipps Otty Savary, K.C., who had come to Alberta in 1909, where he had won universal esteem in his profession. A member of St. Stephen's, Calgary, he had been Chancellor and Solicitor from 1918 up to the time of his death.

After paying tribute to Bishop Pinkham, the Bishop dealt with changes among the clergy of the diocese and remarked upon the special appointments, namely that of Canon R. H. Robinson, as rector of the Pro-Cathedral and Dean of the Diocese; of the Reverend Cecil Swanson as Archdeacon of Lethbridge (a new archdeaconry created out of the area covered by the three rural deaneries of Lethbridge, Macleod and High River), which was not only a personal tribute but also intended to emphasize the growing importance of the city of Lethbridge in the work of the Diocese. The Archdeaconry of Calgary had become coterminous with the Rural Deanery of Calgary, and to it he had transfered Archdeacon Tims. The Honourable Mr. Justice W. L. Walsh had been kind enough to accept the appointment of Chancellor. J. G. Adam, their faithful and efficient Secretary-Treasurer, had been appointed Registrar, and the Bishop desired to express his gratitude for all that he had done, and to assure him of the feeling of security and appreciation that the Synod felt in his integrity, faithfulness and devotion.

The work of the Diocese's theological students was discussed at some length, together with an announcement that the examination requirements of the Diocese were being made more exacting for both deacons and priests. Also stressed was a knowledge of the Bible—"Not of books about the Bible, of the making of which there is no end, but of the Book itself." The Bishop considered knowledge of the Word of God as the primary intellectual condition for ordination. The Kingdom of God was not built with money; it is built with men. He went on to speak of vocation, urging the clergy to prophesy, arouse and persuade in this matter.

The second problem that troubled the Bishop was that of the diocesan policy in filling vacant parishes, the problem of concentration versus expansion; urban centres needed intensive work, rural districts needed extensive work, and one man could not do both well. He then turned to the theme that became linked with his name across the Dominion, that of self-support, beginning with a criticism of the parochial situation in the Diocese. Out of forty parishes only thirteen were self-supporting. "Men and women who can drive to Church in motor cars and who can find money for all manner of other things should not be dependent upon charity from England or eastern Canada for the maintenance of their Services." He also drew the attention of the Synod to the increasing expense of clergy transportation. Among the sundry matters with which he dealt was the launching of a *Diocesan Gazette*, the need for more branches of the W.A., a better system of insurance for church property, and the very important one of parochial assessments.

The first issue of the *Calgary Diocesan Gazette* appeared at Easter, 1928, with Canon W. J. Merrick of Red Deer as Chairman of the Editorial Board. It came out quarterly until September, 1935, when it was overcome by financial difficulties. To its pages, Archdeacon Tims contributed an interesting history of the early years of the Diocese.[23]

Synod journals are apt to be factual and concise, but a diocesan journal is often revealing about parochial progress and intimacies. In 1928, for example, the Reverend Canon Willis G. James, who had been rector of St. Stephen's Church since 1921, left for St. Thomas' in St. Catharines, Ontario. Under his inspiring guidance, St. Stephen's had become the second most important church in Calgary, and the Diocesan Board of Religious Education had succeeded, in co-operation with other religious bodies, in establishing a course in Religious Education in the Provincial Normal School. He was to be followed at St. Stephen's by the Reverend F. H. Wilkinson, who had been Professor of Old Testament at Emmanuel College, Saskatoon, and about twenty years later was to be elected Bishop of Toronto. The canonry vacated by Mr. James was filled by the appointment of the Reverend W. R. Haynes, one of the pioneer Indian missionaries of the Diocese, who had been in charge of the Peigan Mission for twenty-six years.

[23]Archdeacon Tims' statements in these articles appear to be based upon contemporary sources, and any errors in them are rare.

The Anniversary Appeal, 1928

The *Diocesan Gazette,* in its Chrismas number, said that *the* item of diocesan news was the phenomenal success of the fortieth anniversary appeal, "gingered up" by a most energetic and persistent committee of Calgary laymen. The whole diocese had responded in a marvellous way; instead of $40,000, $50,000 was obtained and the Diocese stood out of debt.

The Synod of the Diocese met February sixth, 1929. The *Diocesan Gazette,* in its Easter number, remarked that "all Synods are disappointing according to the way one looks at them, this one was no exception to the rule." The reporter said, "People attended Synods for the following purposes: 1. To fight over money matters; 2. To fight over standards of churchmanship; 3. To enjoy fellowship with one another; 4. To criticize everything that has been done; 5. To get what is called 'inspiration.'" The writer went on to say there was no fighting over anything at all, "it isn't done in this Diocese at present," over money or churchmanship. As for inspiration, "the average Anglican thought of the work of the spirit as that of producing order out of chaos, and sees his work in the quiet, steady growth of the soul of the individual or of the Church, and this kind of inspiration was abundantly present."

As to what the Synod accomplished, first the Finance and Property Board was reconstructed and all trust funds were brought under its jurisdiction; some revision of the Canons and Constitution was made to bring them more in line with those of the older dioceses, and a provision was inserted for the appointment by the Bishop of three clerical and three lay delegates to the executive committee; an assessment commission was set up to find some method of apportionment that would operate on a flat rate basis, yet be capable of local adjustment. The matter of clergy transportation received animated discussion, but it was felt to be primarily the concern of the parishes. Another report that provoked a good deal of criticism was that of the Diocesan Council of Social Service, which did not concern itself with immigration, but was much worked up over the relation of country and city work, at least so it appeared to the observer who wrote for the *Diocesan Gazette.* But the report itself shows that the council was much concerned about a new scheme of farm immigration that had been proposed by the Church of England Empire Settlement Board. In 1928, 10,000 miners had been sent out from England to Canada for harvest work; it was hoped that many would become good settlers. The plan also mentioned the establishment in Calgary of a Church Army hostel for boys about fifteen years of age.

Between 1927 and 1928 new churches were erected at Waterton Lakes, Nanton, and St. Michael's and All Angels, Calgary. St. Augustine's at Lethbridge was moved and rebuilt. The Diocese at this period undertook a scheme of group insurance for clergy, students and other workers. This was a pioneer step as far as western Canada was concerned.

The *Calgary Diocesan Gazette,* in its Trinity number of 1929, carried an unsigned article under the caption "When, Canada? When?" that created a sensation. It was reprinted in the *Church Messenger,* the *A.Y.P.A. Monthly, The Canadian Churchman,* and was mentioned in the English *Church Times.* This dealt in forthright and somewhat caustic language with the constant appeals being made to the English missionary organizations to assist the Canadian Church, ascribing such appeals to tradition, ignorance and western lack of ambition, and suggesting remedies. Most readers attributed it to Bishop Sherman, but actually it was admitted later to have been written by Archdeacon Cecil Swanson of Lethbridge, the Literary Editor of the *Gazette.* When the Provincial Synod of Rupert's Land met in Calgary in September, this article was adversely criticized in both Houses with some heat, and in the Upper House one Bishop, who became angry when he discovered its authorship, remarked, "Well, Bishop, the only thing for you to do is to exercise more supervision of your editorial staff." Bishop Sherman replied, "Not at all. You can't get good men to do the work if they always feel the presence of the big stick over their heads."[24] The Archdeacon remained unrepentant and followed the article, in the Michaelmas number, with a scathing indictment of the Provincial Synod itself.

In 1931 Bishop Sherman met his Synod on February fourth. He had been to the Lambeth Conference in 1930 and at the same time had attended the S.P.G. Conference of those Bishops whose Dioceses received grants from that Society. In characteristic phrase, he told the Synod that he went "dutifully and came away ashamedly." He went because he was conscious of the great generosity of the Society to the Diocese, but when he had heard of the demands upon it for expansion in other parts of the world, he knew better than ever that the Diocese of Calgary should not be a beneficiary. "The fact is that we have outgrown the S.P.G.," and he added, "some day, I have the faith to believe, we're going to begin proudly to pay for our religion ourselves." By "ourselves" he meant the Dominion of Canada, and he had an unshakable faith in the Canadian Church as a whole, but it

[24]*Calgary Diocesan Gazette* (Michaelmas, 1929), 6. O. R. Rowley, "Pillars of the Church, ix—The Dean of New Westminster," *Canadian Churchman* (October 10, 1940), 564.

was not until the Stratford meeting of the Executive of General Synod in 1940 that he saw this accomplished.

The Bishop indicated the continued expansion and consolidation of the Church's work in the Diocese; new churches had been erected at Carbon, Rocky Mountain House and St. Paul's on the Blood Reserve. The executive reported that all claims on the Diocese respecting St. Hilda's College had been settled for a payment of $6,000, to be spread over three years. In 1930 Mr. Justice W. L. Walsh resigned as Chancellor upon his appointment as Lieutenant-Governor of the Province of Alberta. He was succeeded by Mr. J. C. Brokovski.

About this time, 1930, radio broadcasting began to receive the serious consideration of the Church. Reference to its increasing importance was made by the Bishop in his Charge to the Synod, noting the Prime Minister's first broadcast to the nation on New Year's morning of 1931. He suggested that the Church must be ready to accommodate itself to meet new revelations, to alter methods to meet changed conditions, to greet the unseen and the unexpected with a cheer. Actually, reports in the *Calgary Diocesan Gazette* indicate that evening services were being broadcast from the Pro-Cathedral of the Redeemer as early as 1928, and there were occasional broadcasts from St. Stephen's. By 1931 these seem to have increased to once a month from St. Stephen's and twice a month from the Pro-Cathedral. Religious broadcasts during the next ten years increased in number, over both the C.B.C. and private stations, on Sundays and week-days. A detailed study, particularly in southern Alberta, might show that in no other part of Canada was the impact of broadcasting so widely felt as in this area. In the later years of his episcopate in Calgary, Bishop Sherman's own broadcasts came to be very highly regarded.

Depression Years in Calgary

The depression years called for increased economy, and after 1931 the Bishop's Charges ceased to be published in the Synod journals. Most of the Charge to the Synod of 1934, however, was published in the *Calgary Diocesan Gazette* of that year, and was noteworthy for its demonstration of Bishop Sherman's skill in dealing with matters of finance. Beginning with the Restoration and Maintenance Fund, in which the Diocese of Calgary was only concerned through its interest in the Clergy Superannuation Fund and the Clergy Widows' and Orphans' Fund, he went on to discuss problems in the Diocese of Calgary. Here, the Church had 20,000 members, of which 7,500 were communicants from 5,500 families. "We have average ability, average incomes, average congregations, average collections. But at the present second, in this area of 65,000 square miles, with our 20,000 members, if we had to depend on ourselves there wouldn't be more than six clergy outside the city of Calgary." There were only four self-supporting parishes outside the city, with two on the border line, and of the four, one had paid nothing on assessment for two years. This was the extent of the security that had been won in practically fifty years. The Bishop asked whether or not they could pay their way. Should they take a strong line, close churches right and left and let the clergy look for work elsewhere, or should they conclude that people were doing all they could and go on living dangerously?

The second problem was the standing of the Diocese with the M.S.C.C.; the disposition of funds was reviewed. In 1931 they had received, as a Missionary Diocese, $4,200, and had paid the General Synod Boards on apportionment their full quota of $4,185. In 1932 neither the M.S.C.C. grant, nor the Diocesan apportionment, had been paid in full, but their percentage of payment was much larger than the percentage they had received in grant. The question was whether the work on the prairies was a Canadian responsibility, rather than a purely diocesan one; whether their grant for the next triennium should be greatly increased, or their apportionment remitted altogether.

Then he came to the matter of support from England. The S.P.G. had been having an extremely hard time. Home expenditures had been reduced drastically. The Society had been obliged to promise only three-quarters of its grant, but one could count on that. It had been magnificent, but after a conference between Canon Waddy, its Secretary, and diocesan representatives, following the last General Synod, the S.P.G. had decided that in future it would give no more to any Canadian diocese than that diocese received from its own missionary society.

After dealing with changes of clergy, the customary statistics, vacancies and problems, the Bishop proceeded (as he often did) to work in "from the circumference to the centre." He saw the matter of international relationships and the support of peace as a major religious question of the day, and pleaded for increased study of the League of Nations and its work by their missionary and W.A. groups. In times of unparalleled suffering through economic catastrophy, with the resultant spectre of unemployment, people ought to be much less hidebound and satisfied concerning theories of government, industry and finance. It was the human factor that mattered.

Two years passed and the Church in the Diocese of Calgary maintained its position in spite of adversity. Services were maintained in vacant parishes by other clergy, regardless of the long distances to be travelled. The publication of the *Diocesan Gazette* had to be abandoned. The equalization of the S.P.G. grants, with those received from the M.S.C.C., was a matter of great anxiety, and the Synod that met in Calgary on February 18, 1936, urged parochial exchanges of short duration between clergy of eastern and western Canada so that the needs of the western dioceses might be better known and supported.

A suggestion by the Bishop that a joint committee of the Diocesan W.A. and the Diocesan Synod might be formed to unify diocesan financial efforts, did not find acceptance and finally was toned down to an approval of parochial church councils. A resolution sponsored by Archdeacon Swanson and Dean Ragg urged that the time was ripe for the re-establishment of the Prairie Brotherhood, which would work along the lines of the Archbishops' Western Canada Fund of past days. But in spite of the financial difficulties of the moment, a scheme was launched to inaugurate a Fiftieth Anniversary Fund to raise $50,000 by 1933, which would increase the Bishop's Endowment Fund to $70,000, and augment the Clergy, Mission and Sustentation Fund.

Jubilee celebrations began on February 15, 1938. The twenty-seventh meeting of the Synod opened the following morning and Synod agreed to petition the Canadian Broadcasting Corporation to restore the weekly Vesper Hour on Sunday afternoons.[25] An inquiry was made under the report of the Indian Missions as to whether missions in the Diocese had every produced a candidate for ordination. Archdeacon Tims replied that Bishop Pinkham's policy had been that he did not feel he should ordain a man unless the candidate had a good knowledge of the English language.[26]

The years 1938 to 1942 seem to have brought little that was dramatic to the Diocese of Calgary. The Synod met again on January 31, 1940, but its concerns were with the war and needs of the ministry due to the absence of chaplains in the armed forces, and the prospect of finding young men when the war was over.

The Synod heard with deep regret that Mrs. Pinkham had died on February first, and put on record its appreciation of her work for the betterment of social conditions in the city, and the inspiration which she had been to the younger members of the Church.

In 1942 the Synod endeavoured to revive the Diocesan Layman's Association, which nominally consisted of the church wardens and lay

[25]It never was. The service came from St. George's Church, Winnipeg, and was conducted by Rev. Henry D. Martin, who in 1939 became Bishop of Saskatchewan. The C.B.C. changed its religious broadcasting policy about this time.
[26]This seems curious when one considers the exceptionally high educational standards that have been achieved in schools on the Calgary Indian Reserves, the obvious success Bishop Pinkham had with native clergy and catechists in the Diocese of Saskatchewan, and their place in the Diocese of Moosonee.

delegates to Synod, to give it a special work of raising $1,000 a year towards the episcopal stipend, and of increasing clerical stipends to the amount of $1,500 per annum. This latter item was referred to the executive committee. The Synod also took up the matter of daily Bible readings in the public schools and suggested that the Cambridgeshire Syllabus should be made the basis of religious instruction by the clergymen in the public day schools. An attempt was made to elect women to the vestries, owing to the shortage of men during the war, but the motion was declared unconstitutional and the subject was dropped.

The Election of Bishop H. R. Ragg

Bishop Sherman was elected Metropolitan of the Province of Rupert's Land on February 11, 1943, and the Synod met on June 15 under the presidency of the Very Reverend H. R. Ragg, Dean of Calgary, as administrator. After the nominating ballots had been received, H. E. Howard made a report on behalf of a sub-committee of the executive committee of the Diocese respecting the Bishop's stipend. It showed that the endowment fund amounted to $60,965, which brought in $2,586 a year, to which was to be added $27,000 from the Hull Estate, which brought in $828 per annum. It was noted that it had been customary in recent years to make the annual stipend of the Bishop $3,600 in addition to the income from the Hull Estate. The committee thought it very undesirable that any part of the Bishop's stipend should be included in the general budget. It was determined to leave further discussion until after a Bishop had been elected, and balloting proceeded, resulting in the election of the Very Reverend H. R. Ragg. He was consecrated in the Pro-Cathedral Church of the Redeemer in Calgary on the Feast of St. Bartholomew (August 24), by the Metropolitan of Rupert's Land (Sherman). His enthronement took place the same day.

Born in a suburb of Birmingham, Bishop Ragg was educated at Hereford Cathedral School, later proceeding to St. John's College, Cambridge. He was ordained deacon on January 2, 1912, by Bishop Chavasse of Liverpool. He came to the Diocese of Kootenay in 1914, and had been in Calgary as Rector and Dean of the Pro-Cathedral since 1932. Besides proving himself a devoted parish priest, his wide range of interests had included the work of Toc H. and the problems of St. John's College, Winnipeg, during its difficult years.[27]

[27]A. R. Kelley and D. B. Rogers, *The Anglican Episcopate of Canada and Newfoundland*, II, 96-97. O. R. Rowley, "Pillars of the Church, xvi—The Dean of Calgary," *Canadian Churchman* (July 10, 1941), 420. "Bishop Ragg," *Canadian Churchman* (November 15, 1941), 353.

Bishop Ragg presided over his first Synod in June, 1945. For the first time in the history of the Diocese Archdeacon Tims was unable to be present and a message of appreciation was sent to him; a vote of thanks was recorded to Chancellor Brokovski for his long service. Mr. Brokovski was succeeded by Hugh C. Farthing, K.C. A committee reported on the appointment of a secretary-treasurer to the Diocese, a post which, since the resignation of J. G. Adam in 1937, had been filled by Miss D. K. Benbow. The proposal that the office should be filled by a clergyman was approved and Canon R. Axon was elected, shortly afterwards being appointed Archdeacon of Calgary. The Synod agreed to a proposal that a minimum stipend of $1,500 a year be paid to chaplains in the armed forces, now on temporary leave from the Diocese, when they returned to work in the Diocese. It also strongly endorsed the suggestion that an information pool be created to supply information about returning chaplains to every Bishop, diocese and vacant parish across Canada. Concern was expressed regarding the mission field, and a motion by the Reverend J. W. House of the Old Sun School, and Archdeacon Middleton of the Blood Reserve, asked that General Synod take steps to establish a missionary college, the sole purpose of which should be the training of missionaries for native races both in Canada and foreign lands. This was carried, but there is no evidence that any further action was taken.

The Government of Alberta was urged to establish a separate jail for persons serving a first jail sentence, and to use the Borstal System in dealing with juveniles.

The Synod also formulated a strong resolution with regard to current and post-war absorption of loyal Japanese Canadian citizens, which it felt should be considered in a friendly attitude, and expressed the hope that after taking safeguards, loyal citizens of Japanese descent should be entitled to the ordinary rights of work, wages and assistance, comparable to those given to other law-abiding citizens. Synod affirmed that people of proven loyalty to the Dominion should not be forcibly dispossessed of their property, pending decision of the courts, nor eventually prohibited from holding residential or business premises. Some of these people had been removed from the west coast and had been settled in the southwest part of the Diocese.

The Bishop, in his Charge of 1949, referred to the work being done among these Japanese, and the Synod of that year reaffirmed the resolution of 1947. In this Charge the Bishop also stated that he had raised the Pro-Cathedral Church of the Redeemer to the status of Cathedral Church of the Diocese, and the Synod placed on record its deep appreciation of the great and lasting work that had been carried on by the Venerable Samuel Middleton for forty years on the Blood

Reserve; although he was retiring as Principal of St. Paul's School, it was hoped that he would be able for many years to continue his work as a missionary on the Reserve.

A strong resolution declaring its uncompromising opposition to Marxian Communism was carried on motion of Mr. Chancellor Farthing, seconded by A. Beaumont of Lethbridge, and was sent on to General Synod. That body was also informed of the Synod's disapproval of the proposal to appoint a Canadian ambassador or minister to the Vatican, because such an appointment would constitute a breach of the principle of the equality of all religious communions in their relations with the state.

The Synod held its thirty-fourth meeting on June 12, 1951. Bishop Ragg's Charge dealt with a number of things outside the actual Diocese, including the changes that had taken place in the episcopacy in the Province of Rupert's Land during the previous two years. This prompted an interesting discussion on a motion, which followed a suggestion in the Bishop's Charge, that General Synod should "give study to the advisability of the election of Diocesan Bishops, with the view to making it mandatory upon Dioceses to choose their Bishops from outside their own Diocese." But in the end the motion that passed simply called upon the House of Bishops to study the question of the present method of electing Diocesan Bishops.

The Bishop, himself a distinguished amateur athlete, drew attention to the increasing amount of commercialized sport, but the committee on his Charge felt this was a matter for parental or private solution and was also linked with the major question of Sunday observance. Attention was drawn to a report to the last Synod, which read: "The Church must be careful not to surround the Lord's Day with too many rules and regulations and to make it a day of 'Shall nots'." The same committee also agreed with the Bishop that people's attitudes and actions on the liquor question should be governed by self-discipline, moderation and self-control, but it felt that the provincial liquor laws were not conducive to the cultivation of these virtues, and the Church ought to press for a rational revision of the liquor laws and commended their study to the Diocesan Council for Social Service.

A genuine step forward was the decision to co-operate fully with the Every Member Canvass Committee of General Synod. The Executive Committee, in its endeavour to reach an understanding with the M.S.C.C. and the Budget Committee of General Synod, looking towards the time when the diocese might become self-supporting, pledged the Synod to this end.

The Election of Bishop G. R. Calvert

Bishop Ragg resigned at the end of 1951 due to ill health, and the Synod of the Diocese of Calgary convened in Paget Hall on February 20, 1952, under the chairmanship of the Dean, the Very Reverend J. H. Craig, as administrator. The Very Reverend George Reginald Calvert, rector of Christ Church Cathedral, Victoria, B.C., and Dean of British Columbia, was elected as the new Bishop.

A native of Kingston, Ontario, a graduate of the University of Toronto and Wycliffe College, he was ordained deacon by Bishop Clarke of Niagara for the Archbishop of Rupert's Land, in the Church of the Ascension, Hamilton, on April 27, 1924. He came to the Diocese of Rupert's Land in the fall of 1925 as incumbent of Snowflake, then served in the Diocese of Brandon from 1928 to 1932. In 1933 he became rector of St. Matthew's Church, Winnipeg. In 1949 he moved from Rupert's Land to become rector of Christ Church Cathedral in Victoria, B.C., and Dean of British Columbia.

Bishop Calvert was consecrated on St. Mark's Day, April 25, 1952, in the Cathedral Church of the Redeemer in Calgary, by the Metropolitan of Rupert's Land (Sherman). He was enthroned the same day.[28]

[28]Kelley and Rogers, *op. cit.*, 128-129.

CHAPTER FOURTEEN

The Upper Saskatchewan Valley
Since the 1890's: The Diocese of Edmonton

⊷⊰⊱⊷⊰⊱⊷⊰⊱⊷⊰⊱⊷⊰⊱⊷⊰⊱⊷⊰⊱⊷

From 1896 very little development took place but individual congregations were growing and developing an independent personality and soul which afterwards became a matter to be reckoned with. In 1902 a missionary was stationed at Beaver Lake, and later on the Sturgeon, while a new point was opened at Vegreville and Leduc received its first regular clergyman. But a new advance was about to begin. In January, 1906, with the thermometer at 47 degrees below, I visited a district north-west of Edmonton then known as the forks of the Paddle River. In this country in every direction settlers of many nations were gathering, from Edmonton to the Pembina and still onward to the Macleod and the Athabasca Rivers the stream of settlers kept slowly moving in. Then the construction of the G.T.P. and C.N. Railways (imperishable monument to the unprincipled methods to which our politicians are devoted) brought still further developments until the situation became critical from a church standpoint, and the Archdeacon of Edmonton knew it better than any.

Bishop Henry Allen Gray:
FAREWELL ADDRESS TO SYNOD, 1931.

⊷⊰⊱⊷⊰⊱⊷⊰⊱⊷⊰⊱⊷⊰⊱⊷⊰⊱⊷⊰⊱⊷

The development of the Edmonton district, or central portion of the Province of Alberta that is now incorporated in the Diocese of Edmonton, can hardly be made into a continuous story. Edmonton was still a fairly isolated, though important Hudson's Bay Company post when Dr. Newton arrived there in 1875. Its connections with distant Winnipeg were either by prairie trail or the Saskatchewan River and Lake Winnipeg. The coming of the C.P.R. through Calgary a few years later changed things. First there was a trail from Calgary to Edmonton that became the recognized route between the two points; then in 1891 the C.P.R. got as far as the south side of the Saskatchewan River, and around its terminus grew the town later known as Strathcona, now merged into the City of Edmonton. It was by the use of this old Calgary-Edmonton trail that settlement first began to creep north from the main C.P.R. line, and the Church came with the settlers. Two years later there was sufficient settlement in the neighbourhood of Wetaskiwin for services to be held there by the Reverend C. H. Andras, and by 1899 there was a church at Leduc in charge of the Reverend J. J. Jones.

The first few years of the twentieth century saw a policy of intensified immigration sponsored by the Dominion government under the inspiration of the Honourable Clifford Sifton. The Canadian Northern Railway reached Edmonton in 1905 and that part of the country began to be occupied by homesteaders. The first services at Vegreville were held there by the Reverend G. Card in 1904, St. Mary's Church being built in 1907. In the meantime the rolling lands to the northwest of Edmonton, which had attracted settlement more than twenty years previously, once more drew attention. The work in the Pembina Valley Mission was begun in 1906 by the Reverend A. A. Cramp and taken over the following year by a young lay worker named Walter Leversedge who, after his ordination by Bishop Pinkham in 1910, continued his work in the Diocese until he retired in 1948 as its senior Archdeacon, greatly honoured and beloved by the whole Church. The Grand Trunk Pacific Railway, which took a course across the Province of Alberta to the south of the C.N.R., reached Edmonton in 1909, and from there began to make its way through the foothills to the Yellowhead Pass. By this time the problem of settlement brought by the railways had reached northern Alberta and was strongly felt by the Church, which earnestly tried to serve newcomers in this district, as it had already endeavoured to serve them under similar conditions in the Dioceses of Saskatchewan, Calgary and Qu'Appelle.

The work accomplished by the Archbishops' Western Canada Fund, in what is now the Diocese of Edmonton, was so noteworthy that it demands special attention. The scheme launched under this name in the spring of 1910, by a vigorous appeal under the joint signatures of Canterbury and York, was the result of many months of consultation between the Church in Canada and in England. It was decided to establish three separate mission centres: at Regina, under the Reverend D. Ellison; at Lethbridge and Cardston, under the Reverend W. H. Mowatt; and at Edmonton, under the Reverend W. G. Boyd, a former chaplain to the Archbishop of Canterbury, who had been a prime mover in the matter. The appeal was so successful that between Easter, 1910, and Easter, 1913, some £78,000, roughly $390,000, was raised for the purpose.

Mr. Boyd arrived in Edmonton in May, 1910, accompanied by six others and took over a large piece of land in northeast Edmonton. Out of the surrounding area was created St. Faith's parish, probably so dedicated in recollection of St. Faith's, Stepney, London, England, where Mr. Boyd had formerly ministered. The first building erected was a stable, and the hayloft constituted the sleeping quarters for the first members of the Mission. The following year the Edmonton Mission House was built, which was destined to serve the Diocese for thirty-five years as a spiritual centre, for after its original purpose was fulfilled it became the diocesan synod office and a place where conferences of the clergy were held, as well as being partly devoted to the work of the Sisters of St. John the Divine. The beautiful chapel was added to this building by Sir Henry Pellatt about 1911; the original chapel became St. Faith's Parish Church.[1] About the same time another house was built on the property to house women workers, and in it lived Miss Warden, who acted as matron and housekeeper of the Mission, and became a veritable godmother to many young men on the staff. She was assisted by Sister Mary who did much to develop the parish work.

The country work of the Mission took it along the new Grand Trunk Pacific line, destined to go through the Yellowhead Pass to the coast, and in the area farther north towards the Edson Trail into the Peace River country. Mission houses were established at Wabamun, Lac la Nonne, Westlock, Paddle River, Edson, Onoway, Entwistle, Danderand, Greencourt, Stony Plain and Telfordville. A small hospital was eventually erected at Onoway and churches were built. The names of some of the men who went into these sparsely populated districts and laboured unselfishly for their people, are still recalled with appreciation: Bailey, Dallas and Ball, Mercer and Provis, Trench and Whitaker, Creighton and Swan, Boustead and Simmons, among others. It is doubtful if the Diocese could have been formed so soon had it not been for the men of the Edmonton Mission and the cordial co-operation of their leader. As J. Burgon Bickersteth says in his book *Land of Open Doors*: "In time to come, the Church in the West will be able to look back and see that she was helped by the Archbishops' Mission to traverse a period in her history which posterity will judge to have been unprecedented in the life of this or any nation. For the vision of these leaders, for the indefatigable leadership of Canon Boyd, and the self-sacrificing work of these great men, we should thank God, and take courage to go forward."

The demands upon the Church in and around Edmonton itself grew in proportion at the same time, and it was during this period that a number of new parishes were formed. The Edmonton Mission increased its staff to nine clergymen and eight laymen in 1910, one of these being the Reverend J. J. Robinson, then recently resigned

---

[1] A new St. Faith's Church was built upon the same site and opened in December, 1956.

as Dean of Belfast, Ireland. Also in 1910, the churches of St. Luke's, St. Faith's, St. Andrew's, St. Michael and All Angels were dedicated, as well as the Church of the Good Shepherd in Edmonton, and St. Catherine's in Edson. All Saints' Home for Girls was built about this time through the generosity of Mrs. Humphrey Lloyd, who for some years had been an honoured worker in the city. It is recorded that in 1913 there were thirty clergy working in the Archdeaconry of Edmonton, eight of whom were entirely supported by their congregations.

The Formation of the Diocese of Edmonton

By 1913 Bishop Pinkham felt that the formation of the Archdeaconry of Edmonton into a diocese had become a pressing necessity and at the Synod at Calgary in July of that year he proposed to ask the Provincial Synod to make that part of the Diocese of Calgary lying north of the line dividing townships forty-two and forty-three into a new diocese to be called Edmonton, to be administered by the Bishop of Calgary until such time as a bishop could be elected and consecrated. In doing this he added: "The only difficulty in the way of the appointment of a new Bishop is that the Metropolitan and the Provincial Bishops will not consecrate anyone, even if he were chosen, until his stipend is forthcoming. I am in hopes that this difficulty will be soon overcome.... I am willing ... to organize it (the diocese) in the autumn, and for such time as may be necessary to have again charge of two dioceses, as I had from 1888 to October 1903, because I feel that every moment during which there is the postponement of new organization means precious time lost." The Bishop was also hoping at that time to form the southern part of the Diocese of Calgary into a separate diocese with Lethbridge as the See City.

The Synod endorsed the Bishop's proposals, and the Provincial Synod adopted them unanimously. The Bishop's stipend, however, seems to have been a rather complicated matter, and temporarily to have been provided by grants from the S.P.G., the Diocese of Calgary and the M.S.C.C.

The First Synod of the Diocese of Edmonton

The first meeting of the Synod of the new Diocese of Edmonton was held on November 12, 1913, with thirty-one clergy and thirty-five laymen present. The Synod opened with Holy Communion in All Saints' Church, at which an address was delivered by the Very Reverend E. C. Paget of Calgary, who also preached at the service in the evening. The Dean bid his brethren of the new Diocese to go forth in their new life and their new strength to do their old work, that of bringing the life of the Church of Christ home to every soul entrusted to their care, the noblest work in the world.

Bishop Pinkham's Charge outlined the history of the formation of the diocese, its financial problems, its opportunities and the necessity of training candidates for Holy Orders. The Reverend W. E. Edmonds seems to be the only clergyman present at that Synod who is still left in the Diocese (1960).

The work of this first Synod was, necessarily, devoted largely to organization; the Rules and Canons finally adopted were very much based on those of the Diocese of Calgary. J. H. Gamble of Edmonton was appointed Secretary-Treasurer. The Synod, from the first, exhibited a keen interest in religious education, and passed a resolution urging all rural lay members to use their influence to secure from school trustees in their districts the right of entry of local religious ministers. It also authorized its Committee on Sunday Schools to approach other religious bodies to seek their co-operation in a determined effort to have the fundamental principles of Christianity taught in the public schools.

The Election of the First Bishop of Edmonton

"The highest public responsibility committed to the ordinary citizen is to choose his representative in the legislature. The possession of a vote is a most solemn trust—an education in itself, so to speak— so suggestive is it, to observation, reflection and the thoughtful exercise of a personal responsibility, for honest minds. And surely a specially great and precious responsibility rests upon you, the clergy and canonically-elected lay delegates from organized parishes in this new Diocese, to choose the man who is to be your Father-in-God, the Bishop and Pastor of Christ's Flock committed to him, in this portion of our Church." With these words, the Right Reverend William Cyprian Pinkham, Bishop of Calgary and Edmonton, opened his brief Charge to the second Synod of the Diocese of Edmonton on January 29, 1914, when it met to select a Bishop of the new and independent Diocese. The choice, which was made unanimous after the fifth ballot, on the motion of the Reverend G. H. Webb, seconded by the Reverend W. G. Boyd, fell upon the Venerable Henry Allen Gray, Archdeacon of Edmonton, who was consecrated as Bishop on March 25, 1914, by the Metropolitan (Matheson).[2]

Bishop Gray held his first Synod on February first, 1916, (the third of the Diocese). Two years of war had darkened the skies and put a stop to any substantial development in the general machinery of the Diocese. No new districts had been occupied, but none had been

[2]O. R. Rowley, *The Anglican Episcopate of Canada and Newfoundland,* 180-181.

vacated. An increasing shortage of men was laying a heavier burden on the staff of the clergy. The Bishop said that on the previous Trinity Sunday it had been his privilege to hold his first Ordination, admitting G. Boustead to the diaconate. He added, "Here let me say that there is a grave need of a change in the attitude of the laity towards the Ministry as a vocation for their sons. Our people have not been selfish or backward in giving their sons to the service of their country, or asked the question, 'What is there in it?' The duty, as well as the privilege, has been sufficient attraction, the honour of serving or even dying for one's country, enough reward. Is the service of God of lesser attraction?" The Bishop also commented on the absence of any organized men's work in the parishes, and the fact that the Church was too often made to take a second place to the lodge or the club.

This Synod accomplished much useful work. It instituted the financial arrangements that still exist between the Synod and country missions, reviewed the Constitution, Canons and Rules of Order of the Diocese, spent much time considering religious instruction in the provincial schools, rejoiced in the progress made in regulating the liquor traffic, besides giving attention to the organization of Sunday School work.

The Edmonton Mission: Its Closing Years

The work of the Edmonton Mission was carried on with some difficulty after 1914 owing to the war. The number of workers was reduced by enlistments, and in 1918 the Reverend R. H. Robinson (later Dean of Calgary), who had been in charge of the work since 1916, reported that nine clergy were serving as chaplains, eleven laymen were serving as combatants, and seven had been killed. Only five clergy and one layman remained on the staff, but the work was being maintained and new work had been started along the Alberta Coal Branch at Mile 22 and at Mountain Park by the Reverend H. B. Stavely. At St. Faith's House, Miss Warden was the only remaining member of the original mission staff; St. Barnabas' Nursing Home at Onoway, which had been built by the Mission in August, 1913, at a cost of $10,000, had been incorporated on November first, 1918, and was then known as the Onoway Hospital. It was being managed by a board of trustees, of whom three were appointed by the Mission. By 1920 the Mission staff had become reduced to four, who were keeping in touch with no less than twenty-seven places. The Onoway Hospital had been handed over to the Onoway District and was being operated as a municipal hospital. Bishop Gray, in his Charge, said that in 1920 the A.W.C.F. would complete its period of work in the Diocese and would then hand over to it the property it held, and a sum of money by way of endowment. During the ten years the Mission had been working it had established four parishes in the city, built twenty-two churches in the country, and provided fourteen mission houses. The Mission had come to the aid of the Diocese at a time of extreme necessity, and the value of its work could be estimated by the love and affection with which the members were regarded in those districts where they had laboured long after they had left them. He expected that during the year the mission staff and plant would become an integral part of the Diocese.

To the Synod of February, 1922, Bishop Gray reported in his Charge that the members of the mission staff, with the exception of the Reverend W. Mather, had left, and that he himself had assumed responsibility as head of the Mission, with the Reverend R. M. Swan in charge of the Mission House. This arrangement had continued until July first, 1921, when the Central Board of Finance in England failed to remit the balance of income due; the Bishop had been compelled to close the House altogether. Subsequently, after correspondence with the Archbishop of Canterbury, the balance had been remitted, but in the meantime Mr. Swan had gone to England and had conferred with the Reverend Malcolm Buchannan, Vice-Principal of the Missionary College at Burgh in Lincolnshire, and later with Bishop King of the S.P.G., which meeting had resulted in Buchannan's offer to re-establish the work of the Mission on lines similar to those before, but under different conditions. The property and endowments of the Mission were now invested in the Synod, and the new organization would be completely under the control of the Bishop. Under this new organization the work of the Church was reopened at Lac la Nonne in July, 1922, at Westlock in September, at Greencourt in the summer of 1923. But the experiment did not work out, largely owing to the inability of men who joined the mission staff to stay with it. The Mission House was again about to be closed, apparently in 1925, when Mr. Buchannan resigned. At this juncture Archdeacon Burgett came forward with a very generous offer to take over the Mission House at his own expense, taxes, insurance and usual repairs excepted, and the House was from that time maintained by the Archdeacon, and a welcome was extended to the clergy and others as his guests.

St. Aidan's College

In 1915 the civil Province of Alberta was barely ten years old, but Edmonton had become both the centre of government and the seat of the University of Alberta. The Anglican Church, with a noteworthy record in the educational field, naturally looked to possibilities of establishing a college in connection with the latter. In his Charge to the Synod of 1916, Bishop Gray said: "We have secured an assurance from the University authorities that a site will be available for us as soon as we are ready to apply for it. For this purpose a sum of money has been collected by Mr. J. B. G. Bickersteth from friends in England and placed in the hands of the Reverend Canon Boyd and myself as trustees at the wish of the donors."

In 1918 the Bishop again referred to the matter in his Charge, and from what he said appeared to have in mind the founding of a theological college in connection with the university, for he spoke of the possibility of training men for the ministry even before the college was built, but by 1920 this view was beginning to fade. When he emphasized in his Charge to the Synod of that year that there was a responsibility resting upon the Anglican Church to contribute whatever it could to the moulding influences of the university, he asked all the members of Synod to note, and many others outside the Diocese who might read these words, "It is not my desire to multiply Theological Colleges. Indeed we have sufficient for our needs in the Dominion to-day, but the University being here we must see to it that our sons and daughters are given the opportunity for spiritual training as well as mental. Our present intention is to establish a residential building on the University Campus, which will serve as a residence for our Church members, in which the religious side of life will be preserved."

Nothing more about this matter appears in the Synod report until 1926, when Bishop Gray revived the subject in his Charge, but the Committee on the Charge commented on his remarks rather coldly, and could only suggest that an appeal be made to the Carnegie Foundation for assistance in establishing the college, if it was to become a reality.

The last full report on behalf of the trustees appears in the Journal of the Synod of 1928, which indicated that there was then $10,485 capital on hand. Bishop and Synod were possibly more concerned at the time with the extension of the Diocese to the eastern boundary of Alberta, and the matter of the college seems to have lapsed until 1938, when, although Bishop Burgett made no reference to it, two reports were presented: one under the signature of the secretary of the trustees, indicating that the capital on hand was approximately $14,500, and the other under the signature of Canon G. G. Reynolds, which stated that St. Aidan's Club had come into being in May, 1935, through the statesmanlike foresight of Bishop Burgett and the generosity of Mr. Attenborough (the legal representative of the Anonymous Donor). This club was housed in a small bungalow on Ninetieth Avenue, opposite the Arts building of the university, and was in charge of two hostesses, the Misses M. E. I. and M. E. Smith. The register showed that more than two hundred students were making use of the club, which was about the proportion of Anglicans in the university. How long this was carried on is not apparent; possibly the outbreak of war in 1939 altered the circumstances. After that date the chief charge on the Attenborough Fund seems to have been grants towards the moving expenses of clergy coming into the Diocese. No more is heard of St. Aidan's Hostel until the 1951 Synod when Bishop Barfoot traced some of the previous history of the St. Aidan's College Fund, and said that the trustees had recently decided to provide accommodation for The Canterbury Club of the university, an organization of Anglican students aiming at the maintenance of sound churchmanship during their college days. A large house had been bought close to the university, and this would become the home of the club.

The General Missionary

The difficulty of maintaining the Edmonton Mission, and the natural extension of rural work due to increased settlement after World War I, brought with it the difficulty of providing ministrations and supervision in outlying districts. Gradually it became apparent that the appointment of a travelling or general missionary in the Diocese was a pressing necessity, although some such work was being carried out to a certain extent by Archdeacon Howcroft. But living in Camrose, he was not centrally situated. It was the hope of the executive committee of the Diocese that some grant towards the expenses of a general missionary might be secured from the M.S.C.C., but little progress was made in this direction. The executive did, however, decide to advertise in the *Canadian Churchman* for a diocesan missionary. By 1924 the whole situation had changed, and in his Charge to the Synod in June, Bishop Gray said: "Early this year I received a communication from Rev. Archdeacon Burgett of Qu'Appelle which resulted in his offering to come to this Diocese, as General Missionary without stipend other than travelling expenses, and to undertake the work we had in mind, and which he had been doing successfully for over ten years in Qu'Appelle. I very cordially accepted this very generous offer, and Archdeacon Burgett is now at work as our General Missionary." In the 1924 Journal of the Synod there is an extensive report from the Archdeacon in which he states that he had arrived in Edmonton on March first, and, after consultation with the Bishop, had left for Toronto on March 5, where he had interviewed the M.S.C.C.; this had secured for the Diocese an assurance that a special grant to the diocese of $2,000 would be paid during 1924, and would be considered for 1925. He sailed from New York on March 15 and arrived in England on the twenty-fifth. He had persuaded the C. and C.C.S. to increase its grant for 1924 by £50; the S.P.C.K. had offered to send the interest on £1,000 (the amount of their potential grant to the Bishopric Endowment Fund) if the S.P.G. would do the same. His appeal to the S.P.G. for special consideration in 1925, and an extra grant for five years for extension work, had been favourably recommended to the Missionary Council of the Society by the recommendations committee, and he had made an appeal to the Council of the Colonial Bishoprics Fund. As the Archbishop of Canterbury was away, he had arranged for Archbishop Matheson to write to him direct concerning the Edmonton Bishopric Fund. On his way back he had again seen Canon Gould of the M.S.C.C., Burgon Bickersteth of Hart House in Toronto, and Archbishop Matheson in Winnipeg. As the Archdeacon arrived back in Edmonton on May 17, he appeared to have had a profitable time.

The activity of the new Archdeacon of North Edmonton (Mr. Burgett was made Archdeacon when he took up the post of general missionary) was consistent and remarkable in the mileage and work he covered in the extension of the Church in the Diocese, and the improvement of its finances. In his report to the Synod of 1929, he remarked that at the time of his original appointment, a layman had described him as "A Floating Archdeacon," but he felt that as a result of his constant travelling much progress was made possible in the northern half of the Diocese, where conditions were less favourable than in the south. In 1924 only one new church was reported built, and that encumbered with debt. By 1928 thirteen churches had been built, twelve outside the city, free from debt, with one exception. Whereas in 1924 only one student was preparing for Holy Orders, the Diocese now had fourteen. In 1931 the Archdeacon reported eight more churches built; ministrations had been provided and every parish in the Diocese had been visited, many of them frequently. One of the most interesting parts of this report is quoted here: "Since last Synod the General Missionary was appointed as Collector for the Bishopric Endowment Fund, and with the permission and approval of the Primate and the Bishops visits were made to eastern Dioceses to collect money for the fund. Altogether the General Missionary succeeded in obtaining personally the total sum of $29,600 towards the Bishopric Endowment Fund, of which $27,000 was collected by house to house personal canvass in eastern Canada." Before proceeding with some account of this fund, we must turn to the matter of the enlargement of the Diocese.

Extension of the Diocese Eastward

The Provincial Synod of 1887, which agreed to the division of the Diocese of Saskatchewan and the setting up of the Diocese of Calgary, simply described the area of the latter as the civil territory of Alberta, but when the civil province of Alberta was brought into being in 1905, its eastern boundary was defined as the Fourth Principal Meridian, and this lay considerably east of the one designated in 1887. Moreover, at that time, much of the Saskatchewan valley west of Prince Albert was still undeveloped prairie. But with the establishing of the Barr Colony, under the direction of Archdeacon Lloyd of Saskatchewan, a large part of this territory, which a year or two later was to be in the Civil Province of Alberta, became regarded as part of the Diocese of Saskatchewan, and continued to be so regarded for more than twenty years. The Diocese of Edmonton was originally defined by the Provincial Synod of 1913 as: "That portion of the present Diocese of Calgary north of the line dividing Townships 42 and 43," the boundaries of the Diocese of Calgary still being assumed to be those of 1887.[3] Public opinion in the Diocese of Edmonton gradually began to ask why the eastern boundary of the Diocese was not coterminous with that of the civil province, and the Diocese presented a memorial petitioning that this be made the case to the Provincial Synod of Rupert's Land in October, 1920, but no action was then taken, except to refer it to the Boundaries Committee.[4] When the Provincial Synod met in Saskatoon in September, 1923, the Boundaries Committee reported this to be only one of several possible changes in the boundaries of Dioceses, and again no action was taken.[5] In 1926 the Provincial Synod agreed to the change and it was decided that "that part of the Province of Alberta bounded on the east by the fourth Principal Meridian; on the south by the line between Townships 34 and 35; on the west by that between Ranges 10 and 11 west of the Fourth Meridian; and the one north by the line between Townships 63 and 64 should be added to the Diocese of Edmonton."[6]

The new area added to the Diocese seems to have been about 26,000 square miles, and brought in the towns of Vermilion, Wainwright, Hardisty, Clandonald, Provost, Kitscoty, Marwayne and Edgerton, but, as Bishop Gray said to his Synod of 1928 when he announced

[3] *Journal of the Provincial Synod of Rupert's Land, 1913*, p. 33.
[4] *Ibid.*, 1920, p. 28.
[5] *Ibid.*, 1923, p. 32.
[6] *Ibid.*, 1926, pp. 45-46. Concurrence of the House of Delegates with Message "Y" from the House of Bishops, which incorporated the Report of the Boundaries Committee, clause one of which recommended the transference of certain townships that were west of the Saskatchewan-Alberta boundary to the Diocese of Edmonton. *Ibid.*, Act 2 of this Synod.

the completion of the transfer of the territory, while it contained fifty new parishes, little financial assistance had yet been forthcoming. He pleaded for the means to train clergy. Some assistance actually was received from the M.S.C.C., the Anonymous Donor gave generous help, and the vigour of Archdeacon Burgett stimulated a new sense of responsibility for increased giving in the local parishes.

The Bishopric Endowment Fund

When the Diocese of Edmonton was formed in 1913 steps had to be taken to provide an income for the Bishop. The Provincial Synod required that until $50,000 had been raised and invested, an assured income of $3,000 a year had to be guaranteed before an election took place. Part of the endowment was expected to come from the English societies and the Colonial Bishoprics Endowment Fund, part from the Diocese itself or outside subscription. In the meantime the S.P.G. promised a grant over a period of three years from its American Colonial Bishoprics Fund, and the Diocese of Calgary agreed to provide half of the residue if the Diocese of Edmonton would provide the other half. The Bishopric Endowment Fund of the Diocese of Calgary was administered under a trust deed that made no provision for any partition of the diocese, and hence Calgary was not in a position to surrender any part of its capital fund to the Diocese of Edmonton, but it was willing to share any block grants that were being made by the S.P.G. and the C. and C.C.S. The M.S.C.C. also agreed to provide $5,000 for work in the new Diocese. In 1918 the Bishop told the Synod that his stipend had been met in full hitherto owing to the ready assistance of the S.P.G. and the M.S.C.C., and seemed assured for the current year. He felt it unreasonable that he should be asked to go to England to raise funds until he was able to say what the Canadian Church was prepared to do. In 1922 a special report was submitted to the Synod on the subject.[7]

The Diocese of Calgary seemed to look upon its annual payment towards the stipend of the Bishop of Edmonton as a burden, and the committee had received, on March 3, 1921, a letter from Calgary asking for a joint meeting with representatives of Edmonton, with a view to terminating the agreement at an early date. The meeting took place but reached no definite decision;[8] however, on May 26 the Edmonton Committee wrote to the Calgary Committee and pointed out that the matter of establishing the endowment of the Bishopric of Edmonton might be the responsibility of the whole

[7]*Proceedings of the Synod of the Diocese of Edmonton, 1918*, p. 29. *Ibid.*, *1920*, p. 25. *Ibid., 1922*, pp. 30-31.

[8]*Proceedings of the Synod of the Diocese of Calgary, 1922*, pp. 64-65.

Church, but Calgary and Edmonton had a special share in it, and it had always been considered that $20,000 should be raised locally. The Edmonton Committee, therefore, suggested that the Diocese of Calgary should undertake to raise $10,000 of the capital required, and when that was paid the annual contribution should cease. The same committee proposed to the Edmonton Synod that steps should be taken to raise $10,000 in the Diocese of Edmonton in order to strengthen the position of the Diocese in an appeal to eastern Canada. At that time there was little more than $10,000 in the fund. By the end of 1925 this had grown to more than $17,000, and at the end of 1927 close to $24,500. In 1931, when Bishop Gray presided over his last Synod, he was able to announce that the endowment of the Bishopric had been completed and stood at $90,000. Of this approximately $35,600 had been raised in the Diocese itself, $28,000 had come from England (of which $11,250 was a gift from the Anonymous Donor), with $26,350 raised by Archdeacon Burgett in eastern Canada. The Bishop said they owed this success first of all to the organizing ability and persevering work of G. R. F. Kirkpatrick, and to the Archdeacon.[9]

Bishop Henry Allen Gray

Bishop William Cyprian Pinkham presided over the first Synod of the Diocese of Edmonton, but it is not very clear as to whether he was the first Bishop, though he claimed in his Charge to be in a similar position to that he held with respect to the Diocese of Calgary in 1887; that Diocese was formed five days after he had been consecrated Bishop of Saskatchewan. For thirty-five years, however, the official Year Book of the Anglican Church in Canada has named the Right Reverend Henry Allen Gray as first Bishop of Edmonton, and the circumstances of his election have already been related. As a young man he lived in southern Alberta, and as a lay delegate attended the two first Synods of the Diocese of Calgary; he was acting as a lay reader on the Sarcee Reserve. About 1891 he went to St. John's College, Winnipeg, and graduated from the University of Manitoba in 1895; in the same year he was ordained deacon by Bishop Pinkham, and appointed curate of the church in south Edmonton. When priested in 1896 he became incumbent, but only remained on the south side of the river another year as he then took charge of All Saints' Church, the Mother Church of Edmonton (later to become the Cathedral of the Diocese). He remained there until his election as Bishop, but was made Archdeacon of Edmonton in 1907.

The years of his episcopate were ones of great difficulty, and the preceding pages have already dealt in some detail with this work. Bishop Gray's Charges to his Synods over the years are conspicuous for his emphasis upon the spiritual life of the diocese, but he had a wide outlook: "Missionary work must be the first duty of every diocese in this Dominion," he told the Synod of 1918. The social work of the Church was a matter of great importance and the Bishop continued, "If we have no contribution to make to the great questions of the day; no part to take in the social work calling for our attention, we have grave cause for anxiety as to the future . . . bend your efforts to the study and consideration of some of these for the betterment of our social conditions upon the best and surest principles of human relations and obligations as taught us by Jesus Christ." In this work he himself took a very practical interest in the city of Edmonton (he was for some years Judge of the Juvenile Court).

After he had formally concurred in the Acts of the Synod of 1931, Bishop Gray took the unusual step of giving an address in which he outlined the history of the work of the Church, from Canon Newton's arrival in Edmonton in 1875 to their own time. Speaking of the period of the Great War, he said:

The ten years of war and its aftermath were ten years of strenuous and anxious endeavour, not hoping for progress but thankful as year by year went on to find ouselves still existing.

To add to our difficulties All Saints' Pro-Cathedral was burnt on December 21st, 1919, and with it went much that represented the work and associations over twenty-two years. Then came hard times, low prices, drought and in its track a poverty that has been disastrous, not only to the farmer, but crippling the work of our Church.[10]

The dark days of our history are nearly over and I hope by this year's end the diocese will have materially increased its staff of clergy and re-occupied most of our mission districts. To be prepared for a fresh advance into hitherto unoccupied territory is our next task.

In taking leave of you, for this is the last time I shall preside over the Synod, I want to say that words fail to express my appreciation of the affectionate loyalty with which you have co-operated with me in this diocese—some of you since the beginning. . . . I can only say as I dismiss you . . . I thank you from the bottom of my heart.

The Election of Bishop Arthur Edward Burgett

The Synod of the Diocese of Edmonton met again on October 14, 1931, under the presidency of the administrator, the Venerable George Howcroft; after the usual formalities nominations were received by ballot for the new Bishop, and eight names were submitted. On the first ballot by Orders, the Venerable Arthur Edward Burgett was elected.

[10]*The Cathedral Church of All Saints, Edmonton, 1875-1935*, pp. 40-42. *Diocesan Annual (Silver Jubilee), 1914-1939. Proceedings of the Synod of the Diocese of Edmonton, 1931*, pp. 38-40.

Born in Calcutta, India, in 1869, Bishop Burgett was educated at Radley School and Trinity Hall, Cambridge, but after completing his course he obtained a commission in the army. In 1896 he resigned his commission, offered himself as a candidate for the ministry, and went to Cuddesdon Theological College for a year; he was ordained deacon in 1897 by Bishop Creighton of London in St. Paul's Cathedral. He came to Canada in 1906 as Domestic Chaplain to the Bishop of Quebec, and began his missionary work in frontier outposts, travelling many miles along the inhospitable coasts of Quebec and Labrador.

In 1913 Mr. Burgett came west and undertook the work of general missionary in the Diocese of Qu'Appelle under Bishop Harding, and in 1917 he was appointed one of the Archdeacons of the Diocese. The author of the brief biography of him in the *Edmonton Diocesan Annual* for 1941 said: "The needs of a prairie diocese afforded ample scope for his restless energy, and for ten years he worked unremittingly, with great generosity building up the Church in every part of the territory under his supervision"; the same words might be used with justice about his years as Archdeacon of North Edmonton. His election ensured that the second Bishop of Edmonton would be a man indefatigable in his work, far-sighted in his judgments, most generous and kindly in disposition.

Bishop Burgett was consecrated in All Saints' Pro-Cathedral, Edmonton, on January 13, 1932, by the Metropolitan of Rupert's Land (Stringer).[11] The years of his episcopate were those of the great depression in western Canada, but he continued the same vigorous policy that he had maintained as Archdeacon. His interest in the Sunday School by Post led to the enlargement of that work; at one time there were more than 4,000 children enrolled. The summer camp at Kapasawin, with its fine set of buildings, was made possible when he arranged for the purchase of the site, and through his personal efforts a See House was bought and maintained. Always missionary minded and eager to extend the boundaries of the Church, no call was ignored by the Bishop; a favourite phrase was, "I will see what can be done about it." He only held two Synods (1935 and 1938). His Charges to both were brief, practical, and very frank in places, as when he spoke in 1935 in opposition to raising money for the Church by dances, raffles and draws. In 1938 he reported that no parish or mission had been closed since the last Synod. Clergy in the country districts had ministered to their flocks faithfully and without complaint, even if reduced stipends had made it difficult to do so, and not

[11] A. R. Kelley and D. B. Rogers, *The Anglican Episcopate of Canada and Newfoundland*, II, 40-41. *Diocesan Annual, 1941* (Edmonton), 5-7.

without considerable sacrifice on their part. But all financial obligations of the Diocese had been met; there were no debts, no overdraft at the bank. He wished to acknowledge the self-sacrificing efforts of clergy and laity that had enabled this to be done.

It was with deep regret that the Diocese of Edmonton learned of his resignation on December 15, 1940, following a lengthy illness. His unwavering energy, sense of duty and courage in difficult situations, and his assumption of heavy responsibilities in the service of the Church he loved were characteristic of his ministry. Bishop Burgett retired to the west coast, where it was hoped his health would improve, but he died on December 13, 1942.[12]

The Election of Bishop Walter Foster Barfoot

The Synod of the Diocese of Edmonton met on January 28, 1941, under the direction of the Administrator, the Venerable S. F. Tackaberry, to elect a new Bishop. On the fourth ballot the Very Reverend C. E. Riley, Dean of St. James Cathedral, Toronto, was elected, but the following day word was received from the Dean that he could not see his way to accept. A proposal that the Synod should be adjourned to February 25 was defeated and new nominations were called for. On the third ballot the Reverend Walter Foster Barfoot, Warden of St. John's College, Winnipeg, was declared elected and later in the day his acceptance was received. At this Synod it was learned that the Chancellor of the Diocese, William Dixon Craig, had died only a few hours before it had opened. General regret was felt that the Church had lost one who had been generous and ardent in its service.

Bishop Barfoot was consecrated in All Saints' Pro-Cathedral, Edmonton, on April 25, 1941, by the Metropolitan of Rupert's Land (Harding).[13] A native of Collingwood, Ontario, he graduated from the University of Toronto in Arts (1922) and took his theology at Wycliffe College, his studies having been interrupted by his service overseas during the First World War. He was ordained by Bishop Sweeney of Toronto in 1922. In 1926 he became Professor of Apologetics and New Testament History in Emmanuel College, Saskatoon. In September, 1934, he joined the staff of St. John's College, Winnipeg, as Professor of Ecclesiastical History, and in May, 1935, was appointed Warden of the College by Archbishop Harding.

[12]Bishop Burgett is buried in Jasper Park Cemetery, this being his own desire. He had a great affection for Jasper and its beautiful Church of St. Mary and St. George, built there in 1928 by the Anonymous Donor as a memorial to her son, who had looked forward to joining the Archbishops' Western Canada Fund Mission in the Diocese of Edmonton, but was prevented from doing so by the outbreak of World War I, in which he was killed. The original log church at Jasper, now demolished, was built in 1914, by the A.W.C.F. missionaries.

[13]Kelley and Rogers, op. cit., 88-89.

Bishop Barfoot came to the Diocese of Edmonton with a wide experience in the educational and administrative fields of the Church. He was an excellent scholar, very interested in modern social philosophies. Always a hard worker, he never spared himself.

By the middle of 1941 the Diocese of Edmonton was faced with a number of problems from the depression days, and the impact of the early war years. In ten years the staff of the Diocese had decreased from forty-eight to twenty-five, partly because a number of its clergy had become chaplains to the armed forces, partly due to inadequate stipends that made it impossible for clergy to meet their expenses, partly for a reason the Bishop expressed in his Charge to his first Synod in 1942, in the words: "It is one of the major sins of the Church that country work is often regarded as small potatoes. God forgive us for our disloyalty to Him and to the work of the Church if we entertain the suspicion that the Church's work is only worthwhile when it can be carried on under the inspiration of large numbers and to the accompaniment of a pipe organ and a vested choir. . . . But the Achilles heel of our local diocesan work is the rural rectory. There are quite a few parishes in the diocese to which it is impossible for me to appoint a married priest without subjecting him and his family to grave discomfort, and in some places there is no provision whatever for a married priest."

Two years later the Bishop was able to announce that through the assistance of H. R. Milner, K.C., a fund of nearly $10,000 had been raised to put the rural rectories in order upon a "revolving" loan basis; the minimum stipend had been raised to a guaranteed $1,200, and clergy were receiving assistance towards transportation. Two other matters came before this Synod of 1944 that had far-reaching effects upon the work in the Diocese and considerable influence outside it. The first of these was in the matter of propaganda, a word which the Bishop said had acquired a sinister connotation, but which the Church should restore to its rightful use and service in the propagation of the faith. The monthly *Church Messenger* became *The Edmonton Churchman,* which, with a circulation of five thousand copies a month, quickly became a powerful influence in the affairs of the Diocese under the editorship of Canon W. M. Nainby. The second was the establishment in Edmonton of a home for elderly women, to be administered by the Sisters of St. John under the financial responsibility of an independent group of women. This eventually resulted in the old Edmonton Mission House being remodelled for this purpose in 1946, and the Synod Office being removed to a house immediately south of the Pro-Cathedral where its quarters, though rather limited in space, were much more accessible and convenient for meetings.

The founding of Elizabeth House, as this home for elderly women was called, owed much to the inspiration and enthusiasm of Mrs. Barfoot. She had come as a bride to the See House in 1942, and by her charm and friendly personality had made it a centre of hospitality. She had had a brilliant career in business, and other organizations in Edmonton outside the Church profited by her help. Although she had not been well for several years, the whole Church was shocked when on October 22, 1952, it was learned that she had died after a very brief illness. The expressions of sympathy and sorrow reflected the sincere regret of the Church across Canada.

The close of the war in 1945 brought to the Diocese of Edmonton an extension of some problems, but solutions to others. A number of vacant parishes were filled, a number of young men returning from war service offered themselves for the ministry and began their training, and the generally increased prosperity of the country began to solve some of the financial problems. In Edmonton new churches were built in the parishes of St. John's and St. Paul's, and in the country at Camrose and Fort Saskatchewan. The overpayment by the Diocese of its share of the Anglican Advance Appeal cleared the way for a new effort to complete the Cathedral, and an appeal was made to the Diocese for funds. An agreement was made on March 11, 1945, between the Bishop and the Parish of All Saints', Edmonton, whereby the latter was to be the Cathedral Church of the Diocese and function as such, with certain rights appropriated to the Dean and Chapter and the congregation. The appeal was partially successful, but later further action had to be postponed because more immediate problems were pressing.

An extension of building in the suburbs and the discovery of oil at Leduc and Redwater produced situations of grave concern which, only briefly touched on at the Synod of 1947, became matters of serious consideration at the Synod of 1949, when at an early point in his Charge, the Bishop said:

I would remind you that we are called upon to live and work in a Diocese which is changing so fast, that the manners and methods of yesterday will not be adequate to the conditions of tomorrow . . . at the moment I am thinking of two particular types of problems. First, how to meet the spiritual needs of this City of Edmonton. The answer to that question is far from easy. For instance we know that we must build a Cathedral Church . . . whether or not we should project our thoughts and plans forward to the Edmonton of the future, or permit them to be controlled by the insistent demands of the immediate present or near future, is one which requires the most careful thought. There is also the question of providing, at the right time and the right place, for the rapidly increasing population. . . . There is, on the other hand, our problem of ministering to the people in the smaller towns and villages and to the scattered rural families. Nothing gives me greater concern. There is no easy solution . . . we face a tragic shortage of clergy . . . whole large areas which are without the regular ministrations of the Church. The clergy who are in the field tend to be overwhelmed by the size of the Parishes committed to their charge.

The establishment of All Saints' Church as the Cathedral in the Diocese of Edmonton was followed by the appointment of Canon Alick McDonald Trendall as first Dean of the Diocese. Dean Trendall had begun his work in 1928 as incumbent of Wainwright, and later was rector of Wetaskiwin, which he resigned in 1936 to go to the parish of St. Mary the Virgin, South Vancouver. He had returned to Edmonton as rector of the Pro-Cathedral in January, 1940, and there his work was particularly successful with young people and in the field of marriage counselling; in fact, he was keenly interested in any work that concerned the welfare of the younger generation, and following the tradition set by Bishop Gray and Canon C. F. A. Clough, from 1942 to 1946, he was Judge of the Juvenile Court. Dean Trendall resigned in 1950 to return to Vancouver to the parish of St. John's, Shaughnessy Heights.

Early in 1950 a special convocation of St. John's College, Winnipeg, was held in All Saints' Cathedral to confer an Honorary Fellowship upon Vernon Barford, who had just completed fifty years' service as organist and choirmaster there and was the dean of musicians in the city.

On November 20, 1950, to the great regret of the Anglican Church in Canada, Archbishop George Frederick Kingston, Primate of All Canada, died after a very brief illness. He had only held this office since 1947 when he was elected to succeed the equally beloved Derwyn Trevor Owen, but even in this short space of time he had made a great impression on the life of the Church.

When the Executive of General Synod met in Victoria, B.C., in 1951, its first business was to select a new Primate, and on September seventh Bishop Barfoot of Edmonton was elected to this most important office, which thus returned, after twenty years, to a western bishop, and for the first time the Primatial See was west of Winnipeg. The new Primate was duly enthroned the same evening in Christ Church Cathedral, and the appointment was received with wide approval. As the *Canadian Churchman* pointed out in its issue of September 20, "His experience in parish work and with students has provided an insight to many of the problems of the Church, and his contacts with the east and with the west qualify him for the high office to which he has been called."

The new work, of course, entailed much absence from the Diocese of Edmonton on his part, beginning with an extensive tour of Korea and a visitation of the Canadian armed forces there, and also of India to gain a closer knowledge of the work in the Diocese of Amritsar, for which the Anglican Church in Canada had for so long, and so largely, been responsible. These added duties and responsibilities, however, made no appreciable difference to the work in the Diocese, which had celebrated in September of 1950 the seventy-fifth anniversary of the coming of Canon Newton to Edmonton with a great service of witness.

At Trinity, 1951, seven young clergy were ordained, which helped to fill vacant country parishes. Some of these were men returning from the forces, others had had their homes in the Diocese and had grown up with it. An appeal by the Bishop for $5,000 a year for three years for the purpose of training candidates for Holy Orders had received a prompt and warm response, and will always stand as a testimony to the great usefulness of the *Edmonton Churchman,* through which it was made.

In spite of the many changes amongst the clergy, which can be noted in lists of the Proceedings of the Synods, the Diocese of Edmonton seems to have always been fortunate in having a number who gave it long and devoted service: Archdeacon George H. Webb, Archdeacon George Howcroft and Archdeacon Walter Leversedge were among those of the early years. Archdeacons F. C. Cornish and S. F. Tackaberry were successively Secretary-Treasurers of the Diocese, and as such showed great business ability through difficult periods.

The progress of the Church, however, depends less upon central administration than upon parochial ministrations, and the long years of service by Canon Pierce-Goulding at the Pro-Cathedral; Canons C. Carruthers and W. M. Nainby at Holy Trinity; Canons C. McKim and E. S. Ottley and the Reverend J. Comyn-Ching at Christ Church, and Canon (later Archdeacon) C. F. A. Clough at St. Luke's and St. Faith's; Canons J. C. Matthews and C. E. F. Wolfe at St. Stephen's, all made a great contribution to the growth of the Diocese. Outstanding among laymen was Mr. Justice Frank Ford, Chancellor of the Diocese from 1913 to 1933 and again from 1941 to 1957, the trusted counsellor of Bishops and Synods.

Archbishop Barfoot called the twentieth Synod of the Diocese of Edmonton, and the sixth over which he presided, on November 18, 1952, and as the first business of his Charge, placed before the members a formal request that the Synod should empower him to seek permission from the Provincial Synod of Rupert's Land for a Bishop Coadjutor or Bishop Suffragan. In a sense this was a precautionary request made because General Synod had under consideration the matter of the Primacy and a fixed Primatial See, and the Archbishop did not want the work of the Diocese to suffer during his tenure of the Primacy. There was a prolonged discussion and it was finally decided to ask for the assistance of a Bishop Suffragan. The Provincial Synod of Rupert's Land, when it met in Winnipeg at the end of April, 1953, readily agreed to the request, but it was never implemented.

The Archbishop told the Synod that since its last meeting the clergy staff had a net increase of eleven men, and four parishes, Winfield, Hardisty, Westlock and Kitscoty, had resident priests after a lapse of nearly ten years. The missionary giving in the Diocese had increased by almost $14,000. Church extension in Edmonton was still the biggest problem and he appealed to the clergy and people of existing parishes to extend their work to include new areas adjacent to them, noting that a Sunday School would often hold the fort until a church could be established. After speaking of the Missionary Year that would commemorate the fiftieth anniversary of the M.S.C.C., the Archbishop had a word of praise for the Diocesan Board of Religious Education and the G.B.R.E. Western Field Secretary (Rev. F. A. Peake), regarding their work in adult education, and said that he had great hopes for the future of the Church in the Diocese if their programme could be carried through.

This Synod received a report from its committee on transportation, and after long discussion decided to enter into the rural transportation scheme proposed by the M.S.C.C., and empowered the committee to reassess each parish so that the additional $2,000 needed might be found. A report from the committee on rural work also drew much interest, especially in its suggestion that it should be authorized to investigate the possibility of establishing a Bible School in the Diocese with the same object as the various schools operated by the sectarian groups, whose work was obviously succeeding. It also recommended that a committee should be appointed to investigate the possibility of organizing a Savings and Credit Union on a diocesan scale. The Rural Work Committee was constituted then as one of the standing committees of the Diocese.

The death of Archbishop Louis Ralph Sherman of Rupert's Land on July 31, 1953, made necessary the election of a new Metropolitan for the Province, and a meeting of the Electoral College was held in Winnipeg on October seventh, the Right Reverend Henry D. Martin of Saskatchewan presiding as Senior Bishop. Only three nominations were received, and on the first ballot Archbishop Barfoot was elected as Metropolitan. The Archbishop resigned the See of Edmonton on October 30 and was enthroned in St. John's Cathedral, Winnipeg, on

January fourth, 1954. Thus after a lapse of twenty-three years the Primate of All Canada was once again the Metropolitan and Bishop of Rupert's Land. During the twelve years Archbishop Barfoot had occupied the See of Edmonton, the Diocese had grown stronger, the members of the Church were knitted more closely together, the work in the rural parts had been restored, very largely by his own unceasing efforts, and the whole work of the Church extended.[14]

The Election of Bishop Howard Hewlett Clark

The twenty-first Synod of the Diocese of Edmonton met on November 18, 1953, under the presidency of the Very Reverend J. Grant Sparling, who pointed out that the new Bishop would have to lead them into further fields of new work and guide them in raising the necessary funds to meet expansion. They were pledged to take a further step towards self-support, with a view to gradually relinquishing the grants from the M.S.C.C. After three ballots the Administrator declared that the Very Reverend Howard Hewlett Clark, Dean of Ottawa, was elected.

Bishop Clark was consecrated in All Saints' Cathedral, Edmonton, on January 25, 1954, by the Metropolitan of Rupert's Land (Barfoot), and enthroned the same day.[15] Born at Macleod, Alberta, Bishop Clark was educated in the public schools of Toronto, Thorold and St. Catharines, Ontario. He graduated in Arts from the University of Toronto in 1932, having previously received the Divinity Testamur from Trinity College in 1930, and was ordained deacon in 1930 by Bishop Roper of Ottawa. He became assistant curate at Christ Church Cathedral, Ottawa, in 1932, priest in charge in 1938, rector in 1939, was made a Canon of the Diocese in 1941 and Dean of Ottawa in 1945.

[14]T. C. B. Boon, "Anglican Archbishop W. F. Barfoot retires from Rupert's Land," *Winnipeg Free Press* (December 31, 1960), 25.
[15]Kelley and Rogers, *op. cit.*, 140-141.

CHAPTER FIFTEEN

The Subdivision of the Diocese of Rupert's Land: The Diocese of Keewatin

⬦⬧⬦⬧⬦⬧⬦⬧⬦⬧⬦⬧⬦⬧⬦⬧⬦

Bishop Lofthouse contributes to the Moosonee (and Keewatin) Mailbag an interesting account of his three months' visitation through his Diocese last summer (1904), which included a canoe journey of 2,400 miles. Of one Sunday spent in camp with the Indians, he says: "I had an opportunity of seeing something of the consistency of the Indian as regards the Sunday. In the afternoon as we were sitting in the tent, a splendid large moose came right across the river, and we could have shot it with the greatest ease, but the Indians made not the slightest attempt to get hold of a gun, but calmly sat and watched it swim off. Anyone who knows Indian nature will well understand what a test this is. I have travelled much with white men in this country, and I know that not one white man in a hundred would have let that moose alone. At the time we had no fresh meat of any kind, but were living on salt pork and flour.

THE NEW ERA,
August, 1905.

⬦⬧⬦⬧⬦⬧⬦⬧⬦⬧⬦⬧⬦⬧⬦⬧⬦

Keewatin, "The Land of the North Wind," was the name given to a district north of the original Province of Manitoba that took in part of what we now call the Northwest Territories. Like the section of southern Saskatchewan that was known as Assiniboia, before the province was established, it was largely thought of only as a name on a map. Not until the name was chosen for the new diocese erected in 1899 by the Ecclesiastical Province of Rupert's Land did the name Keewatin really mean something. As a diocese, it was designed to effect two purposes: the first, to remove from the supervision of the Bishops of Rupert's Land and Moosonee those parts of their Dioceses that it was becoming increasingly difficult for them to visit and administer; and, secondly, to provide for the administration of a large area that was still mainly Indian territory, but was beginning to show signs of settlement and development in its southern parts, through which passed the main line of the Canadian Pacific Railway. Geographically, it might be termed the "Diocese of the Pre-Cambrian Shield," a land of rock, turbulent rivers, small lakes, forests, muskeg, and little arable land; one where life still depended on hunting and fishing, canoe transport, trading and lumbering. The prospect of mineral resources was still a dream of the future.

Some of the work of the Anglican Church in this area was commenced before the Diocese of Rupert's Land was established. Much of it was begun by the Wesleyan Methodist missionaries who were brought in by Sir George Simpson of the Hudson's Bay Company in 1840. The work of James Evans at Norway House was most successful, but that at Lac la Pluie, begun at the same time by the Reverend William Mason, proved unsuccessful. In 1843 he joined and later replaced Mr. Evans at Norway House.[1]

Mr. Mason was succeeded at Lac la Pluie by the Reverend Peter Jacobs, a full-blooded Indian from eastern Canada, who remained there until 1854 and was followed by the Reverend Allan Salt. But the mission was closed in 1858. The work at this point was peculiarly difficult and remained so for a number of years, even after it was reopened by Anglican missionaries. In his *Methodism in the Middle West,* Dr. J. H. Riddell ascribes this want of success to the "bitter and unseemly rivalry of Christian Churches," but makes no suggestion as to its sources. Certainly the charge cannot be brought against the Anglican Church, for it had no missionaries in the area, nor did it even begin to penetrate the district until 1851; in fact, the area to the east of the Red River and Lake Winnipeg was left to evangelization by the Wesleyan Methodists, and Bishop Anderson appreciated their efforts. It is more probable that it was the natural obduracy of the Ojibways and Salteaux about accepting the Christian life, so often mentioned in reports of the Reverend Robert Phair and his fellow workers in this district, which was the cause of the failure of the Wesleyan Methodist missions.

The initial advance of the Anglican Church in Rupert's Land to the east was a journey of "exploration" made by the Reverend Robert James of St. Andrew's, Red River, in the summer of 1851, up the

[1]Methodist Missionary Society Archives, London, *Wesleyan Missionary Notices,* X, New Series (October, 1842). A letter from James Evans, Norway House, July 7, 1842, states: "II. Lac la Pluie has been deserted all the winter, part of which Mr. Mason has spent at Bas de la Riviere and part at the Red River Settlement. . . . III. Henry Steinhour has been at Rat Portage. A useful and indefatigable worker. . . . IV. At Norway House Mr. Jacobs has been teaching 40 scholars." *Ibid.* (January, 1843), 225-235: "James Evans Letters and Journals: I. Norway House station includes York Factory, Oxford House, Moose Lake, Cumberland House, Bering's River and Nelson River. Reports 193 Baptisms, 77 adults and 27 marriages on the register." The present writer tried to locate these registers, but has so far failed to find them. Besides keeping their own registers, which survive and can be consulted, Anglican missionaries who were chaplains to the Hudson's Bay Company were required to transmit copies to the Company. These, with a detailed analysis of their contents that has been admirably indexed, are in the Company's Archives in Beaver House, London, England.

Winnipeg River as far as its junction with the English River, a place for many years known to the Indians as White Dog, but usually called Islington in the Church's records. There had been a Roman Catholic mission at this point but it had been abandoned. The Corresponding Committee of the C.M.S. at Red River at its meeting on July 9, 1851, put on record that it had

heard with much interest the account of Mr. James' visit to White Dog, and looked forward to it as a spot likely to be blessed by God, and of great importance as being on the route to [eastern] Canada and Moose Factory. It is but a trial, and if they succeeded where others failed they will make much cause for thankfulness. For the first year they will be mainly responsible themselves. £100, the gift of a friend by the Rev. J. Stevenson, is placed at their disposal; £30 from local contributions, to which others may yet be added. After the perusal of Mr. James' journal, they hope the Society will not think they asked too much in requesting a grant of £50 for the current year to meet the £130 raised above.

Mr. James' journey must have been made immediately after the spring break-up of the ice, because in a St. Andrew's Register he entered three baptisms at Fort Alexander (where the Winnipeg River enters Lake Winnipeg) on May 23, 1851.

Bishop Anderson, in his journey to Moose Factory in the summer of 1852, called at White Dog each time he passed, and in *The Net in the Bay* relates the discussion he had with Philip Kennedy, who was acting as catechist. The Bishop was so impressed with possibilities of the work that having ordained Robert McDonald on December 19, 1852, he sent him to the White Dog mission in the spring of 1853, where McDonald remained until 1862, when he went to open the farthest northwest mission of the Church at Fort Yukon.[2]

There is no immediate record of what happened at Islington after Mr. McDonald left, but in the minutes of the Corresponding Committee of the C.M.S. of May second, 1864, there is a reference to the appointment of the Reverend Robert Phair to Fort Alexander, about which some misunderstanding seems to have arisen with the Parent Committee in England, which had apparently doubted the wisdom of his being placed so close to Winnipeg. Noting this, the Committee recorded: "The sphere, it is submitted, is in itself a very wide one; it was intended to comprise Islington and Lac Sal [Seul], connecting these with Albany and Moose; and in the direction of Canada, there is no missionary at present, between Fort Alexander and Lake

[2]S.P.G.A., Bishop David Anderson to S.P.G., November 22, 1852: It was recommended that the Society agree to place Robert McDonald at York, after he had been ordained (December 19, 1852). The Society would contribute £50 a year, and McDonald's salary as an H.B.C. chaplain would be £100. However, the Society seems to have thought that McDonald was too young.

Superior. Mr. Phair may in this way, meet as large a number of Indians as any missionary in the country." Robert Phair devoted the larger part of his active ministry to this eastern area of the Diocese of Rupert's Land, becoming the Archdeacon of Islington in 1888 and succeeding Archdeacon Cowley as Superintendent and Secretary of the C.M.S. affairs in the Diocese until he retired in 1915.

The Islington mission itself was again stirred into activity by the appointment of the Reverend Baptiste Spence in 1869. Mr. Spence was a native of St. Peter's Reserve, Dynevor, and one of the earliest graduates in theology of the reorganized St. John's College. He was in charge of this mission until he retired in 1893 to live again in the surroundings of his boyhood. He died on February fourth, 1896, and is buried on the north side of St. Peter's Church. Mr. Spence was followed by another missionary of native ancestry, this time a Sioux Indian, the Reverend John Albert Maggrah, who carried on the work there until 1901, when he took charge of the Sioux Mission at Griswold.

Apart from the single reference quoted, the minutes of the Corresponding Committee of the C.M.S. at Red River contain no financial references to the Islington Mission. The explanation for this is to be found in Volume XII of the *Church Missionary Intelligencer,* published in 1861, in which is printed a report from Bishop Anderson: "This mission is at present sustained by a munificent gift from Mrs. Landon of Bath, of £1,000 sterling for its establishment, and £100 a year for its maintenance. Its present prospects are favourable, and it will eventually become an important station in the wilderness by which it is surrounded." The Bishop also noted that "Below Islington the river precipitates itself down a succession of falls to Lake Winnipeg. Some of these are exceedingly beautiful."[3]

The building of the C.P.R. across the southern tract of the country diminished the importance of the Islington Mission and its work was absorbed into that of Lac Seul farther east. It was named at the request of Mrs. Landon to commemorate the Church Missionary Society's Training College, long known as the Islington Institution.

The Reverend Robert Phair struggled with the work at Fort Frances, but finally the Indian population became too scattered and as a white mission it failed; by the time the Diocese of Keewatin was constituted, work there was at a standstill.

At Long Sault on the Rainy River, some work was begun by Mr. Phair in 1874, but without much success. To the east of Islington,

[3]These falls, between the junction of the English and Winnipeg Rivers and Fort Alexander, have become the powerhouse of the metropolitan area of Winnipeg during the past fifty years. Their natural beauty has consequently disappeared, but Winnipeg and the Province of Manitoba have profited economically.

Lac Seul itself was visited by Phair in 1866, but there is no record of any permanent work there until more than twenty years later. The Reverend Thomas Hill Pritchard became missionary at Lac Seul in 1890 after his ordination by Bishop Machray. Lac Seul was his sole charge, for he died there in 1903 at the age of thirty-eight. His brother, "E.C.R.," also pioneered in the missionary work of this part of Ontario, his first post being Dinorwic to the east of Rat Portage (now Kenora), where he was stationed for three years.[4]

The Long Sault Mission, Rainy River, was begun again in 1896 by the Reverend Jeremiah Johnston, a native of St. Peter's Reserve, Dynevor, and he was still in charge when the district became part of the Diocese of Keewatin.

Fort Alexander, at the mouth of the Winnipeg River, was opened by Henry George who went there as a schoolmaster in the spring of 1855. At Fort Alexander he was succeeded by Henry Cochrane, who taught school there until he was priested on December 27, 1859. (He had been ordained deacon on August first, 1858.) The work of the Reverend Robert Phair at Fort Alexander has already been mentioned. In 1865 his bride came out from England; they were married in St. Peter's, Dynevor, then were at Fort Alexander until 1874. The Phairs moved to the new mission at Fort Frances and lived there until 1886; in 1889 they settled in Winnipeg, a more central point from which to conduct the affairs of the Archdeaconry. A devoted mission worker herself, Mrs. Phair had the gifts of inspiring others with her enthusiasm. Her death on February sixth, 1903, was deeply regretted.

York and Churchill

For many years after 1820 no definite work was undertaken by the Church at either York Factory or Churchill. For the first twenty years of the Church Missionary Society's efforts in Rupert's Land, York Factory only received the casual visits and ministrations of such Hudson's Bay Company chaplains, Anglican missionaries or Wesleyan Methodist ministers as happened by in the course of their travels. Archdeacon Faries, who was at York Factory for more than fifty years,

[4]There were three Pritchard brothers, differing in age by about ten years. Taken in order of seniority, their early records may be found as follows: *Crockford's Clerical Directory, 1898*, p. 1101. John Francis Pritchard and Thomas Hill Pritchard. *Ibid.*, 1908, pp. 1163-1164. Edward Charles Radigar Pritchard. J. F. Pritchard, "The Rev. J. F. Pritchard's Recollections of Red River and Prince Albert Days," *Canadian North-West Historical Society Publications*, I (1927), 29-36. The eldest and the youngest spent the greater part of their lives in the service of the Protestant Episcopal Church in the U.S.A. Thomas Hill Pritchard died when he was only thirty-eight, spending his entire ministry at Lac Seul, Ontario.

states that some baptisms were taken by the Reverend James Evans there on one of his visits.[5]

The arrival of Bishop David Anderson in the new Diocese of Rupert's Land in 1849 brought definite direction and fresh inspiration to the work of the Church in Northwest Canada. Realizing the importance of York Factory as the gateway of the west, he made strenuous efforts to establish a mission there, going to considerable trouble to secure the support, first of the S.P.G. and later of the C.M.S. in the matter, but it was not until after the ordination of the Reverend William Mason in the summer of 1854 that the Bishop was able to carry out his plans and ambitions. Mr. Mason was responsible for the establishment of the mission at Fort Severn, farther south along the coast of the Bay. He was succeeded by the Reverend William West Kirkby, who, when he returned from his furlough in England in 1869, found the Mackenzie River brigade had left, and so returned to York Factory from the Red River to fill in there, as Mason had gone back to England. Mr. Kirkby stayed at York Factory until 1881,[6] and left an outstanding record of work both there and at Churchill, where he made a great impression upon the Chipewyans. It was during his time that the Hudson's Bay "Districts of Churchill, York, Oxford and Severn," became part of the Diocese of Moosonee. Kirkby himself, in 1876, was appointed Archdeacon of York, the first Archdeaconry constituted in that Diocese.

For the next twenty years York and Churchill belonged to the Diocese of Moosonee, and the work of Archdeacon G. S. Winter has been related in connection with it. When he and his very energetic wife left in 1893 they had been saddened by the great changes that had taken place at York Factory due to new economic conditions. They were succeeded by the Reverend Richard Faries in 1898. Mr. Faries was a native of the Moose region, who was educated by Bishop Horden, and through the interest of Bishop Newnham went to Montreal Diocesan College, from which he graduated and was ordained in 1894. After a year as assistant at Moose Factory, he was at Fort Hope from 1895 until he was priested in 1898. He devoted the rest of his active life to York Factory and became Archdeacon of York in 1917.

The coming of the Canadian Pacific Railway through western Canada diminished the importance of York Factory to such an extent

[5] See n. 1 of this chapter.
[6] *Crockford's Clerical Directory, 1898*, p. 783, states that Kirkby was at Fort Simpson until 1868, and removed to York Factory the same year. In 1868 Kirkby and his family went to England for their first furlough since coming to the Red River in 1852, and in those days of the sailing ship they could not have returned until the summer of 1869.

that the Hudson's Bay Company found itself in great difficulty. Faries, in an article for *The New Era* in June of 1907, said that because of the C.P.R. "York Factory received its death blow as a sea port. Consequently the Hudson's Bay Company had to reduce the number of its servants and working men, and all the Europeans went 'home' or up to Winnipeg, seeking employment. The Company's business was confined to simple bartering with the Indians for the raw fur pelts, and the number of servants left for maintenance for the fur-trade made an English-speaking congregation of about twenty persons. About two or three hundred [Indians]—perhaps more—migrated to Split Lake, a large lake in the interior on Nelson River and settled there." The migration from York Factory seems to have started in the early eighties, but the Split Lake settlement, three hundred miles from York Factory, occurred about 1890. These Indians were all Christians, most of them had been baptized at York Factory, but the inaccessibility of this part of the country placed them beyond the reach of the missionary, and they found their spiritual welfare left in their own hands. They asked for help, but it was difficult to do anything; from 1893 to 1898 there was no clergyman at York Factory and the whole of this part of the country was left to what ministrations the Reverend Joseph Lofthouse, then stationed at Churchill, could give.

At the request of Bishop Newnham, Mr. Lofthouse communicated with Joseph Kitchekesik, the catechist at York, and arranged for him to come to Churchill. From the latter they started in the middle of February, 1896, with a team of five huskies and an Indian half-breed boy as driver. They had twelve days' provisions. On this journey they struck bad weather, lost their way, ran out of food for both themselves and their dogs, but finally did reach Split Lake after eighteen days. After ten days there they went to York Factory, and from there to Churchill, where they arrived home on April 20, after ten weeks absence. Some years later another group of York Indians moved to Norway House, where a school was begun in 1901 on the Jack River and a church was built in 1906 by the Indians themselves, under the direction of the schoolmaster, Mr. C. Wilkins. In 1899 Lofthouse was appointed Archdeacon of York by Bishop Newnham, but before he left the work on the west side of the Bay he was able to take a young clergyman, the Reverend C. G. Fox, and establish a permanent mission at Split Lake. They went in from Norway House by the difficult and treacherous route down the Nelson River, and had a miserable journey owing to heavy rain all the way. The Archdeacon has recorded, "Mr. Fox afterwards proved himself one of the very best missionaries we ever had in the north, and put in some fifteen years of most devoted service. He got a remarkable hold of the Cree language, in which he could both think, speak and even dream."[7]

The Formation of the Diocese of Keewatin

From what has already been written it will easily be gathered that the Reverend Joseph Lofthouse was an experienced missionary in the work of the northern part of the new diocese, with experience gained the hard way in those intermediate years between the regime of the Hudson's Bay Company and the modern era of transportation, years that left the missionaries dependent almost entirely upon their own resourcefulness. Mr. Lofthouse had been born December 18, 1855, at Wadsley in Yorkshire (just outside Sheffield) England, educated at the local school and at the Islington Institution of the Church Missionary Society. Apart from his three years on the east side of Hudson Bay, all his experience in the Canadian north was centred at Churchill. After furlough in England he returned to Canada in July, 1899, as Archdeacon of York, "an honour which I had refused when the Bishop was in the north in 1895." Mr. Rowley[8] describes him in 1900 to 1901 as C.M.S. missionary travelling across Baffin Land, but this is a misprint for the Barren Lands, for during this period he was a member of J. W. Tyrell's expedition that traversed northern Canada from Edmonton to Marble Island in Hudson Bay, a 5,000 mile journey by snowshoe and canoe during which members of the party never slept in a bed in the ten months they were away.

The financial foundations of the Diocese being at last assured, the Standing Committee of the Province on the Election of Bishops met at Bishop's Court, Winnipeg, on April ninth, 1902, and gave its assent to the nomination by the House of Bishops of the Venerable Joseph Lofthouse as first Bishop of Keewatin, but the election was not formally reported to the Provincial Synod until its fourth session on August 22.

The consecration of the new Bishop took place in Holy Trinity Church, Winnipeg, on Sunday, August 17, 1902. In the absence of Archbishop Machray, due to illness, the Right Reverend Richard Young of Athabasca acted as Metropolitan. The fact that it took place before the Synod met enabled the Diocese of Keewatin to be represented for the first time by delegates. The clerical ones were the

[7]Thompson, Manitoba, the new mining development (1960) of the International Nickel Company, is on the south bank of the Burntwood River, about sixty miles southwest of Split Lake.
[8]O. R. Rowley, *The Anglican Episcopate of Canada and Newfoundland*, 126-127. Rowley dates the appointment as archdeacon in 1896, also an error.

Reverends J. W. B. Page, T. H. Pritchard, the Venerable Archdeacon Phair, and the lay representative was R. D. Richardson.

In the winter of 1902 Bishop Lofthouse returned to England and succeeded in completing the Endowment Fund, also in raising £1,500 for the purchase of a See House. In addition he received the promise of support for two missionaries, and £1,000 for the beginning of the Clergy Sustentation Fund. The required amount of the Endowment Fund, £10,000, was provided by £5,000 from the Diocese of Moosonee, £4,000 from the S.P.C.K., S.P.G. and Colonial Bishoprics Fund, and the remaining £1,000 from the Diocese of Rupert's Land. In 1913 the Colonial Bishoprics Fund made a further grant of £500, and this with other sums raised by the Bishop brought the endowment up to $60,000.

The first Synod of the Diocese of Keewatin met on June 29, 1905. Bishop Lofthouse began his Charge by outlining in detail the boundaries of the Diocese, the sources and amounts of its Endowment Fund, See House Fund and Clergy Sustentation Fund. In its life of three years the number of mission stations had grown from eighteen to thirty, the number of priests serving them from eight to eleven, of deacons from one to three, of catechists from six to eight. There were also now two licensed lay readers. The only self-supporting parish in the Diocese was Kenora. The missions were existing on grants, but, said Bishop Lofthouse, "Each Parish or mission receiving a grant should seek to reduce that grant every year." To clergy who did not like appealing for money, he said, "There are and always will be many things in the Master's service that are disagreeable but they are duties to be done for Him and will bring their reward."

He took a practical view of the situation respecting Indians: "Many of our Indians, especially in the southern parts of the Diocese, are in as good a position as their white brethren, and are very well able to give large support to the work but unfortunately they have been led in the past to look to the mission for everything and asked to do little or nothing in return." He spoke of the prospects of new work having to be opened up because of plans for the transcontinental Grand Trunk Pacific Railway. The Diocese had 1,200 communicants, 500 Indians, 700 whites. Rat Portage (Kenora) headed the list with a roll of 280. "It may not be known to all or even to very few that the Diocese of Keewatin is more than half missionary and that we have more mission work, more missions and more Indians and Eskimo than in any Diocese of the Province of Rupert's Land unless it be the Diocese of Saskatchewan. . . . It seems strange to me to come from uncivilized and wild parts of the north into the midst of civilization and there to meet for the first time with heathen Indians. In the north where our missions are often four or five times the size of missions in the south we have not one heathen."

The Bishop mentioned the assistance the Diocese received from the Church Missionary Society and the newly-formed Missionary Society of the Church of England in Canada. Dr. Norman Tucker, the first Secretary of the M.S.C.C., still busily engaged in organizing the work and securing the co-operation of the Canadian Dioceses, was present at this Synod and spoke to it on the new missionary scheme. He laid great stress on the fact that the Missionary Society *was* the Church, not a part of the Church. The fundamental considerations in determining apportionments were first to find out the need; second, to find out the giving power of the people.

Bishop Lofthouse was a practical and plain-spoken man, and when the Synod met the next morning, he called its attention to the use of the title "Lord Bishop," saying that it should be confined to Bishops who sat in the House of Lords. He wished that clergy would omit the phrase when addressing him. He would be quite satisfied to be addressed as "Bishop." At this session the Synod took up legal matters and decided to petition the Legislature of Ontario that it be incorporated and given the necessary power to make amendments to its own Constitution. Actually, the Bishop of Keewatin was incorporated by an Act of the Legislative Assembly of Manitoba, given assent on February 13, 1907, but the Act to incorporate the Synod of the Diocese of Keewatin was a Dominion one passed by the Senate of Canada on May 22, 1908.

To the Synod of 1907 the Bishop expressed regret that Archdeacon Page had had to return to England because of his health: "No man was ever more sincerely loved, not only by his own people but by the whole diocese." The Venerable J. W. B. Page was one of a singularly brilliant group of students at St. John's College between 1886 and 1892; he was ordained both deacon and priest in 1888. In 1892 he became rector of St. Alban's, Kenora, and was appointed Archdeacon of Keewatin in 1906.

Churches had been built at Whitemouth, Lac du Bonnet, Emo, Barwick, Split Lake and Jack River, nearly all of them free from debt. Progress had been made towards self-help. Rainy River, under the Reverend M. H. Jackson, had asked that the grant from diocesan funds be reduced by $100. The continued kindness and liberality of friends in England had nearly doubled the Sustentation Fund. It seemed to the Bishop that with the withdrawal of C.M.S. aid many of the missions in the far north would have to be abandoned, unless the Diocese had something to fall back on. "It certainly seems to me that the M.S.C.C. and our own Church in Canada does not seem inclined to assume any responsibility for the Indian work. . . . . I maintain very strongly that as a Church we have no right to take up mission work in foreign lands, and expect others to carry on our own work, which is as distinctly missionary work as any, for there are still heathen in Canada, and even in the Province of Ontario." The general missionary, the Reverend Arthur A. Adams, reported that during 1906 he had travelled 4,000 miles, and to the end of June, 1907, nearly 7,000. Fort Frances was making great progress under the Reverend C. Wood. With the completion of the international power dam and the prospect of new settlers, it was hoped that Fort Frances would soon cease to require any grants from the mission fund. The work in the camps along the C.P.R. and G.T.P. lines was a problem that had to be met; nothing had been done for the men except occasional visits from Archdeacon Page and Mr. Wood, but a worker had been found who would spend the summer months traversing the camps.

Another feature of this Synod was a missionary meeting that was addressed by the Reverends R. Faries of York Factory, G. G. Fox and Chief Kitchekesick of Split Lake, W. Dick of Trout Lake, and E. Thomas of Fort Alexander, who told of their work at the missions they served. The general missionary, the Reverend Arthur A. Adams, spoke on the "white work." This was the first time Chief Kitchekesick and the Reverend William Dick had been into civilization.

By 1911 some changes had taken place. Archdeacon Page was succeeded as rector of St. Alban's, Kenora, by the Reverend C. W. McKim, and as Archdeacon by the Reverend Horace Davis Cooper, who died on June 15, 1909, at the age of seventy-three. Mr. Cooper was a graduate of Trinity College, Toronto, and was ordained in that diocese in 1861. After spending thirty-two years in mission stations in eastern Canada, he had gone to Holland, Manitoba, in 1893, and four years later had undertaken missionary work in the Dryden district to the east of Kenora. There, in spite of the fact that he was well over sixty years of age, he was most successful as a pioneer church builder, and largely responsible for the foundation of the mission at Dryden, where he built the church in 1901, doing most of the work himself. This church was the first one consecrated in the Diocese in 1905. Missions at Wabigoon and Dinorwic also were largely his work. Whenever other means of transportation failed, Mr. Cooper would "walk the ties," and only a short time before his death he walked twenty-two miles over bush trails to take a service.

Two extensions were mentioned at the Synod held in August, 1911. A new mission had been established at Graham, or the Sioux Lookout, on the Grand Trunk Pacific Railway, and a good church had been

built there, nearly free from debt, through the efforts of the Reverend
J. H. Atkinson. The Indian missionary work at Jack River, Norway
House, had been taken over by the Reverend J. F. J. Marshall, whom
the Bishop welcomed as the first real Canadian to enter into their
Indian missionary work. Mr. Marshall spent sixteen years at the
Jack River mission, then fourteen years as Principal of the Indian
Residential School at Sioux Lookout. Commenting on the fact that
the Diocese had lost one clergyman to another diocese because the
people would not do their part, the Bishop stated, "Here I would
like to say publicly I will never help any Parish where the people
are not willing to do their share. I will never attempt to build up
Parishes on the English system where the people expect the Church
and clergyman to do everything for them and they do nothing."

The mission at Churchill had been re-established in 1904 when the
Reverend F. C. Sevier went there, and by 1911 the Bishop was anxious
to secure a second worker so that a new mission might be opened
to the Eskimos, either at Chesterfield Inlet or Repulse Bay.

When the Synod met for the fifth time on June 24, 1913, Bishop
Lofthouse reviewed the previous ten years. The Reverend H. V.
Maltby had just left Keewatin to take charge of Fort Frances. At
that time Keewatin was the only potential industrial centre in that
part of Ontario. Church of England services had been held in the
Methodist Church up to 1903, but with the appointment of Mr.
Maltby in 1902, the first church was opened on November 8, 1903,
at a cost of $1,000, and was consecrated on June 16, 1907. Maltby
had gone to Fort Frances in 1908, and become Archdeacon of
Keewatin in 1914. There seemed to be indications that other towns
along the railways would become self-supporting, and the Bishop
tried to encourage this by telling the Synod, "I may say for your
benefit that Kenora was forced by Rupert's Land to become a self-
supporting Parish when she had a smaller population than two out
of the three mentioned."

Bishop Lofthouse held strongly that to talk about unity among the
Churches and then find them competing in smaller towns was an
absurdity: "To find three and sometimes four protestant Churches,
all striving, not so much for the Kingdom of God, as for their own
little sect, and often paying their ministers, even with the help of
Mission Boards, what is nothing better than a starvation wage, is to
my mind not only a sin against Christ, but also a crime against reason."
This comment was caused by the appearance of a second protestant
church in Sioux Lookout. The Bishop also complained of the number
of students of various bodies working during the summer in such

places as Redditt, Minaki and Malachi, where there was only room for one.

The sixth Synod of the Diocese was delayed for a year owing to the First World War, and did not take place until June 13, 1916. In the meantime some changes had occurred. In October of 1915 Canon Joseph Lofthouse, the Bishop's nephew, had been called into Kenora to become general missionary and Secretary-Treasurer of the Synod. Mr. Lofthouse had been working in the Diocese since 1907, in the Wabigoon and Rainy River district. He had come from England in 1904 and spent four years at Wycliffe College, Toronto, with two summers at Split Lake. He was well acquainted with the work in the Diocese and was appointed Canon in 1914. His place at Rainy River was taken by the Reverend Joseph Milner. The previous Good Friday, the Diocese had been shocked by the news that the Reverend J. B. Clark of Lac du Bonnet had died suddenly. It was a great loss, for he had done five years of good and faithful service there. The Reverend F. C. Sevier and his family had had a very hard time at Churchill for two years, and in the winter of 1915 had been very close to starvation.

The question of women voting at the annual meetings for church-wardens, or vestrymen, or in dealing with parochial funds, was to be brought up at the Synod. The Bishop was concerned that they should safeguard themselves so that they did not shut out the men, "for we need them as much or more than the women." In discussion that followed, section twenty-five of Canon X was amended by striking out the word "male" in the eighth line, thereby allowing women to have a vote at parishioners' meetings. This was carried by a standing vote.

The Diocese of Keewatin was perennially worried by its small population, large area, and the difficulties of travel in getting to Kenora for meetings. There were, at the end of 1917, fifteen clergy in the diocese; three of them had left. The Reverend A. A. Adams had resigned Sioux Lookout and retired from the ministry; the Reverend C. G. Fox, who had spent nearly seventeen years at Split Lake and had built up one of the strongest and best Indian Missions in the country, had gone overseas in August of 1916; the Reverend R. E. Lemon of Lac du Bonnet and Pointe du Bois had received a call from Rupert's Land.

The vacancies had been filled. The Reverend W. H. J. Walter had had to give up his work at Nelson Harbour at the end of 1917, as all construction work there had been stopped and the men withdrawn.[9] He was going to Split Lake. The Reverend R. F. Widdows was taking

[9]The government changed its policy with respect to the Hudson's Bay Railway; having determined that the mouth of the Nelson River was unsuitable for a harbour, the track was later swung north to Churchill, where terminal facilities were constructed.

up work at Sioux Lookout, and the Reverend L. A. Todd was going to Lac du Bonnet and its associated points. Fort Frances, by this time, had become the second self-supporting parish in the diocese.

An interesting point respecting the annual financial statements is the high proportion of giving on the part of the Indian Missions, seven of them providing more than one-third of the total amount of $1,500 raised in the Diocese, about half of which went to the Home Mission Fund, and the rest to what are now called the General Synod Departments. (In 1917: St. Alban's, Kenora, $340; White Missions, $627; Indian Missions, $516.)

In 1917 the Diocese of Keewatin received a heavy blow when St. Alban's Church, Kenora, was burned down. This church had stood on top of the hill high above the C.P.R. railway lines, but the new church was built on the present site near the Court House, almost on the lake front, at a cost of $30,000.

The last Synod over which Bishop Lofthouse presided, and eighth of the Diocese, met on August 17, 1920, eighteen years to the day after his Consecration. In his Charge the Bishop said he had tendered his resignation last year to the Metropolitan, who had begged him to keep on for another year at least, and he had consented to do this. Bishop Lofthouse paid a generous tribute to many of those who had served the Diocese in the past. With regard to the Rainy River district, which extended some two hundred miles from Atikokan to Sprague along the two main railway lines, he noted: "In the whole of this country there was no Church of England work being done when I came to the Diocese (except one Indian Mission at the Long Sault, with an occasional service at Beaver Mills—now Rainy River town)." He appreciated the work done at Fort Frances by the Reverend J. W. B. Page, Charles Wood and Archdeacon Maltby, the climax of which was that the congregation, with a communicants' list of less than half that of Kenora or Dryden, had recently pledged more than $1,000 to the Anglican Forward Movement. The churches at Barwick and Stratton had been built by the Reverend F. Cousins, who went there in 1903, almost with his own hands, and he had stayed for fifteen years. At Rainy River town the church had been built in 1904 through the efforts of John Hodges, then churchwarden, who raised $1,500. It was to the credit of the congregation that they had kept this church entirely free from debt for many years, because the removal of the lumber mills and other industries had been a heavy blow to the neighbourhood. Lac du Bonnet, Point du Bois and Pinawa were all making steady progress due to electric power plants that had been established at those points.

The Bishop then turned to the Indian Missions in the north, and after speaking of York Factory, mentioned the work of the Reverend W. Dick, a pure Cree native pastor who had remained for nearly thirty-five years at his post and won all the Indians, nearly 1,000, for Christ. In 1918 Mr. Dick had had to give up the work and had gone to live at York Factory, where he died quite suddenly in August of 1919. He spoke with a good deal of personal feeling about the mission at Churchill, described by one Bishop as "the last house of the world, the dumping off place t'other side of nowhere." The Jack River mission at Norway House was prospering under the Reverend J. F. J. Marshall, a real "master builder." The Reverend C. H. Fryer had been doing steady work since 1911 at Fort Alexander, one of the oldest established missions in the Diocese. The missions on the Winnipeg River at The Dalles and White Dog, and on the Rainy River at Long Sault, had been closed because there were no Indians any longer on the Reserves. To keep a man at such stations meant that "having no one to feed with the Bread of Life, his own soul starved and died, for only as we feed others can we sustain our own spiritual life." Since 1915 it had been impossible to keep a man in Lac Seul, and the large band of Indians there had been neglected, but it was hoped soon to remedy the situation by placing an ordained man in charge.

The Synod listened to the usual reports dealing with the finances of the Diocese and then went into a long discussion about the budget system. The resolutions authorizing this and bringing it into effect on January first, 1921, were carried unanimously. It was also resolved to raise the stipends to $1,500 for married men and $1,200 for unmarried parochial clergy.

The business of the Synod being ended, the Reverend R. Diamond, rector of St. Alban's, Kenora, said, "This being the last Synod over which the Bishop will preside I feel we cannot allow the opportunity to pass without saying a few words with respect to the time and labour our Bishop has given to this part of God's field. I would move there-fore, that we extend to the Bishop, as the Synod representing the Diocese, our heartfelt thanks for all that he has done to build up the Diocese on a solid foundation. The Diocese stands second to none in this respect." In reply, the Bishop said, "I thank you most sincerely. . . . I have felt for some time that a younger man should take up the work. . . . Speaking officially, I wish you every blessing, temporal and spiritual, that a father can give to every individual son."

In his book *A Thousand Miles from a Post Office*, which was published two years later, Bishop Lofthouse dealt exclusively with his experience as a missionary before becoming Bishop of Keewatin, but he did refer to this later work at the end: "It was with much pain and sorrow that I gave up my work, but during the last four years of that period [which ended December 31, 1920] I lost both my wife and only daughter, and my own health was beginning to give way under the strain." Bishop Lofthouse retired to England, where he spent thirteen years before he died at Dawlish, South Devon, on December 18, 1933, on his seventy-eighth birthday, in the fiftieth year of his ministry and the thirty-first year of his episcopate.

The Episcopate of Bishop A. D. A. Dewdney

Following the resignation of Bishop Lofthouse at the end of 1920, his nephew, Canon Joseph Lofthouse, was appointed Administrator of the Diocese, a tribute to his work as general missionary and secretary-treasurer.

A meeting of the Standing Committee on the Election of Bishops in the Province of Rupert's Land was called for March 31, 1921, but seems to have reached a deadlock for no election was made. The Diocese at that time did not have, nor has it now, the requisite number of self-supporting parishes to hold its own election. No report of the proceedings of this committee, or of the committee that did elect Bishop Dewdney, appears in the printed proceedings of the next meeting of the Provincial Synod itself, which was held in Saskatoon on September 11, 1923. Consequently one is dependent upon Bishop Dewdney's own statements, made in his Charge to his first Synod (the ninth of the Diocese), which met on July 19, 1922.

The second meeting of the Electoral Committee had been held immediately following the General Synod.[10] At the time he had been on his way to Prince Albert to take up the duties of administrator of the Diocese of Saskatchewan, just become vacant due to the resignation of Bishop Newnham. Just before reaching Kenora he had received a telegram informing him of his election and requesting an answer.

I did not know much about the Diocese, except that there was a good deal of Indian work scattered over an immense area and that the country was mostly rough and rocky . . . very thinly peopled. I had laboured for nearly sixteen years on the prairie. I had but little experience in Indian work. If my experience fitted me, for anything, certainly it was not for the kind of work here in Keewatin. Besides, I had no opportunity to consult anyone, not even my wife. My first inclination was to decline, I decided to consult the Metropolitan; and then, on further thought, I decided to consult the Metropolitan; and I may say that what decided me was the conviction expressed by him, in which he assured me the other Bishops concurred, that the election

[10]O. R. Rowley, op. cit., 191, states that Bishop Dewdney was "elected to the Missionary See of Keewatin, on the 19th October, by the Bishops and Electoral Committee of the Synod of the Province of Rupert's Land in session at Winnipeg." General Synod met in Hamilton, Ontario, on October 5, 1921.

had been made under the Divine guidance. If it were, indeed, the will of God and also the will of the Church I dared not decline; and so I am here today as your Bishop to serve you as far as I may in this office.

He went on to say that the position of the Bishop of Keewatin was in a sense strategic. The Diocese divided Canada into two, extending as it did from the extreme south to the North Pole, but it was also the connecting link; through their territory passed all travel and commerce between east and west. It was similar ecclesiastically. With a Metropolitan on the east (Thorneloe of Algoma) and a Metropolitan on the west, he was in distinguished company, and they might well aspire to be a unifying factor in the life of the Church and also in the national life.

Enough has already been said about the earlier ministry of Alfred Daniel Alexander Dewdney in connection with the Diocese of Saskatchewan. When he was elected Bishop of Keewatin he was more than fifty-eight years of age. He was consecrated in St. Alban's Pro-Cathedral, Kenora, on December 11, 1921, by the Metropolitan (Matheson).[11] Bishop Dewdney was enthroned the same evening, and thus began a useful episcopate that was to extend through seventeen years.

Although Bishop Dewdney disclaimed any particular experience with the work of Indian Missions, his Charge to the Synod of 1922 indicated a very considerable familiarity with their problems, as well as a deep sympathy with the condition of the Indian people themselves. He was very concerned about missions in the Diocese of Keewatin that had been closed, and emphasized that without missionaries and without schools the Indian people were bound to deteriorate. In the northern part of the Diocese education was to some extent being carried on through day schools at the mission stations, but many of them had been closed in the southern area, and he felt the only solution was to provide a residential school. He was not quite satisfied with the present system and felt that education should be adapted to the life the child would have to live: "The training ought to be such that the boy will be a more independent and therefore a better trapper and the girl a better homemaker."

The general missionary's report spoke with appreciation of the assistance received from the Reverend J. J. Roy who had filled in by taking services at a number of different places when there was a shortage of clergy. Mr. Roy, for the thirty-three years previous to his retirement in 1919, had been rector of St. George's Church in Winnipeg, and was then living in Kenora. It was also noted that the

[11]*Ibid.*, 190-191.

Diocese had been fortunate in securing the services of the Reverend Maurice Sanderson to take charge of the Lac Seul mission, where he had won many of the people back to the Church. Following this Synod a two day conference was held, the second day of which was largely devoted to the discussion of Indian missions and education.

By 1924 the Bishop had completed his first visitation of the Diocese and was better acquainted with its problems. He told the Synod that met on July second that they had had difficulty filling their northern missions, and that his efforts to do more for the Eskimos north of Churchill had so far failed because he could not get men for the work.[12] But in the south the appointment of Mr. Sanderson had enabled them to open up White Dog and Lac Seul, services had been resumed at Atikokan in the extreme southeast (later to become an important mining town), and they had been able to place a summer student at Badger in the extreme southwest. The Anglican Forward Movement had provided some funds for this, which had been helpful in easing losses suffered through the withdrawal of the C.M.S., and the Bible Churchman's Missionary Society had undertaken the support of three of their Indian missionaries.

In his Charge Bishop Dewdney spoke at length about the M.S.C.C., and the Indian and Eskimo work. The failure of the M.S.C.C. to provide adequately for this work had caused criticism and misunderstanding. The task undertaken by the Church, to provide for the native work in Canada, was much greater than many realized. It involved educational and evangelistic work, the support of schools and missions. Two-thirds of the amount required had been provided, one third had not, and the shortage had affected the missionary work. In Keewatin, as a consequence, they had gone behind at the rate of $1,500 a year, which had wiped out what credit balance they had. He also pointed out that the only funds available for distribution by the M.S.C.C. were those provided by the apportionments subscribed by the Dioceses; but the whole matter was now bound up with the budget system, almost universally adopted, and this made it difficult to make specific appeals. The Bishop had spent two winters in eastern Canada as a special missionary deputation; he found people deeply interested, and if it were the only problem he was satisfied that the Indian and Eskimo work would be amply provided for.

Advance in another direction was taken on January 18, 1923, when the Bishop called the organization meeting of the Diocesan Board of

---

[12]The ordination of Rev. D. B. Marsh on June 20, 1926, and his appointment to Eskimo Point the same summer, brought about the long desired extension of mission work to Eskimos in the area north of Churchill, Manitoba. The original suggestion that work should be done north of Churchill was made by Rev. John West in 1823, but more than a hundred years elapsed before it became possible to do anything practical.

Religious Education. This board received a request asking that the Sunday School by Post be established in the Diocese, and it was agreed to ask Miss H. S. Carpenter to superintend this work with Miss Evelyn Smith as her assistant. They had begun with seven pupils and now had fifty-three. In the same month a Diocesan Council for Social Service had been set up.

During the next few years there was considerable industrial development in the southern part of the Diocese of Keewatin. Near Atikokan mining camps were at work at Mine Centre and Foley Mine, and hydroelectric development was beginning nearby to the north. The Church sent a student in there each summer. At Pine Falls a new pulp mill was being erected and the Reverend C. H. Fryer of Fort Alexander had interested himself in the people engaged in its construction. A new town was being established at Hudson near Sioux Lookout, to the northwest of Lac Seul there was a new gold mine at Red Lake, and the Central Manitoba Mines farther west were providing new opportunities for religious ministrations. The Anglican Church was the first to commence work in the places named.

In the summer of 1927 Bishop Dewdney had a serious illness, but fortunately made an excellent recovery. By 1928 the prospect of easier, faster travel by air was beginning to appeal to him, but at the time the cost proved prohibitive. He made his visitation that year by the long hard route up the east coast of Lake Winnipeg, through Island Lake to Trout Lake, then down to Fort Severn, where a motor-schooner took him to York Factory, Churchill, Eskimo Point and other places on the coast. During this visitation he dedicated a memorial tablet in the church at Churchill to Pastor Rasmus Jensen Aarkus and sixty-two other members of the Danish Expedition that had wintered there in 1619. All of them had died of scurvy, leaving only Captain Munck and two others to return home. The tablet was provided by an unnamed Danish pastor of New York.

1927 saw the Diocese reach twenty-five years of age, and though no particular celebrations seem to have been held, Bishop Dewdney marked it by creating a third Archdeaconry to which he appointed Canon Lofthouse. Boundaries of the Archdeaconries were realigned so that the new one extended from the C.P.R. line to the Jack River Mission at Norway House, and the former one of Keewatin had a smaller district and a new name, that of Rainy River. The Archdeaconry of York was to take in all the missions accessible from the Hudson Bay railway or Hudson Bay shore-line. The vacant Canonry was filled by the appointment of the Reverend Maurice Sanderson, "as a representative of a race which from time immemorial has occupied this land, as one who has done faithful work in the Church for a quarter of a century, as one whose gifts of personality and speech do credit to himself and to the Church and make his ministry acceptable not only amongst his own people, but with all, and as one who has endured hardness in the Master's service and is still ready to endure." To this might be added that there are few better written or more informative documents among diocesan papers in the Province of Rupert's Land than those submitted to the Synods of the Diocese of Keewatin by Canon Sanderson.

At the end of January, 1929, Archdeacon Lofthouse resigned as treasurer of the Synod owing to his appointment as rector of St. Alban's, Kenora, though he continued as secretary, and Bishop Dewdney temporarily undertook the duties of treasurer, which he was to continue for the rest of his active episcopate.

In 1932 the Diocese began to feel the effects of the depression, and while mining developed in both the Red Lake and Central Manitoba districts, work was made difficult at places like Pine Falls, Redditt, and in the neighbourhood of Ignace. The establishment of relief camps in connection with the construction of the Trans-Canada Highway brought 5,000 men into the eastern part of the Diocese. The Anglican Church co-operated with other Churches and the government of Ontario in ministering to the social and spiritual life of these men; this work was under the care of Captain Alp of the Church Army in the area between English River and Ignace.

During the year a second canonry was instituted, to which the Reverend F. C. Sevier was appointed to represent the clergy engaged in "white work" in the Diocese. He was also senior in ordination at the time; his work at Churchill and later at Sioux Lookout had been both devoted and successful.

When the Synod next met on May 19, 1932, there had been a considerable number of changes in clergy. Vacancies had been filled for the most part, and there had been some ordinations, notably W. J. R. James, who went to Baker Lake, W. M. Clarke to Churchill, and G. C. Cowley to Split Lake.

The last weeks of August, 1932, produced a critical situation for the Diocese of Keewatin, due to the financial disaster involving the firm of Machray and Sharpe in Winnipeg, which had been the financial agent of the trustees of two major endowments of the Diocese, the Endowment of the Bishopric and the Clergy Endowment Fund. On September 13 the executive committee received a report that these had been depleted to the extent of about $100,000, and a special committee was immediately set up to watch the proceedings in bankruptcy of the company. Steps were also taken to raise within the Diocese the sum of $1,500 for the year, so that the Bishop might at least have a missionary income. Relief soon came, however, when the Diocese was advised by Canon Gould, Secretary of the M.S.C.C., that the income of the Bishop, together with four per cent of the Clergy Endowment Fund, would be provided for three years. In the meantime, early in March of 1933 the Restoration Fund had been organized by the General Synod of the Church and a strong diocesan committee was appointed, with Archdeacon Lofthouse and Mr. E. L. Carter as joint chairmen, to organize and carry out the appeal in the diocese itself. Up to May 31, $5,219 had been pledged and $2,837 paid in cash. St. Alban's, Kenora, had over-subscribed its quota.

The outstanding change since the Synod had last met had been the creation of the Diocese of The Arctic, which had taken from the Diocese of Keewatin the last vestige of the territory of that name.[13] Consequently, to the Bishop, the name seemed no longer appropriate and he suggested that it be changed to that of the See City, Kenora; but to this the committee on his Charge failed to agree, saying that the expressed majority opinion was that the merging of the territory with the Diocese of The Arctic provided an added reason why the historic name should be retained, not obliterated.

In 1936 the current financial position of the Diocese of Keewatin was still one of anxiety, for the receipts of the M.S.C.C. had dwindled from $254,000 in 1929 to $160,000 in 1935. Grants to the missionary dioceses had had to be cut *pro rata* by 45 per cent, and their own quarterly grants had dropped accordingly. This was the more serious because there was likewise a fall in interest received from all new investments, which affected to an alarming extent the income from restored funds. The Bishop spoke strongly upon the subject of increased giving by the parishes, and in defence of active participation in the work of the W.A., especially with respect to help the Diocese received from the Dominion Board of the W.A. for the Sioux Lookout School.

About this time the Diocese was deeply affected by the death of the Reverend C. H. Fryer who had cared for the Fort Alexander Mission for some twenty-five years, extending its work along the shores of Lake Winnipeg as far as Hole River and into the interior, besides founding the prospering parish of Pine Falls. Mr. Fryer was succeeded by the Reverend W. H. J. Walter, who previously had been at Norway House.

[13]The Bishop was wrong. It is true that the boundaries of the District of Keewatin are rather indeterminate according to the map issued by the Department of the Interior to December 31, 1882, especially respecting the eastern boundary of Manitoba and the western boundary of Ontario. Yet the Diocese of Keewatin has always had the portion of the old District lying south of Latitude 60°N, and this line is considerably north of Churchill, Manitoba.

On June ninth, 1938, when Bishop Dewdney met the Synod for the last time, he had to chronicle two other deaths, that of A. J. Gardiner of Eagle River, who had been churchwarden there for many years, and of C. H. Carpenter, for over forty years organist and choirmaster of St. Alban's Pro-Cathedral. A new feature connected with the Sunday School by Post was a visit by Misses Hasell and Sayle to the southeast portion of Rupert's Land and the southwest portion of Keewatin, which secured a large number of new members for the Sunday School by Post as well as finding lost members of the Church. Miss Hasell's visit to the Keewatin area was an inadvertent and unpremeditated one, as she did not know she had crossed the diocesan boundary. But having made this discovery in 1937, she offered to repeat her visit in 1938, and the Bishop thought that with the increasing number of better roads there was an opportunity for caravan work.

In closing his Charge Bishop Dewdney spoke of the fifty-two years he had spent in the ministry and what he had tried to accomplish, especially during the seventeen and a half years he had been their Bishop. He felt that at his time of life it was in their interest and his own to leave the active work of the Diocese to a younger man, and so he had sent his resignation to the Metropolitan, effective September thirtieth. He ended, "I have enjoyed the years I have spent in the Diocese of Keewatin . . . and I have valued the opportunities of its service. I acknowledge that in all the past thirty-five years I have been supported by my partner in life who has aided me in every possible way. . . . But especially I acknowledge the Grace of Him for whom the Church exists and whose is the Kingdom, and the Power and the Glory. May He be with you in the days that are to come and crown with success the labours of him who will be called to be my successor."

In her own report, Mrs. Dewdney, as retiring President of the Diocesan Board of the W.A., said that the thirteen years she had held that office had been ones of happy fellowship with her fellow officers.

Bishop Joseph Lofthouse II

The Standing Committee of the Province on the Election of Bishops met at St. John's Cathedral, Winnipeg, on September 29, 1938. There never seems to have been any question as to who should be the third Bishop of Keewatin; the House of Bishops submitted the name of the Venerable Joseph Lofthouse, Archdeacon of Kenora, to the Standing Committee and this was accepted at once by a large majority. He was consecrated in St. Alban's Pro-Cathedral, Kenora, on November 30, by the Metropolitan (Harding). Bishop Lofthouse was then fifty-eight years of age, having been born at Wadsley, Sheffield, England, March 17, 1880.[14]

In his Charge to the eighteenth Synod of the Diocese, held on June 13, 1940 (his first), the new Bishop said of himself:

In 1904 the present Bishop came to the diocese as a student in training. . . . On May 12th, 1907, he was ordained deacon in St. Alban's, then on the hill overlooking the railway, and was appointed to Wabigoon and Gold Rock. The following year . . . he became incumbent of St. James Church, Rainy River. . . . He was made a Canon of St. Alban's Pro-Cathedral in 1914, and in September 1915 removal was made to Kenora to become General Missionary . . . until 1928 when he was appointed rector of St. Alban's, Kenora, having previously been instituted as Archdeacon of Kenora. . . . Thus the whole of my ministry has been exercised in the diocese of which I have the honour to be Bishop. . . .

In the meantime, it must be recorded that the Executive Committee of the Diocese met on September 8, 1938, and that at this meeting J. A. Kinney, K.C., was congratulated on his appointment as Chancellor of the Diocese. This was the last appointment made by Bishop Dewdney. Mr. Kinney, a leading solicitor of Kenora, had been a member of the executive since November, 1910, and had been appointed legal advisor to the Diocese on May 20, 1915. In 1943 Kinney was appointed one of the assessors to General Synod, an honour much appreciated by his friends in Keewatin.

The new Bishop was succeeded as rector of Kenora by the Reverend F. J. Boyd, who was inducted on April 2, 1939. Another interesting addition to the staff of the Diocese at the time was the Reverend R. F. Gibson, who, having been ordained on May 19, was appointed to the mission at Churchill. He was the son of the Reverend Canon Gibson who was rector of Kenora from 1913 to 1917.

Bishop Lofthouse, in his Charge, said that since his consecration he had confirmed 316 candidates and had visited all the northern missions except York. His own account of part of this visitation is an exceptionally interesting illustration of the way in which a Bishop gets around:

In June, 1939, I visited Trout Lake where the Rev. L. Garrett ministers to his people in a widely scattered mission, containing at that time by record, 1,059 Indians, practically all of our Church. Space does not permit me to go into details of the journey made by air, except to say, that as an effort towards economy, I travelled by plane 300 miles in company with two 500 pound steers. One side trip of some 100 miles to Round Lake was made by plane from Trout Lake, which took one hour. The return journey to Trout Lake by canoe

[14]A. R. Kelley and D. B. Rogers, *The Anglican Episcopate of Canada and Newfoundland*, II, 68-69.

took four long days of hard travel with 29 portages, many of them through swamp deep in water. After various services return was made direct to Kenora by plane. After a few necessary days at home I left for our missions in the Hudson Bay area, spending a long week-end at each mission, visiting Thicket Portage, Pikwitonei, Natawanan and Gillam in company with the Rev. H. S. Hughes-Caley. . . . From Gillam I retraced my steps by railway to Landing River where I was met by the Rev. G. C. Cowley, with whom I proceeded by canoe with outboard engine to Split Lake. . . . Leaving Split Lake we returned to Landing River. After spending a night at a hospitable bachelor home I took train for Churchill, where services were held for both the towns-people and the Indians, who had all, with the exception of two families, come in. A few Eskimo were also in from the north, and they attended some of the services.

About this time the Indian Affairs Branch of the Department of Mines and Resources began to cut its grants to the Indian schools on the grounds that the academic year was being reduced from ten months to nine, and in the case of the school at Jack River from $650 to $175 because of the smaller percentage of Indian children in attendance. These together meant a loss of $1,100 to the Diocese.

Then the new Pension Fund required greatly increased payments on behalf of the Diocese, which fell not only upon the Synod but also on the parishes. The S.P.G. and the C. and C.C.S. of England were continuing their grants for the current year, but the former might have to impose reductions the following year. These grants were not large and were reduced in any case by the adverse rate of exchange, though they were still essential to the work of the Diocese. The B.C.M.S. was continuing to support the Reverend L. Garrett at Trout Lake by direct payment to him, but here again the position was uncertain. Further, the General Synod apportionments were being increased with a view to eliminating special appeals, and this was producing another problem they would have to face. At that time there was rather soul-searching discussion in the General Synod area as to whether the Anglican Church in Canada should any longer accept grants from the missionary societies in England. This question was to be decided the same September at the meeting of the executive council in Stratford, in the declaration that the Church would no longer do so.

The Bishop of Keewatin, perhaps, saw this coming, for he wondered if they realized that the missionary societies of England provided $250,000 a year for church work in Canada, fully $50,000 more than they themselves normally raised each year through the M.S.C.C. apportionments. If those funds from England were withdrawn, the Anglican Church in Canada would be required to raise $450,000 a year to maintain the present work it was doing. Actually, after

General Synod had assumed full responsibilities, the dioceses and their parishes voluntarily accepted assessments that met the new situation.

One small but interesting item about Indian Missions appears at this time. The Mackay School at The Pas was destroyed by fire in 1933 and efforts had been made by the M.S.C.C. to have it replaced, but these had failed. The Diocese was appealing to the Indian Branch of the Department of Mines and Resources for a school farther north to benefit the Split Lake and York Factory areas. The department had acknowledged the receipt of this and filed it for future reference. A situation that arose in 1933 was not remedied until a new residential school, also bearing the name of Mackay, was opened at Dauphin, Manitoba, in 1957, several hundred miles away from the area it was supposed to serve.

The Bishop announced that he had appointed Canon F. C. Sevier, who had served the Diocese since 1903, as Archdeacon of Kenora.

The new approach of the Church to the matter of financial support after the Stratford meetings was marked by the visit of Bishop Sherman to the executive of the Diocese, which met on November 13, 1940. The minutes reveal that "three members of the W.A. joined us to hear the Bishop of Calgary give us an outline of the new budget plan, and after his forceful address, we accepted the M.S.C.C. Apportionment for the Diocese of $1,466.67. The diocesan budget assessment of $2,665, including the above for 1941, was approved." It was loyally supported by the parishes to the extent of over ninety-five per cent.

On December 29, 1940, the Reverend J. F. J. Marshall of Sioux Lookout died after a long illness. He had spent more than thirty years in the Diocese, first at Jack River mission, Norway House, where, in the words of Bishop Lofthouse, "he laboured with diligence and distinction" for sixteen years. He was appointed the first Principal of the new Indian Residential School, in which position he served, again to quote the Bishop, "with marked devotion and good judgment." The school was highly commended.

In 1942 the fortieth anniversary of the Diocese was commemorated at the Synod held on June 18. The Bishop pointed out that in 1902, "The Diocese consisted of eleven parishes or missions with eight priests and one deacon, together with six school teacher catechists, Rat Portage, now Kenora, being the only self-supporting parish. At this date in 1942 our full staff is nineteen clergy and five stipendiary and thirty honorary lay readers and catechists. We had for some years four self-supporting parishes or rectories, but changed conditions have reduced these to three, and one of these requires financial assistance. We now have twenty-two parishes and missions with thirty-six outstations where active work is carried on."

In order to give recognition to clergy who had readily assumed additional responsibilities in a diocese where advancement or promotion was limited, two new canonries were instituted to which were appointed the Reverends G. W. Plumridge of Dryden, who was the Bishop's Examining Chaplain, and F. J. Boyd, rector of St. Alban's Pro-Cathedral. The Reverend T. H. Broughton of Keewatin, who had succeeded the Bishop as Secretary of the Synod, was made Rural Dean of Kenora, an office that had lapsed for a number of years.

Archdeacon Sevier died suddenly on February 20, 1943. With the exception of a period from 1916 to 1918, during which he was on leave working in the Diocese of Nova Scotia, the whole of his ministry had been exercised in the Diocese of Keewatin. The Synod that met on June 20, 1944, expressed its appreciation of his diligent and faithful stewardship.

The Diocese was made very happy when St. John's College conferred the degree of D.D. upon Canon Maurice Sanderson. He had completed forty years service in the mission field the previous year. The removal of the Reverend R. T. Gibson from St. Paul's, Churchill, was viewed with regret. He had given outstanding service, both in the increasing "white work" there and with the Chipewyan people at North Knife River and Duck Lake, one hundred fifty miles northwest across the Barren Lands. He had gone to the residential school at Aklavik, work for which he was well qualified, and which it had always been his ambition to undertake.

Bishop Dewdney died at his home in Toronto on April 21, 1945, at the age of eighty-two, in the fifty-ninth year of his ministry and the twenty-fourth of his episcopate. The Diocese learned the news with sorrow, for it appreciated the efficient and devoted leadership that had been part of a life spent in diligent and faithful service in the cause of Christ and his Church.

The Synod, which met on June 11, 1946, was told of the impending retirement of the Venerable Richard Faries, who had resigned the incumbency of York Factory, which he had held since 1899. That summer, however, after spending the winter in Toronto, the Archdeacon and Mrs. Faries returned to York Factory, and his name does not actually appear on the retired list until 1952. The Venerable Henry Vaughan Maltby, Archdeacon of Rainy River, did retire on June 30, 1946, after spending the whole of his ministry since 1902 in the Diocese. He had been at Fort Frances for thirty-eight out of those fourty-four years.

Bishop Lofthouse spoke with force and eloquence on the Anglican

Advance Appeal for rededication and thanksgiving, of which the Diocese had been allotted $21,000 as its share, and outlined the organization being set up to achieve the objective.

The Bishop announced the appointment of two new Canons: "Our clergy in Indian work carry on with great zeal and devotion and are worthy of our grateful recognition. They are deprived of many facilities and social advantages considered by city and most town dwellers to be essential to a well-ordered life." This had led to his decision to appoint the Reverends W. H. J. Walter and G. C. Cowley as Honorary Canons of St. Alban's Pro-Cathedral. Canon Walter had been trained under the C.M.S. and had the L.Th. from Durham. Ordained in 1913, he had spent a short time in the Rainy River district before volunteering for work in the north. The main parts of his ministry had been at Split Lake, Norway House and Fort Alexander, covering twenty-eight of his thirty-three years in the Diocese. Canon Cowley had received his training in England but had not come to Canada until after the First World War, when he served on the staff of the Indian residential school at Elkhorn. During the sixteen years of his ministry at Split Lake he had been also teacher at the Indian day school.

In 1949 the Synod met for the first time outside Kenora, an invitation having been accepted to St. Luke's Church, Dryden, to mark the year of the dedication of this new church. It was also hoped that the meeting would provide a stimulus for the work of the Church in the parish, the Diocese and the Dominion. The Synod concurred in the regret expressed by the Bishop in the deaths of James Arthur Kinney, K.C., on February 18, 1947, at Gore Bay, Manitoulin Island, where he was Crown Attorney, and also of his Honour Judge William Woodworth Crow, K.C., of Fort Frances, who had been appointed Chancellor on June 15, 1947, in succession to Mr. Kinney, but never had the opportunity of exercising his office.

Among the changes in staff reported by Bishop Lofthouse was the ordination of L. C. Fryer, younger son of the late Reverend C. H. Fryer, who had been appointed to Norway House. In July of 1947 Sandy Clippings was ordained. A Chipewyan Indian, for many years he had ministered to his people as lay reader, and had been made deacon in the mission church at Duck Lake, one hundred and fifty miles northwest of Churchill. As far as was known, he was the first Chipewyan Indian to receive Holy Orders, a leader among his people, doing most faithful work.[15]

At the end of July, 1951, the Reverend T. H. Broughton retired.

[15]J. A. Davidson, "He served his People and his God," *Winnipeg Free Press* (January 9, 1959).

From 1922 to 1930 he had served at Lac du Bonnet, and from 1930, at Keewatin. Since 1940 he had been Secretary of the Synod.

The regular visitations of the Bishop to the northern missions well indicate the extent and success of work in a diocese where communications were often primitive. Those of 1949 to 1950 are worth recording in his own words; they were the last this Bishop Lofthouse made during his episcopate:

Shortly after our Synod of 1949 the Bishop left for Churchill where several days where spent. From thence he went to Duck Lake, our Chipewyan Indian Mission, 150 miles to the north-west, to return later to Churchill, from whence he journeyed by air to York Factory to join Archdeacon Faries who accompanied him to Shammattawa, where the Archdeacon remained for several days. Returning again to Churchill the Bishop took train to Landing River, and from that point he took canoe to Split Lake where a happy weekend was spent with Canon and Mrs. Cowley. Returning to the railway, train journey was taken to Gillam, thence south to Pikwitonei where the Rev. H. S. Hughes-Caley awaited him. By gravel train the Bishop journeyed to Waboden, and from thence across country to the Jack River Mission, Norway House, and later to Warren's Landing by canoe. At the nine mission centres visited, 156 candidates received the Laying on of Hands in Confirmation, and in most centres other services were held.

In the summer of 1950 visitations were made by air from Sioux Lookout to Big Trout Lake, from whence, accompanied by the Rev. Leslie Garrett visits were made to Sashige Lake, Bearskin Lake, Fort Severn on the shore of Hudson Bay with return to Trout Lake, thence to Kasabanekok, Big Beaver House, Round Lake, Nekip Lake, Cat Lake and Pickle Lake, the two latter being Ojibway Indian Missions, and the former eight Cree Indian Missions. In all 155 persons received Holy Communion, with some 1,200 in attendance, counting only one service at each place, there being often three services. Conferences were also held with groups of native catechists. Total offerings presented, and handed to the Bishop amounted to $696.00, and one elderly man handed to me an envelope containing $29.00 with which to purchase two large pictures for the Church at Bearskin Lake, which pictures, "The Light of the World" and "The Good Shepherd" were later purchased and sent. A visit was later made to the Lac Seul Mission where 12 candidates were confirmed, 46 persons receiving Holy Communion, 3 Marriages were solemnized; attendance at the morning service being 107.

He met the Synod of the Diocese of Keewatin for the last time as Bishop on June 16, 1953, and in his Charge spoke once again of the work of Archdeacon Faries.

The Ven. Archdeacon Faries, D.D., was appointed Missionary at York Factory in the year 1898 by Bishop Newnham, and there served for 53 years. He was appointed Archdeacon of York in 1917, being honoured by St. John's College, Winnipeg, in 1938 with the degree of Doctor of Divinity. He did a noble work among our Cree Indian people, and took a leading part in the production of a Cree Dictionary which is widely used. He also wrote a number of hymns in the language of the Cree Indians and saw a new Hymn Book through the press. In addition to his spiritual ministrations he was a master builder. He rebuilt the Church at York Factory (in 1934), and also the Church of St. Peter at Fort Severn, 200 miles down coast from York Factory, which Church was consecrated by the Bishop in 1943. Mrs. Faries, who had shared her husband's life and work at York Factory for upwards of forty years, passed away at Fort William on July 10th, 1951. On October 1st, 1951, Archdeacon Faries retired . . . at the ripe age of 82 years.

The Bishop also spoke of an innovation, as far as the Diocese was concerned, when he welcomed to the Synod Miss Margaret A. Etter as Bishop's Messenger and part-time secretary. Her services to the Diocese had been made possible by a special grant from the Dominion Board of the Woman's Auxiliary. Miss Etter later became Secretary-Treasurer of the Diocese.

In the spring of 1951 St. Mary's Church at Pointe de Bois had been destroyed by fire; a new church had been built by voluntary labour on a more suitable site. The chancel of the church at White Dog had been damaged by burning grass and had to be rebuilt. The foundations of the church at Dinorwic had been completely replaced by the Diocese.

At the close of the Synod, Bishop Lofthouse announced that he had submitted his resignation to the Metropolitan of Rupert's Land, to be effective December 30. He had been nearly fifty years in the Diocese, forty-six in Holy Orders, but he now felt no longer able to undertake the exacting duties and extensive travel required in a diocese such as Keewatin. The members of the Synod told him that his long and faithful service, devoted Christian witness, and missionary zeal throughout the years would long be remembered with profound love and affection. The Bishop was then in the seventy-third year of his age, the forty-sixth of his ministry, and the fifteenth of his episcopate.

Bishop H. E. Hives

The Electoral Committee of the Ecclesiastical Province met on October 8, 1953, under the presidency of the new Metropolitan, the Most Reverend W. F. Barfoot, elected to this position only the day before. On the sixth ballot the Venerable Harry E. Hives, Archdeacon in charge of Indian Missions in the Diocese of Saskatoon was elected Bishop of Keewatin. He was consecrated in the Pro-Cathedral, Kenora, on January 6, 1954, by the Metropolitan (Barfoot), and enthroned the same evening.

Bishop Hives brought to his work a singularly wide experience in Indian mission work, to which practically the whole of his ministry had been devoted. An excellent Cree scholar, he was able to speak and write the language fluently. Ordained deacon in 1926 by Bishop Lloyd of Saskatchewan, upon his graduation in Arts from the University of Saskatchewan and in Theology from Emmanuel College (where he took honours in Licentiate of Theology), he was at Cumberland House from 1926 to 1929, and then moved north to Lac la Ronge, where he remained from 1929 to 1938. In that year he left the Diocese of Saskatchewan for that of Saskatoon, and was for two years at Paynton, and then again for two years at Lashburn, both parishes in the Battle River Valley. In 1943 he removed to Battleford, at the centre of a number of Indian Reserves in that part of the country, and in 1945 became the Bishop's Commissary in Indian work. His election was evidence of the rising feeling of responsibility in the Church with regard to its Indian Missions, which form such a large part of the work carried on in the Diocese of Keewatin.[16]

[16]Kelley and Rogers, *op. cit.*, 138-139.

CHAPTER SIXTEEN

The Subdivision of the Diocese of Rupert's Land: The Diocese of Brandon

••◆❄❄◆••◆❄❄◆•••◆❄❄◆•••◆❄❄◆•••◆❄❄◆•••◆❄❄◆•••◆❄❄◆•••◆❄❄◆••

The present Session is one of profound and momentous importance, for we have gathered for the first time as Bishop, Clergy and Laity for the management of the temporal affairs of a new Diocese, and we are also charged in the Providence of God, with the solemn responsibility of laying the foundation of what, in due time, we hope may prove one of the most progressive Dioceses in Western Canada. "The lot has fallen to us in a fair ground, yea we have a goodly heritage," and I feel that our ambition should be to maintain with fidelity the great traditions and standards of Rupert's Land while reaching upward to achievement and standards of our own.

BISHOP THOMAS: FIRST CHARGE TO THE
SYNOD OF THE DIOCESE OF BRANDON.
November 10, 1925.

••◆❄❄◆••◆❄❄◆•••◆❄❄◆•••◆❄❄◆•••◆❄❄◆•••◆❄❄◆•••◆❄❄◆•••◆❄❄◆••

It was stated in chapter eleven that the first proposals for the division of the Diocese of Rupert's Land originated in its western part, and were discussed at the Synod of 1911. At the Synod of 1912, the required application for such a division was approved and placed before the Provincial Synod of Rupert's Land at its meeting on August 27, 1913, which in turn gave its approval and set up the boundaries of the new diocese, but left it under the jurisdiction and administration of the Bishop of Rupert's Land until such time as he, as Metropolitan, was satisfied that funds had been provided sufficiently to support a bishop.

The First World War postponed all further discussion and action in the matter, and for ten years the western part of the Diocese was almost completely administered by Archdeacon W. W. H. Thomas. After the war, the Diocese of Rupert's Land was rather more concerned with doing its share in the Anglican Forward Movement, and commemorating the centenary of the founding of the work of the Anglican Church in western Canada, but by 1924 matters were sufficiently advanced for definite action to be taken to establish the Diocese of Brandon.

On June 4, 1924, Archbishop Matheson opened the first Synod of the Diocese of Brandon in St. Matthew's Church, Brandon.[1] Clergy and lay delegates represented the parishes within the boundaries stated by the resolution of the Provincial Synod of Rupert's Land in 1913. In his Charge the Archbishop explained the long delay in the actual separation of the Diocese from Rupert's Land; it had seemed more prudent to him to continue the administration of the area within Rupert's Land until the endowment had been completed, and he cited the cases of Calgary and Kootenay as examples that justified his action.

In the formal records and journals of the Dioceses of both Rupert's Land and Brandon there is singularly little information on some points of interest. For example, there is no statement as to the origins or amount of the endowment for the new bishopric; some indication of its source is to be found in later journals, but even these have nothing specific. Presumably, this arises from the fact that a bishop is often incorporated as a "Corporation Sole"; this provides for continuity in the office of bishop, but appears to remove all outside and lay concern for its maintenance. It seems unfortunate that in an age when the real value of money is unstable this reticence about such funds should be maintained; the more so because it has produced from time to time what may be unjustifiable criticism respecting the Church's funds and accounting, and has placed some bishops in an embarrassing situation when the value of their stipend deteriorated.

The formal business of the session opened with the reading of the resolution of the Provincial Synod of 1913, setting up and describing the boundaries of the new Diocese of Brandon. The Synod then proceeded to elect its Bishop; on the third ballot, the Venerable W. W. H. Thomas was declared elected; his name had been the first choice in each of them.

Wilfrid William Henry Thomas
First Bishop of Brandon

Bishop Thomas was consecrated in St. Matthew's Church, Brandon, on September 7, 1924, by the Metropolitan (Matheson). Bishops Harding and De Pencier, who took part in the consecration, were both former rectors of St. Matthew's, Brandon. Bishop Thomas was enthroned the same evening in St. Matthew's Church, later to be formally declared the Pro-Cathedral of the diocese.

Wilfrid William Henry Thomas was born at Tenby on the Pembrokeshire coast of South Wales on April 6, 1875, and educated in the church schools there; later he attended St. Paul's Missionary

---

[1]*Journal of the Synod of the Diocese of Rupert's Land, 1924.* The Minutes of the First Synod of the Diocese of Brandon are incorporated in this. They have not otherwise been published.

College at Burgh in Lincolnshire and completed his training at St. Augustine's College in Canterbury. In pursuit of his vocation to missionary work, he came to Canada late in 1897, but being under canonical age when he arrived at Hamilton, Ontario, he was ordained on January 2, 1898, by Bishop DuMoulin of Niagara in Christ Church Cathedral, under a special faculty from Archbishop Frederick Temple of Canterbury. He came west to Winnipeg in 1899 as second rector of St. Luke's Church. From 1901 to 1916, Bishop Thomas was rector of Christ Church, Selkirk, Manitoba, and after that spent eight years as general missionary and Archdeacon of Western Manitoba in the Diocese of Rupert's Land. He therefore brought to his work a very intimate knowledge and experience of the area that comprised the new Diocese, for, with the exception of the episcopal function of confirmation, its supervision and development had largely been in his hands during that time. He was the trusted friend and adviser of the people.[2]

The new Diocese was a curious mixture, geographically, economically and ethnically, of the old and the new. One hundred and twenty miles east and west, its northern boundary, at the time of its formation, was on the northern boundary of Township 44, 264 miles north of the International Boundary; the southern portion, of which the city of Brandon is approximately at the centre, is for the most part rolling prairie that has been settled between forty and fifty years, and is largely devoted to grain growing. North of the Riding Mountain Reserve, which ten years later was to be developed as a national park, there were several pockets of excellent agricultural land. Between the Riding Mountain Reserve and the Duck Mountain Reserve was the Dauphin-Gilbert Plains country on the east side of the Diocese, with an area of about 2,500 square miles. On the west side of the Reserves was a smaller pocket (which might be termed the Roblin district) of about 800 square miles; still farther north, between the Duck Mountain Reserve and the Porcupine Mountain Reserve, there was a 1,000 square-mile tract in the Swan River valley. In the southern area, the railway lines of the C.P.R. and the C.N.R. ran chiefly east and west, while the line of the Hudson's Bay division pursued its twisted route west of Lakes Manitoba and Winnipegosis along the eastern edge of the forest reserves, breaking out lines to the west from Dauphin and Swan River in between them.

Few of the northern roads were more than dirt trails, for in 1924 the government programme of road improvement was still in its infancy, and even in the well-settled southern part of the province

[2]O. R. Rowley, *The Anglican Episcopate of Canada and Newfoundland*, 194-195.

only a few of the roads were gravelled. The rest of the Diocese consisted of 13,000 square miles of forest reserves and lakes. Thus, at the outset, Bishop and Diocese were not only faced with the problem of communications, but the further problem that except for Brandon itself, the whole Diocese was an agricultural community, and still a pioneer and lumbering one in the northern section. In one respect, the Diocese of Brandon was unique; Diocese and physical resources development had not grown up together.

The Second Synod: Organization

The second Synod of the Diocese of Brandon was held November 10, 1925, with thirty out of thirty-five listed clergy, and seventy out of one hundred and thirty-two lay delegates, present. Bishop Thomas was an eloquent speaker with a facility of phrase that is still delightful to read. He began his Charge by apologizing for calling the Synod so late in the year, but unavoidable delay had been caused by the necessity of organizing the Diocese. The Bishop then cheerily remarked that its date would be a test of the often expressed wish for winter Synods. (All Synods of the Diocese after that were held in the summer.)

Bishop Thomas told the Synod that his preliminary visitation would be completed by the end of November; by then he would have visited every parish in the Diocese at least once. He had confirmed 1,012 candidates, 229 of them adults, and dedicated churches at Bowsman, Miniota and Makinak. Eight clergy had left the Diocese, but had been replaced by five from other dioceses, and three ordinations. He had appointed Mr. G. B. Coleman, K.C., of Brandon as Chancellor, and Mr. H. L. Rixon as Registrar. The Diocese had been reorganized into seven rural deaneries, this being necessitated by the revision of boundaries upon becoming independent. St. Matthew's, Brandon, would be the Pro-Cathedral, and the W.A. had been reorganized on a diocesan basis. The Bishop announced a forward movement in mission work within the Diocese; Miss Eva Hasell had offered in the winter of 1924-1925 to raise enough funds in England to provide the cost of a Sunday School van, and had placed herself and a fellow worker at their disposal to work for a whole summer at no cost. The van, dedicated to St. David, had travelled 2,867 miles in the northern part of the territory, 506 homes were visited, eighteen Sunday School by Post Sunday Schools started, and 1,068 children were placed on the Sunday School by Post roll. The van was to be theirs as long as they could use it, and the Bishop had applied to the

Dominion Board of the W.A. for assistance in carrying on the work in 1926.

The report of the executive committee mentioned that St. Matthew's parish was asked to increase the published number of the *Pro-Cathedral Magazine* by one hundred as a preliminary to establishing a diocesan one. This hope was realized in the spring of 1927; the circulation rapidly increased to twelve hundred copies, and it continued to prosper for many years under the skilful management of John Popkin.

The Synod, which met in June, 1927, was largely concerned with Canons and Constitution, but steps were also taken to provide a See House at a cost not exceeding $15,000.

The Bishop commented on conditions in the Deaneries of Dauphin and Swan River, and asked for the establishment of a fund of $40,000 to set up an Archdeaconry of Dauphin and so provide a much needed travelling priest in the northern area. He had already appealed to the National Assembly of the Church of England and the S.P.G. for some assistance in handling this missionary work. The Episcopal Endowment Fund was reported to have reached the sum of $80,500, most of which had been invested in fully-registered government bonds, and he was himself treasurer of the fund, which was now a Trust of the Synod of the Diocese. The work of the Reverend H. L. Roy in connection with the diocesan budget was warmly commended. Mr. Roy, rector of Rapid City, had worked for many years in Rupert's Land as assistant general missionary.

The Anglican Commission

The year 1928 saw the beginnings of a new approach to the problems of the Anglican Church in Canada, in the appointment of three Field Commissioners (Bishop Owen of the Diocese of Niagara, Canon Gould, Secretary of the M.S.C.C., and Chancellor F. H. Gisbourne of Ottawa), whose duty it was to visit every diocese and bring before General Synod an over-all picture of present work and future needs of the Church. They began their visitation with the Diocese of Brandon, where, according to Bishop Thomas, they were welcomed with open arms. "We endeavoured to make clear to them some of the problems that confront us, and we hope they carried away a correct impression of our real position. Their visit was one of great stimulation to the Diocese generally, and we trust that the supreme object of the survey, which is to develop a deeper and more fruitful sense of corporate unity and responsibility throughout the whole Church will be abundantly blessed. . . ." When he met the fourth Synod in June,

1929, one of the problems he had to present to the members had already been discussed with the Commissioners.

The Bishop stated that it was common knowledge that a proposal had been made to add to the Diocese a large section of northern Manitoba that lay north of Township 44 and comprised about 250,000 square miles. This territory was actually in the Diocese of Saskatchewan, but boundaries set up in 1873 were rather indeterminate: "The Diocese of Saskatchewan is to consist of the Districts of the Saskatchewan and English River, with the sub-district of Fort la Corne in the Cumberland District." This had made the Diocese of Saskatchewan extend from the mouth of the Saskatchewan River as far west as the town of Vermilion in Alberta, a reasonable and accessible piece of country at that time when rivers were the highways of travel, but out-dated fifty years later by railways and settlements.

In 1926 the Provincial Synod of Rupert's Land had agreed to the transfer of the portion of the Diocese of Saskatchewan that lay in Alberta to the Diocese of Edmonton. Bishop Lloyd of Saskatchewan wished to release that portion of his diocese that lay in Manitoba to either Rupert's Land or Brandon, or both.

One would gather from the Synod journals that Bishop Lloyd approached Bishop Thomas in the matter after it had been discussed with the Field Commissioners of General Synod, with a view to securing an agreement between the Dioceses as to the resolution to be placed before the Provincial Synod at its meeting in 1929. After outlining the Indian work and mining developments that might be brought under his jurisdiction by this scheme, Bishop Thomas said, "The position I took at that time, and still maintain, is that the Diocese will be ready to accept responsibility for the increased area if the M.S.C.C. is willing to assist the project financially during the initial years and makes some permanent provision for the maintenance of the Indian work within the area. A study of the situation, as outlined by the Bishop of Saskatchewan, reveals the fact that, apart from the self-supporting Parish of The Pas, the existing work requires considerable financial support, and that a great deal of new work awaits commencement. . . . The cost to the Diocese for the maintenance of this work, that is the work now in hand, would be in the neighbourhood of $4,000 per annum, which amount would be increased as the work enlarges."

When the Provincial Synod met in Calgary on September 11, 1929, a memorial was presented by the Diocese of Saskatchewan asking that its Manitoba section be handed over to the Diocese of Rupert's Land, Brandon, or both as of October first. The Synod passed this on to the Committee on Boundaries with an attached request that the House of

Bishops be asked to arrange a joint session to discuss the committee's report. Before this was received, Chancellor Ford introduced a lengthy amendment to the Constitution of the Provincial Synod that would have set up a form of judicial commission to settle matters pertaining to diocesan boundaries. The House of Bishops felt that the amendment should be referred back to the Committee on Constitutions and Canons, and brought up again at the next Synod. In the meantime, the report of the Committee on Boundaries was presented. It included a recommendation, which had been carried in committee by ten votes to nine, that this Manitoba section of Saskatchewan should be added to the Diocese of Rupert's Land if that Diocese would accept it before January first, 1930, but that if it failed to do so the section should become part of the Diocese of Brandon. Upon reception of this report, the Bishop of Saskatchewan informed the Synod that this disposition was not agreeable to him; therefore, he had ordered the original petition of his Diocese to be withdrawn. Referring to this in his Charge to the Synod of the Diocese of Brandon in June of 1931, Bishop Thomas said:

Two months later, namely in November 1929, I was urged by the Bishop of Saskatchewan to administer the whole area for a period of six months under his commission, and with the consent of the Metropolitan [Matheson] and the approval of our own Executive Committee [November 15], I agreed so to do . . . looking at the matter from every point of view, I am still of the opinion that this area on account of its location falls naturally to our lot. . . . We can, I think, justly claim that our temporary administration of the area has been beneficial to it. . . . This eminently satisfactory state of affairs is the result of the splendid work and management of our Superintendent of Northern Missions, Rev. W. Brailsford, who, at my request "went in and possessed the land."

Mr. Brailsford was rector of Christ Church, The Pas, from 1919 to 1927. In 1931 he became rector of Dauphin, but continued the superintendency of the area "North of 53" until he returned to England in 1935.[3]

The Provincial Synod next met in Winnipeg in September, 1933, and a lengthy report was presented to it by the Committee on Boundaries. By this time the loss of many of the endowment funds of the West through the Machray defalcations had necessarily changed the thinking of the delegates, and the report of the committee contained four definite recommendations, three of which were specifically agreed to by the Synod: the transfer of the Diocese of Moosonee to the Ecclesiastical Province of Ontario, the transfer of the

[3]*Crockford's Clerical Directory, 1936*, p. 145.

Diocese of the Yukon to the Ecclesiastical Province of British Columbia,[4] and the division of the Diocese of Saskatchewan within the limits of the civil province of that name, whereby it was continued as the Diocese of Saskatoon and the new Diocese of Saskatchewan was set up. The transfer of the Manitoba section of the original Diocese of Saskatchewan was never specifically made by definite resolution of the Synod, but agreed to, apparently, by the acceptance of the report of the Boundaries Committee and the concurrence of the House of Bishops with that report.[5]

In between the Synods of 1929 and 1933, the Bishop of Brandon, at the request of Bishops Lloyd and Hallam of Saskatchewan, continued to administer and develop the work of the Church in the area as though it properly belonged to the Diocese of Brandon. The western boundary, which coincided with that of the Province of Manitoba, was always fixed, but the eastern boundary remained indeterminate as to any exactness, until the Provincial Synod of 1956.[6].

The situation with regard to the northern section of the original diocese, particularly the districts of Swan River Valley and Duck Mountain, was a much happier one, and in 1929 the Bishop was able to report very real progress. In the summer of 1928 Mrs. Holland, the Overseas Secretary of the Mothers' Union in the Diocese of Worcester, England, made a tour of part of western Canada, including the Diocese of Brandon. She spent a month in the Diocese, accompanied the Bishop when he visited the Elkhorn Indian School, and Sioux Mission, and journeyed more than four hundred miles in the Sunday School caravan, St. David.

Mrs. Holland sponsored an appeal for the Pioneer Priest Endowment Fund, with and through the S.P.G., and pledged herself to provide for the expense of maintaining a travelling priest during the five years it would take to raise such an endowment. The first step was taken by using the town of Swan River as a centre, and the

[4]The transfer of the Diocese of Yukon to the Ecclesiastical Province of British Columbia was not completed until December 8, 1941.
[5]*Journal of the Provincial Synod of Rupert's Land, 1933*, p. 45; Message 24 from the House of Delegates to the House of Bishops. *Ibid.*, 49: Message "T" from the House of Bishops to the House of Delegates. *Ibid.*, 106-109; Appendix vi, Report of Committee on Diocesan Boundaries, Clause B5, p. 107.
[6]*Ibid.*, 1899, pp. 33-34. The western boundary of the Diocese of Keewatin is defined as being coincident with the western boundary of the District of Keewatin, apparently as shown on the map issued by the Department of the Interior "to December 31st, 1882," which was made the basis of all diocesan boundaries in the Province of Rupert's Land by the Provincial Synod of 1883. On this map the junction of the northern and eastern boundaries of the old District of Saskatchewan appears to be on a township line just north of Latitude 55°N. The subsequent extension of the northern boundaries of the prairie provinces to Latitude 60°N, and the adjustment of the eastern boundary of Saskatchewan to the line between Ranges 29 and 30 West of the First Principal Meridian, produced more complications in the determination of the limits of this part of the old Diocese of Saskatchewan.

Reverend Ivor A. Norris was appointed to the post. He also served the district between Lake Dauphin and Lake Manitoba, a large area with a small scattered population. In addition he superintended the work of lay readers and students from St. John's College, who were placed at convenient railway centres during the summer months.

Bishop's Messengers

Bishop Thomas told the Synod of 1929 that he was able to record some advance in solving the problem of the northern portion of the Diocese being deplorably undermanned. The exploratory work of their St. David's van during four summer seasons had revealed that in the Riding Mountain area there were twenty-two settlements, in none of which had the Church of England any footing; in the inter-lake district (between Lakes Dauphin and Winnipegosis), there were seventy-four settlements, in only four of which could they claim to be definitely engaged; in the Swan River Valley there were fifty settlements, but in only twenty of them had they a mission. So far they had tried to carry on with seven lay readers and priests at Dauphin and Swan River, but there still remained much to do:

In the spring of last year [1928] Miss Fowler volunteered to come to the Diocese and serve as a voluntary missionary in our outlying parts. On her arrival in Canada, and after appointing her Bishop's Messenger I sent her forth to the Swan River Valley to labour in the districts hitherto untouched by the Church. She has now completed one year of work, the results of which have been so remarkable that I have decided to establish an Order of voluntary Messengers, and to extend their operations over the whole northern field. For this purpose we intend as soon as we are able, to build a central home for the voluntary Messengers at Swan River, and also to build mission shacks at selected centres of their work. This is a great forward movement, and I trust it will be blessed by Him in whose Name this venture of faith is being made.

Miss Marguerite D. Fowler, in a little book published in 1950 by the S.P.G., about what has become known as St. Faith's Mission, says that in 1926 she paid a long promised visit to the United States and Canada. During the summer she stopped off at Winnipeg to visit a family she had known since her childhood, who many years before had taken up a homestead about one hundred and twenty-five miles north of the city. They told her how much they missed the Church, and the following Sunday there came to her the sudden inspiration that she might work for God in some isolated district in western Canada. Upon her return to England, she asked the advice of Canon Stacy Waddy of the S.P.G., who told her that if she trained at St. Christopher's College, Blackheath, he was sure some western Canadian bishop would accept her for the work she wanted to do. At St. Christopher's she heard for the first time of Miss Eva Hasell and her Sunday School caravans, and later Miss Hasell put her in touch with the Bishop of Brandon, who accepted her offer to work. Miss Muriel Secretan had offered to come out and help her for a couple of years. Miss Fowler suggested the name of "Bishop's Messengers" as it had been used for groups of women in England who had taken part in the Mission of Repentance and Hope during the First World War. Her licence from the Bishop was similar to that of a lay reader and included "the taking of Services and administering comfort to the isolated and sick." Also, "in the absence of a Priest or Deacon to baptize children in danger of death and to bury the dead."

Swan River thus became, in the summer of 1928, the centre of the greatest effort in missionary work by women in any diocese in western Canada, for the work did not stop on the northern boundary of Township 44 but eventually was extended to the mining developments north of the town of The Pas, and within a few years what might be termed "subsidiary houses" were founded just over the borders of the Diocese at Fort Pelly in the Diocese of Saskatchewan and Eriksdale in the inter-lake region of the Diocese of Rupert's Land.

The work of the Bishop's Messengers took its first step outside the immediate district of Swan River by establishing a mission, in 1929, at Birch River, a small town on the railway line about twenty-five miles to the north. Here a house was secured and converted into suitable premises, which included a small chapel. This work was completed by December of 1930, through generous help given by the children's congregation of Sherborne Abbey in Dorset, England. In the spring of 1932, a Messenger, Miss R. F. Pennell, was permanently located at this town. Later, in March of 1936, Birch River became probably the first pioneer village to hold a parochial mission, conducted by a young priest, the Reverend L. F. Wilmot, then rector of Swan River. Subsequently he was for some years travelling priest in the northern part of the Diocese, an army chaplain overseas who did conspicuous service in the Italian Campaign of World War II, Western Field Secretary of the General Board of Religious Education, and finally Warden of St. John's College, Winnipeg.

Some brief reference may be made to some general matters in the life of the Diocese, to be found in the minutes of the executive committee. November 15, 1929: a gift of £300 to the Parish of McCreary, and £400 for the church at Kenville was announced. St. Michael's, McCreary, was built through the interest of Mrs. Holland. April 24, 1930: the last payment of its share in the income of the endowment funds of the Diocese of Rupert's Land was received, and a grant of

$1,500 from the M.S.C.C. for the work north of Township 44 was announced; at the meeting on November 21, word came of the formation of a Brandon Diocesan Association in England.

Women's Work in the Church

When Bishop Thomas met his Synod again in June of 1933, he devoted a considerable portion of his Charge to the work of women in the Church, particularly concerning the status of deaconesses. This matter had been discussed several years before at a meeting of General Synod, and also formed part of the report of the National Anglican Commission, which had recommended that women should be admitted to those councils of the Church to which laymen were admitted, and on equal terms. The Diocese of Brandon had already made much larger use of the services of women than most Canadian dioceses in work of the Church for which they were specially fitted, and for which the Bishop felt the opportunities were unparalleled. It is a matter of record that the Diocese of Saskatchewan had for more than twenty-five years recognized the Order of Deaconesses, established a house for them in Saskatoon, which had become the centre of Sunday School by Post and of social service work, but it had not used them out in the rural parts the way that the Diocese of Brandon had used its valiant Bishop's Messengers. The Synod of the Diocese of Brandon deferred action, and after twenty years the situation appears to be little changed; the status of the Order of Deaconesses or of Bishop's Messengers has never been settled, though now at Synods it has been customary to give them "the courtesy of the floor of the House."

The Synod of 1946 by unanimous decision gave to all Bishop's Messengers the status of lay delegates to the Synod, but the Synod of 1948 was informed by the Chancellor that the vote on this point had been unconstitutional; in the estimation of the executive it was meaningless, as lay delegates were required to be elected. After further discussion section two of the constitution was amended by adding, "It is provided, however, that Bishop's Messengers attached to St. Faith's and commissioned by the Bishop may be elected as Lay Delegates by the congregation to whom they are ministering." This being carried unanimously by both orders voting separately, it became effective immediately.

Indian Work in the Diocese of Brandon

Compared with other western dioceses, it seems strange to find very little about Indian Missions in the Journals of the Synods of Brandon during the first ten years of its existence as an independent Diocese.

There were several points where work among the Indians had been long established. The oldest of these was probably the Kinosota (originally known as Staggville) district, which lay on the west side of Lake Manitoba, with the small Reserves of Sandy Bay to the south and "Ebb and Flow" to the north. This district was originally served from the Fairford Mission, about fifty miles away to the northeast, on the other side of the lake. Fairford was established by the Reverend Abraham Cowley in 1842, but the work on the west side of Lake Manitoba will always be associated with the names of the Reverend William Stagg and James Settee.

With the coming of settlers in the early seventies, this part of Manitoba ceased to be country through which the Indian could roam. Gladstone, for example, originally known as Palestine, was a town of some size by 1881. Plumas, further north, was settled only a few years later, and there was enough grain to be hauled out of the lakeshore district to justify construction of a railway line to Amaranth about the turn of the century.

How the countryside received its ministrations is somewhat obscure, as the presence of an ordained clergyman at Plumas, the nearest point, seems to have been irregular, and probably most of the credit should go to the Scrase family who farmed a few miles to the south at Bluff Creek for a great many years. H. H. Scrase, ably assisted by his wife, carried on the work of the Church in this district from 1913 to 1940, and he was succeeded in December of that year by the Reverend George Snape, who was there until 1943. For some time Bishop Thomas had planned to place Bishop's Messengers in this district, and in November of that year Miss Frances Wilmot, who had been Messenger for a number of years at Birch River, moved to Kinosota. Most of the time, until she was transferred in 1950 to the supervision of youth work in the Diocese under the W.A., she carried on the work at Kinosota by herself.

A new mission house was built in 1944, and Kinosota became the centre for vocational schools, missions and other activities in the district. The ministrations during these years were conducted by Archdeacon Norris, and each year the Bishop had large Confirmation classes, a great achievement in a district noted for its bad roads. At the time of writing, the work is still in the hands of the Bishop's Messengers.

The second point was at Shoal River Reserve, on the south side of Dawson Bay at the north end of Lake Winnipegosis, where the Swan River, having traversed Swan Lake, flowed into the larger body of water. The details of this mission, which lay on the borders of the Saskatchewan valley, are missing. It is stated in *One Day Telleth*

Another[7] that it was commenced about 1879 by the Reverend George Bruce of Fairford, who was in charge of that mission from 1868 for forty-three years, with the assistance of the Hudson's Bay Company post manager and Keuper Garrioch, who was still alive in 1934. Recording from what is available, one learns that from 1898 to 1906 it was served by a young clergyman named Alfred Thomas Norquay.[8] A note in the report of the rural dean of Dauphin to the Diocese of Rupert's Land in 1917 states that a new church was under construction at that time. A student of St. John's College, Winnipeg, T. D. Conlin, was then in charge. After his ordination in 1918 Conlin gave the first ten years of his ministry to Indian work (Fairford 1918-1923, Scanterbury, 1923-1928).[9] The Reverend C. E. Cooke, who was ordained by Bishop Thomas in 1925, was at the mission until he retired about 1940; he died in 1948. Cooke was followed by Gilbert Hicks as stipendiary lay reader, who was ordained by Bishop Thomas in 1949.

The third, and most important, was the Indian School at Elkhorn that was founded in the 1880's by the same Reverend Edward Francis Wilson who had been responsible for the foundation of the Shingwauk School in the Diocese of Algoma. The intimate history of this school is difficult to trace; practically no references are made to it in the Journals of the Synod of Brandon and no indication as to who were its principals. In the Journal of the Provincial Synod of 1896, it is listed as one of the three industrial schools, with ninety pupils. In 1899 the only entry is under the title "Washakada Homes, Elkhorn, Principal, Mr. A. E. Wilson, 70 pupils, largely supported by the government," which puts it in practically the same category as the Middlechurch, Manitoba, Battleford, Saskatchewan and Calgary, Alberta, industrial schools.[10] Archdeacon Tims, who became Permanent Secretary of the Provincial Synod Indian Missions Committee, reported in 1926[11] that in Brandon the Elkhorn Residential School had been reopened, the only such school in the Diocese of Brandon, and the figure of one hundred twenty-six pupils would seem to apply to it. This school, however, had come under the management of the

[7]C. E. Cooke, "Shoal River Indian Mission," *One Day Telleth Another* (Brandon, Synod Office, 1934), 66-67.

[8]*Crockford's Clerical Directory, 1925,* p. 1119.

[9]*Ibid.,* 1957-1958, p. 235.

[10]S. J. Wickens, "Indian Residential Schools, Elkhorn," *One Day Telleth Another,* 58-60.

[11]*Journal of the Provincial Synod of Rupert's Land, 1923,* p. 69, Appendix 4. *Ibid.,* 1926, pp. 25-28, 68. The absence of the "triennial report" for so long a period was explained as due to the death of Canon W. A. Burman in 1910, and no election of anyone in his place until 1916, when Canon E. K. Matheson was appointed secretary.

Indian Schools Commission of the M.S.C.C., and in the report of 1950 it is not listed.

During the years when it was open, Elkhorn School did excellent work. It had been relocated on a new site in 1897 and performed useful service until 1918, when it was closed. In the summer of 1923 the buildings were repaired and extended and reopened in 1924. When the Diocese of Brandon celebrated its tenth anniversary in 1935, one hundred forty-two boys and one hundred twenty-eight girls had passed through the school in the previous eleven years; there were thirty-two boys and sixty-seven girls currently enrolled, who had come chiefly from the Dioceses of Brandon, Rupert's Land and Keewatin, representing the four tribes of Cree, Sioux, Ojibway and Salteaux. The school raised much of its own food on its half section of land, and the training of the pupils was on the practical side to make them better farmers.

Its closing was probably determined by the policy of the Indian Department, after the Second World War, to educate Indian children in their natural surroundings on their own Reserves, and as many of the children came from Reserves where trapping and fishing were the main occupations, it seemed a reasonable policy. This change was welcomed by many of the missionaries engaged in Indian work who felt that they had a better opportunity to approach the Indian in the natural environment of the family.

The fourth centre of Indian work in the Diocese of Brandon was the Sioux Mission on the sandy hills north of the Assiniboine valley at Griswold. These Indians were really Dakotas who had come across the Canadian border as refugees following the Indian war in 1876. This was a very natural move on their part as they had long been accustomed to travel a trail that passed through Portage la Prairie to Lake Manitoba, though in the earlier years of the Red River Colony their visits to the Canadian side had been anticipated with trepidation and anxiety because of their warlike nature. After 1876 they were settled by the Dominion government on four Reserves, Portage la Prairie, Pipestone, Deloraine and Griswold, and took to agricultural life very well. There seems to have been no question of their loyalty to their adopted country, for there was no indication of any thought on their part in 1885 to participate in the Riel troubles in Saskatchewan. The largest settlement at Griswold attracted the attention of Bishop Machray, and through his efforts an old student of St. John's College, the Reverend W. A. Burman, just ordained deacon, was sent to the Reserve in 1879.[12] He made arrangements for the establishment of a permanent mission, and returned in the summer of 1880

[12]*Crockford's Clerical Directory, 1908,* p. 210.

by the steamship *Marquette*, accompanied by his wife, household goods, a year's supply of provisions, a cow, pony, plow, harrows and a buckboard. A new house had been built on the flats by the Assiniboine River, as the government frowned upon any white inhabitants on a Reserve, but the flooding of the river at this point forced the Burmans to live in a tent on the high ground of the Reserve most of the summer. In 1882 the house was pulled down and rebuilt where they had been camping.

The first church was commenced in 1887 and was just framework covered with canvas, but good progress was made in the mission, particularly with the children attending Sunday School. The influx of settlers, accompanying construction of the Canadian Pacific Railway about 1883, produced a change in the country, especially to the north and south of the mission. The town of Griswold was established and a church was built, about the same time as the church on the Reserve.

There is little information about the Sioux Mission for the next sixteen years, but in 1906 the Reverend John A. Maggrah was appointed to the mission, where he stayed until 1914. Mr. Maggrah was a graduate in Theology of St. John's, Winnipeg, and is said to have been of Sioux ancestry. After his ordination in 1893 he had worked at the White Dog, or Islington, Mission, at the junction of the English and Winnipeg Rivers in Ontario, until 1901.[13] During his eight year incumbency at Griswold, the old church was dismantled and the present St. Luke's was built about 1910. About the same time a commodious mission house was erected just to the northwest of the church; as both are on a hilltop they are almost as conspicuous on the landscape as the old cemetery itself, which is dominated by a large wooden cross.

The story of this mission is again obscure until after 1925. Bishop Thomas appointed Deaconess Winifred H. Stapleton to the Sioux Reserve in the spring of 1927, who brought with her Miss Lena Wilkins as co-worker. Miss Stapleton had come to Canada in 1912 after training at the C.M.S. Institution in London, received her deaconess's orders from Bishop Newnham of Saskatchewan shortly after her arrival, and had been sent by him to the Lac la Ronge Indian School, then under the direction of Archdeacon J. A. Mackay. Miss Wilkins had joined the staff of the same school later and together they had gone to the Peigan School in southern Alberta. For five years they had been responsible for the Peguis Mission, north of

[13]*Ibid., 1925*, p. 992. J. A. Maggrah was at Moose Factory Indian School from 1927 to 1929, then returned to Russell, Manitoba, in the Diocese of Brandon, where he died in the spring of 1930.

Hodgson, Manitoba. Both were experienced workers, understanding well the Indian temperament and getting on well with them.[14] An undated pamphlet, which probably belongs to the middle thirties, written by Marjorie Pearman (now Mrs. Hughes-Caley), says, "While the Deaconess takes charge of services, teaches in school, visits the people, Miss Wilkins runs the home and cooks and cans in addition to caring for garden, cows and poultry and acting as chauffeur to the Deaconess! . . . The school, which is recognized officially by the Indian Department, provides a hot dinner every day, presumably cooked by Miss Wilkins too!"[15]

In 1934 Deaconess Stapleton reported that 114 baptisms had taken place in the previous six and a half years, that there was scarcely an unbaptized person among the three hundred people on the Reserve. Sixty children were attending the Elkhorn School.

These two women remained at the Sioux Mission until 1943, at which time Miss Stapleton retired and they went to live close to St. Peter's, Dynevor, where their work was unofficially continued with equal success. After their removal from the Sioux Mission, the work there was taken over for a time by the Bishop's Messengers.

North of 53: Indian Work

When the Bishop of Saskatchewan invited the Bishop of Brandon to assume the administration of that part of the Diocese of Saskatchewan lying in Manitoba, and the agreement by the Bishops was accepted by the Diocese of Brandon, the latter Diocese assumed responsibility for a large area of long and well-established work among the Indians, the story of which has been told in connection with the Diocese of Saskatchewan. The biggest centre was at The Pas in the Devon Mission on the north side of the river. Here was the Mackay Indian School, administered by the Indian Residential Schools Commission, of which the Reverend Albert Fraser was Principal. This school, unfortunately, was completely destroyed by fire on March 19, 1933, and was never replaced in any way until the fall of 1957, when the Department of Indian Affairs opened its new centre for the education and training of Indians at Dauphin, the staff of which is under the direction of an Anglican principal.

There were three churches on the Devon Mission Reserve, St. Michael and All Angels, the Church of the Messiah and the Church of the Redeemer. The first was built in 1918 as a memorial to a

[14]W. H. Stapleton, "The Sioux Mission," *One Day Telleth Another*, 63-65.
[15]Marjorie Pearman, *Autumn Adventure at the Sioux Mission* (Diocese of Brandon, n.d.).

former president, Mrs. Caroline Green, by the Ottawa Diocesan W.A.; the second was built on the north side of the river by the Indians themselves as a replacement (and replica) of the original Christ Church; the Church of the Redeemer was built at the other end of the Reserve, also by the Indians, but it is somewhat larger. In 1929, in addition to Mr. Fraser at the school, there was a devoted and experienced missionary at the Devon mission in the person of the Reverend Charles William Morris, a graduate of St. Paul's College, Burgh, Lincolnshire, and Emmanuel College, Saskatoon. Ordained deacon in 1912, Mr. Morris' whole ministry was devoted to Indian work.[16] He was succeeded at the Devon mission by the Reverend R. B. Horsefield, who had graduated from the University of Saskatchewan in 1921 and been ordained in the Diocese of Saskatchewan in 1926. After that he spent five years as missionary on the Reserve at Grand Rapids at the mouth of the Saskatchewan River. By his enterprising work and his expert command of the Cree language, Mr. Horsefield made a noteworthy contribution to the Indian work north of the Saskatchewan River. When radio broadcasting became possible, the services and addresses he gave in the native language achieved a tremendous popularity throughout the north, and he continued this work after becoming rector of the mining parish of Flin Flon, about 100 miles north of The Pas, on the Saskatchewan border.

Between The Pas and Grand Rapids there were two other missions of some note, one at Moose Lake, which had been refounded in the eighties by the Reverend J. R. Settee. It was he who originated the work at Chemhawin, where the Saskatchewan River loses itself in the broad and shallow expanse of Cedar Lake. The first church at Cedar Lake was built in 1890 by the Reverend John Sinclair, who continued his work there until his death in 1897. He is buried there. A year later the Reverend J. F. Pritchard built the second church at Cedar Lake while he was incumbent from 1898 to 1906. At the time the Diocese of Brandon took over this area, Horace P. Barrett was the stipendiary lay reader in charge, and he continued there after his ordination by Bishop Thomas in 1936. Barrett remained at this isolated point, where he was the only permanent white resident, until 1945 when he was forcibly removed from his mission by a doctor because of his physical condition; he died before the end of 1946 at the age of seventy-one, another example of the devotion of older men in the service of the Church.

[16]*Crockford's Clerical Directory, 1936*, p. 933. C. W. Morris was at the Peguis Reserve, Hodgson, Manitoba (Diocese of Rupert's Land) from 1928 to 1935, and then returned to England.

The mission at Grand Rapids was seldom without a regular minister. St. James' Church in the village was built by the Reverend John Hines in 1902. The tower of the church was said to have been built in 1905 by the Reverend J. Brown, a native clergyman and expert carpenter, in a single day. The Reverend John Hines asserts in *Indians of the Plains* that Mr. Brown was eventually worn out by the work of building churches in the Diocese of Saskatchewan. The church on the Reserve, known at St. John's, is a substantial building of logs and was the work of the Indians themselves.

Mr. Horsefield was succeeded at Grand Rapids by the Reverend W. P. Mason in 1931, who in turn was followed by the Reverend G. M. Armstrong, who remained there until his transfer to Rivers in 1939. He was followed by the Reverend F. H. J. Donaghy, a graduate of St. John's College, who for the previous six years had served the parish of Somerset in the southeast part of the Diocese. An excellent scholar, but of a retiring nature, Donaghy became singularly devoted to the work with the Indian people. He remained at Grand Rapids until 1946, when the difficulty of finding men for this kind of work caused the Bishop to transfer him to the Devon mission, which in the report of the rural dean of The Pas to the Synod of that year was described as still the brightest spot in the deanery. He said that Francis Donaghy was spending himself without stint, trying to minister to the three churches of the Reserve, the two out-stations, and the tuberculosis sanatorium for Indians fourteen miles away. "His faithful assistants are Mrs. Donaghy and the two day school teachers, Miss Montgomery and Mr. Sam Waller, the latter an experienced Indian missionary who kept the mission going single-handed for three years from the time I left it to the arrival of Mr. Donaghy. There are seven native lay readers also."[17]

The Synod was meeting on this occasion for the first time since 1939, and Rural Dean Horsefield complained rather bitterly about the way in which the Indian Missions had been neglected. There was no one at Cedar Lake and at Moose Lake they had only one layman, Percy Pryke:

a faithful man, diligent and kind, but not trained for his position. As well as he can he teaches the fifty odd children in the little one room day school; visits homes where the language is one he is trying hard to master though he has perhaps begun too late to hope for any real success; tends the sick; advises about buildings and gardens and cattle and questions of law; directs and shares in the work of the four honorary lay readers (his tact and genuine kindness his only authority); and tries to keep alive in the village the conviction that

[17]*Ibid.*, 1957-1958, p. 320. Canon Donaghy died on November 12, 1958.

the Church still yearns over them like an affectionate mother, although she sends no priests to baptize their children or to give the Lord's Supper to the dying.

This situation was not corrected until 1950, when Mr. Pryke was ordained.[18]

North of 53:
The Mining Country

In addition to the Indian work, taking over the territory north of 53 from the Diocese of Saskatchewan brought to the Diocese of Brandon the problem of new mining developments, for this country was at once the oldest explored and the last developed part of the Province of Manitoba. Roughly, it lies in a great triangle to the north of The Pas; the west side angles to the north-northwest through Cranberry Portage to Flin Flon; the east side follows the Hudson Bay Railway's main line as far as Waboden; the area is about 12,000 square miles.

The first large mining developments in the district north of The Pas were at Flin Flon and Sherridon, the former about ninety miles away on the lake of the same name that straddles the Manitoba-Saskatchewan border, and the latter about the same distance but more to the northeast.[19] Serious mining operations had begun at Flin Flon in September of 1926, after the railway had gone in. The Synod journal records the Reverend R. F. Dawson was in charge. The Reverend Canon Stacy Waddy of the S.P.G. visited the camp the same year, with the result that the Society made a grant to purchase two lots in the townsite; a parish hall was built and opened in July. In 1933 Dawson returned to England and was succeeded by the Reverend E. A. Syms, who gradually began to furnish the hall as a church, and to develop the work of the Girls' Auxiliary and Junior Branch of the W.A., Church Boys' League, and similar work in the pioneer community. The Flin Flon branch of the W.A. started with a membership of two, at a time when there were only seven women in the construction camp.

Flin Flon, which proved to be the largest mining development in the Province, expanded so rapidly that in 1939 it was the third largest town in Manitoba. St. James' parish seems to have been firmly established, and was reported to the Synod in Brandon that year, by the rural dean of The Pas, as one of the two self-supporting parishes in his deanery north of 53. The Reverend J. H. R. Percy was then incumbent.

[18]Rev. F. J. Pryke died at Moose Lake in 1954.
[19]Mining was pushed two hundred miles farther north to Lynn Lake in 1957, and the Sherridon property was then closed.

There were no Synods in the Diocese of Brandon between 1939 and 1946, by which time the Reverend R. B. Horsefield had been there for only a few months, but as rural dean of The Pas he reported to the Synod in that year:

I come next to my own parish of Flin Flon. . . . In a town of 10,000 people, where 1,100 call themselves Anglicans, where we have been holding Services occasionally since 1919 and regularly since 1928, we have not even a Church; only a parish hall where we hold Services on Sunday and social events during the week. It is true that in all mining communities there is a spirit of "make do," a feeling the people are merely camping out for as long as the vein of ore lasts, and will then have to move on to another place. But Flin Flon has long passed the experimental stage; its mine, which is its life, is assured of half a century more of operations, and probably much longer than that. So we have a building project in hand now. But we need more than buildings, we need a curate or at least a Church Army Captain; no one priest can look after this parish and hope ever to go to bed feeling he has finished the work of the day.[20]

The completion of a road from The Pas into the Flin Flon made it less isolated. Mr. Horsefield did finally secure a curate in the person of the Reverend W. H. Jones, who appears in the Brandon Clergy List of 1951 as a deacon.

To this area, "North of 53," in October of 1931, Bishop Thomas sent two of the Bishop's Messengers, Miss Elsie Marriott, a trained and experienced nurse, and Miss Ena Harrold. They first tackled the small settlement of Cormorant on the northeast side of the lake of that name, at about mile 42 on the Hudson Bay Railway. They began their work by gathering together the mothers and children, beginning with Sunday services and Sunday School in the schoolhouse.

After spending three months at Cormorant they moved off to Herb Lake, about forty miles farther on. This point was less accessible as the railway has to be left at Wekusko, from which there was a rough thirty-five mile road into the mines. They began their work in an unused store, which they were also able to use as a church, clubroom and home. While settling down at Herb Lake, they managed to keep contact through the Sunday School by Post with the children at Cormorant Lake; only one child there failed to send in the weekly assignment. At the end of three months they returned again to Cormorant and there began, under the determined leadership of Miss Marriott, to build a church in the summer of 1932. They started with five dollars, the thank-offering gift of a woman patient, and within eight months the fund had risen to $1,777, of which the Cormorant people themselves contributed nearly $300. Practically every man

[20]*Journal of the Synod of the Diocese of Brandon, 1946*, p. 39.

woman and child served in some way in the building of the church, which was dedicated by the Bishop on November 19, complete and free of all debt.

Mining at Herb Lake is of a marginal nature, and whether the mines are open or not depends on the current price of gold. In 1934 there were about two hundred people there, making a rather precarious living by trapping, fishing and prospecting. Here the work was continued on an intermittent basis by the Bishop's Messengers from Cormorant, with the aid of the travelling priest.

By 1936 the Bishop had placed the Reverend W. A. Gilbert at Cormorant and Herb Lakes, and the Messengers were free to go about sixty miles farther up the line to Waboden. This was not considered a mining community, but chiefly an Indian country, within a few miles of that expanse of the Nelson River north of Lake Winnipeg where there are a number of small Indian Reserves. To the west are the swampy lands of the Grassy River, which drains the country north of The Pas from Cormorant Lake. In the winters there is a good deal of tractor hauling between the railway line and Cross Lake. Waboden itself was one of the two divisional points on the railway between The Pas and Churchill. This was, therefore, a different kind of town. Miss Fowler says,

Many of the railway people and traders were quite sophisticated, with nice steam-heated houses, electric washers and bridge clubs, but over on the point of the lake there were the settlements of Indian trappers. Some of these had quite nice homes, too, but trapping is a very fluctuating means of livelihood. In 1935, Miss Olive Thomson joined the team at Cormorant to enable them all to take turns in working at Waboden. The Indians were very glad to attend Services as they have a real love of worship, but many of the white people were apathetic and few attended regularly, though they were glad for the children to go to Sunday School.

In 1936, under Elsie Marriott's able direction, a church and cottage were built, and Olive Thomson went to live there with Mrs. Baldwin as a fellow worker. It was hard going at first, but gradually she won their friendship and the congregation improved. She wrote in December, 1940, "A full church on Christmas Morning . . . a contrast to 1937, when we had only four people." The cottage was burned down in 1946, but the local people rallied around the mission and worked to supplement the insurance till there was enough to build a new and better cottage.

During the war the work at Herb Lake had to be closed down, but after 1947 it was placed in charge of the Messengers at Waboden.

Miss Marriott had to resign her work before 1940 owing to ill health, and she died on May 22 of that year. She is remembered as the pioneer Bishop's Messenger who built three churches "North of 53."[21]

Some Noteworthy Clerics of the Time

One of the problems of the Church in the Ecclesiastical Province of Rupert's Land, a problem common to all dioceses on the prairies at least, has been the constant movement of the clergy from one parish to another. It would be difficult to assign any particular reason for this. It is refreshing to recall men who stayed, for western Manitoba, in which the Diocese of Brandon lies, has never been an easy place in which to maintain this continuity of effort. Brandon itself has been an ambitious little city whose economic fortunes have varied. Two of its earlier rectors, Harding and de Pencier, went further west to end their careers as Archbishops; another, Quainton, became Dean of Christ Church Cathedral in Victoria. Two other men of note followed him in Brandon. In 1924 the rector of St. Matthew's, Brandon, was Edward Albert Anderson, who had been there since 1917; the following year he was made the first Archdeacon of the Diocese. Irish by birth, and educated at Trinity College, Dublin, he came to Canada in 1897 to be ordained in the Diocese of Ottawa. An excellent scholar and organizer, St. Matthew's, Brandon, prospered under his ministry, and the Synod profited by his work as first clerical secretary of its executive, a post he held for about five years. He relinquished his work as rector in 1932, but continued to serve the diocese as archdeacon for another six years, retiring to Ottawa in 1939, where he spent the rest of his life.[22] His successor at St. Matthew's was the Reverend Percy Heywood, an exact, serious-minded and scholarly man, who had spent his early years in the diocese at Waskada and Boissevain, before undertaking urban work in Winnipeg for about ten years. He had been at Trenton, Ontario, before coming to Brandon. Appointed Archdeacon of Brandon in 1938, he remained sixteen years in the diocese, doing steady and faithful work until he retired in 1948.[23] Two years before, Canon W. J. Finch had retired after spending twenty years as rector of Birtle; previously he had been at Pierson,

---

[21]"The Bishop's Messengers," *One Day Telleth Another*, 25-31. F. E. Pennell, "St. Aldhelm's," *ibid.*, 32-34. E. Marriott and E. C. Harrold, "Hudson's Bay Railway," *ibid.*, 35-38. R. B. Horsefield, "The Church in Willowland," *ibid.*, 49-53. W. A. Gilbert, "Mining Camps," *ibid.*, 68-70. E. A. Syms, "Flin Flon," *ibid.*, 71-72. M. Fowler, *The Story of St. Faith's* (London, S.P.G., 1950). R. B. Horsefield, "Willows and Hard Rocks," *Journal of the Canadian Church Historical Society*, III (February, 1958).

[22]*Crockford's Clerical Directory*, 1936, p. 22.

[23]*Ibid.*, 1957-1958, p. 530.

Melita and Elkhorn. The whole of his ministry since 1915 had been in the area of the Brandon Diocese.[24]

Some reference has already been made to the work done for the diocese by the Reverend H. L. Roy. In 1925 he became rector of Rapid City, a place of considerable size, and optimistic about its future, though quite close to Brandon. When he retired about 1935, Bishop Thomas said of Canon Roy: "In countless ways [he] contributed to the success of our early years. Canon Roy regarded church finances as a definite element in Christian worship, and conscientiously held that money given for the maintenance of the church 'was held in remembrance in the sight of God.' Added to this, he was endowed with a great gift of appeal. . . . His removal . . . was a . . . deep personal regret to me, for it brought to a close an intimate association of twenty-four years."[25]

The Depression Years

Like the rest of western Canada, the Diocese of Brandon felt the impact of the depression years. The Synod of 1931 was informed that the financial position of the Diocese was as good as could be expected, and that careful management had closed the year without a deficiency, though the working balance was impaired. It was their good fortune that the synod officials were all voluntary workers, and that the synod office was the Bishop's study; also that they had no stipendiary travelling agents. Bishop Thomas doubted if there was another diocese with lower overhead expense than Brandon. This meant, however, that retrenchment began with grants to the clergy. The Synod of 1931 was urged to meet its apportionments in full.

There was little said about the matter in the Synod of 1933, but in the minutes of the executive committee it was noted that the matter of stipend arrears was given a great deal of attention and new figures were set as a minimum for newly-ordained clergy: $80 a month for deacons and $90 for priests. Also arrangements were made for two winters' work in the Riding Mountain relief camps. These camps were Dominion government projects to assist the unemployed, and were used to develop the area as a national park. About the same time discussions also began about commencing summer work at Clear Lake, which was to be the centre of this project. This work was placed to some extent under the direction of H. Gordon Walker, then a student at St. John's College. About 1,500 men had been placed in the five camps near Clear Lake, a cosmopolitan group from every walk of life. Although many of them had not been regular attenders at

[24]*Ibid.*, 1947, p. 440.
[25]*Ibid.*, p. 1143. He died September 20, 1953.

any church, the majority respected the Christian life, and in camp they learned to live as a brotherhood of men.[26]

The journal of the Synod held in June, 1939, indicated a disposition on the part of the Diocese to take a fresh look at itself. Possibly some credit for this should be given to the Reverend I. A. Norris, who was appointed Secretary of the Synod at the meeting of the executive committee on January 20, 1937. Another factor may have been the ratification by the same committee on February second, 1938, of a new division of the rural deaneries in the diocese to make them more compact. First among these new reports was one from the Social Service Committee. It reported that the clergy were making regular visitations to government institutions in Brandon— the provincial jail, general and mental hospitals—and that St. Mary's (church) Brotherhood of St. Andrew was doing special work at the Immigration Hall, then chiefly used as a home for about sixty old men. The rector of Belmont had made himself responsible for visiting and ministration at Ninette Sanatorium.

The report of the Diocesan Board of Religious Education was a lengthy document dealing with Sunday School, young people's work and follow-up work regarding the confirmed. It urged the local clergy to take advantage of their rights and privileges in connection with religious education in the day schools. A sub-section dealt with the work of the summer school that had been held at "Y-Point" at Pelican Lake. This had begun in 1935 with twenty in attendance and each year since had had an increased attendance, reaching eighty-three in 1938.

The report of the Board of Missions summarized the state of the Home Mission Fund from 1928 to 1938 in a way that confirms what has already been said about the effect of the drought and depression years. The Home Mission and General Synod Funds in 1928 amounted to $14,159, and from that year showed a decline until 1935, when the amount received was $5,174. After that there was a slight recovery, and in 1938 the amount had risen to $6,968, approximately sixty per cent of the sum required to maintain the work in the right way. Grants to clergy stipends had been reduced from $1,762 in 1929 to $1,017 in 1938. How soon this situation was able to right itself is hard to say, but the financial statements presented to the Synod at its meeting in 1946 show that the diocesan collections for these funds at the end of 1944 had risen to $10,585.

The rearrangement of the rural deaneries was based on the fact that railways were becoming much less important, and roads much more

[26]H. G. Walker, "Unemployed Relief Camps," *One Day Telleth Another*, 73-76.

so, in the Diocese of Brandon; under the old arrangement, some of the deaneries dependent upon the former had followed the east-west line. Under the rearrangement, the old rural deanery of Souris disappeared and the new one of Tiger Hills came into being.

The reports of the rural deans to the Synod of 1939 revealed more effectively the troubles of the depression years than the proceedings of the Synod itself. Most of what is said in these reports concerning the deaneries of The Pas and Swan River has already been dealt with. With respect to the others, the reorganized deanery of Turtle Mountain in the southwest part of the province had been perhaps the most seriously affected by the years of drought, hoppers, rust and depression. But by 1939 there was evidence that the weather was changing and prosperity was beginning to return; there was increased response to the work and needs of the Diocese, and six congregations had paid their full apportionments for 1938.

The adjoining deanery of Tiger Hills had paid seventy-one per cent of its diocesan obligations, with one congregation over-paying its assessment. The rural dean of Birtle complained about the handicaps to church attendance in the form of radio and recreation. The report from the deanery of Minnedosa gave account of successful retreats at Clear Lake, which lay within the deanery, and of arrangements made for services for visitors at that lake during the summer season. Its problem was to minister to the scattered Anglican families in the large and fast developing area to the south of the national park.

All rural deans were united on two points: the difficulties that arose from the shortage of clergy and consequent problem of maintaining parish services, and the great usefulness of the work of the St. David's van and the Sunday School by Post in keeping Anglicans and their children in touch with their Church.

In 1946 nearly every parish in the Turtle Mountain deanery reported improved attendance, greatly improved finances, much success with the Anglican Advance Appeal, and improvements to their churches and parish halls. The rural dean of Birtle felt that things were improving, though their troubles were not over, and in his report made some recommendations: (1) That summer schools should be deanery rather than diocesan efforts; (2) That laymen's banquets should be re-established in order to get the men to work again; (3) That Sunday School deanery meetings should be restored, because the Sunday School seemed to be the weakest of the deanery activities; (4) That incumbents should pay much more attention to the condition of the church grounds, which in many cases were not attractive.

The Brandon deanery reported, in 1946, extensive repairs and improvements at Rivers, Alexander and St. George's Church, Brandon, but its greatest satisfaction lay in the fact that it was able to tell the Synod that St. Matthew's Church in Brandon, the Mother Church of the Diocese, had freed itself of all indebtedness and been consecrated on Ascension Day, 1945. There was one note of regret, "The Church of St. Michael and All Angels, Katrine, once a delightful sanctuary and notable as the smallest church in the diocese, is dismantled."

The deanery of Minnedosa briefly complained of the shortness of clergy, but thankfully recorded the help of lay readers who had maintained services at Gladstone, Plumas, McCreary, Kelwood, Bethany and Clan William.

The deanery of Tiger Hills had much the same story. In its area of 1,600 square miles, there were nineteen towns and five missions to be served, and the diocese was trying to do this with the aid of only four clergy, two students and several very faithful lay readers. As with other deaneries, the twenty-four branches of the Senior W.A. were doing a splendid service in their unfailing work.

In the deanery of Swan River, four new churches had been built since 1939 at Renwer, Mafeking, Dunkinville and Swan River itself. The population was changing, owing to the removal of Anglicans and the arrival of persons of other denominations and nationalities. It was urged that the Anglican Church should endeavour to offer a spiritual home to these new Canadians; the chief problem perhaps was the lack of work among young adults. The house-to-house visitations on behalf of the Anglican Advance Appeal had brought very beneficial results to the spiritual life of the parish, where carried out.

Actually, a great effort had been made in the Diocese to welcome returning men. In September of 1944 the Bishop had appointed the Reverend E. A. Syms and Canon W. H. Powell as a liaison committee between the Church and the forces. They had received splendid co-operation from the Army and Air Force, and had been able to reintroduce 1,500 persons to their parishes in the diocese.

When the Brandon Synod met again in January of 1948, economic conditions in the Province of Manitoba were on the upturn. Most of the things about which people had been afraid at the end of the war had not materialized, and the Diocese was sharing in the general prosperity and optimism common across Canada. The diocesan apportionments reflected this situation by again mounting to over $10,000, and the Diocese had paid to the Anglican Advance Appeal more than $29,000 out of the $30,500 pledged. The Missions Committee had begun consultations with parishes it felt were underassessed and asked for authorization to continue, also for an increase in the total amount, which it claimed was needed for three reasons:

(1) The general increase in cost of diocesan missioners; (2) The increased assessment on the Diocese for the General Synod departments; (3) The lowering of interest rates on endowments, particularly affecting those of the Episcopal Endowment Fund. The Synod agreed to an increase of apportionments on the basis of ten per cent of current expenditures.

Two other matters of interest were the setting up of a standing committee on broadcasting, with a view to making such things as regular mid-week Lenten services available in rural parts, and the other to proceed with the establishment of a summer camp for young people at Clear Lake. The appeal for funds to carry this out met with a ready response and the Diocese was able to complete the first part of the project before three years were up. A similar appeal on behalf of the Episcopal Endowment Fund was also successful, and the fund was again restored to an adequate amount.

A new church, St. John's, at Moose Lake was consecrated on September 28; this was built by the Indian congregation to replace the old log one, and much credit was due to the Reverend F. J. Pryke in stimulating the work. About the same time a new church was built at Flin Flon to serve that growing community, another in the new mining town of Snow Lake, and a building was converted into a church by the congregation at Neelin. The most notable change took place at the end of 1949 when Miss M. D. Fowler, O.B.E., the senior Bishop's Messenger, resigned. She was succeeded by Miss M. F. Hooper.

The Resignation of Bishop Thomas

Bishop Thomas resigned the See on January first, 1950, after an episcopate of a few months more than twenty-five years. He retired to his own house in Brandon, the grounds of which had been landscaped by subscription throughout the Diocese, as part of its farewell gift to him. The time of his retirement, however, was short. Mrs. Thomas died on June fourth, 1951, and the Bishop himself on July second, 1953; he was just over seventy-eight years of age, and in the fifty-fifth of his ministry. A great traveller for more than forty years, it was said of him that he was always ready to take his turn with the paddle, carry his full share of the load, and make himself thoroughly at home wherever he might be. His quiet manner and slow speech often concealed the alertness of the mind behind the heavy glasses; the readiness with which the Diocese met its problems was often a tribute to his foresight.[27]

[27]"Loved Rugged Northland," *Winnipeg Free Press* (July 2, 1953).

The Election of Bishop Ivor Norris

A diocesan Synod met on February 15, 1950, under Archdeacon H. E. Bridgett as Administrator, and elected the Venerable Ivor A. Norris as Bishop on the first ballot. Born in London, England, Bishop Norris had received most of his education in Winnipeg, had taken his Arts course at the University of Manitoba as a student of St. John's College, and his Theology at King's College, London. He had been ordained deacon in St. Paul's Cathedral, London, for Rupert's Land, in 1926. With the exception of a two-year curacy at All Saints', Winnipeg, and the years 1941 to 1945 as a chaplain in the R.C.A.F., the whole of his ministry had been spent in the Diocese of Brandon. Bishop Norris was consecrated in St. Matthew's Pro-Cathedral, Brandon, on Sunday, April 16, 1950, by the Metropolitan (Sherman), and he was enthroned the same day.[28]

[28]A. R. Kelley and D. B. Rogers, *The Anglican Episcopate of Canada and Newfoundland*, II, 114-115.

CHAPTER SEVENTEEN

Diocese of The Arctic

··+《logo》+···+《logo》+···+《logo》+···+《logo》+···+《logo》+···+《logo》+···+《logo》+···+《logo》+··

Friday, the 27th [August, 1909] was what I may call the day of
days. . . . We fortunately met an Eskimo who was out hunting in his
canoe, . . . who guided us to our new field of labour. . . . We soon
heard from him that the Eskimo were not living now at Ashe Inlet,
but at a place called Lake Harbour. . . . We sailed past various islands,
and at last sailed into a sheltered bay almost shut in with hills. Here
we cast anchor and were soon welcomed by a large party of Eskimo.
. . . The reason for such a welcome . . . [was that] some of our old
friends who had been instructed at Blacklead Island had travelled to
Lake Harbour, and had taught . . . their fellow countrymen to read
the Gospels. . . . On Sunday, August 29th, we held our first service in
central Baffin Land. . . . Stones were used for seats, and my pulpit
was a rock. . . . On Monday we commenced to build the Arctic house.

REV. E. J. PECK,
"The New Era," January, 1910.

··+《logo》+···+《logo》+···+《logo》+···+《logo》+···+《logo》+···+《logo》+···+《logo》+···+《logo》+··

The incident recounted above marks the beginning of a new direction
in the work of the Church among Eskimos, for when Mr. Peck and
his companions landed at Lake Harbour they were not only on Baffin
Land itself, but had made a first step towards closing the gap between
the missions of the eastern and western Arctic, to the formation of an
archdeaconry, and then of a new diocese in 1933, which lay almost
completely north of latitude 60.

The early history of the Anglican Church among the Eskimos in the
eastern Arctic is part of the history of the Diocese of Moosonee, and
has been related in connection with that diocese where it properly
belongs. Contacts with the western Eskimos were made rather later,
but became increasingly regular after the Reverend William Carpenter
Bompas was made Bishop of Mackenzie River in 1884; however,
it was not until 1896 that the first permanent mission to them was
established by the Reverend I. O. Stringer on Herschel Island. It is
to the history of Mackenzie River, particularly during the episcopates
of Bishops Reeve and Lucas, that one must look for the real development of the western Eskimo missions. The events between 1890 and
1933 have been outlined in connection with the Mackenzie River
Diocese, the critical area in missionary work among the native races

living in the Province of Rupert's Land during these years. But it was not until after 1920 that serious suggestions were made, leading to the reorganization of the northern work across the Canadian Arctic.

The Years of Discussion

The primary object of the Anglican Forward Movement appeal that was launched after the end of World War I in 1918 was to raise funds necessary to replace the annual grants of the Church Missionary Society, for these were to be withdrawn in 1920. It was recognized that the problem of mission support after that would have to be met by the M.S.C.C. Out of this fund $300,000 was invested for work among the Indians and Eskimos, and $100,000 was designated as the Indian and Eskimo Equipment Fund. By 1925 the M.S.C.C. was able to report that the original fund had been completed, $45,000 had been applied to the reorganization and support of schools, $44,000 to the support of Indian and Eskimo missions, and $1,500 from the Equipment Fund had been expended on them.[1] In the east, Lake Harbour was firmly established with a church of its own; native catechists were carrying on there, at Blacklead Island, and at a new point on Cumberland Sound (later called Pangnirtung). Blacklead Island was closed in 1926, and the work transferred to the latter point. The Colonial and Continental Church Society was still supporting the Fort Chimo mission at Ungava, begun in 1899 by the Reverend S. M. Stewart. Southampton Island had been first visited in 1924, and a missionary was sent there in 1926. The same year a mission was established by the Diocese of Keewatin at Eskimo Point, north of Churchill on the west side of Hudson Bay.

This progress drew attention to the possibility that there might be a need for centralized organization of the Arctic work, but it was some time before the Province of Rupert's Land, the four dioceses concerned (Moosonee, Keewatin, Mackenzie River, Yukon), and the M.S.C.C. viewed the matter with a common mind. To the Provincial Synod of 1923 Archdeacon Woodall, on behalf of the Diocese of Moosonee, presented a memorial that the Synod "proceed at as early a date as possible towards the creation of a purely Eskimo diocese, which will release the portion of work of this nature now attached to this diocese." The Lower House agreed, but the House of Bishops declined action on the ground that "just now it would be premature." At the 1926 Synod, Moosonee responded by affirming that it would be to the advantage of the Indian and Eskimo work "to be under a more central and unified control," which could be accomplished by a rearrangement of diocesan

---

[1]*From East to West* (Toronto, M.S.C.C., *ca.* 1924), 6-7. **Disposition of Anglican Forward Movement Funds.**

boundaries. The resolution relating to this was passed by the Lower House. However, it would also appear that the House of Bishops in a sense got there first, for its "Message B" on the Monday afternoon said that the proposal had been made more than once for setting up a diocese to cover such Eskimo work. But it felt this called "for very careful consideration and investigation by those who are familiar with the topography of the districts affected, their relation to one another, the facilities for transportation between them, etc.," and suggested the appointment of a special committee to consider this and report to the next Synod. This move was agreed upon.

When the Provincial Synod met in Calgary in 1929, the subject was dealt with in the Metropolitan's Charge.[2] The committee had not viewed the setting up of an Eskimo diocese favourably, as it did not seem practicable to unite the work in the eastern and western Arctic. The Metropolitan thought it would be appropriate for the Synod to note and express its appreciation of the work initiated by the M.S.C.C. and accomplished through its Arctic Mission Committee. The executive part in this was being carried on by the Venerable A. L. Fleming, as Archdeacon of the Arctic, under commission by the Bishop of Moosonee, and operating in the Diocese of Keewatin with the sanction of its Bishop. "Archdeacon Fleming is not only a man of commanding devotion and aggressiveness but a gifted advocate of the cause which he has in hand, who commends it with wonderful effectiveness wherever he visits." The appointment of such an organizing Archdeacon of the Arctic was really a signal victory for the diplomacy of Canon Gould, and was one of his two great achievements in Canada as Secretary of the M.S.C.C., the other being his organization of the Restoration Fund in 1933. While it might be said that Canon Gould was not the creator or founder of the Diocese of The Arctic, it must be admitted that he was the instigator of circumstances that made it impossible *not* to set the diocese up.

To the Synod of 1929 a report on Indian missions was presented by Archdeacon Tims, which also covered those to the Eskimos, and commented upon the remarkable success attending the evangelization of these people. It drew attention to the stress that the Anglican Church had always laid upon the value of literacy in extending the work, and reviewed its early history in this respect, remarking on the place the use of syllabics had taken in promoting the Gospel amongst the Eskimos. Besides the reprinting of Dr. Peck's *Eskimo Grammar* in 1920, and the more recent publication of the *Memorial Dictionary,* the Reverend H. Girling's *Gospel of St. Mark* in Coppermine Eskimo had

[2]*Journal of the Provincial Synod of Rupert's Land, 1929,* p. 19: Archbishop Matheson's Charge.

been published in 1920 by the Bible Society. The S.P.C.K. had produced a revised and enlarged Service Book in western Eskimo, compiled by Archdeacon Whittaker, Canon Hester of Aklavik and Mr. Girling.

The same report recorded the death of Mr. Girling in 1920, and that of the Reverend W. H. Fry in 1921. Both had shared responsibility for the extension of evangelization to the east of the Mackenzie River delta, and the experiences they endured had permanently affected the health of each of them.

Archdeacon A. L. Fleming

Archdeacon Fleming, when he accepted his new work in the Arctic, was rector of the Old Stone Church in St. John, N.B., a position he had held since 1921. Previous to that he had been Chaplain and Financial Secretary to Wycliffe College, Toronto, for three years, and consequently was quite well known and an experienced organizer.[3] A native of Greenock in Scotland, the son of a sea captain, he had become interested in the Eskimos at an early age. Upon leaving school he had entered the firm of John Brown and Company, the famous shipbuilders of Clydebank, and it was during his years in Glasgow that he became concerned about mission work. In 1906 his attention was directed to an appeal by Bishop George Holmes of Moosonee for a young man to work in Baffin Land; that fall he entered Wycliffe College in Toronto. A year later he sailed for Baffin Land with Bilby and Peck; their arrival at Lake Harbour forms the introductory paragraph of this chapter. Two years later Fleming returned to college, and was ordained deacon in 1912 and priest in 1913 by Bishop John George Anderson of Moosonee. He went back to Baffin Land until 1916, but on coming out on furlough his health was unsatisfactory and he was only allowed to undertake light work. He did, however, visit Baffin Land again in the summer of 1920.

1927: A Year of Advance

Besides the establishment of the Archdeaconry of the Arctic, the year 1927 saw advances made at four different places. At Port Harrison, three hundred miles north of Great Whale River, much easier contacts were made possible with people still farther north. Bishop Marsh remarks in his *Arctic Century*: "In earlier days, they had travelled once a year down the coast to Great Whale River, or Fort George, in order to partake in the Easter celebrations and it sometimes took several months to make this journey." In the western Arctic an influenza epidemic was fatal to more than half the people at Bernard Harbour,

---

[3]A. R. Kelley and D. B. Rogers, *The Anglican Episcopate of Canada and Newfoundland*, II, 48-49.

where in 1916 Mr. Girling had taken over the buildings of the Canadian Arctic Expedition, and the mission was moved in 1928 to Coppermine, its present site. But in the year before, 1927, a new mission was opened at Cambridge Bay on the south side of Victoria Island, through the generosity of the Anonymous Donor. In 1927, also, there was added to the church and house at Shingle Point a small residential school, the first to be built for the Eskimos, and Thomas Umaok was ordained deacon by Bishop Stringer, acting as commissary for the vacant Diocese of Mackenzie River. Thomas Umaok was the first native Eskimo to enter the ministry. He was a native of the Mackenzie River delta, and had some boyhood recollections of the coming of a white man, possibly Bishop Bompas, who told his father and uncle of the Gospel. In 1908 a mission was opened at Kittigazuit on the east side of the delta, where Mr. Fry was catechist for three years. It was eighteen years before any Eskimos were baptized, but Thomas Umaok and his wife, Susie, were one of the first couples to receive baptism. In 1934 Mr. Umaok was moved to Tuktoyaktuk, where he built a log cabin that was used as a house and church; in 1945 this became the present church, and it now contains many of the furnishings originally at Herschel Island and Shingle Point.[4]

Inland to Baker Lake

In 1927 the work of the Arctic was for the first time moved away from coastal waters. Baker Lake is about two hundred miles in from Chesterfield Inlet, and was chosen because it was a trading post for Eskimos who crossed the Barren Lands in pursuit of caribou. This mission was commenced by Mr. Fleming when he made his first journey to the Arctic as Archdeacon, and he took with him the Reverend B. P. Smyth, who had volunteered to work there. When their ship called at Lake Harbour, the Archdeacon spoke to his old friends about this new project and asked for helpers. The congregation decided to send Joseph Pudlo, a catechist he had trained himself, regarded by him as a great friend. At Baker Lake itself, the officers of the Hudson's Bay Company and Revillon Frères were very co-operative; Joseph Pudlo, although a stranger, was accepted by the Eskimo community, and the mission was successfully established.[5]

The Archdeaconry of the Arctic

Mr. Fleming undertook his new work as Archdeacon of the Arctic with a high sense of duty and a feeling that it was God's will that he

[4]D. Robinson, "Rev. Thomas Umaok," *The Arctic News* (Toronto: Diocese of The Arctic, June, 1960), 3-13.
[5]A. L. Fleming, *The Hunter—Home* (Toronto, M.S.C.C., 1931), 33-39.

should do so. He faced a number of difficulties: technically, he was Archdeacon of the Diocese of Moosonee, a missionary diocese that had always interested itself in the evangelization of the Eskimo, but had accomplished its work in this respect through the support and co-operation of the Church Missionary Society, which support had been lacking since 1920. His work with the Bishops of Keewatin and Yukon was of a permissive nature, and much of the Arctic coastline in the west lay in the Diocese of Mackenzie River, which, in 1927, had no bishop, except in so far as the Bishop of Yukon was able to fulfil the function of commissary. His relation with these bishops was, there-fore, rather a long distance one, and while their attitude was sym-pathetic, he had only small hope either of consultation or practical support. A further personal responsibility of Archdeacon Fleming was emphasized by the fact that the General Synod had set up a committee of seven to direct the work, but it only met once a year. The committee had informed him that in addition to his work in the Arctic field he would be expected to raise $5,000 a year in Canada, and the equivalent of the same amount in England.

A room was found for him in the Church House, Toronto, where he set up an office, and for some years he visited what missions he could in the summertime. During the winter months he travelled through Canada, the United States and to England, trying to interest people in the work with the Eskimos, founding and expanding The Arctic Fellowship, and appealing for funds. Many of these journeys were rather discouraging, because he found in a number of cases that a dollar given to the work of the Arctic was regarded as a dollar taken away from a local diocese or parish. Gradually, through admirable publicity with voice, pen and picture, Archdeacon Fleming overcame these difficulties and The Arctic Fellowship was firmly established. His books on the Arctic people, often written for church study groups, attracted public interest. His pictures of Arctic scenes (many appeared in The Beaver of the H.B.C.) caught the public imagination, and later, when he began using the airplane to visit mission posts, he became good newspaper copy as the "Flying Bishop."

Archdeacon Fleming went to England in the winter of 1929, and after that made a point of visiting there every two years. The Diocese of The Arctic received much whole-hearted support from the Bible Churchman's Missionary Society, which not only provided funds but also some of the most outstanding men among its workers.

In 1929 the Church moved farther north along the coast of Baffin Land, and a mission was established at Pond Inlet. In 1930 a small hospital, known as St. Luke's, was built at Pangnirtung. This was really an extension of the pioneer medical work that had been done for many years on Blacklead Island by Greenshield and Bilby. Strongly impressed with the necessity for this work, the Archdeacon had successfully pleaded for help both in England and eastern Canada, as well as securing government support. The hospital was built under the practical direction of the Reverend George Nicholson, who had been specially trained for pioneering work in the mission field, and had gained experience by working for a building firm for a year (incidentally, without pay). The first nurse-in-charge at Pangnirtung was Miss Prudence Hockin of Winnipeg, who remained there until 1946, and then took charge of the larger hospital at Aklavik.

Archdeacon Fleming made his first trip to the western Arctic in 1928, and saw for the first time the large and important area that had come under his supervision. Unfortunately, an epidemic of influenza, ending in many cases of pneumonia, seemed to follow the ship down the river. Proceeding to Shingle Point and Herschel Island, the Archdeacon's party found that they had to deal with a similar situation there. The whole journey was, to the new Archdeacon, a terrible and challenging experience; thereafter he was very conscious of the necessity of increased hospital accommodation and medical services in the Arctic.

From Herschel Island on the west, Archdeacon Fleming sailed for thirty-one days on the *Bay Chimo* to Bernard Harbour in the east, the scene of Girling's early work, and spent a short time in the district with the Reverend J. H. Webster. There were navigating difficulties on the return trip, due to weather and magnetic conditions, but Shingle Point was reached again in time to get back to Aklavik and make the return trip on the *Distributor*.

Archdeaconry to Diocese

The twenty-second meeting of the Provincial Synod of Rupert's Land took place on September 13, 1933, in Winnipeg, and the erection of the Diocese of The Arctic was finally determined, but not until after long discussion. The Metropolitan (Stringer) referred to the prospect of its foundation in his Charge, pointing out that Dr. E. J. Peck had earnestly advocated it in his time, that the Arctic Mission Fund Committee had considered it for some years and recommended it, and that the Anglican National Commission had approved the plan. At the Thursday evening session the Lower House received a message from the Bishops, recommending that the area in the four Dioceses of Yukon, Mackenzie River, Keewatin and Moosonee, then being administered by the Arctic Mission Committee (in other words, by Archdeacon Fleming), should be set apart as the Diocese of The Arctic, and that the Diocese of Mackenzie River should cease to exist.

The resolution of concurrence, however, was held up, first by a request for a joint meeting of the two Houses, which took place on the Friday afternoon, and then by the request of the Diocese of Athabasca that a vote be taken by Orders, then by dioceses. In each case there was a large majority in favour of concurrence, with the exception of Athabasca, whose delegates voted against it. This opposition may have been due to the fact that obliteration of the Mackenzie River Diocese was to leave with the Diocese of Athabasca the problem of what later became known as the Mackenzie River Deanery.

It was felt by some of the delegates that the maintenance of the Diocese of The Arctic was too big a problem to be handled by the Province of Rupert's Land, and should be handed over to the General Synod to be dealt with by that body as an extra Provincial Diocese, similar to those of Honan in China and Mid-Japan. But the motion moved by the Reverend G. A. Wells of Rupert's Land and A. H. Hanson of Saskatoon, which recommended General Synod should amend its constitution and undertake this new responsibility, was defeated.

While the report of the Committee on Diocesan Boundaries was being presented, a message was received from the House of Bishops that set up the boundaries of the new diocese. Later in the afternoon the House of Delegates received a further message, informing the members that the Upper House had selected the Venerable A. L. Fleming as Bishop of The Arctic, and asking for concurrence. Unanimous consent was given to both these messages.[6]

The new Bishop was consecrated in St. John's Cathedral, Winnipeg, on December 21, 1933, by the Metropolitan (Stringer). This was the last consecration in which Archbishop Matheson took part, and it seems fitting that he was able to be present at this final division of Rupert's Land into dioceses. A second link with the past was in the presence of the Reverend Alfred C. Garrioch, now bent with age, who had been one of the original clergy of the undivided Diocese of Athabasca, before the formation of Mackenzie River.

New Diocese: New Efforts

For a time economic development took place faster in the western part of the new diocese than in the east, probably due to increased prosperity in the fur trade, and the prospect of mining and oil develop-

[6]Archbishop Stringer, "The Arctic Mission," *Journal of the Provincial Synod of Rupert's Land*, 1933, pp. 21-22. *Ibid.*, 32: Message "B", House of Bishops to the House of Delegates. *Ibid.*, 40-42: Formation of The Diocese of The Arctic. *Ibid.*, 42-43: Determination of the boundaries of The Diocese of The Arctic. *Ibid.*, 44-45: Message "R" from the House of Bishops to the House of Delegates, and the election of Bishop A. L. Fleming. *Ibid.*, 50-51: Acts of The Synod, Nos. 2 and 16.

ments in the lower Mackenzie around Great Bear and Great Slave Lakes. A small hospital had been built at Aklavik in 1926, which had done useful service in the community, especially during the epidemic. Unfortunately this was completely destroyed by fire in 1936. At the time, a new residential school to accommodate one hundred and fifty children was being built there, and work on it was delayed while the hospital was reconstructed on a larger scale (fifty beds) with improved equipment. The school was completed and opened in 1937, and it carried on something of a new experiment. Schools at Shingle Point and Hay River were closed and the children all transferred to Aklavik, and so a younger generation of Loucheux Indians and Eskimos, whose ancestors were traditional enemies, began a common education in a Christian atmosphere. By this time the original church at Aklavik, built in 1920, had become inadequate, and after much consideration it was decided to build a new one rather than enlarge the old, though the matter was complicated for the Diocese by the recent erection of the new school and new hospital.

When Bishop Fleming visited Aklavik in 1936 he received $100 from the Loucheux Indian women as the first gift towards the new church, a second one of $25 from a fur-trader, and further contributions were made by Indian, Eskimo and white people before he left for the south. These amounted to a considerable sum, which was encouragingly increased by gifts from others in the Arctic, Canada and England. The new All Saints' Church was consecrated on June 29, 1939, by Archbishop Owen, Primate of All Canada, and immediately constituted the Pro-Cathedral of the Diocese of The Arctic.[7] Its builders are commemorated by a brass plate with the inscription: "This tablet is erected to record the devoted leadership given by Thomas Summers, Master Carpenter, to the Indians who, under his direction, built All Saints' Residential School, All Saints' Hospital and this Church 1935-37." There is only one nail in the chancel that was not driven by an Indian, and that was hammered into its middle step on the morning of August second, 1937, by Lord Tweedsmuir, Governor-General of Canada.

All Saints' Pro-Cathedral is a treasure house of beautiful gifts that have come from many places in England and Canada. The oil painting over the Communion Table is "The Epiphany in the Snows," by the Australian artist, Miss Violet Teague. Three of the singularly beautiful hangings are of local interest. A set made of caribou skins and moose hide, embroidered with silk and porcupine quill work, was the gift of the Loucheux people; another is a set made of brown

[7]All Saints' Cathedral, Aklavik (Toronto, Diocese of The Arctic, 1949), 20. The Architects were Molesworth, Secord and Savage of Toronto.

squirrel, caribou and coloured thread hangings, worked by Coast Eskimos in the Mackenzie River area; a third is of sealskin work, in pattern by the Senior Branch of the Woman's Auxiliary at Pangnirtung in Baffin Land. Every effort has been made to preserve associations of historic and local interest, and there are memorials connected with the Reverends E. J. Peck, E. W. T. Greenshield and J. W. Bilby of the eastern Arctic, and with Bishop Lucas, the Reverend Herbert Girling of the western (or Mackenzie River) part of the diocese, the Hudson's Bay Company, and Mrs. R. J. Loiselle of Montreal, the wife of the first president of the Fellowship of the Arctic in that city.[8]

The Travelling Bishop

That summer (1937) the Bishop travelled 4,144 miles by land, 5,250 miles by air, 880 miles by water, a total of 10,274 miles. In spite of difficulties the work of the Church slowly expanded during the next few years, and outstations of existing missions were established at Fort Ross, a year after the Hudson's Bay Post went there, and at Tavanne in 1940. By this time the Bishop's visitations to the eastern Arctic on the Hudson's Bay Company ship *Nascopie* were being complicated by the war, which now involved the threat of submarines in the Gulf of St. Lawrence and along the Labrador coast. This made sailings uncertain, navigation often difficult, supplies hard to get in to both missionaries and traders; some posts had to remain unvisited. It was also hard to maintain some missions owing to the shortage of men.

The constant strain of travel, which must be endured by a missionary bishop, is both a mental and physical hazard, particularly when one is required to continue his journeys during what is normally the off-season of winter, as Bishop Fleming had to do in order to secure the necessary financial support and public interest. The Bishop eased his work a little after 1939 by the appointment of the Reverend Donald Ben Marsh as Archdeacon of Baffin Land. Mr. Marsh was a native of Enfield, near London, where he was educated, and had spent a summer at Livingstone College, a missionary training school in England. In 1922 at the age of nineteen he had entered Emmanuel College, Saskatoon, graduated in 1926, been ordained by Bishop Dewdney of Keewatin, and had opened the new mission at Eskimo Point. Here, he and his wife had stayed and worked, with brief furloughs, for seventeen years. Marsh is an example of the persistence with which the missionaries in the Arctic held consistently to their work over long years, and thus followed the tradition of the pioneer days of Rupert's Land.

[8]*Ibid.*, 17-19.

In 1943 the residential school at Fort George was destroyed by fire, but was rebuilt and opened again the following year. The Reverend E. J. Peck had been succeeded there in 1892 by the Reverend W. G. Walton, who carried on for thirty-two years; then had come the Reverend Fred Mark, followed in 1927 by the Reverend J. T. Griffin, who organized the first residential school, in place of the day school that had been conducted at Fort George since 1907. The new school was opened in 1933 on February first with thirteen girls in residence. Incidentally, St. Philip's school has always arranged its curriculum so that the children trained there would be able to resume ordinary life in the district when they left it.

Bishop and Mrs. Fleming, with Canon L. A. Dixon of the M.S.C.C., had a very uncomfortable journey to Moose Factory early in July, 1944, and this was only the beginning of a series of misfortunes, the culmination of which was a serious accident to the Bishop during the service of dedication of the school on Sunday, July 8. He was not able to resume his work until the middle of August; the experience left him shaken, and he began considering a successor more seriously. The energy, personality and comparative youth of Archdeacon Marsh greatly appealed to him, but the Archdeacon did not know the western Arctic, and so in 1944 Bishop Fleming transferred him to Aklavik as Archdeacon and missionary in charge.[9]

In 1945 the Bishop apparently attempted no more than a visitation of the western Arctic, that in the east on the *Nascopie* being made by Bishop Henry D. Martin of Saskatchewan. In the following year he was able to make this visitation himself, but it was for the last time. On December 21, 1946, Bishop Fleming suffered a severe heart attack; however, after some months, he was able to return to some of his administrative duties.

The issue of *The Arctic News* for November, 1947, contains an appreciation of the work of those associated with the Bishop in the administration of the Diocese. The Honorary Secretary, G. L. Foster, had held this position since 1933 and had carried on in spite of ill-health for the past two years, until he was compelled to resign at the end of October. His resignation had ended a partnership of more than thirteen years, during which Bishop and Diocese had profited by his broad knowledge of affairs and discriminating mind. The Bishop also wrote appreciatively of Miss Mildred Johnson, who had been his secretary. Mr. Foster was being succeeded by H. L. Alcorn.

The same number reported the opening of the first full-time day school in the Arctic at Tuktoyaktuk, which had been placed under Miss Dorothy Robinson, formerly at the Aklavik school. The church

[9]A. L. Fleming, *Fort George* (Toronto, Diocese of The Arctic, 1944).

at Tuktoyaktuk, in charge of the Reverend Thomas Umaok, had been remodelled and re-equipped, the work being done by the Eskimos themselves with logs washed down the Mackenzie River, and found by them on the Arctic coast. Bishop Renison of Moosonee had visited Fort George and Great Whale River, and Bishop Barfoot of Edmonton was to be at the Coppermine Mission at Easter in 1948.

The death of Archdeacon Whittaker on February first, 1947, was mentioned with great regret; he had given twenty-two years of service to Indian and Eskimo work, and promoted interest in it through his writing for years during his retirement.

The Diocese of The Arctic: Problem to the Province

The Provincial Synod of Rupert's Land met on April 23, 1947, under the presidency of Archbishop Sherman. This was its first meeting in five years, and the Metropolitan in his Charge drew attention to two important questions. The first was the future of the Deanery of Mackenzie River, which had been referred to the Province by the M.S.C.C. three years before. The second was linked with this in some respects, for the Bishop of The Arctic had been concerned, but his illness had deprived them of his help and advice. The Bishop had made an application "for the election of either a coadjutor or suffragan bishop of the Arctic as the Provincial Synod may see fit." For a right decision on this request it must be remembered that the Board of Management of the M.S.C.C., had agreed in September, 1944, "that the full support of the Diocese of The Arctic by the Church, through M.S.C.C., be assumed as soon as possible," and on November 19, 1946, had decided that "the church [will] assume such support as from January 1st, 1948." This involved an increase in the annual grant by the M.S.C.C. to the Diocese of The Arctic of $15,000 per annum, and the Budget Committee of General Synod had been asked to increase the M.S.C.C. apportionment accordingly.

Through Archbishop Sherman, the procedures of the Synod were modified so that more joint sessions could be held by the two Houses. It was to a joint evening session on April 23 that Bishop Ragg of Calgary presented the report of the Metropolitan's special committee on the Mackenzie River Deanery. At this point, the Metropolitan presented the request of the Bishop of The Arctic for a coadjutor or suffragan, and considerable discussion took place before the debate was adjourned at 10 p.m., when a resolution was under consideration to the effect that the final decision on this application should be deferred until after the proposed conference had taken place between the Metropolitans of Rupert's Land and British Columbia on the whole work of the Church in northern Canada. The following morning the

Metropolitan was asked to appoint a special committee to consider the resolution moved the previous evening. When the debate was resumed in the afternoon, permission was given to withdraw the original motion and substitute another, and this may be summarized. Because of the death of Bishop Geddes of Yukon, the fact that the Synod had placed the Deanery of Mackenzie River under the temporary jurisdiction of the Metropolitan, and because the Synod deemed it advisable that a comprehensive policy should be formulated with respect to the work of the Church in the whole of northern Canada, the Synod was of the opinion that it would not be advisable to grant the application of the Bishop of The Arctic. This was carried unanimously and no further synodical action was taken until 1950.[10]

Bishop Fleming's immediate reaction was to arrange for Archdeacon Marsh to take over administrative details in the Toronto office. On October 21, 1948, a somewhat inconspicuous article entitled "The Arctic Calling" appeared in the *Canadian Churchman*, written by Bishop Fleming at the request of the editor. In this the Bishop remarked that the objections set forth by the Provincial Synod in 1947 had no real bearing on the matter that he had submitted. When he had asked the Provincial Synod to elect an assistant bishop, he had guaranteed his stipend and a suitable dwelling; the money had actually been on hand, and had not come either directly or indirectly from the M.S.C.C., the W.A. or any other Canadian source. If an assistant bishop had been appointed, it would have given the Church time and opportunity to find out how best to deal with the situation, and there would have been no additional cost to the Synod or the M.S.C.C. If after that consideration it had been decided wise to divide or rearrange diocesan boundaries, this assistant bishop could have entered upon whatever sphere might have been allotted to him. Bishop Fleming went on to say, "The Diocese of The Arctic differs from an ordinary diocese in that it has many features that call for special attention on the part of the Bishop. The divergent needs of the various missions, schools and hospitals with their staffs, and the adjustment of relationships between the various groups of Eskimo, Indians and Whites, requires an extensive and intimate knowledge of conditions in that far-away region. It is only a matter of common sense that the man who shall succeed me should be given an adequate opportunity of understanding something of the problems which will confront him." During the summer of 1949 Bishop Fleming tendered his resignation of the Diocese of The Arctic, to become effective September 18. In

[10]*Journal of the Provincial Synod of Rupert's Land, 1947*, pp. 32-36: The Mackenzie River Deanery and application of the Lord Bishop of The Arctic. *Ibid.*, 18-19: Archbishop Sherman's opinion regarding these matters.

October the House of Bishops conferred with the Standing Committee on the Election of Bishops. Having concluded that the whole future of the Church in the north depended upon the decision to be made by the Provincial Synod, further action was postponed so that consultations might be held with the Metropolitans of British Columbia and Ontario.[11] In the meantime, following this October meeting, the Metropolitan appointed the Venerable D. B. Marsh as Commissary in the Diocese of The Arctic.

The Provincial Synod of Rupert's Land met on April 19, 1950, and in his Charge the Metropolitan again reviewed the situation respecting Canadian northern territories. He particularly welcomed "Canon J. H. Webster who had been stationed at Coppermine for some twenty-two years, and who last year in ministering to his huge area—which now included Cambridge Bay as well—travelled 3,400 miles by dog team. He has come out at my personal request to represent the clergy of the Diocese of The Arctic at first hand—something I think never done before—to give them a voice and at the same time help us in our important decision." He had also invited the Reverend Tom Greenwood of Yellowknife in the Deanery of Mackenzie River to attend the Synod as a guest, that they might have first hand knowledge of that area. The rest of the first day was taken up with the consideration of changes in the Constitution and Canons dealing with the election of missionary bishops, and, in the event of a vacancy at the time of Synod, of providing for the election of the new bishop by the whole body.

On the Thursday morning, according to the report in the *Canadian Churchman* of May fourth,

The most careful consideration was given to the whole problem of the work of the Church in the Arctic . . . [the] matter which was the main purpose of the meeting of the Synod. The Rev. Canon Webster of Coppermine spoke of the work amongst the Eskimo in the Western Arctic and presented the problems in that field; the Rev. Tom Greenwood of Yellowknife dealt in detail with conditions and problems in the Mackenzie River Deanery, and the Venerable D. B. Marsh explained the working of the Diocese of The Arctic from the point of view of administration and the relationship between its eastern and western parts. The substantive motion that we proceed to the election of a Bishop of the Diocese of The Arctic which shall also include the Deanery of Mackenzie River was moved by the Bishop of Saskatchewan. An amendment which proposed to set up at the same time an Assistant Bishop, whose chief duty would be to exercise a pastoral care over the Western Arctic and Deanery of Mackenzie River areas, was defeated only after prolonged debate, but there seemed to be a feeling that this was only being delayed because of present financial

[11]"Letter to the Archbishops and Bishops of the Church of England in Canada from the Metropolitan of the Province of Rupert's Land," October 21, 1949. *The Arctic News* (Toronto, November, 1949), pp. 2-3.

difficulties. The delegates from the Dioceses of Athabasca and Edmonton, the nearest adjacent to the area concerned, warmly supported the proposal.

On Friday morning the election was proceeded with in joint session in accordance with the rule established under the new Canon. The Venerable Donald Ben Marsh was elected with a clear majority in both Houses on the second ballot, and expressed his willingness to accept the call.

Bishop Marsh was consecrated in St. John's Cathedral, Winnipeg, on the Tuesday in Whitsun Week (May 30, 1950), by the Metropolitan of Rupert's Land (Sherman), and was enthroned in All Saints' Cathedral, Aklavik, on June 18.[12] Tuesday in Whitsun Week was the same day in the Church's Calendar as that on which the first Bishop of Rupert's Land (David Anderson) had been consecrated in 1849, one hundred and one years previously.

Arctic Missionaries:
Some Personal Records

In recording the events of the Provincial Synod at which the election of Bishop Marsh took place, a comment by the Metropolitan was quoted in which he welcomed Canon J. H. Webster to that meeting. Canon Webster had worked in the Diocese of The Arctic only one year less than Bishop Marsh, for after having been ordained deacon in 1927 by Bishop Stringer of the Yukon, then Commissary of the Diocese of Mackenzie River, he had gone to Bernard Harbour and had been responsible for moving that mission to the Coppermine River a year later. After a year at Shingle Point, he had returned to Coppermine in 1934, and remained there until his appointment as Archdeacon at Aklavik in 1951. Archdeacon Webster came to Emmanuel College, Saskatoon, in 1923 under the C. and C.C.S. For eleven of the years he was at the Coppermine, he averaged 3,200 miles a year by dog-team, besides travelling between 2,000 and 3,000 miles every year by the annual supply ship. When he left the Coppermine, eighty per cent of the people in the area were members of the Anglican Church, and he was one of the first Honorary Canons appointed when All Saints' Church in Aklavik was consecrated and made the Cathedral of the Diocese of The Arctic.[13]

Canon Henry Arthur Turner came out from England in 1928 as a missionary supported by the Bible Churchman's Missionary Society,

[12]Kelley and Rogers, *op. cit.*, 116-117.
[13]*Crockford's Clerical Directory, 1957-1958*, p. 1377. *The Arctic News* (Toronto, October, 1958). Archdeacon Webster retired from work in the Diocese of The Arctic in 1958.

and was a graduate of their college in Bristol. He began his work at Pangnirtung and except for occasional furloughs and the years of 1938 to 1940, which he spent at Port Harrison, the whole of his life was devoted to this mission. His death on April 21, 1953, was a great loss to the Church. He and his wife were married in 1931, and the *Arctic News* commented in its memorial notice that Pangnirtung had seemed to them their only home, "and indeed their daughter, Jean, had known no other."[14] For some years Canon Turner could not travel in comfort owing to arthritis of the spine, but he refused to leave his work; in 1951 heart trouble kept him in bed for several months, but he taught from his bedside, and continued to direct the work of the mission and hospital. His translational work never stopped; his aim was to have the whole of the Bible translated into Baffin Land Eskimo.

Canon Turner's brother, Canon John Hoodspith Turner, also a graduate of the B.C.M.S. College in Bristol, came to the Arctic only a year later than he did, and from 1929 to 1945 was at Pond Inlet, the most northerly mission station in Baffin Island. In August of 1944 he was married to Miss Joan Hobart, who had come out from Felixstowe, England, the native place of both of them. His wife had had some training as a nurse. They moved to Moffet Inlet, which they thought was a better point for their work. On September 24, 1947, when Canon Turner was returning from a hunt for meat, he stopped to help an Eskimo girl who was carrying a bucket of ice to their house. But as he was taking it through the kitchen door, the rifle he was carrying under his arm discharged, the shot fracturing the base of his skull and traversing his brain.

The difficulties and delays of communications and weather greatly hindered the organization of relief, and hampered the efforts of the Army and Air Force for two months. It was not until November 22 that the plane carrying him reached Winnipeg, and Canon Turner was taken to the General Hospital; recovery, however, was not possible and he died on December ninth. Canon Turner loved the Arctic and the Eskimo, and regarded his years there as the best of his life.[15] Among other things, he had revised and completed a translation of the eastern Arctic Prayer Book. Originally the work of Dr. E. J. Peck and the Reverend W. G. Walton, the special type of their edition had been lost in the London bombings during the war. Bishop Fleming announced in *The Arctic News* of October, 1948, that the final revision of this new translation was in the hands of Canon H. A.

---

[14]"Rev. Canon H. Arthur Turner," *The Arctic News* (October, 1954), 9-10.
[15]H. M. Speechley, "Canon John H. Turner of Moffet Inlet (1929-1947)," *Canadian Churchman* (March 4, 1948), 9-10.

Turner, and it would be printed as a memorial to his brother, a special fund being raised for the purpose.

Another of the clergy who had served the diocese for several years, while the area was still an archdeaconry, the Reverend William John Rundle James went to Baker Lake in 1930, taking over the work begun by the Reverend B. P. Smyth and Joseph Pudlo, the catechist from Lake Harbour. Mr. James had the L.Th. degree of Wycliffe College, Toronto, and was ordained by Bishop Dewdney of Keewatin in 1930. Like all pioneer missionaries he had been pastor, doctor, nurse, teacher and dentist to his people. When he first went there all the Eskimos at Baker Lake only made a twenty-member congregation. In 1958 the congregation averaged ninety and there were seldom absentees. Canon James still travels his parish a week at a time by dog-team. His canonry was conferred in 1951. Now, with the opening of the Arctic to scientific research and defence operations by the Army and Air Force, he is well known and appreciated by the armed services. Concerning this impact of "civilization" Canon James feels that missionaries will continue to be needed to help Eskimos grasp the good things offered, above all to retain their faith in God, and to reject those things that would destroy their spirit of independence and self-reliance.[16]

A graduate of the B.C.M.S. College in Bristol, Tom Daulby was ordained deacon and priest in 1942 by Bishop Fleming, and then followed the Reverend J. H. Turner at Pond Inlet. Here he has remained, doing steady and unspectacular work ever since. The Reverend B. P. Smyth left Baker Lake in 1930 for college and ordination. After a number of years in the Diocese of Toronto, in 1953 he volunteered once more for work in the Arctic, and when Canon H. A. Turner died that year, Mr. and Mrs. Symth returned to take over the mission at Pangnirtung. At that time about six hundred and fifty Eskimos lived in the vicinity of this mission.

In 1949 the Reverend H. C. and Mrs. Quartermain resigned after ten years in the Arctic, nine of which had been spent at Lake Harbour. Their five children had all been born in the north. Mrs. Quartermain had also spent some time as a nurse at Aklavik Hospital before her marriage. Their successor, the Reverend G. A. Ruskell, was a young Irishman who had been an outstanding athlete at Trinity College, Dublin. He had come to the Diocese of The Arctic in 1946, and was taken to Fort Chimo in Ungava by Bishop Fleming that year. The Bishop's letter in *The Arctic News* of October, 1948, said that Mr.

---

[16]"Honor Minister for 28 Years At Baker Lake," *Winnipeg Free Press* (October 15, 1958). Canon James received an honorary D.D. the previous day from Wycliffe College, Toronto. "Baker Lake and Chesterfield Inlet," *The Arctic News* (April, 1949), 7.

Ruskell had spent seven months out of the twelve living and travelling with the Eskimos. He had journeyed by sledge and dog-team down the west coast to Port Harrison. He had visited all the Eskimo encampments, spent Christmas in an igloo, and held services in igloos, shacks, trading and wireless posts and in the beautiful little chapel at Port Harrison, where he had stayed for three weeks. "It was only fair to Mr. Ruskell that it should be said that none of the six missionaries who had preceded him at Fort Chimo had ever spent so much time with the people or travelled as far in one winter as he had done." The Bishop felt this was one more proof that if they had the spirit the young men of today were able to do just as much as did the pioneers, indeed they could do more because the north was now opening in a way undreamed of forty years before.

The mention of wireless stations in the north is a reminder that 1949 saw the beginning of a new experiment in communication. Through the efforts of the late Canon J. E. Ward of Toronto, himself a pioneer in broadcasting, the services of Morning and Evening Prayer in western Eskimo and Loucheux had been recorded and broadcast by the community-owned station at Aklavik, CHAK. Duplicate recordings had been provided for the Charles Camsell Hospital in Edmonton, where patients from the western Arctic and Mackenzie underwent treatment for tuberculosis. Later, similar recordings were made in eastern Arctic dialects, and also of sermons, for the benefit of patients in similar hospitals in the east.

In 1952 the centenary of the mission at Fort George was celebrated, and as it was also the jubilee year of the M.S.C.C. The services were made part of a commemorative film prepared for the latter event by Crawley Films of Ottawa. The founding of this mission has been dealt with in the early history of the Diocese of Moosonee. Bishop Marsh, in looking at its oldest register, was surprised to find that the first baptism was dated October 20, 1852, and that there were several more recorded in the same month; it seemed strange because the Reverend E. A. Watkins could only have been there a few weeks. The Bishop learned, however, that the wife[17] of the Hudson's Bay Company Factor at Fort George at that time was an earnest Christian, who spent time and trouble in instructing the natives, and had some of them prepared for baptism and Christian marriage when Mr. Watkins arrived.

Conditions have changed at Fort George in the course of years, but the tents of the Indians are still teepees, though the skin covers

[17]D. B. Marsh, "Through the Century," *The Arctic News* (July, 1952), 8. This was Mrs. John Spencer (Anne, daughter of William Sinclair and Nahoway), elder sister of Mrs. Robert Miles (Elizabeth), the wife of Chief Factor Robert Miles of Moose Factory.

of bygone days have given place long since to canvas. The church in 1952 was about seventy years old, a log structure, pinned together with great wooden pegs. The school was about to close for the season when Bishop Marsh was there. He remarked upon the happiness in the children's faces, and said in his account of the proceedings: "If there was ever any doubt in the minds of people as to the value of two of our residential schools, I would suggest that they go either to Fort George or Aklavik." Of the services, Mrs. Marsh added, "The interior of the church is very beautiful. The people kept coming in and where I thought it impossible for another to sit, lo, another and yet another seemed just to melt into a place. They sat upon the floor, upon the chancel steps, by the Communion rail and everywhere. And I understood that many of the Inlanders had not yet come into the post. Finally, with the ringing of the last bell, the seven catechists arrayed in surplices, preceded the Canon and the Bishop. There were wonderful faces to gaze upon, wonderful voices to listen to, wonderful lives witnessing daily in their communities for the Lord."

The Reverend Canon Henry Sherman Shepherd, who had been in charge of the school and mission for the preceding five years, was on the point of ending his twenty-five year association with the Arctic. A graduate of King's College, Nova Scotia, ordained in the Diocese of Fredericton, he had left that diocese in 1929 to take charge of the school at Shingle Point, remaining there until 1936, the year before it was closed and the children moved to Aklavik. After nine years at All Saints' School, Canon and Mrs. Shepherd were at Port Harrison on the east side of the Bay for a couple of years, going to Fort George in 1947.[18] (Canon Shepherd was one of the first residentiary Canons of the Cathedral at Aklavik in 1939; the other was its rector, the Reverend Trevor Jones.)

One other name must be associated with this mission, that of Miss Bessie Quirt. In the summer of 1944, when Bishop Fleming found himself well enough to be able to return to his office, he discovered that although they had a new school at Fort George, the Indian and Eskimo Residential Schools Commission had been quite unable to find workers to go there, and that the Diocese had less than two weeks in which to secure a staff, outfit the members and get them off in time to join the Hudson's Bay Company's schooner at Moosonee. However, through the efforts of Mrs. W. C. White, wife of the retired Bishop of Honan, they were able to obtain two supervisors and a registered nurse, but they still lacked a necessary teacher. At this point Miss Quirt, who was assistant secretary in the office of the Diocese,

[18]*Crockford's Clerical Directory, 1957-1958*, p. 1054. Canon Shepherd spent a year as Principal of the Horden School at Moose Factory before he retired from the ministry.

offered to go to Fort George. She made an outstanding contribution, not only in the school, but in what might be termed the parish. When Miss Quirt came out on furlough in 1949 she was presented with a life membership in The Arctic Diocesan W.A. by the president, Mrs. Henry Marsh; it was the gift of St. Philip's W.A. at Fort George in recognition of her service, and she continued to serve this mission for another three years.

Expansion after World War II

The war years, 1939 to 1945, made it difficult to find new men to replace older missionaries, and a number of mission posts were left in the care of native catechists, who did splendid work in conducting services and holding the people together. Canon Webster, at the Coppermine Mission, was left with a huge area to serve, but it was not possible to find any relief for him until 1951 when two young men were ordained by Bishop Marsh. The first of these was the Reverend John R. Sperry, who came from Leicester in England and joined Canon Webster that year. A young man of energy, he quickly made himself at home in his surroundings. At Easter, 1952, he was married at Coppermine to Miss Elizabeth MacLaren, a young nurse who had come out from England at the same time as himself and for the previous year had been on the staff of the hospital at Aklavik.

The other young missionary was the Reverend D. H. Whitbread, who was stationed at Port Harrison where he did excellent work with the help of two Eskimos, Willie and Adam, in building a new mission house and converting the old house into a new church. In the meantime, farther west it had been possible to reopen the mission at Cambridge Bay, and the Reverend J. R. Sperry was able to visit Spence Bay on the Boothia Peninsula, which had not seen a missionary since Bishop Marsh had been there in 1950. Mr. Whitbread took charge of Spence Bay in 1955. This proved the most expensive mission to operate in the Diocese, but a most important point, for it links the Eskimos of the west with those of the east. A year later it was possible to open up an outstation of this mission at Gjoa Haven on King William Land to the southwest.[19]

Mackenzie River Deanery
Restored to the Diocese of The Arctic

The varying problem of the Church's work in the southern part of the valley of the Mackenzie River has been studied previously, as

[19]Freight via Waterways, Alberta, the Mackenzie River, and along the Arctic coast at this time cost over $200 a ton.

far as possible in the contemporary environment of the Diocese of Athabasca, the Diocese of Mackenzie River, and its three years as a deanery under the Metropolitan of Rupert's Land. In 1947, when the area was designated as a Deanery, the old mission points of Fort Norman, Fort Simpson and Fort Smith were all vacant; Hay River was in charge of Miss Neville carrying on at the hospital; Fort Rae and Fort Resolution had passed into history, but the new mining town of Yellowknife, not far from the site of the former, was beginning to make progress in Church life under the Reverend J. D. Batten. In 1949 there was an improvement when the Reverend S. J. and Mrs. Bell went to Fort Simpson, and about the same time the Reverend Tom Greenwood left Fort McMurray, where he had been since 1946, to take charge of Yellowknife. The addition of the area to the Diocese of The Arctic brought a welcome from *The Arctic News* in June of 1950 and the remark: "They [Bell and Greenwood] are the only protestant missionaries in an area of approximately 4,000 square miles, with a population of some 7,000. Ordained men are urgently needed at two important centres in this area—Hay River and Fort Smith." By 1951 Mr. Bell was serving the river from Fort Wrigley to Fort Norman; a new church had been built at Yellowknife. That mission was on its way to the position of self-support, which it was the first parish to achieve in the Diocese of The Arctic. The Reverend R. S. and Mrs. McKinnel were at Fort Smith, a key point on the Mackenzie River. But Hay River, old mission and new town alike, was to be a problem for some time.

Fort McPherson: Old and New meet

Little has been said about Fort McPherson, at least not since Archdeacon Whittaker left there in 1918. It was the second oldest mission in this part of northwest Canada; after that date the importance of Aklavik as the trading point of the Mackenzie River delta grew, and that of Fort McPherson diminished. Not much is heard of it for the next six years. The work of the Church during this period seems to have been kept alive very largely through the efforts of the Reverend Edward Sittichinli, the second Loucheux Indian ordinand of Bishop Reeve, who made Fort McPherson the centre of his work from 1903 to 1928.[20]

In 1924 the Reverend S. C. Deacon went to Fort McPherson. An Emmanuel College graduate, who had served in both Paraguay and Argentina, he returned to South America after two years. In 1924,

---

[20]Edward Sittichinli was ordained by Bishop Reeve in 1903, after working as a catechist for 35 years. His son, John Edward Sittichinli, who was educated at the Hay River school, was ordained by Bishop Fleming in 1943, and ever since then has been attached to All Saints' Cathedral at Aklavik.

another Loucheux ordinand, the Reverend John Martin, was appointed to assist Mr. Sittichinli, with whom he worked until 1927, when he was moved to Aklavik. Most of John Martin's ministry was spent at Ross River and Mayo in the Diocese of Yukon, however. Another Emmanuel College man, the Reverend John Morris, was at Fort McPherson from 1928 to 1932, and then went to the Coppermine Mission until he returned to England two years later. Mr. Morris was followed by the Reverend J. W. Johnson, who also stayed for only two years. After that there seems to be no record until 1937, when the Reverend A. S. and Mrs. Dewdney took up residence there and spent the next ten years in restoring the old Fort McPherson Mission to its original standard of usefulness. Bishop Fleming remarked in the account of his four day visit there in 1945 that he had attended a "Tribe Council," at which serious discussion took place on the need of a school for the children who could not be sent to Aklavik. This seems to have been regarded as a church problem rather than a government one at the time, and the people gave the Bishop $600 towards the project. The school was actually built about the same time as the one at Tuktoyaktuk (1947), and this project was followed by an attempt to convert the old mission house into a hostel, a new mission house having been built.[21] Obstacles arose, however, and the project did not come into being until some years later.

In the *Canadian Churchman* (May 17, 1945) Mrs. D. B. Marsh wrote of her experiences the previous year when she was travelling down to Aklavik for the first time to take up residence there: "Something about McPherson seemed temporarily to lift the gloom and depression of this long heart-aching trip down the Mackenzie River. It was wonderful to find our Church alive and strong and manned, (the only missionary all the way from McMurray to McPherson, 1,561 miles). One felt the consolidation of years of faithful service." She found a church "seeping with atmosphere and beauty," and had

[21]C. E. Whittaker, "Recollections of an Arctic Parson," *Canadian Churchman* (March 17, 1938). Robert McDonald retired from Fort Youcon in 1871, when it was closed by the H.B.C., and settled at Fort McPherson on the Peel River. The first mission house was built in 1872; St. Matthew's Church there was begun the same year, and the cemetery was laid out alongside it. This mission house was twenty-five feet by forty, built of squared logs in Red River style. The roof was made of close-laid spruce logs, covered thickly with clay and then with spruce bark, held by riders lengthways. Still in good condition in 1907, it deteriorated rapidly and was replaced in 1914 by the mission house mentioned in the text. Much of the material used in the latter was shipped in from Ontario; it was of split-log construction in Ontario style, built under the direction of W. D. Young. Archdeacon Whittaker lived in the original house from 1897 to 1901 and 1907 to 1914; in the second house from 1914 to 1918. From 1901 to 1906 he was posted at Herschel Island. J. E. Sittichinli, "Fort McPherson Centenary," *The Arctic News* (October, 1960), 4-8.

never seen one with such exquisite frontals and hangings, all the work of the finest Loucheux seamstresses. Mrs. Marsh gave great credit to Mrs. Dewdney for encouraging this work.

After the Dewdneys left on furlough in the summer of 1947, the mission was again vacant for two years, but then was supplied by a young Irishman from Emmanuel College, who came back as an ordained missionary in 1951. The Reverend S. P. A. Timmons received a hearty welcome from the people who had come to know him. The fortunes of this, the second oldest mission station on the Mackenzie River, have varied over the years, but the name of its real founder, Archdeacon Robert McDonald, has always been revered. The loyalty of the Loucheux Indians to the principles of Christianity he taught them, and to the branch of the Holy Catholic Church into which he brought them, has never wavered.

Epilogue

It has been thought fitting to terminate this history of the Anglican Church in Rupert's Land as close to the year 1950 as possible. This date almost coincides with the centenary of the foundation of the original Diocese (1849), and is the seventy-fifth anniversary of the organization of the Provincial Synod of Rupert's Land itself. By 1950 the usefulness of York Factory as a trading post had long ceased, and within a few years it was to be abandoned by the Hudson's Bay Company. Gone now is the gateway of the fur trade to Rupert's Land, but it will always remain in the honoured recollection of the Anglican Church. It was through York Factory that the first missionaries came; here the first Bishop of Rupert's Land first trod upon the soil of his new diocese, and preached his first sermon within its boundaries. It was from York Factory, too, that James and Jean Hunter set out to get the first translations of Scripture, prayers and hymns in the Cree language printed, and William and Sophia Mason sailed with the text of the first Bible in Cree syllabics, now in circulation for nearly a hundred years.

The year 1950 also marks the end of an era, for in that year five new Bishops were consecrated to serve dioceses within the Province, and before Easter, 1954, four other changes had taken place in the Provincial Episcopate. By that time, too, the whole environment had changed. Many of the hardships, difficulties of travel and discouragements of isolation experienced by the pioneer missionaries had disappeared. The dioceses in the southern part of the Province were now well organized parochially, beginning to look to self-support, and the possibility of programmes of extension based upon their own resources. Economic conditions had improved in the northern Dioceses of Athabasca and Saskatchewan, because of better roads, modernized agriculture and new policies bringing government aid to further development. Only in the Dioceses of The Arctic and Keewatin (and some remote parts of the Diocese of Brandon) did traces of the original situation with regard to mission work remain, and even here the prospect of impending change was imminent.

And so, as each Diocese, during or after 1950, has received a new Bishop and the Province of Rupert's Land a new Metropolitan, the story has been closed. These pages relate events and achievements for which we should be humbly thankful and sincerely proud. The writer has sought to show how the devoted zeal and work of many men and women, all of diverse gifts but with one hope of their calling, have built up the Kingdom of God through the expansion of His

463

Church in that part of western Canada known by the time-honoured
name of Rupert's Land.

> Thou wast their rock, their fortress and their might;
> Thou, Lord, their Captain in the well fought fight;
> Thou, in the darkness drear, their one true light.
>
> Alleluia
>
> O blest communion! fellowship divine!
> We feebly struggle, they in glory shine;
> Yet all are one in Thee, for all are Thine.
>
> Alleluia

Select Bibliography

Allan, W. O. A. and McLure, Allen, *Two Hundred Years of the S.P.C.K.* (London, 1898).

Anderson, David, *The Net in the Bay; or the Journal of a Visit to Moose and Albany* (London, 1854 and 1873).

Anderson, David, *Notes on the Flood at the Red River* (London, 1854 and 1873).

Arctic Research (Ottawa, 1955).

Ballantyne, R. M., *Hudson's Bay: or Every-Day life in the Wilds of North America during Six Years Residence in the Territories of the Honourable Hudson's Bay Company* (Edinburgh and London, 1848).

Batty, Beatrice, *Forty Years among the Indians and Eskimo* (London, 1893).

Begg, Alexander, *The Great Canadian North West*, 3 vols. (Toronto, 1881).

Bickersteth, J. G., *The Land of the Open Doors* (London, 1915).

Bryce, George, *John Black, Apostle of the North* (1898).

Buckland, A. R., *John Horden, Missionary Bishop* (London and Toronto, n.d., *ca.* 1895).

Camsell, Dr. Charles, *Son of the North* (Toronto, 1954).

Clarke, B. F. L., *Cathedrals outside the British Isles* (London, 1958).

Cnattingius, Hans, *Bishops and Societies* (London, 1948).

Cody, H. A., *The Apostle of the North* (Toronto, 1908).

Fleming, Rt. Rev. A. L., *Archibald The Arctic (The Flying Bishop)* (Toronto, 1956).

Garrioch, A. C., *The Correction Line* (Winnipeg, 1933).

Garrioch, A. C., *The Far and Furry North* (Winnipeg, 1925).

Garrioch, A. C., *First Furrows* (Winnipeg, 1923).

Gordon, Rev. Charles W. ("Ralph Connor"), *Life of James Robertson* (undated).

Griesbach, W. A. (The Hon.), *I Remember* (Toronto, 1946).

Gunn, D., and Tuttle, C. R., *History of Manitoba from the Earliest Settlement* (Ottawa, 1880).

Hargrave, J. J., *Red River* (Montreal, 1871).

Healy, W. J., *Early Winnipeg Days* (Winnipeg, 1927).

Healy, W. J., ed., *Women of Red River* (Winnipeg, 1923).

Heeney, W. Bertal, *John West and his Red River Mission* (Toronto, 1920).

Heeney, W. B., ed., *Leaders of the Canadian Church*, second series (Toronto, 1920).

Heeney, W. Bertal, ed., *Rupert's Land Centenary Papers* (Winnipeg, 1921).

Herklots, H. G. G., *Frontiers of the Church* (London, 1961).

Hill, R. B., *Manitoba: History of its Early Settlement, Development and Resources* (Toronto, 1890).

Hines, John, *The Red Indians of the Plains* (London, 1915).

Hughes, Katherine, *Father Lacombe, The Black-Robe Voyageur* (Toronto, 1911).

Jessett, Thomas E., *Chief Spokane Garry* (Minneapolis, Minn., U.S.A., 1961).

Kelley, A. R. and Rogers, D. B., *The Anglican Episcopate of Canada and Newfoundland*, II (Toronto, 1961).

Laut, A. C., *The "Adventurers of England" on Hudson Bay* (Toronto, 1915).

Lewis, Arthur, *The Life and Work of E. J. Peck Amongst the Eskimo* (London, 1904).

Lofthouse, Rt. Rev. J., *A Thousand Miles from a Post Office* (1922).

"M. E. J.," *Dayspring in the Far West* (London, 1875).

Machray, Robert, *Life of Robert Machray: Archbishop of Rupert's Land* (Toronto, 1909).

MacKay, Douglas (revised by Alice MacKay to 1949), *The Honourable Company: A History of the Hudson's Bay Company* (Toronto, 1949).

Macoun, John, *Manitoba—The Great North-West* (Toronto, 1882).

McCormick, J. H., *Lloydminster* (London, 1920).

McElheran, Irene Brock, *That's what I'm here for: A Biography of Archdeacon R. B. McElheran* (undated).

McLean, John, *James Evans: Inventor of the Syllabic System of the Cree Language* (Toronto, 1890).

Metcalfe, J. H., *The Tread of the Pioneers* (1931).

Mockridge, C. H., *The Bishops of the Church of England in Canada and Newfoundland* (Toronto, 1896).

Montgomery, Rt. Rev. H. H. (Secretary, S.P.G.), *The Church on the Prairie* (London, 1910).

Morton, A. S., *A History of the Canadian West to 1870-71* (Toronto, 1939).

Morton, A. S., *Sir George Simpson, Overseas Governor of the Hudson's Bay Company* (Toronto, 1944).

Morton, W. L., *"Introduction," London Correspondence Inward from Eden Colvile, 1849* (London, 1956).

Morton, W. L., *Manitoba: A History* (Toronto, 1955).

Morton, W. L., *One University* (Toronto, 1957).

Mountain, Armine W., *Memoir of George Jehoshaphat Mountain, Lord Bishop of Quebec* (Montreal, 1866).

Mountain, G. J., *The Journal of the Bishop of Montreal During a Visit to Church Missionary Society, North West America Mission* (London, 1845).

Newton, William, *Twenty Years on the Saskatchewan* (1897).

Oliver, E. H., ed., *The Canadian North-West: Its Early Development and Legislative Records,* 2 vols. (Ottawa, 1914).

Peck, E. J., *The Eskimo* (Toronto, 1920).

Renison, R. J., *One Day at a Time* (Toronto, 1957).

Rich, E. E., *Hudson's Bay Company 1670-1870;* Vol. II, *1763-1870* (London, 1960).

Rich, E. E., ed., *John Rae's Correspondence with the Hudson's Bay Company on Arctic Exploration 1844-1855* (London, 1953).

Riddell, J. H., *Methodism in the Middle West* (Toronto, 1946).

Ross, Alexander, *Red River Settlement: Its Rise, Progress and Present State with Some Account of the Native Races, and Its General History to the Present Day* (London, 1856).

Rowley, O. R., *The Anglican Episcopate of Canada and Newfoundland* (London, 1928).

Ryerson, John, *Hudson's Bay, or a Missionary Tour of the Territories of the Hudson's Bay Company* (Toronto, 1855).

Shearwood, F. P. (Mrs.), *By Water and the Word* (Toronto, 1943).

Skelton, O. D., *The Railway Builders,* Chronicles of Canada, Vol. XXXII (Toronto, 1915).

Stock, Eugene, *History of the Church Missionary Society* (London, 1899).

Taylor, Fennings, *The Last Three Bishops Appointed by The Crown* (1870).

Thompson, Norman and Edgar, J. H., *Canadian Railway Development* (Toronto, 1933).

Tucker, Norman L., *Western Canada* (Toronto, 1907).

Tucker, Sarah, *The Rainbow in the North* (London, 1856).

Two Hundred Years of the S.P.G. 1701-1900 (London, 1901).

West, John, *The Substance of a Journal During a Residence at the Red River Colony, British North America: and Frequent Excursions among the North-West American Indians in the Years 1820, 1821, 1822, 1823* (London, 1824).

Wood, L. A., *The Red River Colony*, Chronicles of Canada, Vol. XXI (Toronto, 1916).

PERIODICALS:

The Arctic News (Toronto, The Arctic Fellowship). Now published twice each year. It goes back to *ca.* 1930.

Canadian Church Magazine and Mission News, C. H. Mockridge, ed. (Toronto, Domestic and Foreign Missionary Society of the Ecclesiastical Province of Canada, 1886-1893).

Church Messenger (Toronto, G.B.R.E.). A monthly insert for parish magazines, which ceased publication about the end of 1960. (Particularly useful for its "One Hundred Years Ago" page selected by the late Prof. Young of Toronto and the late Canon A. R. Kelley.)

The New Era (Toronto, M.S.C.C., 1904-1914). A monthly edited by L. N. Tucker (1904-1911), and S. Gould (1911-1914).

The Western Churchman, R. C. Johnstone, ed. (Winnipeg, 1896).

ABBREVIATIONS
used in text and footnotes

B.C.M.S. *Bible Churchman's Missionary Society*

C.M.S. *Church Missionary Society, London, England*

C.M.S.A. *Church Missionary Society Archives, London, England*

C. AND C.C.S. *Colonial and Continental Church Society*

G.B.R.E. *General Board of Religious Education (Anglican Church)*

H.B.C.A. *Hudson's Bay Company Archives, London, England*

M.S.C.C. *Missionary Society of the Church in Canada (Anglican Church)*

M.M.S.A. *Methodist Missionary Society Archives, London, England*

P.A.C. *Public Archives of Canada, Ottawa*

P.A.M. *Public Archives of Manitoba, Winnipeg*

Q.D.A. *Quebec Diocesan Archives (in Public Archives of Quebec)*

R.L.A. *Rupert's Land Archives (in Legislative Library, Winnipeg)*

S.P.C.K. *Society for Promoting Christian Knowledge, London, England*

S.P.C.K.A. *Society for Promoting Christian Knowledge Archives*

S.P.G. *Society for the Propagation of the Gospel, London, England*

S.P.G.A. *Society for the Propagation of the Gospel Archives*

U.C.A. *United Church of Canada Archives, Victoria University*

Index

469